Employment Law for Business and Human Resources Professionals

THIRD EDITION

Kathryn J. Filsinger

CONSULTING EDITOR
Daryn M. Jeffries
Filion Wakely Thorup Angeletti LLP

emond

Toronto, Canada
2015

Emond Montgomery Publications Limited
60 Shaftesbury Avenue
Toronto ON M4T 1A3
http://www.emond.ca/highered

Printed in Canada.
Reprinted July 2015.

We acknowledge the financial support of the Government of Canada.
Nous reconnaissons l'appui financier du gouvernement du Canada.   Canadä

Publisher: Mike Thompson
Acquisitions editor: Lindsay Sutherland
Managing editor, development: Kelly Dickson
Director, editorial and production: Jim Lyons
Copy editor: David Handelsman
Production editor & coordinator: Laura Bast
Proofreader & indexer: Paula Pike
Permissions editor: Monika Schurmann
Typesetter: Shani Sohn
Cover designer: Tara Wells
Cover image: iStockphoto.com/Svetl

Library and Archives Canada Cataloguing in Publication

Filsinger, Kathryn J., author
    Employment law for business and human resources professionals / author, Kathryn J. Filsinger. — Third edition.

Includes index.
ISBN 978-1-55239-595-0 (pbk.)

    1. Labor laws and legislation—Ontario.   I. Title.

KEO629.F54 2015   344.71301   C2014-905033-X
KF3320.ZB3F54 2015

Contents

PART I

LEGAL FRAMEWORK

1 Overview of Legal Framework

PART II

HIRING

2 Human Rights Issues: Hiring

3 Common Law Issues

4 The Employment Contract

PART III

DURING THE COURSE OF EMPLOYMENT

5 Human Rights Issues: Duty to Accommodate, Harassment, Accessibility Standards

6   Employment Standards Act

7   Occupational Health and Safety Act

PART IV

THE END OF THE EMPLOYMENT RELATIONSHIP AND BEYOND

12 Resignation and Retirement

13 Dismissal With Cause

14 Termination and Severance Pay Requirements Under the Employment Standards Act

15 Dismissal Without Cause

16 Post-Employment Obligations

APPENDIXES

Preface

From the initial recruitment stage to the end of employment, the law potentially affects every aspect of the employment relationship. As a human resources professional, you will not be expected to become an expert in all areas of employment law. However, you will be expected to have sufficient understanding of employment law so that, wherever possible, you can minimize legal risks and liabilities, be aware of the implications of actions proposed or taken, and—most important—know when to seek expert legal advice.

The purpose of this book is to provide you with a fundamental and practical understanding of the key legal issues that arise between employers and non-unionized employees. The book contains an extensive review of the content and interpretation of relevant employment-related statutes. It also examines the underlying contractual relationship between the workplace parties, and the implications of applying general principles of contract law to that relationship. Throughout the book, case summaries are used to help clarify and explain ideas and to provide you with a sense of how courts and administrative tribunals interpret the relevant laws.

This text focuses on non-unionized employees—individuals whose terms and conditions of work are based on an individual contract of employment. It does not, for the most part, cover unionized employees, whose terms and conditions of employment are collectively bargained for and governed by a collective agreement. Generally speaking, however, most employee rights contained in statutes apply to unionized and non-unionized employees alike, while common law (judge-made) rights and remedies, such as the right to sue for wrongful dismissal, apply only to non-unionized employees.

The text is divided into four parts. Part I (Chapter 1) provides an overview of the legal and judicial framework within which Ontario's employment laws are created and interpreted. It explains the sources of employment law, both statutory and judicial; the relevance of the *Canadian Charter of Rights and Freedoms*; and the issues related to constitutional jurisdiction in the employment area. It also provides an overview of current employment-related statutes that apply in Ontario. The chapter concludes by discussing the distinction between an employee–employer relationship and that of independent contractor–principal, and the legal implications of that distinction.

Subsequent chapters are organized according to the chronology of the employment relationship. Part II (Chapters 2 to 4) addresses key legal issues surrounding the hiring process. Chapter 2 focuses on the significant impact that Ontario's *Human Rights Code* has on selection and recruitment. Unlike most employment laws, the Code applies to pre-employment conduct, as well as to all subsequent aspects of the employment relationship, and an understanding of its requirements is crucial for anyone involved in the hiring process.

Chapter 3 examines common law issues related to hiring, including areas of potential liability for employers. It also discusses different categories of employees. Chapter 4 considers the benefits of written contracts of employment over oral ones, reviews common contractual terms, and examines the main enforceability issues that can arise.

Part III (Chapters 5 to 11) focuses on laws that apply during the course of an employment relationship. Chapters 5 to 10 provide an overview of the principal statutes that govern human rights, employment standards, occupational health and safety, workplace safety and insurance (formerly known as workers' compensation), equity, and privacy, respectively. Chapter 11 covers contractual issues, such as performance reviews and changes in the terms of employment agreements during the course of employment, as well as issues surrounding vicarious liability.

Part IV (Chapters 12 to 16) reviews the key legal issues that arise at the end of an employment relationship. Chapter 12 deals with resignation and retirement. Chapter 13 reviews dismissal with cause under the common law. Chapter 14 covers statutory termination and severance requirements under Ontario's *Employment Standards Act, 2000*. Chapter 15 reviews the common law concerning dismissal without cause, and related issues. Finally, Chapter 16 looks at post-employment obligations.

In the five years that have passed since the second edition of this text was published, there have been a significant number of developments in the employment law field. These include several important legislative changes. The *Employment Standards Act* has been amended to provide three new statutory leaves: family caregiver, critically ill childcare, and crime-related child death or disappearance, all effective October 29, 2014. (Under Bill 18, which received second reading in October 2014, further proposed amendments include removing the $10,000 cap on ministry orders, extending the time limits on recovery of wages, and making temporary help agencies and their clients jointly liable for unpaid wages owing to agency employees.) In 2012, two new grounds—gender expression and gender identity—were added to the list of prohibited grounds of discrimination under Ontario's *Human Rights Code*. Also since the publication of the second edition, the requirements under the *Accessibility for Ontarians with Disabilities Act* have started being implemented. As well, Bill 160 made wide-ranging changes to Ontario's health and safety system, including requiring basic health and safety awareness training for all workers and supervisors, effective July 1, 2014.

This edition also examines key employment law–related decisions made over the past five years. These include *Bowes v. Goss Power Products Ltd.* (duty to mitigate), *Jones v. Tsige* (new tort of intrusion upon seclusion), *R v. Cole* (employee's reasonable expectation of privacy on employer-owned technology), and *Piresferreira v. Ayotte* (rejection of tort of negligent infliction of mental suffering in the employment context). Other major developments include a series of cases highlighting the need to ensure that termination clauses match statutory requirements at all times and in all regards (for example, *Stevens v. Sifton Properties Ltd.*) and the Supreme Court of Canada decision in *Boucher v. Wal-Mart*, where an unprecedented level of special damages was upheld in a constructive dismissal case.

Acknowledgments

There are a number of people I would like to acknowledge and thank for their support and assistance in the preparation of this book. First and foremost is Daryn M. Jeffries of the law firm of Filion Wakely Thorup Angeletti LLP, the consulting editor. I am deeply indebted to him for his ongoing and generous help and insightful guidance during the preparation of this, as well as the previous, editions.

Thank you also to the reviewers of the third edition: Pnina Alon-Shenker, Ryerson University; Shiyamala Devan, Humber College Institute of Technology and Advanced Learning; Veronique Henry, Centennial College of Applied Arts and Technology; Lavinia Inbar, Sir Sandford Fleming College; and Bob Thompson, Seneca College of Applied Art and Technology.

I also want to thank Anneli LeGault of Fraser Milner Casgrain LLP and summer students at the same firm, Kelly Griffin and Cristiano Papile, as well as Ted Shaw of the Ontario Human Rights Commission, for their kind assistance with several chapters of this book. My sincere appreciation goes as well to my sister, Ruth Owens, who reviewed an early draft of the text and wisely counselled me to "give lots of examples."

Finally, I thank my husband, Nick, and our children, Caitlin, Rachel, and Francesco, for their patience and support through the many, many hours that it took to bring this book to completion.

This book is dedicated in loving memory to my parents, Norman and Ella Filsinger.

Kathryn J. Filsinger

PART I

Legal Framework

Overview of Legal Framework

1

LEARNING OUTCOMES

After completing this chapter, you will be able to:

- Identify the three main sources of employment law and their respective roles.

- Understand how and why employment law changes.

- Understand jurisdiction over employment law.

- Understand the relevance of the *Canadian Charter of Rights and Freedoms* to employment law.

- Identify key employment-related statutes, with particular focus on Ontario and federal law.

- Understand the judicial and administrative systems that interpret employment laws.

- Locate relevant statutes and case law.

- Distinguish between an employee and an independent contractor.

Introduction

Although most of this book looks at specific employment laws, Chapter 1 provides you with an overview of the legislative and judicial framework within which those employment laws are created. Knowing who makes, interprets, and enforces these laws is essential to understanding and applying them in the workplace. This chapter is intended to provide a context for everything else that you will learn in this book.

As an employment law text, the focus is on non-unionized employees—individuals whose terms and conditions of work are based on an individual contract of employment between them and their employer. Issues specific to unionized employees, whose terms and conditions of employment are collectively bargained for and governed by a collective agreement, are not, for the most part, covered.

Sources of Employment Law

There are three main sources of employment law in Canada: **statute law** (legislation passed by the government), **constitutional law** (the *Canadian Charter of Rights and Freedoms*), and **common law** (judge-made law). The relative importance of each source depends on the particular area of law under consideration. Wrongful dismissal actions, for example, are based on the common law, while minimum employment standards and anti-discrimination laws are provided through statutes, though the common law gradually adopts many statute-based principles. A discussion of statute, constitutional, and common law is set out below.

Generally speaking, most employee rights contained in statutes apply to unionized and non-unionized employees alike, while common law (judge-made) rights and remedies, such as the right to sue for wrongful dismissal, apply only to non-unionized employees.

Statute Law

What Is a Statute?

A statute is a law passed by the federal or provincial government. Statutes are sometimes referred to as "legislation" or "acts." The Ontario *Human Rights Code*, found in Appendix E, is an example of a statute.

Why Are Statutes Passed? Why Are They Amended?

Employment statutes are usually passed because the government decides that employees require protections or rights beyond those that currently exist. Historically, employment legislation has provided minimum acceptable standards and working conditions, such as minimum wages and vacation entitlements. More recently, governments have implemented statutory requirements and protections, such as anti-discrimination legislation, that affect many facets of the employment relationship.

There is a wide range of factors that can lead to changes in employment law. One of these is a change in the political party in power. For example, in 2001 the Ontario

Progressive Conservative government amended the *Employment Standards Act, 2000* (ESA) to allow employees to work up to 60 hours per week. This was one of the first laws targeted by the Liberal Party for change when it formed the government in 2003.

New legislative requirements also often relate to demographic shifts in society and changing social values. For example, the dramatic increase in the number of women in the paid workforce has led to significant new statutory requirements over the past 25 years, such as pay equity and increased pregnancy and parental leave. Similarly, changes in technology have led to enhanced privacy protection laws while shifts within the economy and the nature of work have resulted in laws to better protect workers hired through temporary agencies.

As various employment laws are discussed in this book, consider the policy issue that the law is meant to address, the goal of the legislation, and then the extent to which the law has been, or probably will be, effective in achieving that goal.

FYI

How Ontario Obtained Pay Equity

The mid-1970s to the mid-1980s witnessed a dramatic increase in the number of women in the paid workforce. However, despite their increasing levels of education, working women found that they continued to earn considerably less money than working men. There was extensive public discussion and debate about this wage gap. Various lobbying groups, including many trade unions and organizations representing women, argued that existing laws ensuring "equal pay for equal work" were ineffective because men and women typically performed different jobs. The real problem was the historical undervaluation of "women's work." To remedy the situation, proponents of pay equity argued that Ontario needed "equal pay for work of equal value" legislation, requiring employers to evaluate totally different jobs within their organization and assess whether they were of equal "value."

Proponents of pay equity adopted an effective multi-pronged strategy, convincing the public through a media campaign and members of provincial Parliament (MPPs) through direct lobbying that such a change was desirable and necessary. In 1985, the Ontario government passed the *Pay Equity Act*, which requires Ontario employers with ten or more employees to provide equal pay for work of equal value. It is one of the most far-reaching pieces of legislation of its kind in the world. Pay equity is discussed more fully in Chapter 9.

FYI

Before There Were Employment Statutes ...
and Freedom of Contract Reigned Supreme

During the 19th and early 20th centuries, there were very few employment statutes; the relationship between an employer and employee was based almost entirely on the common law of contract. Under the common law, the parties were free to negotiate whatever terms of employment they could mutually agree on. But because typically an employee has much less bargaining power than an employer, in practice this freedom of contract usually meant that the employer was free to set the terms it wanted. The employer was also free to select or discriminate against anyone it chose. Moreover, when legal disputes between an employer and employee arose, courts saw their role as strictly one of interpreting the existing employment agreement, not as one of trying to achieve a fairer balance between the parties' interests.

Over time, governments became convinced that leaving the employment relationship entirely to labour market forces (supply and demand, with an individual's labour treated as a commodity) was unacceptable, and they intervened by passing laws in a broad range of areas. These included laws setting minimum employment standards; regulating workplace health and safety; prohibiting discrimination based on key grounds; and creating a labour relations system that established the right of employees to join a union so that they could bargain with the employer collectively.

Today, although the non-union employment relationship is still premised on the basic principles of the common law of contract, the relationship between employers and employees is a highly regulated one, with numerous statutes affecting that relationship.

SOURCE: Based on lecture notes by Professor David Doorey as part of his Employment Law 3420 course, 2009, York University, Toronto.

How Statutes and Regulations Are Made: The Legislative Process

A statute first takes the form of a written bill. To become a provincial statute a bill must pass three readings in the provincial legislature. To become a federal statute, a bill must pass three readings in the House of Commons and must also be passed by the Senate in Ottawa. The following description of the legislative process concerns provincial legislation because the provinces pass most laws related to employment.

There are three types of bills. Although the majority of bills of general application are public bills, there are two other kinds of bills: private bills and private members' bills.

1. *Public bills.* Public bills are introduced in the legislature by the Cabinet minister who is responsible for the relevant subject matter. For example, bills concerning employment law are typically put forward by the minister of labour. A bill may contain either proposed amendments to a current statute or an entirely new piece of legislation. First reading introduces the bill. On second reading, members of provincial Parliament debate the principles of the bill. If the bill passes second reading through a vote in the legislature, it goes to a committee of the legislature. Committees may hear witnesses and consider the bill clause by clause before reporting back to the legislature. Sometimes the bill is revised (amended) before its third and final reading to take into account input from the public or from opposition parties. After third reading, there is a vote in the legislature, and if a majority of MPPs vote in favour of the bill, it is passed.

2. *Private bills.* Private bills cover non-public matters, such as changing corporate charters, and so are of limited scope and relevance.
3. *Private members' bills.* Private members' bills may deal with matters of public importance, but they are put forward by a private member of the legislature, not by a Cabinet minister. Therefore, typically they do not have much chance of becoming law and are often tabled to stimulate public debate on an issue or to make a political point. They usually, but not always, "die on the order paper," which means that they don't become law.

A bill becomes a statute once it receives royal assent. A statute may come into force in one of three ways:

- on royal assent: the statute comes into force without the need for additional steps;
- on a particular date: the statute itself names the date on which it comes into force; or
- on proclamation: the statute comes into force on a date to be announced later. Different sections of the statute may come into force at different times. For example, when additional time is required to prepare the regulations necessary to implement certain provisions of the law, those provisions may be proclaimed at a later date or the date may be set out in the statute.

When you are reading a statute, make sure that you have the current version. Statutes can be amended extensively, and sometimes entire sections are repealed (deleted) or added. The Ontario Ministry of Labour's website (www.labour.gov.on.ca) and the Canadian Legal Information Institute (CanLII; www.canlii.org) are two good places to find the most up-to-date version of employment-related statutes and Canadian cases.

While statutes contain the main requirements of the law, detailed rules on how to implement or administer a statute are often found in its regulations. **Regulations** (also known as delegated legislation) are rules made under the authority of a statute. For example, Ontario's *Employment Standards Act, 2000* states that there is a minimum wage for most occupations in Ontario. However, the exact dollar amount of that minimum wage for various occupations is found in the regulations that accompany the Act.

Although regulations are as legally binding as the statute that enables them, they are not made by a legislature. They are made by government officials and published (for example, in Ontario in the *Ontario Gazette*) to ensure public awareness. Therefore, they are more easily made and amended than the actual statute itself.

Statutory Interpretation

Judges or members of administrative tribunals (adjudicators appointed pursuant to a statute) interpret legislation while adjudicating cases. They have developed a number of rules—such as the mischief rule—to help them. When using the mischief rule, they examine the problem or mischief that a statute was intended to correct and apply the corrective rationale to the issue. *Jantunen v. Ross* provides a good example of this approach to statutory interpretation.

Court Uses Mischief Rule to Interpret Statute

Jantunen v. Ross (1991), 85 DLR (4th) 461 (Ont. Div. Ct.)

Facts

Ross, a waiter, borrowed money from the Jantunens, the plaintiffs. He never paid it back. The plaintiffs sued for repayment and obtained a judgment in their favour. Under Ontario's *Wages Act*, the plaintiffs had the right to garnishee (seize) 20 percent of Ross's wages; the other 80 percent was exempt from garnishment. Because Ross earned minimum wage, tips constituted a large portion of his earnings. The plaintiffs argued that they should be able to garnishee his tips, without regard to the 20 percent limit, since tips were not wages paid by his employer and therefore were not covered by the *Wages Act*. Ross argued that he needed his tips to pay his living expenses.

Relevant Issue

Whether tips qualify as wages for the purposes of the *Wages Act*.

Decision

Although tips are not mentioned in the *Wages Act*, they qualify as wages and are therefore protected. The court interpreted the term "wages" in accordance with the "underlying intent and spirit" of the *Wages Act*—that is, to allow debtors to pay off creditors while still being able to support themselves. Since tips were a significant portion of Ross's earnings, garnishing them entirely would undermine Ross's ability to support himself. Thus, the court's decision to include tips in the definition of "wages" addressed the mischief that the legislation was aimed at.

Note that this decision only addresses whether tips are part of "wages" for the purposes of the *Wages Act*; for the purposes of the *Employment Standards Act*, and the prohibition in that statute against employers deducting money from wages except in very limited circumstances, the term "wages" does *not* include tips and other gratuities (French, 2013, p. 19).

Courts and tribunals also use "internal aids" found in the statute itself to assist in its interpretation. Sections of a statute that define important terms, or an introduction or preamble that explains a statute's purpose, can help the court in its interpretive role. For example, the broad preamble to Ontario's *Human Rights Code*, which includes as its aim "the creation of a climate of understanding and mutual respect for the dignity and worth of each person," has led to an expansive interpretation of the rights contained in that statute.

"External aids," such as legal dictionaries and scholarly articles, are also used in interpreting statutes.

What Levels of Government Can Pass Employment-Related Statutes?

Canada is a federal state with three levels of government: federal, provincial, and municipal. Municipalities have no jurisdiction over employment, although they can pass bylaws on matters that affect the workplace, such as smoking.

The federal government has authority over only about 10 percent of employees in Canada. This is because in 1925 the court ruled in *Toronto Electric Commissioners v. Snider* that the federal government's legislative authority was limited to industries of national importance, such as banks and interprovincial communications. As a result of this decision, approximately 90 percent of employees in Canada are covered by provincial employment legislation. For this reason, this text focuses primarily on provincial employment legislation (with particular emphasis on Ontario) rather than on federal employment laws.

Although employment laws in all the provinces are similar in principle, they vary in detail and should be referred to specifically when issues related to employees outside Ontario arise.

Key Ontario Employment Statutes

The following are the key employment statutes in Ontario:

- The *Employment Standards Act, 2000* sets out minimum rights and standards for employees, including minimum wages, overtime, hours of work, termination and severance pay, pregnancy and parental leave, vacation, and public holidays.
- The *Human Rights Code* is aimed at preventing and remedying discrimination and harassment based on specified prohibited grounds.
- The *Labour Relations Act, 1995* deals with the rights of employees to unionize and the collective bargaining process.
- The *Occupational Health and Safety Act* (OHSA) outlines the requirements and responsibilities of parties in creating a safe workplace and preventing workplace injuries and accidents.
- The *Workplace Safety and Insurance Act, 1997* (formerly the *Workers' Compensation Act*) provides a no-fault insurance plan to compensate workers for work-related injuries and diseases. It also allows employers to limit their financial exposure to the costs of workplace accidents through a collective funding system.
- The *Pay Equity Act* addresses the issue of gender discrimination in compensation. It requires employers with ten or more employees to provide equal pay for work of equal value.
- The *Accessibility for Ontarians with Disabilities Act, 2005* provides the legal basis for the development of accessibility standards in five key areas: customer service, information and communications, employment, transportation, and the built environment (design of public spaces).

FYI

Why Most Employees in Canada Are Governed by Provincial, and Not Federal, Employment Law

When Canada became a nation on July 1, 1867, its founding document, the *Constitution Act, 1867*, set out the division of powers between the federal and provincial governments. However, it made no specific reference to employment matters. In the 1920s, a federal employment law was challenged in the courts in *Toronto Electric Commissioners v. Snider* on the basis that the federal government did not have the constitutional authority to pass it. The court held that employment law fell within the provinces' jurisdiction over "property and civil rights." As a result, federal jurisdiction over employment law became limited to industries of national importance, such as national transportation and communication. Industries that are federally regulated include

- navigation and shipping,
- interprovincial communications and telephone companies,
- interprovincial buses and railways,
- airlines,
- television and radio stations,
- the post office,
- the armed forces,

- departments and agencies of the federal government,
- Crown corporations, and
- chartered banks.

All other employers are provincially regulated.

Whether a company is federally or provincially incorporated does not determine whether it is provincially or federally regulated. Nor does a company's location affect the source of its regulation. Banks are federally regulated, and therefore a bank in Ontario is governed by the same federal employment statutes as a bank in Saskatchewan. In contrast, a provincially regulated employer that operates businesses throughout Canada will have its Ontario employees covered by Ontario's employment laws and its Saskatchewan employees covered by Saskatchewan's employment laws.

All of these statutes, except for the *Labour Relations Act*, are covered in this text. The *Labour Relations Act* deals with unionized workplaces and thus is beyond the scope of this book. However, for organizations that are unionized or face the real possibility of unionization, an understanding of the law setting out how unions organize, of employee rights during an organizing drive, and of the collective bargaining process is of critical importance.

Several different laws may apply to a single situation. For example, an employee who is injured in the workplace and who wants to return to her pre-accident job may have remedies under both workers' compensation and human rights legislation against an employer who refuses to allow her to return. However, an employee may be required to choose which law she will proceed under. For example, the Human Rights Tribunal has the power to defer hearing an **application** where the fact situation is the subject matter of another proceeding. Moreover, the Tribunal may dismiss an application if it decides that the substance of the application has already been appropriately dealt with in another proceeding.

Federal Employment Statutes

As noted above, federal employment law covers employees who work for a federally regulated company, such as a bank or airline. The two main federal employment statutes are

- the *Canada Labour Code*, which covers employment standards, collective bargaining, and health and safety; and
- the *Canadian Human Rights Act*, which covers human rights and pay equity.

These statutes are similar in principle to their provincial counterparts, but there are some differences in the rights and protections granted. This text does not discuss these two statutes in detail because only 10 percent of employees in Canada are covered by them.

The following two federal statutes do not have provincial counterparts in Ontario. However, they are discussed in Chapters 9 and 10, respectively, because their concepts and requirements are relevant to provincially regulated employers:

- the *Employment Equity Act*, which requires affirmative action initiatives for visible minorities, women, people with disabilities, and Aboriginal people; and
- the *Personal Information Protection and Electronic Documents Act* (PIPEDA), which establishes rules concerning how organizations may collect, use, and disclose personal information. For federally regulated employers, this includes the personal information of clients, customers, suppliers, contractors, and employees. In Ontario, and in the other provinces where there is no provincial legislation comparable to PIPEDA, provincially regulated employers must follow PIPEDA with regard to the personal information of their clients, customers, suppliers, and contractors (that is, commercial relationships) but not for employees. For reasons relating to the constitutional division of powers, PIPEDA's requirements apply to the personal information of such employees only in narrow circumstances, such as where personal employee data are sold across provincial borders. In contrast, in Alberta, British Columbia, and Quebec, where there is comparable provincial legislation, employers must comply with their own province's, rather than PIPEDA's, privacy requirements for all groups, including employees.

The following federal laws apply to both federally and provincially regulated industries:

- the *Canada Pension Plan*, which provides qualifying employees with pension benefits on retirement and permanent disability; and
- the *Employment Insurance Act*, which provides qualifying employees with income replacement during periods of temporary unemployment.

Constitutional Law

The Canadian Charter of Rights and Freedoms

GUARANTEED RIGHTS AND FREEDOMS

One special statute that affects employment law in Canada is the *Canadian Charter of Rights and Freedoms*, which was adopted as part of the Constitution in 1982. Although the Charter does not address employment law specifically, it does set out guaranteed rights and freedoms that can affect the workplace whenever government action is involved. They include freedom of religion, association, and expression; democratic rights; mobility rights; legal rights; and equality rights.

As a constitutional document, the Charter is part of the "supreme law of the land." This means that other statutes must accord with its principles. If a court finds that any law violates one of the rights or freedoms listed in the Charter, it may strike down part or all of the law and direct the government to change or repeal it. Before the Charter, the only basis on which the courts could overturn a law passed by a legislative body was a lack of legislative authority on the part of that body. The Charter has therefore greatly expanded the courts' role in reviewing legislation. From an employment law perspective, the most important guarantee in the Charter is the equality rights provision in s. 15:

> 15(1) Every individual is equal before and under the law and has the right to the equal protection and equal benefit of the law without discrimination and, in particular, without discrimination based on race, national or ethnic origin, colour, religion, sex, age or mental or physical disability.
>
> (2) Subsection (1) does not preclude any law, program or activity that has as its object the amelioration of conditions of disadvantaged individuals or groups including those that are disadvantaged because of race, national or ethnic origin, colour, religion, sex, age or mental or physical disability.

Note that s. 15(1) includes the words "in particular" before the list of protected grounds. Consequently, these grounds have been found not to be an exhaustive list of groups protected under the section; as seen in the *Vriend v. Alberta* case below, courts will add analogous (or comparable) grounds to protect members of groups who are seen as being historically disadvantaged.

The equality rights set out in s. 15 go beyond conferring the right to "formal" equality—that is, the right to be treated the same as others. The Supreme Court of Canada has repeatedly stated that the goal is "substantive equality": in deciding if a law or government action is discriminatory it is the effect, not the intent, that matters. The test is whether the government has made a distinction that has the effect of perpetuating arbitrary disadvantage on someone because of his or her membership in an enumerated or analogous group. In short, if the government action "widens the gap between an historically disadvantaged group and the rest of society rather than narrowing it, then it is discriminatory" (*Quebec (Attorney General) v. A*).

In one of the leading decisions on s. 15, *Vriend v. Alberta*, the Supreme Court of Canada had to decide whether the failure of Alberta's human rights legislation to include sexual orientation as a prohibited ground of discrimination was itself an infringement of the Charter's equality rights guarantee. This decision also illustrates the difference between "substantive" and "formal" equality rights.

CASE IN POINT

Supreme Court of Canada Takes Expansive Approach to Equality Rights

Vriend v. Alberta, 1998 CanLII 816 (SCC), [1998] 1 SCR 493

Facts

Vriend was employed as a laboratory coordinator by a Christian college in Alberta where he consistently received positive evaluations and salary increases. However, shortly after he disclosed that he was gay, the college requested his resignation and, when he refused, he was terminated. His subsequent attempt to file a complaint with the Alberta Human Rights Commission was unsuccessful because the province's human rights legislation (the *Individual's Rights Protection Act* (IRPA)) did not include sexual orientation as a protected ground. Vriend filed a motion for declaratory relief that the

IRPA violated s. 15 of the Charter due to its failure to include this ground. The trial judge agreed, but on appeal that decision was overturned. Vriend successfully applied to have his case heard by the Supreme Court of Canada.

Relevant Issue

Whether the omission of sexual orientation as a prohibited ground of discrimination under Alberta's human rights legislation violated s. 15 of the Charter and was therefore unconstitutional.

Decision

The Supreme Court of Canada allowed Vriend's appeal, holding that "sexual orientation" should be "read into" Alberta's human rights law as a protected ground. In reaching this conclusion, the court rejected the Alberta government's formal equality argument that the IRPA was not discriminatory because it treated homosexuals and heterosexuals equally since neither one was protected from discrimination based on sexual orientation. The court noted that, looking at the social reality of discrimination against gays and lesbians, the omission of sexual orientation from the human rights statute clearly was far more likely to impact homosexual persons negatively than heterosexual persons. As a result, gays and lesbians were denied "the right to the equal protection and equal benefit of the law" as guaranteed by s. 15(1), on the basis of a personal characteristic that was analogous to those grounds enumerated in the provision.

In *Vriend* the Supreme Court actually "read in" to a human rights law a category of people (based on sexual orientation) that a provincial legislature had previously excluded. In taking this activist approach, the court commented that "[t]he denial by legislative omission of protection to individuals who may well be in need of it is just as serious and the consequences just as grave as that resulting from explicit exclusion."

While the *Vriend* decision involved the courts "reading in" words to a statute, most successful challenges based on s. 15 equality rights result in the courts striking down (nullifying) parts of legislation. One example is the Supreme Court of Canada's decision in *M. v. H.* Although the facts of *M. v. H.* had nothing to do with the workplace, the case has had a significant impact on employment law. As a result of this ruling, the Ontario and federal governments were forced to change the definition of "spouse" to include same-sex partners in many pieces of legislation, including employment-related statutes. Same-sex partnership status was added as a prohibited ground of discrimination under Ontario's *Human Rights Code* in 1999, although it was later removed after same-sex marriage became legal in Ontario and it was therefore no longer required as a separate ground.

CASE IN POINT

Definition of "Spouse" in Family Law Act Violates Section 15 Charter Rights

M. v. H., [1999] 2 SCR 3

Facts

Two lesbian women, M and H, lived in a spousal relationship for several years. When they separated, M sought support payments based on the role she had played in managing the home and assisting H with business entertaining during their years together. The Ontario *Family Law Act* provided that a spouse is entitled to support payments when a relationship ends. However, the definition of "spouse" was limited to married or cohabiting heterosexual couples.

Relevant Issue

Whether the *Family Law Act*'s definition of "spouse" contravened M's equality rights under s. 15 of the Charter.

Decision

The Supreme Court of Canada held that the definition of "spouse" discriminated against same-sex partners and violated their equality rights. The purpose of the *Family Law Act* was to provide financial support for spouses whose relationships broke down, and excluding same-sex partners was contrary to the purpose of the law.

IMPACT OF THE CHARTER ON PRIVATE SECTOR EMPLOYERS

The Charter directly applies only to government actions and conduct, such as passing legislation, or where the employer is itself part of the public sector. It does not apply to the actions of individuals or private sector employers and employees. It is essentially a restraint on government power. Therefore, an employee cannot use the Charter directly to challenge a private sector employer's employment decision or policy. However, an employee may be able to achieve the same result if the employer's decision or policy is based on, or allowed by, legislation (that is, government action) that is found to contravene the Charter. For example, in *Ontario Nurses' Association v. Mount Sinai Hospital*, a disabled employee whose employer relied on a statutory exemption to refuse to pay her severance pay under the *Employment Standards Act* (now the *Employment Standards Act, 2000*) used the Charter to successfully challenge that exemption.

CASE IN POINT

Disabled Employee Challenges Denial of Statutory Severance Pay

Ontario Nurses' Association v. Mount Sinai Hospital, 2005 CanLII 14437 (Ont. CA)

Facts

Christine Tilley was hired as a nurse in the neonatal intensive care unit at Mount Sinai Hospital in 1985. Ten years later she seriously injured her knee in a waterskiing accident. Because of subsequent complications, including depression, she was unable to return to work and in 1998 the hospital terminated her employment on the ground of innocent absenteeism. The employer refused to pay Tilley statutory severance pay under the *Employment Standards Act* (ESA) because the Act contained an exception for employees whose ability to remain on the job has been "frustrated" (made impossible) as a result of an illness or injury. Tilley challenged this refusal, arguing that the exception violated her s. 15 equality rights under the Charter. The employer countered that the legislation was not discriminatory because the main purpose of statutory severance pay is prospective—to compensate employees as they move on to find new employment. It contended that employees whose employment has become frustrated because of severe injury or illness are unlikely to return to the workforce, and therefore it is not discriminatory to deny them this form of compensation.

Relevant Issue

Whether s. 58(5)(c) of the *Employment Standards Act*, which creates an exception to an employer's obligation to pay severance pay to employees whose contracts of employment have been frustrated because of illness or injury, contravenes s. 15 of the Charter.

Decision

The Ontario Court of Appeal found that the denial of ESA severance pay to employees whose contracts have been frustrated because of illness or injury violated the Charter's equality rights provision. The court held that even if it accepted the employer's argument that the dominant purpose of severance pay is prospective—to compensate those employees who will return to the workforce—this exception still contravenes s. 15. This is because differential treatment based on disability is premised on the inaccurate stereotype that people with severe and prolonged disabilities will not return to the workforce. The court concluded that this stereotype "can only have the effect of perpetuating and even promoting the view that disabled individuals are less capable and less worthy of recognition and value as human beings and as members of Canadian society."

As a result, s. 58(5)(c) of the ESA was struck down and Tilley was entitled to statutory severance pay.

As a result of this decision, the Ontario government amended the ESA to allow employees whose employment is frustrated because of disability to receive both severance pay and pay in lieu of notice. These changes affect all employees, regardless of whether their employer is in the public or the private sector. For two other examples of Charter challenges to employment-related legislation, see the In the News box below.

SECTION 1: CHARTER RIGHTS SUBJECT TO REASONABLE LIMITS

The rights and freedoms guaranteed by the Charter are not unlimited. The courts may uphold violations of Charter rights if they fall within the provisions of s. 1 of the Charter:

> The *Canadian Charter of Rights and Freedoms* guarantees the rights and freedoms set out in it subject *only to such reasonable limits prescribed by law as can be demonstrably justified in a free and democratic society* [emphasis added].

In the watershed case of *R v. Oakes*, the Supreme Court of Canada set out a two-part test (that is, an "ends" and a "means" part) for determining when a law that limits a Charter right is a reasonable limit and therefore saved by s. 1. A limitation of Charter rights is justifiable if

FYI

In *R v. Oakes*, a criminal case, the "R" is an abbreviation of Regina, meaning the Queen or Crown.

1. the law relates to a pressing and substantial government objective (the "ends" part of the test); and
2. the means chosen to achieve the objective are "proportional" in that:
   a. they are rationally connected to the objective;
   b. they impair the Charter right or freedom as little as possible (minimal impairment); and
   c. the benefits of the limit outweigh its harmful effects—in other words, the more severe the harmful effects of a measure, the more important the objective must be to justify it (the "means" part of the test).

Unless a law passes both parts of the *Oakes* test, the portion of the law that violates the Charter will be found to be unconstitutional. The burden of proof is on the party (that is, the government) arguing that the infringement is justified.

For example, in the *Ontario Nurses' Association* decision discussed above, the employer argued that even if the ESA's exemption that denied statutory severance pay to disabled employees whose contracts of employment have been frustrated contravened s. 15 of the Charter, it was saved by s. 1. In the employer's view, it was a reasonable and justifiable limit because the government is entitled to balance the interests of employers and employees by limiting the availability of severance pay. However, the court rejected this argument. First, it held that this objective was not sufficiently compelling to override the right of disabled persons to equal treatment in employment. Second, it found that there was no rational connection between the objective of granting severance pay to those employees who will rejoin the workforce and the law denying severance pay to employees whose contracts have been frustrated because of illness or injury.

IN THE NEWS

Charter Challenges to Employment Laws

In a unanimous decision, the Supreme Court of Canada decided that workers' compensation legislation in Nova Scotia infringed the Charter's equality rights by limiting benefits for chronic pain. The legislation provided sufferers of chronic pain with a treatment program that lasted only four weeks, after which time benefits were stopped. The court found that this differential treatment, based on the nature of the disability, was discrimination on an enumerated ground (disability) because it dealt with chronic pain differently from other injuries. The Supreme Court's declaration of invalidity was postponed for six months from the date of judgment, to allow the Nova Scotia legislature an opportunity to change the law. (See *Nova* *Scotia (Workers' Compensation Board) v. Martin; Nova Scotia (Workers' Compensation Board) v. Laseur*, 2003 SCC 54, [2003] 2 SCR 504.)

In 2002 the United Food and Commercial Workers Union launched a legal challenge to the exclusion of agricultural workers from coverage by Ontario's health and safety legislation. It claimed that this exclusion infringes the equality provisions of the Charter because it denies rights to farm workers that are available to almost every other worker in Ontario. A regulation extending OHSA coverage to farming operations took effect on June 30, 2006. It appears that this change in the government's position was a direct result of the Charter challenge.

In contrast, in the 1990 decision of *McKinney v. University of Guelph*, the Supreme Court of Canada found that an otherwise discriminatory provision was saved by s. 1 of the Charter. In that case, several university professors challenged the constitutionality of Ontario's *Human Rights Code* because (at that time) it failed to prohibit age-based discrimination in employment after age 64. They argued that this contravened the Charter's equality rights provision. The Supreme Court found that, although allowing mandatory retirement policies violated the equality rights section of the Charter, such policies served a legitimate social interest—including opening up teaching positions—and were therefore a reasonable limit to those rights under s. 1.

SECTION 33: THE NOTWITHSTANDING CLAUSE

A second potential limit on the Charter's rights and freedoms is found in s. 33, the override provision. Section 33 allows the federal or provincial governments to enact legislation "notwithstanding" (in spite of) a violation of the Charter. To invoke s. 33, the government must declare that the law in question will operate notwithstanding the Charter, and this declaration must be renewed every five years. This section has rarely been invoked because few governments want to admit to knowingly infringing Charter rights. One of its rare uses occurred when the Quebec government passed a law requiring signs to be in French only and invoked s. 33 to avoid a Charter challenge in the courts.

Common Law

What Is the Common Law?

The third source of employment law is the common law, which is that part of the law that has developed over the years through court decisions. The common law is applied where there is no statute covering a particular area or where a governing statute is silent on a relevant point. For example, because most employment-related statutes define the term "employee" in general terms, judges and tribunals often look to previous **case law** to determine when an employment relationship exists and whether an individual is entitled to the statutory protections afforded employees. (See under the heading "Defining the Employment Relationship" in this chapter for a further discussion of this topic.)

You can think of the sources of employment law as forming a pyramid, with the Constitution (including the Charter) at the top, because all statutes must conform with it. Regular statutes are in the middle. Common law is at the bottom since statute law takes precedence over judge-made law. Figure 1.1 illustrates this hierarchy.

Within the bottom tier, law formulated by the Supreme Court of Canada is the most significant, followed (in Ontario) by law formulated by the Ontario Court of Appeal, then the Ontario Superior Court of Justice and the Ontario Court of Justice. More detail about Canadian courts is provided below under the heading "Judicial Framework."

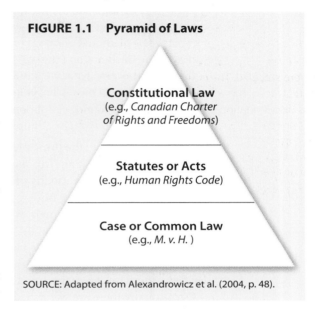

FIGURE 1.1   Pyramid of Laws

Constitutional Law
(e.g., *Canadian Charter of Rights and Freedoms*)

Statutes or Acts
(e.g., *Human Rights Code*)

Case or Common Law
(e.g., *M. v. H.*)

SOURCE: Adapted from Alexandrowicz et al. (2004, p. 48).

Common Law Rules of Decision Making

English-speaking Canada inherited the common law system from the British legal system, where it evolved over centuries.

To understand how the common law is applied, it is important to understand several principles of judicial decision making. Under the common law, cases are decided by judges on the basis of **precedent**—that is, what previous courts have decided in cases involving similar circumstances and principles. Decisions made by higher courts are **binding** on lower courts in the same jurisdiction if the circumstances of the cases are similar. This principle is called *stare decisis*, which means "to stand by things decided." A decision is considered **persuasive**, rather than binding, when a court is persuaded to follow a precedent from another jurisdiction or from a lower court, although it is not bound to do so.

In considering the weight to be given to previous cases, recent decisions tend to have more authority than older ones, and higher courts have more authority than lower ones.

Where a lower court decides not to follow a previous decision from a higher court in the same jurisdiction, it may do so on the basis that the earlier case is **distinguishable**. In other words, it finds that the facts, or other elements in the previous case, are so different from those of the current case that the legal principle in the previous decision should not apply.

FYI

Where the "Common Law" Comes From

In the 12th century, King Henry II of England tried to bring greater consistency and fairness to the justice system. He trained a group of circuit judges who went from place to place and held assizes, or travelling courts, to hear local cases. Over time, these judges noted similarities in certain types of cases that allowed for similar judgments to be made and penalties to be assigned. At some point they began to write down their decisions and the reasons for them, so that other judges could consult them. This became what we know today as case law or common law, because it allowed the law to be applied in a common fashion throughout the country (Alexandrowicz et al., 2004, p. 42).

Generally speaking, the principle of *stare decisis* promotes predictability and consistency in decision making. This means that when a legal issue arises, a lawyer knowledgeable in the field can usually predict the outcome (or range of outcomes) of the case based on the existing body of case law. However, consistency is not always achieved. For example, seemingly minor factual differences may lead to different legal results. Where, in a court's view, the application of case law would lead to an inappropriate result, the court may try to circumvent legal precedent, thus leading to apparent inconsistencies. When decisions are appealed to higher courts, the law may be clarified; otherwise, it remains unsettled until a similar case reaches an appellate court.

Occasionally there are watershed cases where a high court decides to expand the boundaries of previous rulings or to depart entirely from a line of cases because, for example, it believes the cases no longer reflect social norms or economic realities. On occasion, a higher-level court may even decide to establish an entirely new **cause of action**. The FYI entitled "Ontario Court of Appeal Creates New Tort" discusses a case in which Ontario's appeal court explicitly recognized a new legal claim for "intrusion upon seclusion." (The legal concept of a "tort" is discussed later in this chapter.)

FYI

Ontario Court of Appeal Creates New Tort

In pre-digital times, privacy was much less of a pressing issue than it is today. In fact, until recently the common law did not recognize "invasion of privacy" as the basis for a distinct legal claim. This changed, however, in 2012 when the Court of Appeal awarded Sandra Jones $10,000 in damages against a fellow bank employee who inappropriately accessed her personal banking records at least 174 times over a five-year period. In creating this new common law claim for "intrusion upon seclusion," the court stated that recognition of such a cause of action amounts to "an incremental step that is consistent with the role of this court to develop the common law in a manner consistent with the changing needs of society." (*Jones v. Tsige*, 2012 ONCA 32.)

Changes in the composition of higher courts through the appointment of new judges may also lead to changes in the direction of case law.

Branches of the Common Law That Affect Employment

Two branches of the common law that affect employment are contract law and tort law.

CONTRACT LAW

The common law of contracts is fundamental to employment law because the legal relationship between an employer and a non-unionized employee is contractual. An employer and a prospective employee negotiate the terms and conditions of employment, and subject to legislative requirements, their agreement forms the basis of their employment relationship. General principles of **contract law** determine whether an employee–employer relationship exists and what remedies apply to a breach of the employment agreement.

One contract principle that has a significant impact on employment law in Canada relates to dismissal. All employment contracts, whether written or oral (unless the parties expressly agree otherwise), contain an implied term that an employee is entitled to reasonable notice of dismissal, or pay in lieu of notice, unless the dismissal is for **just cause** (very serious misconduct). In other words, the employer must provide advance notice of dismissal or pay instead of notice. Economic necessity does not relieve the employer of this obligation; employees who are laid off because of a shortage of work are entitled to reasonable notice or pay in lieu as well. This implied contractual term affects the Canadian approach to the entire non-union employment relationship, including hiring, using written employment contracts, and managing job performance (Gilbert et al., 2000, p. 15). It can be contrasted to the American approach, where in many states employees are employed "at will," meaning that employment can be terminated without notice or cause.

In a successful lawsuit based in contract, **damages** in the form of monetary compensation are awarded so that the **plaintiff** (the party suing) is placed in the same position that she would have been in if the **defendant** (the party being sued) had not breached the contract. In a wrongful dismissal action, for example, damages are awarded to reflect the wages and benefits the plaintiff would have received had the employer provided reasonable notice of the termination.

TORT LAW

A tort is a wrong for which there is a legal remedy. **Tort law** is a branch of **civil law** (non-criminal law), and covers wrongs and damages that one person or company causes to another, independent of any contractual relationship between them. A tort can be either a deliberate or a negligent action. To establish a negligent tort, the plaintiff must show that (1) the defendant owed the plaintiff a **duty of care**, (2) the defendant breached that duty, and (3) the plaintiff suffered foreseeable damages as a result.

An intentional tort is committed, for example, when an employer deliberately provides an unfair and inaccurate employment reference for a former employee. In this case, the former employee can sue the employer for committing the tort of defamation. A negligent tort occurs, for example, when an employer carelessly misleads a prospective employee about the job during the hiring process, and the employee suffers losses as a result of relying on the misrepresentation.

In a successful tort action, damages are awarded to the plaintiff for losses suffered as a result of the defendant's conduct. In the negligent misrepresentation situation, damages can be awarded to compensate the plaintiff for the costs of relocation (including losses on real estate) if the new job involves moving to a different city, the costs of a job search, and the emotional costs of distress.

Judicial Framework

The Court System

The court structure in Canada is hierarchical, as indicated in Figure 1.2. There are various levels of courts, the lowest being provincial courts and the highest being the Supreme Court of Canada. Parties who dislike the decision they receive in a lower court may appeal that decision under certain circumstances. The appeal system assists in the creation of consistent laws because a higher court may overturn the decision of a lower court that has failed to follow precedent.

FIGURE 1.2   The Structure of Federal and Ontario Courts

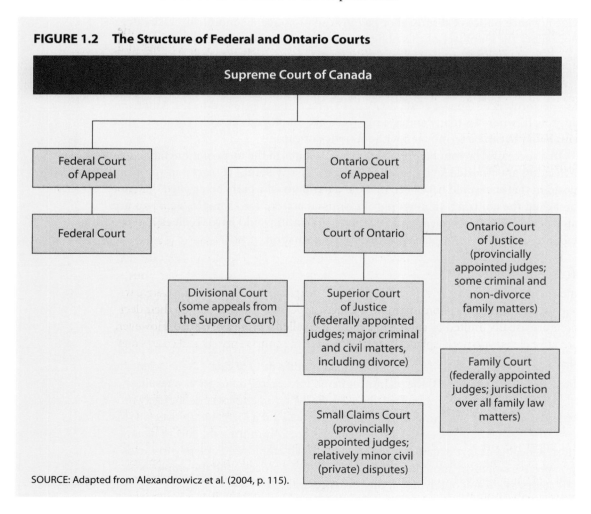

SOURCE: Adapted from Alexandrowicz et al. (2004, p. 115).

The Supreme Court of Canada

Located in Ottawa, the Supreme Court of Canada is the final court of appeal. It hears cases from the various provincial court systems, the Federal Court of Appeal, and the Court Martial Appeal Court. However, it hears appeals only if it has granted leave to appeal. Because of its heavy workload, it grants leave to appeal only when a case is of general public importance or where the law requires clarification. Decisions of the Supreme Court of Canada bind all lower courts across Canada.

Other Courts

Each province has a court of appeal that hears appeals from decisions of the provincial superior courts. In Ontario, for example, it is called the Ontario Court of Appeal. Ontario's superior court consists of two divisions: the Superior Court of Justice (formerly the Ontario Court—General Division) and the Ontario Court of Justice (formerly the Ontario Court—Provincial Division). The Superior Court is the primary trial court in civil and most criminal matters and generally hears cases involving claims that exceed $25,000.

Each province also maintains courts of special jurisdiction. These courts preside over matters such as small claims, family law, juvenile offences, traffic violations, and trials of less serious criminal offences (Gilbert et al., 2000, p. 11).

In Canada, judges are not elected. They are appointed by the federal or provincial government, depending on the level of court.

The Administrative System

Administrative Tribunals

Administrative tribunals have been established to make decisions in specialized areas, such as employment standards or discrimination. In employment law, administrative tribunals have primary jurisdiction over most matters. The main exception is the common law of wrongful dismissal, where disputes are heard in the traditional court system.

Tribunals act in a quasi-judicial manner, meaning that they observe the rules of procedural fairness and provide a full hearing, but they are less formal than courts, and their members are experts in employment matters. Although administrative tribunals are technically subordinate to the courts, appeals to the courts from their decisions are usually limited by statute in a provision called a **privative clause**. However, privative clauses do not displace the jurisdiction of the courts entirely and courts may also overturn a tribunal's decision if it exceeded its jurisdiction, showed bias, or denied a party natural justice (Gilbert et al., 2000, pp. 11–12).

A request to a court to review the decision of an administrative tribunal is called an application for **judicial review**. In Ontario it is the Divisional Court, a special branch of the Superior Court of Justice, that reviews the decisions of administrative tribunals. The court will overturn a decision based on questions of fact or applying the facts to the law only if the decision was "unreasonable" (not simply incorrect). As the Supreme Court of Canada stated in *Dunsmuir v. New Brunswick*, a decision will be found to be unreasonable only if it falls outside "a range of possible, acceptable outcomes which are defensible in respect of the facts and law." In other words, the reviewing court does not have to agree with the tribunal's decision as long as it is justifiable and supported with reasoning. This is a very deferential **standard of review** that recognizes the experience and expertise of specialized administrative bodies and the authority conferred on them by the legislature. However, for those relatively few cases that turn on a question of law that is outside the tribunal's area of expertise, such as constitutional law, reviewing courts will apply the "correctness" standard. This means that the court will substitute its own view if it does not agree with the tribunal's result.

Because most decisions of employment-related administrative tribunals attract the "reasonableness" standard of review, significant judicial deference is given to these tribunals' decisions.

More information concerning specific administrative processes and tribunals can be found in the chapters of this book dealing with particular employment-related statutes.

Administrative Agencies

Below tribunals in the administrative hierarchy, there are usually **administrative agencies** empowered to investigate complaints, make rulings, and sometimes issue orders. These agencies, or commissions, usually issue policy guidelines and have an educational role in furthering the goals of a statute. For example, the Ontario Human Rights Commission plays a key role in educating the public about human rights issues.

Individual employees may gain access to an administrative agency at no monetary cost to themselves; once a claim is initiated, the agency pursues the claim on behalf of the employee. An agency may have an internal appeal procedure, usually with the possibility of a further appeal to a board or tribunal (Gilbert et al., 2000, p. 12). For example, there is an internal appeal procedure within the Ontario Workplace Safety and Insurance Board.

FYI

Solicitor–Client Privilege

Solicitor–client privilege refers to the right to have communications between a lawyer and her client kept confidential. The purpose of this privilege is to promote open communications by ensuring that an individual can seek legal advice without being concerned that the information exchanged will have to be disclosed later to a third party, be it the opposing party, or an adjudicative body. However, solicitor–client privilege does not automatically apply to all communications between lawyer and client. For it to apply, four conditions must be met:

1. The communication must be *between* a lawyer and her client (for example, merely copying a lawyer on a communication to another party will not be enough unless the client and the lawyer have both specifically agreed the

lawyer will be copied on all relevant communications for the purpose of receiving legal advice on the file).

2. The communication must be connected to obtaining *legal* advice (as opposed to business or non-legal advice). Adjudicators will also look at the dominant purpose for which the lawyer is retained. In one case, an arbitrator ordered disclosure of a lawyer's investigation report into allegations of bullying and harassment on the basis that the lawyer was retained to conduct the investigation and make findings of fact, not to provide legal advice. (*North Bay General Hospital v. Ontario Nurses' Association*, 2011 CanLII 68580 (Ont. LA).)

3. The communication must be confidential (for example, the requirement to show an intention to maintain confidentiality may be undermined where communications are forwarded or copied to individuals beyond those directly involved in the decision-making process on the file).

4. There must have been no waiver of confidentiality. Waiver may be voluntary, such as where a client decides to rely on a privileged communication as part of her claim or defence, or it may be involuntary. Involuntary communication includes inadvertently sending an email or text to someone who should not have received it. In that case, a court or arbitrator will look at factors such as how many of these communications were accidentally sent, whether the client immediately tried to retrieve them, and whether preserving solicitor–client privilege in the circumstances would be unfair to the opposing party.

Given the importance of preserving solicitor–client privilege and the challenges of doing so in an era of electronic messaging, you should keep in mind the following:

- Where a lawyer is retained as part of an investigation into workplace misconduct, the retainer agreement should clearly indicate that its dominant purpose is to provide legal advice and that any investigating done by the lawyer is only for the purpose of determining facts as part of providing that advice. A legal opinion letter, based on that investigation, should be provided by the lawyer (Emond Harnden, 2012).

- Only send, copy, or forward messages to those individuals for whom it is reasonably necessary.

- Make sure those individuals are aware that the information is confidential. Prominently indicate this with a statement such as "Privileged and Confidential—Solicitor & Client Communication." This statement is not a guarantee of privilege but it will indicate your intention.

- State clearly on every communication that the communication must not be forwarded.

- Confirm to whom you are sending the communication—one last time—before hitting the "Send" button (Sherrard Kuzz LLP, 2011).

Decision-Making Processes Under Ontario's Employment Statutes

Figure 1.3 sets out the decision-making processes for appeals and requests for judicial review under Ontario's employment-related statutes.

FIGURE 1.3　Decision-Making Processes Under Ontario's Employment Statutes

Statute	Initial decision	Appeal	Judicial review
Employment Standards Act, 2000	Employment standards officer, Ministry of Labour	Hearing before the Ontario Labour Relations Board (OLRB)	Limited right to Divisional Court
Human Rights Code	Human Rights Tribunal	Divisional Court on questions of law and fact	See Appeal (previous column)
Labour Relations Act, 1995	Ontario Labour Relations Board (OLRB)	Discretionary reconsideration by OLRB	Limited right to Divisional Court
Occupational Health and Safety Act	For routine inspections and investigations of accidents: Ontario health and safety inspector, Ministry of Labour; for reprisals for work refusals: OLRB	OLRB (although occupational health and safety offences involving injuries and deaths are litigated in the courts)	Limited right to Divisional Court
Pay Equity Act	Review services officer or Pay Equity Commission	Pay Equity Hearings Tribunal	Limited right to Divisional Court
Workplace Safety and Insurance Act	Claims adjudicator of Workplace Safety and Insurance Board (WSIB)	Hearings officer of WSIB and externally to Workplace Safety and Insurance Appeals Tribunal (WSIAT)	Limited right to Divisional Court

SOURCE: Compiled in part from information contained in Gilbert et al. (2000, pp. 394–397).

Where to Find Employment Laws

Common Law

Court decisions are found in a number of case reporters—national, regional, provincial, and topical. These are periodical publications containing judges' written decisions. Because it is expensive to purchase case reporters, the Internet is now used more frequently to conduct legal research (Alexandrowicz et al., 2004, pp. 62–63).

Discussions of case law can be found in encyclopedic digests, textbooks, loose-leaf reporting series, and newsletters.

Reading and interpreting case citations is an important skill for researching legal cases. A **case citation** tells you how to locate a specific case. It sets out the style of cause (case title), year, volume number of the case reporter, series number (where applicable), page number, and court. Consider the following style of cause:

McKinney v. University of Guelph, [1990] 3 SCR 229.

- *McKinney v. University of Guelph*. McKinney is the plaintiff, and the University of Guelph is the defendant. In an appeal case, the first party named is the

appellant (the party requesting the appeal), and the party named after the "v." (versus) is the **respondent** (the party opposing the appeal).

- [1990]. Square brackets indicate the year that the case reporter volume was published. Sometimes parentheses are used in case citations to indicate the year in which a case was decided.
- 3 SCR. This refers to the case reporter volume and name. It indicates that the case can be found in the third volume of the 1990 Supreme Court Reports.
- 229. This is the page number.

In the example above, the court is indicated in the name of the case reporter, Supreme Court Reports. Where the name of the court is not contained in the case reporter's name, an abbreviation of the court's name appears in parentheses at the end of the citation. For example, the citation for *Jantunen v. Ross* (1991), 85 DLR (4th) 461 (Ont. Div. Ct.) indicates that the case was heard by the Ontario Divisional Court. Note also that "(4th)" indicates that this is the fourth series of the case reporter.

A case may be published in several different reports, so you may see several alternate citations.

Many Canadian courts have adopted a new method of citing judicial decisions. Since 2001, cases are assigned a neutral citation, which gives a unique identifier but does not refer to any case reporter. This neutral citation standard has three main parts: the traditional style of cause; the core of the citation, containing the year of the decision, a court or tribunal identifier, and a number assigned to the decision; and possible optional elements, such as paragraph numbers or notes. Consider the following example:

Starson v. Swayze, 2003 SCC 32.

In this example, "*Starson v. Swayze*" is the style of cause, "2003" is the year the decision was rendered, "SCC" (Supreme Court of Canada) is the court identifier, and "32" is the number of the decision. The numbering sequence usually restarts each January 1. Neutral citations are very helpful when conducting searches through online service providers such as CanLII (Brian Dickson Law Library, 2014).

Statute Law

The federal and provincial governments each publish their statutes and regulations. These can be purchased from the Queen's Printer and found in most public libraries and on the Internet.

Three useful Internet search sites are:

1. The Canadian Legal Information Institute
   - www.canlii.org
     CanLII is a good source for federal and provincial statutes and cases. The site is run by the Federation of Law Societies of Canada, which is the umbrella organization of Canada's 14 law societies. (For example, to locate a provincial statute or regulation, choose the desired province under Browse, and then "Statutes and Regulations" under Legislation.)

2. e-Laws
   - www.e-laws.gov.on.ca
     e-Laws is a good source for Ontario statutes and regulations. The site is run by the Ontario government.
3. Justice Laws Website
   - http://laws.justice.gc.ca
     This Department of Justice Canada website is a good source for Canadian federal statutes and regulations.

Staying Current

It is important to keep abreast of changes in the law. Newsworthy cases are often reported in newspaper articles, but you need legally focused sources as well, such as law firm newsletters, industry association publications, and employment reporting services. One example of a reporting service on employment law is *Canadian Employment Law Today*, published by Thomson Reuters Canada.

Defining the Employment Relationship

Before discussing particular employment laws, one threshold question must be addressed: when is an individual who is hired to perform work actually an "employee"? As noted above, for this question we look primarily to common law cases, rather than statute law, for the answer.

Independent Contractors Versus Employees

Although an employee–employer relationship is the most common one when someone is hired to perform work, it is not the only possibility. Sometimes the organization hiring an individual decides that an independent contractor–principal relationship is better suited to its needs than a traditional employee–employer relationship.

In contrast to an employee, an **independent contractor** is a self-employed worker engaged by a **principal** to perform specific work. In some cases the distinction between an independent contractor and an employee is obvious. For example, if a homeowner hires an individual to paint his house, he is not hiring that person as an employee but rather as a self-employed contractor. However, there are other situations where it is much more difficult to make the distinction. For example, is a delivery driver who owns his own truck but delivers for only one business an employee of that business or an independent contractor? Despite the difficulty in some cases of distinguishing an employee–employer relationship from one of independent contractor–principal, the two relationships are treated very differently in law.

The hallmarks of an independent contractor–principal relationship are discussed below. Also examined are the numerous legal pitfalls that the parties may encounter if they do not identify their relationship accurately. The legal rights and responsibilities of the parties depend on the nature of their relationship: a worker is not an independent contractor simply because the parties intend it to be so.

Indeed, there is always a risk that a relationship characterized by the parties as an independent contractor–principal relationship will be found to be an employee–employer relationship by a court or tribunal.

What Are the Advantages of an Independent Contractor–Principal Relationship?

There is an increasing trend for organizations to hire individuals as independent contractors rather than as employees. Many organizations like the fact that this relationship presents fewer ongoing legal obligations, less paperwork, and less expense than the employee–employer relationship. Reducing the "head count" is also a goal of many larger organizations.

Consider the following obligations that employers have to employees but not to independent contractors:

1. *Providing statutory benefits*, such as vacations and overtime pay, and protections, such as pregnancy and parental leave, for employees. Independent contractors generally are not entitled to employee statutory benefits. The terms of their contract determine their entitlement to benefits.

2. *Paying premiums for workplace health and safety insurance.* Independent contractors must arrange their own coverage.

3. *Providing reasonable notice of termination or pay in lieu* (unless the employment contract states otherwise). Independent contractors are entitled to notice of termination only if their contract so provides. There is no implied right to reasonable notice. (It should be noted that courts now recognize an intermediate category of worker, referred to as a "dependent contractor." Dependent contractors, while not employees, are entitled to receive reasonable notice of termination by virtue of having worked exclusively (or almost exclusively) and for a long period for a single organization. Courts have decided that their financial dependence on that single organization creates the duty to provide reasonable notice (*McKee v. Reid's Heritage Homes Ltd.*; *Marbry Distributors Ltd. v. Avrecan Int. Inc.*).)

4. *Remitting appropriate health and income taxes, and contributing to and remitting Canada Pension Plan and employment insurance premiums.* Independent contractors remit their own statutory deductions and taxes. This reduces both costs and paperwork for the hiring organization. Also, the organization does not have to pay the "employer's" portion of CPP and EI premiums for independent contractors.

5. *Assuming liability for an employee's deliberate or negligent acts during the course of employment.* In contrast, independent contractors are generally liable to both the third-party victim and the hiring organization for misconduct or negligence while on the job (Levitt, 2002, pp. 1–23).

The individual being hired may also prefer independent contractor status over that of employee. There are tax benefits available to the self-employed: deducting expenses against income, no withholding of income tax at source, and fewer statutory deductions (such as employment insurance premiums). Independent contractors also have greater flexibility in working for organizations other than the principal.

Why Is the Independent Contractor–Principal Designation Challenged?

If both parties agree that they want to create an independent contractor–principal relationship, how does the nature of their relationship become a legal issue? The parties' initial characterization may be challenged before a court or tribunal in several ways. A government agency may question the parties' characterization because it thinks that statutory premiums for such programs as employment insurance, workplace safety and insurance, and the Canada Pension Plan should have been remitted. An individual initially designated as an independent contractor may subsequently wish to claim statutory benefits or protections that depend on employee status, such as employment insurance benefits, workplace safety and insurance coverage, or employment standards benefits. This issue may also arise when an individual is terminated and seeks wrongful dismissal damages. Only in an employment relationship (or as a "dependent contractor," as discussed above) do courts find an implied duty to provide reasonable notice of termination or pay in lieu of notice.

What Happens if a Tribunal Finds an Employee–Employer Relationship?

If a court or tribunal finds that the parties created an employment relationship, the "employer" may have to remit thousands of dollars to various government agencies for outstanding statutory premiums (potentially including those owed by the "employee"). It may also have to pay the individual significant amounts of money for employment standards benefits, such as vacation and overtime premium pay or wrongful dismissal damages. At the same time, the individual will be liable for outstanding statutory premiums and income tax not deducted at source.

What Tests Establish an Employee–Employer Relationship?

As noted above, although several employment-related statutes contain a definition of "employee," the definitions are so brief that courts and tribunals fall back on the common law tests for distinguishing between an employee–employer and an independent contractor–principal relationship. The fundamental issue is whether the individual is an independent entrepreneur in business for herself or under the control and direction of the employer. The following tests have evolved under the common law to distinguish between an employee and an independent contractor. No single fact determines the matter; the facts of the case are assessed as a whole.

1. *Control test.* Does the organization control the individual's work, including where, when, and how it is performed? Is the individual free to hire others to perform the work or to have many clients? Does the individual report to the organization during the workday? If the individual does not have autonomy, and day-to-day control over the work is maintained by the organization, the individual is probably an employee.

2. *Risk test.* Does the individual have any expectation of profit (other than fixed commissions) or bear any risk of financial loss? For example, does the individual face the risk of not receiving payment for services performed? If not, that person is more likely to be considered an employee.

3. *Organization or integration test.* Are the services rendered by the individual an integral part of the business? For example, an individual who writes a manufacturing company's newsletter is less likely to be an employee than a tool and die maker whose duties are central to the company's operations.

4. *Durability and exclusivity of relationship test.* Courts consider the permanence and exclusivity of the parties' relationship. Where an individual performs work over a long period of time and has no other clients, courts are more likely to find an employment relationship.

5. *Tools test.* Does the individual provide his own tools? If so, this weighs in favour of independent contractor status, especially if a significant capital investment is involved, as in the case of a truck driver supplying his own truck. The tools test is probably the least significant of the tests, but it is still relevant.

In applying the common law tests, courts assign much greater weight to the substance of the relationship (what happened in practice) than to its form (what the written contract says). For example, the fact that an individual incorporates and declares herself self-employed for tax purposes is considered because it indicates her intent to be an independent contractor. However, this fact is not determinative if the other facts point to an employment relationship. *Belton v. Liberty Insurance* demonstrates how courts look at the specific facts of a case and are not limited by the terms of a contract when deciding whether there is an employment relationship.

CASE IN POINT

When Is an Independent Contractor Not an Independent Contractor?

Belton v. Liberty Insurance Co. of Canada, 2004 CanLII 6668 (Ont. CA)

Facts

The plaintiffs were sales agents for Prudential Insurance. Although they were restricted to selling Prudential property and casualty insurance products, they had signed representative agreements acknowledging their status as independent contractors. After the defendant insurance company bought Prudential, it introduced a new compensation agreement for its sales agents. The plaintiffs refused to sign the new agreement. They were fired, and they subsequently sued for wrongful dismissal.

Relevant Issue

Whether the plaintiffs were employees, and thereby entitled to reasonable notice of termination, or independent contractors.

Decision

The court found that the plaintiffs were employees, not independent contractors, on the basis of the facts of the case, and not the terms of the contract. It applied the following tests in considering the status of a commissioned agent:

1. *Was the agent limited to the exclusive service of the principal?* This factor was ambiguous because the plaintiffs sold life insurance for London Life and property and casualty insurance for the defendant. The plaintiffs, however, were not permitted to sell any property and casualty insurance other than that of the defendant.

2. *Was the agent subject to the control of the principal not only as to the product sold but also as to when and how it was sold?* The agents reported to managers at the insurance company.

3. *Did the agent have an investment or interest in the tools required for service?* The defendant provided the plaintiffs with office facilities, telephones, and fax machines.

4. *Did the agent undertake any business risk or have any expectation of profit (as distinct from receiving a fixed commission)?* The plaintiffs did not own their book of

business and had no legal or other entitlement to their customers. That is, the customers belonged to Prudential, not them.

5. *Was the activity of the agent part of the business organization of the principal?* The plaintiffs' activities were integral to the defendant's business.

How to Maintain an Independent Contractor–Principal Characterization

The list below outlines several ways to minimize the risks of having an independent contractor relationship subsequently characterized by a court or government agency as an employment relationship. Keep in mind that no single fact alone determines status. All the facts will be viewed together. In a large majority of cases, relationships that are purported to be independent contractor–principal relationships will, if challenged, be found to be employee–employer relationships.

1. A clearly written contract should confirm the individual's independent contractor status. Although this statement is not conclusive, it indicates the original intent of the parties.

2. The contract should cover a fixed term and should include a fair mutual termination clause, because independent contractors are typically hired for a specific project or period, while employees are usually hired on an indefinite basis. Be specific about the compensation to be paid, the work to be done, and where it will be done.

3. The organization should not take any statutory deductions or remittances for income tax, Canada Pension Plan contributions, and employment insurance contributions. The individual should acknowledge in the contract that the organization is not making these deductions and remittances.

4. The contract should include an indemnity provision stating that the independent contractor is responsible for any statutory remittances, such as for employment insurance or workplace safety and insurance premiums.

5. The contract should state that the independent contractor has no authority to create obligations on behalf of the organization, endorse cheques, or accept returns (Israel, 2003, p. 2997).

6. The organization should not provide vacation, holiday, or overtime pay; health care benefits; or employee benefits, such as stock options or bonuses. Similarly, the organization should not provide a company uniform; business cards; company car; bookkeeping services; or office equipment, such as a computer, desk, or other facilities.

7. The contract should not restrict the independent contractor from working for other clients, although it may require that the contractor dedicate a certain number of hours to the work being contracted for. (A contractor who works fewer than full-time hours, and on a non-exclusive basis, is also less likely to be considered a "dependent" contractor to whom reasonable notice of termination is required.)

8. The contract may have a non-disclosure provision if protection of confidential information is an issue but it should not include a non-competition clause because this could restrict the individual's ability to have other clients (Landmann, 2012, p. 4).

9. The organization should avoid reimbursing the independent contractor for expenses.

10. The organization should avoid setting, in terms of scheduling, hours of work.

11. The independent contractor should work offsite as much as possible. This is not, however, a guarantee of independent contractor status if the contractor works for only one employer and reports on a regular basis, electronically or otherwise.

12. The independent contractor should be entitled to accept or decline work when it is offered by the organization.

13. The independent contractor should purchase her own liability insurance.

14. The contract should not provide for performance reviews or disciplinary measures.

15. An individual who is incorporated, has a GST number, and makes the appropriate tax returns is more likely to be seen as an independent contractor.

16. An individual who has the ability to assign others to do all or part of the work is more likely to be seen as a contractor.

17. The contract should reflect the reality of the relationship. If, for example, the organization exercises day-to-day control over the individual's work, that practical reality will undermine all the effort that went into preparing the contract.

Differing Results Possible in the Determination of the Relationship

In some cases, an individual may be considered an independent contractor for the purposes of taxes and government remittances and be designated an employee for the purpose of a wrongful dismissal action. This occurs when the facts of the case are not clearcut, and various agencies weigh those facts and the common law tests somewhat differently. Some government agencies may also tend to find that individuals are employees because it is easier to collect remittances from one employer than from hundreds of independent contractors.

Similarly, courts may be reluctant to characterize an individual, especially one with long years of service, as an independent contractor if it means that he may be terminated without any notice. In *Dynamex Canada Inc. v. Mamona*, an individual who successfully claimed to be an independent contractor for income tax purposes also successfully claimed to be an employee for the purposes of claiming holiday and vacation pay under employment standards legislation.

Agents

Another type of relationship is that of agent and principal. An **agent** is someone who represents another person (the principal) in dealings with a third party (Yates, 2010, p. 131). Agents can bind an organization to a contract with customers or other parties, even without the organization's knowledge. Common examples are real estate agents, travel agents, and insurance agents. An agent may be an independent contractor or an employee. For example, salespersons, buyers, and human resources managers who recruit employees are agents because they have the capacity to bind an organization in contracting with others. However, despite their agency status, they are usually categorized as employees and thus are eligible for reasonable notice of termination. Moreover, merely having a job title that includes the term "agent" does not make that individual an independent contractor. To determine whether an agent is an employee or an independent contractor, courts would look at the established tests discussed above.

REFERENCES

Accessibility for Ontarians with Disabilities Act, 2005. SO 2005, c 11.

Alexandrowicz, G., et al. *Dimensions of Law: Canadian and International Law in the 21st Century*. Toronto: Emond Montgomery, 2004.

Belton v. Liberty Insurance Co. of Canada. 2004 CanLII 6668 (Ont. CA).

Brian Dickson Law Library. Legal Citations—The Neutral Citation. Last updated September 10, 2014. Principles of Legal Research. http://web5.uottawa.ca/www2/rl-lr/eng/legal-citations/1_17-neutral_citations.html.

Canada Labour Code. RSC 1985, c. L-2.

Canada Pension Plan. RSC 1985, c. C-8.

Canadian Charter of Rights and Freedoms. Part I of the *Constitution Act, 1982*, RSC 1985, app. II, no. 44.

Canadian Human Rights Act. RSC 1985, c. H-6.

Dehmel, Trish. Criminal Background Checks Not So "Clear." *Canadian HR Reporter*. March 25, 2013, p. 11.

Dunsmuir v. New Brunswick. 2008 SCC 9, [2008] 1 SCR 190.

Dynamex Canada Inc. v. Mamona. 2003 FCA 248.

Emond Harnden. Arbitrator Holds Lawyer's Investigation Report Not Protected from Disclosure by Solicitor-Client Privilege. February 2012. http://www.ehlaw.ca/whatsnew/1202/Focus1202.pdf.

Employment Equity Act. SC 1995, c. 44.

Employment Insurance Act. SC 1996, c. 23.

Employment Standards Act, 2000. SO 2000, c. 41.

Fairley, John, and Philip Sworden. *Introduction to Law in Canada*. Toronto: Emond Montgomery, 2014.

Farm Workers Want Protection. *Canadian HR Reporter*. July 14, 2003, p. 2.

Forsey, Eugene. *How Canadians Govern Themselves*, 5th ed. Ottawa: Her Majesty the Queen in Right of Canada, 2003.

French, Shana. What Does Your Tip-Out Policy Say About You? *Canadian HR Reporter*. October 21, 2013, p. 1. http://www.sherrardkuzz.com/pdf/kuzz_HRReporter_Oct_21_tipout.pdf.

Gilbert, Douglas, Brian Burkett, and Moira McCaskill. *Canadian Labour and Employment Law for the US Practitioner*. Washington, DC: Bureau of National Affairs, 2000.

Human Rights Code. RSO 1990, c. H.19.

Ilaris Corporation v. Gadzevych. 2007 CanLII 19192 (Ont. LRB).

Israel, Peter. Ensuring Independent Contractors Are Not Really Employees. *Canadian Employment Law Today*. Issue no. 384, March 5, 2003, p. 2997.

Jantunen v. Ross. (1991), 85 DLR (4th) 461 (Ont. Div. Ct.).

Jones v. Tsige. 2012 ONCA 32.

Kapp, R v. 2008 SCC 41, [2008] 2 SCR 483.

Labour Relations Act, 1995. SO 1995, c. 1, sched. A.

Landmann, Jeff. Case in Point: Dependent Contractors and Unforeseen Notice Requirements. *Canadian Employment Law Today*. March 7, 2012, p. 4. http://www.sherrardkuzz.com/pdf/eCELT%20March%207%202012.pdf.

Levitt, Howard. *Quick Reference to Employment Law*. Toronto: International Reference Press, 2002.

M. v. H. [1999] 2 SCR 3.

Mackie, Richard. Ontario to Get Tough on "Bad Employees." *Globe and Mail*, April 27, 2004.

Marbry Distributors Ltd. v. Avrecan Int. Inc. 1999 BCCA 172, 171 DLR (4th) 436.

Marcus, Joseph. Sometimes Help Hurts: Imagining a New Approach to Section 15(2). *Appeal: Review of Current Law and Law Reform*. Volume 18, no. 1, 2013, p. 121. http://journals.uvic.ca/index.php/appeal/article/view/12120/3610.

McKee v. Reid's Heritage Homes Ltd. 2009 ONCA 916, [2009] OJ no. 5489.

McKinney v. University of Guelph. [1990] 3 SCR 229, 76 DLR (4th) 545.

North Bay General Hospital v. Ontario Nurses' Association. 2011 CanLII 68580 (Ont. LA).

Oakes, R v. [1986] 1 SCR 103, 26 DLR (4th) 200.

Occupational Health and Safety Act. RSO 1990, c. O.1.

Ontario Justice Education Network. Section 1 of the Charter and the Oakes Test. *In Brief*. 2013. http://ojen.ca/sites/ojen.ca/files/resources/In%20Brief_Section%201%20and%20Oakes_0.pdf.

Ontario Nurses' Association v. Mount Sinai Hospital. 2005 CanLII 14437 (Ont. CA).

Pay Equity Act. RSO 1990, c. P.7.

Personal Information Protection and Electronic Documents Act. SC 2000, c. 5.

Quebec (Attorney General) v. A. 2013 SCC 5.

Rubin, J. Calling All Independent Contractors! *RT Blog*. January 18, 2010. http://www.rubinthomlinson.com/blog/independent-contractors/.

Ryder, Bruce. *Doctrinal Plasticity, Continued*. (n.d.) Institute for Feminist Legal Studies. http://ifls.osgoode.yorku.ca/2013/05/eric-lola-1-bruce-ryder-doctrinal-plasticity-continued/.

Ryder, Bruce. R. v. Kapp: Taking Section 15 Back to the Future. July 2, 2008. The Court (Osgoode Hall Law School). http://www.thecourt.ca/2008/07/02/r-v-kapp-taking-section-15-back-to-the-future.

Sherrard Kuzz LLP. Between You and Me: Email and Solicitor-Client Privilege. *Management Counsel: Employment and Labour Law Update*. Volume X, no. 5, October 2011, p. 3. http://www.sherrardkuzz.com/pdf/Vol_X_5.pdf.

Silliker, Amanda. More Firms Hiring Contract Workers. *Canadian HR Reporter*. May 7, 2012, p. 1. http://www.hrreporter.com/articleview/13016-more-firms-hiring-contract-workers.

Toronto Electric Commissioners v. Snider. [1925] 2 DLR 5, [1925] AC 396, 1 WWR 785 (UKPC).

Vriend v. Alberta. 1998 CanLII 816 (SCC), [1998] 1 SCR 493.

Waddams, Stephen. *Introduction to the Study of Law*. Toronto: Thomson, 2004.

Wages Act. RSO 1990, c. W.1.

Workplace Safety and Insurance Act, 1997. SO 1997, c. 16, sched. A.

Yates, Richard. *Legal Fundamentals for Canadian Business*, 2nd ed. Toronto: Pearson Canada, 2010.

RELATED WEBSITES

- http://www.canlii.org
- http://www.e-laws.gov.on.ca
- http://laws.justice.gc.ca

REVIEW QUESTIONS

1. Name a significant current demographic trend, and discuss the effect that it might have on employment law in the future.

2. In your opinion, what are some of the strengths and weaknesses of the common law system?

3. The *Canadian Charter of Rights and Freedoms* applies only where government is involved. However, the Charter can indirectly affect private sector employers. How?

4. Describe two possible tools or rules that a judge may use in determining how to interpret a statute in a particular case.

5. Go to the Legislative Assembly of Ontario website: http://www.ontla.on.ca/web/bills/bills_all.do?locale=en. Locate a current public bill that relates to employment law. Is it in first, second, or third reading? What is the significance of each reading?

6. Although the Ontario *Human Rights Code* was amended in 2006 to prohibit age-based discrimination against anyone aged 18 years or older, it also expressly stated that the right to equal treatment on the basis of age was not infringed by benefit plans that complied with the *Employment Standards Act*. The ESA in turn continued to allow employee benefit plans that discriminated against workers age 65 or over. In 2008 the Ontario Nurses' Association filed a grievance against the Municipality of Chatham-Kent because, under the negotiated collective agreement, employees over the age of 64 received inferior benefits (for example, no long-term disability coverage) compared with those received by employees under that age. The union argued that the statutory provisions that allowed these discriminatory distinctions violated the *Canadian Charter of Rights and Freedoms*.

    Based on the tests the courts use to interpret ss. 15 and 1 of the Charter, discuss whether you think the union's argument would be successful.

7. Joanne and her husband were unable to have children and they decided to adopt. When their adopted baby daughter came into their care, Joanne applied for both pregnancy benefits (17 weeks) and parental benefits (35 weeks) under the federal government's employment insurance program. She was given parental benefits but denied pregnancy benefits on the basis that she was never pregnant. Joanne challenged this denial on the basis of the equality rights provision in the Charter.

    a. In your opinion, was denial of pregnancy benefits to an adoptive parent fair?

    b. Did it contravene s. 15 of the Charter? Explain your answer.

8. You are hired for the summer to paint houses for CK Inc. As part of your arrangement with CK, you sign a contract that states you are an "independent contractor"—you're agreeing that you operate your own painting business. CK will advertise and bid for the painting jobs, as well as provide the materials, and you will perform the work in exchange for a fixed amount per contract. This arrangement works out for a while but after completing one major job, CK refuses to pay you because it alleges that your work is substandard. You tell CK's manager that you intend to file a complaint with the Ministry of Labour under the *Employment Standards Act*. She responds, "How are you going to do that when you're not even an employee?" What are your rights in this situation?

9. Why might an employer prefer to hire an individual as an independent contractor rather than as an employee?

10. Why might an individual choose to work as an independent contractor rather than as an employee?

11. List ways that parties who want to create an independent contractor–principal relationship can minimize the risk that their relationship will be viewed as that of employee–employer.

12. Brad began working at Lay-Z-Guy in 1981 as a customer service manager. In 1995 his employer started requiring him and other salespeople to sign a series of one-year agreements that stated they could be terminated on 60 days' notice. Three years later it required Brad to incorporate, and from that point forward, the agreements were between Lay-Z-Guy and Brad's corporation. The agreements defined Brad, and later his corporation, as an "independent marketing consultant" and expressly stated that the relationship was not one of employment, but rather of an independent contractor–principal. Brad paid for his own office space and remitted his own income taxes and workers' compensation premiums. At the same time, Lay-Z-Guy set prices, territory, and promotional methods and Brad was limited to servicing Lay-Z-Guy exclusively. In 2003, Lay-Z-Guy terminated the agreement with 60 days' notice. Brad sued for wrongful dismissal damages, alleging that he was an employee.

a. What arguments could Brad make to support his position that he was an employee?

b. What arguments could Lay-Z-Guy make to support its position that Brad was an independent contractor?

c. Which side do you think would be successful?

PART II

Hiring

You may be surprised to learn that a number of legal issues can arise even before an employer hires an employee. Employers must satisfy several legal obligations under both statute and common law during the recruitment, selection, and hiring process. The most significant obligations arise from human rights legislation because the employer must ensure that no discrimination occurs while it selects and hires an employee. The protection afforded by human rights law extends from the pre-employment stage to the end of the employment relationship.

Chapter 2 discusses Ontario's *Human Rights Code* as it relates to the hiring process. The chapter begins with a brief discussion of the scope of prohibited conduct under the Code and a review of the 16 prohibited grounds of discrimination. It also considers the limited circumstances where discrimination is allowed. The chapter then reviews the provisions in the Code that relate to advertisements, applications, interviews, testing programs, and conditional offers of employment.

Chapter 3 addresses the key common law issues that arise during the hiring process. The most basic of these is the employer's obligation not to mislead candidates about the job that it is offering. The chapter also reviews the different categories of employees, including full-time, part-time, temporary (or contract), and agency employees.

Chapter 4 discusses the benefits of a written employment contract and reviews common contractual terms.

Human Rights Issues: Hiring

2

LEARNING OUTCOMES

After completing this chapter, you will be able to:

- Trace the development of human rights law in Ontario.

- Identify the key features and requirements of Ontario's *Human Rights Code*.

- Identify the 16 prohibited grounds of discrimination under the *Human Rights Code*.

- Understand the requirements of the *Human Rights Code* in relation to hiring, including job advertisements, applications, interviews, and conditional offers of employment.

- Understand the human rights issues raised by pre-employment testing, including medical and drug and alcohol testing.

Introduction

There was a time when even the most blatant forms of discrimination were legal in Canada. Under the common law, stores could refuse service, landlords could refuse housing, and employers could refuse to hire individuals for whatever reason they chose, including race, gender, or marital status. The 1939 case of *Christie v. York Corp.* provides a striking illustration of how accepted discrimination once was (see the Case in Point feature below). However, the days of *Christie v. York Corp.* are long gone. Over the past 55 years, every jurisdiction in Canada has enacted human rights legislation that prohibits discrimination in key social areas, including employment, services (such as stores, restaurants, hospitals, and schools), and accommodation (housing).

CASE IN POINT

Freedom of Commerce Eclipses Human Rights

Christie v. York Corp., [1940] SCR 139

Facts

One evening in 1936, the plaintiff went with some friends to the Montreal Forum to see a hockey game. After the game, they all went to the Forum's tavern, where the plaintiff ordered a beer. The barman refused to serve him because the "house rules" prohibited serving "coloured persons." Christie brought an action against the corporate owners of the tavern, claiming $200 for the humiliation that he suffered. The defendant corporation claimed that it was merely protecting its business interests and was free to serve whomever it chose.

Relevant Issue

Whether it is illegal to refuse to serve an individual in a public establishment on the basis of race.

Decision

The Supreme Court of Canada found that the refusal to serve an individual on the basis of race was legal. The court ruled that in the absence of a law specifically forbidding a company from refusing service, the general principle of freedom of commerce prevails, and merchants are free to deal as they choose with individual members of the public.

FYI

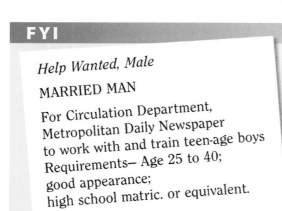

Help Wanted, Male

MARRIED MAN

For Circulation Department, Metropolitan Daily Newspaper to work with and train teen-age boys Requirements— Age 25 to 40; good appearance; high school matric. or equivalent.

To arrange for interview, telephone *The Telegram*.

This ad appeared in a Toronto newspaper in June 1962.

Advertisements such as this are now illegal in Canada.

Unlike the *Canadian Charter of Rights and Freedoms*, which directly applies only to government actions, human rights statutes apply to the actions of individuals and corporations as well. Moreover, the scope of human rights law has been steadily expanding. Ontario's first comprehensive human rights statute, passed in 1962, prohibited discrimination on only 6 closely related grounds: race, creed, colour, nationality, ancestry, and place of origin. In contrast, Ontario's current *Human Rights Code* prohibits discrimination in employment on 16 grounds.

The definition of "discrimination" has also expanded since the first human rights laws were enacted in Ontario. Initially, discrimination was limited to intentional acts, such as an employer's refusal to hire an individual because of his religious beliefs. Today, however, the effect of a rule or action matters as much as the intention behind it. For instance, a seemingly neutral and business-related rule, such as a retail store's requirement that all full-time employees be available to work on Saturday, may infringe the Code if it has a negative effect on someone who is unable to work on Saturday for religious reasons.

Today, a rule or qualification that has a negative effect on a protected group is discriminatory, and thus illegal, unless an employer can demonstrate that it is a **bona fide occupational qualification (BFOQ)**. To be considered a BFOQ, a contested job requirement must pass the three-part test set out by the Supreme Court of Canada in *British Columbia (Public Service Employee Relations Commission) v. BCGSEU* (known as the *Meiorin* case). *Meiorin* involved a female firefighter who, after three successful years on the job, was terminated when she failed to meet one aspect of a new physical fitness test imposed by the employer. The court held that to be a BFOQ, the discriminatory rule or requirement must be

1. adopted for a purpose rationally connected to the performance of a job;
2. adopted in an honest belief that it was necessary to satisfy a legitimate business purpose; and
3. reasonably necessary to accomplish that purpose. To establish this, the employer must show that it was impossible to accommodate the individual or group without creating undue hardship for itself.

In the 2008 case of *Hydro-Québec v. Syndicat des employé-e-s de techniques professionnelles et de bureau d'Hydro-Québec, section locale 2000 (SCFP-FTQ)*, the Supreme Court of Canada further clarified the third part of the *Meiorin* test by stating that the employer does not have to show that accommodation itself is impossible but rather that it is impossible to accommodate the individual or group without undue hardship. However, despite this clarification, the third part of the test continues to set a high standard for employers in justifying a discriminatory job requirement or rule. A detailed discussion of the duty to accommodate and of the characteristics of undue hardship is presented in Chapter 5.

Overview of Ontario's Human Rights Code

The Ontario *Human Rights Code* opens with a preamble that sets out the spirit and intent of the legislation. Inspired by the 1948 Universal Declaration of Human Rights, it recognizes the "inherent dignity and the equal and inalienable rights of all members of the human family" and provides for equal rights and opportunities without discrimination to create a climate of understanding and mutual respect.

> WHEREAS recognition of the inherent dignity and the equal and inalienable rights of all members of the human family is the foundation of freedom, justice and peace in the world and is in accord with the Universal Declaration of Human Rights as proclaimed by the United Nations;

AND WHEREAS it is public policy in Ontario to recognize the dignity and worth of every person and to provide for equal rights and opportunities without discrimination that is contrary to law, and having as its aim the creation of a climate of understanding and mutual respect for the dignity and worth of each person so that each person feels a part of the community and able to contribute fully to the development and well-being of the community and the Province;

AND WHEREAS these principles have been confirmed in Ontario by a number of enactments of the Legislature and it is desirable to revise and extend the protection of human rights in Ontario …

As a statement of principles, the preamble does not contain specific legislative requirements. However, it affects the interpretation of the Code. Where a provision is silent or ambiguous about an issue, courts and tribunals often use the preamble as an internal aid in deciding to interpret the Code in its broadest sense. For example, in *Rocha v. Pardons and Waivers of Canada*, the Human Rights Tribunal pointed to the preamble in its decision to give a liberal and expansive interpretation to the category of "employment" by finding that it includes unpaid internships.

Another factor that has encouraged a broad and liberal interpretation of rights in the Code is its role as **remedial legislation**. This means that it exists to right a societal wrong and give the affected person or group a remedy, not to allocate blame or punish an offender.

Finally, the Code is a quasi-constitutional law. This means that where there is a conflict between the Code and another Ontario law, such as the *Employment Standards Act, 2000*, the Code prevails unless the other law specifically states that it applies despite the Code (see s. 47(2)).

FYI

Key Features of Ontario's Human Rights Code

1. The Code applies to both the private and the public sector and to the conduct of individuals. Unlike the *Charter of Rights and Freedoms*, its application is not limited to the actions of government.

2. Discrimination in employment is prohibited on 16 grounds: race, ancestry, place of origin, colour, ethnic origin, citizenship, creed, sex, sexual orientation, gender identity, gender expression, age, record of offences, marital status, family status, and disability. The Code also prohibits sexual harassment as well as harassment based on other prohibited grounds of discrimination in the workplace.

3. To infringe the Code, it is not necessary to intend to discriminate. The effect of an employer's action or rule matters as much as the intent. The employer has a duty to accommodate the special needs of protected individuals or groups unless doing so would create undue hardship for the employer.

4. No one can contract out of the Code. For example, the negotiated terms of a collective agreement or individual employment contract do not override obligations under the Code.

5. The Code provides for civil remedies, such as ordering an employer to compensate employees for lost wages or mental suffering or ordering it to change

its employment policies. The Code does not provide for criminal penalties, such as imprisonment.

6. The Code is quasi-constitutional legislation in that if there is a conflict between its provisions and those of another statute, its requirements prevail unless the other statute specifically states that it applies despite the Code.

7. The Code applies to every stage of the employment relationship, from recruitment through to termination.

Areas Covered

The Code provides that everyone has the right to be free of discrimination in five areas of social activity:

- services, goods, and facilities;
- accommodation (housing);
- contracts;
- employment; and
- membership in vocational associations and trade unions.

Although employment is only one of the five areas covered by the Code, over 75 percent of human rights complaints arise in the workplace (Pinto, 2012, p. 214). The term "employment" has been interpreted broadly to include full- and part-time employment, contract work, temporary work, probationary periods of employment, unpaid internships, and in some cases volunteer work.

Prohibited Grounds of Discrimination in Employment

Section 5 of the *Human Rights Code* provides that every person is entitled to equal treatment with respect to employment without discrimination on the basis of race, ancestry, place of origin, colour, ethnic origin, citizenship, creed, sex, sexual orientation, gender identity, gender expression, age, record of offences, marital status, family status, or disability. Note that only some of the grounds are defined in the Code. Definitions are given in s. 10 for age, disability, family status, marital status, and record of offences but no definitions are given in the Code for race, colour, ancestry, place of origin, ethnic origin, citizenship, creed, sex, sexual orientation, gender identity, or gender expression. However, courts and tribunals have considered how many of the grounds that are not defined in the Code should be interpreted and have thereby provided guidance on their scope.

Each of the 16 prohibited grounds is considered in the list below, together with any applicable statutory exemptions. Exemptions are discussed more fully in the section "Exemptions: Where Discrimination Is Allowed" below.

1. *Race.* Race is not a defined ground but it can often be related to other grounds, such as colour or ethnic origin.

   An exemption exists for **special service organizations** (non-profit social and other organizations that serve a protected group). For a discussion of the special service organization exemption, see the heading "Special Service Organizations," as well as Figure 2.2, below.

2. *Colour.* Colour refers to skin colour.

   An exemption exists for special service organizations.

3. *Ancestry.* Ancestry refers to family descent and is closely related to place of origin.

   An exemption exists for special service organizations.

4. *Place of origin.* Place of origin refers to a country or region of birth, including a region in Canada.

   An exemption exists for special service organizations.

5. *Ethnic origin.* Ethnic origin has more of a cultural component than ancestry. Protection is not limited to people who have recently arrived in Canada; it can apply to third- or fourth-generation Canadians.

   An exemption exists for special service organizations.

   Although "language" is not explicitly listed as one of the prohibited grounds, it can be an element of a complaint based on the related grounds of ancestry, ethnic origin, place of origin, or race. Similarly, because a person's accent is usually related to those same grounds, the Code can be infringed when someone is discriminated against because of an accent. In *Gajecki v. Surrey School District (No. 36)*, a supply teacher who was originally from Poland found out that the reason he was not receiving any temporary assignments was because there was a note attached to his file which said that he did not speak English. His human rights application was successful: the Tribunal found that he had been discriminated against because of his accent, which was directly related to his ancestry or place of origin (Ontario Human Rights Commission, 1996).

6. *Citizenship.* Citizenship refers to discrimination on the basis of citizenship status, including status as a permanent resident, refugee, or temporary resident.

   Exceptions are set out in s. 16 of the Code. Discrimination on the basis of citizenship is allowed in the following cases: where the law requires or authorizes citizenship as a qualification or requirement; where the requirement for Canadian citizenship or permanent residence in Canada has been adopted to foster participation in cultural, educational, **trade union**, or athletic activities; and where an employer imposes a preference that the chief or senior executive is, or intends to become, a Canadian citizen.

7. *Creed.* This ground protects people from discrimination on the basis of their religion or faith, but historically it has not covered discrimination based on political convictions. For example, someone who is discriminated against because she is a member of a particular political party probably cannot file an application. However, the 2012 case of *Al-Dandachi v. SNC-Lavalin Inc.* has opened the door to a possible broadening of this interpretation. In that case, the Ontario Superior Court of Justice dismissed the employer's motion to

strike down an employee's human rights application on the basis that his claim that he was terminated for his political views on the Syrian civil war was not protected by the Code. The court commented that it could not conclude that the plaintiff's views could not amount to creed (Gorsky, 2013, p. 6).

The Code provides two types of protection based on creed. First, it prohibits one person from attempting to force another to accept or comply with a particular religious belief or practice. Second, it may require an employer to take positive measures, such as allowing breaks for prayer at certain times. Religious beliefs and practices are protected, even if they are not essential elements of a particular religion, provided that they are sincerely held.

An exemption exists for special service organizations.

8. *Sex.* Discrimination on this ground extends to sex (male or female), gender identity, and (under s. 10(2)) pregnancy. This category also protects the right to breastfeed in public areas.

Exemptions exist for special service organizations and BFOQs under s. 24(1)(b).

Mottu v. MacLeod and others illustrates an employer's discriminatory conduct in insisting that its female employee wear a bikini top for a special event at its nightclub.

CASE IN POINT

Discrimination Based on Sex

Mottu v. MacLeod and others, 2004 BCHRT 76, [2004] BCHRTD no. 68

Facts

Mottu started work at MacLeod's nightclub in March 2000, when she was 21 years of age. She usually wore a black top and skirt or pants at work. In April 2001, there was an annual fundraiser with a beach theme at the nightclub. The employer informed Mottu that if she wanted to work that evening, she must wear a bikini top and surfer shorts. She decided to work, but she wore a top and sweater over her bikini top. She also contacted her union about the matter. The employer appeared to be annoyed with her, and over the next several days tension increased between them. The employer cut Mottu's hours, and relegated her to selling drinks in a dark corner at the back of the club. She eventually quit her job and filed a human rights complaint based on sex discrimination.

Relevant Issue

Whether the employer's conduct constituted discrimination on the basis of sex.

Decision

The British Columbia Human Rights Tribunal found that the employer's actions constituted discrimination on the basis of sex. The fact that the female servers were required to wear a gender-specific outfit that was sexual in nature while the male bartenders and door staff wore their usual attire constituted discrimination. The Tribunal also found that the employer's subsequent attitude and actions were retaliatory and intended to force Mottu to resign. The Tribunal awarded the employee almost $3,000 for lost wages and tips, plus $3,000 for injury to her dignity and self-respect. It also ordered the employer to refrain from committing similar contraventions of human rights legislation in the future.

Another, surprisingly common, type of sex-based discrimination occurs when an employee is fired after her boss finds out she is pregnant. This occurred in *Maciel v. Fashion Coiffures*, where the employer let Maciel go on her first day on the job as a receptionist after she disclosed that she was four months pregnant. The Human Rights Tribunal found that the employer's explanation that Maciel herself had changed her mind and only wanted to work part-time, while they needed a full-time receptionist, lacked credibility. The employer was ordered to pay Maciel more than $35,000 in general damages, lost wages, and benefits as a result of its discriminatory actions against her.

9. *Sexual orientation.* Sexual orientation concerns a person's sexuality and includes lesbian, gay, bisexual, and heterosexual people.

10. *Gender identity.* This ground refers to a person's intrinsic sense of self, especially with respect to their sense of being male or female.

11. *Gender expression.* This ground refers to a person's external attributes, such as behaviour, appearance, and dress, that are socially perceived as being masculine or feminine (Edmonds and Ip, 2013, p. 8).

In 2012, the Code was amended to add both gender identity and gender expression to the prohibited grounds of discrimination. Before that time, transgendered and transsexual individuals could file claims of discrimination but they had to do so under the grounds of sex or sexual orientation. However, on the basis of evidence of persistent and severe discrimination against these groups, the Ontario legislature decided to make their protection explicit. Although there is little case law on these two new grounds to date, it is possible to get a sense of their potential scope by looking at relevant arbitral decisions (from unionized workplaces) and several related Tribunal decisions. For example, rules in unionized workplaces that prohibit males from having longer hair, wearing earrings, or having facial jewellery have been struck down where the policy is based on sex stereotyping. As with other prohibited grounds of discrimination, employer arguments that the requirements are based on "customer preference" will not be successful. Gender-neutral dress codes, such as requiring all employees to dress "professionally" (rather than requiring males to wear dress pants and females to wear skirts), are the safest (Edmonds and Ip, 2013, pp. 15–16).

In the case of *XY v. Ontario (Government and Consumer Services)*, the Tribunal found that legislation requiring a person to have "transsexual surgery" before they can change the sex designation on their birth registration is discriminatory because it reinforces the stereotype that transgendered persons must have surgery to live in their felt gender (Ontario Human Rights Commission, 2013, p. 10). In light of this finding, employers should not insist that an employee who is transitioning to become a woman, for example, be treated as a man until her sex reassignment surgery is complete. Similarly, employers should not require medical documentation before accommodating an employee on the basis of gender identity: how the employee self-identifies is the determining factor. Once an employee decides to make the changed gender identity known in the workplace, it is up to the employer to update its records: internal documents, business cards, email signatures, and the like. It must also respect the employee's preferences, up to the point of undue hardship, regarding whether, when, and how they want their decision to transition to be known to others in the workplace (Edmonds and Ip, 2013, p. 17). It is the employer's responsibility to provide a workplace that is respectful and harassment-free. Proactively implementing a gender transition policy, before there is an immediate need, and sensitizing employees to issues faced by transgendered people, will lay the groundwork for a harassment-free workplace (Edmonds and Ip, 2013, p. 16).

FYI

Gender Identity, Gender Expression, and Gender-Specific Facilities

One workplace issue related to gender identity and expression is in the area of washroom usage. The Law Society of Upper Canada's model policy (2013) for law firms on LGBT (lesbian, gay, bisexual, and transgender) inclusion provides the following:

> Washroom and other Gender-Specific Facilities—The Firm respects the needs of those who identify as transgendered regarding the use of washrooms and gender-specific facilities. It is that person's right to use a washroom that is in accordance with their gender identity and presentation (Edmonds and Ip, 2013, p. 19).

---

12. *Age.* Age is defined as 18 years or older. For example, this ground protects a 19-year-old who is denied a position because of negative stereotypes about teenagers as well as a 67-year-old who is rejected because he does not "fit the company's youthful image."

According to the definition of "age," someone under 18 cannot make an age-based application related to employment. However, that person could use the Code to challenge discrimination based on another prohibited ground, such as sex or race.

Before December 2007, "age" was defined in the Code as being between the ages of 18 and 64, which allowed employers to have policies requiring employees to retire at age 65. As a result of a legislative change removing the ceiling of age 64 in the definition, mandatory retirement at age 65 was effectively eliminated in Ontario. However, according to Ontario Human Rights Commission policy, some discrimination against persons age 65 or older is permissible. For example, employers are not required to provide the same health benefits to employees age 65 or older as they do to those under the age of 65.

The following case, heard under Alberta's human rights legislation, illustrates the type of age-based discriminatory behaviour that the law seeks to eliminate, as well as the extent of remedies available.

CASE IN POINT

The Dangers of Making Assumptions About Age

Cowling v. Her Majesty the Queen in Right of Alberta as represented by Alberta Employment and Immigration, 2012 AHRC 12

Facts

Cowling was first hired on contract as a provincial labour relations officer in 1999 when she was 59 years old. Her contract was renewed every two to three years and she received positive performance reviews and bonuses every year for eight years. Just before her final contract ended in 2007, Cowling was told that her department was restructuring and her position was being downgraded. It would become a permanent "growth" or "developmental" position. When Cowling applied for the new position, she found that the responsibilities were virtually identical to her former position; however, she wasn't hired. The new position was never filled and the job description was then upgraded. Cowling filed a complaint with the Alberta Human Rights Commission.

Relevant Issue

Whether the employer's actions constituted age-based discrimination.

Decision

The Tribunal held that the employer's actions did constitute age-based discrimination. Given the non-renewal of the contract after eight years of strong performance reviews, Cowling's exemplary qualifications, her ongoing pursuit of training opportunities, and her consistent achievement of bonuses, it was reasonable to infer that age was a factor in denying her continued employment (para. 169). Furthermore, the language used ("growth" and "developmental") to describe the "new" position created the inference that the employer was looking for someone younger to fill Cowling's duties and that she was being targeted because of her age (para. 188). As the Tribunal stated, "[D]iscrimination is rarely practiced openly. Accordingly, it is appropriate to draw reasonable inferences based on circumstantial evidence" (para. 166). Cowling was awarded $15,000 in general damages, plus five years' pay (minus 30 percent to reflect the more tenuous nature of contract employment), interest, and costs. It also ordered that Cowling, now aged 72, be reinstated.

The *Cowling* case illustrates how the burden of proof operates in human rights cases. Cowling, as the applicant, initially had to prove a ***prima facie*** (on the face of it) case of discrimination on a protected ground. To do this, three elements are required. The applicant has to show that she is a member of a group protected by the Code (in this case, a member protected on the ground of age); that she was subject to adverse treatment (here, job loss); and finally, that there was a connection between the adverse treatment and the ground of discrimination. Once this threshold is reached (and it is a fairly low bar), the evidentiary burden then shifts to the respondent employer to show that, on a **balance of probabilities**, there is a credible and acceptable explanation for its conduct. In other words, once the inference of discrimination has been shown to be more probable than not, the respondent has to "explain or risk losing" (*Peel Law Association v. Pieters* (para. 73)). Here, the employer was unable to meet this burden of proving that age-based discrimination did *not* play a part in its decision to not renew the employee's contract. This reversal of the burden of proof after a *prima facie* case has been shown makes it imperative that employers carefully document the reasons behind their hiring and other employment-related decisions and that those reasons not touch on a prohibited ground of discrimination.

Exemptions exist for special service organizations and BFOQs under s. 24(1)(b).

The In the News feature below, "Is 'Youth' a BFOQ?," concerning a 44-year-old exotic dancer, is another example of an age-based discrimination application. It's one that has not been previously dealt with by a tribunal in Ontario.

IN THE NEWS

Is "Youth" a BFOQ?

EXOTIC DANCER FILES AGE DISCRIMINATION COMPLAINT

Kim Ouwroulis doesn't believe her age should be a barrier in her chosen career: exotic dancing.

In an unusual test of age discrimination laws, the 44-year-old Toronto-area woman filed a complaint last month with the Human Rights Tribunal of Ontario, alleging the owner of a strip club fired her because she was too old.

Ouwroulis says she and three other women at the New Locomotion club in Mississauga were fired last summer, allegedly for the same reason.

"I was told by a manager, 'Your time is up here,'" she said. "At first I was speechless. And I said, well, 'Why am I being fired—my age?'"

"I was told they were going in a new direction with younger girls," said Ouwroulis.

A tribunal official confirmed that a second complaint has been filed against the same employer but did not provide details.

The club owner has not returned phone calls from CBC News.

Ouwroulis started her exotic dancing career four years ago, and says she raked in thousands of dollars each week. Since her dismissal, Ouwroulis, who lives in the town of Whitchurch-Stouffville, has found work at another establishment in the Toronto area.

"I'm a bubbly blond with a good personality. The boobs and the blond hair, usually you can't go wrong in a strip club with those two things," she said.

SEX APPEAL ARGUMENT "TRICKY"

Denise Reaume, a University of Toronto professor who specializes in discrimination law, says the complaint explores uncharted territory.

"These kinds of cases don't get litigated very often, and so there's not a lot of hard thinking about them," says Reaume.

Under the Ontario Human Rights Code, employers are barred from treating a worker differently because of their age.

But while age discrimination cases typically examine the person's ability to perform their job, this case will look at how appearance, as it relates to age, plays a part.

Reaume says the respondent's underlying objection doesn't have to do with the quality of the dance, but rather the general appeal and look of the dancer.

"The question is going to be whether this employer can defend the argument that sex appeal is the essence of the job. ... This is tricky because sexual response is as variable as human beings are."

SOURCE: CBC News, "Exotic Dancer Files Age Discrimination Complaint," November 3, 2008. CBC Licensing. Used with permission.

13. *Record of offences.* Record of offences means provincial offences or pardoned federal offences. This ground means that, unless one of the exceptions applies, employers cannot discriminate against prospective or current employees because they have been convicted of a provincial offence (typically

a less serious offence) or a criminal offence for which they have received a pardon. Conversely, it is legal to discriminate on the basis of a criminal offence for which no pardon has been obtained. Moreover, the Code does not prohibit discrimination in employment as a result of being charged with a crime (*de Pelham v. Mytrak Health Systems*).

An exemption exists for BFOQs under s. 24(1)(b).

In *Quebec (Commission des droits de la personne et des droits de la jeunesse) v. Maksteel Québec Inc.*, the Supreme Court of Canada examined the scope of this ground in relation to a person who lost his job because he had been incarcerated.

CASE IN POINT

Discrimination Based on Incarceration

Quebec (Commission des droits de la personne et des droits de la jeunesse) v. Maksteel Québec Inc., 2003 SCC 68, [2003] 3 SCR 228

Facts

In 1989, the employee pleaded guilty to charges of fraud and breach of trust. His sentencing was postponed. By the time that he was sentenced to a prison term of six months less a day, he was employed as a maintenance mechanic with Maksteel. The employer dismissed him the day after he failed to report to work because of his incarceration. The employee was released on parole after several days of imprisonment and attempted to return to work. When the employer refused to hire him back, he filed a complaint with the Quebec Human Rights Commission, claiming that he had been discriminated against because he had been convicted of a criminal offence, contrary to Quebec's human rights legislation. The Human Rights Tribunal ruled in favour of the employee, maintaining that the employer failed in its duty to accommodate his incarceration. It awarded the employee lost wages and $5,000 in damages. The case was eventually appealed to the Supreme Court of Canada.

Relevant Issue

Whether the employer's termination of the employee constituted discrimination on the basis of criminal record.

Decision

The Supreme Court of Canada ruled in favour of the employer. It held that the protection against discrimination on the basis of a criminal record protects employees only in cases where the criminal record is the cause of the employer's actions. The purpose of the legislation is to shield employees from an "unjustified social stigma" that tends to exclude people with criminal convictions from the labour market. However, here the dismissal resulted from the employee's failure to report for work because of his prison sentence, not from his criminal conviction.

14. *Marital status.* Marital status refers to a person's being married, single, widowed, divorced, separated, or living in a common law relationship. The Supreme Court of Canada has held that this ground also includes the identity of the complainant's spouse (see the discussion of family status below).

Exemptions exist for special service organizations, BFOQs under s. 24(1)(b), and **nepotism policies** (policies that allow the employer to discriminate either in favour of or against specified close relatives of employees).

15. *Family status.* The Code defines "family status" as "the status of being in a parent and child relationship." Given that human rights legislation is interpreted liberally, adopted children, stepchildren, and foster children qualify although it is not yet known whether this definition would apply to grandparents and grandchildren.

In *B v. Ontario (Human Rights Commission)*, the Supreme Court of Canada held that this ground does not only cover a person's status as being in a parent and child relationship. It also includes the *identity* of the complainant's family members.

An exemption exists for nepotism policies.

CASE IN POINT

Discrimination Based on Family Status

B v. Ontario (Human Rights Commission), 2002 SCC 66, [2002] 3 SCR 403

Facts

The employee, A, had worked for the employer for 26 years when his superior, B, who was also his brother-in-law, fired him. The reason for the termination was that A's daughter and wife had accused B of sexually abusing the daughter. On the first workday after the confrontation between B and A's wife and daughter, B shouted at A about the allegations and told him that he was terminated. A filed a complaint with the Ontario Human Rights Commission, alleging that he had been discriminated against on the basis of family and marital status.

Relevant Issue

Whether discrimination on the basis of family and marital status includes discrimination on the basis of the identity of the family member or spouse.

Decision

The Supreme Court of Canada found in favour of A. It gave the *Human Rights Code* a broad interpretation by deciding that the grounds of family and marital status not only protect employees from being discriminated against on the basis of whether, for example, they are married or single or have children; they also protect employees who are adversely affected because of the identity of their spouse or child. In this case, A was dismissed because of who his family members were, so he was arbitrarily disadvantaged on the basis of his marital and family status. The matter was returned to the Board of Inquiry (the predecessor to the Ontario Human Rights Tribunal) to determine the appropriate remedy.

16. *Disability.* Disability is extensively defined in s. 10 to cover a spectrum of disabilities, including

    a. physical disability or disfigurement caused by injury, illness, or birth defect;

    b. psychiatric disability;

    c. disability for which benefits were claimed or received under the workers' compensation system;

    d. substance abuse (addiction to drugs or alcohol); and

    e. a "perceived" disability, a subject examined in *Quebec (Commission des droits de la personne et des droits de la jeunesse) v. Montréal (City)*.

CASE IN POINT

What Constitutes a Perceived Disability?

Quebec (Commission des droits de la personne et des droits de la jeunesse) v. Montréal (City),
2000 SCC 27, [2000] 1 SCR 665

Facts

The job applicant was a horticulturalist who applied for a job in the employer city's parks department. She was hired subject to passing a pre-employment medical test. The results of this test showed that she had a slight curvature of the spine that might lead to physical impairment in the future. The applicant was not aware of this condition, experienced no symptoms, and would have been able to perform the usual duties of the job. However, the employer decided not to hire the applicant because it believed that she was at greater risk than other candidates of having future costly back problems.

Relevant Issue

Whether the employer's refusal to hire the applicant on the basis of a perceived back problem constituted discrimination on the basis of disability.

Decision

The Supreme Court of Canada decided that the employer had discriminated against the applicant on the basis of disability. What matters is how a person experiences and is affected by a disability, not its precise nature or cause.

Despite the breadth of the term "disability," it has been interpreted, in *Ouimette v. Lily Cups Ltd.*, not to include a minor, temporary illness to which the general public is susceptible, such as the flu or common cold.

Exemptions from the obligation not to discriminate on the basis of disability exist for special service organizations. The Code also recognizes that there will be situations where the nature of a disability prevents an individual from performing a job. For example, an employer is not required to hire someone who is blind to drive a school bus. However, the Code places strict limits on an employer's ability to claim that an employee is unable to perform a job. Under s. 17, the employer must eliminate the non-essential requirements of the job and modify the existing job requirements to enable a disabled person to carry out the **essential job duties** unless this causes undue hardship to the employer. Modifications include providing specialized equipment or services to allow the person to do the job. Chapter 5 contains a more detailed discussion of the duty to accommodate in cases of disability.

Additional Grounds of Discrimination

Discrimination Because of Association

In addition to the 16 listed prohibited grounds of discrimination, the Code protects an individual from being discriminated against because of her relationship with people *identified by a prohibited ground*. For example, an employee cannot be denied a position because she associates with a person of a certain religious belief (s. 12). On the other hand, if an employee is discriminated against because of her association with a particular political party, for example, that situation would *not* be covered because political conviction is not currently one of the prohibited grounds of discrimination.

Discrimination Through Reprisal

The Code also provides that people have the right to enforce their rights under the Code without reprisal (s. 8). An employer who retaliates against someone for asserting his rights or for refusing to discriminate against another person on the basis of a prohibited ground infringes the Code. For example, if a recruiter is demoted for refusing to discriminate against an applicant on the basis of her sexual orientation, that recruiter could file a human rights application under s. 8 of the Code.

Discrimination Not Covered by the Code

To engage the protection of the Code, the discriminatory treatment *must be based on one of the 16 prohibited grounds.* Although the prohibited grounds of discrimination are numerous and broadly defined, they are not exhaustive. Someone who is discriminated against on the basis of a ground not covered in s. 5, such as political conviction or social status, cannot file an application under the Code. Similarly, discrimination on the basis of physical appearance does not infringe the Code unless it touches on a prohibited ground. For example, a person who wears a nose ring as a fashion statement does not engage the protection of the Code, but a person who wears the same nose ring for religious reasons does.

The prohibited grounds of discrimination in other provinces are similar, but not identical, to the grounds in Ontario. For example, some provinces, such as British Columbia and Manitoba, prohibit discrimination on the basis of political belief or opinions. Others do not include all the grounds found in Ontario. For example, New Brunswick's human rights legislation does not include family status as a prohibited ground of discrimination.

Exemptions: Where Discrimination Is Allowed

The right to be free of discrimination in employment on the basis of the 16 grounds is not absolute; the Code sets out specific exemptions where even intentional discrimination is permissible.

However, these exemptions are of limited application and are interpreted narrowly. Furthermore, in many cases, the employer cannot explore whether the exemptions apply until later in the hiring process, usually at the job interview stage or possibly after it makes a **conditional offer of employment**. This is because the Code restricts the types of questions that an employer may ask at the job application stage in order to encourage an employer to consider a broad range of qualified job applicants early in the hiring process.

The statutory exemptions are set out below.

1. Special Service Organizations

Under s. 24(1)(a), the right to equal treatment in employment is *not* infringed where a special service organization—a religious, philanthropic, educational, fraternal, or social organization that primarily serves people identified by their race, ancestry, place of origin, colour, ethnic origin, creed, sex, age, marital status, or disability—gives employment preference to members of that group. However, this exemption is limited to situations where the preference is a reasonable and bona fide requirement for the job in question. For example, a faith-based organization can stipulate that counsellors must be of the relevant faith; however, it probably cannot stipulate that janitors be of that faith because such a requirement is not related to job function. This exception is one of the rare instances under the Code where the hiring organization is not required to accommodate the person or group negatively affected by the job requirement.

Note that to fall within the special service organization exemption, the organization *cannot* be operated for private profit. Moreover, it must serve, as well as hire, people identified by a particular enumerated ground, although as shown in the case of *Ontario Human Rights Commission v. Christian Horizons*, the courts are willing to take a broad interpretation of this requirement if it falls within the spirit of the legislative exemption.

CASE IN POINT

Court Takes Broader View of Special Service Organization Exemption

Ontario Human Rights Commission v. Christian Horizons, 2010 ONSC 2105

Facts

Christian Horizons was an evangelical Christian organization that operated residential homes for people with developmental disabilities. It required all of its employees to sign an employment contract that included a lifestyle and morality statement that, among other things, prohibited homosexual relationships. Most of its employees were categorized as "support workers," whose job functions included cooking, cleaning, doing laundry, taking residents on outings and to appointments, as well as participating in prayer, Bible reading, and hymn singing (para. 104). After one employee, a support worker named Heintz, confided to two co-workers that she was a lesbian, she received uncharacteristically poor performance reviews and criticism and eventually she quit because of stress. Heintz filed a human rights complaint on the basis of sexual orientation. The employer argued that as a religious organization it had the right to restrict employment to those who followed its values, which were clearly stated. However, the Ontario Human Rights Tribunal found that Christian Horizons' actions were not protected by the special service

organization exemption for two reasons. First, it did not restrict its activities to serving only those who shared its creed. It was a government-funded general residential care provider and provided its services to people with developmental disabilities regardless of creed, so it fell outside that exemption. Second, the organization was unable to show that following the lifestyle requirements prohibiting homosexual relationships was a BFOQ for Heintz's position as a support worker. It ordered the employer to pay Heintz $23,000 for its discriminatory conduct against her and ten months' salary for wrongful dismissal. It also ordered the employer to stop imposing the lifestyle statement on employees. Christian Horizons appealed the decision.

Relevant Issue

Whether the employer's actions regarding Heintz were protected by the special service organization exemption.

Decision

The Ontario Divisional Court disagreed with the Tribunal on the first issue but not on the second. It stated that the

Tribunal's interpretation of the requirement for a charitable organization to serve only individuals who shared its beliefs ignored the exemption's underlying purpose: to allow such organizations to join together, share their views, and carry out their joint activities (Smith, 2010, p. 3). To deny the Code's exemption for organizations that broaden the scope of their charitable activities to serve individuals outside their faith is an unnecessarily narrow view of the exemption:

> In the case of the members of Christian Horizons, the charitable work they do is an exercise of their religious beliefs and values. The Tribunal's interpretation of s. 24(1)(a) has the effect of severely restricting the manner in which that religious activity will be carried out, as the Tribunal's interpretation would require them to confine their charitable work to members of their faith group, when they see their religious mandate as to serve all of the needy without discrimination.

On the second issue, however, the court agreed with the Tribunal that Christian Horizons was unable to show that not being in a homosexual relationship was a BFOQ for Heintz's position as a support worker. Although support workers engaged in some of the Christian practices, they were not engaged in actively promoting an evangelical Christian way of life. The court upheld the damage award but ruled that the lifestyle statement could be retained, as long as the prohibition on homosexual relationships was removed.

The *Christian Horizons* decision underscores the need for employers that fall within the special service organization exemption to also direct their minds as to whether the discriminatory requirements are a BFOQ for a particular position. Tribunals and courts will scrutinize such claims carefully; a BFOQ has to be "tied directly and clearly to the execution and performance of the task or job in question" (para. 90).

2. Bona Fide Occupational Qualifications

Under s. 24(1)(b), an employer may discriminate on the basis of age, sex, record of offences, or marital status, if these are genuine requirements of the job. For example, a shelter for abused women may choose to hire only women as counsellors. Similarly, a recreational club may hire only male attendants to work in the men's locker room. However, in such instances, the employer must consider whether accommodation could be made under s. 24(2) to enable a female to work in the position. For example, if working in the men's locker room is a minor part of the job, could the job be redefined to eliminate that element and thus accommodate a female candidate? The employer's general duty to accommodate is discussed more fully in Chapter 5.

3. Nepotism Policies

Under the nepotism policy exemption in s. 24(1)(d), an employer may choose to hire or not hire, or to promote or not promote, her spouse, child, or parent or the spouse, child, or parent of an employee. A nepotism policy whereby an employer gives preference for student employment to the children of its employees is permitted. Conversely, employers may discriminate against spouses, children, or parents of employees if they prefer not to have closely related employees working in the same area. Section 24(1)(d) therefore authorizes both nepotism and anti-nepotism policies.

Where this limited exception applies, the employer is not obligated to accommodate the person or group negatively affected by the job requirement.

4. Medical or Personal Attendants

The medical or personal attendant exemption in s. 24(1)(c) applies to all 16 prohibited grounds of discrimination. A person may refuse to employ someone on the basis of any of the prohibited grounds where the primary duty of the job is attending to the medical or personal needs of the person or to those of an ill child or an aged, infirm, or ill spouse, same-sex partner, or relative of the person. This exemption covers home care and does not apply to conduct by or within an institution, such as a nursing home. For example, a person who wants to hire someone to look after his infirm grandfather in the grandfather's home can discriminate against an applicant on the basis of any of the grounds set out in the Code, including sexual orientation or ethnic origin. This exception presumably reflects the personal nature of the care and the fact that the applicant comes into the person's home. However, the same person may not stipulate in a hospital setting that the grandfather is to be cared for only by people of a certain sexual orientation or ethnic background. This exception also does not apply to persons hired as nannies of healthy children.

There is no duty to accommodate a person or group negatively affected by this exception.

5. Special (Affirmative Action) Programs

Like the medical or personal attendant exemption, the **special programs** exemption in s. 14 of the Code applies to all 16 prohibited grounds. Under this exception, an employer may implement a special program to relieve or promote the status of disadvantaged groups or persons to help them achieve equal opportunity. This exemption allows an employer to prefer or promote people who typically suffer from employment discrimination on the basis of one or more of the prohibited grounds. These special programs are often referred to as **affirmative action** programs. For example, where the employer has a bona fide affirmative action program to hire youth from economically disadvantaged backgrounds, the employer may discriminate in favour of people who fall within this category. Upon application, the Ontario Human Rights Commission will review a program to decide whether it qualifies for the exemption. However, even if it is not "pre-approved," the Tribunal could still find that a particular program that is being challenged is a special program protected by s. 14.

The Code gives the Ontario Human Rights Commission the right to review the employer's special program to ensure that it is operated in good faith.

Recruitment, Selection, and Hiring

It has been said that the selection process is probably responsible for more discrimination than any other area of employment practice. At the hiring stage, assumptions, often subconscious, about certain groups of people and their abilities can come into play. Recruiters are required to make a decision quickly on the basis of information in a job application form and one or two interviews. Unspoken assumptions and first impressions lend themselves to subtle forms of discrimination.

The Code protects job applicants from discrimination by requiring that advertisements, application forms, interviews, and pre-employment testing programs comply with human rights law. At each step of the hiring process, an employer should document all decisions made and include the reasons for each decision. Clear and careful documentation, prepared at the time that a decision is made, provides an employer with a credible basis to defend against allegations that the decision was made on discriminatory grounds. *The Code is infringed even if a discriminatory ground is only one of several reasons for an employment decision.* For example, in *Derksen v. Myert Corps Inc.*, a tribunal found that an employee's dismissal violated the Code even though his absence for a religious leave was only one reason, along with poor job performance, for his dismissal.

The following is a discussion of the human rights issues raised at each step of the recruitment, selection, and hiring process.

Essential Requirements of the Job

An employer should ensure that a job description is current and accurately reflects its needs and expectations. Particular duties or structures that made sense when the job was last filled may have changed in the interim.

The employer should review the job carefully to determine which requirements are *essential* for the job. Under s. 17 of the Code, only essential job duties or requirements can be considered in deciding whether someone is physically capable of performing the job.

Job duties or requirements that are both essential and relate to a prohibited ground of discrimination should be scrutinized carefully. For example, requiring a driver's licence for a job that entails only a minor amount of driving would unnecessarily bar a candidate who is unable to obtain a driver's licence because of physical disability, and therefore would infringe the Code. Similarly, if the job involves a lot of communication with the public, it is reasonable to require fluency in English, but it is unacceptable to discriminate against someone who speaks English with a non-Canadian accent. (Recall that although "language" is not a prohibited ground of discrimination under the Code, it is directly linked to other grounds, such as place of origin.)

Where an essential job requirement negatively affects a person or group on the basis of a prohibited ground of discrimination, an employer has a duty to accommodate the individual or group, unless this causes undue hardship. An employer who alleges undue hardship must prove it on a balance of probabilities. For example, an employer who maintains that a pregnant job applicant is not capable of performing the job because it is too physically demanding must have significant information to back up such a view. This is difficult but not impossible, as *Mack v. Marivtsan* demonstrates.

Employer Refuses Pregnant Applicant Because of Job's Physical Demands

Mack v. Marivtsan (1989), 10 CHRR D/5892 (Sask. Bd. of Inq.)

Facts

The job applicant, who was seven months pregnant, applied for a job as a kitchen helper in a restaurant. The prospective employer refused to hire her because the position involved considerable heavy lifting and she was in the later stages of her pregnancy.

Relevant Issue

Whether the prospective employer infringed the human rights legislation by discriminating on the basis of sex.

Decision

The Saskatchewan Board of Inquiry found that the employer did not infringe the Code. The applicant was not aware of the extent of the physical demands of the kitchen position because she had never worked in such a position before. The employer was able to show that the job was strenuous. Not being in the later stages of pregnancy was a BFOQ.

Use of Employment Agencies

Section 23(4) provides as follows:

> The right under section 5 to equal treatment with respect to employment is infringed where an employment agency discriminates against a person because of a prohibited ground of discrimination in receiving, classifying, disposing of or otherwise acting upon applications for its services or in referring an applicant or applicants to an employer or agent of an employer.

Sometimes employers use employment agencies to hire people temporarily. These workers are often referred to as "temps." In some situations, the agency remains the employer.

The Code prohibits employment agencies from accepting or acting on requests to hire people on the basis of preferences related to prohibited grounds of discrimination. It also forbids employers from making hiring requests that contravene the legislation. For example, an employer cannot legally ask an employment agency to send only "young blondes" to fill a position. An employment agency that accepted this illegal directive would also be in contravention of the Code.

To ensure that it is not implicated in any discriminatory practices, an employer should include a term in its contract with the employment agency requiring the agency to comply with all human rights requirements. Similarly, the agency should make it clear that it will not accept or act on discriminatory directions.

Advertising a Job

Many jobs are filled through advertisements. It is the intention of the Code that an employer consider many qualified candidates in the early part of the recruitment process so that suitable candidates are not eliminated inadvertently. This intention affects both where and how a position is advertised, as well as the contents of the advertisement.

Where and How Is a Job Advertised?

Jobs are often advertised informally, using the "old boys' network" or "word of mouth." The human rights problem with such informality is that it tends to perpetuate the current composition of the workforce. For example, if most of the current employees come from a certain ethnic background, filling the position by internal posting or word of mouth may perpetuate the ethnic status quo.

It is not illegal to advertise by word of mouth or in an ethnically based community paper. However, if there is a subsequent complaint about discrimination, an employer's hiring practices may affect a tribunal's view of the case. Broadly based advertising using a variety of media is best because it provides access to the largest pool of applicants. Senior or highly skilled positions may need to be advertised over a larger geographic area than other jobs.

Contents of Advertisements

Section 23(1) of the Code provides as follows:

> The right under section 5 to equal treatment with respect to employment is infringed where an invitation to apply for employment or an advertisement in connection with employment is published or displayed that directly or indirectly classifies or indicates qualifications by a prohibited ground of discrimination.

The Code states that advertisements should not contain qualifications that directly or indirectly discourage people from applying for a job on the basis of a prohibited ground of discrimination. An advertisement should be geared to the qualifications and skills required for the position.

Advertisements should always use non-discriminatory language when describing a job. For example, gender-neutral words, such as sales clerk (rather than salesman) or server (rather than waitress), should be used. Reference to preferred applicants as "mature" and descriptions of an employer as having a "youthful" culture tend to exclude candidates on the basis of the prohibited ground of age.

Employers should also avoid qualifications that, while not obviously biased, touch on a prohibited ground. For example, if the advertisement states that Canadian experience is preferred, a qualified candidate whose work experience is largely outside Canada might be deterred from applying. Such a qualification could touch on the prohibited ground of place of origin. According to the OHRC's 2013 *Policy on Removing the "Canadian Experience" Barrier*, a strict requirement for "Canadian experience" is *prima facie* discrimination and can only be used in very limited circumstances.

The onus is on employers to show that a requirement for prior work experience in Canada is a bona fide requirement. Previous work experience may be canvassed at the application and interview stage to the extent that it is relevant. Sometimes an essential job duty unavoidably touches on a prohibited ground. For example, because a school bus driver needs a special driver's licence, this requirement may be stated in the advertisement even though it bars applicants who are unable to obtain such a licence because of a disability. Similarly, an employer may indicate that fluency in a particular language is required as long as it can demonstrate that this requirement is a BFOQ. But employers must make sure that they state the essential job requirements rather than refer to personal characteristics. For example, where strenuous physical work is necessary, the advertisement should state that "heavy lifting is required," rather than that "the applicant must be physically fit."

An advertisement can indicate that an employer is an equal opportunity employer or that candidates from diverse backgrounds are encouraged to apply.

Job Applications

Section 23(2) of the Code provides as follows:

> The right under section 5 to equal treatment with respect to employment is infringed where a form of application for employment is used or a written or oral inquiry is made of an applicant that directly or indirectly classifies or indicates qualifications by a prohibited ground of discrimination.

The Code prohibits questions and requests for information on the application form that directly or indirectly classify candidates by prohibited grounds. The wording of s. 23(2) is similar to that of s. 23(1) related to job advertisements. Once again, the intent is to avoid discouraging potential applicants from applying by creating the impression that they would not be acceptable. Appropriate questions are limited to establishing the applicant's name, address, education, and previous employment history. The purpose of the job application form is to gather information on job qualifications and skills and to avoid eliciting information that directly or indirectly excludes individuals on non-job-related grounds.

Figure 2.1 sets out most of the 16 prohibited grounds of discrimination and provides examples of questions that the Commission believes should be avoided because they directly or indirectly touch on those grounds. This list is not exhaustive. In some cases, acceptable alternative wording is suggested. The list of acceptable questions that are not directly job-related is short.

FYI

Sample Job Application Form from the Ontario Human Rights Commission

The following is a sample application form prepared by the Ontario Human Rights Commission that suggests the information that an employer may ask on a job application.

Position being applied for   Date available to begin work

PERSONAL DATA

Last name   Given name(s)

Address   Street   Apt. no.   Home telephone number

City   Province   Postal code   Business telephone number

Are you legally eligible to work in Canada?   ☐ Yes   ☐ No

Are you 18 years or more?   ☐ Yes   ☐ No

Are you willing to relocate in Ontario?   ☐ Yes   ☐ No   Preferred location: _____

To determine your qualification for employment, please provide below and on the reverse,
information related to your academic and other achievements including volunteer work,
as well as employment history. Additional information may be attached on a separate sheet.

EDUCATION

☐ SECONDARY SCHOOL   ☐ BUSINESS OR TRADE SCHOOL

Highest grade or level completed: Name of program: _____

_____   Length of program: _____

Licence, certificate or diploma awarded?   ☐ Yes   ☐ No   ☐ Honours   Type: _____

☐ COMMUNITY COLLEGE   ☐ UNIVERSITY

Major subject: Name of program: _____

_____   Length of program: _____

Degree, diploma or certificate awarded?   ☐ Yes   ☐ No   ☐ Honours   Type: _____

Other courses, workshops, seminars: _____

Licences, certificates, degrees: _____

WORK-RELATED SKILLS

Describe any of your work-related skills, experience, or training that relate to the position being applied for.

_____

_____

_____

(Continued on the next page)

(Continued)

EMPLOYMENT

Name of present/last employer: _____ Job title: _____

Period of employment (includes leaves of absence related to maternity/parental leave, Workplace Safety & Insurance claims, disability, or human rights complaints):   From: _____   To: _____

Salary: _____ Type of business: _____

Reason for leaving (do not include leaves of absence related to maternity/parental leave, Workers' Compensation claims, handicap/disability, or human rights complaints):

_____

Functions/responsibilities: _____

_____

Name of previous employer: _____ Job title: _____

Period of employment (includes leaves of absence related to maternity/parental leave, Workers' Compensation claims, handicap/disability, or human rights complaints):   From: _____   To: _____

Salary: _____ Type of business: _____

Reason for leaving (do not include reasons related to maternity/parental leave, Workplace Safety & Insurance claims, disability, or human rights complaints):

_____

Functions/responsibilities: _____

_____

For employment references we may approach:

Your present/last employer?   ☐ Yes ☐ No   Your former employer(s)?   ☐ Yes ☐ No

List references if different than above on a separate sheet.

PERSONAL INTERESTS AND ACTIVITIES (CIVIC, ATHLETIC, ETC.)

_____

_____

Have you attached an additional sheet?   ☐ Yes ☐ No

I hereby declare that the foregoing information is true and complete to my knowledge. I understand that a false statement may disqualify me from employment, or cause my dismissal.

_____

Signature   Date

FIGURE 2.1 Job Application Form Questions

Prohibited grounds	Unacceptable questions	Acceptable questions
Race *Colour* *Citizenship* *Place of origin* *Ethnic origin* *Ancestry*	• Are you a Canadian citizen? • What is your social insurance number? (This may indicate place of origin or citizenship status, and it should be requested after a conditional offer of employment.) • Where are you from originally? • What schools have you attended? (This may indicate place of origin.) • Are you a member of any clubs or other organizations? (This could indicate sex, race, or religion.) • What is your height and weight? • What is your Canadian work experience?	• Are you legally entitled to work in Canada? • What is the highest level of education that you have reached? • What professional credentials or diplomas have you received? • Are you fluent in English, French, or another language? (Acceptable only if this is a BFOQ.)
Creed	• Are there any days of the week when you are unable to work? Are you willing to work Saturdays? (If these questions are asked, they may raise human rights issues and the employer should be prepared to accommodate up to the point of undue hardship.) • What is your religion? • What religious holidays or customs do you observe?	• None
Sex	• What was your surname before marriage? • What form of address do you prefer (Mr., Mrs., Miss, or Ms.)? • What is your relationship with the person to be notified in case of emergency?	• None
Sexual orientation	• Are you participating in Pride Week?	• None
Marital status	• Are you married? • What was your surname before marriage? • What form of address do you prefer (Mr., Mrs., Miss, Ms.)? • Is your spouse willing to transfer? • What is your relationship with the person to be notified in case of emergency?	• Are you willing to travel or relocate? (Acceptable only if travel or relocation is a BFOQ.)
Family status	• Are you married, divorced, single, or living in a common law relationship? • What is your birth name? • What form of address do you prefer (Mr., Mrs., Miss, Ms.)? • Do you have children? • How many children do you have? • Do you plan to start a family soon? • Are you pregnant? • Do you have appropriate childcare arrangements? • Is your spouse willing to transfer? • What is your relationship with the person to be notified in case of emergency?	• Are you willing to travel or relocate? (Acceptable only if travel or relocation is a BFOQ.)

FIGURE 2.1   Job Application Form Questions   *continued*

Prohibited grounds	Unacceptable questions	Acceptable questions
Record of offences	• Have you ever been convicted of a crime? • Have you ever been arrested? • Have you ever spent time in jail?	• Have you ever been convicted of a criminal offence for which a pardon has not been granted?
Age	• What is your date of birth? • Attach a copy of your driver's licence. • Provide an educational transcript. (This could include dates or age of the applicant.)	• Are you 18 years of age or older?
Disability	• Do you have any handicaps? • Have you ever claimed or received Workplace Safety and Insurance benefits? • Do you have a history of substance abuse? • Are you physically or mentally capable of performing this job? • Do you require any accommodation to perform this job? • This job requires heavy lifting. Will you be able to do it? • Are you a member of Alcoholics Anonymous?	• None

SOURCE: Compiled in part from information contained in Ontario Human Rights Commission (1999, pp. 3–6).

Job Interviews

Section 23(3) of the Code provides as follows:

> Nothing in subsection (2) precludes the asking of questions at a personal employment interview concerning a prohibited ground of discrimination where discrimination on such ground is permitted under this Act.

At the job interview stage, the Code allows an employer considerably more latitude in questioning an applicant than at the previous stages in the hiring process. In a face-to-face meeting, a candidate has a better chance of countering any assumptions or stereotyping that could arise as a result of her response to an employer's inquiries. The employer may expand the scope of job-related questions to include questions that touch on prohibited grounds if they relate to a BFOQ or if an exemption to the Code applies under s. 14, 16, or 24. For example, if the employer is a religious organization hiring an executive director, it may question an applicant's religious affiliation. However, under several of the exemptions, an employer is still obligated to accommodate an employee unless doing so would cause undue hardship (s. 24(2)).

The job interview process poses unique human rights challenges, and everyone who participates in the process should be knowledgeable about human rights requirements. For instance, when meeting a candidate, an interviewer may be tempted to chat informally to create a relaxed atmosphere and to get to know the candidate. During such a conversation, information may be elicited that touches on a prohibited ground. For example, the interviewer may ask whether the candidate prefers to be addressed as Mrs., Ms., or Miss during the interview. Even if this information is elicited without intent to discriminate, it may raise questions about whether the candidate's marital status played a part in the eventual hiring decision. A candidate who is not hired could file a claim of discrimination on the basis of marital status, and an employer would need to expend time and effort in responding to it.

Similarly, it is common for job candidates to comment about family pictures displayed in an interviewer's office. The interviewer should refrain from eliciting information regarding the candidate's family, even though it would be normal to do so in conversation.

The interviewer should resist any urges to form subjective impressions or observations that relate to prohibited grounds. The interviewer should be conscious of human rights issues when placing notes on the interview file that are intended to help him remember a particular candidate. From a legal point of view, notes referring to an "older guy with a slight lisp" or a female candidate wearing a "tight rainbow sweater" will not be helpful.

There are several ways to limit the potential for human rights problems arising from the interview. These include the following:

1. *Accommodate disabilities.* If a job applicant is unable to attend an interview because of a disability, an employer must accommodate the candidate so that he has an equal opportunity to be interviewed.

2. *Have a standard set of questions.* Standardizing an interview keeps it on track and avoids the perception that candidates were treated differently on the basis of a prohibited ground. For example, do not question only female candidates about their ability to travel or relocate or question only certain candidates about whether their race would present difficulties in getting along with staff or clients.

3. *Use interview teams.* Teams allow interviewers to compare impressions and can reduce the impact of individual biases. If a candidate subsequently alleges discrimination, there are several people to recall what took place during the interview. There should be at least one interviewer knowledgeable about the position being offered.

4. *Beware of prohibited grounds.* An interviewer should not ask questions that relate to a prohibited ground unless the elicited information can legally form the basis of a hiring decision. If a response cannot be used in making a hiring decision, the employer takes a risk in asking it. The candidate may perceive that the information played a part in the decision not to hire and it may be difficult to prove otherwise.

   For example, there is some debate about whether an interviewer should raise the issue of physical ability to perform the job at the interview stage. If the disability is obvious and relevant to the essential requirements of the job or if the candidate raises the issue, the employer should discuss the disability and possible accommodations. Otherwise, the candidate may get the impression that the employer has no serious interest in understanding how she can perform the job. However, if the disability is not obvious or is not raised by the candidate, it is probably safer for the employer not to introduce it. Once the employer is aware of the disability, an unsuccessful candidate could allege that that information played a part in denying her the job. The Ontario Human Rights Commission suggests that issues of accommodation should be discussed only after a conditional offer of employment is made unless the candidate requests accommodation at the interview stage or the disability is obvious (Ontario Human Rights Commission, 2008, p. 108).

Generally speaking, a job applicant is under no obligation to voluntarily disclose during an interview a medical condition that qualifies as a mental or physical disability under human rights legislation.

Similar considerations apply to discussions about the accommodation of religious practices. For example, if the position requires that the successful candidate work Friday nights and Saturdays, the employer would be wise not to discuss the candidate's availability for those shifts because this could elicit information concerning a prohibited ground, such as creed. Even if shift work is an important part of the job, an employer is obliged to accommodate an employee unless accommodation would create undue hardship. Therefore, there is little to be gained by raising the issue during the interview stage and risking a discrimination claim unless accommodation is virtually impossible because of the employer's size or hours of operation. If accommodation is virtually impossible, it could be raised at the interview because the employer can justify its discriminatory rule under the three-part *Meiorin* test.

Figure 2.2 sets out the prohibited grounds of discrimination and indicates the circumstances when questions touching on those grounds are acceptable at the interview stage. Other than questions directly related to these circumstances, questions that are prohibited in the job application (see Figure 2.1) are also prohibited during the job interview.

Employers must be careful not to screen out job applicants from the testing or job interview process for discriminatory reasons. In the 2013 case of *Reiss v. CCH Canadian Limited*, a 60-year-old lawyer applied to be a commercial legal writer at CCH, a legal publishing firm. When he was not selected for an interview, he contacted the external human resources consultant who was helping the employer with its recruitment processes. The consultant explained that it looked like the employer was "moving toward candidates that are more junior in their experience and salary expectation." Seeing this as age-based discrimination, Reiss filed a complaint with the Ontario Human Rights Tribunal. The Tribunal held that, although the evidence did not show that age was probably a factor in the employer's decision not to interview him, the human resources consultant's comments were "suggestive of a stereotyped assumption that an older person would necessarily want a higher salary and would therefore not be a good candidate." The Tribunal ordered the employer to pay Mr. Reiss $5,000 "for injury to dignity, feelings and self-respect" as a result of the discriminatory assumptions made. Note that although the external consultant was not an employee of CCH, he was acting as its agent (he'd been given authority to act on its behalf) and therefore the employer was legally responsible for his actions (Rubin Thomlinson LLP, 2013).

A related point to note is that, whether it is at the time of receiving a job application or resumé, during the interview, or after the interview, an employer should be cautious about automatically screening out applicants on the basis that they are overqualified for the position (Miedema and Hall, 2012, p. 39). As shown in the following case of *Sangha v. Mackenzie Valley Land and Water Board*, rejecting an applicant who is an immigrant because he is "overqualified" may be found to be discrimination on the basis of national or ethnic origin.

FIGURE 2.2   Job Interview Questions

Prohibited grounds	When questioning is acceptable
Race *Colour* *Ancestry* *Place of origin* *Ethnic origin*	• The employer is a special service organization that serves the needs of a particular community, and membership in that community is a BFOQ (for example, a social club for a particular ethnic group wants to hire an events coordinator from that ethnic group). • Multilingualism is a BFOQ (for example, a legal aid clinic serving an ethnically diverse population wants to know what languages a candidate speaks).
Creed	• The employer is a special service organization that serves the needs of a particular religious community, and membership in that community is a BFOQ. • The applicant raises the issue and the questions directly relate to the applicant's ability to perform the essential duties of the job and the nature of any necessary accommodation (for example, the job requires a uniform, and the candidate wears a head covering for religious reasons).
Citizenship	• Citizenship or permanent resident status is required by law (see s. 16 of the Code). • Citizenship or permanent resident status is required to foster participation in cultural, educational, trade union, or athletic activities by citizens or permanent residents (see s. 16 of the Code). • The job is a chief or senior executive position (see s. 16 of the Code).
Sex	• The employer is a special service organization that serves the needs of a particular community and being a particular sex is a BFOQ (for example, a woman's shelter wants to hire a female therapist). • Sex is a BFOQ (for example, a residential institution wants to hire male attendants to assist male residents with personal hygiene).
Sexual orientation	• There is no specific exemption. However, if the job is, for example, a helpline counsellor for gay youth in crisis, the employer could still argue that being gay is a BFOQ based on the three-part test in *Meiorin*.
Record of offences	• An applicant's capacity to be bonded is a BFOQ (for example, a security service wants to hire a security guard). • Driving is an essential job duty, and the questions relate to any convictions under the *Highway Traffic Act*.
Disability	• The applicant raises the issue or the disability is obvious, and the questions directly relate to the applicant's ability to perform the essential duties of the job and the nature of any necessary accommodation (for example, Braille readers or ramps). • The employer is a special service organization that serves a particular community and membership in that community is a BFOQ (for example, an organization serving the needs of the hearing impaired wants to hire a community liaison officer who has a hearing impairment).
Age	• The employer is a special service organization that serves the needs of a particular age group and being of that age group is a BFOQ (for example, a youth group wants to hire a social coordinator under a certain age). • Age is a BFOQ under s. 24(1)(b) because of the nature of the employment.
Marital status	• The employer is a special service organization that serves the needs of a particular community, and membership in that community is a BFOQ (for example, an organization that serves single women hires a single woman as its director). • Marital status is a BFOQ under s. 24(1)(b) because of the nature of the employment. • The employer has a nepotism policy that falls within s. 24.
Family status	• The employer has a nepotism policy that falls within s. 24.

SOURCE: Compiled in part from information contained in Ontario Human Rights Commission (1999, pp. 7–10).

CASE IN POINT

Is Overqualification a BFOQ?

Sangha v. Mackenzie Valley Land and Water Board, 2007 FC 856; 2006 CHRT 9

Facts

Sangha had a PhD in environmental science and extensive work experience in this field. After he immigrated to Canada from India, however, he was unable to get a job in keeping with his employment background. Desperate to find a job in his field, he applied for one of four entry-level environmental positions advertised by the employer, Mackenzie Valley. Although Sangha was one of the best-qualified candidates, the employer's interview team decided he was unsuitable because he was overqualified for the position. The team felt he would be easily bored with the job and leave as soon as he found something better and they already had a problem with high turnover. When Sangha found out that he did not get the job, given his credentials and how well he believed the interview had gone, he filed a complaint of discrimination based on race, national or ethnic origin, colour, and religion.

Relevant Issue

Whether rejecting a job candidate who is an immigrant on the basis that he is overqualified is contrary to the Code.

Decision

The Canadian Human Rights Tribunal found that Sangha had been discriminated against on the basis of national and ethnic origin. The Tribunal noted that on the face of it, the employer's hiring process was non-discriminatory and neutral. There were no questions that touched on personal characteristics, such as race, colour, national or ethnic origin, religion, or age, and the interview was conducted professionally. However, relying on expert testimony at the hearing, the Tribunal found that the experience of applying for a job for which one is overqualified is disproportionately an immigrant experience. Visible minority immigrants are disproportionately excluded from the higher levels of the job market because of barriers to employment at this level. They therefore seek employment at lower echelons where their qualifications exceed the job requirements. The Tribunal held: "Thus, a policy or practice against the hiring of overqualified candidates affects them differently from others to whom it may also apply." As such, it is *prima facie* discriminatory.

Sangha was awarded $9,500 for pain and suffering. However, his request for compensation for three years' worth of lost earnings ($55,000 per year) and for an order that Mackenzie Valley hire him when a position became available was denied. In the Tribunal's view, Sangha had not established that his being hired was more than just a "mere possibility" had there not been discrimination. However, on appeal, the Federal Court found that Sangha had in fact shown that there was a "serious possibility" that he would have been hired but for the discriminatory overqualification standard. It therefore sent the decision back to the Tribunal for reconsideration as to the appropriate remedy.

As noted in this decision, an employer should not screen out candidates who are "overqualified" simply because the employer assumes they will be dissatisfied and leave as soon as another position is found. It must make some inquiry into the candidate's motives for applying for the job, in order to obtain a more accurate prediction of the candidate's behaviour if hired.

Special Programs and Medical or Personal Attendants

Under the exemption in s. 14 of the Code, an employer with a bona fide special (affirmative action) program may question an applicant concerning his membership in the group that the program is aimed at.

Similarly, an employer may question a candidate regarding any of the prohibited grounds where the primary job is attending to the medical or personal needs of the employer or of an ill child or an aged, infirm, or ill spouse or relative of the employer. This exemption is narrowly focused on the in-home care of the employer or a close relative under s. 24(1)(c). See above under the headings "Medical or Personal Attendants" and "Special (Affirmative Action) Programs" for more information about these exemptions.

Conditional Offers of Employment

The Ontario Human Rights Commission recommends that certain questions be left until after a conditional offer of employment is made. The Commission believes that this "avoid[s] a misapprehension of discrimination" because the employer obtains the information only after it has offered a job to a candidate.

The following are examples of information that the Commission suggests should be requested only after an employer makes a conditional offer:

- a copy of a driver's licence, which contains information such as date of birth;
- a work authorization from immigration authorities, which contains information regarding date of arrival in Canada;
- a social insurance card, which may contain information regarding immigration status;
- a transcript or copy of professional credentials, which often indicate place of origin; and
- requests for medical examinations or health information necessary for pension, disability, life insurance, and benefit plans, all of which may indicate physical disabilities (Ontario Human Rights Commission, 2008, p. 109).

Another piece of information that an employer should not request until after making a conditional offer relates to Ontario's *Consumer Reporting Act*. Under this Act, information, such as a credit report, can only be provided by a credit-reporting agency in response to an employer's request if a candidate has been told about the request. Details about the request and penalties for failure to comply are set out in Chapter 3 under the heading "Background Checking: Negligent Hiring." Similarly, any police record checks should be done after a conditional offer of employment is made.

Pre-employment Medical or Fitness Examinations

The Commission takes the position that medical tests to determine a candidate's ability to perform the essential duties of a job should take place only after a conditional offer of employment is made. The examination must be directly relevant to the job as well as objectively necessary and appropriate. For example, a back X-ray may be appropriate for a job that involves heavy lifting but not for a managerial job. The results cannot be used to disqualify a candidate unless they directly undermine his ability to perform the essential duties of the job. Even then, the employer is obliged to accommodate the employee unless this would create undue hardship.

If medical testing is required, all candidates must be tested; employers who test only certain candidates may be vulnerable to allegations of discrimination. The results of medical tests must be maintained in confidential medical files, separate from human resources files, and accessible only to qualified medical personnel.

The Commission recommends that where medical testing is appropriate, candidates should be so notified at the time that an offer of employment is made. Arrangements must be made for the competent handling of test materials and for keeping them properly labelled and secure at all times. Test results should be reviewed with the employee by the physician.

Pre-employment Drug and Alcohol Testing

Human rights legislation in Canada considers alcoholism and drug dependency, as well as perceived dependency, to be forms of disability and therefore prohibited grounds of discrimination. As a result, workplace alcohol and drug testing has been severely restricted in this country. However, such testing continues to be an important issue, especially in workplaces that are safety sensitive or that are affiliated with companies operating in the United States where such testing is far more common. The Commission takes the position that testing for drug and alcohol use is *prima facie* discrimination and therefore allowable only in limited circumstances. In its view, drug and alcohol testing is very difficult to justify at the recruitment or hiring stages. The Commission notes that pre-employment drug testing does not measure current impairment, and pre-employment alcohol testing, while measuring impairment at the time of testing, does not predict a candidate's ability to perform the essential job requirements. However, this area of the law is somewhat unsettled. For example, the case of *Weyerhaeuser Company Limited v. Ontario (Human Rights Commission)* (known as the *Chornyj* case) suggests that pre-employment safety-certification drug testing by urinalysis may be acceptable as long as accommodation is provided should the applicant test positive.

CASE IN POINT

Pre-employment Drug Test Not Prima Facie Discriminatory

Weyerhaeuser Company Limited v. Ontario (Human Rights Commission), 2007 CanLII 65623 (Ont. SCDC)

Facts

Weyerhaeuser offered Chornyj a position as a stationary engineer at its Kenora, Ontario plant. The position was considered "safety sensitive" and the offer was conditional on his passing a drug test. Chornyj took the drug test (urinalysis) and the result came back positive for marijuana.

After receiving the positive drug test result, Ms. Argue, from the employer's HR department, spoke with Chornyj. She asked him whether he had ever used marijuana; he initially denied it but finally admitted that he had. Argue expressed serious concerns about Chornyj's honesty, and the next day the offer of employment was withdrawn. Acknowledging that he was not an addict, Chornyj filed a human rights complaint based on perceived disability with the Ontario Human Rights Commission. The Commission referred the complaint to the

Ontario Human Rights Tribunal. The employer brought a motion to the Tribunal to have the complaint dismissed without a hearing on the basis of lack of jurisdiction. It argued that the *Human Rights Code* does not protect a right to lie and there was no evidence that Weyerhaeuser perceived Chornyj to be suffering from a disability. The Tribunal dismissed the motion and Weyerhaeuser applied to the court for an order preventing the Tribunal from hearing the complaint (a very rare occurrence).

Relevant Issue

Whether the employer's pre-employment drug testing is *prima facie* discriminatory on the ground of perceived disability.

Decision

The court found that the employer's policy was not *prima facie* discriminatory because none of the evidence supported a conclusion that the employer perceived Chornyj as being disabled. All of the evidence from Weyerhaeuser's representatives indicated that they saw him as dishonest, not disabled. Moreover, the consequences of a positive drug test under the employer's policy did not support an inference of perceived disability. Under that policy, a positive result for marijuana use did not automatically result in revocation of an offer of employment. The consequences included having a negative drug retest and signing an agreement that prohibited certain conduct for five years, such as using controlled substances (including marijuana) or refusing to submit to an alcohol or drug test. Even then, a positive drug test would not automatically result in dismissal; specific circumstances would be examined and the need for further accommodations evaluated. The court concluded that the Code was not engaged and the Tribunal lacked jurisdiction to hear the matter.

The *Chornyj* decision states that the mere existence of a pre-employment drug-testing policy is not *prima facie* discriminatory on the ground of perceived disability. Rather, it is the effect of the particular policy in each particular case that must be examined. In addition to ensuring that a positive drug test does not automatically disqualify an applicant, an employer must be able to show that such testing assesses an applicant's ability to perform the essential duties of the job (for example, meeting safety-related requirements) and is not merely a test of whether the candidate uses drugs or alcohol. Furthermore, as happened in *Chornyj*, the testing must be carried out only after a conditional offer of employment has been made.

Where such testing is legitimately necessary, the employer should make job applicants aware of the requirement when they make a job offer. On-the-job drug and alcohol testing is discussed in Chapter 5.

Other Forms of Pre-employment Testing

In the Commission's view, tests that seek to assess personal interests, personality traits, and attitudes (psychometric tests) may raise human rights issues if they tend to screen out individuals on the basis of a prohibited ground (Ontario Human Rights Commission, 2008, p. 111). Tests that measure job-related skills, such as typing, mechanical, electrical, and computer skills, are acceptable.

Employers should administer any assessments at the same point in the selection process for all candidates; obtain the candidate's written permission before conducting the testing; investigate the reliability and validity of any tests administered; and ensure that the confidentiality of test results is protected (Hemeda and Sum, 2011, p. 23).

Employers must be prepared to accommodate a job candidate during any testing. In *Mazzei v. Toronto District School Board* (TDSB) the Human Rights Tribunal found that the TDSB had contravened the Code by not accommodating a job applicant's learning disability. The applicant had requested he be provided with a calculator and a separate room to write the pre-employment test but was refused. Once the applicant provided sufficient information about his disability, the employer had a duty to investigate the options for accommodation, and failure to do so was *prima facie* discrimination. The employer was ordered to pay $7,500 for injury to his dignity, feelings, and self-respect. It was also ordered to distribute its guidelines on accommodation to all managers and staff with hiring power as well as a reminder that the duty to accommodate applies "at all stages of the hiring process."

In contrast to other forms of pre-employment testing, pre-employment fitness tests have been frequently challenged under human rights legislation. *Meiorin*, for example, arose out of a fitness test that failed to take into account the different physiological capacities of males and females. *Canadian Union of Public Employees, Local 4400 v. Toronto District School Board*, a more recent case, shows how sensitive employers must be to this issue.

CASE IN POINT

Discrimination on the Basis of Sex Found in Pre-employment Fitness Test

Canadian Union of Public Employees, Local 4400 v. Toronto District School Board (2003), OLAA no. 514 (Howe)

Facts

The employer school board offered three women part-time cleaning jobs on the condition that they pass a physical demands assessment. They began work but were dismissed when they failed to complete the part of the assessment that required them to lift 50 pounds from bench to shoulder height. The employees filed grievances challenging the lifting requirement. They got their jobs back after they were given strength training that helped them meet the lifting requirements, but they pursued their grievance, claiming that the requirement was discriminatory.

Relevant Issue

Whether the lifting requirement contravened the *Human Rights Code* by discriminating on the basis of sex.

Decision

The arbitrator found that the lifting requirement indirectly resulted in the exclusion of a group identified by a prohibited ground (sex) because evidence showed that female candidates initially failed the strength test 16 times more often than male candidates. Because the job requirement had a *prima facie* discriminatory effect, the onus shifted to the employer to show that it was a BFOQ. The employer failed the third part of the *Meiorin* test because it could not demonstrate that it could not accommodate the employees without incurring undue hardship. For example, the employer could have ordered supplies in smaller containers, reduced the height to which supplies are stacked, or arranged for the heavier lifting to be done by others.

Employers must keep human rights requirements in mind throughout the hiring process. Human rights issues that arise after the employee begins to work are discussed in Chapter 5.

REFERENCES

Al-Dandachi v. SNC-Lavalin Inc. 2012 ONSC 6534.

Alexandrowicz, G., et al. *Dimensions of Law: Canadian and International Law in the 21st Century*. Toronto: Emond Montgomery, 2004.

B v. Ontario (Human Rights Commission). 2002 SCC 66, [2002] 3 SCR 403.

British Columbia (Public Service Employee Relations Commission) v. BCGSEU. [1999] 3 SCR 3.

Canadian Union of Public Employees, Local 4400 v. Toronto District School Board. (2003), OLAA no. 514 (Howe).

Christie v. York Corp. [1940] SCR 139.

Consumer Reporting Act. RSO 1990, c. C.33.

Cowling v. Her Majesty the Queen in Right of Alberta as represented by Alberta Employment and Immigration. 2012 AHRC 12.

de Pelham v. Mytrak Health Systems. 2009 HRTO 172.

Derksen v. Myert Corps Inc. 2004 BCHRT 60, [2004] BCHRTD no. 57.

Dobson, S. Smokers Need Not Apply. *Canadian HR Reporter*. May 6, 2013, p. 1.

Edmonds, Ryan, and Jennifer Ip. *An Employer's Guide to Gender Identity and Gender Expression in the Workplace*. Montreal: Heenan Blaikie, 2013.

Focus on Canadian Employment and Equality Rights. Volume 6, no. 35, p. 281. Toronto: CCH Canadian.

Gajecki v. Surrey School District (No. 36). (1989), 11 CHRR D/326 (BCCHR).

Gilbert, Douglas, Brian Burkett, and Moira McCaskill. *Canadian Labour and Employment Law for the US Practitioner*. Washington, DC: Bureau of National Affairs, 2000.

Gorsky, Thomas. Political Beliefs the Next Protected Ground? *Canadian Employment Law Today*. January 9, 2013, p. 1. http://www.sherrardkuzz.com/pdf/kuzz_eCELT _jan_2013_politics.pdf.

Heintz v. Christian Horizons. 2008 HRTO 22.

Hemeda, Y., and J. Sum. Understanding Pre-employment Testing. *Canadian HR Reporter*. November 21, 2011, p. 23.

Human Rights Code. RSO 1990, c. H.19.

Hydro-Québec v. Syndicat des employé-e-s de techniques professionnelles et de bureau d'Hydro-Québec, section locale 2000 (SCFP-FTQ). 2008 SCC 43.

Israel, Peter. Ask an Expert: Can Employers Conduct Drug Screening on Job Applicants? *Canadian Employment Law Today*. Issue no. 384, March 5, 2003, p. 2996.

Law Society of Upper Canada. *Sexual Orientation and Gender Identity: Creating an Inclusive Work Environment—A Guide for Law Firms and Other Organizations*. October 2013. http://www.lsuc.on.ca/WorkArea/DownloadAsset .aspx?id=2147487143.

Maciel v. Fashion Coiffures. 2009 HRTO 1804.

Mack v. Marivtsan. (1989), 10 CHRR D/5892 (Sask. Bd. of Inq.).

Mazzei v. Toronto District School Board. 2011 HRTO 400.

Miedema, Adrian, and Christina Hall. *HR Manager's Guide to Background Checks and Pre-employment Testing*, 2nd ed. Toronto: Carswell, 2012.

Morra, Michelle. Talent Management: Psychometric Testing—Peering Beneath the Surface. *HR Professional*. March/April 2012.

Mottu v. MacLeod and others. 2004 BCHRT 76, [2004] BCHRTD no. 68.

Ontario Human Rights Commission v. Christian Horizons. 2010 ONSC 2105.

Ontario Human Rights Commission. *Annual Report 2003–2004*. Toronto: Government of Ontario, 2004. http://www.ohrc.on.ca/sites/default/files/2003-04.pdf.

Ontario Human Rights Commission. *Annual Report 2008–2009*. Toronto: Government of Ontario, 2009. http://www.ohrc.on.ca/sites/default/files/attachments/ Annual_report_2008-2009.pdf.

Ontario Human Rights Commission. *Annual Report 2012–2013*. Toronto: Government of Ontario, 2013. http://www.ohrc.on.ca/sites/default/files/2012-2013 _accessible_1.pdf.

Ontario Human Rights Commission. *Hiring? A Human Rights Guide*. Toronto: OHRC, 1999.

Ontario Human Rights Commission. *Human Rights at Work 2008*, 3rd ed. Toronto: Carswell, 2008.

Ontario Human Rights Commission. *Policy on Discrimination and Language*. 1996. http://www.ohrc.on.ca/sites/ default/files/attachments/Policy_on_discrimination _and_language.pdf.

Ontario Human Rights Commission. *Policy on Removing the "Canadian Experience" Barrier*. 2013. http://www.ohrc .on.ca/en/policy-removing-%E2%80%9Ccanadian -experience%E2%80%9D-barrier.

Ouimette v. Lily Cups Ltd. (1990), 12 CHRR D/19 (Ont. Bd. Inq.).

Peel Law Association v. Pieters. 2013 ONCA 396.

Pinto, Andrew. *Report of the Ontario Human Rights Review 2012*. Toronto: Ontario Ministry of the Attorney General, 2012.

Quebec (Commission des droits de la personne et des droits de la jeunesse) v. Maksteel Québec Inc. 2003 SCC 68, [2003] 3 SCR 228.

Quebec (Commission des droits de la personne et des droits de la jeunesse) v. Montréal (City). 2000 SCC 27, [2000] 1 SCR 665.

Reiss v. CCH Canadian Limited. 2013 HRTO 764.

Rocha v. Pardons and Waivers of Canada. 2012 HRTO 2234.

Rubin Thomlinson LLP. Is Age Discrimination the Next Frontier? *Employers' Alert*. Issue no. 51, November 2013, p. 1. http://www.rubinthomlinson.com/wp-content/uploads/2012/05/Employers-Alert-November-2013-Age-Discrimination.pdf.

Rudner, S. Ask an Expert: Human Rights—Career Development Program for Younger Workers. *Canadian Employment Law Today*. April 6, 2011, p. 2.

Sangha v. Mackenzie Valley Land and Water Board. 2007 FC 856; 2006 CHRT 9.

Seale, Donna. Using Social Networking Sites in the Hiring Process: Smart Move or Human Rights Trap? Part One. January 26, 2009. http://donnaseale.ca/using-social-networking-sites-in-the-hiring-process-smart-move-or-human-rights-trap-part-one/.

Shaw v. Levac Supply Ltd. (1990), 14 CHRR D/36 (Ont. Bd. of Inq.).

Sherrard Kuzz LLP. Accommodation of Family Status: What Does It Mean? *Management Counsel: Employment and Labour Law Update*. Volume VII, no. 1, February 2008, p. 1. http://www.sherrardkuzz.com/pdf/Vol_VII_No_1.pdf.

Silliker, Amanda. Memo to Winnipeg Hospital Staff: Speak English Only, Please. *Canadian HR Reporter*. April 22, 2013, p. 3.

Silliker, Amanda. US Hospital Balks at Hiring Obese Workers. *Canadian HR Reporter*. May 21, 2012, p. 1.

Sinberg, Laura. Think Looks Don't Matter? Think Again. *Forbes*. December 5, 2009. http://www.forbes.com/2009/12/05/appearance-work-pay-forbes-woman-leadership-body-weight.html.

Smith, Jeff. Organization Must Prove Religion Is a Job Requirement to Discriminate. *Canadian Employment Law Today*. Issue no. 563, August 25, 2010, p. 3.

Special Test Conditions for Learning-Disabled Job Applicant: Tribunal. *Canadian Employment Law Today*. August 24, 2011, p. 7.

Treash, A. Your Toughest HR Question: Accents, Language Issues in the Workplace. *Canadian HR Reporter*. August 2010, p. 23.

Weyerhaeuser Company Limited v. Ontario (Human Rights Commission). 2007 CanLII 65623 (Ont. SCDC).

Wilson, Peter, and Allison Taylor. *The Corporate Counsel Guide to Employment Law*, 2nd ed. Aurora, ON: Canada Law Book, 2003.

XY v. Ontario (Government and Consumer Services). 2012 HRTO 726.

Zeilikman, A. Partner Not an Employee: BC Court: Law Firm Partner Claimed Firm Discriminated Against Him Based on Age. *Canadian HR Reporter*. September 24, 2012, p. 23.

RELATED WEBSITES

- http://www.ohrc.on.ca   The Ontario Human Rights Commission's website. This site contains Commission policies and public education resources.
- http://www.hrto.ca   The Ontario Human Rights Tribunal's website. This site contains application and response forms and materials to assist in working through the application/response process.
- http://www.interfaithcalendar.org   A site that sets out sacred days for various faiths.

REVIEW AND DISCUSSION QUESTIONS

1. Azar worked as a nurse for five years in various temporary positions for the same employer. She applied for a temporary position that was available from September 2009 to June 2010. Before the hiring decision was made, Azar advised the employer that she was pregnant and expected to commence her pregnancy leave in February 2010. Although she was the most qualified applicant for the job, the employer awarded the job to someone else because of her lack of availability to complete the short-term contract. Azar filed an application with the Ontario Human Rights Tribunal.
   a. What is the alleged ground of discrimination?
   b. In your opinion, did the employer contravene the Ontario *Human Rights Code*? Explain your answer.

2. Monique applied for a position as a cashier at a cafeteria. The employer's dress code requires employees to be "neatly groomed in appearance" and to avoid displaying body piercings or tattoos. The employer refused to hire Monique because she wears a nose ring. Monique filed an application with the Human Rights Tribunal.
   a. What is the alleged ground of discrimination?
   b. In your opinion, did the employer contravene the Code? Explain your answer.

3. Joe applied for a position in a daycare centre. The centre refused to interview him because it thinks that parents would be uncomfortable with having a man take care of their young children. Joe filed an application with the Ontario Human Rights Tribunal.

   a. What is the alleged ground of discrimination?

   b. In your opinion, did the employer contravene the Code? Explain your answer.

4. During his job interview, Zhou mentioned that he was recovering from an addiction to cocaine. The employer refused to proceed with the interview because the position being applied for was in a safety-sensitive area. Zhou filed an application with the Ontario Human Rights Tribunal.

   a. What is the alleged ground of discrimination?

   b. In your opinion, did the employer contravene the Code? Explain your answer.

5. The employer interviewed a number of candidates for a position in a nursing home that involves lifting patients and other physically demanding work. One of the candidates, Joan, had limited mobility in her arm, which was obvious at the interview. The employer did not address the issue, and the interview was brief. Joan was not hired and filed an application with the Ontario Human Rights Tribunal.

   a. What is the alleged ground of discrimination?

   b. In your opinion, did the employer contravene the Code? Explain your answer.

6. Joe has a medical degree from a university outside Canada. He applied for a position as an orderly because his degree is not recognized in Canada. The employer refused to give him the job because she felt that he was overqualified and would leave as soon as he found a position more in keeping with his education. Joe filed an application with the Ontario Human Rights Tribunal.

   a. What is the alleged ground of discrimination?

   b. In your opinion, did the employer contravene the Code? Explain your answer.

7. In 2005 Martha was charged with, and pleaded guilty to, shoplifting. She received a conditional discharge and according to the law in that province (Quebec), she automatically received a pardon after the passage of a certain period of time. Four years later, Martha applied to be a police officer in Montreal but because of her past charge, her application was rejected on the ground that she did not meet the Montreal police service's strict hiring standards, which required that candidates must be of "good moral character." Martha filed a human rights application, alleging that her rights had been violated. The police responded that the misconduct itself, not the charge, brought her moral character into question. Assuming that this fact situation had taken place in Ontario:

   a. What is the alleged ground of discrimination?

   b. Discuss possible arguments that Martha could make to support her claim. Discuss possible arguments that the police could make to support their position.

   c. In your opinion, would Martha succeed in her claim? Explain your answer.

8. The Ontario *Human Rights Code* was first enacted in 1962 to end discriminatory practices in five social areas. It has been argued, however, that this law has not been very effective. Critics have asserted that racist and sexist employers have found ways to circumvent the law. Discuss whether Ontario's human rights law has achieved its objective of eliminating discrimination based on the 16 prohibited grounds. If not, how could it be made more effective?

9. Increasingly, employers are using social networking sites to find out more information about job candidates in the hiring process and basing their hiring decisions in part on this information. Is this a smart move or a human rights trap? What are some of the upsides and downsides of this approach?

10. Sarah, a salon owner, operates a trendy salon in London, Ontario. She advertises for a stylist. Nia calls in response to the ad and seeks an interview. At no time does Nia mention she covers her head for religious reasons. Nia attends the interview, which lasts only ten minutes. During the interview, Nia makes it clear that she will not remove her headscarf while at work and Sarah tells her that in that case, she cannot hire her. Sarah has a policy requiring all stylists to show their hair. She doesn't allow baseball caps or other hats to be worn by staff because, in her view, a stylist's hair is her "calling card" and that of the salon's.

   As a result of Sarah's reaction to her headscarf during the interview, and the ultimate decision not to offer her the job, Nia files a human rights application alleging discrimination. (She's been turned down by numerous salons and she's tired of it.) Sarah says she's a small salon and the costs of responding to this complaint will put her into financial ruin.

   Assume that you are on the Human Rights Tribunal deciding this case. On the basis of Ontario's *Human Rights Code*, what would your decision be? Support your conclusions.

11. You are the newly hired HR manager at a medium-sized bottling plant. A supervisor tells you that one of his employees, George, has just told him that he is in the process of transitioning to a female and would like co-workers to refer to him by his new name: Gina. The supervisor thinks the other employees will simply find this a joke, and make fun of George. How would you advise the supervisor?

12. Is it a violation of the Code for an employer to require proficiency in English?

13. McCormick was an equity partner at a prestigious law firm in British Columbia. As per the terms of the partnership agreement, he was due to retire during the year in which he turned 65. When he and the firm were unable to reach an agreement that would allow him to work beyond this age, he started a proceeding under British Columbia's human rights legislation, alleging age-based discrimination. The law firm challenged the Tribunal's jurisdiction on the basis that McCormick was a partner, not an employee, of the firm. The British Columbia Court of Appeal agreed: unlike a corporation, a partnership is not a separate legal entity. Therefore, McCormick, as a partner, could not be an employee of the partnership because he cannot employ himself.

    If this fact situation occurred in Ontario, instead of British Columbia, would the result likely be different?

14. Can an employer can have a "non-smokers only" hiring policy? Discuss.

15. You've just started your new job as an HR manager at a retail chain that sells teen clothing. A supervisor calls you with a question. She's been getting complaints from a couple of employees that other employees are speaking with each other during work hours in a language other than English (even though they speak English well). This seems rude because it makes them feel left out of the conversation. The supervisor is wondering whether she can insist that all employees speak English during working hours. Advise the supervisor.

16. Ontario's *Human Rights Code* currently lists 16 prohibited grounds of discrimination. Although weight discrimination is one of the most common forms of discrimination in the workplace, weight is not one of the 16 prohibited grounds. Should it be added?

17. Your employer tells you she would like to establish a mentorship program for employees under age 35 but wonders whether this would be illegal under the Ontario *Human Rights Code*. Advise her.

18. Mary was hired by Good Value Shop in 2004. She has suffered from, and been treated for, depression most of her life. Mary is seen as a difficult employee: her supervisor describes her as short-tempered, manipulative, and disruptive. One behaviour that is particularly resented by her manager is her habit, after receiving directions from a manager, of checking with other managers and co-workers in the store to see whether those directions are being consistently applied. In 2012 Mary goes off work on stress leave for depression. The supporting documentation sent to the disability insurance provider makes it clear that her depression relates to her work situation. It indicates that several friends and co-workers have quit because of stress, she has had four different managers in less than two years, and there is frequent bullying and verbal abuse by managers. When she returns to work two months later, she continues with the behaviour that had most upset her supervisor: questioning instructions and checking with other managers to see whether those instructions are being consistently applied. Her supervisor repeatedly tells her not to do this but she continues. As a result, her employment is terminated for insubordination, four months after she returned from stress leave. In your opinion, has the employer infringed the *Human Rights Code*? Explain your answer.

Common Law Issues

3

LEARNING OUTCOMES

After completing this chapter, you will be able to:

- Understand key common law issues related to hiring, including negligent misrepresentation.

- Understand the effect of using executive search firms in the recruitment process.

- Explain the legal implications of using background checks, including conducting Internet and social media-based searches.

- Identify the various categories of employees, including full-time, part-time, and temporary.

Introduction

Although issues arising under human rights legislation present the most significant challenges facing employers during the hiring process, common law issues arise as well. This chapter begins by looking at the main areas of potential common law liability for both parties during the recruitment, selection, and hiring phases. These include misrepresentations by job candidates, the employer, and executive search firms; inappropriate inducements by employers to lure a job candidate; negligent hiring where an employer fails to conduct proper background checks; and anticipatory breach of contract.

The chapter concludes by briefly discussing different categories of employees. Although in most situations the law does not distinguish one group of employees from another, categories such as full- and part-time employees are commonly used by employers and are noted here for clarification.

Areas of Common Law Liability

1. Misrepresentation by Job Candidates

There is no legislation that requires job candidates to be honest during the application process. However, courts have held that misrepresentations made by **employees** before they are hired may justify dismissal if the misrepresentations go to the root of their qualifications for the job. In other words, if a false statement related to qualifications or work experience has a significant impact on the hiring decision, an employer can terminate an employee as a result of that misstatement, even if the employee is performing the job satisfactorily.

This principle also applies to false statements that are not necessarily material to the hiring decision but that suggest an inherent lack of honesty, especially where the job requires a high degree of trust. If, for example, a candidate indicated that she had obtained a particular academic degree when in fact she had completed most of the course work but never graduated, dismissal may be justified. In *Cornell v. Rogers Cablesystems Inc.*, the court found that dismissal was justified where the applicant misled the prospective employer into believing, among other things, that he was still employed with his former employer when in fact he had been dismissed.

On the other hand, minor or negligent misstatements do not customarily justify dismissal without notice. For example, if an applicant unintentionally misstated the length of time that he had worked in a previous job and that misinformation was not significant to the employer, the employer probably could not dismiss the employee without reasonable notice. In *Earle v. Grant Transport*, the employer was unsuccessful in defending an action for wrongful dismissal by an employee who had misled the employer during an interview into thinking that he was earning more at his current job than what the employer was offering. The court found that the employee's "innuendo" was not sufficiently misleading to support his dismissal without notice.

To emphasize the importance of honesty in filling out application forms, and to buttress its legal position, an employer should include an **attestation clause** at the end of all job application forms. This clause should state that the information provided is true and complete to the applicant's knowledge and that the applicant realizes that a false statement may disqualify her from employment or be the cause for her dismissal. Thus, if the employer subsequently discovers a serious misrepresentation, it can establish that the employee was forewarned about the possible consequences, including dismissal without notice. Similarly, if an employer believes that a certain educational or professional qualification is necessary for a particular job, it should state this in its job posting or hiring policy (Miedema and Hall, 2012, p. 43).

2. Wrongful Hiring: Negligent Misrepresentation

Misrepresentation by an Employer

An employer also may be legally liable for inaccurate statements made during the hiring process. If the employer makes a misrepresentation that is relied on by a prospective employee and that employee suffers damages because of it, the employer may have to compensate the employee. It is irrelevant that the employer sincerely believed that the misleading or inaccurate statements were true. The employer has an obligation to ensure that material statements made during the recruitment process are accurate.

The leading case in the area of **negligent misrepresentation** in hiring is *Queen v. Cognos Inc.* It demonstrates the potential liability that exists when an employer fails to ensure the accuracy of statements made during the hiring process.

CASE IN POINT

Negligent Misrepresentation in Hiring

Queen v. Cognos Inc., [1993] 1 SCR 87

Facts

Queen was living with his family in Calgary, where he had been practising as a chartered accountant for approximately eight and a half years, when he responded to the employer's advertisement for a position in Ottawa. During the interview, the employer's representative told him that the job involved a major project that was going to be developed over the next two years and that would be maintained by the individual hired. Although the representative was aware at the time of the interview that senior management had not yet approved funding for the project, he did not advise Queen that the job was dependent on the funding approval. Queen accepted the job, leaving a position that was well paying and secure. He signed a written contract of employment under which he could be terminated without cause on one month's notice or pay in lieu of notice. He moved his family from Calgary to Ottawa. However, funding for the project failed to materialize, and he was dismissed shortly thereafter. He brought an action for negligent misrepresentation in hiring.

Relevant Issue

Whether the employer was liable for negligent misrepresentation.

Decision

The Supreme Court of Canada held that the employer and its representative breached the duty of care owed to Queen during the hiring process. The court found that to establish a negligent misrepresentation, the following test must be met:

- there must be a duty of care based on a special relationship between the party making the representation and the candidate;
- the representation must be untrue, inaccurate, and misleading;
- the party making the representation must have acted negligently in making the misrepresentation;

- the candidate must have reasonably relied on the negligent misrepresentation; and
- the reliance must have caused harm to the candidate.

The Supreme Court found that an employer owes a duty to a job candidate beyond merely being honest; it must also be careful that it does not mislead potential employees. It was apparent to the employer's representative that Queen was relying on the information provided during the interview in deciding to take the job. To meet the duty of care, the representative should have informed Queen of the precarious nature of senior management's financial commitment to the project.

Queen was entitled to damages of $50,000 for loss of income, the cost of obtaining other employment, and the loss incurred on the sale of his Ottawa home, and general damages of $5,000 for emotional stress.

Actions for negligent misrepresentation in hiring are uncommon in Canada because employees recruited under false pretenses generally claim wrongful dismissal. However, in *Queen v. Cognos*, the candidate had signed a written contract of employment that limited his notice of termination to one month. The court found that the fact that he had signed an employment contract did not remove the employer's liability for the misrepresentation made during pre-contract discussions. The written contract did not prevent the negligent misrepresentation action because the misrepresentation went to the "nature and extent" of the employment opportunity, and the contract did not cover this issue.

There are a number of steps that an employer can take to avoid liability. It should ensure that all information given at the pre-employment stage is accurate and complete. It should ensure that the job description is accurate and that all interviewers know what the prospective job and compensation package involve. The employer's representatives must be candid about the job. Attempts to make the job sound as attractive as possible should be avoided if they involve misleading a candidate in any way. If the interviewer does not know the answer to a question asked by a candidate, the interviewer should undertake to contact the candidate with the correct answer.

When a candidate is chosen, the employer should prepare a written employment contract that sets out the terms of employment. The contract should include a clause that states that all oral representations are void on the signing of the contract. Such a clause may override inaccurate statements and simple misunderstandings made in the hiring process.

There are limits to when an employer will be held liable for misstatements made during the hiring process. Employers will not be found liable, for instance, where an employee's reliance on an employer's information is unreasonable. Where a reasonable person would have detected the inaccuracy or where the employee was in a position to verify the facts of a statement but failed to do so, the plaintiff will not be successful. Reliance on opinions or idle comments does not constitute grounds for a negligent misrepresentation claim, and misstatements that result in mere inconvenience do not establish a claim (Gilbert, 2000, p. 109).

Executive Search Firm Misrepresentations

Employers often use executive search firms to recruit potential candidates. Most representations made by a recruitment firm are the legal responsibility of the employer. For example, if an overly zealous search firm recruiter promises a job candidate annual pay increases of 20 percent, that representation could bind the employer. If the pay increases do not materialize, it is possible that the employee could successfully sue the employer for breach of the employment contract.

Therefore, the employer's contract with the search firm should specify the position, compensation, and career potential for the job and restrict the firm to providing only that information to job candidates. Representations about the job should be limited to those authorized by the employer. The contract should also contain an indemnity clause establishing the search firm's liability in the event that it makes a misrepresentation to a candidate that the employer is subsequently held liable for.

As shown in the following case of *The Treaty Group Inc. v. Drake International Inc.*, an executive search firm may also be legally responsible if it is negligent in the way it conducts its search and the employer suffers damages as a result.

CASE IN POINT

Executive Search Firm Liable in Both Contract and Tort

The Treaty Group Inc. v. Drake International Inc., 2007 ONCA 450; (2005), 36 CCLT (3d) 262

Facts

Treaty retained Drake, a global personnel and training firm, to fill a position that involved bookkeeping and banking duties. Drake's marketing material promised that it would provide the "highest calibre of professional screening, evaluation and reference-checking," and Treaty hired Drake's recommended candidate, Ms. Simpson. However, when Simpson resigned from her position two years later, Treaty discovered that she had defrauded the company of over $263,000. It turned out that Simpson had been twice criminally convicted of defrauding former employers but Drake had not uncovered that information. In addition to taking action against Simpson, Treaty sued Drake, claiming damages on the basis of both breach of contract and tort for negligent misrepresentation concerning the quality of its service and negligence in failing to conduct proper reference checks.

Relevant Issue

Whether the executive search firm is liable for losses sustained by Treaty as a result of the employee's fraud.

Decision

The trial judge, upheld by the Court of Appeal, held that Drake was liable for Treaty's losses on the basis of both the tort of negligence and breach of contract because it was clear that, had Drake properly checked Ms. Simpson's background, Treaty would not have hired her. However, damages were limited to 50 percent of the total amount of $263,324 on the principle of contributory negligence because Treaty could have avoided the losses if it had supervised Simpson more carefully.

3. Inducement: Aggressive Recruiting

A tort known as "inducement," "allurement," or "enticement" occurs when an employee is lured from her current position through aggressive recruiting or inflated promises. Aggressive recruiting involves more than advertising a position. It requires a significant degree of pursuit, such as repeatedly contacting the candidate and encouraging her to leave her current job. The tort of inducement may also occur when the recruiter promises such things as promotions, salary increases, job security, or other benefits that never materialize.

As shown in the decision of *Egan v. Alcatel Canada Inc.* below, where the tort of inducement is committed and the new employee is subsequently dismissed by the employer, the employee may be entitled to a larger award for wrongful dismissal damages than if there had been no inducement. Usually, in determining the length of notice of termination that a dismissed employee is entitled to, the court looks at length of service, age, position, and the availability of similar employment. However, where it finds that the employee was lured to a new job from a secure job, it considers additional factors in determining reasonable notice. It may extend the notice period on the basis of such factors as how secure the previous job was, whether the employee rejected other job offers that provided greater benefits, and whether the new job involved relocating. The rationale for this is that where a person is enticed to leave a secure position, it is unfair to wrongfully dismiss her after a short period of employment and then rely on a short notice entitlement.

CASE IN POINT

Luring a New Recruit Can Be Costly

Egan v. Alcatel Canada Inc., 2004 CanLII 2553 (Ont. SC)

Facts

Egan was a senior-level employee who had worked for Bell Canada for close to 20 years when she was contacted by two former Bell employees who were now working for Alcatel. They both encouraged her to interview for a position with their new employer. Although they never advised Egan of this, the two former colleagues would share an $8,000 recruitment bonus if they successfully recruited her to Alcatel.

Initially Egan was not particularly interested in leaving her secure job at Bell but she finally agreed to let them submit her resumé and she later attended an interview. The position offered a large pay increase, a signing bonus, and stock options. Although no express promises were made about job security, both sides anticipated a lengthy period of employment. Egan finally agreed to take the job at Alcatel. Less than two years later Egan was let go as part of a mass termination. She was offered a severance package of 12 weeks' pay in lieu of notice. Egan sued for additional severance moneys, alleging that she was entitled to receive enhanced common law reasonable pay in lieu of notice because she had been "lured" from her secure position.

Relevant Issue

Whether the employee's common law notice period should be extended to reflect the manner in which she had been recruited.

Decision

The court held that her common law reasonable notice period should be extended. Although it found that there was nothing "untoward" in Alcatel's or her former colleagues' approach, Egan was unaware that the latter had a financial incentive to induce her to take the job at Alcatel. She was thus put at a disadvantage in judging the weight she should put on their assurances about the position at Alcatel. The court awarded her nine months' pay in lieu of notice, a significantly greater amount than would normally be given to an employee with less than two years' service.

An employer that overstates the features of a job may find that it has also committed the tort of negligent misrepresentation. Inducement and negligent misrepresentation are separate torts, but they can both arise from the same situation.

In summary, honesty and openness about the job being offered, especially in the area of job security and the possibilities for career advancement, are essential. It is never advisable for an employer to make specific promises with respect to long-term job security, such as "I guarantee you'll be in this job for at least five years."

The issue of the termination notice period should be addressed by the employer and employee in a written employment contract before an employee starts the job. For example, if the prospective employee is leaving a secure job of 18 years, the parties should state whether, or to what extent, this service will be recognized in determining reasonable notice of termination. It is better for both parties to negotiate this sensitive issue while they are on positive terms.

4. Restrictive Covenants

Many written employment contracts restrict the ability of employees to compete with their former employer, to solicit employees or customers, or to use the former employer's confidential information. Before hiring an applicant, an employer should find out whether the applicant is subject to a **restrictive covenant**—that is, a promise not to engage in certain types of activities during or after employment—that might affect her ability to perform the new job.

Restrictive covenants are seen as a "restraint of trade" and are enforceable only if they are reasonable in the circumstances. The courts do not like contractual terms that inhibit or prevent someone from earning a living in his own field. Therefore, they uphold a restrictive covenant only if an employer can show that the covenant does not go beyond what is necessary to protect its legitimate interests. For example, restricting a regional sales manager from competing in her own region for a short period of time after employment ends may be reasonable, but restricting her from competing beyond that region is not.

An employer that is interested in recruiting a candidate who is subject to a restrictive covenant should obtain legal advice concerning the covenant's enforceability and the limits that it could place on the candidate's ability to perform the job. This is especially true if the new employer is a competitor of the former employer. The written employment contract should designate which party is legally responsible if the former employer successfully enforces this covenant. Restrictive covenants are discussed at greater length in Chapter 4 under the heading "Restrictive Covenants."

5. Anticipatory Breach of Contract

An anticipatory breach of contract occurs when one party repudiates (rejects) the employment contract—through either its statements or its conduct—after the offer of employment is accepted but before employment begins. Although in principle this cause of action applies to both employer and employee, typically the employer is sued for wrongful dismissal damages when it changes its mind about an employment contract. For example, the employer may change its mind about the candidate's suitability or decide to eliminate a position after hiring someone to fill it because of changed circumstances. During the financial crisis in 2008, for instance, Ford Canada revoked hundreds of job offers made just before the crisis began, arguing that because of the rapidly deteriorating economy, it could no longer proceed with those hires. (See the FYI box "Ford Revokes Hundreds of Job Offers.") However, an employer's changed circumstances generally are not a defence against a claim for anticipatory breach of contract. At a minimum, an employee whose employment contract is revoked before starting the job will be entitled to "reasonable notice" damages, similar to the amount payable if an employee had already started work and been employed for a very short period. Moreover, where the individual has quit a secure job, relocated, or made some other change because of the job offer, the damage award will typically reflect these additional expenditures (Stefanik, 2010, p. 4).

To be successful in an action for anticipatory breach of contract, the hired employee must show that

- an offer of employment was made,
- the offer was accepted,
- the contract was then repudiated by the employer (by either word or conduct), and
- the employee suffered damages as a result.

To protect itself against an action for anticipatory breach of contract, an employer should hire with care by determining the suitability of the candidate *before* an offer is made. Where the position depends on a particular set of circumstances unfolding in a certain way, the offer should be made conditional upon those circumstances occurring. Where an anticipatory breach *has* occurred as a result of changed circumstances, the employer may choose to help the employee find another, comparable job as quickly as possible to minimize the damages suffered, and should certainly do nothing to hinder such a search. Finally, it is helpful to the employer to have a written employment contract that includes a reasonable termination notice clause that restricts the amount of wrongful dismissal damages the employee is entitled to. These clauses often provide for limited notice in the first few months of employment, and likely could be relied upon to reduce damages in an anticipatory breach situation (Stefanik, 2010, p. 5).

That said, there may be situations in which an employer's repudiation of the employment contract is justified, and the employer will not be liable for damages for anticipatory breach of contract. For example, if driving is an essential part of the new position and the hired employee loses his licence after the job offer is made and accepted, the employer may, subject to any human rights obligations, be justified in refusing to honour the employment agreement.

FYI

Ford Revokes Hundreds of Job Offers

In the spring of 2008, Ford Canada made job offers to about 350 individuals to work on its assembly lines. However, before the newly hired employees could begin work, the economic crisis hit and Ford decided that it had to revoke those offers. The hired individuals, many of whom had resigned from other positions as a result of Ford's job offer, launched a class action against Ford for anticipatory breach of contract. Claims included damages for loss of income and employment benefits, as well as loss of tenure with their former employers. The class action was **certified**, and in 2011, Ford settled the claim for $835,000.

6. Background Checking: Negligent Hiring

How important is it to investigate the information supplied by a job candidate? One large study found that 46 percent of the employment, education, and reference checks performed revealed inconsistencies between the information provided by the job applicant and the information uncovered through background checks (Miedema and Hall, 2012, p. xi). Common misrepresentations found in resumés include listing family members as former supervisors; gaps in employment not shown on the resumé; incorrect start and end dates and job titles; and false academic credentials.

As noted above in the section "Misrepresentation by Job Candidates," an employer may (in rare cases) be able to dismiss an employee for cause for serious misrepresentations made during the hiring stage. However, the time and effort expended in doing so, as well as the costs of a "bad hire," underscore the desirability of verifying the information supplied and doing a background check *before* someone is hired. The costs of a bad hire can include potential liability for **negligent hiring** if that employee later causes foreseeable harm to a **third party** (someone other than the employer or employee).

Reference Checks

Asking an applicant to supply references is a common and recommended practice. It is advisable to get references from a variety of sources, including past supervisors, co-workers, and teachers, to get a well-rounded picture of the job candidate.

Although there have not been many Canadian cases on negligent hiring, there have been instances where an employer has been found liable to a third party when its failure to check references has resulted in harm to that third party. For example, in *Downey v. 502377 Ontario Ltd.*, two doormen employed at a bar beat a patron severely and caused serious brain injuries. One of the doormen had a history of violent actions. The employer was found liable for failing to properly check its employees' references.

The more a job exposes others to the risk of harm, the stronger the employer's duty to investigate becomes. The **standard of care** (the level of diligence one is expected to exercise) imposed on employers is the common law duty of reasonable care—the level of diligence that is reasonable under the circumstances. Hiring an employee who will be in a position of trust, such as a daycare provider, or who may be required to use force, such as a security guard, requires a high standard of care. What that level of care is has not been firmly settled by the courts. However, in the *Drake* case discussed above, one expert suggested that standard practice in the executive search firm industry is to check the last five years of employment and/or the last three references (Miedema and Hall, 2012, p. 21).

Before checking references, an employer should obtain the written permission of the applicant. This authorization may be obtained through a statement on the application form where the applicant's signature indicates that permission has been given. The consent should be general enough that it allows the employer to contact any person who it believes is able to provide relevant information about the applicant. The employer should not be limited to making decisions based on only references named by the applicant. Note that if the applicant's current employer is to be contacted, specific consent should be obtained for that employer since the applicant may not have told the current employer that he is searching for another job. One way of handling this is to only obtain a reference from the current employer after a conditional offer of employment has been made (Miedema and Hall, 2012, p. 22).

Employers should record the details of all steps taken when investigating candidates so that they will have a written record to use as evidence in the event of a lawsuit. A detailed paper trail should include references who did not respond and the information provided by those who responded. The same inquiries should be made of all applicants to ensure consistency and thoroughness and to avoid perceptions of discrimination. All information obtained should be kept confidential. The reference checker should not share the comments of one reference with other references, or tell references who the other references are (Miedema and Hall, 2012, p. 22).

If a reference voluntarily offers information about the applicant that relates to a prohibited ground of discrimination, such as race or sexual orientation, the reference checker should indicate that she is not interested in that information. In addition, foreign references should not be treated as less valuable than Canadian references because this could lead to a claim of discrimination (Miedema and Hall, 2012, p. 26).

A common problem with reference checking is that former employers are hesitant to criticize a candidate, fearing that a negative reference could result in a lawsuit. In reality, former employers are rarely sued for giving negative references. Still, many employers have adopted a "no references" policy or they confirm only basic facts such as the individual's job title, and start and end dates of employment. Despite this difficulty, an employer should conduct reference checks, especially where the position is one of trust and could reasonably result in harm to a third party. Moreover, even a reference that only confirms dates and job title can be helpful in revealing inconsistencies on a candidate's resumé (Miedema and Hall, 2012, p. 23).

Education and Professional Credentials Checks

Another type of background check relates to education and professional or trade certification. Failure to perform these checks could also result in negligence claims where a negligently hired employee causes harm or loss to a third party in the course of her employment because she lacks the educational requirements necessary for her job. This is especially true where the applicant is required by law to hold a particular degree or certification, as in the case of engineers, accountants, and nurses (Miedema and Hall, 2012, p. 31). Given the growth of "diploma mills" and fake degrees, the checker should call the institution cited on the resumé and speak directly with the records department or registrar's office to confirm a candidate's degree and date of graduation or, where relevant, contact an independent source that evaluates educational institutions.

IN THE NEWS

Yahoo CEO Scott Thompson Resigns After Scrutiny of His Resumé

NEW YORK—Yahoo CEO Scott Thompson left the company four months into the job Sunday after more than a week of scrutiny into inaccuracies on his resumé and in company filings. ...

Thompson's exit was encouraged by Third Point, the activist hedge fund that owns nearly 6 per cent of Yahoo shares. Third Point claimed that Thompson had padded his resumé with a degree in computer science from Stonehill College. Thompson did earn an accounting degree from Stonehill, a Catholic school near Boston, in 1979, a fact that Yahoo correctly lists. But he did not earn a computer science degree.

SOURCE: Christina Rexrode, "Yahoo CEO Scott Thompson Resigns After Scrutiny of His Resumé," The Associated Press, May 13, 2012. Used with permission.

Credit Checks

Laws dealing with credit checks are common throughout Canada. For example, if an employer in Ontario wants to check the candidate's credit situation, Ontario's *Consumer Reporting Act* requires that the employer notify the applicant, in writing, of its intention before the check. The employer should include the request for authorization to conduct the credit check and provide notification on the application for employment. (The request and notification must be in boldface type or underlined and in at least 10-point print.) If the candidate requests it, the employer must notify her of the name and address of the credit-reporting agency supplying the report. If the candidate is not hired, wholly or in part because of the credit check, the employer must advise the candidate of the reasons for her rejection and of her right to request information concerning the credit-reporting agency within 60 days. There are significant fines of up to $100,000 for failure to comply with this legislation (Israel, 2003, p. 2996).

Checking an applicant's credit history may be prudent where the position requires, for example, handling customers' money. However, it should be noted that, based on the wording of the *Consumer Reporting Act*, a legal argument can be made that the Act requires an employer who rejects an applicant to advise the applicant of *all* information that the employer considered in the job application process, not just the credit report (s. 10(7)), where the applicant requests it. This is true even where the information in the credit report played no part in the decision not to hire that individual. Therefore, it may be wise for an employer to only conduct credit checks where credit information is reasonably necessary for the position in question (Miedema and Hall, 2012, p. 53). In Canada, most jobs do not require a credit check.

Police Records Checks

Where the position being applied for requires an employee to work with vulnerable people such as children or people with disabilities, or involves substantial trust, employers should require candidates to provide a police records check. Such checks are actually required by law in certain industries or sectors or for certain jobs. For example, in Ontario an employer who operates a group home for persons with developmental disabilities must, before hiring an employee or volunteer who will work directly with residents, obtain a police records check. Similarly, a teacher applying for a teaching certificate must provide a "criminal record declaration" (Miedema and Hall, 2012, p. 103). All police records checks require the prospective employee's informed consent.

Where a police check is required, this should be clearly stated on the application form, and the offer of employment should be made conditional on the employee's providing the results—and those results being acceptable—to the employer. The employer should also be specific about the kind of search involved (Miedema and Hall, 2012, p. 105). There are three main levels of police records checks: a "police criminal records check," which shows unpardoned criminal convictions; a broader "police information check," which shows unpardoned convictions as well as other contact with police; and finally a "police vulnerable sector check," which, as the broadest search, can also include records of pardoned criminal convictions. Before implementing a police records check policy, an employer should ask its local police department about its practices and procedures (Miedema and Hall, 2012, p. 105).

Over the past several years, the process of obtaining a police records check has become more restricted. There are now two ways to have a police records check completed: through a third-party background-screening firm (except for a vulnerable sector check, where the results will be released to the applicant only), or by sending the job applicant to a police station in the area where he resides (Miedema and Hall, 2012, p. 109). The police will not provide details about what offence a job applicant was convicted of to a background-checking firm, even with written consent from the applicant. However, where an applicant is asked to identify conviction details on the background-checking consent form, the police can confirm whether those conviction details are accurate (Miedema and Hall, 2012, p. 102).

In most Canadian jurisdictions, an employer may refuse to hire someone who has a criminal record, even if the record does not relate to the job being applied for. The exceptions are British Columbia, Yukon Territory, Quebec, and Prince Edward Island, where the record does have to relate to the job being applied for (Miedema and Hall, 2012, p. 101). However, best practice in this area points to only conducting a criminal check where it is necessary for the position, documenting reasons for the hiring decision, and keeping the results confidential (Sherrard Kuzz LLP, 2012, p. 2).

As noted in Chapter 2, employers in Ontario are prohibited from discriminating against a person because she has been convicted of a provincial offence (for example, speeding) unless it is a bona fide occupational qualification (BFOQ) for the job. Similarly, an employer may not discriminate because of a criminal conviction for which a pardon has been granted unless it is a BFOQ for the position, such as where it involves working with young children. On the other hand, where the job applicant was charged with a criminal offence but not convicted, this does not fall within the specific definition of "record of offences" under the Ontario *Human Rights Code*. However, there is always a risk that an applicant will file a human rights application if she was not hired because of the charge, so an employer needs to approach this area with caution (Miedema and Hall, 2012, p. 127).

Internet and Social Media Searches

A recent addition to the list of background checks that employers can perform relates to Internet and social media-based searches. The ease with which an employer can simply "Google" candidates' names or check out their social media footprint makes this a tempting strategy. In fact, according to one UK study, 91 percent of employers now use Internet sites to screen applicants and assess qualifications and fit ("How Employers Use Social Media," n.d.). However, there are several potential pitfalls that an employer should be aware of if performing these types of searches. First, there is the possibility of mistaken identity, especially if the applicant has a relatively common name. Second, there is no "quality control" on the information located through a web-based search; anyone with a grudge or who is simply misinformed can post material on the Internet that is wrong, misleading, or one-sided. It is obviously unfair to reject someone on the basis of incorrect information, and an employer that relies on such information misses out on a potentially great candidate. Third, web-based searches often reveal information that touches on prohibited grounds of discrimination: for example, photographs posted can reveal religious affiliation or family status. As discussed in Chapter 2, having this type of information before the hiring decision is made opens an employer up to claims that the discriminatory information played a part in that decision (Miedema and Hall, 2012, p. 172). One way to address this concern is to have someone other than the decision-maker perform the search and ensure that that person is aware of, and abides by, human rights requirements. In addition, an employer should carefully document its reasons for any hiring decision. However, given the pitfalls discussed above, employers may soon conclude that the bad outweighs the good with this method of checking references.

Internet and social media searches also present potential privacy issues. However, to date, in the handful of cases where an employee's social media profile has been at issue, courts have found that individuals have no reasonable expectation of privacy where they have posted comments on sites to which hundreds of people have been given access (Miedema and Hall, 2012, p. 172).

FYI

Social Media Searches Can Both Help and Hurt Job Prospects

A job candidate's social media profile can have a positive, as well as negative, effect on one's employment prospects. For example, a search on LinkedIn, Twitter, and other sites can confirm applicants' experience, qualifications, and connections within a particular industry, as well as convey their social media savvy. Sixty-eight percent of the employers surveyed in the study noted above indicated that they had hired a candidate because of what they saw on the individual's social networking site. At the same time, a similarly high percentage indicated that they had rejected candidates based on their social media profile. Reasons given include the posting of inappropriate photographs or comments (including disparaging comments about a former employer and discriminatory statements), posts that demonstrated poor communications skills, and posts that revealed criminal conduct.

When Background Checks Should Be Done

Like the pre-employment medical examination discussed in Chapter 2, most types of background checks should be done only after a conditional offer of employment is made. The exception is job reference checks, and even then usually the *current* employer should be contacted only after a conditional offer. Conducting background checks at the very end of the process reduces the risk of allegations of discrimination by unsuccessful job applicants. For example, credit checks require an applicant to provide her social insurance number, which can reveal information about citizenship, one of the prohibited grounds of discrimination under the *Human Rights Code*.

It is easier to defend against an allegation of discrimination if the information was not obtained before a conditional offer of employment was made (Miedema and Hall, 2012, p. xv). In addition, many organizations now use third parties to carry out background checks, after a conditional offer of employment has been made. With the applicant dealing directly with the third party, there is less risk that the employer will obtain information that touches on a prohibited ground of discrimination (Rudner, 2010, p. 2).

Different Types of Employment Relationships

As discussed in Chapter 1 under the heading "Defining the Employment Relationship," not all individuals hired to perform work for an organization are hired as "employees." They may be hired as independent contractors, performing work as self-employed business persons, instead. Moreover, even where an organization decides to hire someone directly as an employee, it still has the option of choosing or negotiating which type of employment relationship there will be. For example, the person could be hired full-time or part-time, as a permanent or as a fixed-term (contract) employee. The arrangement chosen is a matter of contractual agreement between the parties. For the most part, statute law in Ontario does not distinguish between different types of employees. Both full-time employees (those who work a full week) and part-time employees (those who work less than a full week) are entitled to statutory benefits and protections, although the monetary amount of benefits (such as the amount of vacation or termination pay) reflects the number of hours worked.

Temporary (fixed-term) employees and casual employees are generally entitled to statutory benefits and protections as well. However, individuals who fall within the definition of "temporary employee" under the *Employment Standards Act, 2000* are not entitled to termination notice or pay in lieu of notice, because these workers are aware of the temporary nature of their employment. Qualifications to the temporary employee exemption, such as that where the term is greater than 12 months, are discussed in Chapter 14 under the heading "Exceptions to Individual or Mass Notice of Termination Requirements."

To be eligible for benefits under the employment insurance system, an employee must have worked a minimum number of qualifying hours in insurable employment during the qualifying period. Thus, part-time or casual employees who have worked less than the minimum number of hours in the qualifying period are not eligible for benefits. However, where an employee has more than one job during the qualifying period, all insurable employment hours are added together to determine whether an employee qualifies for benefits.

Employees are commonly categorized by employers as follows:

1. *Permanent full-time employees.* These employees are hired for an indefinite period—that is, with no predetermined end to the employment relationship—and usually work 35 to 40 hours per week. If a specific term of employment is not stipulated in an employment contract, the term of employment is assumed to be indefinite.

2. *Permanent part-time employees.* These employees are hired for an indefinite period to work less than full-time hours. There is no statutory definition of what constitutes a "part-time employee," although for the purposes of collective bargaining, part-time employees are usually those who work 24 hours per week or less.

3. *Temporary employees (or contract workers).* These employees work either full-time or part-time, but they are hired for a specific period or task rather than for an indefinite period like permanent employees. They may be called "fixed-term employees" because their employment contract is for a fixed period of time, such as six months. They may also be referred to as "contract workers." However, temporary employees are not independent contractors. Likewise, they are not "temps" or "agency employees," who remain employees of an employment agency.

4. *Casual employees.* These employees form a special category of temporary employees and work intermittently as work is offered. Both temporary and casual employees are sometimes referred to as "contract employees." Casual employees used to be exempt from public holiday pay and termination and severance entitlements under the *Employment Standards Act, 2000* if they were able to refuse a work assignment without any negative consequences. Effective November 2009, these exemptions for elect-to-work employees were removed, so they are now covered by those standards.

5. *Agency employees or temps.* These employees work for an employment agency at various places as arranged by the agency. The contract of employment is between the agency and the agency employee. An organization that uses the services of an agency employee pays the agency directly. The agency remains responsible for employment standards entitlements, such as vacation and public holiday pay, as well as termination and severance pay. This topic is discussed further under the heading "Temporary Employment Agencies" in Chapter 6.

REFERENCES

Balogun v. Canada, 2010 FCA 29.

Cathcart, Cindy. Haste Makes Waste—And Bad Hires. *Canadian HR Reporter*. July 13, 2009, p. 16.

CBC, 99.1 FM Radio One. *Equal Work, Unequal Treatment*. Metro Morning, September 9, 2008.

Consumer Reporting Act. RSO 1990, c. C.33.

Cornell v. Rogers Cablesystems Inc. (1987), 17 CCEL 322 (Ont. Dist. Ct.), [1987] OJ no. 2047.

Dobson, Sarah. Temp Industry Given More Than Passing Glance. *Canadian HR Reporter*. September 8, 2008, p. 1.

Downey v. 502377 Ontario Ltd. [1991] OJ no. 468 (Gen. Div.).

Earle v. Grant Transport. [1995] OJ no. 3593 (Gen. Div.).

Echlin, Randall, and Christine Thomlinson. *For Better or For Worse: A Practical Guide to Canadian Employment Law*, 3rd ed. Toronto: Canada Law Book, 2011.

Egan v. Alcatel Canada Inc. 2004 CanLII 2553 (Ont. SC).

Employment Standards Act, 2000. SO 2000, c. 41.

Employment Standards Amendment Act (Temporary Help Agencies), 2009. SO 2009, c. 9 (Bill 139).

Gilbert, Douglas, Brian Burkett, and Moira McCaskill. *Canadian Labour and Employment Law for the US Practitioner*. Washington, DC: Bureau of National Affairs, 2000.

How Employers Use Social Media to Screen Applicants. *Undercover Recruiter*. (n.d.) http://theundercoverrecruiter.com/infographic-how -recruiters-use-social-media-screen-applicants.

Israel, Peter. Ask an Expert: Can Employers Conduct Credit Checks on Job Applicants? *Canadian Employment Law Today*. Issue no. 384, March 5, 2003, p. 2996.

Israel, Peter. Ensuring Independent Contractors Are Not Really Employees. *Canadian Employment Law Today*. Issue no. 384, March 5, 2003, p. 2997.

Israel, Peter. How Can Employers Guard Against Wrongful-Hire Suits? *Canadian Employment Law Today*. Issue no. 394, July 23, 2003, p. 3076.

Levitt, Howard. The Cost of Lying on Your Resumé Can Be High. *Financial Post*, May 7, 2013. http://business.financialpost.com/2013/05/07/cost-of -lying-on-your-resume-can-be-high/.

Lublin, Daniel. Employing Temporary Workers Comes with Its Own Legal Responsibilities. *Canadian Employment Law Today*. Issue no. 485, 2007, p. 3.

MacDonald, Natalie. Who's the Boss? *Canadian HR Reporter*. November 4, 2002, p. 15.

Miedema, Adrian, and Christina Hall. *HR Manager's Guide to Background Checks and Pre-employment Testing*, 2nd ed. Toronto: Carswell, 2012.

Mistry, Heena. Independent Contractors Can Have Their Cake and Eat It Too. *Canadian Employment Law Today*. Issue no. 394, July 23, 2003, p. 3077.

Ontario Ministry of Labour. *A Consultation Paper on Work Through Temporary Help Agencies*. May 2008. Toronto: Author.

Queen v. Cognos Inc. [1993] 1 SCR 87.

Rubin Thomlinson LLP. Inducement. *Employers' Alert*. Issue no. 32, February 2011, p. 1. http://www.rubinthomlinson .com/employers-alerts/documents/ DiasvParagonGamingECCompany EmployersAlertFebruary2011.pdf.

Rudner, Stuart. Ask an Expert: Human Rights—Requesting Information for Background Checks. *Canadian Employment Law Today*. Issue no. 558, June 2, 2010, p. 2.

Rudner, Stuart. Reference Letters Not So Risky. *Canadian Employment Law Today*. Issue no. 539, July 29, 2009, p. 3.

Sherrard Kuzz LLP. Criminal Record Checks: Managing Liability and Getting the Information You Need. *Management Counsel: Employment and Labour Law Update*. Volume XI, no. 4, August 2012, p. 1. http://www.sherrardkuzz.com/pdf/Vol_XI_4.pdf.

Stefanik, Thomas. Case in Point: Wrongful Dismissal, You're Hired! Wait, Check That … *Canadian Employment Law Today*. Issue no. 555, April 21, 2010, pp. 4–5.

The Treaty Group Inc. v. Drake International Inc. 2007 ONCA 450; (2005), 36 CCLT (3d) 262.

Wilson, Peter, and Allison Taylor. *The Corporate Counsel Guide to Employment Law*, 2nd ed. Aurora, ON: Canada Law Book, 2003.

REVIEW AND DISCUSSION QUESTIONS

1. Describe the circumstances in which an employee may be terminated, without reasonable notice, for having provided inaccurate information on a job application form or during an interview. Is it fair that an employee may be terminated in these circumstances, even where he or she has been performing the job satisfactorily for some time? Why or why not?

2. During the interview, the interviewer assures Giselle, the job candidate, that the position is a secure one and on that basis she accepts the job. However, shortly after Giselle starts work, the employer hires a new CEO, who decides to undertake a total reorganization of the firm. As part of that reorganization, Giselle's position is eliminated and she sues for negligent misrepresentation. Will her action be successful?

3. Connor applied to be an officer in the Canadian Forces but his application was denied because of his poor credit rating. He filed a human rights complaint on the basis that the requirement to provide a credit check was discriminatory. Do you think his human rights complaint will be successful?

4. Greg had worked for two years as a sales manager in an IT firm when he was terminated for a serious incident of insubordination. Greg sued for wrongful dismissal damages. During his testimony at trial, Greg told the court that he had a degree from Arizona State University and that he had played football there. Counsel for the employer noticed that Greg seemed rather small for a football player and he asked Greg to name the coach of the football team or the team's nickname. At that point, Greg admitted that he had never in fact attended Arizona State even though he said he had on his resumé. In your view, would this misrepresentation on his resumé constitute just cause for his dismissal?

5. Fiona has been offered a job as a marketing representative in a prestigious cosmetics firm called Beauty R Us. However, one week before she is to start her new job (and two weeks after she gave notice to her current employer) she receives a phone call from Beauty R Us stating that it has to withdraw its job offer. The firm tells Fiona that it just found out that she is a high-profile activist for an animal rights group and some of its customers (such as those who sell fur coats) would be extremely uncomfortable dealing with her as a Beauty R Us marketing representative. Fiona is very upset and wants to know what her legal rights are in this situation. Advise her. Explain your answer.

6. Daniel had worked for Classy Casino for 14 years, first as a dealer and eventually as a games manager, when he was approached by the owners of Lucky Stars, a casino that would soon open. Looking to staff the new casino with the "best people in the business," they offered him more money and better benefits, a larger bonus, and greater opportunities for promotions than he currently had. Daniel eventually accepted. However, 18 months after Daniel started working at Lucky Stars he was terminated, without just cause, and given two weeks' pay as required under the *Employment Standards Act*. Considering this amount insufficient, Daniel sued for wrongful dismissal damages under the common law. The court found that, based on the factors normally taken into consideration in determining "reasonable notice" under the common

law—his age (41) at the time of dismissal, his mid-management position, his length of service (relatively short), and the availability of similar employment—it would have awarded him two months' pay in lieu of notice. However, Daniel argued that he was entitled to more, based on the employer's pre-hiring statements. Do you think a court would agree?

7. Coney was hired by a well-known consulting firm. Although the firm had expected great things of him based on his past experience and academic achievements (including having a PhD from the University of Illinois), he exceeded even its expectations. After three very successful years with the firm, Coney applied for partnership and, as part of the admission process, he was asked to provide evidence of his PhD. After Coney claimed to have moved so many times that he lost the documentation, the firm called the University of Illinois, only to be told it had no record of Coney—at all. When confronted, Coney said it was an honorary degree. Now probing further, the employer offered to fly to Chicago with him to verify his honorary degree, but Coney declined. The firm concluded that the PhD was fabricated (in fact, it turned out he did not have a university degree at all) and it fired him for cause—meaning no advance notice or severance package. Coney sued for wrongful dismissal. Do you think he will be successful?

8. "It should be illegal for an employer to ask job applicants for their Facebook passwords." Discuss.

9. Some employers prefer to hire employees as contract, rather than as permanent, workers. Taking this approach to staffing has several potential benefits for employers. Are there any disadvantages for employers and if so, what are they?

The Employment Contract

4

LEARNING OUTCOMES

After completing this chapter, you will be able to:

- Identify the legal requirements for a valid employment contract.

- Understand the advantages of a written employment contract over an oral contract.

- Identify common contractual terms and understand why they must be clearly drafted.

- Understand factors affecting the interpretation and enforceability of employment contracts, including lack of consideration, inequality of bargaining power, failure to meet statutory standards, and obsolescence.

Introduction

Every employment relationship is based on a contract, regardless of whether the contract is oral or written. Under the common law, three things are necessary to create a contract: an offer, acceptance of the offer, and **consideration** (something given or promised in exchange). A binding legal employment contract is created, therefore, wherever there is a job offer (covering essential terms), an acceptance of that offer, and the promise to exchange wages for work performed (the consideration). An oral contract that contains these elements is just as binding as a written one.

FYI

Occasionally a Written Contract Is Required ...

There are two exceptions to the rule that oral and written contracts are equally binding. The first of these is found under the Ontario *Statute of Frauds*, a law that requires certain types of contracts to be in writing. An employment contract that is for a definite period of time (that is, a fixed-term contract) that exceeds one year must be in writing. The second exception is where the parties negotiating an agreement clearly intend to have a signed contract before their agreement becomes enforceable. In *Ross v. Christian & Timbers Inc.*, the offer letter specifically stated that employment was conditional on the employee's executing a formal contract. In that case, the court found that there was no employment contract even though the employee had worked for several weeks because no formal agreement had been signed (Mitchell, 2012, p. 2).

Written Employment Contracts

Advantages of a Written Employment Contract

Despite the validity of an oral employment contract, a well-drafted written contract offers a number of significant benefits, which are set out below.

1. *Reduces Risk of Misunderstandings*

By specifying the rights, obligations, and expectations of both the employer and the employee, a written contract reduces the risk of misunderstandings that could lead to disputes and lawsuits later on. It reflects a common understanding of the terms and conditions of employment that can always be referred to, even if the passage of time or staff changes make it difficult to recall the actual agreement made by the parties.

2. *Addresses Contentious Issues Early*

A written contract encourages the parties to deal with potentially contentious issues early in their relationship, when they are usually positively disposed to one another. Furthermore, because both the employer and the employee have a strong incentive to reach an agreement that is mutually satisfactory, contentious issues are likely to be dealt with in a constructive manner.

3. Reduces Uncertainty

If a dispute arises and the parties take the matter to court, a well-drafted written contract provides the court with a clear record of the terms and conditions of employment. In contrast, the terms of an oral agreement are those that a court finds the parties agreed to and those that are implied by law. Where the matter in dispute relates to terms agreed to, and an oral agreement was made, both parties will have the problem of convincing the court that on a balance of probabilities their version is the truest. For example, the employer and employee may, after the start of employment, disagree on how sales commissions are to be calculated. If the formula is not in writing, the parties may end up in court trying to prove that their own recollection of the agreement is more accurate than that of the other party.

Implied Terms

Where the issue in dispute was *not* addressed in an oral contract, or was left out of a written contract, a court imports **implied terms** into the agreement. This means that the court considers what terms the parties would likely have agreed on had they put their minds to the issue; it then deems those terms to be part of the contract. The courts have also developed a set of standard implied terms that reflect what they perceive the parties' rights and obligations ought to be, unless expressly stated otherwise in the agreement. For example, in the absence of an express term relating to the contract's duration and termination notice, the courts will find that the contract implies an obligation on the employer to provide the employee with reasonable notice of termination in the absence of serious misconduct. What is "reasonable" depends on the particular facts of each case. Similarly, as reconfirmed in 2008 by the Supreme Court of Canada in *RBC Dominion Securities Inc. v. Merrill Lynch Canada Inc.*, employees have an implied duty to provide reasonable notice of resignation and can be liable for damages suffered if such notice is not given. Another implied term is that, unless otherwise specified, an employee owes a duty of "good faith" to the employer. An employee cannot, for example, compete with the employer during the currency of the employment relationship or make improper use of the employer's confidential information.

How Formal Should a Written Contract Be?

When a job is a senior position or when special issues are involved, the parties may want a written contract that is formal and comprehensive. For example, in the high-tech sector, it may be important to address confidentiality, non-solicitation, and non-competition obligations.

However, for most employment relationships, the written contract can be more basic. It often consists of a letter from the employer offering the employee a job and setting out the key terms and conditions, such as salary, benefits, start date, title, and job duties. Another essential element is the termination clause since this can eliminate costly **litigation** regarding reasonable notice. The offer letter should specifically refer to the employer's policy manual, so that the employer's policies covering such matters as discipline, probationary periods, absence, safety, and harassment are incorporated by reference into the employment contract, and thereby become part of the terms of employment.

Common Contractual Terms

In addition to being clearly drafted, written employment contracts should be customized to reflect the issues that are important to both the employer and the employee. The temptation to use a single, standard contract for all employees should be avoided.

All employment contracts rest on the same general principles; however, the level of formality and detail varies. As noted above, for less-skilled jobs, a letter of hire that sets out key terms and expressly incorporates the employer's policy manual may be sufficient. Key terms include the names of the parties, the date that the job begins, a job title and description, the duration of the contract (if it is for a fixed term), the compensation offered, and the termination clause. For managerial positions, positions that involve a high degree of skill, and positions that require specific contractual terms (such as a non-competition clause), a formal contract is advisable. Executives and skilled employees may require the inclusion of details about bonuses, pension arrangements, stock options, and specifically negotiated perks.

The written contract provides both parties with the opportunity to set out their expectations, thereby reducing the risk of misunderstandings that can later lead to disputes and litigation. In setting out its expectations, the employer may want to maintain sufficient flexibility so that, as circumstances change, it can make adjustments without risking a claim from the employee that it has fundamentally breached the contract. For example, the contract may stipulate that hours of work may vary from time to time.

A sample indefinite-term contract is set out in Appendix A to this text, and a sample fixed-term contract is set out in Appendix B.

An employment contract may include any terms that are not prohibited by law. The following are some of the more important topics that may be addressed in a written contract, as well as suggestions for minimizing the risk of legal problems associated with them.

1. Job Description

Setting out the job duties clarifies the expectations of both parties and reduces the potential for misunderstandings. However, in the absence of contractual language that allows the employer to modify responsibilities, the employee is entitled to refuse to perform duties that fall outside the original agreement.

This problem can be lessened (but probably not eliminated entirely) by language in the contract that expressly allows the employer to change the duties of the job. For example, the contract could state that the employer may assign "any and all other duties as may be required from time to time."

2. Remuneration

The terms of an employment contract must at least match statutory minimum requirements. For example, a contract cannot contain a term that allows for overtime premium pay that is less than that required under the *Employment Standards Act, 2000* (ESA). If it does, the term is null and void. (See Chapters 6 and 14 for a discussion of the ESA requirements.)

There is no obligation to provide for future pay increases in the contract. It may be safer to remain silent on this point or simply to state that the employee's remuneration may increase or decrease in future, based on performance evaluations. Contracts for executives may also contain details of bonus structures and stock options.

3. Term

If an employment contract is to cover a fixed period of time or a particular task, it must state the term or task. Otherwise, the contract is considered to cover an indefinite period. Hiring for a fixed term or task (as long as the task is well defined and of limited duration) eliminates the employer's obligation to provide reasonable notice of termination, because at the end of the term or task, employment simply ends. Creating a fixed-term or task contract limits the employer's liability and provides both parties with an opportunity to evaluate their working relationship.

However, there are several caveats for employers that use this approach. First, where the contract is, in substance, an indefinite one and the employer uses a series of rolling, fixed-term contracts simply to avoid statutory and common law termination requirements, courts are unlikely to enforce the term, as shown in *Ceccol v. Ontario Gymnastic Federation*.

CASE IN POINT

Series of Fixed-Term Contracts Really an Indefinite-Term Contract

Ceccol v. Ontario Gymnastic Federation, 2001 CanLII 8589, 55 OR (3d) 614 (CA)

Facts

Ceccol worked for a gymnastics club over a nearly 16-year period under a series of 1-year contracts. Each of these contracts stated that the agreement was subject to renewal if she received a favourable performance review and the parties agreed on renewal terms. When the employer decided not to renew Ceccol's contract, it claimed that the relevant notice period was based on 1 year's employment, rather than 16 years. Consequently, it provided severance pay based on 1 year's employment. The trial court looked at the parties' reasonable expectations. It held that Ceccol was entitled to reasonable notice of 12 months because her employment relationship was to be characterized as one lasting for an indefinite term rather than for a series of 1-year fixed terms. The employer appealed.

Relevant Issue

Whether termination notice or pay in lieu of notice should be based on a 1-year employment contract or on a 16-year period of employment.

Decision

The Ontario Court of Appeal stated that employers should not be able to evade the traditional protections of the *Employment Standards Act, 2000* and the common law by resorting to the label "fixed-term contract." This is especially true where the underlying reality of the employment relationship is actually one of continuous service by the employee for many years. The employer's conduct and its verbal representations to Ceccol indicated an indefinite-term relationship. The court concluded that reasonable notice should be based on her 16 years of employment, which the trial judge appropriately determined was 16 months (although it was reduced to 12 months owing to her failure to properly mitigate her damages).

In these circumstances, the employer would have been wiser to negotiate a fair termination provision in an indefinite-term contract than to attempt to frame it as a series of fixed terms.

The second caveat with fixed-term or task contracts is that monitoring and renewing them pose an administrative challenge for employers, especially if the contracts expire at different times. If a renewal date is missed, a fixed-term contract becomes a contract for an indefinite term, which requires an employer to provide the employee with common law notice or pay in lieu. One solution is to provide for automatic renewal of the contract. However, if the employer intends to terminate or alter the relationship at the end of the contract, it must do so in a timely manner because the contract will otherwise be renewed automatically for the same fixed term.

Finally, employees hired on a fixed-term or task basis generally are required to be employed for the entire term or task. If an employer terminates an employee before the end of that period, damages are based on the remainder of the term, which might prove more costly to an employer than pay in lieu of common law notice for an indefinite-term employee. For example, if the employee's contract is for 12 months and the employer terminates the contract after only 2 months, the employer may be liable for the remainder of the contract (10 months) rather than for common law notice for a 2-month employee.

These problems can be solved by including a termination clause in the fixed-term contract stating that either party is entitled to terminate the contract by giving the other party two (or three or four) weeks' written notice.

One interesting side note on fixed-term contracts is that according to s. 2 of the Ontario *Employers and Employees Act*, fixed-term contracts with a term of greater than nine years are not binding. The Ontario *Employers and Employees Act* is the successor legislation to the 19th-century *Master and Servant Act*, which codified the common law of contract.

4. Termination

The amount of notice due to an employee on termination (without cause) is typically the most contentious issue in the employment contract. However, the benefits of dealing with the thorny issue up front, while the relationship between the parties is positive, can be significant. Otherwise, the common law presumption of "reasonable notice" applies, and such notice is both more generous and less predictable than that provided for in most employment contracts. That said, as will be seen below, there are downsides to including a termination clause, particularly if it is not carefully drafted.

To safeguard the enforceability of its termination clause, the employer should review its obligations regarding written contracts (those discussed under the heading "Enforceability and Interpretation of Written Contracts" below), especially the requirement to meet or exceed the statutory minimum notice requirements. As illustrated by the decision in *Stevens v. Sifton Properties Ltd.* (also discussed below), termination clauses that fail to meet the statutory minimum standards *in every aspect and at any point in the employment relationship* are likely to be found to be invalid.

In addition, the termination clause should be clearly expressed because *clear language is required to rebut (override) the common law presumption that an employee is entitled to reasonable notice.* Furthermore, the termination clause should be specifically brought to the employee's attention and both parties should sign off on it before the employment relationship commences. This advice applies whether the termination clause is found in a formal written contract, a letter of hire, or an employer's policy manual incorporated into the employment agreement. *Christensen v. Family Counselling Centre of Sault Ste. Marie and District* shows the importance of clarity in rebutting the common law presumption that an employee is entitled to reasonable notice.

CASE IN POINT

Termination Provisions Insufficiently Clear to Rebut Common Law Presumption

Christensen v. Family Counselling Centre of Sault Ste. Marie and District, 2001 CanLII 4698 (Ont. CA)

Facts

Christensen had worked as a therapist for the employer counselling centre for seven years when her employment was terminated as a result of funding cuts. On termination, she received ten weeks' pay. Her employment contract was the initial letter of offer, which did not address termination, except as it related to the probationary period. The contract referred to the staff manual, which was not sent with the letter of offer but which the employee received during her first week of work. The termination provisions in the manual were never explained to her. The trial judge found that the termination clauses were capable of at least four interpretations, and the court applied the interpretation most favourable to the employee under the *contra proferentem* rule.

Relevant Issue

Whether the termination provisions limited Christensen's common law entitlement to reasonable notice or pay in lieu.

Decision

The Ontario Court of Appeal held that the key factor was whether the provision was sufficiently clear to rebut the common law presumption of reasonable notice. To rebut this presumption, the employer should have expressed its intention clearly and brought the clause to Christensen's attention when she was hired. An ambiguous notice provision cannot rebut the common law presumption in favour of reasonable notice. The court awarded Christensen eight months' pay in lieu of reasonable notice of termination.

A contrasting problem is found in *Freudenberg Household Products Inc. v. DiGiammarino*. There, the termination clause was clear; unfortunately for the employer, the court found that it clearly said something that the employer did not intend it to say.

CASE IN POINT

Cardinal Rule of Interpretation: Parties Intend What Agreement Says

Freudenberg Household Products Inc. v. DiGiammarino, 2012 ONSC 5725

Facts

The employer signed an employment agreement with the employee in late 2010 that contained the following clause:

> In the case that the Company would decide to terminate the contract with the employee in the first 4 years after the signature, the Company will pay to the employee an indemnity compensation of two (2) years' salary including the bonuses. …

> After these 4 years, this indemnity compensation will be no more applicable.

In the summer of 2011, the employer decided to terminate DiGiammarino's employment. However, in light of the contractual obligation to provide a two years' lump-sum severance package if she was terminated within the first four years of employment, it also resolved not to let her know about this decision until she had completed four years' work. At the end of the four-year period, DiGiammarino's employment was terminated, without payment of the two-year lump-sum severance payment. DiGiammarino sued the employer, arguing that the termination provision had been triggered.

Relevant Issue

Whether the contractual severance pay obligation was triggered based on when the decision to terminate was made or on when the termination occurred.

Decision

The court agreed with DiGiammarino that the words "would decide to" meant that the employer's severance pay obligation was triggered on the date it *made the decision* to terminate the contract, not on the date of the actual termination. The court noted that the cardinal presumption of interpretation is that the parties intended what the agreement says. "If the Applicant intended for the indemnity provision to apply based on the date of termination as opposed to the date of the *decision* to terminate, then the Applicant should have said so in the employment contract. It did not."

Termination Clauses and the Duty to Mitigate

The *Freudenberg* decision also touched on another important issue related to termination clauses: does an employee still have a duty to mitigate (that is, to try to lessen damages suffered by looking for a comparable job) where the contract specifically sets out the amount of notice, or pay in lieu, required upon termination and is silent on the duty to mitigate?

As noted above, the duty to mitigate refers to the obligation placed on a dismissed employee to look for a job that is comparable to the one from which he has been dismissed during the common law reasonable notice period. If the dismissed employee is successful, earnings from that new job will reduce any wrongful dismissal damages owed by the employer. (See Chapter 15 under the heading "The Duty to Mitigate.") This duty clearly applies where there is no enforceable termination provision in the employment contract and the period of reasonable notice is established as an implied term of the contract under the common law. However, until recently, case law has been mixed about whether the duty to mitigate applies where an employment contract specifically sets out the length of termination notice (or a specific amount of termination pay) and *is silent on the duty to mitigate*. However, in the 2012 case of *Bowes v. Goss Power Products Limited*, the Ontario Court of Appeal confirmed unequivocally that where an employment contract contains a stipulated entitlement on termination without cause and *is silent as to the obligation to mitigate*, the employee will not be required to mitigate. In the court's view, in the context of the employment relationship, deciding otherwise would be unfair. As Chief Justice Winkler notes (at para. 55):

> It is worthy of emphasis that, in most cases, employment agreements are drafted primarily, if not exclusively, by the employer. In my view, there is nothing unfair about requiring employers to be explicit if they intend to require an employee to mitigate what would otherwise be fixed or liquidated damages. In fact, what is unfair is for an employer to agree upon a fixed amount of damages, and then, at the point of dismissal, inform the employee that future earnings will be deducted from the fixed amount.

Following the *Bowes* decision, the court in *Freudenberg* held that the employee did not have a duty to mitigate during the two-year severance period.

To avoid the result in *Bowes*, an employer must make sure that its contractual termination provisions expressly establish a duty to mitigate. This applies whether the employment contract is for a fixed term or an indefinite period (Thompson and Lambert, 2013).

Other Terms Related to the Termination Clause

In addition to specifying the termination notice owed to the employee on dismissal without cause—and the duty to mitigate—the parties may decide to include other terms related to termination. For example, the employer may want to include a definition of "just cause" to establish the conduct that would justify dismissal without notice or pay in lieu of notice.

The termination clause may also set out the method by which termination pay is to be paid. For example, it could provide for payment by lump sum, salary continuance, or a combination of the two. The employer may also want to stipulate that salary continuance ends when the employee finds a comparable job.

Finally, the parties may want to address the issue of the employee's obligation to provide advance notice of resignation. This is especially important for an employer if the employee has specialized skills or holds a key position. Depending on the difficulty involved in finding a suitable replacement for such employees, resignation notice of a few weeks to a month is typical. For most other employees, two weeks' notice is usually sufficient.

5. Probationary Period

Employers often want a period of time at the beginning of the employment relationship during which they may dismiss an employee without being obliged to provide reasonable notice under the common law. This gives the employer a window of time in which to evaluate the new employee's suitability for the position. Under the common law, however, a probationary period is not an implied term of an employment contract. Therefore, to incorporate a probationary period, the contract *must* expressly provide for it.

It is somewhat unclear under the case law whether an employee may be summarily dismissed (that is, dismissed without notice) during the probationary period at the employer's sole discretion, or whether the employer must provide objective reasons for its decision in order to avoid paying termination pay. In this regard, it is helpful if the contractual provision concerning the probationary period expressly allows the employer to terminate the employee at any time, and for any reason, within the first three months of employment without having to provide any notice or pay in lieu of notice (Israel, April 2, 2003, p. 3012).

Probationary periods are typically three to six months, depending on the nature of the position. The assessment period is usually shorter for people employed to perform simple and repetitive tasks than it is for people who are employed in more demanding and varied positions (Echlin and Thomlinson, 2011, p. 64).

Under Ontario's *Employment Standards Act, 2000*, employees who work less than three months are not entitled to statutory notice of termination or pay in lieu. However, statutory notice is required after three months' service. Therefore, where the probationary period under a contract exceeds three months, the employer must give statutory notice to an employee who is dismissed after three months unless the dismissal occurs for reasons exempted from the statutory notice requirement. For example, if the contract calls for a probationary period of six months and the employee is terminated after four months because the employer is dissatisfied with her performance, the employer must provide one week's statutory notice of termination because dismissal for poor job performance is not an exemption (unless it constitutes "wilful neglect of duty").

This notice is necessary even though the termination occurs during the contractual probationary period and no "reasonable notice" is required under the common law. It is essential that the contractual provisions regarding notice of termination during any probationary period longer than three months take this statutory requirement into account; otherwise, the entire provision may be found unenforceable.

6. Relocation

If a transfer to another city or region is a potential issue, the parties should address the matter in the contract. Otherwise, if the employer decides to transfer the employee, they could become embroiled in an unnecessary dispute about whether the right to relocate is an implied term of the contract. An employee could argue, for example, that the relocation constitutes a fundamental breach of contract and therefore amounts to constructive dismissal. (For more information about constructive dismissal, see Chapter 15.) However, if having the discretion to transfer the prospective employee is not significant to the employer but is a serious concern for the employee, the contract can expressly provide that there is no employer right to require relocation (Echlin and Thomlinson, 2011, p. 65).

7. Benefits

Employment contracts can provide the details of benefit entitlements, including medical and dental benefits, vacation, and use of a company car or laptop computer. Some benefit entitlements may not come into effect until several months after work begins. If this is the case, the delay should be set out in the contract so that the employee is not caught unaware.

The parties may also choose to establish how benefits will be dealt with in the event of dismissal or resignation.

8. Restrictive Covenants

Restrictive covenants are clauses that protect an employer's business interests by restricting what an employee can do during, and especially after, employment with regard to such matters as confidential information and customer lists. The three main types of restrictive covenants are set out below.

1. *Non-disclosure clauses.* These clauses prevent a departing employee from using and disclosing confidential information related to the employer after employment ends.
2. *Non-solicitation clauses.* These clauses prevent a departing employee from soliciting the employer's customers, clients, or possibly employees. For example, an employee may agree that she will not initiate contact with her employer's customers for one year after employment ends.

3. *Non-competition clauses.* These clauses prevent a departing employee from competing with the employer. They are typically drafted to restrict competition for a specific time within a specific geographic area. For example, an employee could agree that he will not start up a business that competes with the employer's business in the city of Toronto for 12 months after employment ends.

Non-disclosure clauses that simply limit the employee's use of the employer's confidential information are usually enforceable. The employer should clarify with its employees what information it considers confidential and consistently enforce those guidelines. Confidential information usually includes such things as customer lists and information, intellectual property, and marketing plans.

FYI

New Frontiers—Who Owns the Customer Contacts on LinkedIn?

It is a long-standing principle in employment law that an employee cannot print a customer list, take it home (or email it to himself), and then use it to compete against his former employer (Pugen, 2013). But what if the competitive information is on LinkedIn? The law in this area is still developing. A 2013 decision in the United Kingdom found that the traditional obligation of an employee to not steal an employer's confidential or proprietary information applies to an employer's contacts on a LinkedIn page. However, this case did not deal with an employer's interest in an employee's personal LinkedIn account (Pugen, 2013). In *Eagle Professional Resources v. MacMullin*, the Ontario Court of Appeal decided that three employees who allegedly contacted their former employer's customers did not breach the non-solicitation provision in their employment contracts. The employees successfully argued that they relied only on "publicly available" information taken from social media sites such as LinkedIn, and the employer did not have a proprietary interest over the content (Stam, 2013).

Employees, especially those in sales, are often encouraged to use social media sites (for example, Twitter, Facebook, and LinkedIn) to connect with customers and prospective customers. Given the ease with which former employees can now reconnect with contacts made with or for an employer online, courts are having to make "awkward distinctions … between information that could be memorized or in the public domain and information committed to writing or electronic storage" (Kempf, 2013).

To try to protect its interests in this unsettled area of the law, an employer should consider doing the following:

- Ensure that its databases and LinkedIn presence are maintained on its premises by employees who use only the employer's equipment and receive compensation for doing so (as per their job descriptions).
- Set clear privacy and confidentiality policy guidelines on the employer's LinkedIn networking information that is available to everyone who has access to this information.
- Make all employees aware of the employer's proprietary interest in all contact management software, including LinkedIn.
- Keep the employer's LinkedIn groups and networking separate from employees' personal LinkedIn profiles or groups (Pugen, 2013).

Courts are more suspicious of non-solicitation and non-competition clauses. This is because they affect a former employee's ability to earn a living in her area of expertise and limit competition. In the case of a dispute over a non-solicitation clause, the court will examine the clause carefully to ensure that it is reasonable in the circumstances. The onus is on the employer to show that the clause is reasonable in the circumstances because, for example, the employee's job involved significant contact with, and knowledge of, customers and suppliers.

Courts take the most stringent approach with non-competition clauses. This is because they actually prevent former employees from working in a particular area for a fixed time. These clauses are viewed as a restraint of trade, and they are presumed invalid unless the employer shows that

- the non-competition clause is necessary to protect the employer's legitimate business interests,
- the non-competition clause covers a reasonable length of time and geographic area, and
- a non-solicitation clause would not adequately protect the employer's legitimate interests in the circumstances (Israel, 2004, p. 3196).

The key to creating enforceable restrictive covenants is to be clear and to go no further than is necessary to protect the employer's legitimate business interests. For example, in industries where state-of-the-art information changes rapidly, a non-competition clause that extends beyond 12 months is probably unenforceable. There must also be a reasonable link between the employee's expertise or position and the scope of the clause. It is an error to use a standard clause for all employees.

Another consideration is whether the duration and scope of the clause are the industry norm. Clauses that are more restrictive than those typical of the industry are less likely to be enforced by the courts. *Mason v. Chem-Trend Limited Partnership* provides an example of a court weighing both the duration and scope of the non-competition clause in determining reasonableness.

CASE IN POINT

"Less Is More" in Non-Competition Clauses

Mason v. Chem-Trend Limited Partnership, 2010 ONSC 4119

Facts

Mason was a salesman at a chemical products manufacturer who after 17 years was dismissed, allegedly for cause. His employment contract contained the following non-competition clause that prohibited him from competing with the employer for one year after termination—with no geographic restriction.

I agree that if my employment is terminated for any reason by me or by the Company, I will not, for a period of one year following the termination, directly or indirectly, for my own account or as an employee or agent of any business entity, engage in any business or activity in competition with the Company by providing services or products to, or soliciting business from, any business entity which was a customer of the Company during the period in which I was an employee of the Company, or take any action that will cause the termination of the business relationship between the Company and any customer, or solicit for employment any person employed by the Company.

After being dismissed, Mason applied to the court for a declaration that the non-competition clause was unenforceable. The application judge upheld the restriction, finding that the unlimited geographic scope was reasonable: the employer's business was global, as a salesman Mason had extensive access to confidential customer information, and one year was a relatively short period of time for non-competition clauses within the industry. The court also noted that the clause was clearly worded and understood by the employee when he signed it. Mason appealed the court's decision.

Issue

Whether the non-competition clause was enforceable.

Decision

The Court of Appeal found that although the non-competition clause was clearly written, and the one-year limit was well within the industry norm for salespeople, the clause was overly broad in other respects. Completely prohibiting Mason from competing for one year anywhere in the world constituted an unreasonable geographic scope. Furthermore, preventing him from doing business with "any business entity which was a customer of the Company" was an unworkable restriction. Mason had no way of knowing every customer the employer had had during his 17-year tenure. Finally, the employer's legitimate interest in its trade secrets and other confidential information was already protected by the non-disclosure clauses within the agreement (Emond Harnden, 2011).

As noted above, in addition to being reasonable, a restrictive covenant's wording must also be unambiguous. In *Shafron v. KRG Insurance Brokers (Western) Inc.*, the restrictive covenant prohibited the defendant insurance broker from competing with the employer within the "Metropolitan City of Vancouver" for a period of three years after leaving its employ. The trial judge refused to enforce the agreement, finding that the term "Metropolitan City of Vancouver" was ambiguous because there was no such legal municipal entity. The British Columbia Court of Appeal agreed that the term was ambiguous but decided that it could be made enforceable if the court notionally "severed" part of that term from the agreement and "read down" the geographic scope so that it would be reasonable. On appeal, the Supreme Court of Canada overturned that decision. Noting the potential power imbalance between employees and employers, it reasoned that employers should not be allowed to negotiate overly broad non-competition clauses and then rely on the courts to read them down to the broadest scope that it considers reasonable. The court concluded that restrictive covenants should be strictly construed; an ambiguous covenant is, by definition, unreasonable and unenforceable.

Some employers have started to include language in employment contracts that specifically allows for non-competition clauses to be "read down" by the courts. It remains to be seen whether the courts will find these contracts to be unenforceable as well.

Given the long-standing reluctance of courts to enforce non-competition clauses in employment contracts, it makes sense, wherever feasible, for employers to also use non-solicitation clauses. Not only are non-solicitation clauses more likely to be enforced (although as noted above they too have to pass the "reasonableness" test), but they also enable former employees to look for work in the same industry as part of mitigating their losses (Levitt, 2013).

It should be noted that restrictive covenants that are negotiated as part of a purchase agreement (that is, as part of an agreement to purchase the seller's business) are more likely to be found enforceable than those found in an employment contract. In a commercial purchase agreement, there is no presumed imbalance of power between the parties, and a restrictive covenant will be considered enforceable unless the plaintiff can show that it goes beyond what is necessary to protect the legitimate interests of the purchaser. For example, in the 2010 case of *Guay inc. c. Payette*, the court found that five-year non-competition and non-solicitation clauses were reasonable given the highly specialized and mobile nature of the purchaser's business activities, which involved crane rentals (Wendel, 2013).

9. Ownership of Intellectual Property

Intellectual property, such as inventions, patents, and copyright, is important for many companies, including those that develop electronics or computer software. An ownership clause deals with the ownership of intellectual property or inventions developed by the employee in the course of employment. It is useful to establish ownership of intellectual property early in the employment relationship to avoid potentially bitter disputes later if the employee develops a commercially viable product. The ownership clause typically provides that intellectual property that the employee invents or develops during the normal course of employment belongs to the employer.

10. Choice of Law

A choice of law clause specifies the jurisdiction whose laws govern the contract. Often the jurisdiction is obvious. An employment contract between an Ontario-based employer hiring an Ontario-based employee is interpreted according to the laws of Ontario. However, where an employer hires an employee to work in another province or country or where someone from another jurisdiction is hired to work in Ontario, jurisdiction is an issue.

One consideration in determining which law should govern the contract is costs. A party who becomes involved in a legal dispute in another jurisdiction can incur significant additional litigation costs. On the other hand, where the employment contract has some connection with the United States—if, for example, an employee is hired to work in the United States—an Ontario employer may prefer that the contract be governed by US law. This is because, unlike Ontario, most US states do not require employers to provide reasonable notice of termination but allow termination at will.

However, for a choice of law clause to be upheld, there needs to be a reasonable connection between the employment contract and the chosen jurisdiction. Where there is no choice of law clause, a contract is interpreted according to the law of the jurisdiction that is most closely connected to the employment relationship.

11. Corporate Policies

In most circumstances, an employer wants a new employee to be contractually bound by its general policies, which are usually found in an employer policy manual. The employer should arrange for a candidate to receive a copy of the manual some time before signing the contract so that he has time to review it. The employee should acknowledge, in writing, that he has read the policies and agrees to be governed by them. The best approach is for the written employment contract to include a provision that recites this agreement. If there are certain policies from which the employee wishes to be exempt, and the employer agrees, these should be specified in the written contract.

12. Entire Agreement Clause

This clause states that the signed contract constitutes the entire agreement between the parties. Previous conversations, negotiations, and promises that may have been made during the hiring process are not binding on either party. The entire agreement clause is intended to ensure that in case a dispute arises, a court is restricted to the words of the contract in settling the dispute. The decision in *McNeely v. Herbal Magic Inc.* demonstrates the impact that this clause can have.

CASE IN POINT

Entire Agreement Clause Prevents Reliance on Earlier Representations

McNeely v. Herbal Magic Inc., 2011 ONSC 4237

Facts

McNeely had been a senior executive at Herbal Magic, a weight loss management company, for two years when it was purchased by TorQuest. During the sales negotiations, Tor-Quest's president told McNeely that he was a vital part of the deal and he would become the president and CEO of the new firm, Herbal Magic Inc. In light of these oral representations, McNeely invested $2.5 million in the new company's stock. However, only seven months after he became president and CEO, McNeely's employment was terminated. Although the employer paid him severance pay according to his employment agreement, McNeely argued that the representations made to him before the purchase created a "collateral agreement" and he was entitled to damages for its breach. The employer countered that the entire agreement clause in McNeely's employment contract precluded him from relying on any and all oral representations made that were not part of the signed contract.

Relevant Issue

Whether the contract's entire agreement clause precluded the employee from claiming damages for oral statements made during pre-contractual discussions.

Decision

The court held for the employer. The inclusion of an entire agreement clause showed that the parties intended the contract documents to be the whole of their agreement, notwithstanding any prior oral representations or discussions regarding the subject matter of the agreement. Negotiated by commercially sophisticated parties, the entire agreement clause explicitly covered "all prior agreements, understandings, representations or warranties, negotiations and discussions, whether oral or written." As a result, the employee could not rely on any statements made during such discussions to claim damages for negligent misrepresentations.

The *McNeely v. Herbal Magic Inc.* decision illustrates the potential impact of an entire agreement clause. Although such a clause does not guarantee that a court will ignore evidence of all previous discussions, especially in the face of serious or fraudulent misrepresentations on the part of the employer, it provides a legal basis for an argument to exclude prior discussions from a court's consideration.

13. Inducement

This clause addresses whether the employee's service with a previous employer is recognized by the contracting employer for severance purposes. If the employee was arguably induced to leave secure employment, the parties should negotiate and expressly state whether those previous years of service will be recognized for the purpose of benefits and calculating termination notice in the event that employment is terminated.

14. Independent Legal Advice

This clause states that the employee has had the opportunity to seek independent legal advice before signing the contract. The statement must, of course, be true. An employee who has had an opportunity to obtain independent legal advice will find it difficult to challenge the contract on the basis that he was unaware of its terms or of their legal meaning. Such a provision may be less important for senior management employees, who are assumed to have the requisite knowledge and leverage to protect themselves during negotiations.

15. Severability Clause

This clause provides that if a court invalidates part of the employment contract, it will not affect the validity of the remainder of the agreement. An unenforceable clause will simply be severed from the rest of the agreement. A severability clause may be especially important where there is a non-competition provision in the contract, to ensure that if the non-competition clause is found invalid, the rest of the contract will remain in force.

16. Golden Parachute

A unique feature that has evolved in executive employment contracts is the "golden parachute." Golden parachutes provide for substantial economic compensation in the event that an executive's employment is terminated under certain specified circumstances. Typically, the triggering event is a change in the ownership or control of the employer, as a result of which the executive loses her job or is justified in leaving the employer.

The rationale behind the golden parachute is to permit the executive to act in the interests of the employer during the transitional period without being distracted by its effect on her personally.

Enforceability and Interpretation of Written Contracts

Even after agreement on the terms is reached and the contract is signed, there are a number of issues that can affect the enforceability and interpretation of written employment contracts. A party who is unhappy with the terms of an employment contract may challenge the contract's enforceability by raising one of the issues described below. For example, a written contract may restrict the amount of notice of termination that an employee is entitled to. If terminated, the employee may argue that the notice term is unenforceable because it does not meet minimum statutory standards and therefore common law notice—which is usually much more generous than the notice specified in a written employment contract—should apply. Employers need to be aware of the issues set out below so that they can avoid these pitfalls.

1. Lack of Consideration

It is a basic principle of contract law that for a contract to be enforceable there must be an offer, acceptance, and consideration. Your uncle's promise to give you $1,000, without your doing anything in exchange, is a gratuitous promise. Because there is no consideration, you cannot successfully sue your uncle to enforce the terms of this promise.

In the employment context, consideration is usually provided by the promised exchange of payment for work performed. However, problems can arise where an employee begins working before the contract is finalized. The employee may allege that the final contract, signed after work began, is unenforceable because no new consideration was provided in exchange for the new terms. In *Francis v. Canadian Imperial Bank of Commerce*, the employee had already accepted employment and started work with the bank before signing the bank's contract. The court found that the employer could not rely on the 3 months' notice clause in the contract because there was no new consideration for the added term. The employee was therefore entitled to common law notice of 12 months. A similar problem can arise if an employer wants to add a new term to a contract during the course of the employment relationship.

To prevent this result, employers should ensure that the formal written employment contract is finalized before the hiring process is completed or before the employee is allowed to begin work. Once the employee begins work, it is too late to ask her to sign a contract containing new terms that are disadvantageous to her, unless the employer is prepared to provide some new consideration, such as a signing bonus.

2. Inequality of Bargaining Power

Written employment contracts can be challenged on the basis of the parties' alleged inequality of bargaining power at the time that the contract was negotiated. Courts have been sympathetic to these arguments where the terms of a contract are **unconscionable** (unreasonably one-sided) and the employee did not understand them. This could occur, for example, where the employee has little education or the employer applied undue pressure.

To minimize the risk of this problem, there are several things that the employer can do:

- Ensure that the terms of the contract represent a reasonable balance between the interests of both parties.
- Provide the candidate with a written copy of the proposed contract and give her time to read it and obtain independent legal advice before signing. This allows the person time to carefully review the terms of the contract so that they can be finalized before employment begins.
- Include a provision in the contract stating that the candidate had the opportunity to obtain independent legal advice before signing.
- Draw the candidate's attention to key terms such as non-competition, non-solicitation, and termination notice clauses and have the candidate initial them.

However, apparent inequality in bargaining power does not in itself render a contract unenforceable. For example, in *Wallace v. Toronto-Dominion Bank*, the Ontario Court of Appeal rejected the argument that a termination clause that provided for only four weeks' notice of termination or pay in lieu for a senior manager with eight years' service was invalid because of the parties' unequal bargaining power. Although the termination provision was not brought to the employee's attention at the time of hiring, the court found that no special circumstances, such as lack of understanding of the terms of the contract or oppressive conduct by the employer, undermined the contract.

3. Obsolescence

A contract may be challenged on the ground of obsolescence where its terms no longer reflect the realities of an employee's position within the organization. In *Lyonde v. Canadian Acceptance Corp.*, the employee had been promoted over a 24-year period from a junior position to vice-president, administration. The court refused to enforce a termination provision that provided no notice of termination. It found that his position within the organization had changed so dramatically that the essence of the employment contract was now fundamentally different. He was awarded 21 months' notice of termination.

More recently, the Ontario Court of Appeal, in *Irrcher v. MI Developments Inc.*, examined a termination clause in a ten-year-old contract where an employee's responsibilities and remuneration had changed substantially since the time the contract was signed.

CASE IN POINT

"Simply Not the Same Job": Employment Contract Found to Be Obsolete

Irrcher v. MI Developments Inc., 2003 ONCA 10675, 2003 CanLII 27685

Facts

In 1990, Irrcher signed a new contract of employment that restricted his termination notice period to six months. Subsequently, he accepted a number of responsibilities that were not outlined in his employment contract. The employer dismissed him in 2000 after several concerns arose with respect to his performance. The employer provided him with six months' notice of termination, as outlined in the 1990 contract.

Relevant Issue

Whether the termination provisions of the 1990 contract of employment should apply in light of the change in Irrcher's job function.

Decision

The Court of Appeal found that the termination provisions of the 1990 employment contract did not apply because the "substratum [foundation] of the written contract had disappeared." Irrcher had experienced a fundamental change in the nature of his job since signing the 1990 contract. His responsibilities had increased dramatically, as had his remuneration. Consequently, he was entitled to damages for reasonable notice corresponding to his new job, not the 1990 job.

To ensure that old contracts do not become invalid, the parties should update the employment agreement whenever there is a promotion or other significant change in duties. Promotions or salary increases could be made conditional on the execution of an amended employment contract (Israel, May 28, 2003, p. 3044). Similarly, the employment contract could include a provision that allows it to be reviewed and updated periodically.

The termination clause usually states that the employee is entitled to a certain number of weeks' notice for each completed year of service, with a certain maximum and minimum total notice period. This type of clause protects against obsolescence in most cases. For greater certainty, the clause could also state that it applies despite any changes in duties that arise over the life of the contract.

4. Failure to Meet Minimum Statutory Standards

Employers must ensure that the terms of an employment contract at least meet minimum statutory standards. Otherwise, the contract term that addresses the same issue will be null and void. In *Machtinger v. HOJ Industries Ltd.*, the Supreme Court of Canada examined a contract that specified a notice of termination period that failed to meet the statutory minimum notice requirements of the *Employment Standards Act, 2000*. The court held that the provision was invalid and required the employer to provide not merely the statutory minimum, but full reasonable notice under the common law.

CASE IN POINT

Employment Contract Fails to Meet Statutory Termination Requirements

Machtinger v. HOJ Industries Ltd., [1992] 1 SCR 986

Facts

The severance provisions in the written employment contract provided for two weeks' termination notice or pay in lieu whereas the Ontario *Employment Standards Act, 2000* required four weeks' notice or pay in lieu for someone with Machtinger's length of service. The employee argued that the provision was invalid for failing to meet the statutory minimum. He sued for common law damages for pay in lieu of reasonable notice. The trial judge agreed, ruled the provision invalid (effectively making the contract silent on the issue of termination notice), and awarded reasonable notice pay of seven months. The Court of Appeal allowed the employer's appeal, holding that the employee was entitled only to the statutory minimum. The employee appealed to the Supreme Court of Canada.

Relevant Issues

1. Whether the employer's attempt to contract out of the termination provision of the ESA nullified the termination provisions of the employment contract.

2. Whether an employee is entitled to common law damages for pay in lieu of reasonable notice when an employment contract is silent on the issue of termination notice.

Decision

The Supreme Court of Canada held that the employer could not contract out of the minimum statutory notice requirement. Furthermore, it refused simply to substitute the legislative requirement of four weeks' notice. The contractual termination provisions were void for all purposes, and the employer was liable for pay in lieu of reasonable notice under the common law. The employer was required to provide the employee with seven and one-half months' notice rather than the four weeks' notice set out in the contract.

The court held that to rebut the common law presumption of pay in lieu of reasonable notice on termination, the contract of employment must clearly specify another period of notice. If a contract does not comply with the statutory requirements for termination notice, the common law presumption is not rebutted.

More recently, courts have gone even further to find that just the possibility that a contractual termination clause could provide an employee with less than what she would be entitled to under employment standards legislation will render the clause unenforceable. For example, if the termination clause meets the statutory requirements at the time of termination, but would not meet them if the employee had been terminated at a later point, the clause will be found null and void from the outset. Another example of this rigorous approach is found in *Stevens v. Sifton Properties Ltd.*, where the court considered the enforceability of a termination clause that was silent on the continuation of benefits during the statutory notice period.

CASE IN POINT

Courts Provide Added Incentive to Draft Termination Clauses That Comply with ESA

Stevens v. Sifton Properties Ltd., 2012 ONSC 5508

Facts

Upon taking the position of head golf professional, Stevens signed an employment letter that contained the following termination provision: "The corporation may terminate your employment without cause at any time by providing you with notice or payment in lieu of notice, and/or severance pay, in accordance with the *Employment Standards Act*." Three years after signing the agreement Stevens was terminated, without cause, and she was given three weeks' pay in lieu of notice, as required by the ESA. The employer also continued her group benefits during those three weeks. Nonetheless, Stevens sued for wrongful dismissal damages, arguing that the termination clause was unenforceable because, as written, it did not specifically require the employer to provide benefit coverage during the statutory notice period, which is contrary to the *Employment Standards Act, 2000*.

Relevant Issue

Whether the termination clause was null and void because it did not expressly require the employer to continue the dismissed employee's statutory benefits during the notice period.

Decision

The court held that the contract's termination clause was null and void from the outset because it did not expressly meet the minimum requirements of the ESA with respect to benefit continuance. The fact that the employer actually continued to provide benefit coverage during the statutory notice period did not save the provision. As a result, Stevens was not limited to ESA entitlements on termination; she was entitled to damages based on the much more generous reasonable notice period under the common law. (See the discussion of common law principles in determining reasonable notice in Chapter 15.)

The intent behind this strict approach appears to be to motivate employers to comply with statutory requirements on termination. Employers are on notice that termination clauses will be scrutinized carefully; they therefore must be drafted with great care to ensure that they can satisfy minimum statutory standards *in every aspect and at any point in the employment relationship* (Chsherbinin, 2013, p. 1). Analogously, a contract (likely drafted prior to the 2006 amendments that effectively abolished mandatory retirement at age 65) that provides for mandatory retirement at age 65 or any other age could be argued to be unenforceable even if the termination of employment occurs well before that age.

To safeguard against changes to the termination requirements in the ESA, the termination clause could state that the employee is entitled to the greater of the entitlements specified in the contract and the entitlements required by the Act. Another approach is for the parties to revisit employment contracts at regular intervals to ensure that they still meet or exceed statutory requirements.

5.   Use of Ambiguous Language: Contra Proferentem Rule

In preparing an employment contract, employers should use clear and unambiguous terms. If a court finds that the terms of a contract can bear two possible interpretations, it may apply a rule called **contra proferentem**. Under the *contra proferentem* rule, ambiguous language may be interpreted against the party who drafted the agreement because that is the party who could have avoided the problem by being clearer.

Because the drafter is usually the employer, most contractual ambiguities are interpreted to benefit the employee. However, *Foreman v. 818329 Ontario Limited* shows that the principle of *contra proferentem* can operate in favour of an employer as well.

CASE IN POINT

Contractual Ambiguities Work to the Disadvantage of Drafter

Foreman v. 818329 Ontario Limited, 2003 CanLII 57401 (Ont. CA)

Facts

When Foreman, a 32-year-old manager of two bingo halls, found out that ownership of the bingo halls was being transferred, she asked the current owner to prepare an employment contract that would provide her with "some security." The contract stated that the employer "shall not dismiss" Foreman. When she was terminated nine months later, she sued for wrongful dismissal, alleging that she had a fixed-term contract for her working lifetime because only she could terminate it. At trial, she was awarded $712,000, representing the income that she would have earned over the remainder of her 33-year working life.

Relevant Issue

Whether the employment contract guaranteed employment for life.

Decision

The Ontario Court of Appeal found that it is possible to have a fixed-term employment contract for the lifetime of an employee. However, it stated that a contract for life requires greater clarity than other fixed-term employment contracts "given the profound financial responsibility of such a guarantee." The court found that the contract contained no explicit language that unequivocally guaranteed employment for life. Therefore, because the contract was drafted on behalf of Foreman, the ambiguity was interpreted against her. The order of the trial judge was set aside, and Foreman was awarded $30,800 in lieu of the 12 months' reasonable notice to which she was entitled.

Employers should keep the following tips in mind when drafting employment contracts to reduce the risk that a contract, or a term of a contract, will be ruled unenforceable by a court:

1. *Use clear, straightforward language.* The *contra proferentem* rule may result in ambiguous language being interpreted in favour of the other party. (And make sure that the clear language says what you intend it to mean.)
2. *Be fair when negotiating terms.* Evidence of unfairness or undue influence in negotiating terms may render the contract void.
3. *Give the other party time to read, understand, and seek independent legal advice about the contract before signing it.*
4. *Meet or exceed the minimum statutory standards.*
5. *Bring critical terms to the other party's attention.* For example, an employer who drafts an agreement should bring clauses related to a probationary period to an employee's attention and have the employee initial those clauses.
6. Provide additional consideration if the employer wants a new term included in the contract after it is signed or after employment begins.
7. *Customize contracts rather than using a standard form.* It is important that the parties consider special issues that need to be addressed.

REFERENCES

Bowes v. Goss Power Products Limited. 2012 ONCA 425.

Ceccol v. Ontario Gymnastic Federation. 2001 CanLII 8589, 55 OR (3d) 614 (CA).

Christensen v. Family Counselling Centre of Sault Ste. Marie and District. 2001 CanLII 4698 (Ont. CA).

Chsherbinin, Nikolay. Employment Contracts: Say What You Mean. *Canadian HR Reporter.* December 3, 2012, p. 1. http://nclaw.ca/testing/wp-content/uploads/2012/12/employment-contracts.pdf.

Chsherbinin, Nikolay. Finding the Right Words. *Canadian Employment Law Today.* May 15, 2013, p. 3. http://nclaw.ca/testing/wp-content/uploads/2013/05/Finding-Right-Words.pdf?edc861.

Dimson v. KTI Kanatek Technologies Inc. 2013 ONCA 454.

Eagle Professional Resources v. MacMullin. 2013 ONSC 2501.

Echlin, Randall, and Christine Thomlinson. *For Better or For Worse: A Practical Guide to Canadian Employment Law,* 3rd ed. Toronto: Canada Law Book, 2011.

Emond Harnden. Court of Appeal Strikes Down Unreasonable Non-Competition Clause. *What's New.* June 2011. http://www.ehlaw.ca/whatsnew/1106/Focus11062.shtml.

Employers and Employees Act. RSO 1990, c. E.12.

Employment Standards Act, 2000. SO 2000, c. 41.

England, Geoffrey. *Individual Employment Law,* 2nd ed. Toronto: Irwin Law, 2008.

Foreman v. 818329 Ontario Limited, 2003 CanLII 57401 (Ont. CA).

Francis v. Canadian Imperial Bank of Commerce. (1994), 120 DLR (4th) 393 (Ont. CA).

Freudenberg Household Products Inc. v. DiGiammarino. 2012 ONSC 5725.

Global Foreign Exchange Corporation v. Kelcher. 2011 ABCA 240.

Guay inc. c. Payette. 2010 QCCS 2756.

Irrcher v. MI Developments Inc. 2003 ONCA 10675, 2003 CanLII 27685.

Israel, Peter. Ask an Expert: Are Employment Agreements Valid if the Position and Salary Change? *Canadian Employment Law Today.* Issue no. 390, May 28, 2003, p. 3044.

Israel, Peter. Ask an Expert: Does an Employer Have the Right to Terminate Probationary Employees Without Pay in Lieu of Notice? *Canadian Employment Law Today.* Issue no. 386, April 2, 2003, p. 3012.

Israel, Peter. Ask an Expert: Preventing Former Employees from Competing. *Canadian Employment Law Today.* Issue no. 409, March 17, 2004, p. 3196.

Jamieson, Elisha. OCA Affirms Termination Clause in Employment Contract Does Not Violate ESA. July 24, 2013. Hicks Morley. http://www.hicksmorleycaseinpoint.com/2013/07/24/oca-affirms-termination-clause-in-employment-contract-does-not-violate-esa/.

Kempf, Alfred. Social Media and Trade Secrets. November 29, 2013. Pushor Mitchell LLP. http://www.pushormitchell.com/law-library/article/social-media-and-trade-secrets.

Levitt, Howard. Managers Have Duty to Remain Loyal to Employer. *National Post.* November 12, 2008. Levitt & Grosman. http://www.levittgrosman.com/resources/articles/managers-have-duty-to-remain-loyal-to-employer.

Levitt, Howard. Too Long Non-Compete Periods Risk Being Overturned by Courts. *Financial Post.* December 10, 2013. http://business.financialpost.com/2013/12/10/too-long-non-compete-periods-risk-being-overturned-by-courts.

Lyonde v. Canadian Acceptance Corp. (1983), 3 CCEL 220 (Ont. HCJ).

Macchione, Paul. Restrictive Covenants—Context Matters! *The Employers' Edge.* October 3, 2013. http://www.ccpartners.ca/blog/details/the-employers-edge/2013/10/03/restrictive-covenants-context-matters!.

Machtinger v. HOJ Industries Ltd. [1992] 1 SCR 986, 91 DLR (4th) 491; rev'g 1988 CanLII 4645 (Ont. CA), 55 DLR (4th) 401.

Mason v. Chem-Trend Limited Partnership. 2010 ONSC 4119.

McNeely v. Herbal Magic Inc. 2011 ONSC 4237.

Mitchell, T. Ask an Expert: Employment Contracts—Changes to Oral Contract. *Canadian Employment Law Today.* May 2, 2012. http://business.financialpost.com/2013/12/10/too-long-non-compete-periods-risk-being-overturned-by-courts/.

Payette c. Guay inc. 2013 CSC 45.

Pugen, Daniel. Customer Contacts on LinkedIn = Property of the Employer. *Ontario Employer Advisor.* September 24, 2013. McCarthy Tétrault. http://www.ontarioemployerlaw.com/2013/09/24/an-employees-linkedin-network-is-property-of-the-employer/.

RBC Dominion Securities Inc. v. Merrill Lynch Canada Inc. 2008 SCC 54.

Reeve, Connie. Case Summaries: RBC Dominion Securities Inc. v. Merrill Lynch Canada Inc., 2008 SCC 54. *The Six-Minute Employment Lawyer.* The Law Society of Upper Canada, June 17, 2009.

Ross v. Christian & Timbers Inc. 2002 CanLII 49619 (Ont. SC).

Rudner, Stuart. Can You Negotiate a Job for Life? *Canadian Employment Law Today*. Issue no. 398, October 1, 2003, p. 3107.

Rudner, Stuart. Enforceability of Termination Clause in Employment Agreement. *First Reference Talks*. June 7, 2013. http://blog.firstreference.com/2013/06/07/enforceability-of-termination-clause-in-employment-agreement/.

Shafron v. KRG Insurance Brokers (Western) Inc. 2009 SCC 6.

Smith, J. Contract Not Fixed-Term Without Definite End Date: Court. *Canadian Employment Law Today*. Issue no. 582, June 15, 2011, pp. 1, 7.

Stam, Lisa. Who Owns "Publicly Available" Social Media Content? *Employment and Human Rights Law in Canada*. October 22, 2013. http://www.canadaemploymenthumanrightslaw.com/2013/10/articles/social-media/who-owns-publicly-available-social-media-content/.

Statute of Frauds. RSO 1990, c. S.19.

Stevens v. Sifton Properties Ltd. 2012 ONSC 5508.

Thompson, Martin, and Kyle Lambert. "You Can't Have Your Cake and Eat It (Part) 2": An Update on Mitigation and Employment Contracts. *Employment and Labour Bulletin*. December 2013. McMillan LLP. http://www.mcmillan.ca/You-Cant-Have-Your-Cake-and-Eat-it-Part-2-An-Update-on-Mitigation-and-Employment-Contracts.

Treash, Andrew. Case in Point: Restrictive Covenants. Piling on the Restrictions. *Canadian Employment Law Today*. October 5, 2011, p. 4.

Wallace v. Toronto-Dominion Bank. (1983), 41 OR (2d) 161 (CA); leave to appeal to SCC refused 52 NR 157n.

Wendel, Cristina. Latest from the Supreme Court of Canada on Restrictive Covenants in the Commercial Context. *Employment and Labour Law*. October 8, 2013. Dentons. http://www.employmentandlabour.com/latest-from-the-supreme-court-of-canada-on-restrictive-covenants-in-the-commercial-context.

Wilson, Peter, and Allison Taylor. *The Corporate Counsel Guide to Employment Law*, 2nd ed. Aurora, ON: Canada Law Book, 2003.

REVIEW AND DISCUSSION QUESTIONS

1. What are the advantages of a written employment contract over an oral one? Are there any disadvantages?

2. If a dispute arises out of an oral employment contract, how does a court establish the terms and conditions of the contract?

3. What are the main legal issues that can affect the enforceability of an employment contract?

4. What is the *contra proferentem* rule of interpretation? Does this rule seem fair to you? Why or why not?

5. Explain the difficulties that an employer may face with a fixed-term contract.

6. Why are courts generally wary of restrictive covenant clauses?

7. What standard contractual terms do you think an employee may have the most difficulty with?

8. An employee may challenge the enforceability of an employment contract on several grounds. Review the sample indefinite-term employment contract in Appendix A. Identify three ways in which the employer has drafted this contract to help it successfully defend a challenge to its enforceability based on the grounds discussed in the chapter. Explain your answer.

9. The morning Maria started her new job the employer handed her a copy of the firm's employer policy manual and told her to look it over, informing her that its terms and conditions would apply to her employment contract. This was the first time the manual had been mentioned to her. Four months later Maria was terminated without notice on the basis that she was not suitable for the job. The employer stated that it did not owe her any notice of termination or pay in lieu because the policy manual established a probationary period of six months during which time she could be terminated for any reason without notice. Explain whether you think Maria is bound by the terms set out in the policy manual and provide reasons for your answer.

10. In a non-competition clause, a martial arts instructor was restricted from teaching at, owning, or operating a martial arts school within a ten-mile radius of his employer's business for one year after leaving employment. The instructor quit within two months and opened a martial arts school half a block from his former employer. Is the non-competition clause enforceable? Discuss.

11. The following clauses were found in Mark's employer's policy manual, which formed part of his employment contract:

    > Termination notice must be in writing from the Executive Director, and professional staff will receive one month's notice … and/or notice as established by legislation.

This Personnel Code is to be considered a guideline for the minimum expectations of employment and benefits obtaining therefrom.

When Mark was terminated without cause, the employer argued that according to the termination clause, it only had to meet the termination requirements of the *Employment Standards Act, 2000*. Mark sued for wrongful dismissal damages under the common law. In your opinion, which party would likely be successful? Explain your answer.

12. Simardeep's negotiated severance letter contained the following terms:

> (a) The Employer will provide you with 2 weeks' pay in lieu of notice plus 2 days per year of service severance as required by the *Canada Labour Code*. [statutory entitlements]
>
> (b) *In addition to the amount provided in (a) above*, on the condition that you provide a signed copy of this letter and a signed release, the employer will continue to pay you your regular salary until the earlier of the date on which you obtain new employment or May 28, 2010, the date on which your salary continuance period ends. If you obtain new employment during the salary continuation period, the employer will stop the salary continuance and pay you 50 percent of the remaining amount in a single lump sum. [common law entitlements]

When the employer discontinued salary continuation payments earlier than Simardeep expected it to, the parties realized that they disagreed on the proper interpretation of these two clauses. Simardeep sued her former employer for the additional amount, arguing that the common law severance compensation set out in paragraph (b) was to be *in addition to* the statutory severance described in paragraph (a). The employer countered that the benefits and salary negotiated in paragraph (b) were clearly to include the statutory entitlements set out in paragraph (a) because any other interpretation would be unfair and provide the employee with severance pay well in excess of the 24-month "cap" that typically applies to common law awards.

Which interpretation do you think the court will choose?

13. When Serena was dismissed without cause from her position as vice-president, she received only her entitlements under the *Employment Standards Act, 2000*.

Her compensation package was variable so, as required by the ESA, the employer averaged her last 12 weeks of employment in calculating her entitlements to statutory termination and severance pay. No bonus amounts were included in this calculation because she had not received a bonus in the previous 12-week period.

In limiting Serena to her statutory entitlements, the employer relied on the termination clause contained in her employment contract. It read as follows:

> 18(c) In addition, the Employer may terminate this Agreement at its sole discretion for any reason, upon providing the Employee all payments or entitlements in accordance with the standards set out in the Ontario *Employment Standards Act*, as may be amended from time to time.
>
> 18(d) If at any time the Employer provides you with a bonus, it will not be included in the calculation of payment for the purpose of this Article or as otherwise agreed to or required by the *Employment Standards Act*.

Serena sued for wrongful dismissal damages under the common law, arguing that the termination clause was unenforceable.

a. What legal argument might Serena use to say that this termination clause was unenforceable?

b. Do you think this argument would be successful? Explain your answer.

14. It's been said that courts do not like termination clauses that displace the common law presumption that an employee who is dismissed without "just cause" is entitled to reasonable notice (or pay in lieu of notice). What evidence can you find in this chapter that this statement is accurate?

15. Beatrice was hired as a manager in a specialized area of IT in 1999. Her employment contract contained a statement that her employment could be terminated without cause on 30 days' notice. In 2012, the employer terminated her without just cause. At the time Beatrice was 54 years old and earning $200,000 per year including salary, bonus, car allowance, and benefits. Beatrice brought a motion for summary judgment (which can be brought when one of the parties believes that there is no real dispute on the facts and therefore no need for a trial).

Was the termination clause enforceable? (See Chapter 14 to determine Beatrice's statutory entitlements in this situation.)

During the Course of Employment

Part III examines key employment statutes that apply, and common legal issues that can arise, during the course of the employment relationship. As you have seen in Part II, the contractual agreement between an employer and a non-union employee sets out the principal terms and conditions of employment. It forms the base, or heart, of the employee–employer relationship. Around this contractual base, however, there are a number of statutes that affect, often significantly, the rights and obligations of the workplace parties. Unlike contractual obligations, these statutory requirements are non-negotiable: the parties cannot contract out of them.

In Ontario the main employment-related statutes are the *Human Rights Code*, the *Employment Standards Act, 2000*, the *Occupational Health and Safety Act*, the *Workplace Safety and Insurance Act, 1997*, the *Pay Equity Act*, and the *Accessibility for Ontarians with Disabilities Act, 2005*. These statutes are examined in this part in Chapters 5 through 9, respectively. The *Labour Relations Act, 1995*, which focuses on the rights and responsibilities of unionized employees and the methods by which employees may become unionized, is another significant employment-related statute. However, because this text focuses on the non-union employee–employer relationship, discussion of that Act is beyond the scope of this text.

That being said, this part of the text frequently does refer to unionized workplaces for several reasons. First, and most importantly, employment-related statutes, unlike the common law of individual employment contracts, apply to unionized and non-union employees alike. Therefore, how a particular legislative requirement affects the parties in the unionized context generally illustrates how it applies in non-union workplaces as well. Second, where there are requirements that are unique to unionized workplaces, such as a union's duty to support accommodation measures under the *Human Rights Code*, briefly canvassing those requirements provides a broader understanding of the overall legislative framework. Finally, for a small number of issues, such as workplace drug testing and privacy-related questions, the text touches on how these matters are typically dealt with by arbitrators under collective agreements to provide additional context and contrast in certain areas of special interest.

Two federal statutes are also dealt with in this part. The *Employment Equity Act* is considered in Chapter 9 because of its direct relevance to equity in the provincially regulated workplace. Chapter 10 focuses on the evolution of law related to privacy for employees, both on and off an employer's premises. The federal *Personal Information Protection and Electronic Documents Act* is relevant in this regard.

Finally, significant issues that are not covered by statute but that have legal implications under the common law, such as contractual amendments, performance management, discipline, and vicarious liability, are discussed in Chapter 11.

Human Rights Issues: Duty to Accommodate, Harassment, Accessibility Standards

5

LEARNING OUTCOMES

After completing this chapter, you will be able to:

- Determine what constitutes discrimination under the Ontario *Human Rights Code*.

- Understand the practical implications of the Code's duty to accommodate, focusing on the grounds of disability, creed, sex (pregnancy), and family status.

- Grasp the concept of undue hardship.

- Determine the legality of drug and alcohol testing in the workplace.

- Outline the employer's obligations with respect to workplace harassment, sexual harassment, and sexual solicitation.

- Identify an applicant's remedies under the Code.

- Understand how the Code is administered and enforced.

- Understand how the *Accessibility for Ontarians with Disabilities Act, 2005* relates to employment standards.

Introduction

Human rights requirements are a key consideration during the hiring process, and they continue to play a central role throughout the employment relationship. The Ontario *Human Rights Code* requires an employer to maintain a workplace that is free from discrimination and harassment. It must make all employment decisions, including those related to training, transfers, promotions, apprenticeships, compensation, benefits, performance evaluations, discipline, layoffs, and dismissals, on a non-discriminatory basis.

What Constitutes Discrimination?

The term **discrimination** is not defined in the Code. As noted in Chapter 2, initially the courts interpreted it to mean an intentional act of exclusion—for example, the placement of an advertisement specifying that individuals of a certain ethnic background need not apply. This behaviour is known as direct discrimination and is easy to identify. Many acts of discrimination, however, are hidden or even unintentional. For example, the weight and height restrictions formerly attached to some jobs, such as firefighter and police officer, often had an adverse impact on women and members of certain ethnic groups who, on average, were unable to meet those "job requirements." This type of discrimination is sometimes referred to as **adverse impact discrimination** or **constructive discrimination**.

Over time, the idea evolved that employers have a duty to accommodate people affected by this form of discrimination. Thus, even where a job requirement is justifiable, if it affects certain individuals or groups adversely and touches on a prohibited ground of discrimination, an employer has an obligation to accommodate that employee or group if possible. For example, a requirement that retail workers be available to work on Saturdays is a neutral job-related rule imposed in good faith. However, a strict application of that rule bars from employment people whose religion prevents them from working on that day. The duty to accommodate requires the employer to modify the rule for those negatively affected unless doing so would create **undue hardship** for the employer.

In 1985, the Ontario government amended the Code to expressly include the notion of constructive discrimination. Section 11 provides that a rule that *results* in discrimination infringes the Code unless it is a bona fide occupational qualification or requirement (BFOQ) or it falls within one of the limited exemptions discussed in Chapter 2 under the heading "Exemptions: Where Discrimination Is Allowed." The section further states that a rule or qualification will *not* be considered a BFOQ unless it is shown that the needs of that person or group *cannot* be accommodated without imposing undue hardship on the employer. Thus, the duty to accommodate is now an integral part of an employer's obligations under the Code. Although the duty can arise on several grounds, it is most likely to arise in the case of an employee with a disability. The duty to accommodate for disability is specifically covered in s. 17 of the Code.

FYI

Section 11: Constructive Discrimination

11(1) A right of a person under Part I is infringed where a requirement, qualification or factor exists that is not discrimination on a prohibited ground but that results in the exclusion, restriction or preference of a group of persons who are identified by a prohibited ground of discrimination and of whom the person is a member, except where,

(a) the requirement, qualification or factor is reasonable and *bona fide* in the circumstances; or

(b) it is declared in this Act, other than in section 17, that to discriminate because of such ground is not an infringement of a right.

(2)   The Tribunal or a court shall not find that a requirement, qualification or factor is reasonable and *bona fide* in the circumstances unless it is satisfied that the needs of the group of which the person is a member cannot be accommodated without undue hardship on the person responsible for accommodating those needs, considering the cost, outside sources of funding, if any, and health and safety requirements, if any.

FYI

Systemic Discrimination: What Is It?

"Systemic," or institutional, discrimination is one of the more complex and subtle forms of discrimination. It refers to the web of employer policies or practices that are neutral on their face but that have discriminatory effects. For example, a company may have a culture that encourages informal mentoring through sports-related activities that take place after working hours. Employees who are disabled, or whose family responsibilities make it more difficult for them to participate after hours, may be less successful at building internal networks as a consequence. The existence of systemic discrimination is sometimes identified through numerical data. For example, data may show that there are few women in high-level positions in a particular advertising firm compared with the representation of female executives in the labour force in general.

In 1999, the Supreme Court of Canada further broadened the scope of prohibited discrimination in the watershed decision of *British Columbia (Public Service Employee Relations Commission) v. BCGSEU* (the *Meiorin* case). This case established a three-part test for determining when a discriminatory rule or standard is justified. This test is the same whether the discrimination is direct or constructive.

Three-Part Test Established for Justifying Discriminatory Rule

British Columbia (Public Service Employee Relations Commission) v. BCGSEU, [1999] 3 SCR 3

Facts

Meiorin was a forest firefighter who had performed her job in a satisfactory manner for three years when her employer, the British Columbia government, implemented a new policy under which all firefighters were required to pass a series of fitness tests. A team of researchers at the University of Victoria had designed the tests using a sample group of participants that consisted of many more men than women. To measure aerobic capacity, the test required employees to run 2.5 kilometres in 11 minutes or less. Meiorin tried to pass this part of the test on four separate occasions, but her best time was 49 seconds over the 11-minute limit. As a result, the government terminated her employment as a forest firefighter.

Relevant Issue

Whether Meiorin's termination amounted to discrimination and thus violated British Columbia's human rights legislation.

Decision

The Supreme Court of Canada found that the rule was discriminatory because Meiorin was able to show that the aerobic requirement screened out more women than men on the basis of their differing physical capacities. The issue was whether the discriminatory rule or standard could be justified. Reversing previous case law, the court ruled that there should

not be separate categories of discrimination: direct and constructive. Whatever form discrimination takes, job rules or qualifications that detrimentally affect people or groups on the basis of a prohibited ground of discrimination should be subject to the same analysis. The court set out the following three-part test to determine when a discriminatory rule or qualification is justifiable. To successfully defend a discriminatory standard or rule, the employer must

1. demonstrate that a *rational connection exists* between the purpose for which the standard was introduced and the objective requirements of the job;
2. demonstrate that the standard was *adopted in an honest and good-faith belief* that it was necessary for the performance of the job; and
3. establish that the standard was *reasonably necessary* to accomplish that legitimate work-related purpose. To establish this, the employer must show that it was impossible to accommodate employees who share the characteristics of the claimant without imposing undue hardship on itself.

The employer met the first two tests, but failed the third one. It was unable to prove that the aerobic standard was reasonably necessary for a forest firefighter to perform the job safely and efficiently or that accommodation was impossible without undue hardship.

Under the third part of the *Meiorin* test, a discriminatory standard will be found reasonably necessary, and therefore justified, only if the employer can show that it was impossible to accommodate the individual or group negatively affected by the rule without suffering undue hardship. This is a very high standard for an employer to meet and one that requires it to consider differing needs when setting or creating a standard or rule. (This approach is called *inclusive design*.) For example, in *Meiorin*, the employer established the standard by looking at the aerobic capacity of its (mostly male) workforce. The Supreme Court expressly rejected this approach, holding that an employer cannot create a workplace rule based on a perceived norm and then be prepared to make exceptions for individuals who cannot satisfy the rule. Instead, the question of reasonable accommodation must be taken into consideration *from the beginning, as part of setting the rule or standard*. The British Columbia government should have developed standards of aerobic fitness that recognize the different capacities of women and men and established requirements accordingly.

In *Meiorin*, the court suggested some factors that should be considered when assessing whether the duty to accommodate has been met.

1. Did the employer investigate alternative approaches that do not have a discriminatory effect, such as individual testing?
2. Were there valid reasons why alternative approaches were not implemented? What were they?
3. Can the workplace accommodate different standards that reflect group or individual differences and capabilities?
4. Can legitimate workplace objectives be met in a less discriminatory manner?
5. Does the standard ensure that the desired qualification is met without placing an undue burden on those to whom it applies?
6. Have other parties who are obliged to assist in the search for accommodation (for example, the union representing an affected worker) fulfilled their roles?

Meiorin thus places a heavy onus on employers to ensure that the workplace is sensitive to the needs of individuals and groups that are protected by the Code. Undoubtedly, this was the court's intention when it set out the *Meiorin* test. However, since that decision was made, some tribunals and lower courts have interpreted this very high standard for justifying a workplace rule that is *prima facie* discriminatory to mean virtual impossibility. That is, can the employer show that it is *impossible* to accommodate the individual or group? If not, it has to accommodate. In its 2008 decision in *Hydro-Québec v. Syndicat des employé-e-s de techniques professionnelles et de bureau d'Hydro-Québec, section locale 2000 (SCFP-FTQ)*, the Supreme Court of Canada clarified the third part of the *Meiorin* test. It confirmed that the test is not whether it is impossible to accommodate the protected individual or group, but rather whether it is impossible to do so *without undue hardship*.

CASE IN POINT

"Impossibility" Is Not the Standard

Hydro-Québec v. Syndicat des employé-e-s de techniques professionnelles et de bureau d'Hydro-Québec, section locale 2000 (SCFP-FTQ), 2008 SCC 43

Facts

Laverriere, a clerk with Hydro-Québec, missed 960 days of work over a seven-year period because of an array of physical and psychiatric conditions. These included a personality disorder that made her relationships with supervisors and co-workers difficult. Her employer made numerous accommodation attempts, including assigning lighter duties, providing a gradual return to work program, and changing her departments. None was successful. The employer had obtained a psychiatric assessment indicating that Laverriere would not be able to attain regular and continuous attendance in the future and it was clear that accommodation would

have to be constantly adjusted. At that point Hydro-Québec fired Laverriere. The union grieved her termination, arguing that accommodation was not impossible. She could work if the employer provided her with a new work environment, new supervisors, and new co-workers on an ongoing basis. Although the initial arbitration decision held that this degree of accommodation constituted undue hardship, the union appealed. The Québec Court of Appeal found that being required to frequently change accommodation requirements was not an "undue hardship" for a large company like Hydro-Québec because it was not "impossible."

Relevant Issue

Whether the employer proved undue hardship.

Decision

The Supreme Court of Canada found that the employer had shown undue hardship. In its words, "the purpose of the duty to accommodate is to ensure that persons who are otherwise fit to work are not unfairly excluded where working conditions can be adjusted without undue hardship." However, the duty to accommodate does have limits and an employer is not required to "completely alter the essence of the contract of employment, that is, the employee's duty to perform work in exchange for remuneration." Where an employer has taken all reasonable measures to accommodate an employee and enable her to do her work but the employee still remains unable to do so in the reasonably foreseeable future, the employer has established undue hardship. The standard of reasonable accommodation is not whether accommodation is impossible but whether accommodation short of undue hardship is impossible.

The *Hydro-Québec* decision provides some welcome clarification of the third branch of the *Meiorin* test. However, given the employee's extraordinary amount of absenteeism in the case, as well as the numerous attempts at accommodation made by the employer, this decision does not support the proposition that proving that a rule is a BFOQ has become easy for employers. The standard remains high—some or moderate effort is not enough—but in the right circumstances, exclusion is permitted. The decision also underscores the bedrock principle that an exchange of work for remuneration remains at the heart of the employment relationship.

The Duty to Accommodate

The duty to accommodate has been part of an employer's obligation under the Code for many years. The principle that underlies the duty is the belief that it is unfair to exclude people on the basis of a prohibited ground of discrimination because their needs are different from those of the majority.

The essence of **accommodation** lies in tailoring the workplace to meet the needs of the individual employee. According to the Ontario Human Rights Commission's *Policy and Guidelines on Disability and the Duty to Accommodate* (2000), the principle of accommodation involves three factors:

1. *Individualization.* There is no formula to determine when the duty to accommodate has been satisfied. Each person's needs are unique; a solution that meets one person's requirements may not meet another's.
2. *Dignity.* People must be accommodated in a manner that most respects their dignity, including their privacy, confidentiality, comfort, and autonomy. For example, a wheelchair entrance over the loading dock or garbage room is unacceptable.
3. *Inclusion.* Job requirements and workplaces must be designed with everyone in mind. An employer cannot base systems or requirements on "normal employees" and then make exceptions as people or groups request them.

The employer has primary responsibility for initiating accommodation. However, other parties have responsibilities as well: it is a shared obligation. The party requiring accommodation should make his needs known to the employer and supply information regarding the assistance required. Unions also have a responsibility to help find solutions when accommodation conflicts with the collective agreement. The Commission's *Policy and Guidelines on Disability and the Duty to Accommodate* addresses the parties' responsibilities.

The obligations of the employer are as follows:

- accept the employee's request for accommodation in good faith, unless there are legitimate reasons for acting otherwise;
- obtain expert opinion or advice where necessary;
- ensure that alternative approaches and accommodation solutions are investigated;
- keep a record of the accommodation request and the action taken;
- maintain confidentiality;
- limit requests for information to those reasonably related to the nature of the limitation or restriction;
- grant accommodation requests in a timely manner unless they create undue hardship, even when the request is not made formally;
- bear the cost of acquiring necessary medical information or documentation such as doctors' notes; and
- explain to an employee why a request would cause undue hardship, if this is the case.

The obligations of an employee who seeks accommodation are as follows:

- request accommodation;
- explain why accommodation is required, so that all needs are known;
- answer questions or provide information regarding relevant restrictions or limitations, including information from health-care professionals;
- participate in discussions regarding possible solutions to accommodation needs;
- cooperate with any experts whose assistance is required;
- meet agreed-upon performance and job standards once accommodation is provided;
- work with the employer on an ongoing basis to manage the accommodation process; and
- discuss accommodation requirements only with persons who need to know them (possibly including a supervisor, a union representative, or human rights staff).

The obligations of unions are as follows:

- take an active role as a partner in the accommodation process;
- share responsibility with the employer to facilitate accommodation, including suggesting and testing alternative approaches and cooperating when solutions are proposed;
- respect the confidentiality of the person requesting accommodation; and
- support accommodation measures irrespective of collective agreements, unless to do so would create undue hardship.

Bubb-Clarke v. Toronto Transit Commission shows the extent of a union's obligation to assist in accommodation efforts.

CASE IN POINT

Union Violates Its Duty to Accommodate

Bubb-Clarke v. Toronto Transit Commission, 2002 CanLII 46503, [2002] OHRBID no. 6

Facts

In July 1990, approximately four years after commencing employment with the employer transit commission, Bubb-Clarke went on short-term sick leave for a then-undiagnosed medical condition. In February 1991, while working as a rear-door loader, the employee was diagnosed with narcolepsy, a sleeping disorder. Consequently, his driver's licence was downgraded, and it was determined that he should neither work nights nor drive the employer's vehicles off the employer's property. As a result, Bubb-Clarke could no longer perform his job. The employer attempted to find suitable employment for him and eventually transferred him to the position of subway janitor. However, the union took the position that he could only transfer a portion of the seniority rights he had previously held as a rear-door loader.

Relevant Issue

Whether the union's decision not to transfer Bubb-Clarke's full seniority rights amounted to a violation of the *Human Rights Code*.

Decision

The Board held that Bubb-Clarke's transfer was a result of a disability, and his loss of seniority was a result of discrimination. To allow him to transfer all earned seniority would not constitute undue hardship to either the employer or the union. The fact that he was to start with reduced seniority in the maintenance division put him at a disadvantage as a result of his disability. The Board ordered the union to pay Bubb-Clarke $22,000 in general damages and damages for mental anguish. It also granted him full seniority in whatever position he might occupy at the TTC as a result of his disability.

What Constitutes Undue Hardship?

Once an employee makes a ***prima facie* case** of discrimination, the onus shifts to the employer to present evidence showing that the financial cost of the accommodation—even with outside sources of funding—or the health and safety risks would create undue hardship. Under the Code, three factors—costs, outside sources of funding, and health and safety requirements—are specifically recognized as being relevant to a discussion of undue hardship (see ss. 11(2) and 17(2)). However, in *Central Okanagan School District No. 23 v. Renaud*, the Supreme Court of Canada held that there may be other relevant considerations, provided that the difficulties they present are substantial and not merely inconvenient. These include the potential disruption of a collective agreement, morale problems with other employees, and problems relating to the interchangeability of the workforce and facilities and the size of the employer's operations.

Costs

The Ontario Human Rights Commission's *Policy and Guidelines on Disability and the Duty to Accommodate*, while not binding on the Tribunal, can be or will often be taken into consideration in its decisions and therefore is relevant. According to these guidelines, costs constitute undue hardship only if they are quantifiable (not merely speculative), directly related to the accommodation, and "so substantial that they would alter the essential nature of the enterprise, or so significant that they would substantially affect its viability." This is an extremely high standard, and most large businesses will rarely be able to meet it. Business inconvenience and customer preferences are not relevant considerations. Moreover, costs are based on the budget of the whole organization, not the branch or unit where the person works or has made a job application. On the other hand, the capacity of an organization to get a loan to pay for the costs of accommodation or to spread costs over time is relevant. For example, the cost of building a ramp or elevator can be spread over a number of years and tax write-offs and depreciation are factored in.

Employers must be able to produce actual evidence of undue hardship. Speculative risks and conditions that may arise in the future are not valid considerations. For example, if an employee has multiple sclerosis and further deterioration is expected over time, the fact that further accommodation may be necessary in the future cannot be used as a basis for assessing the employer's current ability to accommodate. Similarly, the unpredictability and extent of future disability does not affect the current duty to accommodate.

Finally, the availability of outside sources of funding, such as grants, subsidies, or tax credits, is considered. For example, an employer's eligibility for tax incentives to make the workplace more accessible is factored in when determining whether the point of undue hardship has been reached.

As noted above, the duty to accommodate requires the parties to consider each situation individually and not apply an automatic "rule" concerning when undue hardship has been reached. In the 2008 decision of *McGill University Health Centre (Montreal General Hospital) v. Syndicat des employés de l'Hôpital général de Montréal*, the Supreme Court of Canada held that the parties to a collective agreement can negotiate clauses that set a maximum period of time for absences, after which an employee can be terminated. However, it also held that the time period allocated in the collective agreement cannot be less than what the employee is entitled to under human rights legislation. In other words, the parties can bargain over the time limit but it is still an individualized process and the negotiated limit must, in the end, meet human rights requirements. Although this decision relates to workplaces covered by a collective agreement, it does illustrate the general principle that the Code's requirements represent a "minimum" set of rights that the workplace parties cannot contract out of.

Health and Safety Concerns

For health and safety to constitute undue hardship, the Commission's guidelines state that the employer must show that the risks, evaluated after all accommodations have been made to reduce them, are still serious. The nature, severity, probability, and scope of risk are all relevant considerations. If the potential harm is minor and unlikely to occur, the risk is not considered serious.

Similarly, if the risk is only or primarily to the employee seeking accommodation, the employee's willingness to assume that risk, once it is explained by the employer, will also be taken into account. If there are means to reduce the safety concerns—for example, through the use of medication—undue hardship is unlikely to be found.

Fulfilling the Duty to Accommodate

The duty to accommodate applies to all grounds of discrimination, but it is most likely to arise in the context of disability, creed, sex (including pregnancy and breast-feeding), and family status, because these are the areas where special needs are most common. The following discussion considers the scope of the duty to accommodate in each of these areas and the types of accommodation that employers typically must consider. Although the exact scope of the duty is still unclear in some areas, the general trend is toward the expansion of an employer's obligation to accommodate.

1. Accommodating Employees with Disabilities

Methods of Accommodation

The Code contains a specific provision, s. 17, with respect to the duty to accommodate for disability. It recognizes that individuals with a disability may not be able to perform every part of every job. Section 17 states:

> (1) A right of a person under this Act is not infringed for the reason only that the person is incapable of performing or fulfilling the essential duties or requirements attending the exercise of the right because of disability.
>
> (2) No tribunal or court shall find a person incapable unless it is satisfied that the needs of the person cannot be accommodated without undue hardship on the person responsible for accommodating those needs, considering the cost, outside sources of funding, if any, and health and safety requirements, if any.

Under s. 17, the employer may require an employee with a disability to perform only job duties that are "essential." For example, if a sales job depends on an employee's driving to customers' premises, then having a valid driver's licence is an essential job duty. However, if customers come to the employer's premises and a driver's licence is needed only to get to an occasional meeting, the requirement for a valid licence is not justifiable because it unnecessarily disqualifies individuals who are unable to get a licence as a result of a disability.

Once the essential job duties are determined, s. 17 also requires an employer to accommodate a person with a disability, up to the point of undue hardship, to enable the employee to perform those essential duties. Accommodations may include making changes to the layout of the workplace to make it barrier-free, such as building ramps and wheelchair-accessible washrooms or modifying equipment and vehicles. It may also require changing the way that work is done. This may involve providing stools, special software, or technical aids; modifying work hours; or reassigning disabled employees to vacant jobs that they are able to perform. Episodic disabilities (for example, arthritis, multiple sclerosis, and migraines) may require accommodations such as flex-time, providing a private area in the workplace in which to rest or take medications, project-based work (where the longer time frame allows for periods of disability), and ergonomically designed equipment.

For non-physical disabilities such as learning disabilities, accommodation may include allowing the employee to work in a quieter area, providing clearer and/or written instructions, and providing specialized training.

Manager and supervisor training are also crucial: front-line supervisors need to be aware of how to respond to employees who disclose a disability; they need to be sensitized to the supports required and understand the types of accommodation available; and they need to be prepared for any co-worker issues that may arise. This latter point relates to addressing possible co-worker perceptions of favouritism toward the employee who is being accommodated. Where appropriate, employee education sessions may be helpful (Silliker, February 13, 2012, p. 19).

Workplace accommodations need not be expensive. According to one American study, the average cost of a reasonable accommodation is about US$500, while 49 percent of accommodations cost nothing. Often the largest investment is in taking the time to understand what the employee needs and being flexible in the range of accommodation possibilities considered. However, there may be situations where extensive changes are required. In some circumstances, performance standards or productivity targets may have to be modified.

As a result of *Meiorin*, employers now know they must consider employees' special needs when actually designing their policies and workplace structures. For example, when constructing or renovating buildings, buying equipment, or establishing new policies and procedures, employers should choose products or designs that do *not* create barriers for people with disabilities. For instance, when upgrading a computer and phone system, an employer could incorporate large fonts, bright lighting, and volume control into its design. An employer must also be sensitive to the duty to accommodate in preparing and applying its attendance policy. Requiring a specific level of attendance is discriminatory if it has a negative effect on an employee because of his disability. The employer's attendance policy should establish whether an absence is the result of a medical condition and, if so, assist the employee in meeting its requirements.

Employers are required to test disabled people individually to determine whether their disability affects their ability to perform the duties of the job. For example, an employer may have a general rule that truck drivers must not be epileptic. However, where the job involves only occasional driving, the applicant's epilepsy is controlled by medication, and the applicant's personal physician permits her to drive, a more individualized assessment is required (Gilbert et al., 2000, p. 229).

Although employer size is a relevant factor in determining when the point of undue hardship has been reached, case law makes it clear that even smaller employers have a positive obligation to seriously consider how a disabled employee can be accommodated. As a point of interest, it is possible that a unionized employer that has met its duty to accommodate under the Code will be found by an arbitrator to have not met its duty under the collective agreement if the wording in that agreement sets a higher standard. This was the case in *Canadian Blood Services v. O.P.S.E.U.*, which concerned an employee who was unable to perform his job duties because of carpal tunnel syndrome. The arbitrator found that the employer's initial tardiness in finding the employee modified duties violated the collective agreement even though the time lag was understandable and not a failure to accommodate under the legislation. This result was reached because the collective agreement contained language that required the employer to "make every effort to create an adaptive work environment for employees who sustain injuries at work" and the employer's efforts fell short of that negotiated standard.

In other words, where negotiated provisions exceed human rights requirements, employees are entitled to those higher standards. On the other hand, where negotiated provisions fall below human rights requirements, employees are entitled to the standards set by the Code.

Providing Alternative Work

How far must an employer go to meet its duty to accommodate a disabled employee? Must it, for example, create a new position that the employee is able to perform? *Essex Police Services Board v. Essex Police Association* suggests that, at least where long-term employees are involved, the duty to accommodate may require the employer to create a position. This would involve taking lighter job duties that other people currently perform and putting them together to make a new job. In practice, the employer's obligation to accommodate an incumbent employee returning to work after an injury is probably greater than its obligation to accommodate job applicants.

CASE IN POINT

Employer Must Create New Position for Disabled Employee

Essex Police Services Board v. Essex Police Association (2002), 105 LAC (4th) 193

Facts

Horoky was a 27-year veteran of the police force. In 1999, he was diagnosed with a herniated disc and spinal degeneration. As a result of his disability, he experienced severe pain and back spasms. After a particularly bad episode, Horoky's doctor told him that he could not return to work; the duration of his disability was specified as "unknown." In 2001, after he was refused long-term benefits, he tried to return to work with accommodation for his disability. However, the employer determined that he was incapable of performing any of the existing jobs on the police force because of his disability. Two options for accommodation were advanced by the police association: placing him in one of two occupied positions that he was physically capable of performing or creating a new position out of the duties of several existing positions.

Relevant Issues

1. Whether an employer is required to create a new job based on the reassigned duties of other jobs in order to satisfy its duty to accommodate.

2. Whether an employer can be required to place the employee who needs an accommodation in a position that is currently occupied by another employee.

Decision

The arbitrator held that the employer must create a first-class constable's position from the physically less-demanding tasks performed by other officers. Placing Horoky in the assembled job proposed by the association would not amount to undue hardship because the job was composed of valid job duties and was not a "make-work project." Thus, the employer's failure to accommodate Horoky was a breach of the Ontario *Human Rights Code*.

With respect to the second issue, the arbitrator stated in *obiter dicta*—that is, commentary apart from the main decision—that the fact that a job is filled does not create a legal bar to accommodation. The decision to displace an incumbent employee is based on the following factors: how the position is filled (seniority or discretion), how long the position has existed, and whether displacement would end the incumbent's employment.

The decision in *Essex Police Services Board* extends the scope of the duty to accommodate by requiring the employer to create a job if necessary. However, there is no legal requirement to create a job out of tasks not currently being performed. The employee must be able to perform a useful and productive job for the employer; otherwise, the situation would constitute undue hardship. In the words of the arbitrator:

> It cannot be overstated that the job must be a productive one. ... It would in my opinion, be an undue hardship to require an employer to provide make-work. In our society, the burden of such disabilities is borne in other ways, typically through the provision of long-term disability plans ... . The tasks must be ones that the employer has itself identified as being required to be performed, not ones that it might wish to perform in an ideal world or that the union might hope that it would perform. In most workplaces it remains an employer prerogative to determine what work needs to be done.

In *Human Rights at Work* (2008), the Ontario Human Rights Commission suggests that the following questions be considered in determining whether providing alternative work is appropriate when accommodation in the pre-disability job is not possible:

- Is alternative work available now or in the near future?
- If not, can a new position be created without causing undue hardship?
- Does the new position require additional training, and does the training impose undue hardship?
- Does the alternative work policy contravene the collective agreement?
- What are the terms of the collective agreement or individual contract of employment?
- What are the past practices of the workplace?
- How interchangeable are workers? Do employees frequently change positions, either permanently or temporarily, for reasons other than disability accommodation?

Note that where an employee is placed permanently in a lower-paid, lower-ranked position as a result of accommodation, and all other alternatives have been exhausted, an employer can pay that individual the same as other employees who are performing the same work.

How Diligently Must an Employer Pursue Its Duty to Accommodate?

According to the Commission's guidelines, there is no set rule. An employer's obligation depends on the circumstances, the nature of the disability, and the predictability and frequency of an employee's absences. The prognosis is especially important: is the employee likely to return to work in the foreseeable future? The better an employee's prognosis, the greater the employer's duty to accommodate.

The employer's duty to accommodate is ongoing and must be pursued actively. An employer must not simply decide that an employee with a particular disability is incapable of performing a job. It must seek information, in an objective manner, to help it make that determination and to identify reasonable alternatives. Failure to make proper inquiries undermines an employer's contention that it attempted accommodation or that accommodation constitutes undue hardship. It can also result in significant liability for wages lost during the period that the employee should have been accommodated and for the employee's mental suffering. As the *Fair* case below illustrates, it can even result in reinstatement.

CASE IN POINT

Employer Ordered to Reinstate Non-Union Employee Almost Nine Years After Termination

Hamilton-Wentworth District School Board v. Fair, 2014 ONSC 2411

Facts

Fair had worked as the supervisor of the employer's hazardous material team for about seven years when she developed a generalized anxiety disorder in late 2001. The team was involved in asbestos removal. Evidence showed that her disability was a reaction to her fear that, in making a mistake regarding asbestos removal, she could be held personally liable for a breach of the *Occupational Health and Safety Act*. After being off work and in receipt of disability benefits for two years, her doctor cleared her to return to work but in a role that did not require comparable health and safety responsibilities. Although a number of supervisory positions became available, the employer believed none were suitable because they all involved health and safety responsibilities. In July 2004, Fair's employment was terminated and she subsequently filed a human rights claim, alleging discrimination based on disability and asking for reinstatement.

Relevant Issues

1. Whether the employer school board failed in its duty to accommodate the employee contrary to the Ontario *Human Rights Code*.
2. And, if so, whether reinstatement was an appropriate remedy.

Decision

The Tribunal found that the school board employer had discriminated against Fair by failing to accommodate her medical condition. Contrary to the employer's position, not all supervisory positions were inappropriate given that her personal phobia related specifically to responsibility for asbestos removal. Fair testified that she had been prepared to take at least one of the positions that became available (staff development), and the Tribunal found it likely that she would have been medically cleared for that position had the employer offered it to her.

Noting that the remedial objective of human rights legislation is to make the applicant "whole," the Tribunal ordered the employer to reinstate Fair into a position comparable to the one from which she had been dismissed nine years previously—except it stipulated that it should not involve exposure to personal liability similar to the potential liability caused by working with asbestos. It also ordered the employer to provide up to six months of retraining, if required. In addition, the Tribunal awarded Fair $419,284 (plus interest), representing nine years of lost wages, as well as the pension contributions she would have earned from the date the staff supervisory position was posted in June 2003 until her reinstatement almost ten years later. Finally, she was awarded $30,000 as compensation for the injury to her dignity, feelings, and self-respect. An application for judicial review was dismissed.

The *Fair* decision underscores the employer's duty to diligently pursue possible accommodations and not merely assume that a position is unsuitable without seeking more information. In addition, the nature of the award, including reinstatement and almost ten years' worth of back pay, highlights the Tribunal's intention to issue awards that compensate fully for the losses resulting from the respondent's breach.

Another decision that illustrates the extent of an employer's duty to accommodate disability is *Lane v. ADGA Group Consultants Inc.* There, a consulting firm's cursory investigation of bipolar disorder was found to be insufficient to meet its duty under the Code to accommodate a new employee with that disorder.

Bipolar Disorder and the Duty to Accommodate

Lane v. ADGA Group Consultants Inc., 2007 HRTO 34; [2008] OJ no. 3076 (Div. Ct.)

Facts

Lane, aged 50, was hired by ADGA, an information engineering firm, to be part of a team developing military software. He signed a contract that indicated that he could be terminated at any time during the first 90 days. Before being hired, Lane did not mention that he suffered from bipolar disorder but four days after starting work he told his supervisor about his condition and his need for accommodations. These included monitoring for indicators that he might be moving toward a manic episode; contacting his wife and/or doctor if that occurred; and occasionally allowing him time off work to avert a full-blown manic episode. His supervisor, concerned that the stress of his job (which entailed long hours and high security) could trigger an episode and adversely affect a time-sensitive project, checked informally with the Ontario Human Rights Commission and researched bipolar disorder on the Internet. A few days later, Lane began exhibiting some behaviours that suggested he was going into a manic phase, and his manager decided he was unable to perform the essential job duties. ADGA fired him, saying it couldn't afford him taking long absences and sent him home without contacting his wife or doctor. Lane filed a human rights complaint for discrimination based on disability.

Relevant Issue

Whether the employer failed to meet its duty to accommodate when it terminated Lane.

Decision

The Ontario Human Rights Tribunal found that the employer had not fulfilled its duty to accommodate under the Code. The Tribunal held that the duty to accommodate has two dimensions: procedural and substantive. From a procedural point of view, it found that ADGA's investigation of bipolar disorder was brief and superficial. If ADGA had done further research, it would have found out that although stress can trigger bipolar episodes, usually it is negative stress (for example, difficult working relationships) rather than the stress of challenging work that does so. It also would have found out about the importance of early intervention and the possible negative impact of terminating Lane during a pre-manic episode.

The Tribunal held that the employer, having failed to fulfill the procedural component of the duty to accommodate, did not even get to the substantive component, which required it to consider possible accommodations and whether or not each one would constitute undue hardship.

The Tribunal found that Lane's initial failure to disclose that he suffered from bipolar disorder was understandable given his legitimate concern about being stigmatized. Lane did his part by letting ADGA know about his condition after he was hired and suggesting what the company could do in case of an episode. Furthermore, dismissing Lane during his 90-day probationary period did not relieve the employer of its human rights obligations because the parties cannot contract out of statutory requirements.

Lane was awarded $80,000 in damages: $35,000 for general damages, $10,000 for mental anguish, and $35,000 for loss of earnings.

On appeal to the Ontario Divisional Court, the Tribunal's decision was upheld. The court found that generalized fears, based on false stereotypes and anticipated hardships about the impact of accommodation on the workplace, are not sufficient to discharge an employer's procedural duty to accommodate. The employer should have more fully investigated the nature of bipolar disorder and the employee's own situation as an individual with that disorder, and developed a better-informed prognosis of the likely impact of his condition on the workplace. It also noted that a previous employer—from whom Lane had received excellent performance reviews—had accommodated Lane effectively by contacting his wife when he began to exhibit symptoms of his illness and allowing him time off (Williams and Nave, 2013, p. 4-5).

In making its award, the Tribunal had noted that the employer had no accommodation policy setting up standards for assessing someone with a disability. Moreover, none of the management involved in the decision to terminate Lane had any training in dealing with workplace accommodation issues. As part of the final order, ADGA was ordered to establish a comprehensive, written anti-discrimination policy and to retain a qualified consultant to provide training on its obligations under the Code (Smith, 2008, p. 5). These orders were also upheld on appeal.

Employee's Obligation to Cooperate

Once hired, an employee has an obligation to let the employer know about the need for accommodation. There is also the duty to cooperate with the accommodation process, including responding to reasonable requests for medical documentation in the case of ongoing absences and keeping the employer informed of progress and recovery prospects. In *Al-Saidi v. Brio Beverages Inc.*, an employee's failure to comply with an employer's absenteeism policy by explaining his absences led the Alberta Human Rights Tribunal to find that, despite his disability, the employer had not discriminated against him when it terminated his employment. Similarly, in *Star Choice Television Network Inc. v. Tatulea* an arbitrator dismissed the employee's claim for wrongful dismissal after finding that the employee had repeatedly refused to meet with the employer to discuss a return-to-work process and rejected its offer of reasonable accommodation.

Another case where an employee was found not to have met his duty to cooperate is *Autobus Legault inc. c. Québec (Commission des droits de la personne)* There, an employee gave the employer an ultimatum requiring it to provide a permanent schedule modification within 48 hours. The Quebec Court of Appeal considered this deadline wholly inappropriate and in violation of the employee's obligation to cooperate in trying to find a solution to the accommodation problem.

How Should an Employer Treat Accommodation Requests?

The following are guidelines for employers in handling requests for accommodation for disability (adapted from LeClair, 2003, p. 7). (See the FYI entitled "Attitudes, Legal Expectations, Changing: Accommodating Mental Illness in the Workplace," below, for a discussion of issues specific to mental illness.) Note that regardless of the type of disability, the accommodation process usually starts with a conversation with the employee and, optimally, remains interactive throughout.

1. *Once you have determined that a disability exists, gather information to determine its likely severity and duration, how the disability will affect the essential job duties, and the type of accommodation required.* Determine what the employee's main concerns are at this point. Obtain the employee's written consent for the release of this information. The focus should be on how the current disability affects the essential duties of the job, not on the disability itself. Do not probe for unrelated details about the condition or medications, or ask for a diagnosis.

2. *Evaluate the employee's job to determine its demands and whether they can be altered without causing the employer undue hardship.* As discussed above, the many possible modifications include changing the way in which the work is performed, altering office premises, changing work schedules, or using specialized equipment. Any accommodation must preserve the employee's dignity.

3. *If the employee cannot be accommodated in his pre-disability job, thoroughly review any other available jobs.* Consider placing the employee on a temporary assignment or assembling various tasks that the employee is capable of

performing. The employee is obliged to cooperate in this process by, for example, giving the employer information concerning capabilities and restrictions.

4. *Determine whether the proposed accommodation would cause the employer undue hardship.* Relevant factors include the size of the employer's operations, the cost of the accommodation, the availability of outside sources of funding, and health and safety risks.

5. *Monitor the situation regularly to ensure that it continues to fit the employee's needs.* The employee's limitations may change, for better or worse, over time. Check to see how the employee is adjusting to the accommodation.

6. *Document all facets of the accommodation process.* Include a record of the accommodation options that were considered, reasons why they were or were not implemented, and notes and records of all discussions with the employee and, in the case of a unionized workplace, the union. Create a chronology of events that shows what you did each step of the way.

7. *Maintain confidentiality throughout the process.* Only co-workers who will need to do something differently because of the employee's accommodation should be told about the situation. Similarly, focus only on how the accommodation will affect their duties; don't discuss the details about the disability or a medical diagnosis. Co-workers should be advised that accommodation is a legal right, not a special favour (Merck, 2011).

FYI

Attitudes, Legal Expectations, Changing: Accommodating Mental Illness in the Workplace

Gone are the days when an employer could equate the duty to accommodate for disability with "physical" disability. Given that about 20 percent of Canadians will have a diagnosable mental illness at some point during their lifetime, it's not surprising that the duty to accommodate employees with mental or psychological disabilities is a growing issue in the workplace (Canadian Mental Health Association, 2013). Add to this the financial impact of rising disability costs and productivity losses, as well as heightened legal expectations related to accommodating mental illness (as illustrated by the *Lane* and *Fair* decisions), and it is apparent that employers need to be proactive in this area. Proactive measures include increasing the flexibility in how duties are performed; addressing the stigmatization and social exclusion of people who have mental health issues through awareness education and training; and making sure front-line super-visors and managers are equipped to handle requests for accommodation of mental disabilities, and are supported in the ongoing conversations surrounding it.

An employer also needs to be able to recognize the possible need for accommodations for mental illness even when they are not directly requested (Jurgens, 2013, p. 13). This is because an employee with mental illness may not be able to recognize or articulate the need for accommodation. Also, although awareness and attitudes are changing, there is a lingering stigma that makes some employees hesitant to come forward (Williams and Nave, 2013, p. 4-2). Case law makes it clear that an employer must take the initiative where a problem is apparent: an employer "cannot turn a blind eye to suspicious behaviour and/or other manifestations of an actual disability and then be able to rely upon the absence of direct knowledge to argue that it is under no obligation to accommodate" (Gowlings, 2011).

That said, there are practical limits to what an employer is expected to deduce from an employee's behaviour. In *Stewart v. Ontario (Government Services)*, the applicant was a project manager who was dismissed for poor performance. She filed a human rights application alleging, among other things, that her performance issues were related to her disabilities—a processing learning disorder and adult ADHD—and that her employer's failure to accommodate these disabilities constituted discrimination. Although Stewart admitted that she did not expressly make her employer aware of these disorders, she maintained that it knew or ought reasonably to have known about her disability on the basis of certain workplace behaviours it could readily observe: her preference for visual learning aids, her statements that her children had learning disabilities, her lack of organization, her forgetfulness, her poor time management, and her inability to stay on task. The employer therefore had a duty to make reasonable inquiries concerning possible accommodation.

However, the Tribunal dismissed this portion of the application as having no prospect of success: it found that in the absence of a request for accommodation from the applicant, it was reasonable for the employer to assume that her performance-related difficulties were based on lack of skills rather than a disability. The fact that accommodation requests and plans were common in this particular workplace also supported the employer's position that it would have been receptive to such a request. This decision suggests that it takes more than evidence of poor performance to activate a duty to inquire about possible accommodations based on disability: there also needs to be a clear connection between those problems and a Code-protected ground.

As with physical disability, the primary focus in accommodating a mental illness is job performance. Letting the employee know that certain behaviours have been noticed (for example, the employee seems more stressed or less focused than normal) and that these behaviours are affecting performance can be the starting point. The employer can then ask what the employee needs in order to improve performance and offer ways to find that help (Crisp, 2013, p. 13). This could include, for example, modified duties, flex-time, and access to services, treatments, and supports, including peer support programs (Silliker, June 4, 2012, p. 10). That said, an employer can insist that steps be taken to address the performance-related issues.

Also, a mere assertion that one has a mental disability, or is perceived as having a mental disability, is not sufficient; where there is a legitimate question concerning the existence of a disability, an employer may request relevant medical documentation (*Crowley v. Liquor Control Board of Ontario*).

As part of fulfilling the *procedural* dimension of the duty to accommodate, an employer has the right to obtain a medical prognosis. This refers to information from a medical health professional about the nature of the illness, how it affects the employee's ability to continue or return to work, and the accommodation required to do so (Williams and Nave, 2013, p. 4-5). In *Cristiano v. Grand National Apparel Inc.*, the Ontario Human Rights Tribunal confirmed that the employer's repeated requests for medical information it was entitled to, in the face of the employee's ongoing refusal to provide that information, was not harassment. It stated: "[A]n employer is entitled to know enough to make some assessment of the *bona fides* of the leave request and sufficient information to determine what if any accommodations might be made to return their employee to the workplace, and if that is not possible, some estimate of how long the employee is expected to be absent."

In determining whether an employer has met the *substantive* portion of its duty to accommodate up to the point of undue hardship, health and safety is one possible consideration, usually depending on the employee's specific job duties and the particular conditions of the workplace. For example, medication that makes an employee easily tired presents a significant risk for a forklift driver but a less serious risk for an employee who works in an office environment (Williams and Nave, 2013, p. 4-9).

2. Accommodating Employees Who Abuse Drugs or Alcohol

Canadian law defines alcohol and drug abuse as a disability and therefore considers it to be a prohibited ground of discrimination. Employees who are dependent on these substances are entitled to be reasonably accommodated unless it causes the employer undue hardship. This typically obliges an employer to institute an employee assistance program (EAP) or to allow an employee time off work to attend such a program.

However, accommodating substance abuse does *not* require an employer to accept lengthy, ongoing absences unrelated to rehabilitation. Moreover, as *Chopra* indicates, if an employee does not benefit from rehabilitation efforts, an employer that is fair and consistent in applying its own policies is not required to hold a job open indefinitely.

CASE IN POINT

Employer Terminates Employee for Infringing Drug and Alcohol Policy

Chopra v. Syncrude Canada Ltd., 2003 ABQB 504, [2003] AJ no. 741

Facts

Chopra worked for the employer for 14 years. Although his performance was adequate for most of that period, his alcoholism and depression became a problem eight months from his retirement. In March 1993, Chopra was found to have consumed so much alcohol while on the job that his supervisor had to escort him home. Chopra agreed that he would accept mandatory referral to the EAP, would never again violate the employer's drug and alcohol policy, and would attend supervisory and follow-up meetings as required. Both parties understood that failure to adhere to this plan would result in a termination hearing.

Chopra attended a treatment program but was soon asked to leave for violating its policies. He was, however, admitted into a relapse prevention program to help him deal with his disability. A third incident occurred a short time later, resulting in his absence from work because of intoxication. The employer's response was to require Chopra to submit to a medical tracking process and random drug and alcohol testing. In June 1993, he was again found to be under the influence of alcohol while at work. Consequently, a termination hearing was convened, and he was dismissed. He then filed a wrongful dismissal suit against the employer.

Relevant Issue

Whether the employer had adequately accommodated Chopra's disability.

Decision

The Alberta Court of Queen's Bench found that the employer had fulfilled its duty to accommodate. It had provided Chopra with counselling, allowed several breaches of its policy without resorting to termination, given him a paid leave of absence, and sent him to a treatment facility to receive help. The employer had handled his return to work appropriately. Chopra was not entitled to any further accommodation.

In *Chopra*, the employer fulfilled its duty to accommodate the employee's substance abuse by being both consistent and persistent. It provided the employee with clear, written warnings that he would be dismissed if he did not cooperate in addressing the problem. It got the employee to commit, in writing, to attend therapy or counselling and submit to testing. While accommodating some relapses, it consistently let the employee know that his job was increasingly at risk if he failed to cooperate.

On the other hand, an employer who appears to condone substance abuse by ignoring it, then reacts suddenly in dismissing an employee, is in a different legal situation. To meet its duty to accommodate an alcohol- or drug-dependent employee, an employer should require the employee to undergo counselling or rehabilitation and never create the impression that it is tolerating the abuse (Miller, 2003, p. 3087).

The recreational use of drugs or alcohol does not qualify as a disability. If an employee contravenes an employer's policy by having drugs or alcohol on the employer's property and the employer establishes that the employee does not have a substance abuse "problem," there is no statutory duty to accommodate. In this case, the employer may discipline the employee in the same manner as it would any other employee. Moreover, an employee has to do more than simply say he has a substance abuse problem; there must be convincing, objective evidence from, for example, a credible medical expert who has treated the worker at the relevant time. Excessive drug or alcohol use does not necessarily mean that the individual is an addict.

On the other hand, if an employer dismisses an employee who is subsequently determined to have a drug- or alcohol-related disability, the employee may be entitled to reinstatement and accommodation. In cases where possible drug or alcohol abuse seems a likely contributor in the situation, the employer should inquire about it before termination. Where impairment on the job could cause serious harm to others, such as where the employee is a pilot, medical professional, or train conductor, an employer could make it a term of employment that the individual not consume alcohol or drugs within eight hours of starting a shift (Macleod Law Firm, November 20, 2013).

3. Accommodating Employees' Religious Beliefs and Practices

The requirement to accommodate an employee's creed may arise in a number of areas, including dress codes, break policies, work schedules, and religious leave. According to *Meiorin*, flexibility should be built into an employer's policies. For example, break policies and work schedules should be flexible enough to accommodate daily periods of prayer for employees whose religion requires them. The employer's policy should allow people to deviate from dress codes for religious reasons. If a dress code is designed to address a health and safety issue, the employer should try to modify the requirement. For example, a man who works in food preparation and who is required to have a beard for religious reasons could wear a hairnet over his beard.

The In the News feature "8 Muslims Settle Skirt Dispute with UPS" discusses the settlement of a complaint from eight female Muslim employees after their employer refused to change its dress code policy requiring them to lift their skirts above their knees over their long pants. The employer argued that the ankle-length skirts were a safety hazard in the workplace. The complainants argued that their religion required them to be fully covered and that the employer's dress code was discrimination based on creed and gender. Because the parties reached a voluntary settlement, the Human Rights Tribunal did not make a ruling. Had the complaint gone to a hearing, the Tribunal would have had to consider whether the employer's dress code passed the three-part *Meiorin* test—was it rationally connected to the job; was it imposed in the sincere belief it was necessary; and was it reasonably necessary to job performance? If the dress code had passed the test, the employer still would have had to prove that it was impossible to accommodate the affected employees without creating undue hardship in terms of an unacceptable safety risk.

IN THE NEWS

8 Muslims Settle Skirt Dispute with UPS

BUT WOMEN BEHIND HUMAN RIGHTS COMPLAINT WON'T RETURN TO WORK AT PARCEL FIRM, SOURCE SAYS

Eight Muslim women who filed a human rights complaint against the United Parcel Service (UPS) over a dress code dispute settled with the company yesterday.

But it is unclear whether the company will change its policy, since neither party would discuss the terms of the agreement.

"Everyone is very happy," said Jacquie Chic, lawyer for the complainants, after announcing the agreement at a Canadian Human Rights tribunal yesterday morning ....

The women, all devout Muslims, lost their jobs in 2005 because they refused to hike their skirts above the knee over their long pants.

They argued that Islam requires them to be fully covered for modesty and alleged discrimination on the basis of religion and gender.

UPS said the ankle-length skirts were a safety hazard as workers climb ladders up to six metres high. Only "a gap in the process" allowed the women to work at UPS for up to two years without being told their clothing posed a risk, a UPS manager previously told the tribunal.

In the end, yesterday's settlement means the tribunal did not answer the key question: Was it discrimination, or a legitimate safety concern?

The women's jobs required them to navigate open metal staircases and tall ladders to flip boxes on a conveyor-belt system at a Toronto UPS plant. The company eventually ordered a risk hazard analysis that determined the women's traditional garb—long skirts, hijabs and neck scarves—was unsafe.

Six of the women had brought the company a letter from their mosque confirming their religion insists they wear full-length skirts.

SOURCE: Paola Loriggio, "8 Muslims Settle Skirt Dispute with UPS," *Toronto Star*, November 18, 2008. Reprinted with permission—Torstar Syndication Services.

Religious Days Off

Human rights law requires an employer to accommodate the religious observances of employees who are unable to work on particular days by relieving them from working on those days unless this causes undue hardship.

For example, in *Central Alberta Dairy Pool v. Alberta (Human Rights Commission)*, an employee who refused for religious reasons to work Easter Monday was terminated. Although the employer argued that working on Mondays was an essential job requirement, the Supreme Court of Canada held that the employer had failed to show that it could not accommodate the individual without suffering undue hardship.

However, *Re CANPAR and United Steelworkers of America, Local 1976* shows that the employer's accommodation need not be ideal from the employee's point of view, as long as the employer makes reasonable efforts. In *Re CANPAR*, the employee wanted to leave work early on Friday afternoons to accommodate his religious observance of the Sabbath. The employer discussed several accommodation options with him and eventually transferred him to a more central route where it was convenient for another driver to relieve him of his duties before sunset. As a result of this accommodation, the employee did not lose any meaningful work opportunities, nor were his wages affected. However, after a few months in his new position, the employee became unhappy and grieved his accommodation.

The arbitrator found in favour of the employer because its choice of accommodation was reasonable, alleviating discrimination without impairing the employee's earnings or disrupting operations. The arbitrator stated that an employee cannot expect to receive a perfect accommodation.

A third religious observance accommodation case is *Ontario (Human Rights Commission) v. Ford Motor Co. of Canada* (the *Roosma* case). *Roosma* involved two employees who refused to work their Friday evening shifts after converting to a faith that observed its Sabbath at that time. Although the employer was very large, it successfully argued before the Human Rights Tribunal (in a 71-day hearing) that accommodating the employees by allowing them to not work their Friday night shifts imposed undue hardship on the employer.

In a 2–1 decision, the Ontario Divisional Court upheld the Tribunal's decision, finding that it was reasonable and based on relevant factors. These factors included the high levels of absenteeism on Friday evenings, the disruption of the collective agreement, the negative effect on other workers, safety, and the employer's competitive position. The effect of accommodation on existing seniority rights was a key consideration because of the large number of senior employees. The court also found that the union's unwillingness to advocate for accommodation that significantly prejudiced other workers was not unreasonable.

In some ways, it seems difficult to reconcile *Central Alberta Dairy Pool* and *Roosma*, especially in light of the third test in *Meiorin* under which an employer must show that accommodation, short of undue hardship, is impossible. However, in *Central Alberta Dairy Pool*, the employer was disputing its ability to accommodate the employee's absence for five days per year at most, whereas the employer in *Roosma* was disputing its ability to accommodate many more days. Moreover, in *Roosma* the employer had made several attempts, over a period of many months, to accommodate the employees before concluding that accommodation was not viable in the circumstances.

Another question that arises is whether an employee who takes religious holidays off must be paid for at least some of those days. In the following case of *Markovic v. Autocom Manufacturing Ltd.*, the Ontario Human Rights Tribunal held that the employer did not have to pay the employee for time taken off for religious holidays as long as it offered reasonable options allowing the employee to make up for wages lost through other means such as rescheduling.

CASE IN POINT

No Entitlement to Two Additional Paid Religious Holidays

Markovic v. Autocom Manufacturing Ltd., 2008 HRTO 64

Facts

Markovic, an employee of auto parts maker Autocom, was an Eastern Orthodox Christian who celebrated Christmas on January 7. His employer agreed to let him take the day off but did not pay him for it. As per its policy, it provided him with a menu of options instead that included: making up time at a later date; working

on another holiday if possible; switching shifts with another employee; using paid vacation days; or taking an unpaid leave of absence.

Markovic filed a human rights complaint alleging discrimination on the basis of creed because Western Christians automatically got two paid days off for their religious days (Christmas Day and Good Friday are statutory holidays under the *Employment Standards Act, 2000*) but employees of other faiths had to negotiate from the employer's menu of options for their religious days off. The Ontario Human Rights Commission, which had long taken the position that failure to entitle non-Western Christian employees to at least two paid days off for their religious observances was discriminatory, referred the matter to the Tribunal for a hearing.

Relevant Issue

Whether the employer's policy of providing a menu of options to employees seeking time off for religious holidays that did not include two paid days off infringed the Ontario *Human Rights Code*.

Decision

The Tribunal found that Autocom's policy did not infringe the Code. Offering a menu of options to allow an employee to take time off for religious observances met the employer's duty to accommodate and did not impose an undue burden on employees. It noted that dialogue and negotiation between the employer and the employee are inherent in the accommodation process.

The Tribunal also cited the *Hydro-Québec* decision in acknowledging that the duty to accommodate coexists with the regular contract of employment (that is, services in exchange for pay). The Tribunal stated that "the duty to accommodate is about the design and modification of workplace requirements to enhance the ability of certain employees to participate in the workplace without, at least in the first instance, dislodging the assumption of services for pay."

According to the *Markovic* decision, the duty to accommodate does not require an employer to pay employees for not working on a religious holiday if it offers realistic options for making up the lost time. Furthermore, requiring those seeking time off for religious observance to negotiate from a menu of options is not discriminatory.

When considering the duty to accommodate for a religious observance, there is one threshold question: does the employee genuinely believe that the religious practice is necessary? Whether a particular practice or observance is required by official religious dogma or is in conformity with the position of religious officials of that faith is irrelevant except in extreme cases (for example, where the existing practice is fabricated). Therefore, while an employer may adduce evidence that questions an employee's sincerity about the necessity of a particular religious practice, evidence concerning whether a particular practice is mandatory or even common is not helpful. That said, as with the other grounds, employees seeking accommodation for creed-related needs are required to work with their employers and other affected parties to find solutions to these issues (Krupat, 2013, p. 2-6).

4. Accommodating Employees' Pregnancy and Breast-Feeding Needs

Pregnant employees or employees who are breast-feeding may require temporary accommodation in the workplace. This could include temporary relocation from a work area that might endanger the pregnancy, modification of work duties, a flexible work schedule, increased break time, special parking spaces, accommodating medical appointments, and appropriate workplace support for breast-feeding. *Sidhu* addresses an employer's obligation to modify an employee's duties during pregnancy.

CASE IN POINT

Employer Fails to Meet Duty to Accommodate Pregnant Employee

Sidhu v. Broadway Gallery, 2002 BCHRT 9, [2002] BCHRTD no. 9

Facts

Sidhu became pregnant after working in a nursery for one year. As a result, she found it difficult to pull garbage cans filled with sand and lift heavy objects. She obtained a note from her doctor stipulating that she could not lift objects greater than 40 pounds or spray the trees with pesticide. After she gave the note to her employer, her hours were reduced so drastically that she left her job and filed a complaint under the BC *Human Rights Code*.

Relevant Issue

Whether the employer's failure to accommodate Sidhu by providing alternative work suited to her pregnancy constituted discrimination on the basis of sex.

Decision

The Tribunal held that the employer failed in its duty to accommodate Sidhu during her pregnancy. She established a *prima facie* case of discrimination because, were it not for the doctor's note, the terms and conditions of her employment would not have been altered. She was able to perform her job except for the heavy lifting. Given the nature of the work performed and the size of the workforce, the employer could have accommodated her by providing her with alternative work. Because alternative work existed, the proposed reduction of her schedule, from five days to two, was not a sufficient accommodation.

Pregnancy-related accommodation extends to the area of benefits. An employee who requires time off during or after her pregnancy or parental leave arising from pregnancy-related health concerns is entitled to benefits under an employer's workplace sick or disability plan.

In addition to accommodating pregnancy-related concerns, employers must also accommodate breast-feeding requirements. This may mean allowing the baby's caregiver to bring the baby into the workplace to be fed, making scheduling changes to allow time to express milk, or providing a comfortable, private area for breast-feeding.

5. Accommodating Employees' Family Status

Until recently, there were few cases in this area. The duty to accommodate for family status was generally taken to mean that employers have some obligation to assist employees who are balancing work and family responsibilities and to avoid policies that adversely affect them. For example, an employer may need to provide flexible work hours for an employee who is caring for aging parents or having temporary difficulties arranging child care. Similarly, an employer who consistently holds business meetings after office hours may be contravening the Code because attending these meetings could adversely affect employees with small children (Ontario Human Rights Commission, 2008).

In the past few years, however, courts and tribunals have been increasingly asked also to consider the extent to which employers have a duty to accommodate employees for their general family caregiving obligations. One of the first of these cases was *Health Sciences Assoc. of B.C. v. Campbell River and North Island Transition Society*. In that case, the BC Court of Appeal found that the employer had discriminated against the complainant on the basis of family status when it changed her work hours, inadvertently causing her to be unable to take care of her son, who was a special needs child, after school. Relying on medical evidence that affirmed that the son required his mother's personal care after school, the court distinguished this situation from the commonplace obligation of parents to arrange care for their children. It set down the principle that an employee has proven *prima facie* discrimination on the basis of family status where the employer's rule or requirement "significantly interferes" with a "substantial" family obligation.

More recently, however, a second line of cases on this issue suggests that an employer's duty to accommodate extends to "ordinary," not just "substantial," family obligations. This line of cases criticizes the *Campbell River* approach for applying a different standard to family status than to other prohibited grounds. It posits that concerns about serious workplace disruption should be addressed when determining whether the duty to accommodate has been met up to the point of undue hardship; they should not be used to restrict the definition of "family status" itself.

One case that reflects this second approach is *Johnstone v. Canada (Attorney General)*. Johnstone was a customs inspector at Pearson International Airport who, upon returning from a year's pregnancy and parental leave, requested an accommodation of fixed, rather than rotating, shifts so that she could find proper child care. The employer agreed but the new shift schedule resulted in her working three fewer hours per week (34 instead of 37 hours), thereby affecting her full-time employment status and, consequently, benefit entitlements. Johnstone filed a human rights complaint alleging discrimination on the basis of family status. The Tribunal, and upon appeal the Federal Court, ruled in her favour, finding that the employer had breached both the procedural and the substantive aspects of its duty to accommodate. It had breached the former by dismissing Johnstone's request for accommodation simply based on its "unwritten" policy that fixed daytime shifts were available only to part-time employees. The court noted that the employer allowed fixed shift accommodations for religious and medical reasons but had arbitrarily decided that it would not do the same for family obligations on the basis that they were "merely the result of choices that individuals make, rather than a legitimate need" (Silliker, 2013, p. 12). In rejecting this approach, the court noted that "while family status cases can raise unique problems that may not arise in other human rights complaints, there is no obvious justification for relegating this type of discrimination to a secondary or less compelling status."

The court found that the employer had breached its substantive duty in failing to show that accommodation would create undue hardship. The Tribunal awarded Johnstone her lost wages (the difference between her part-time versus full-time earnings and lost pension benefits), $15,000 for pain and suffering, and $20,000 for wilful and reckless discrimination. The employer was also ordered to develop and implement human rights policies, and to provide related training to all partners and supervisory staff.

It is worth noting that the Tribunal in *Johnstone* carefully reviewed the efforts that the applicant had made to solve her childcare needs *before* seeking help from her employer. These efforts were considerable—she had tried both regulated and unregulated childcare providers and placed unsuccessful ads in newspapers before seeking accommodation from her employer.

On further appeal, the Federal Court of Appeal unanimously upheld this decision and laid out four elements that a complainant must prove to establish a *prima facie* case of discrimination based on family status and the duty to accommodate child-care needs. The four elements are:

1. *The child is under the complainant's care and supervision*—Johnstone's children were clearly under her care.
2. *The complainant's childcare obligations reflect a legal responsibility rather than merely a personal choice (for example, taking the child to extracurricular activities)*—Johnstone had a clear legal obligation to care for her two children.
3. *The complainant has made reasonable efforts to meet those childcare obligations and no alternative solution is reasonably accessible*—Johnstone had made significant efforts, without success.
4. *The workplace in question interferes with the fulfillment of the legal obligation in a manner that is more than trivial or insubstantial*—the employer's shift schedule rule interfered with Johnstone's ability to fulfill her childcare obligations.

To date, this is the highest level of court to deal with this issue and it may point to the end of the *Campbell River* approach. At the same time, it clarifies the point that the duty to accommodate for child care extends only to parental obligations, not to merely personal choices, and that the employee must have made reasonable efforts to self-accommodate before the duty is triggered (Zabrovsky, 2014).

Another important case relating to family status and the duty to accommodate is *Devaney v. ZRV Holdings*. It explicitly recognizes that family status accommodation includes responsibility for eldercare, and underscores the significant onus on an employer to work with employees who are dealing with eldercare issues. Their needs must be assessed and a workable accommodation plan developed, up to the point of undue hardship.

CASE IN POINT

Duty to Accommodate for Family Status Includes Eldercare

Devaney v. ZRV Holdings Limited, 2012 HRTO 1590

Facts

Devaney was an architect with 27 years' service who began working from home frequently when his elderly mother, with whom he lived, became disabled. The employer, noting that much of his work was team-based, became increasingly concerned about this arrangement and started to insist that he be present in the office daily from 8:30 a.m. to 5:00 p.m. Devaney resisted, saying that most of his work could be done remotely from home. Moreover, given his mother's deteriorating condition and variable needs, he had a responsibility to sometimes stay at home to help her. After a series of increasingly stern warnings about his attendance, to no effect, the employer terminated Devaney for cause, on the basis of ongoing absenteeism. Devaney sued for wrongful dismissal, alleging discrimination based on family status.

Relevant Issue

Whether the employer discriminated against Devaney by failing to accommodate his requests to work from home so that he could care for his ailing mother.

Decision

The court found in favour of Devaney. It held that the employer's attendance requirements constituted a *prima facie* case of discrimination because they adversely affected Devaney in discharging his responsibilities as his mother's primary caregiver. Because the employer was unwilling to consider changing those requirements, it breached its procedural duty to make meaningful inquiries and explore accommodation alternatives. It therefore could not prove that accommodation would constitute undue hardship.

The court ordered the employer to pay Devaney $15,000 for failure to accommodate and for injury to dignity, feelings, and self-respect. The employer was also ordered to develop and implement a workplace human rights and accommodation policy, and provide mandatory training for all employees who perform supervisory and/or human resources functions. (No order was made concerning lost wages because Devaney had found a comparable position shortly after being terminated.)

As shown in the *Johnstone* and *Devaney* cases, the duty to accommodate for family responsibilities promises to be a dynamic area of human rights law. However, the case law seems to be moving in the direction of expanding employers' obligations in this area, and an employer needs to take requests for accommodation seriously. Employers need to be prepared to be flexible, and even creative, with respect to requests for accommodation of an employee's family obligations, including eldercare. Each case must be considered on its own merits. An employer should make sure that it understands what the employee is asking for, and why, and it should explore what options are available to meet this need up to the point of undue hardship. That said, the principle that the exchange of work for remuneration lies at the heart of the employment relationship should always be kept in mind.

On-the-Job Drug and Alcohol Testing

Throughout Canada, substance abuse (and perceived abuse) is viewed as a disability protected under human rights legislation. Traditionally this has been interpreted to mean that an employer's ability to administer workplace drug and alcohol testing is severely restricted. According to the Ontario Human Rights Commission, for example, on-the-job testing is unjustified except in limited circumstances—such as in safety-sensitive positions where certain conditions apply or where an employee is involved in a workplace accident that reasonably suggests impairment. Note that despite its similarly stringent view of drug testing, the Canadian Human Rights Commission accepts that Canadian trucking companies operating in the United States must comply with US testing requirements (Gilbert et al., 2000, p. 260).

The seminal decision in the area of drug and alcohol testing in Ontario is *Entrop v. Imperial Oil Ltd.* In that case, the Ontario Court of Appeal drew a distinction between random alcohol testing and random drug testing. It found that Breathalyzers are minimally intrusive yet provide a highly accurate measure of both alcohol consumption and impairment; they may therefore be acceptable in safety-sensitive positions, especially where supervision is impractical. In contrast, drug tests are more intrusive (they require a urine sample) and fail to measure current impairment; therefore, random drug testing is less likely to be acceptable, even in those restricted circumstances when random alcohol testing may be acceptable. *Entrop* also stands for several other propositions: mandatory disclosure of previous substance abuse must be limited to abuse that took place in the recent past; an employer's response to a positive test result must be tailored to the individual circumstances; and an employer must offer reasonable accommodation, such as a rehabilitation program, and not automatically dismiss an employee who suffers from a disability arising from alcohol or drug use.

More recently, however, the Supreme Court of Canada has ruled on the legality of a unilaterally imposed policy requiring universal random testing in a unionized, safety-sensitive workplace. This decision throws into question the previous distinction between drug and alcohol testing, and raises the bar for random substance abuse testing, at least in unionized workplaces and quite possibly in non-union workplaces as well.

CASE IN POINT

Raising the Standard for Random Substance Testing

Communications, Energy and Paperworkers Union of Canada, Local 30 v. Irving Pulp & Paper Ltd., 2013 SCC 34

Facts

In 2006, Irving's unionized paper mill in New Brunswick unilaterally implemented a workplace policy that required, among other things, that all employees in safety-sensitive positions be subject to testing for alcohol (but not drugs) on a random basis. The policy worked as follows: in any 12-month period, 10 percent of the employees in safety-sensitive positions were randomly selected for a Breathalyzer test. A positive result could result in discipline, up to dismissal. One of those randomly selected employees, Perley Day, had not consumed alcohol since 1979. Although his test results, unsurprisingly, showed a blood alcohol level of zero, the union filed a policy grievance challenging the reasonableness of the universal random testing policy under the management rights clause of the collective agreement. It argued that a Breathalyzer test (as an involuntary submission of bodily fluids) is highly intrusive and an unjustifiable breach of an employee's privacy rights.

The arbitration board agreed with the union, finding that although the mill was a dangerous workplace, there was insufficient evidence of alcohol abuse to justify such a privacy-invasive policy. (It noted that in the 15 years prior to implementing the policy, there had been only eight documented cases of alcohol-related impairment and none of these had involved an accident, injury, or "near miss." Moreover, during the 22 months that the policy was in effect, none of the employees had tested positive for alcohol.) Accordingly, it held that a policy requiring privacy-invasive, universal random testing was a disproportionate response.

The employer applied for judicial review, arguing that requiring that there be an accident, incident, or near miss before allowing random testing of all employees in safety-sensitive positions was unreasonable. The New Brunswick Court of Appeal agreed. It held that random mandatory alcohol testing is a reasonable exercise of management rights in workplaces that are inherently dangerous; no further proof of a particular workplace substance abuse problem is necessary. The union appealed this decision to the Supreme Court of Canada.

Relevant Issue

Whether proving that the workplace is inherently dangerous is sufficient to justify unilaterally implementing a universal random alcohol-testing policy.

Decision

In a 6–3 split decision, the Supreme Court of Canada held that, except perhaps in the most extreme safety-sensitive workplaces, showing that the workplace is inherently dangerous is not enough. To warrant such a policy, the employer must demonstrate enhanced safety risks, such as providing evidence of a problem with substance abuse in the workplace. The majority decision found that in this case, the expected safety gains to the employer ranged "from uncertain … to minimal at best," while the impact on employee privacy was much more severe. The onus is on the employer to show that random testing is a proportionate response, based on the particular workplace involved, and the employer had not done this.

It should be noted that the court did uphold the reasonableness of other facets of Irving's drug- and alcohol-testing policy. These included post-incident and for-cause testing, and testing that is part of a return to work protocol when an employee has undergone a substance abuse rehabilitation program.

The majority decision in *Irving* confirms and clarifies certain points, as well as raising others, concerning drug and alcohol testing in safety-sensitive workplaces. These include the following:

1. Selective drug or alcohol testing may be carried out when there is a reasonable suspicion of impairment—for example, when an employee exhibits slurred speech and appears to be under the influence of drugs or alcohol.

2. Selective drug or alcohol testing may be carried out when an employee has been involved in a workplace accident, incident, or near miss where it may be important to determine the root cause of what happened.

3. Random (unannounced) alcohol or drug testing may be carried out as part of an agreed rehabilitation and return to work program of an employee clearly identified as having a problem of alcohol or drug use.

4. The majority decision did not differentiate between the different standards applied to drug testing and alcohol testing that underlay *Entrop*. Instead, it suggests that a policy requiring universal random testing for either drugs or alcohol must be supported by evidence of reasonable cause (Filion Wakely Thorup Angeletti, 2013).

5. There may be a category of workplaces that are so extremely dangerous (for example, a nuclear power facility) that universal random testing is acceptable without further inquiry. This, however, would be the rare exception.

Because the *Irving* decision relates to a unionized workplace, and the reasonableness of the exercise of management rights under a collective agreement, its findings are not directly applicable to non-union employers. However, it is likely that human rights tribunals will look to the *Irving* decision for guidance in trying to balance safety with human rights considerations (Standryk, 2013). Therefore, a union or non-union employer attempting to implement random workplace drug or alcohol testing has to carefully consider both its rationale and scope. First, it should analyze the need for such testing in relation to safety-sensitive positions *and* any indications that on-the-job alcohol or drug use is an actual problem. *If* random testing is implemented, it should be part of a broader, comprehensive substance abuse policy incorporating education, counselling, and rehabilitation. A positive test should not automatically disqualify an applicant or automatically result in termination of a current employee. The test should interfere as little as possible with employee privacy rights and be administered in a respectful way. The policy should also be reviewed regularly to ensure ongoing compliance with developing law (Mitchell, February 27, 2008, p. 2).

Harassment

Ontario's *Human Rights Code* prohibits workplace and sexual harassment in employment. The employer not only has a duty to provide a working environment that is free from harassment and discrimination; it must also deal effectively and efficiently with any allegation of harassment of which it is, or *should be*, aware.

Workplace Harassment

The Code states that employees have the right to be free from abusive or annoying behaviour that is based on one or more grounds in the Code. Section 5(2) of the Code states the following:

> Every person who is an employee has a right to freedom from harassment in the workplace by the employer or agent of the employer or by another employee because of race, ancestry, place of origin, colour, ethnic origin, citizenship, creed, sexual orientation, gender identity, gender expression, age, record of offences, marital status, family status or disability.

Harassment is defined in s. 10 of the Code as "engaging in a course of vexatious comment or conduct that is known or ought reasonably to be known to be unwelcome." Any demeaning or offensive behaviour based on membership or perceived membership in a protected group can be harassment. This includes verbal threats, intimidation, jokes, unwelcome remarks, or offensive pictures and posters.

A "course of conduct" means a pattern of behaviour; therefore, usually—but not always—more than one incident is involved. A single incident may constitute harassment if it is extremely offensive.

The harassing comments or conduct need not explicitly involve a prohibited ground of discrimination to be covered by the Code. For example, if someone who is from a different ethnic background than the rest of her department is singled out for practical jokes, the jokes themselves need not have anything to do with her ethnic background to contravene the Code. Harassment on the basis of ethnic origin may be inferred from other circumstances, such as a lack of employees from visible minorities in the workplace, or a high turnover among these employees.

Where the conduct is known to be, or should have been known to be, unwelcome, the person who is the target of the harassment need not formally object to the behaviour to trigger s. 5(2).

In cases of subtle forms of harassment, or where the harasser does not realize that his conduct is annoying, the harassed employee may need to let him know how his conduct is being perceived. For example, someone may repeatedly tell jokes about a certain ethnic group to an employee from that ethnic group in the honest belief that he is being funny. However, once the recipient of the jokes lets the joke teller know that he finds them offensive, the joke teller has been put on notice that the jokes are unacceptable and must stop. The standard for determining whether harassment has occurred is objective: would a reasonable person think the comment or conduct is inappropriate? It does not require that most people view the behaviour as harassing as long as the recipient does and that perspective is reasonable.

A second type of harassment involves a "poisoned work environment." This refers to a workplace that feels hostile because of insulting or degrading comments or actions related to a prohibited ground of discrimination. It is not necessary that a person who perceives a hostile work environment be the target of the comments or actions in a case where the workplace itself is poisonous. To constitute harassment, the comments or actions must be ones that would influence and offend a reasonable person.

Different workplaces tolerate different comments and conduct. However, when profanity or coarse conduct is directed toward a particular group—even if it is not directed at a particular individual—it is a human rights issue. In *Pillai v. Lafarge Canada Inc.*, the BC Human Rights Tribunal found that racial slurs that were not made directly to the complainant contributed to a poisoned work environment because they were frequent and, like all racial slurs, beyond the bounds of normal social interaction.

An employer has an obligation to monitor, prevent, and respond promptly to harassment that could poison the workplace. For example, an employer that fails to erase offensive graffiti as quickly as possible may be liable for harassment for allowing a poisoned work environment. Similarly, an employer that knew or should have known of harassment, and could have taken steps to prevent or stop it, may be liable. An employer can also be held responsible for harassment that occurs away from the workplace, such as at a company barbecue, conference, or Christmas party.

As shown in the following case of *Smith v. Ontario (Human Rights Commission)*, an employer should carefully monitor the atmosphere of its workplace and take immediate action to prevent any conduct that could result in a poisoned work environment.

CASE IN POINT

Poison in the Workplace

Smith v. Ontario (Human Rights Commission), 2005 CanLII 2811 (Ont. SCDC)

Facts

Smith worked in a junior position for an employer for a year before being promoted to a supervisory position. There was ongoing friction between Smith, who was black, and the acting manager, Jones, who was white and who made racial slurs against Smith. The business owner was aware of the tension between the two, but he stated that he was unaware of the particulars or that the workplace was tainted with racism. About a year after his promotion, Smith was fired for allegedly refusing to assist a junior employee in serving a customer. The business owner did not give Smith a chance to defend himself against the allegation. The Ontario Human Rights Tribunal found that Smith had been subjected to a poisoned workplace, but that the owner did not wilfully or recklessly infringe his rights. It accepted the owner's contention that he was unaware of the discrimination and harassment when he decided to dismiss Smith, and that the dismissal was not racially motivated. Smith appealed.

Relevant Issue

Whether the employer infringed the Code when it fired Smith.

Decision

The court concluded that the business owner was at least reckless in infringing Smith's right to be free from a poisoned atmosphere. It also found that the Tribunal had incorrectly considered the motivation of the business owner, rather than the effect that the discrimination had on Smith, in deciding that race was not a motivating factor in his termination. If an employee is fired from a poisoned work environment, the dismissal must be examined in the context of that environment.

Because race was found to be a factor in the dismissal, the employer was ordered to pay the employee $25,131 in compensation for lost income and $10,000 for mental anguish damages, as well as his legal costs. It also ordered systemic remedies that required the business, under the Ontario Human Rights Commission's supervision, to implement a workplace anti-harassment policy, undertake staff training, implement an internal complaint process, and educate management.

A contrasting situation arose in *General Motors of Canada Limited v. Johnson*, where the Ontario Court of Appeal found that, despite the respondent's genuine belief that the workplace was poisoned by racism, the evidence did not support such a finding and, as a result, the employer was not liable.

CASE IN POINT

"Poisoned Workplace" Based on an Objective Standard

General Motors of Canada Limited v. Johnson, 2013 ONCA 502

Facts

Johnson was a production supervisor in an auto body shop at GM whose role included training group leaders. One group leader, Markov, refused to attend Johnson's training session because he did not like Johnson (who was black). Markov alleged that Johnson had laughed at an insensitive remark made by another GM employee about the death of Markov's brother. Shortly after this incident, another employee claimed that he too could have avoided training by saying he was "prejudiced like the last guy whose brother was killed by a black man." In response to Johnson's concerns that Markov's refusal to train with him was racially motivated, GM conducted three separate investigations, each one concluding that race had not been a factor. (Markov agreed to take the training with another GM employee, who was also a person of colour.) Unhappy with these conclusions, Johnson eventually went on disability leave, alleging that he could not work in a poisoned work environment. After two years, Johnson indicated he would return to work but only at a corporate office because he was concerned about running into Markov. Not having a position available in the office, GM offered him two different plant positions, both a kilometre away from the auto body shop where Markov worked, but Johnson refused, claiming that he should not be required to return to a "poisoned work environment." In the absence of medical evidence supporting Johnson's claim that he was disabled from working in a plant environment, GM took

the position that Johnson had resigned. Johnson sued GM for damages for constructive dismissal and the trial court agreed, awarding him $160,000 in damages, plus legal fees. GM appealed.

Relevant Issue

Whether the employer had tolerated a poisoned work environment and thereby constructively dismissed the employee.

Decision

The Court of Appeal overturned the trial judge's decision, finding that the employer had not tolerated a poisoned workplace and therefore that Johnson had not been constructively dismissed. First, it found that there was no basis for Johnson's allegations that Markov's conduct was racially motivated. Furthermore, it stated that a single incident of this kind, with a single employee, over the course of an eight-year working relationship, cannot objectively support a finding of a poisoned work environment. Noting that discriminatory treatment in the workplace due to racism is a serious claim that implicates the reputational and employment interests of both the claimant and the alleged perpetrators, the court confirmed that a plaintiff's subjective feelings or even genuinely held beliefs are insufficient to establish a claim of racism. The test is an objective one: would a reasonable person find that the workplace is poisoned?

GM's successful defence in this case reinforces the importance of taking complaints of a poisoned work environment seriously, and diligently investigating such complaints when they occur. A contrasting fact situation is found in the case of *Morgan v. Herman Miller Canada Inc.*, where the Tribunal awarded the applicant significant damages even though it found that his allegations of discrimination, while sincerely made, were baseless. It did so because the employer had dismissed his allegations out of hand, without investigating them, and his subsequent termination was found to be retaliation for making those allegations. As such, it was a reprisal contrary to the Code.

Sexual Harassment

Section 7(2) of the Ontario *Human Rights Code* states the following:

> Every person who is an employee has a right to freedom from harassment in the workplace because of sex, sexual orientation, gender identity or gender expression by his or her employer or agent of the employer or by another employee.

Sexual harassment is similar to other forms of workplace harassment in that it refers to a course of vexatious comment or conduct (based on sex, sexual orientation, gender identity, or gender expression) that is known or ought reasonably to be known to be unwelcome. More than one incident is usually required to sustain a human rights complaint; a single incident is sufficient, however, if the conduct is serious enough that the harasser must have known that it was offensive. Sexual harassment may be practised by a male on a female, a female on a male, or between members of the same sex.

Under Canadian case law, the term "sexual harassment" covers a broad range of conduct. The common thread, as discussed in *Janzen v. Platy Enterprises Ltd.*, is that it is "*unwelcome* conduct of a *sexual* nature that detrimentally affects the work environment or leads to adverse job-related consequences for the victims of harassment" [emphasis added]. It can be physical or verbal. The more obvious cases of harassment involve unwelcome physical contact such as touching, patting, pinching, kissing, and hugging. However, it also includes offensive remarks, ostensibly flattering remarks about physical appearance, inappropriate staring, offensive jokes, displays of offensive pictures or other materials, questions or discussions about sexual activities, and paternalistic comments that undermine the recipient's authority.

As in the case of general workplace harassment, there may be instances where the harasser does not realize that her comments are offensive. For example, if she repeatedly questions a colleague about sexual matters, she may think she is simply being open and friendly. However, if the recipient lets her know that her conduct is annoying and inappropriate, she has been put on notice that her questions are unacceptable and should stop. The standard for establishing sexual harassment is objective: would a reasonable person in the recipient's position find the comments or conduct inappropriate? Again, it is not necessary for all men, for example, to view certain behaviour as harassing as long as the recipient does and that perception is reasonable.

Sexual harassment can also include making comments that are not obviously sexual in nature. For example, in *Shaw v. Levac Supply Ltd.*, an employee repeatedly referred to a co-worker as a "fat cow" and said "waddle waddle" when she walked by. The Board held that the comments constituted sexual harassment by implying sexual unattractiveness.

In considering claims of sexual harassment, courts and tribunals recognize that there are different types of workplace culture: what's tolerated as "shop talk" in some workplaces might be considered inappropriate in others with a more formal atmosphere. However, a defence that it was only shop talk will not be helpful to employers who tolerate offensive sexist or racist behaviour. Moreover, an employer that allows questionable shop talk will find it more difficult to dismiss an employee who engages in such conduct for just cause (without notice or a separation package).

At the same time, tribunals have found that where a complainant initiates and willingly participates in sexual banter, co-workers cannot reasonably be expected to know that this type of conduct is no longer welcome unless the complainant communicates that fact. In *Kafer v. Sleep Country Canada and another (No. 2)*, the complainant was unsuccessful because, on the basis of her earlier sexualized banter, the Tribunal found that "no reasonable person would conclude that she found the conduct in question unwelcome." However, it also held that once an employee lets co-workers know that conduct that was previously acceptable is no longer welcome, any continuation would constitute harassment contrary to the Code (Hume and Edstrom, 2013).

Human rights adjudicators have recognized that sending provocative and unwanted text messages ("sexting"), even outside of the workplace and office hours, can constitute sexual harassment as well. In *McIntosh v. Metro Aluminum Products* the applicant filed a human rights complaint after the owner, with whom she had once had a consensual relationship, persisted in sending her sexually explicit, and increasingly nasty, texts after she broke it off. The Tribunal rejected the employer's argument that McIntosh had participated in, and thereby consented to, the ongoing texting, noting that McIntosh's texts were entirely focused on trying to get him to stop sending her his vulgar messages. As a consequence of failing to ensure that McIntosh's workplace was free of harassment, the employer was ordered to pay the applicant approximately $15,000 in lost wages and a further $12,500 for injury to her dignity, feelings, and self-respect.

Sexual Solicitation

Section 7(3) of the Ontario *Human Rights Code* states:

> Every person has a right to be free from,
> (a) a sexual solicitation or advance made by a person in a position to confer, grant or deny a benefit or advancement to the person where the person making the solicitation or advance knows or ought reasonably to know that it is unwelcome; or
> (b) a reprisal or a threat of reprisal for the rejection of a sexual solicitation or advance where the reprisal is made or threatened by a person in a position to confer, grant or deny a benefit or advancement to the person.

This provision refers to unwelcome advances or requests for sexual favours by a person in a position of authority in the workplace, such as a supervisor. The threat of reprisal or promise of reward may be explicit, such as where an employee is denied a promotion because he refuses a sexual advance from his supervisor, but it need not be. It can be implied from the circumstances and the power imbalance between the two individuals. Section 7(3) is also relevant if a co-worker who is in a position to grant or deny an employment-related benefit makes a sexual advance.

Promoting a Harassment-Free Workplace

An employer may greatly reduce the chances of having sexual and other types of harassment occur by devising, communicating, and enforcing a policy against harassment. This policy must include measures that educate employees about their rights and encourage employees to come forward with any complaints. Having and clearly communicating such a policy may also limit the employer's liability for harassment committed by non-management employees.

To be effective, workplace and sexual harassment policies should do the following:

1. Indicate the employer's commitment to eliminating harassment in the workplace. Make it clear to new hires that discrimination will not be tolerated.

2. Explain the types of behaviour that are considered harassment. Communicate this information regularly to staff and managers alike.

3. Include awareness programs to underline the policy's importance. Employees must be encouraged to recognize and report instances of harassment. Supervisors and managers must be able to recognize harassment and respond quickly.

4. Describe the process by which complaints are brought to the employer's attention and investigated, and describe the penalties for violating the policy. An effective complaint and investigation procedure encourages complainants to bring their concerns to the employer's attention and allows the matter to be dealt with internally. (Note that an employee's failure to report alleged harassment to the employer before going to the Tribunal does not automatically undermine his or her credibility. However, the Tribunal may draw a negative inference from a failure to use the internal mechanism unless the employee adduces evidence of a credible reason for failing to use it (Johnston, 2013, p. 2).)

5. Advise employees either to inform harassers that their behaviour is unwelcome or to inform their supervisor of the harassment.

6. Insist that supervisors deal promptly with allegations of harassment.

7. Treat complaints confidentially and inform employees in advance about the confidentiality policy.

8. Require a prompt and thorough investigation by an impartial person who is knowledgeable in human rights law. Critical elements in the investigation include informing the alleged harasser that a complaint has been filed, providing particulars that allow him or her to respond, and conducting separate interviews with both parties, as well as their legal counsel and material witnesses. It is also important to maintain a written record of incidents of harassment and actions taken. Follow through with any disciplinary measures that are warranted.

9. Circulate the anti-harassment policy to all employees, including those who are newly hired, and post it in a prominent spot in the workplace.

The effectiveness of having sound policies and procedures for dealing with harassment is illustrated in the decision of *Ata-Ayi v. Pepsi Bottling Group (Canada) Co.* In that case, the employee quit his job after receiving several negative performance reviews. He alleged that racism and a poisoned work environment forced him to leave. The court found that many of Ata-Ayi's allegations lacked a factual basis and that the employer responded to all concerns raised by him in a fair and objective fashion. Praising the employer's strong workplace policies and practices, the court found that the employee left his job voluntarily.

It should be noted that an employer that fosters an inclusive workplace and trains its managers to recognize and respond promptly to harassment, and to take such complaints seriously, may avoid liability for harassment by non-managerial employees under the Code. This situation differs from workplace *discrimination* where the employer is typically liable for the conduct of its employees.

Investigating Harassment Complaints

The following two cases show the importance of taking harassment allegations seriously and of investigating such complaints promptly, thoroughly, and in a way that is fair to *both* parties involved. In *Harrison v. Nixon Safety Consulting and others (No. 3)*, a female safety officer alleged that she was sexually harassed and that her employer largely ignored her concerns. The *Harrison* case also illustrates the extent to which harassment cases often turn on the credibility of the parties and how issues of credibility are sometimes determined.

CASE IN POINT

Employers Need to Take Harassment Complaints Seriously

Harrison v. Nixon Safety Consulting and others (No. 3), 2008 BCHRT 462

Facts

Harrison, 28, was hired by Nixon Safety Consulting (NSC) to be a safety officer at a condominium construction site. NSC was contracted by Navigator to provide safety services at the site and Navigator, in turn, was contracted to do concrete work by Con-Forte, a construction company in charge of the project. Harrison worked in the site office with Ford, Navigator's project manager, and Goodman, head of onsite operations for Con-Forte.

On her second day of work, Harrison claimed that Ford told her he would "put in a good word for her" at work if she had sex with him. She also claimed that Ford had touched her shoulders and back and slapped her buttocks, as well as shown her pornography on his computer. Harrison spoke to Goodman about Ford's conduct but he simply said she shouldn't worry; she would have her own trailer soon and would be away from Ford.

Harrison then spoke to her supervisor at NSC and he suggested she stay at home the next day. However, almost immediately she received a letter from Ford's lawyer warning her against making "slanderous and defamatory comments" or Ford would take legal action. At this point her NSC supervisor told her that Ford had complained about her, and NSC was worried about its contract with Navigator. Two months into her three-month probationary period, NSC terminated Harrison.

Harrison filed a complaint with the BC Human Rights Tribunal. In Ford's response, he denied making sexual remarks and claimed that Harrison sometimes wore inappropriate clothing to work, such as short skirts and tight jeans, and made inappropriate comments. He admitted there was "sexual banter" but said Harrison usually initiated it. Goodman agreed with Ford's account, adding that Harrison got more demanding and disruptive at the worksite as time went on.

Relevant Issue

Whether the employer's conduct contravened human rights legislation.

Decision

The Tribunal found Ford's and Goodman's version of events not credible. For example, there was no evidence that Harrison wore skirts to work, and their accounts of her other behaviour were unsupported. Ford's quick response with a letter from his lawyer following her complaint to her NSC supervisor seemed extreme for someone who felt he didn't have anything to worry about. Harrison, on the other hand, had made notes in her daily work journal that included records of Ford's behaviour and her complaints to Goodman and her NSC supervisor. Moreover, the Tribunal found the employer's investigation "cursory and superficial."

As a result, the Tribunal ruled that Harrison was subjected to unwelcome sexual misconduct that negatively affected her work environment and employment. Ford should have known his conduct was inappropriate and as a result his conduct constituted sexual harassment. Her termination was directly linked to the harassment and constituted discrimination based on sex. NSC, Ford, Navigator, and Con-Forte were held jointly liable for damages, which were: four months' lost wages ($14,144), plus $15,000 for injury to Harrison's dignity, feelings, and self-respect, plus $3,000 from Ford, Navigator, and Con-Forte for improper conduct in trying to discredit Harrison.

Note that the fact that Harrison was terminated during her probationary period was irrelevant because discrimination and harassment are prohibited regardless of when they occur during an employee's employment. Another interesting point is that although Harrison was officially working for NSC, the Tribunal found that she had an employment relationship with Navigator and Con-Forte as well because Ford and Goodman held positions of authority over her. All of the companies were therefore held jointly liable for the damages awarded.

The Tribunal in *Harrison* specifically criticized NSC for the superficiality of its investigation of its employee's complaint. The following case of *C.R. v. Schneider National Carriers, Inc.* also looks at the importance of a proper investigation, this time from the point of view of the alleged harasser.

CASE IN POINT

Employer's Investigation Must Be Fair to Both Sides

C.R. v. Schneider National Carriers, Inc., 2006 CanLII 532 (Ont. SC)

Facts

C.R. was a training engineer at Schneider, a trucking firm. Her job was to take trainee drivers out on the road for a one- to two-week trip to teach them various aspects of the job. At the end of each trip, trainees were required to complete a critique of the training program; all of C.R.'s reviews were positive. However, six months after she started doing training, management was approached by two of the trainees, Bonnie Cronkwright and Catherine Shaw, who alleged that C.R. had sexually harassed them during their respective training sessions. The alleged harassment included C.R. initiating conversations that focused on sadism, masochism, and domineering behaviour; displaying herself in various stages of nudity; swearing excessively; and inviting each of them to participate in submissive relationships.

Shortly after receiving the written complaints, management called C.R. in for a meeting. She was not told the reason for the meeting, and management, fearing she would retaliate against the complainants, did not tell her their identity or the specific allegations against her. In response to their general allegations, C.R. claimed that she slept nude in the truck's cab because her obesity made it more comfortable but she denied the other allegations. At the end of the meeting the employer terminated C.R. on the ground that she had created a hostile work environment. C.R. sued for wrongful dismissal; the employer responded that it had just cause under the common law.

The employer's policy regarding harassment was brief. It simply stated that "harassment is prohibited and will not be tolerated."

Relevant Issue

Whether the employer had proven just cause for dismissal.

Decision

The court held that the employer did not prove that it had just cause for dismissal. Although C.R.'s conduct was inappropriate at times, there were inconsistencies in the details of the complainants' testimony and serious flaws in the employer's investigation. For example, the two complainants compared notes prior to discussing the matter with management and, in their meeting with management, were allowed to hear each other's allegations. From subtle changes in their testimony over time, it is apparent that these conversations influenced their testimony. Furthermore, C.R. was not given the reason for the management meeting, nor was she given specifics of the allegations made against her, including the names of the complainants. This made it difficult for her to adequately respond to them. Another troubling inconsistency was that both of the complainants had given C.R. a positive evaluation after her training. This discrepancy was never adequately explained and both complainants waited over a month before making their allegations.

In light of these circumstances, the court was reluctant to find that the degree of misconduct warranted dismissal without compensation. Unless harassment is of a very serious nature, lesser sanctions such as a warning or a suspension should be applied first.

Given C.R.'s age (43), total length of service (three years), and her position as training engineer, she was entitled to three months' notice of termination—$15,788.75.

Investigating Harassment Complaints—Doing It Right

1. Investigate in a timely manner

Excessive delay reduces the effectiveness of the investigation (recollection of events gets more difficult, the working environment becomes strained). On the other hand, never rush to the point of undermining the accused's ability to respond to the allegations.

2. Ensure that the investigator is unbiased and properly trained

The investigator should not have a stake in the outcome (as in the case of a supervisor investigating a subordinate). It may be necessary to look externally for someone who is, and who is perceived as being, sufficiently objective. The investigator must be knowledgeable about both human rights laws and due process.

3. Give the accused a chance to adequately respond

Fairness demands that you give the accused an opportunity to defend herself. In particular, provide the accused person with specific information about the allegations (for example, dates and details) because it is difficult to respond adequately to vague or general accusations of harassment.

4. Follow the employer's own policies and procedures

This may seem obvious but failure to follow set procedures (assuming they were well thought through in the first place) undermines the investigation unless there is a good reason to deviate from them. Investigators should be trained in human rights and in how to conduct a proper investigation. In *Schneider*, the court found that the two management members who investigated the allegations were both honest and reliable witnesses who tried their best to be fair but their inexperience led to an unsatisfactory process.

5. Make sure witnesses are interviewed separately

Interviewing witnesses together can influence their statements and lead to collaboration or intimidation. Where there is more than one accuser, they should be warned not to confer when putting their complaints in writing and that their complaint should only reflect their own individual experiences.

6. Ask non-leading questions

Leading questions are those that are phrased in a way that prompts the witness on how to respond (for example, "Did the accused ever look at you in a way that made you feel uncomfortable?"). For example, in the *Bannister* case in Chapter 13, the court noted approvingly that investigators interviewed multiple witnesses and each time started by asking if they had any general information with respect to any human rights or sexual harassment issues. This allowed the investigator to see whether the accused person's name came up unprompted.

7. Interview third-party witnesses

Many harassment issues come down to credibility—he said/she said—so it is important, where possible, to get written statements from third-party witnesses. Moreover, if there is a subsequent wrongful dismissal action, an investigation process that included all of the witnesses that the accused had asked to be interviewed about the situation is more likely to be seen as thorough and fair. At the same time, interview only those people who can contribute to the fact-finding process.

8. Document the investigation

As always, the investigator should thoroughly document each step of the investigation. For example, having a complete record of what witnesses said lends credibility to the investigation. In the *Schneider* case, management recorded only a general synopsis of the meeting and therefore the notes were of minimal value in the subsequent wrongful dismissal action.

9. Keep an open mind

Some employers respond to a complaint by trying to sweep the matter under the rug, while other employers presume the accused must be guilty and overreact by dismissing the accused without a proper investigation. As seen in the *Harrison* and *Schneider* cases, either response can land the employer in legal hot water.

10. Consider the entire context

Where discipline is warranted, keep in mind the entire context in determining the appropriate response. For example, a higher degree of discipline, up to and including dismissal, may be called for where the accused is in a supervisory position, but may be inappropriate for an accused who is not.

SOURCE: Based on information from Bongarde Media Co., "Sexual Harassment: 8 Traps to Avoid When Investigating Harassment Complaints." *HR Compliance Insider.* Volume 5, no. 3, March 2009, p. 1.

During the investigation, the respondent should typically not be suspended without pay because this may suggest guilt; therefore, where warranted, the respondent should be placed on a leave of absence, with pay, until the investigation is complete (Bernardi, 2012, p. 42).

As noted, the Code's harassment provisions are engaged when the harassment relates to one or more of the 16 prohibited grounds of discrimination. Moreover, since 2010, employees in Ontario may also file harassment complaints with their employer under the *Occupational Health and Safety Act* (OHSA). Such complaints do not need to be tied to one of the Code's grounds. (See Chapter 7 for further discussion on the requirements of the OHSA related to harassment.) Where an employee is alleging workplace harassment, the employer should determine whether it is being claimed under the Code, or under the OHSA, and then follow the applicable internal complaint process, which can be similar or even virtually identical (MacLeod, September 6, 2013).

Employee Benefit Plans

Under s. 25 of the Ontario *Human Rights Code*, an employee who is excluded because of a disability from a benefit, pension, or superannuation plan or fund or from a group insurance contract is entitled to compensation from her employer. The amount of compensation must equal the contribution that the employer would have made for an employee without a disability. The compensation may include contributions to benefit premiums or accrual of vacation credits. Employees who are absent from work because of a disability are entitled to receive the same payments that an employer would make to employees who are not working for other reasons.

Employer Liability for Human Rights Violations

Under s. 46.3 of the Code, an employer is **vicariously liable**—that is, legally responsible for the actions of another—for the *discriminatory* acts of its agents and employees in the workplace. It is also directly liable for the actions of management. The situation with harassment is somewhat different. Although an employer's liability for workplace or sexual harassment committed by management employees (as "directing minds" of the organization) is a given under common law principles, an employer may avoid liability for harassment by non-managerial employees if it can show that it was diligent in preventing and responding to the harassment. This applies to harassment that it either knew about or should have known about.

Clients or customers who act in a discriminatory or harassing way toward an employee in the employer's workplace are not liable under the Code. However, an employer may be liable for their behaviour if the following criteria are met: it knew of, or had control over, the situation; it could have done something to prevent or stop the behaviour; and it failed to act (Ontario Human Rights Commission, 2008, p. 52).

Human Rights Applications

In 2008 there were significant changes made to the enforcement provisions of the *Human Rights Code*. One of the most significant of these was the change to the respective roles of the Commission and Tribunal. The Commission no longer accepts or handles individual complaints of discrimination; all new applications (formerly known as "complaints") are now filed directly with the Tribunal. This is referred to as the "direct access model."

The Commission's mandate now is to advocate for human rights and promote public understanding of, and compliance with, human rights requirements. For example, it may file its own application or intervene in an application in particular cases of interest, such as those involving systemic discrimination. The Commission continues its mandate to develop policies on human rights issues. These policies are considered by the Tribunal in making its decisions, so the Commission's numerous policies and guidelines on a wide range of human rights matters remain relevant. (See www.ohrc.on.ca for the Commission's policies and guidelines.)

Without the Commission acting as gatekeeper, the Tribunal now receives an estimated 3,000 applications annually, compared with the 100 to 150 cases that previously reached the Tribunal each year. To satisfy its mandate "to provide for the fair, just and expeditious resolution of any matter before it," the Tribunal has extensive procedural and substantive powers under ss. 43 to 45.2 of the Code to streamline its processes. Under its Rules of Procedure it may:

- examine records it considers necessary;
- direct the order in which evidence will be presented;
- on the request of a party, direct another party to produce a witness when that person is reasonably within that party's control;
- question witnesses and advise when additional evidence or witnesses may assist the Tribunal; and
- narrow issues and limit evidence and submissions to those issues.

In addition to the Commission and the Tribunal, there is a third human rights body in Ontario: the Human Rights Legal Support Centre. The Legal Support Centre's role is to provide free legal advice and assistance to people making a human rights application. It was created to address the concern that, with the change in the Commission's role, applicants would have to represent themselves or incur the expense of hiring counsel. The Legal Support Centre is staffed with lawyers and paralegal support staff in Toronto and several regional centres across the province. It also makes referrals to the private bar and legal clinics.

Unlike Legal Aid, the Legal Support Centre does not require income testing, but only applicants are eligible for the Centre's assistance. Respondents must pay for their own legal representation.

Making and Responding to an Application

The process for making and responding to an application is set out below.

1. An employee who wants to file a claim of discrimination or harassment may obtain an application form (Form 1) from the Tribunal's website and file it directly through that website.

2. Applications should be filed within one year of the date on which the discrimination is alleged to have occurred. If there was more than one discriminatory event, the application should be filed within one year of the last event. Applications filed after one year are not permitted unless the Tribunal finds that there was a good reason for filing late and that the delay will not negatively affect other people involved in the application. In *Garrie v. Janus Joan Inc.*, the Tribunal had to consider the timeliness of an application from a disabled employee who alleged ongoing wage discrimination based on the wage differential between disabled employees (who were paid only $1.25 an hour) and non-disabled employees. In finding for the applicant, the Tribunal held that the wage discrimination was actually a series of separate violations "of the same character." Therefore, because the last pay period fell within the one-year limitation period under the Code, the disabled employee's claim was timely.

3. The application form is extensive. Among other things, it asks the applicant to: identify who they believe is responsible for the human rights violation claimed; provide a detailed first-person account of the situation that led to the claim; and list important witnesses and documents related to the application and explain why each is relevant.

4. The Tribunal will review the application for completeness and jurisdiction. Applications that lack key information will be returned and the applicant will have 20 days to fill in the missing information. The Tribunal does not have jurisdiction to handle an application if:

    a. the application does not relate to a ground of discrimination (for example, race or disability) and an area of activity (for example, housing or employment) covered by the Code;

    b. the events happened outside Ontario;

    c. the organization that is said to have discriminated is federally regulated;

    d. the human rights claim is already before the courts, or the subject of a court decision; or

    e. a complaint related to the same or substantially the same matter had already been filed with the Ontario Human Rights Commission.

    If it appears that the Tribunal may not have the authority to handle the application, the applicant will be notified and has 30 days to respond and tell the Tribunal why the application is within its jurisdiction.

5. Once satisfied as to jurisdiction and completeness, the Tribunal then sends each respondent (for example, employer, supervisor, co-worker) a copy of the application, usually within a week of processing it. (Information about the applicant's witnesses will be deleted.) Respondents must use the Tribunal's response form (Form 2) to respond, and they have 35 days to complete and return it to the Tribunal.

Questions on the response form include:

- Did the applicant tell you about the human rights concern?
- Did you investigate?
- Do you have a human rights policy?
- What is your response to what the applicant says happened and the applicant's proposed remedy?

6. The respondent must also list its important witnesses and documents. If the respondent fails to respond, the application will proceed and monetary as well as other orders may be made against the respondent.

7. In most situations, a respondent must file a complete response. The Tribunal will not consider requests to decide preliminary objections or issues before the complete response is filed unless: the respondent asks the Tribunal to dismiss an application because a court is already dealing with the same matter; there was already a human rights complaint about the same matter; or the applicant and the respondent have already entered into a settlement agreement and the applicant signed a release.

8. The Tribunal sends the applicant a copy of the response, and applicants have 14 days in which to reply. (Information about the respondent's witnesses will be deleted.)

9. The Tribunal offers voluntary mediation services to assist the parties in resolving the application. Any mediation occurs within four to five months of the application. Settlements are voluntary.

10. Where the parties refuse mediation, or mediation does not resolve the application, the Tribunal will issue a Confirmation of Hearing notice. A hearing will be scheduled for a date or dates within five months of the Notice of Hearing. The notice also triggers the obligation to exchange all "arguably relevant documents" within 21 days and sets the hearing dates. Forty-five days before the hearing, the parties must deliver all documents they intend to rely on, a list of witnesses they intend to call, and a brief summary of the anticipated testimony.

11. Prior to the hearing, the Tribunal may issue a Case Assessment Direction, which will identify what the parties need to do to prepare for the hearing. For example, it may identify witnesses who will have to attend on the first day, or the legal or procedural issues that the parties will have to address. The Case Assessment Direction is a decision of the Tribunal and the parties must comply with it.

12. Hearings are typically in person, although procedural and preliminary matters may be heard by conference call, in writing, or in person.

To avoid the time delays common under the old system, timelines are strictly enforced. For example, in *Kearns v. 1327827 Ontario*, the respondent failed to file its response and instead delivered a short letter to the Tribunal advising that it was "on holiday." In its absence, the Tribunal ordered that the respondent would be deemed to have accepted the allegations and given no further notice of proceedings.

In some cases, adjournments and rescheduling of set hearing dates are accommo-dated. For example, accommodation may be made where representatives have pre-scheduled commitments, but only if the party requesting the adjournment does so in a timely manner and provides alternative dates that do not unduly delay the proceedings.

Given the quick and direct access framework of this system, employers that receive an application must focus immediately on developing a thorough response that frames the legal issues in dispute and sets out the facts necessary to make their case. For example, in developing its response, an employer must carefully consider which witnesses and evidence will be required for the hearing, because the Tribunal has broad powers to refuse to allow a party to present evidence or make submissions about a fact or issue not identified in the materials. Closer to the hearing date, rel-evant documents must be delivered to the other party and only those documents can be relied upon in the hearing.

As noted above, there is limited opportunity for a respondent to make preliminary objections under the new system. If, for example, an employer believes that an appli-cation does not set out a *prima facie* case of discrimination, or the application is friv-olous or made outside the time limit, it now must typically raise that issue at a hearing, not before.

Under s. 45.7 of the Code, parties to a Tribunal decision may apply for a recon-sideration of the decision, but this option is only available in limited circumstances. For example, a party may apply where there are new material facts or evidence that could not reasonably have been obtained earlier or where the decision is in conflict with established jurisprudence and it involves a matter of public importance.

It should be noted that human rights issues that arise from a matter covered by a collective agreement are usually heard by an **arbitrator** under the grievance procedure of the collective agreement, rather than by the Tribunal. In fact, most human rights litigation in Ontario is now heard by arbitrators under procedures set out in collec-tive agreements.

Under s. 45 the Tribunal may defer (delay hearing) an application where the same subject matter is being dealt with in another proceeding, such as a labour arbitration. If it defers, the applicant has 60 days to bring the application back once the other pro-ceeding has concluded. (Note that where the same human rights claim is being advanced in a court proceeding, it is not a deferral issue—the Tribunal simply has no jurisdiction.)

Moreover, where the Tribunal finds that human rights considerations have been raised and appropriately dealt with by another body, it will not rehear it. Section 45.1 states that the Tribunal may dismiss an application where "another proceeding has appropriately dealt with the substance of the application." In applying this provision, the Tribunal will look at whether the other decision-making process was a "proceed-ing" (that is, operated under the principles of **natural justice**, was impartial, and pro-vided an opportunity to be heard) and whether the other decision-maker applied human rights principles. An employer's internal complaint process is not considered such a proceeding (Gottheil, 2009).

There has been some uncertainty around how far this provision goes in protect-ing employers from "forum shopping" (where employees go from one adjudication process to another, until successful). However, this issue was canvassed in *Manhas v.*

A.O. Smith Enterprises. There, an employer applied to have its unionized employee's human rights application dismissed on the basis that the issue had already been "appropriately dealt with" at arbitration when his discharge grievance was unsuccessful. The Tribunal held that because the allegations of discrimination on the basis of disability had not been brought before the arbitrator, it could not conclude that the matter had been "appropriately dealt with." Nonetheless, the Tribunal dismissed the employee's application as an abuse of process. It held that although the arbitrator had not dealt with any claims of discrimination, there were no facts set out in the application that were not put before the arbitrator and to allow the relitigation would "violate the principles of judicial economy and the integrity of the administration of justice and amount to an abuse of process."

Remedies Under the Code

Under s. 45.2 of the Code, the Tribunal has broad remedial powers. It can order monetary compensation or order a party to make non-monetary restitution or to "do anything that, in the opinion of the Tribunal, the party ought to do to promote compliance with this Act." Remedies may include an order to hire or reinstate the applicant, compensate the applicant for lost earnings or job opportunities, and pay damages.

Financial Awards

Under the post-2008 system, possible damage awards are significantly broader and larger than they were before. Previously there were three types of damages that could be awarded: specific damages (for example, loss of earnings), general damages (for example, for loss of dignity and self-respect), and damages for mental anguish (capped at $10,000) where the infringement was wilful or reckless. Now the Code simply states that the Tribunal may order (unlimited) monetary compensation for losses arising out of the human rights infringement, including "compensation for injury to dignity, feelings and self-respect" (s. 45.2(i)1). A separate assessment for "mental anguish" damages and the $10,000 cap on those damages under the old system no longer exist.

Non-Monetary Awards

Under ss. 45.2 and 45.3 of the Code, the Tribunal has the power to order one party to make restitution to the other and to do anything that, in its opinion, the party ought to do to promote compliance with the Code. For example, the Tribunal may require an employer to change its policies, implement training programs, establish an internal complaint system, and introduce anti-discrimination and anti-harassment policies. Remedial orders may require an employer to write an apology to an applicant, implement an affirmative action hiring program, promote members of certain groups, and offer educational programs for supervisors and managers. The Tribunal may also order reinstatement of an employee. In the past this remedy was not often used because, given the time delays in the system, many employees had moved on and did not want to return to that employer. However, this seems to be changing. As referred to above in *Fair v. Hamilton-Wentworth District School Board*, the

Tribunal ordered the reinstatement of a non-union employee, with full back pay, almost nine years after her termination, due to her employer's ongoing failure to accommodate her disability. It found in that case that the employment relationship was still viable: the applicant testified that she bore no ill will toward the respondent as a whole, and the individuals who were responsible for the decisions leading to her termination were no longer working for the employer. Moreover, the Tribunal noted that the employer was very large and had a sophisticated management structure, and therefore reinstatement would not cause any hardship.

An application for judicial review has been dismissed. The *Fair* decision may well signal an increased appetite on the part of human rights tribunals to order reinstatement.

New Remedies

Another significant change to the system is the granting of power to the courts to award human rights remedies for civil claims where human rights issues are involved. For example, a plaintiff sues her former employer in court for wrongful dismissal under the common law and claims that the employer's actions also violated human rights law. In that situation, she may now ask the court to award damages (or even reinstatement, previously only available as a statutory remedy) for a violation of the Code.

It is noteworthy that there are, as of yet, no examples of a civil court awarding reinstatement. However, in *Wilson v. Solis Mexican Foods Inc.*, an Ontario court awarded a dismissed employee an additional $20,000 in general damages based on evidence that her back ailment and consequent requests for accommodation were a factor in the employer's decision to terminate. This damage award, higher than those usually awarded by tribunals under the Code, seems to signal the courts' willingness to compensate employees substantially for their loss of dignity and feelings of self-worth for human rights violations (Chu, 2013).

Note that, as was the situation that existed under the old system, an employee only has the ability to pursue an action for discrimination or harassment in the courts if it is tied to a civil lawsuit such as a wrongful dismissal action. As was decided by the Supreme Court of Canada in *Bhadauria v. Board of Governors of Seneca College*, there is no independent tort of discrimination under the common law, so unless there is a human rights element to a civil action, a human rights claim may only be made through the Code.

In those cases where there is a human rights element in a claim, an employee has the option of either going to court or filing an application under the Code. She cannot do both. In making that election, one of the factors to be considered is the possibility of legal costs being awarded against the unsuccessful party. Unlike in the civil courts, there are no provisions for costs to be assessed against an unsuccessful litigant under the human rights system. This factor and the relative informality of the Tribunal's procedures may encourage some applicants to pursue their claim through the human rights system. On the other hand, many who perceive that the main part of their claim is unrelated to human rights may prefer to pursue their remedy in the civil courts, especially in light of the *Wilson v. Solis Mexican Foods* decision.

Examples of Remedies

Gill v. Grammy's Place Restaurant and Bakery illustrates the many factors that a tribunal considers in determining an appropriate remedy—in this case, for sexual harassment.

CASE IN POINT

Damages Awarded for Loss of Dignity from Sexual Harassment

Gill v. Grammy's Place Restaurant and Bakery Ltd., 2003 BCHRT 88, [2003] BCHRT no. 88

Facts

Gill worked as a waitress at a restaurant. She alleged that her employer repeatedly harassed her with unwelcome comments about her body size, lips, and eyes; other inappropriate comments; and unwelcome hugs, kisses, and other physical contact. These actions culminated in an attack one night at the restaurant in which he grabbed her and attempted to kiss her and touch her body. When the employer heard that Gill was confiding in a co-worker about his conduct, he fired both employees. Following termination, the employer started a rumour that Gill was having an affair with the co-worker.

Relevant Issue

Whether the employer's conduct amounted to sexual harassment.

Decision

The BC Human Rights Tribunal concluded that the employer's conduct amounted to sexual harassment and violated the BC *Human Rights Code*. The employer's harassment and discriminatory conduct toward Gill affected every aspect of her life, including her "dignity, and feelings of self-respect" to an extraordinary degree.

In determining the appropriate remedy, the Tribunal concluded that the following factors must be considered: the nature of the harassment (verbal or physical), how aggressive it was, the length of time it lasted, the frequency, the age of the victim, the vulnerability of the victim, and the psychological impact of the harassment on the victim. Gill was entitled to damages for injury to dignity, feelings, and self-respect (as referred to in the BC Code) of $10,000 and specific damages of $7,500 for six months' lost wages plus medical costs for the harm suffered. This was the highest award for injury to dignity ever given under the BC Code, reflecting the devastating effect of the employer's conduct on the complainant.

In *Arias v. Desai*, the manager of the employer hotel sexually harassed an 18-year-old student on her work term. The Ontario Human Rights Tribunal awarded her general damages of $25,000 to compensate for humiliation and loss of dignity. The Tribunal found this amount to be in keeping with the seriousness, frequency, and duration of the repeated infringements, as well as the complainant's youth. It also awarded her $5,000 for her mental anguish, plus special damages of $1,920 to cover six weeks' worth of lost wages after her termination. The manager and employer were ordered to implement a comprehensive workplace anti-harassment and anti-discrimination policy and to obtain anti-harassment training.

Penalties Under the Code

Under s. 46.2 of the Code, every person who contravenes the Code is liable to a maximum $25,000 fine. This could include an individual supervisor or co-worker.

The Accessibility for Ontarians with Disabilities Act, 2005

In 2005, Ontario passed the *Accessibility for Ontarians with Disabilities Act* (AODA). The goal of this legislation is to make Ontario fully accessible to people with disabilities by 2025 by phasing in a series of accessibility standards. In contrast to the *Human Rights Code*'s case-by-case, complaint-driven approach, the AODA obliges organizations to address accessibility issues in a proactive way. It is important to note that the AODA's accessibility standards do not take away from human rights requirements: all employers, regardless of size, still have the duty to accommodate an individual employee who is disabled to the point of undue hardship. The AODA's requirements are intended to complement and supplement those of the Code, not replace them.

Under the AODA, there are now five accessibility standards covering five key areas: customer service, information and communications, employment, transportation, and built environment (design of public spaces). (The last four are combined into the *Integrated Accessibility Standards* regulation, known as the IASR.) The standards covering employment (the Employment Accessibility Standards) apply to all employers in Ontario who employ at least one paid employee. Seven of its eight requirements started coming into effect for the Ontario government and legislature in 2013. (The effective date depends on the employer's size and sector. Private sector organizations with 50 or more employees must be in compliance by January 1, 2016 while private sector organizations with fewer than 50 employees must be in compliance by 2017, although they are exempt from some standards.)

The one workplace standard that came into effect earlier—in January 2012—for *all* employers, regardless of size, relates to the requirement to make workplace emergency procedures accessible. Employers must help employees who are disabled stay safe in an emergency by providing them with individualized emergency response information when necessary. This could involve, for example, designating two co-workers to assist an employee who uses a wheelchair to leave the building in case of fire.

The eight requirements covered by the Employment Accessibility Standards are:

1. Recruitment, assessment, and selection (s. 23)
2. Accessible formats and communication supports for employees (s. 26)
3. Workplace emergency response information (s. 27)
4. Documented individual accommodation plans (s. 28)
5. Return to work process (s. 29)
6. Performance management (s. 30)
7. Career development and advancement (s. 31)
8. Redeployment (s. 32)

Under these employment standards, employers are generally required to establish and implement employment policies, procedures, and training related to accessibility in recruiting, hiring, retaining, and accommodating people with disabilities. For example, when recruiting, an organization has to make applicants aware that accommodations are available to allow them to participate in the recruitment process, and that assessment and selection materials are available in an accessible format on request. Similarly, when an employee with a disability requests it, the employer must work with the employee to make workplace information (for example, its health and safety policy) accessible. This may involve putting it in an accessible format or reviewing it verbally with that employee. Another example relates to performance management: employers must take into account the accessibility needs of employees with disabilities, as well as individual accommodation plans, when applying their performance management process to such employees. This could mean, for instance, providing informal performance feedback in a way that considers an employee's learning disability.

Employers with 50 or more employees are required to develop and have in place a *written process* for the development of documented individual accommodation plans for employees with disabilities. This process-related information will include the way in which an employee can participate in the development of his or her individual accommodation plan, the means of assessment, the measures taken to protect the employee's privacy, as well as how frequently the plan will be reviewed and updated (Ontario Ministry of Community and Social Services, 2012, 2014).

There are several government websites that explain and help employers comply with the accessibility standards' requirements. One good source is the Making Ontario Accessible section on the Ministry of Economic Development, Employment & Infrastructure website at www.mcss.gov.on.ca/en/mcss/programs/accessibility/.

REFERENCES

Accessibility for Ontarians with Disabilities Act, 2005. SO 2005, c. 11.

Al-Saidi v. Brio Beverages Inc. 2001 AHRC 5.

Arias v. Desai. 2003 HRTO 1, [2003] OHRTD no. 1.

Ata-Ayi v. Pepsi Bottling Group (Canada) Co. 2006 CanLII 37418 (Ont. SC).

Autobus Legault inc. c. Québec (Commission des droits de la personne). 1998 CanLII 12534 (QC CA).

BC Human Rights Tribunal Hands Out Record Award. *Canadian Employment Law Today.* Issue no. 404, January 7, 2004, p. 3157.

Bernardi, Lauren. Top 10 Mistakes Investigating Harassment Complaints. *HR Professional.* May/June 2012, p. 42. http://www.nxtbook.com/nxtbooks/naylor/HRPH0412/index.php?startid=42.

Bhadauria v. Board of Governors of Seneca College. (1981), 124 DLR (3d) 193 (SCC).

Bird, Kathryn. The Supreme Court of Canada Strikes Down Random Alcohol Testing Policy. *FTR Now.* June 19, 2013. Hicks Morley. http://www.hicksmorley.com/index.php?name=News&file=article&sid=1879.

Bongarde Media Co. Sexual Harassment: 8 Traps to Avoid When Investigating Harassment Complaints. *HR Compliance Insider.* Volume 5, no. 3, March 2009, p. 1.

British Columbia (Public Service Employee Relations Commission) v. BCGSEU. [1999] 3 SCR 3.

Brown, A. Enabling the Duty to Accommodate. *Canadian HR Reporter.* February 24, 2003, p. 9.

Bubb-Clarke v. Toronto Transit Commission. 2002 CanLII 46503 (Ont. HRT), [2002] OHRBID no. 6.

C.R. v. Schneider National Carriers, Inc. 2006 CanLII 532 (Ont. SC).

Canada (Attorney General) v. Johnstone. 2013 FC 113; 2014 FCA 110.

Canadian Blood Services v. O.P.S.E.U. 2007 CarswellOnt 7999 (Ont. Arb. Bd.).

Canadian Mental Health Association. Fast Facts About Mental Illness. 2013. http://www.cmha.ca/media/fast-facts-about-mental-illness/.

Carriere, Thierry. The Duty to Accommodate: Hype and Reality. *Canadian Employment Law Today.* Issue no. 483, April 11, 2007, p. 1.

Central Alberta Dairy Pool v. Alberta (Human Rights Commission). [1990] 2 SCR 489, 72 DLR (4th) 417.

Central Okanagan School District No. 23 v. Renaud. [1992] 2 SCR 970, 95 DLR (4th) 577.

Chopra v. Syncrude Canada Ltd. 2003 ABQB 504, [2003] AJ no. 741.

Chu, Nicole. Important Decisions from 2013 Employment Law Cases. December 31, 2013. MacLeod Law Firm. http://www.macleodlawfirm.ca/employers/2013/12/important-employment-law-cases-decided-2013/.

Communications, Energy and Paperworkers Union of Canada, Local 30 v. Irving Pulp & Paper, Ltd. 2013 SCC 34.

Communications, Energy, and Paperworkers Union, Local 707 v. SMS Equipment Inc. 2013 CanLII 68986 (Ont. LA).

Conlin, Ryan, and Frank Portman. Is the Sky Falling? Family Status Discrimination and Shift Shopping. *Update.* March 7, 2014. Stringer Management. http://www.stringerllp.com/is-the-sky-falling-family-status-discrimination-and-shift-shopping.

Crisp, Dave. We All Have Everyday Mental Health Issues. *Canadian HR Reporter.* October 7, 2013, p. 13.

Cristiano v. Grand National Apparel Inc. 2012 HRTO 991.

Crowley v. Liquor Control Board of Ontario. 2011 HRTO 1429.

Dobson, Sarah. Bar Raised in Random Drug, Alcohol Testing. *Canadian HR Reporter.* July 15, 2013, p. 1.

Dobson, Sarah. Family Status Accommodation Expanding. *Canadian HR Reporter.* October 8, 2012, p. 1.

Echlin, Randall, and Christine Thomlinson. *For Better or For Worse: A Practical Guide to Canadian Employment Law*, 3rd ed. Aurora, ON: Canada Law Book, 2011.

Emond Harnden. Arbitrator Upholds Termination Where Employee Refuses to Cooperate with Attempts to Accommodate. *What's New.* May 2012. http://www.ehlaw.ca/whatsnew/1205/Focus12051.shtml.

Employment Standards Act, 2000. SO 2000, c. 41.

England, Robert. Supreme Court of Canada Quashes Random Alcohol Testing in Dangerous Workplace. *Canadian Employment Law Today.* June 17, 2013. http://www.employmentlawtoday.com/articleview/18220-supreme-court-of-canada-quashes-random-alcohol-testing-in-dangerous-workplace.

Entrop v. Imperial Oil Ltd. [2000] OJ no. 2689 (CA).

Essex Police Services Board v. Essex Police Association. (2002), 105 LAC (4th) 193.

Filion Wakely Thorup Angeletti. Supreme Court Rules That Random Drug and Alcohol Testing Policies Must Be Supported by "Reasonable Cause." 2013. http://filion.on.ca/supreme-court-rules-that-random-drug-and-alcohol-testing-policies-must-be-supported-by-reasonabl-cause.

Fitzgibbon, Michael. An Expansive View of Dismissing Cases for "Abuse of Process." *Thoughts from a Management Lawyer.* April 4, 2010. http://labourlawblog.typepad.com/managementupdates/2010/04/an-expansive-view-of-dismissing-cases-for-abuse-of-process.html.

Ford, Michael. Safety Issues Raised in Drug Testing Debate. *Canadian Employment Law Today*. Issue no. 497, November 7, 2007, p. 1.

Garrie v. Janus Joan Inc. 2012 HRTO 1955.

General Motors of Canada Limited v. Johnson. 2013 ONCA 502.

Gilbert, Douglas, Brian Burkett, and Moira McCaskill. *Canadian Labour and Employment Law for the US Practitioner.* Washington, DC: Bureau of National Affairs, 2000.

Gill v. Grammy's Place Restaurant and Bakery Ltd. 2003 BCHRT 88, [2003] BCHRT no. 88.

Gorley, Adam. Workplace Accommodation: What About Before Birth? July 10, 2012. First Reference Talks. http://blog.firstreference.com/2012/07/10/workplace -accommodation-what-about-before-birth/.

Gorsky, Thomas J., and Stephen Shore. Family Status: What Should Be Accommodated? *Canadian Employment Law Today*. Issue no. 501, January 16, 2008, p. 4.

Gottheil, Michael. State of the Tribunal. Presented at the Law Society of Upper Canada Six-Minute Employment Lawyer 2009 program, June 17, 2009, Toronto.

Gowlings. Accommodation in the Workplace: Getting It Right. 2011. http://www.gowlings.com/ knowledgeCentre/publicationPDFs/1-%20 Accommodation%20in%20the%20Workplace%20%20 Getting%20it%20Right.pdf.

Great Atlantic & Pacific Co. of Canada Ltd. v. Retail Wholesale Canada, U.S.W.A., Local 414. (1997), 38 CCEL (2d) 291 (Ont. Arb. Bd.).

Hamilton-Wentworth District School Board v. Fair. 2014 ONSC 2411.

Harrison v. Nixon Safety Consulting and others (No. 3). 2008 BCHRT 462.

Health Sciences Assoc. of B.C. v. Campbell River and North Island Transition Society. 2004 BCCA 260.

Human Rights Code. RSO 1990, c. H.19.

Human Rights Tribunal of Ontario. Information Bulletin: Hearings Before the Human Rights Tribunal of Ontario. 2008. http://www.hrto.ca.

Humber, Todd. Mental Health: We Can Do Better. *Canadian HR Reporter*. October 22, 2012, p. 22.

Hume, Kirsten, and Colin Edstrom. Lewd, Sexual Workplace Banter Found Not Discriminatory. December 18, 2013. Harris & Company. http://www.harrisco.com/resources/ legal-news/916.

Hydro-Québec v. Syndicat des employé-e-s de techniques professionnelles et de bureau d'Hydro-Québec, section locale 2000 (SCFP-FTQ). 2008 SCC 43.

Imperial Oil Limited v. Communications, Energy & Paper-workers Union of Canada, Local 900. 2009 ONCA 420.

Israel, Peter. Damages for Human Rights Violations Increasingly Punish Employers. *Canadian HR Reporter*. June 16, 2003, p. 5.

Jansen, Rhonda. A New Approach to Accommodating Family Status. *Canadian Employment Law Today*. Issue no. 530, March 25, 2009, p. 5.

Jansen, Rhonda. Court Addresses Random Drug Testing in Unionized Workplace. *Canadian Occupational Safety*. June 8, 2009. http://www.cos-mag.com/Human -Resources/HR-Stories/Court-addresses-random-drug -testing-in-unionized-workplace.html.

Janzen v. Platy Enterprises Ltd. [1989] 1 SCR 1252.

Johnston, Brian. Ask an Expert: Human Rights—Employee Doesn't Report Harassment. *Canadian Employment Law Today*. August 21, 2013, p. 2.

Johnstone v. Canada (Attorney General). 2008 FCA 101; 2013 FC 113; 2014 FCA 110.

Johnstone v. Canada Border Service Agency. 2010 CHRT 20.

Jurgens, Kathy. Accommodating Mental Illness Strategically. *Canadian HR Reporter*. January 14, 2013, p. 13.

Kafer v. Sleep Country Canada and another (No. 2). 2013 BCHRT 289.

Kearns v. 1327827 Ontario. 2009 HRTO 457.

Kenny, B. Ask an Expert: Employee with Medical Marijuana. *Canadian Employment Law Today*. Issue no. 570, December 1, 2010.

Krupat, Kenneth. Should Religious Employees Have Faith in Workplace Accommodation Law in Canada? Presented at the Law Society of Upper Canada Six-Minute Employment Lawyer 2013 program, June 13, 2013, Toronto.

Lane v. ADGA Group Consultants Inc. 2007 HRTO 34.

LeClair, Ron. The Evolution of Accommodation. *Canadian HR Reporter*. February 24, 2003, p. 7.

Lisi, Lorenzo. Ask an Expert: Employee Who Refuses to Seek Accommodation. *Canadian Employment Law Today*. January 9, 2013, p. 2.

Lublin, Daniel, and Daniel Chodos. Human Rights Damages Without Discrimination: The Consequences of Not Conducting Investigations. *HRPA Today*. March/April 2014. http://hrpatoday.ca/article/human-rights -damages-without-discrimination.html.

MacLeod Law Firm. Navigating Workplace Harassment Complaints. September 6, 2013. http://www .macleodlawfirm.ca/employers/2013/09/workplace -harassment-complaints-an-employers-guide/.

MacLeod Law Firm. The Dangers of Alcohol at Work—How Employers Can Avoid Disaster. November 20, 2013. http://www.macleodlawfirm.ca/employers/2013/11/ dangers-of-alcohol-at-work/.

Manhas v. A.O. Smith Enterprises. 2010 HRTO 659.

Markovic v. Autocom Manufacturing Ltd. 2008 HRTO 64.

McGill University Health Centre (Montreal General Hospital) v. Syndicat des employés de l'Hôpital général de Montréal. 2007 SCC 4.

McIntosh v. Metro Aluminum Products and another. 2011 BCHRT 34.

Merck. Merck Just-in-Time Toolkit for Managers: Effective Accommodation Discussions—The 3 P's: Performance, Productivity & Preventing Turnover. 2011. http://merckdisabilitytoolkit.com/toolkit.cfm?Tool=6.

Miller, Jeffrey. Addiction in the Workplace. *Canadian Employment Law Today.* Issue no. 395, August 6, 2003, p. 3086.

Mitchell, Tim. Health and Safety: Length of Long-Term Disability. *Canadian Employment Law Today.* Issue no. 510, May 21, 2008, p. 2.

Mitchell, Tim. Impairment Testing: Implementing and Administering Testing Policies. *Canadian Employment Law Today.* Issue no. 504, February 27, 2008, p. 2.

Morgan v. Herman Miller Canada Inc. 2013 HRTO 650.

Occupational Health and Safety Act. RSO 1990, c. O.1.

Ontario (Human Rights Commission) v. Ford Motor Co. of Canada. [2002] OJ no. 3688 (Div. Ct.).

Ontario Human Rights Commission. *Human Rights at Work,* 3rd ed. Toronto: Carswell, 2008. http://www.ohrc.on.ca/en/human-rights-work-2008-third-edition.

Ontario Human Rights Commission. *Policy and Guidelines on Disability and the Duty to Accommodate.* November 23, 2000. http://www.ohrc.on.ca/en/policy-and-guidelines -disability-and-duty-accommodate.

Ontario Human Rights Commission. *Policy on Drug and Alcohol Testing.* September 27, 2000. http://www.ohrc .on.ca/english/publications/drug-alcohol-policy.shtml.

Ontario Ministry of Community and Social Services. *A Guide to the Integrated Accessibility Standards Regulation.* April 2014. http://www.mcss.gov.on.ca/documents/en/mcss/accessibility/CombinedEnglishDocumentsIASR-02%20FINAL-s.pdf.

Ontario Ministry of Community and Social Services. Make Performance Management, Career Development and Job Changes Accessible to Employees. 2012. http://www.mcss.gov.on.ca/documents/en/mcss/accessibility/iasr_info/career.pdf.

Pillai v. Lafarge Canada Inc. 2003 BCHRT 26, [2003] BCHRTD no. 26.

Re CANPAR and United Steelworkers of America, Local 1976. (2000), 93 LAC (4th) 208.

Roher, Eric, and Michelle Henry. Duty Extends to a Broad Range of Areas. *Canadian Employment Law Today.* Issue no. 411, April 14, 2004, p. 3214.

Roosma: see *Ontario (Human Rights Commission) v. Ford Motor Co. of Canada.*

Ross, Peigi. Representing Employers Before the Human Rights Tribunal of Ontario. Presented at the Law Society of Upper Canada Six-Minute Employment Lawyer 2009 program, June 17, 2009, Toronto.

Rubin, Janice, and Sharaf Sultan. Drug and Alcohol Testing: Where Are We Now? *Canadian HR Reporter.* March 29, 2009, p. 4.

Rudner, Stuart. Dispelling the Myth of the $10,000 Cap. *Canadian Employment Law Today.* Issue no. 408, March 3, 2004, p. 3187.

Rudner, Stuart. Drug-Testing Picture Gets Murkier for Employers. *Canadian Employment Law Today.* Issue no. 502, January 30, 2008, p. 3.

Seale, Donna. How Can a Human Rights Complaint Come to My Attention? February 6, 2008. http://donnaseale.ca/how-can-a-human-rights-complaint-come-to-my -attention/.

Sexual Harasser Reinstated with Suspension. *Canadian Employment Law Today.* February 6, 2013, p. 11.

Shaw v. Levac Supply Ltd. (1990), 14 CHRR D/36 (Ont. Bd. of Inq.).

Sherrard Kuzz LLP. "Impossibility" Not Standard of Reasonable Accommodation, Says Supreme Court of Canada. *Management Counsel: Employment and Labour Law Update.* Volume VII, no. 6, October 2008, p. 3. http://www.sherrardkuzz.com/pdf/Vol_VII_6.pdf.

Sherrard Kuzz LLP. "Poisoned Work Environment": Must Be More Than a Breakdown of Personal Relationships—Says Ontario Court of Appeal. *Management Counsel: Employment and Labour Law Update.* Volume XII, no. 6, December 2013, p. 1. http://www.sherrardkuzz.com/pdf/Vol_XII_6.pdf.

Sherrard Kuzz LLP. Childcare Obligations Protected Under "Family Status"—So Says Federal Court. *Management Counsel: Employment and Labour Law Update.* Volume XII, no. 2, April 2013, p. 1. http://www.sherrardkuzz.com/pdf/Vol_XII_2.pdf.

Sherrard Kuzz LLP. Court Cheesed Off at Kraft's Non-Enforcement of Workplace Policies. *Management Counsel: Employment and Labour Law Update.* Volume IX, no. 6, October 2010, p. 1. http://www.sherrardkuzz.com/pdf/Vol_IX_6.pdf.

Sidhu v. Broadway Gallery. 2002 BCHRT 9, [2002] BCHRTD no. 9.

Silliker, Amanda. Employers Have Duty to Accommodate Child-Care Needs: Federal Court. *Canadian HR Reporter.* March 11, 2013, p. 12.

Silliker, Amanda. People with Episodic Disabilities Valuable Talent. *Canadian HR Reporter*. February 13, 2012, p. 1.

Silliker, Amanda. Workplaces Have "Role to Play" in Mental Health. *Canadian HR Reporter*. June 4, 2012. http://www.hrreporter.com/articleview/13243-workplaces-have-role-to-play-in-mental-health.

Smith v. Ontario (Human Rights Commission). 2005 CanLII 2811 (Ont. SCDC).

Smith, Jeffrey R. Accommodation: Employer Met Duty but Not Collective Agreement: Arbitrator. *Canadian Employment Law Today*. Issue no. 508, April 23, 2008, p. 7.

Smith, Jeffrey R. Onus on Employer to Start Accommodation. *Canadian HR Reporter*. November 7, 2011, p. 5.

Smith, Jeffrey R. Safety Officer Not Safe from Harassment. *Canadian Employment Law Today*. Issue no. 526, January 28, 2009, p. 1.

Smith, Jeffrey. Bipolar Employee Awarded $80,000. *Canadian HR Reporter*. April 7, 2008, p. 5.

Smith, Jeffrey. Worker Awarded $30,000 in "Sexting" Case. *Canadian HR Reporter*. April 11, 2011, p. 5.

Stam, Lisa. When Does Racism Amount to a Poisoned Workplace? *Employment and Human Rights Law in Canada*. August 21, 2013. http://www.canadaemploymenthumanrightslaw.com/2013/08/articles/discrimination/when-does-racism-amount-to-a-poisoned-workplace/.

Standryk, Leanne. Update on Random Drug Testing in Safety Sensitive Workplace: Supreme Court of Canada Quashes Random Testing. July 5, 2013. Lancaster, Brooks & Welch LLP. http://www.lbwlawyers.com/corporate-bulletins/update-on-random-drug-testing-in-safety-sensitive-workplace-supreme-court-of-canada-quashes-random-testing/.

Star Choice Television Network Inc. v. Tatulea. [2012] CLAD no. 32 (QL).

Stephenson, Kate. Making the Human Rights System Work for Applicants. Presented at the Law Society of Upper Canada Six-Minute Employment Lawyer 2009 program, June 17, 2009, Toronto.

Stewart v. Ontario (Government Services). 2013 HRTO 1635.

Taylor, Kristin. Accommodation of Family Status. Presented at the Law Society of Upper Canada Six-Minute Employment Lawyer 2013 program, June 13, 2013, Toronto, tab 3.

Taylor, Lindsey. No More Human Rights Forum Shopping? *Northern Exposure*. August 25, 2013. http://blogs.hrhero.com/northernexposure/2013/08/25/no-more-human-rights-forum-shopping/.

Todd, Shane, and Kevin MacNeill. Human Rights Tribunal Decision Highlights Difficulties with Adult ADHD and Accommodation Requests. *Workplace Wire*. October 11, 2013. http://www.workplacewire.ca/human-rights-tribunal-decision-highlights-difficulties-with-adult-adhd-and-accommodation-requests/.

Twohey, Alanna. Zero Tolerance of Sexual Harassment in the Workplace. 2013. Bird Richard. http://www.hrinfodesk.com/Articles/onzerotolerancesexualharassmentinworkplacebird13.pdf.

Weyerhaeuser Company Limited v. Ontario (Human Rights Commission). (2007), 279 DLR (4th) 480 (Ont. SCDC).

Williams, Laura, and Dino Nave. Meeting the Challenge: Considerations for Accommodating Mental Illness. Presented at the Law Society of Upper Canada Six-Minute Employment Lawyer 2013 program, June 13, 2013, Toronto.

Wilson v. Solis Mexican Foods Inc. 2013 ONSC 5799.

Wilson, Peter, and Allison Taylor. *The Corporate Counsel Guide to Employment Law*, 2nd ed. Aurora, ON: Canada Law Book, 2003.

Zabrovsky, Andrew. Federal Court of Appeal Upholds Johnstone, Clarifies Nature and Scope of Family Status Protections. *FTR Now*. 2014. Hicks Morley. http://www.hicksmorley.com/index.php?name=News&file=article&sid=2148&catid=6.

RELATED WEBSITES

- http://www.chrc-ccdp.ca/index.html   The Canadian Human Rights Commission website includes *A Place for All: A Guide to Creating an Inclusive Workplace*.
- http://www.hrto.ca   The Human Rights Tribunal of Ontario website contains information on the process of filing an application or response.
- http://www.hrlsc.on.ca/en/welcome   The Human Rights Legal Support Centre website explains the resources available to applicants by the support centre.
- http://www.ohrc.on.ca/en   The Ontario Human Rights Commission website includes guidelines, information, and policies regarding discrimination and human rights in the workplace.

REVIEW AND DISCUSSION QUESTIONS

1. Your employer intends to deny a 64-year-old female employee a training opportunity that is available to everyone else in her department because "she won't be around long enough to use the new information." How would you advise the employer?

2. Your employer is a religious person who seeks your opinion about displaying religious symbols in the workplace. What advice can you offer?

3. Your employer tells you that he's heard that a supervisor in the purchasing department made a pass at two employees at the company picnic. What should the employer do? Why?

4. You are an employer who wants to reinstate an employee who left work with a back injury. However, it's a small workplace and the only job that the employee can perform is one created out of all the "light duties" of the other six jobs. This would require the other employees to perform all of the heavier duties, which might lead to injury. What should you do to meet the requirements of the Ontario *Human Rights Code*?

5. Your employer tells you of a major productivity project that will begin shortly and take six to nine months to complete. Under normal circumstances, he would assign the project to the operations manager, but she is seven months' pregnant and will be on pregnancy leave for most of the project's duration. How would you advise your employer about the human rights issues involved?

6. An employee who has been on pregnancy leave calls you to say that she will need more flexibility in her schedule when she returns to work because of childcare needs. How should you respond?

7. An employee with a history of back problems has applied for a posted job that requires considerable heavy lifting. This employee has more seniority than any other person who has applied for the job. You are concerned that he may be physically unfit to perform the job and could injure himself further. You are the employer. What should you do?

8. Two employees, Joseph and Sean, have come to you complaining about verbal harassment on the job. Both employees are fundraisers for AIDS research, and several of their co-workers routinely tease them about being gay. How would you advise them? What steps would you advise their employer to take?

9. Your co-worker comes into your office Monday morning very angry. She tells you that she is tired of her Uncle Miguel always favouring his nephews over his nieces. At a family gathering on the weekend, he gave each of his nephews $1,000 but gave nothing to his nieces. She wants to know whether she can lodge a complaint against her uncle by filing an application under the *Human Rights Code*. How do you advise her?

10. Julio, a supervisor, continually harasses and ridicules George, who works in his department. No one else in the department believes that Julio's criticisms of George are justified. It appears to them that Julio simply does not like George for a personal reason. Can George file a human rights application? Give reasons for your answer.

11. Datt had worked for McAdams restaurant for 23 years (taking orders, cleaning) when in 2007 she came down with a skin condition on her hands that was made worse by frequent hand washing. She took several short-term disability leaves but her condition always worsened after she returned to work. McAdams said that frequent hand washing was necessary to maintain acceptable sanitary conditions, to meet both government regulations and its own hygiene policies. For example, the restaurant has a timed system where a timer sounds each hour, and all crew members and the manager must wash their hands. Datt's doctor reported that she could not perform any job requiring frequent hand washing but there were duties she could perform, including cash, some food preparation, and some cleaning. However, in August 2009 the benefits provider told Datt she would not be able to return to work because "restaurant work was not good for her" and offered her a three-month job search program. In November 2009, McAdams terminated her. Datt filed a human rights application.

    a. Did Datt have a disability?

    b. Was this a case of *prima facie* discrimination?

    c. Did the employer have a duty to accommodate Datt and if so, did it fulfill that duty up to the point of undue hardship? Explain your answer.

12. Linda was a sales rep whose job involved a lot of driving. After she was diagnosed with cataracts and told that within two years she would be legally blind, her employer advised her to apply for disability leave. Although her vision did deteriorate over the next few years, it was not as severe as the original prognosis so she wrote to her employer, asking to return to perform light duties or take on part-time work. The employer

indicated that nothing was available. Several months later, Linda's disability benefits were terminated because she was deemed capable of returning to work in some occupation. Although her employer was notified of the change and of Linda's wish to return to work, it took no action. Four years later, Linda filed a human rights complaint. The employer argued that it had relied on information from the disability benefit provider indicating that she was unable to perform the available jobs.

Do you think Linda's complaint would be successful? Explain your answer.

13. Clara was hired on a four-month fixed-term contract to perform crisis response work, including responding to calls from area hospitals to assess and provide support for persons who presented as being in crisis. She was terminated after eight weeks in the position because, the employer alleged, she was unable to perform essential parts of the job. For example, she was unable to respond quickly to verbal and non-verbal clues commonly found in individuals who are in crisis. Before her termination, the employer had raised its performance concerns but Clara told them that she was taking medication for epilepsy and among its side effects was an occasional difficulty with words and delays in completing tasks. However, when asked by the employer if she needed accommodation, Clara had said there was no need. When her performance did not improve, despite several poor performance reviews and a final written warning, the employer terminated her contract. Clara grieved her dismissal. Do you think Clara's grievance would be successful? Support your answer.

14. You are the owner of a restaurant. Barney, one of your waiters, tells you that he has government permission to use medical marijuana and needs to smoke during some breaks to relieve symptoms he has for a serious medical condition. You're concerned that his use of marijuana may pose a safety risk. Assuming Barney can prove that he has such permission, what do you tell him?

15. Tiana has been acting strangely at work and her behaviour appears to be alcohol-related. However, she denies that she has a drinking problem. Does the employer have any responsibility to accommodate a disability that the employee denies?

16. David was a machine operator in a cheese factory. After confiding in a colleague that he had had a brief affair with his supervisor's ex-wife, several co-workers began picking on him by making negative comments. This lasted over two years. Despite numerous complaints to his supervisor, who witnessed some of these insults, nothing was done. Despite the employer's zero-tolerance harassment policy, when the employer's HR department became aware of David's allegations, it launched only a superficial investigation: it did not ask who the perpetrators were or gather facts about the specific allegations. It accepted the supervisor's view that it was not a serious problem. After his lawyer's offer to the employer to meet to discuss the matter further was rejected, David filed a lawsuit alleging constructive dismissal, based on the employer's failure to provide a harassment-free environment. The court agreed, finding that in light of both the nature of the comments made and the length of time they continued, it was reasonable for David to leave his job. It awarded him 12 months' notice (a year's worth of compensation).

What lessons does this case hold for employers?

17. Angry that her supervisor had disciplined her for calling him a "dirty Mexican" at work, Danielle posted about the incident on her Facebook page. The supervisor heard about the postings and filed a human rights application against Danielle (but not the employer).

Review s. 5(2) of the *Human Rights Code* and answer the following questions:

a. What is the likely legal basis for the supervisor's application?

b. Can a co-worker be personally named in a human rights application when the employer is not?

c. Can statements made on Facebook, or any other social media forum, be considered "harassment in the workplace"?

d. Given that the employer was not a party to the proceedings, what would be an appropriate remedial order (that is, remedy)?

18. A mailroom clerk's employment was terminated after the employer conducted a brief investigation of a sexual harassment complaint by an employee of its cleaning subcontractor. The alleged misconduct included blowing the cleaner a kiss and sometimes grabbing her buttocks whenever he caught her alone;

this had gone on for five years. The mail clerk grieved his termination, alleging that while the incidents had occurred, they had been consensual. He also pointed to his six years of service, his clean disciplinary record, and testimony from another cleaner that he had stopped his objectionable behaviour with her as soon as she had demanded it (by showing him her fists). The complainant had also indicated that she did not necessarily want the mail clerk to lose his job; she simply wanted an end to the harassment. In this situation, what do you think would be an appropriate remedy?

19. A single mother makes a request to work straight day shifts, rather than rotating day and night shifts, based on the difficulty she is having making suitable childcare arrangements. Is the employer required to accommodate this request?

20. The goal of the *Accessibility for Ontarians with Disabilities Act* is to make Ontario fully accessible to people with disabilities by 2025 by establishing standards in five areas, including employment.

a. Go to the AODA's "Accessibility Compliance Wizard" at https://www.appacats.mcss.gov.on.ca/eadvisor/start.action. (This is a government website set up to help employers and others understand compliance timelines under the AODA's standards.) Choose *one* of the following four scenarios (circle the scenario chosen—A, B, C, or D) and then answer the questions that the Wizard asks about your chosen workplace.

   Scenario A: You own a hair salon with 14 employees in Ontario

   Scenario B: You are a not-for-profit organization with 26 employees

   Scenario C: You own a factory and have 715 employees

   Scenario D: You're in the broader public sector with 1,875 employees

   For your scenario, list the requirements your chosen workplace must be in compliance with as of 2015, 2016, 2017, and beyond 2017 (if any).

b. Go to http://www.mcss.gov.on.ca/en/mcss/programs/accessibility/. (This is a government website set up to explain the accessibility standards' requirements.) Find the Accessibility Standard for Employment by selecting "Employment" from the menu. Locate the policy guidelines and identify one example of how your chosen workplace can comply with that standard.

c. Identify one resource that the website directs the employer to, to assist it with meeting its requirements under the standard.

Employment Standards Act

6

LEARNING OUTCOMES

After completing this chapter, you will be able to:

- Understand the purpose of the Ontario *Employment Standards Act, 2000* in setting minimum rights for employees.

- Identify the minimum standards that apply to wages, hours of work, public holidays, overtime pay, vacation, and statutory leaves.

- Identify the protections available to employees who exercise their rights to statutory leaves, including pregnancy, parental, family medical, and personal emergency leaves.

- Understand the legal relationship between an employee hired through a temporary employment agency and the hiring organization.

- Understand how rights and protections under the Act are enforced.

Introduction

The Ontario *Employment Standards Act, 2000* (ESA) sets out minimum terms and conditions of work, including hours of work; overtime premium pay; public holidays; vacation time and pay; and pregnancy and parental leave. It also establishes minimum requirements with respect to termination notice and severance pay, which are discussed in Chapter 14. An employer is free to exceed these statutory minimum standards, but it cannot, even with the employee's agreement, fail to meet them.

For example, the ESA requires that employees receive overtime pay after working 44 hours in a week. If the employer and employee agree that overtime pay is required after only 40 hours, the parties are bound by this more generous term. However, if they agree that the employer is not required to provide overtime pay until the employee works 48 hours, the agreement contravenes the ESA and is not enforceable. If the employee subsequently files a complaint with the Ontario Ministry of Labour, or the Ministry learns of the statutory contravention in some other way, the employer must pay the employee the overtime premium pay owing, plus interest, and possibly a penalty, payable to the Ministry. The employee's initial agreement to the lower term will not be a defence.

To a certain extent, the ESA displaces the common law principle that the parties are free to negotiate their own terms and conditions of employment. Its rationale is that many employees lack the bargaining power to negotiate acceptable working conditions with the employer. The government is thus setting and enforcing minimum rights that we, as a society, require in the interests of fairness in the workplace.

Although minimum statutory standards apply to all employees, they are most relevant in entry-level positions and lower-paying jobs, where individual employees often lack bargaining power. However, the ESA has evolved over time, and it now contains a range of statutory standards and protections, such as pregnancy and parental leave provisions, that set the standard for most Ontario workplaces. Moreover, legislative changes are ongoing. For example, provisions concerning family caregiver, critically ill childcare, and crime-related child death or disappearance leave have all been added since 2013.

FYI

Key Features of Ontario's ESA

1. The ESA sets *minimum standards*; an employee cannot waive her rights under the ESA and agree to standards of work that are less generous than those in the Act. These standards include minimum wages, hours of work and overtime, vacation entitlement, public holidays, statutory leaves of absence, and termination and severance pay.

2. If an employer promises an employee *a greater benefit* than that provided under the ESA, an employment standards officer (ESO) will enforce the greater benefit if there is a complaint (s. 5(2)). A greater benefit must be related to a specific entitlement under the ESA. An employer, for example, cannot forgo paying employees for public holidays by insisting that the overall compensation scheme is a greater benefit since the employees receive $10 per hour above minimum wage.

3.   The Act covers most *employees*. However, specific exemptions apply to certain occupations and industries. For example, the hours of work standards do not apply to managerial and supervisory employees, and independent contractors are not covered by this legislation.

4.   Enforcement of rights under the ESA is a complaint-based process. Subject to paragraph 5, employees who believe their rights have been infringed under the ESA file a complaint with the Ministry of Labour.

5.   Unionized employees are covered by the ESA. However, they must usually follow the grievance procedure in their collective agreement to pursue their rights under the ESA, rather than file a complaint with the Ministry of Labour.

6.   Except for the personal emergency leave and severance pay provisions, the ESA binds all employers, regardless of size.

General Requirements

Application

The ESA's application is set out in s. 3. Most employees and employers in Ontario are covered. Those not covered include the following:

- employees in federally regulated sectors, such as banks, airlines, and broadcasting;
- secondary school students working in a work-experience program authorized by their school board;
- college or university students working under a program approved by the institution;
- individuals involved in community participation under the *Ontario Works Act, 1997*;
- police officers, except with respect to the lie detector provisions;
- employees of embassies or consulates of foreign nations;
- inmates of correctional institutions taking part in work programs;
- people working in simulated jobs for the purpose of rehabilitation; and
- people who hold political, judicial, religious, or trade union offices.

Certain employees are *exempt only from some parts* of the Act or are subject to special rules. For example, managers and supervisory employees are not covered by the hours of work and overtime pay provisions. To fall within the scope of the exemption, the position must be truly managerial, carrying the power to hire and make independent decisions. Simply giving an employee the title of "manager" will not make her exempt from those requirements. Similarly, professional employees, such as accountants and lawyers, and farm workers directly employed in primary production are exempt from provisions regarding minimum wage, maximum hours of work, overtime pay, paid public holidays, and vacation pay. Government (Crown) employees are exempt from most, but not all, sections of the Act.

Record Keeping

Section 15 of the ESA requires all employers, regardless of size, to keep accurate records about employees and make them available to inspectors from the Ministry of Labour. There are significant penalties for failing to keep these records. Accurate records also can assist the parties in resolving disputes. For example, if an employee alleges that an employer owes him overtime pay and the employer has no reliable records, an adjudicator will usually accept the employee's claim.

Ontario's ESA has specific requirements concerning the information that an employer must record about each employee and the length of time that the records must be kept. Generally speaking, employee records must be kept for three years after the relevant date. For example, an employer must keep the name and address of each employee for three years after employment ends, and must keep the information contained in each wage statement for three years after giving that information to the employee.

Employers must keep copies of employees' agreements concerning overtime hours and average hours of work in calculating overtime pay for three years after work was last performed under the agreement. (See the section entitled "Agreements to Vary" below.) Employers who employ "homeworkers" (employees who do paid work out of their homes for an employer) must keep a register containing the homeworkers' names, addresses, and wage rates for three years after they stop working for the employer.

Posting Information

Section 2 of the ESA requires employers to display, in a conspicuous place in the workplace, a poster prepared by the Ministry of Labour that provides information about the Act and its regulations. This poster contains a brief summary of key standards and includes information about enforcement of the Act, emphasizing that employees cannot be penalized for enforcing their rights under the legislation. The poster can be obtained without cost from the Ministry's website at www.labour.gov.on.ca/english/es/pubs/poster.php.

If English is not the majority language of the workplace, the employer must contact the Ministry of Labour to see whether it has prepared a translation into the majority language. If it has, the employer must post both the English and the translated version of the poster together in the workplace.

At the time of writing, the Ontario government has tabled proposed changes that would require employers to also provide each employee with a copy of the most recent poster published by the Ministry of Labour containing information about rights under the ESA, and to provide material in available translations prepared by the Ministry of Labour if requested (Bill 18, *Stronger Workplaces for a Stronger Economy Act, 2014*).

Wages

Payment of Wages

Section 11 of the ESA requires an employer to establish a regular pay period and payday for employees, and to pay all wages earned during the pay period on or before the regular payday. Payment may be by cash, cheque, or (if certain conditions are met) direct deposit into the employee's account at a bank or other financial institution. Partial payment is prohibited.

When employment ends, all outstanding wages, including vacation pay, must be paid no later than seven days after employment ends or on the employee's next regular payday, whichever occurs later.

Deductions from Wages and Vacation Pay

Section 13 prohibits an employer from withholding or deducting any wages payable to an employee unless it is

1. obliged to do so by statute, as in the case of deductions for income taxes, employment insurance (EI) premiums, and Canada Pension Plan contributions;

2. obliged to do so by a court order, as in the case of a garnishment order requiring the money to be paid to a third party to whom money is owing (for example, a child support payment); or

3. authorized by the employee to do so in writing. The authorization must include specific information concerning the amount of money to be deducted and the method of calculating it. It should be signed, dated, and preferably witnessed. A blanket authorization is not sufficient to allow a deduction from wages. For example, if an employer gives the employee a loan, the written agreement should specify the exact amount owed or a formula by which it can be easily calculated. The written agreement should also include the amount to be deducted each pay period.

Even with a written authorization, an employer *cannot* make a deduction from wages to cover faulty work, such as a broken tool or a mistake made on a credit card transaction. However, with proper authorization, it can make a deduction for a cash shortage or lost or stolen property, but only if the employee is the only one with access to and total control over the cash or property. For instance, if more than one person has a key to a locker where tools are kept, an employee cannot be held financially responsible for loss of the tools from the locker.

On the other hand, employers are permitted to recover a genuine wage advance or an unintentional overpayment. Calculations should be documented and disclosed on the statement of wages. Overpayments should be recovered as soon as possible. *Hutchins v. Atlantic Provincial Security Guard Service Ltd.* shows that employers generally are restricted from making wage deductions unless they fall within one of the specific statutory exemptions. In *Hutchins*, the Board ruled against an employer that deducted money from an employee's wages because of unexplained damage to a rented vehicle in the employee's possession. The Board did so because the damages did not fall within the statutory provisions.

CASE IN POINT

Employer's Ability to Deduct Wages Limited

Hutchins v. Atlantic Provincial Security Guard Service Ltd., 1995 CanLII 8876, [1995] NBLEBD no. 24

Facts

Hutchins, an employee of Atlantic Provincial Security Guard Service, was in possession of a rented minivan during the course of his employment when his shift ended on Friday. He obtained permission from his employer to keep the van for personal use on Saturday and Sunday. The employer failed to inform Hutchins that he would be responsible for the $40 cost of the weekend rental. After another rental in the course of his employment, he returned the vehicle with a damaged back door. The cost to repair the door was $424. Hutchins, who was the only driver of the vehicle, denied all knowledge of the damage. The employer demanded that he pay for the damage through a deduction from wages. When Hutchins refused, the employer terminated his employment. The employer withheld both the $40 and the $424 from his final pay.

Relevant Issue

Whether the employer violated the ESA by deducting $40 and $424 from the employee's wages in these circumstances.

Decision

The Board found that the $40 deduction was appropriate because the employee requested the use of the van and derived a personal benefit from the employer's goodwill. However, the $424 deduction was inappropriate. There was no evidence to suggest that the employee damaged the van negligently or intentionally. Because the New Brunswick ESA (like the Ontario ESA) provides for employer deductions only in the clearest and most carefully defined circumstances, the employer was not entitled to deduct the $424. The appropriate remedy for the employer was to pay the wages owing and to sue the employee for damages.

Wage Statements

Section 12 of the Act specifies the information that an employer must provide on each wage statement and when it must provide it. An employer must furnish the employee with a written statement (or may provide an emailed statement if the employee is able to make a paper copy) on or before the employee's payday setting out

- the period for which the wages are paid;
- the wage rate;
- the gross wage amount and how it is calculated, unless this is communicated in another way, as in a written employment contract;
- the amount and purpose of each deduction;
- the amount paid in respect of room or board; and
- the net wage amount.

Special requirements apply to vacation pay statements.

Agreements to Vary

In 2001, to enhance the flexibility of employment standards, the government introduced **agreements to vary** from the legislated minimum standard. Now employers and employees can agree to vary these standards in the following four ways:

1. to exceed the daily and weekly maximum hours of work;
2. to average hours of work for overtime pay purposes;
3. to compensate overtime hours with time off in lieu of overtime premium pay; and
4. to take vacation time in increments of less than one week.

Agreements to exceed the maximum *weekly* hours of work and agreements to average hours of work for the purpose of calculating overtime pay require the approval of the Director of Employment Standards at the Ministry of Labour.

To be enforceable, agreements to vary must be in writing, unless otherwise specified in the legislation. Agreements by email are enforceable if the employee has signified her acceptance of the agreement (for example, by confirming acceptance by email). An agreement to vary should

- name the parties,
- specify the date it will come into effect and date it will expire,
- specify the employment standard being varied,
- specify the new agreement,
- contain the signatures of both parties,
- pertain only to future events, and
- be understood and freely entered into by the parties.

An employee's consent to the agreement must be informed and voluntary. Consent is informed when the consenting party understands the consequences of giving consent. For example, if an employee does not understand the language that the agreement is written in or if an important term is not prominent, the agreement may not be enforceable. Consent is voluntary when it is freely given. An agreement may be unenforceable, for example, if an employer threatens to fire or reduce the hours or pay of employees who refuse to sign it. An agreement to vary is considered valid unless an employee challenges it.

Minimum Employment Standards

1. Minimum Wage

Section 23 of the ESA addresses minimum wage requirements. Minimum wage is the lowest hourly wage that an employer can pay an employee. Most employees are subject to minimum wage requirements, regardless of whether they are full-time, part-time, or casual workers and regardless of whether they are paid on an hourly basis or on commission, piece rate, flat rate, or salary.

Minimum wage rates are set out in the regulations to the ESA. In the past, rates were typically increased every few years, on an ad hoc basis. In early 2014, the Ontario government announced an increase to the minimum wage from $10.25 to $11.00 effective June 1, 2014 and further promised annual increases tied to the rate of inflation, beginning in October 2015 (Ontario Budget, 2014).

There are several minimum rates, which vary depending on the job category. Most employees are covered by the general minimum wage. Certain employees, such as students who instruct or supervise children or who work as camp counsellors, are exempt from minimum wage requirements.

General Minimum Wage

As noted above, effective June 1, 2014 the minimum wage was increased from $10.25 to $11.00.

Special Wage Rates

Special wage rates apply to the situations listed below.

1. *Liquor service.* Employees who regularly serve liquor directly to customers in licensed premises have a special rate that is lower than the general minimum wage. Effective June 1, 2014, their minimum hourly rate became $9.55.
2. *Full-time students.* Full-time students under 18 who work 28 hours a week or less when school is in session or work during school holidays also have a special rate that is lower than the general minimum wage. Effective June 1, 2014, their minimum hourly rate became $10.30.
3. *Hunting or fishing guides.* The rates paid to hunting and fishing guides are calculated in blocks of time, and not by means of an hourly rate.
4. *Homeworkers.* Homeworkers are entitled to receive 110 percent of the general minimum wage rate. Homeworkers who are students, even those under age 18, are entitled to this premium minimum wage. Effective June 1, 2014, their minimum hourly wage became $12.10.

Special Situations

Special rules apply to the situations listed below.

1. *Room and board.* There are limits on the deductions that may be made for room and board supplied by employers.
2. *Harvesting.* Special rules apply to fruit, vegetable, and tobacco harvesters.
3. *Commissions.* Subject to the exception discussed below under the heading "Commissioned Salespeople Working Outside the Workplace," employees who are paid entirely, or in part, through commissions are entitled to receive at least the equivalent of the minimum wage for each hour worked.

The following is an example of how minimum wages are calculated for an employee who is paid by commission.

> Over the course of a week, Ruth worked 40 hours and earned $320 in commissions. This amounts to $8.00 per hour. If the applicable minimum wage is $11.00 per hour, Ruth's employer owes her the difference between her commission pay ($320) and what her employer would have paid for the same number of hours at the minimum wage ($11.00 × 40 hours or $440).
>
> Therefore, Ruth's employer must pay her an additional $120 ($440 − $320).

Minimum Reporting Pay: The Three-Hour Rule

On occasion, employees who come in to work their scheduled shift are sent home before the end of the shift because, for example, business is slow or an expected shipment does not arrive. In this situation, special rules apply.

An employer must pay an employee who is scheduled to work three hours or more and is sent home after working less than three hours the greater of three hours at the applicable minimum wage and the employee's regular wage for the time worked.

The following example illustrates how the calculation works.

> Yassi is scheduled to work an eight-hour shift at a retail store. Business is slow, and the employer decides to send her home after only two hours. Yassi earns $13.00 an hour, so payment at her regular rate would be 2 × $13.00 or $26.00. If the applicable minimum wage is $11.00 per hour, the three-hour rule means that she is entitled to receive 3 × $11.00 or $33.00 because that amount is greater than $26.00.

This rule does not apply to students or to employees whose regular shift is three hours or less. It is also inapplicable if the employer has no control over the reason that work is unavailable, as in the case of a fire or power failure.

Unpaid Internships

Generally, individuals who perform work for another person or organization are employees (unless they are in business for themselves) and therefore are entitled to the minimum standards set out in the ESA. However, there are a number of exceptions. One is where students perform work under a program approved by a college of applied arts and technology or a university. This exception is meant to encourage employers to provide those students with practical training to complement their classroom learning. A second, very limited exception is where an intern receives training and *all* of the following conditions are met:

- The training is similar to that which is given in a vocational school.
- The training is for the benefit of the intern, such as acquiring new knowledge or skills.
- The employer derives little, if any, benefit from the activity of the intern while he or she is being trained. (The organization cannot profit in any way from the unpaid intern's efforts.)
- The training doesn't take someone else's job.
- The employer isn't promising the individual a job at the end of the training. (Even a suggestion that a paid job could result from the training would be a disqualifier.)
- The individual has been *told* that he or she will not be paid.

Note that simply being called an "intern" is not enough to fall within this exception.

Employers who have inadvertently violated the law by hiring unpaid interns outside of an educational program should immediately offer full payment—that is, provide at least the minimum wage for the hours worked, plus any overtime—including interest, to the intern (Whitten, 2013; Ontario Ministry of Labour, 2011).

Commissioned Salespeople Working Outside the Workplace

Another exception to the requirement to provide minimum wage (and vacation pay) is where the employee is a commissioned salesperson who works outside the workplace. Salespeople over whose hours of work the employer has little or no control fall within this exception. However, this exception does *not* apply to "route" salespeople: these are employees who sell on a particular route and over whom the employer exercises considerable control. In *Schiller v. P & L Corporation Ltd*, the court found that a person who was hired to sell newspaper subscriptions door-to-door and who was driven to the neighbourhood by the employer (who also supplied the list of addresses and a script) was a "route" salesperson and therefore covered by the minimum wage (and vacation pay) entitlements.

2. Hours of Work and Eating Periods

Sections 17 to 21 of the ESA outline the maximum hours that an employer may assign to an employee or that an employee may agree to work in a given time period. "Maximum hours of work" and "overtime" are separate issues. Overtime refers to the threshold when overtime premium pay is required, which is 44 hours per workweek under the ESA.

General Rule

The maximum number of hours that an employee is required to work is

- 8 hours per day (or if the employer has established a regular workday longer than 8 hours, the number of hours in that day), and
- 48 hours per week.

Agreement to Work Excess Hours

In 2001, the hours of work provisions of the ESA were amended to allow more flexibility in work schedules. The employer and employee may agree to vary the statutory maximum hours *if* they follow the procedures set out below.

To vary the maximum *daily* hours the employer must

- give non-union employees the most recent version of an information bulletin from the Ministry of Labour entitled "Information for Employees About Hours of Work and Overtime Pay" (available from the Ministry website at www.labour.gov.on.ca/english/es/pubs/hours/infosheet.php); and
- get the employee's (or union's) *written* agreement to the variation. (See the section "Agreements to Vary," above, regarding requirements for a binding agreement.) The agreement must include an acknowledgment that the employee received the information bulletin referred to above.

To vary the maximum *weekly* hours, the employer must

- comply with both requirements for varying the maximum *daily* hours above; and
- get approval from the Director of Employment Standards at the Ministry of Labour.

Subject to certain limited exceptions (for example, see under the heading "Exceptional Circumstances" below), an employee is not permitted, nor can the employee be required, to work excess hours unless these procedures are followed.

Employers may file an application for excess weekly hours over the Internet or in writing to the Ministry of Labour. Applications must be made using a form provided by the Ministry, available on the Ministry's website, and a copy must be posted in a conspicuous place in the workplace. A copy of the employee's consent must be included in the application. Where the Director has not yet made a decision, the employees may begin working the additional hours up to a maximum of 60 hours a week 30 days after the application is made, if all other conditions are met.

Approvals are given for a maximum of three years, unless the hours in a workweek would exceed 60, in which case the maximum is one year. In making the decision, the Director may consider such relevant factors as the employer's history of compliance with employment standards and with employee health and safety requirements. For example, an employer with a poor health and safety record may find it difficult to obtain approval to have employees work more than 48 hours per week. This is because extra hours pose an additional safety risk in a workplace that is already facing problems in that area.

When the approval or the notice of refusal is received, it must be posted in place of the application.

A non-union employee may revoke the agreement at any time on two weeks' written notice, while the employer may revoke it on "reasonable notice." Reasonable notice is not defined, but what is reasonable will depend on the individual circumstances, including how long the agreement has been in effect. One exception to the right to revoke on two weeks' notice is where an employee has entered into an agreement to work excess *daily* hours when he was hired and that agreement was approved by the Director of Employment Standards. In that case, the employee may be unable to cancel the agreement until the employer also agrees to cancel it, although such employees generally cannot be required to work more than 10 hours in a day (O. reg. 285/01, s. 32(1)).

The Ministry may perform spot checks to ensure that written agreements are in place and that employees have received Ministry information sheets.

Hours Free from Work

Employees are entitled to have a certain number of hours free from work. Specifically, they must have at least

- 11 consecutive hours off work each day (this does not apply to employees who are on call and are "called in" to work when they would usually be off work);
- 8 hours off work between shifts unless the total time worked on both shifts is not more than 13 hours or unless the employer and employee have agreed otherwise in writing; and
- 24 consecutive hours off work every workweek or at least 48 consecutive hours off work every two consecutive workweeks (this requirement cannot be altered, even with the written agreement of both parties).

Eating Periods and Breaks

The employer must provide a 30-minute eating period after five consecutive hours of work. However, an employer and employee may agree, verbally or in writing, that the employee is entitled to two eating periods that together total at least 30 minutes in each consecutive five-hour period instead. An employer does not have to pay for the meal break; however, whether the break is paid or unpaid, the employee must be free from work for the time to be considered a meal break. Meal breaks are not considered hours of work and are not counted toward overtime.

An employer is not required to provide coffee breaks. If it does so, and employees are required to remain at the workplace during the break, they are entitled to payment for this time.

Exceptional Circumstances

Section 19 provides that in exceptional circumstances, an employer can require an employee to work beyond the maximum hours noted above or during a mandatory rest period, but "only so far as is necessary to avoid serious interference with the ordinary working of the employer's establishment or operations." Exceptional circumstances include:

1. dealing with emergencies, such as natural disasters, extreme weather conditions, fires, and floods;
2. ensuring the continued delivery of essential public services such as hospitals, public transit, or firefighting (this could include, for example, an employee of a company that supplies meals to a hospital);
3. ensuring that continuous processes or seasonal operations are not interrupted when something unforeseen, such as an accident or unforeseeable breakdown in machinery, occurs that would prevent others from doing their jobs; and
4. carrying out urgent repair work to the employer's plant or equipment.

Exceptional circumstances do *not* include situations such as rush orders, taking inventory, absenteeism, seasonal busy periods, or routine maintenance.

3. Overtime

General Overtime Pay Rule

Under s. 22 of the ESA, employers must pay employees overtime pay at the rate of 1.5 times their regular rate of pay after they work 44 hours in a workweek. For example, an employee who makes $12 per hour is entitled to overtime pay of $18 (1.5 × $12) for every hour worked after 44 hours. Unless the employment contract states otherwise, overtime is calculated on a weekly, not a daily, basis in accordance with the workplace's established workweek. The purpose of overtime pay is to compensate employees for additional time spent working and to discourage employers from requiring employees to work excessive hours. In many workplaces, overtime is paid after only 40 or fewer regular hours pursuant to a collective agreement or company policy, and this standard overrides the minimum requirements of the legislation.

Under the Act, an employer cannot lower an employee's regular wage to avoid paying overtime. For example, if an employee's regular pay is $18 per hour, the employer cannot lower the rate to $12 per hour and then pay 1.5 × $12 for overtime hours worked. As previously noted, employees cannot give up their right to overtime pay (or equivalent time off in lieu of pay as discussed below) under the ESA.

Some job categories do not qualify for overtime pay under the ESA. The most significant of these exemptions refers to "a person whose work is supervisory or managerial in character and who may perform non-supervisory or non-managerial tasks on an irregular or exceptional basis" (O. reg. 285/01, s. 8). Managerial duties include hiring, firing, and imposing discipline. Employees who do not have supervisory responsibilities but have considerable policy or budgetary authority may also fall within the exception. Some employers mistakenly assume that this exemption covers anyone who is paid on a salary, rather than an hourly, basis. Determining whether an employee falls within this exemption may be a difficult question, as *Tri Roc* illustrates.

CASE IN POINT

Overtime Pay for Managerial Employees

Tri Roc Electric Ltd. v. Butler, 2003 CanLII 11390 (Ont. LRB), [2003] OESAD no. 1002

Facts

Butler began working for the employer in 1999. By the end of 2000, he became involved with several large electrical projects. In addition to his regular duties, he assumed some supervisory and administrative functions. He became responsible for keeping track of all hours worked by the employees at his site. He approved their time sheets, occasionally made recommendations for hiring and firing, and suggested wage rates for the new employees.

Although Butler consistently worked more than 44 hours a week, his employer refused to pay him overtime because it viewed him as being employed in a supervisory capacity.

Relevant Issue

Whether the employee was a supervisory or managerial employee and thus exempt from the overtime pay requirements of the ESA.

Decision

The Board held that under the old ESA, Butler was not entitled to overtime pay because the essential character of the job was managerial. Consequently, he was not entitled to any overtime pay for work performed before September 4, 2001 (the time at which the new ESA came into force).

However, from September 4, 2001 on, Butler's duties could no longer be classified as supervisory or managerial because he "regularly" performed non-managerial duties, such as working with tools and completing electrical work, in the ordinary course of his employment. He was therefore entitled to receive overtime premium pay for work performed after the new statutory wording related to the supervisory/managerial exemption came into force.

Tri Roc establishes that under the current ESA, any employee who regularly performs non-managerial duties is eligible for overtime premium pay. For example, if a retail manager is regularly ringing in purchases and making sales, it is likely that he will be entitled to receive overtime pay, regardless of his title (Loewenberg and Lisi, 2008, p. 5).

Another group of employees who are exempt from the overtime pay requirements are information technology *professionals*. These are employees who use specialized knowledge and professional judgment to work with information systems based on computers and related technologies.

A related situation arises when an employee performs several kinds of work, only some of which are exempt from overtime pay. In this case, the employee qualifies for overtime pay if at least 50 percent of the hours she works are in a job category that qualifies for overtime pay (s. 22(9) of the ESA). For example, Teresa works for a taxi company both as a cab driver (a job that is exempt from overtime pay requirements) and as a dispatcher (a job that is covered). If she works 27 hours as a dispatcher and 23 hours as a driver (a total of 50 hours), she is entitled to overtime pay for all overtime hours. This is because a majority of her time is spent in work that qualifies for overtime pay, and she worked 6 hours beyond the statutory threshold of 44 hours.

Salaried employees, whose wages are not based on the number of hours worked, are entitled to overtime pay if they work more than 44 hours in a week and do not fall within the managerial or supervisory exemption. For example:

> Thuy's salary is $600 per week. Because she worked 50 hours this workweek, she is entitled to 6 hours at the overtime rate. To calculate her overtime pay, divide $600 by 44 hours to determine her hourly rate ($600 (44 = $13.64 per hour). Thuy's overtime rate is therefore $20.46 per hour (1.5 × $13.64). Her total overtime pay is $122.76 ($20.46 × 6 hours).

It should be noted that an employer is legally responsible for paying for any work it permits or suffers to be done, not just for work it specifically authorizes. Accordingly, an employer may still be required to give overtime pay to an employee who works more than 44 hours in a week, even if some of those hours were not specifically authorized (O. reg. 285/01, s. 6(1)). It is therefore important that an employer not simply ignore breaches of a workplace policy that, for example, requires permission to work overtime.

Averaging Agreements

An employer and employee may agree in writing that the employee's hours of work may be averaged for the purpose of determining the employee's entitlement to overtime pay. In order to be valid, such agreements require the approval of the Director of Employment Standards. With a valid agreement, overtime pay is then payable after the employee has worked an average of 44 hours a week over the agreed period. For example:

> Jacob worked 54 hours in week 1 and 36 hours in week 2. Without an averaging agreement, the employer must pay Jacob 10 hours' overtime pay in week 1 and none in week 2. With an averaging agreement, the total number of hours for the two weeks (90 hours) is divided by 2, for an average of 45 hours in each week. In this situation, the employer must pay Jacob for only 2 hours at the overtime rate because Jacob has worked only 1 hour over 44 hours a week in each week.

Averaging agreements have obvious advantages for the employer because they potentially lower the amount of overtime pay. At the same time, employees may find an averaging agreement attractive if they prefer to work excess hours in some weeks and fewer in others. An averaging agreement makes this schedule more practical.

An averaging agreement must be in writing and include an expiry date. If an employee is not represented by a trade union, the expiry date must not be more than two years after the date the agreement takes effect. The agreement should specifically state that its purpose is to specify the method of calculating the employee's entitlement to overtime pay and that it may affect that entitlement.

An expiry date does not prevent an employer and employee from agreeing to renew or replace the averaging agreement. However, the agreement cannot be revoked or cancelled before the expiry date unless both parties agree in writing.

With respect to the Director's approval, if an employer has applied for an approval but the Director has not yet made a decision, the employer may begin to use averaging periods of two weeks, 30 days after the application is made, if the other conditions are met.

FYI

Class Actions and Overtime Claims

Overtime pay is a common source of employment standards claims. The provisions can be complicated to apply. For example, an employer may misclassify an employee as a manager when he is not, or fail to keep track of overtime hours worked. Recently, overtime claims have also become headline news. Two legal developments in Ontario and elsewhere in Canada have contributed to this:

1. Amendments to the law have made it easier to file class action claims. A class action is a form of lawsuit in which a group of plaintiffs who have a common complaint combine their claims and sue the defendant in a single lawsuit (Bongarde Media Co., 2009, p. 3). As a result, the dollar amounts involved in class actions are often in the millions (or hundreds of millions) of dollars.

2. Court decisions have now established that employees are *not* restricted to filing ESA claims, including claims for overtime, through the Ontario Ministry of Labour. They may pursue ESA entitlements through the civil courts, where class actions are heard, instead. This results from the courts' finding that *an employer's obligation to meet the ESA's requirements is an implied part of every employment contract* and thus can be pursued in court as a breach of contract.

A review of recent class action claims based on overtime pay illustrates their potential magnitude. For example, a claim for $600 million was made against CIBC on the basis that the employer routinely refused to pay overtime to tellers and other front-line workers. In *McCracken v. Canadian National Railway Company*, a claim was made for $300 million on the basis that employees were incorrectly classified as supervisors and managers.

Not all class action claims are allowed to proceed. For a class action to be brought, a plaintiff representing the class has to get a civil court judge to "certify" it. This requires the plaintiff to prove that, among other things, there are common issues of law or fact involved, a representative plaintiff will adequately represent the class, and a class action is the preferred proceeding. For example, in the *McCracken* case, the Ontario Court of Appeal held that the court could not certify the class action because determining the managerial status of the employees required an individualized assessment. In that case, there were 70 different job positions that held the same title ("first line supervisor"), with some exercising greater decision-making authority than others, depending on location and other factors (Sherrard Kuzz LLP, 2012).

In contrast, in *Rosen v. BMO Nesbitt Burns Inc.* a class action by a group of investment advisers was certified. There, the employees alleged that they were misclassified as managers and improperly denied overtime pay under the ESA, despite working more than 60 hours a week. The employer countered that the investment advisers were exempt from the overtime requirements for one or both of the following reasons. First, they were employed in a managerial/supervisory capacity. Second, their overall autonomy and potential for high earnings provided them with a greater benefit than the overtime pay provisions of the ESA (s. 5) and therefore overrode the overtime provisions. Although at the time of writing no decision on the merits of the case has been made, it appears possible that having high, commission-based earnings and exercising considerable autonomy over their own work does not mean that employees are necessarily exempt from the ESA's overtime pay requirements (Pugen, 2013).

Moreover, in two separate cases involving thousands of bank employees—*Canadian Imperial Bank of Commerce v. Dara Fresco* ($600 million claimed) and *Bank of Nova Scotia v. Cindy Fulawka* ($350 million claimed)—the Supreme Court of Canada has now certified class action suits based on overtime claims. In both cases, the plaintiff employee class members alleged that, contrary to the *Canada Labour Code*'s overtime provisions, they were required to get pre-approval from a manager before they could be compensated for overtime that they were required or permitted to perform. In certifying these class action suits, the court found that because the key issue is the legality of the banks' overtime policies, an individualized assessment of each individual's claim is unnecessary. (Note that effective August 2014, Scotiabank reached a court-approved settlement with its front-line sales employees in this case. Early estimates of the cost of the settlement are around $95 million) (Canadian Press, 2014).

These class action claims, coupled with the proliferation of smartphones and other electronic devices that enable employees to extend their workday, underscore the need for employers to ensure that their overtime policies and practices comply with the requirements of the ESA.

Employers should take the following steps to ensure compliance:

1. Make sure the overtime rules are fully understood (for example, not all salaried employees are exempt from overtime requirements) and that employees are classified properly so that only those who are truly managers or supervisors are exempt from overtime pay. (Note that even employees who are exempt by statute may be entitled to overtime pay under their employment contract or an office policy.) Job titles do not determine status. Periodically review job duties to ensure that the work being done continues to match their categorization (Piccolo, 2013).

2. If possible, don't schedule non-managerial employees for more than 44 hours a week (or whatever the limit for non-overtime hours is under the terms of their employment agreement) and make sure that employees leave work at the end of those hours. Allowing an employee to stay late, even though it is not required or asked of the employee, potentially makes the employer liable for paying any resulting overtime.

3. Review job descriptions and performance targets to determine whether overtime hours are inherent in the workload.

4. Ensure that agreements to extend the hours of work or to average overtime pay fully comply with the ESA—"almost" in compliance does not count.

5. Monitor and maintain accurate records of the hours worked and the amount paid. Without documentation it will be difficult to prove that legislative requirements were met.

6. Have a clear policy that lets employees know whether they are eligible to work overtime and, if so, what the reporting arrangements are (Sherrard Kuzz LLP, 2012). Such a policy should also specifically address travel time and the amount of electronic work being done during off hours (Loewenberg and Lisi, 2008, p. 5). Some employers ban the use of smartphones or similar devices for work purposes between certain hours or limit them to emergency use.

7. Clearly communicate and consistently enforce the overtime policy.

SOURCE: Based on information from Loewenberg and Lisi (2008, p. 4).

Time Off Instead of Overtime Pay

An employer and employee may agree that the employee will receive paid time off work instead of overtime pay. The agreement must be in writing, and the employee must receive 1.5 hours of paid time off for each hour of overtime worked. For example, if the employee works 48 hours in a week and therefore is entitled to 4 hours at the overtime rate, that employee may agree in writing to take 6 hours (1.5×4 hours) of paid time off in lieu of overtime pay. Without such a written agreement, the employer must provide overtime pay (at 1.5 times the employee's regular rate of pay) to compensate for overtime hours worked.

Paid time off must be taken within 3 months of the week in which the overtime was earned or within 12 months if the employee agrees in writing. On leaving employment, the employee must be paid any overtime pay owing with his final payment of wages.

4. Vacation

Vacation time and vacation pay, which are covered in ss. 33 to 41 of the ESA, are separate entitlements. An employee may be entitled to vacation pay but not vacation time, depending on whether she has worked a full year for the employer.

Vacation Time

Employees are entitled to at least two weeks' vacation time per year after they have worked for an employer for a full 12 months. An employee who resigns before completing a full year of employment is not entitled to vacation time, only vacation pay.

An employee may take her two-week vacation time in either one-week or two-week intervals. Vacation time can be taken in periods of less than one week only if the parties agree in writing. (See the section entitled "Agreements to Vary" above.)

The employer is entitled to decide when vacation time will be taken. For example, the employer can designate a plant shutdown for a week at Christmas, during which all employees take a vacation. However, the employer must give the vacation time within 10 months after it is earned. For example, if Carlos starts work on January 1, 2014, his employer is required to provide him with two weeks' vacation before November 1, 2015 because he earned his vacation time in the 12 months between January 2014 and January 2015 and November 1, 2015 is 10 months after that period.

Periods of inactive service—such as time that an employee is away from work because of layoff, sickness, injury, approved leaves, or statutory leaves such as pregnancy, parental, or emergency leave—are included in calculating the 12 months' employment. An employee who is on a statutory leave does not lose the right to take vacation time, although she may receive no vacation pay. Vacation time may be taken after the statutory leave expires or at a later date if the parties agree. The employee does not have to shorten the statutory leave or risk losing some or all of her vacation time. If any employee, including an employee who has been on leave, wants to forgo vacation time, she may do so with the agreement of the employer *and* the approval of the Director of Employment Standards. An employee cannot agree to forgo vacation pay.

Vacation Pay

Under the legislation, employees are entitled to vacation pay that is at least equal to 4 percent of gross wages earned (excluding the vacation pay) during the 12-month period for which the vacation pay is given. For example, if Eli earns $25,000 a year, he is entitled to receive 4 percent of that amount as vacation pay, which is $1,000. For full-time employees, 4 percent of earnings typically equals two weeks' pay. Where an employee works irregular hours, has worked many hours, or was laid off in the previous 12 months, 4 percent of earnings could be considerably more or less than two weeks' wages. When determining vacation pay, "wages" include overtime pay, public holiday pay, termination pay, and commissions.

The entitlement to vacation pay begins from the first hour of employment. An employee who leaves at any time must be given all vacation pay earned to that point. For instance, an employee who works only three days is entitled to 4 percent of the wages earned during those three days.

Many employers offer more vacation time and pay than the statutory minimum. In fact, employers usually provide at least three weeks' vacation time and 6 percent vacation pay after five years of service. The workplace trend is toward recognizing the importance of leisure time. Even four weeks' vacation at an 8 percent rate is becoming common for employees with as little as three to five years of service.

Vacation pay must be paid in a lump sum before the beginning of the employee's vacation. However, the legislation allows alternative methods where

1. the employee is paid by direct deposit, in which case vacation pay must be paid on or before the payday for the period in which the vacation falls;
2. the employee takes vacation in periods of less than one week, in which case vacation pay must be paid on or before the payday for the period in which the vacation falls;
3. the employer and employee agree that payment is to be made at some other time; or
4. the employee agrees in writing to have vacation pay accrue on each paycheque. In this common situation, the wage statement must show the amount of vacation pay being paid.

Where an employee's employment is terminated, vacation pay must be paid in respect of the statutory notice period but not on severance pay. (See Chapter 14 for discussion of notice and severance pay requirements.)

Vacation Entitlement and Statutory Leaves of Absence

An employee continues to earn credits toward vacation time during statutory leaves of absence, such as pregnancy, parental, and emergency leaves. However, the impact of those leaves on vacation pay depends on the terms of the contract of employment. For example, where either a collective agreement or an individual contract provides that the employee earns two paid vacation days for every month of service, both vacation time and pay are earned through service and therefore continue to accumulate during statutory leaves.

However, where vacation pay is based on earnings, the amount of vacation pay is affected by statutory leaves because it is calculated as a percentage of wages earned, and an employee does not usually earn wages during a leave. For example, an employee on pregnancy and parental leave for the year preceding the vacation time would probably have no earnings from the employer. Therefore, vacation pay would not be owing, although vacation time entitlement would continue to accumulate.

5. Public Holidays

Sections 24 to 32 of the ESA set out the provisions related to public holidays.

Nine Public Holidays

As set out in the definitions in s. 1, the nine paid public holidays, often called statutory holidays, that employees are entitled to each year are: New Year's Day, Family Day (third Monday in February), Good Friday, Victoria Day, Canada Day, Labour Day, Thanksgiving Day, Christmas Day, and Boxing Day (December 26). Many employers also provide the first Monday in August and/or other holidays, but these additional days are not required under the ESA.

When the newest public holiday, Family Day, was first introduced in 2007, many employers questioned whether they had to honour it. This is because, under the ESA, where an employer provides a greater benefit with respect to a particular standard, the ESA provisions on that standard do not apply. This is subject to the specific wording in any written employment contract or policy that may indicate otherwise. For example, if the employment agreement or policy entitles employees to receive two floating personal days in addition to the statutory holidays required by the ESA, the employer may be contractually bound to provide the new holiday (Sherrard Kuzz LLP, 2009). On the other hand, where no such contractual obligation exists, the employer does not have to provide exactly the same public holidays as those found in the ESA (such as Family Day) as long as its public holiday package, in total, provides a greater benefit than the ESA. For example, if an employer provides 11 paid public holidays, it probably does not have to add Family Day because its public holiday package already exceeds the statutory standard.

Qualifying for Paid Public Holidays

Most employees are eligible for public holidays. However, employees who work in certain industries, such as hotels, restaurants, and hospitals, may be required to work on a public holiday. An employee who performs more than one kind of work, only some of which is exempt from paid public holidays, is eligible for a paid public holiday if at least half of the work performed in the week of the holiday is non-exempt work.

Employees must fulfill two conditions to qualify for a paid public holiday. To be eligible, they must *not*

1. fail, without reasonable cause, to work their entire shift on either of their regularly scheduled days of work immediately before or immediately after the public holiday; or
2. fail, without reasonable cause, to work their entire shift on the public holiday if they agreed to work or were required to work that day.

Employees who have a legitimate reason for not working on the regularly scheduled day of work before or after the public holiday, such as illness, are entitled to the paid public holiday.

"Regularly scheduled day of work before or after the public holiday" does not necessarily mean the day right before and right after the holiday. The employee need only work all of her *regularly scheduled shift* before and after the public holiday or provide a reasonable cause for not working. The employee may not be scheduled to work the day right before or right after the holiday for a number of reasons. For example, the employee may not usually work that day, the employee may have obtained the employer's permission to take the day off, or the employee may be on vacation or statutory leave.

Calculating Public Holiday Pay

The amount of public holiday pay that an employee is entitled to is calculated by adding all regular wages (not including overtime) and vacation pay that is owing to the employee in the four workweeks ending just before the workweek with the public holiday and dividing by 20. If an employee chooses to take a substitute day off with public holiday pay, this calculation is based on the four workweeks before the workweek in which the substitute day falls. A workweek is set by an employer, and therefore the calculation is not necessarily based on the four calendar weeks immediately preceding the holiday.

This calculation is meant to provide an employee with an amount equal to his average daily earnings over the month before the public holiday. The following three examples show how it works:

- EXAMPLE 1: Izumi works eight hours a day, five days a week, earning $200 per day and $1,000 per week. She qualifies for the public holiday. She earned $4,000 in the relevant four-workweek period, and so her public holiday pay is $200 ($4,000 ÷ 20). In other words, she receives her typical day's pay.
- EXAMPLE 2: Owen earns $20 per hour working part time on an as-required basis. Some days he works eight hours while others he works two or three hours. In the relevant four-workweek period before the public holiday he earned $1,000. His public holiday pay is $50 ($1,000 ÷ 20). This reflects his average daily wage over the period before the holiday.
- EXAMPLE 3: Joshua is in the middle of his parental leave. Although he receives parental benefits under the federal employment insurance program, he has no wages from his employer in the relevant four-workweek period. He is not entitled to public holiday pay because he did not earn any wages or vacation pay during that period.

When a Public Holiday Falls on a Workday

Unless an employer operates in certain kinds of industries, such as essential services or the hospitality industry, or has continuous operations, an employee may agree, but cannot be required, to work on a public holiday that falls on a regular working day. If the employee agrees to work, the employee may either

- receive regular wages on that day plus a substitute day off, or
- if both parties agree in writing, receive public holiday pay for that day plus premium pay.

Premium pay is 1.5 times an employee's regular rate of pay. Thus, premium pay for an employee whose regular rate of pay is $12 per hour will be $18 per hour. For example:

Luke has agreed to work on a public holiday and receive public holiday pay plus premium pay for all hours worked. His hourly rate is $12 per hour and he earned $1,920 in the relevant four-workweek period. If Luke worked 8 hours on the public holiday, his earnings on that day will be as follows:

Public holiday pay: $1,920 ÷ 20 = $96

Premium pay: $12 × 1.5 = $18 per hour
$18 × 8 hours = $144

Luke's total entitlement for working on the public holiday is $96 + $144 = $240.

If an employee chooses to take a substitute holiday, the holiday must be scheduled no later than 3 months after the public holiday. However, the employee and the employer may agree, in writing, to schedule the substitute day off up to 12 months after the public holiday. Hours worked for premium pay on a public holiday are not included in calculating overtime hours.

When a Public Holiday Falls on a Non-Working Day

When a public holiday falls on a non-working day, an employee may either

- take a substitute day off with public holiday pay within 3 months of the public holiday or, if both parties agree, within 12 months of the public holiday; or
- receive public holiday pay for the public holiday instead of receiving a substitute day off by agreeing to do so in writing.

Special Rules for Certain Industries

Employers in certain businesses, such as hotels, motels, tourist resorts, recreational and amusement services, restaurants, taverns, hospitals, nursing homes, and continuous operations (that is, an operation that does not stop or close more than once a week), may require an employee to work on a public holiday. If so, the employee is entitled to either

- her regular rate of pay for the hours worked plus a substitute day off, or
- public holiday pay plus premium pay for each hour worked.

In these industries, the employer chooses which of these options the employee receives. A substitute day off must be taken within 3 months after the public holiday or within 12 months if both parties agree in writing.

Special Rights for Retail Workers

Most retail workers, other than those in the industries noted above, have special rights to refuse to work on a public holiday. If a retail worker agrees to work on a public holiday, he may subsequently refuse to work on that day if he gives his employer at least 48 hours' notice.

Furthermore, retail workers have special rights related to Sunday employment. Retail workers who were hired before September 4, 2001 may refuse to work on Sundays. An employee who has agreed to work on Sundays may subsequently refuse to do so by giving the employer at least 48 hours' notice. Retail employees hired on or after September 4, 2001 have the right to refuse to work on Sundays unless they agreed, in writing, at the time they were hired to work on Sundays. They can subsequently refuse to work on Sundays only for reasons of religious belief, in accordance with human rights legislation.

6. Statutory Leaves of Absence

The ESA now provides for ten types of statutory leave: pregnancy, parental, personal emergency, family medical, declared emergency, reservist, organ donor, family caregiver, critically ill childcare, and crime-related child death or disappearance leave. An employer is not required to pay employees while they are on statutory leave. However, employees who exercise their right to statutory leave are entitled to certain other statutory rights and protections, discussed below.

FYI

Pregnancy Leave in Ontario

Until the 1960s, pregnancy was considered just cause for termination. The first pregnancy leave provisions came into the *Employment Standards Act* in 1972. In 1975, the Act was amended to require reinstatement of a returning employee to the same or a comparable position, rather than simply entitling her to "resume work." The legislation now provides that an employee returning from pregnancy leave must be returned to the same position and only to a "comparable" position if the pre-leave position no longer exists.

Pregnancy Leave

Sections 46 and 47 govern pregnancy leave. A pregnant employee has the right to take up to 17 weeks' unpaid time off work. The employee may be eligible for employment insurance benefits during this time, but the employer is not required to pay the employee during the leave.

To qualify for pregnancy leave, the employee must have been hired at least 13 weeks before the expected due date. She does not need to have actively worked for the 13 weeks. For example, an employee hired 16 weeks before her due date is eligible for pregnancy leave even if her baby is born prematurely 10 weeks after her hiring.

It is up to the employee, not the employer, to decide when to start her pregnancy leave. However, the ESA does set some parameters on when pregnancy leave may be taken. The earliest a pregnancy leave can begin is usually 17 weeks before the employee's due date, and the latest it can begin is on the due date or when the baby is born.

If an employee needs to leave her job early for health reasons, she does not have to start her leave when she stops working; she may go on sick leave if she chooses. If any portion of an individual's absence before or after the birth of a child is related to a bona fide medical condition, the employee is entitled to whatever short-term disability benefits are available to other employees in the workplace.

A pregnant employee is supposed to give her employer at least two weeks' written notice before beginning her leave. However, there is no penalty for failing to provide this notice. If the employer requests it, the employee must subsequently provide a medical certificate stating the due date and the date of birth, stillbirth, or miscarriage.

For most employees, a pregnancy leave is 17 weeks, although an employee may take a shorter leave if she wishes. However, once pregnancy leave is started, the employee must take it all at once; when she returns to work, she gives up the right to take the remainder of the leave. In the case of miscarriages or stillbirths, the pregnancy leave may slightly exceed 17 weeks because leave ends on the later of 17 weeks after it begins or six weeks after the stillbirth or miscarriage.

If the employee does not specify the date when she will be returning to work, the employer must assume that she is taking the full 17 weeks. An employee who decides to return to work earlier than indicated must provide the employer with at least four weeks' notice before the earlier return date. This allows the employer time to make an alternative arrangement for the person who is taking the employee's place during her pregnancy leave. An employee who decides to resign before the end of her pregnancy leave is required to give the employer at least four weeks' written notice of her resignation.

FYI

Use It or Lose It Paternity Leave

WOULD MORE MEN TAKE A "USE IT OR LOSE IT" PATERNITY LEAVE?
Rather than focusing on ways to bring women back into the work force after having children, it's worth exploring how to provide incentives for men to step out.

In Norway, fathers receive 12 weeks of paternity leave that is non-transferable to the mother: dads must "use it or lose it." In Sweden, fathers get about eight weeks of non-transferable paternity leave. In Quebec, they get five weeks. ...

"Daddy quotas" carry a lingering, positive impact on fathers. A study by Ankita Patnaik, a doctoral student at Cornell University, found that men who took advantage of parental leave spent more time on child care and domestic obligations even years later. And their female partners spent more time working outside the home.

SOURCE: Leah Eichler, "Would More Men Take a 'Use It or Lose It' Paternity Leave?" *Globe and Mail*, April 12, 2013. Leah Eichler is CEO of r/ally and a columnist for The Globe and Mail. Used with permission.

Parental Leave

Sections 48 and 49, the parental leave provisions of the ESA, were passed in 1990, almost 20 years after pregnancy leave was first enacted. Unlike pregnancy leave, which is available only to birth mothers, parental leave is available to any new parent. It is intended to give new parents time to adjust to their new family roles. To qualify, an employee must have been hired at least 13 weeks before the leave begins. As in the case of pregnancy leave, the employee need not actively work for these 13 weeks to be eligible.

The term "parent" is broadly defined to include a birth parent, an adoptive parent, or a person who is in a relationship of some permanence with a parent of the child and who plans on treating the child as his or her own. This includes same-sex couples who give birth to or adopt children. A birth mother who takes pregnancy leave must usually start her parental leave as soon as her pregnancy leave ends. An exception is made if the child has not yet come into her care, such as when a baby remains hospitalized.

All other parents must begin parental leave within 52 weeks after the child is born or first comes into their care, custody, and control. A father's parental leave does not necessarily have to start immediately after a mother's pregnancy leave ends, for example.

Parental leave for birth mothers who take pregnancy leave can last up to 35 weeks. For all other new parents, parental leave can last up to 37 weeks. Parental leave must be taken at one time. An employee does not have the right to take part of the leave, return to work, then go back on parental leave, unless the employer agrees.

Employees are required to give their employer at least two weeks' written notice before beginning a parental leave or before changing the proposed leave date. However, there is no penalty for failing to give this notice. An employer cannot require an employee to return from leave early. An employee who decides to return to work earlier than the previously scheduled date must provide the employer with at least four weeks' written notice. An employee who decides to resign on or before the end of the parental leave is required to give the employer at least four weeks' written notice of resignation as well.

Both parents are entitled to take the full period of parental leave. If the mother and the mother's partner, for example, both work for the same employer, the employer is required to provide 52 weeks of combined pregnancy/parental leave for the mother and 37 weeks of parental leave for the mother's partner. Their leaves may overlap or the mother's partner could begin parental leave as the mother is returning from her leave. Alternatively, both the mother and her partner could take their leaves at the same time.

For employment insurance benefit purposes, one or both parents may apply for the 35 weeks of EI parental benefits. However, if they both apply, their combined benefits claim cannot exceed 35 weeks. At the same time, only one 2-week waiting period need be served before benefits begin.

Personal Emergency Leave

First introduced in 2000, s. 50 of the ESA entitles employees to up to ten unpaid days of leave each calendar year to deal with certain emergency situations. To qualify, an employee must work for an employer that regularly employs at least 50 people. The emergency leave provision is one of only two employee entitlements under the ESA (the other being severance pay provisions, discussed in Chapter 14) that depend on the size of the employer's organization. This presumably recognizes that small employers typically are less able to absorb unscheduled absences. The Ministry has developed a policy to explain how it determines whether the 50-employee threshold has been reached when employment has fluctuated throughout the year.

Emergency leaves are allowed for any of the following reasons:

1. personal illness, injury, or medical emergency; or
2. death, illness, injury, medical emergency, or another urgent matter relating to
   a. a spouse or same-sex partner of the employee;
   b. a parent, step-parent, foster parent, child, step-child, foster child, grand-parent, step-grandparent, grandchild, or step-grandchild of the employee, the employee's spouse, or the employee's same-sex partner;
   c. a spouse or same-sex partner of an employee's child;
   d. a brother or sister of the employee; or
   e. a relative of the employee who is dependent on the employee for care or assistance. For example, if an employee has primary responsibility for the care of an aging uncle, the emergency leave provisions may be applicable.

According to Ministry policy, an "urgent matter" that relates to individuals other than the employee must be unplanned or out of the employee's control and involve the possibility of serious negative consequences, including emotional harm, if left unattended. The test of urgency is objective: would a reasonable person in the employee's circumstances feel that the matter is urgent? Urgent situations include a cancellation call from an employee's babysitter where no one else is available to care for the employee's child or an unexpected call from the school of an employee's child asking the employee to pick the child up.

The employer may request proof that the leave is required, and the employee must provide proof that "is reasonable in the circumstances." According to the Ministry's policy, proof may consist of doctor's notes, death certificates, notes from a school or daycare facility, or receipts. However, an employer cannot require detailed medical information concerning a diagnosis or treatment. Where the emergency relates to a relative's medical emergency, the employer cannot require a medical certificate because the relative has no obligation to share her medical information. In these circumstances, the employee must disclose only the relative's name and her relationship to the employee. The employee must also provide a statement that the absence is required because of an illness, injury, or medical emergency.

The ten emergency days need not be taken consecutively, and a partial day is counted as a full day. An employee who requires emergency leave must inform the employer beforehand if possible; otherwise, the employee must inform the employer as soon as possible afterward.

The entitlement to emergency leave applies equally to part-time, full-time, and temporary employees. An employee who starts work partway through the calendar year is entitled to the full ten days in that year. However, emergency days cannot be carried over from one calendar year to the next.

The emergency leave provisions do not apply where leaving work would constitute an act of professional misconduct or a dereliction of duty for persons employed in certain professions, such as architecture, law, professional engineering, teaching, or dentistry. For example, a dentist cannot insist on using the emergency leave provisions if it means leaving a patient in the middle of corrective surgery.

As with the other provisions of the ESA, if the terms of an individual employment contract or a collective agreement provide the employee with a greater benefit, those terms prevail over the emergency leave provisions of the ESA. According to Ministry policy, an example of this would be a contract that entitles employees to ten days of paid personal sick leave each year but does not allow time off for emergencies involving relatives. It prevails over the ESA, even though it is less generous than the statutory leave in some regards. In this situation, an employee who takes all ten days of paid personal sick leave in a calendar year cannot insist on taking additional unpaid days under the emergency leave provisions to care for a sick family member.

If an absence qualifies as a leave under both an employment contract and the ESA, it is counted against both entitlements. For example, a personal sick day taken off will count both as one of the ten statutory emergency leave days and as one of the employee's personal sick leave days if these entitlements are provided for under the employee's contract of employment. However, these emergency leave provisions do not remove an employer's ongoing obligations under human rights legislation.

Family Medical Leave

Under amendments made to the ESA in 2004, employees are now entitled under s. 49.1 to take up to 8 weeks of unpaid leave to care for a gravely ill family member. To qualify, an employee must provide a certificate from a qualified health practitioner indicating that the family member has a serious medical condition and that there is a significant risk of death within a 26-week period. Family medical leave may be taken for the following family (or people like family) members:

- an employee's spouse, including a common law or same-sex partner;
- an employee's parent, step-parent, or foster parent;
- a child, step-child, or foster child of the employee or the employee's spouse;
- a (step) brother or sister of the employee;
- a (step) grandparent of the employee or of the employee's spouse;
- a (step) grandchild of the employee or of the employee's spouse;
- a (step) father-in-law or mother-in-law of the employee;
- a (step) brother-in-law or sister-in-law of the employee;
- a son-in-law or daughter-in-law of the employee or of the employee's spouse;
- an uncle or aunt of the employee or of the employee's spouse;
- the nephew or niece of the employee or of the employee's spouse;
- the spouse of the employee's grandchild, uncle, aunt, nephew, or niece;
- a foster parent of the employee's spouse; or
- a person who considers the employee to be like a family member (O. reg. 476/06, s. 1(1)).

The purpose of the leave must be to provide "care or support" to the sick family member. This includes providing emotional support and taking time to arrange care by a care provider. A "qualified health practitioner" is an individual who is qualified to practise medicine under the laws of the jurisdiction where the family member is being treated, whether inside or outside Canada. In Ontario only medical doctors can currently issue a certificate.

Family medical leave is available to employees irrespective of the size of their employer. It operates in addition to emergency leave, so employers with 50 or more employees must provide both emergency leave and family medical leave to employees who qualify. For example, an employee who has a sick parent may take up to ten days' leave under the emergency leave provisions and up to 8 weeks of family medical leave to provide care if a qualified health practitioner issues the requisite medical certificate. All employees, regardless of length of service or number of hours worked in a week, are eligible for family medical leave.

Employees wishing to take family medical leave are required to provide advance notice in writing, if possible; otherwise, notice should be provided as soon as possible after the leave begins. The employee is responsible for obtaining and paying for the certificate, and the employer is entitled to receive a copy of it.

Under the ESA, the 8 weeks' leave need not be taken consecutively, but the time may be taken only in periods of full weeks. Where more than one employee takes leave to care for the same family member, the total leave cannot exceed 8 weeks during a 26-week period. For example, if one spouse takes 5 weeks' family medical leave to take care of her child, the other spouse can take only 3 weeks. This rule applies whether or not the spouses work for the same employer.

These ESA provisions are meant to complement compassionate care benefits under the federal *Employment Insurance Act*, and employers should issue a record of employment for any employee going on family medical leave. However, because there are minimum hour requirements for employment insurance benefits, some employees who are eligible for leave are not entitled to employment insurance benefits.

If the sick family member survives the 26-week period, the employee may be entitled to take a second leave of up to 8 weeks in a second 26-week period if another medical certificate is issued. The employee may or may not be eligible for employment insurance benefits, depending on the hours of work they have accumulated in the intervening period.

Family medical leave ends on the earlier of

- the last day of the week in which the family member dies,
- the last day of the week in which the 26-week leave period ends, or
- the last day of the 8 weeks of family medical leave.

FYI

Ontario's Three Newest Job-Protected Leaves

On October 29, 2014, three new job-protected leaves, all of which build on the existing family medical leave, came into effect. They are as follows:

1. *Family caregiver leave.* Employees can take up to eight weeks of unpaid leave to provide care and support to a family member (including someone who is like family) with a "serious medical condition." This leave requires a certificate from a health practitioner (which can include a registered nurse or psychologist, not just a physician) indicating that the family member has a "serious medical condition."

2. *Critically ill childcare leave.* Employees with at least six months' service can take up to 37 weeks of unpaid leave to provide care or support to a critically ill child (someone under 18 years of age) whose life is at risk because of illness or injury. A qualified health practitioner must certify that the child is critically ill and requires the care or support of one or more parents; the certificate should also indicate the time period for which the care or support is required.

3. *Crime-related child death or disappearance leave.* Employees with at least six months' service can

take up to 52 weeks of unpaid leave if they are parents of a missing child where it is probable that the child's disappearance was a result of crime. Similarly, such employees can take up to 104 weeks of unpaid leave if they are parents of a child who has died and it is probable that the death was a result of a crime.

These leaves are in addition to the current family medical leave, which is available only when a family member has a serious medical condition *with a significant risk of death occurring within 26 weeks*. Moreover, unlike personal emergency leave, which only applies to employers with 50 or more employees, these leaves would apply regardless of the size of the employer (Whitten & Lublin Employment Lawyers, 2014).

Declared Emergency Leave

Declared emergency leave is distinct from, and in addition to, personal emergency leave. Employees are entitled, regardless of length of service, to an unpaid leave of absence if they are not performing the duties of their position because of a *declared* emergency under s. 7.0.1 of the Ontario *Emergency Management and Civil Protection Act*—for example, a SARS- or H1N1-type epidemic or a power blackout—and one of certain other eligibility criteria is met. For example, if the employee is needed to give care or assistance to any one of a list of individuals set out in s. 50.1(8) during a declared emergency, the eligibility criteria are met. This list includes: the employee's spouse; a parent, step-parent, or foster parent of the employee or the employee's spouse; a child, step-child, or foster child of the employee or the employee's spouse; the spouse of the employee's child; the employee's sibling; or a relative of the employee who is dependent on the employee for care or assistance.

The employer may require an employee taking this leave to provide reasonable evidence of his entitlement to it. The leave will last as long as the employee is not performing his job duties because of the declared emergency *and* the employee continues to be needed to care for or assist someone in the above list, for example.

An employee may also be entitled to declared emergency leave when there is a declared emergency and the medical officer of health has taken certain measures to prevent, or deal with, the outbreak of a communicable disease.

Reservist Leave

As of December 3, 2007, employees who are reservists in the military and who are deployed, either internationally or domestically, are entitled to unpaid leave for the time required to engage in the operation. These engagements could include search and rescue operations, national disaster relief, or military operations. For international operations, the leave includes pre-deployment and post-deployment activities. To be eligible for reservist leave, an employee must have worked for her employer for at least six consecutive months. Generally, leave is only available to reservists who provide their employer with reasonable written notice, including the dates on which they will begin and end the leave.

One special feature of reservist leave is that an employer may postpone the employee's reinstatement for two weeks after the end of the leave or one pay period, whichever is later.

Organ Donor Leave

People who donate all or part of an organ to another individual are entitled to unpaid statutory leave. To be eligible, donors have to be employed by the same employer for at least 13 weeks before taking the leave. If required by the employer, they must provide a medical certificate as evidence of their eligibility for the leave. The leave itself is for 13 weeks, with a possibility of extension of another 13 weeks where a qualified medical practitioner provides a certificate stating that the employee is not yet able to resume his duties because of the organ donation. Again, two weeks' written notice (or as soon as possible if circumstances do not permit two weeks' notice) is required.

Employee Rights During Statutory Leaves

Employees who take leave under the ESA have considerable rights and protections. These are found in ss. 51 to 53. They are designed to ensure that employees are put in the same position that they would have been in if they had not taken leave. This reflects the public policy that no employee should suffer negative consequences because he exercises the right to take a statutorily guaranteed leave. The following rights are guaranteed under the ESA.

1. *Right to reinstatement.* When a statutory leave ends, an employer must reinstate the employee in the *same* position if it still exists or in a comparable position if it does not exist. Employers should be aware that the employee may be brought back to a "comparable" job only if the pre-leave job truly no longer exists. For example, an employer may find that the individual hired to replace the employee on leave is doing a much better job and it wishes to keep him or her instead. Knowing that the returning employee has a right to reinstatement, the employer may want to bring the employee back to a different but "comparable" job. It may even try to "reorganize" the workplace so that the original position no longer exists. If the returning employee files a complaint in such a circumstance, an employment standards officer will review the employer's claim that the returning employee's position no longer exists. If any employee is still performing the returning employee's pre-leave duties, or if those duties have been distributed to a number of other employees (unless it is part of a more general restructuring), the returning employee's job may be deemed to still exist, and the employee must be returned to it.

    Where the pre-leave job no longer exists, the employer may bring the returning employee back to a comparable job. For a job to be "comparable," the salary must be at least equal to what the employee received before taking leave. There should be no significant change in duties, level of responsibility, location, hours, job security, and opportunity for promotion.

    An employer is relieved of the obligation to reinstate a returning employee only if his employment is terminated for reasons unrelated to the leave, such as elimination of his job because of downsizing, and there is no comparable position. The onus is then on the employer to prove that there was no connection between the leave and the termination of employment. For example, in

Moday and Bell Mobility Inc., the employer was able to show that Moday's job category had been eliminated as part of a much larger reorganization. The adjudicator held that the employer did not have to reinstate Moday to the same or a comparable position after her pregnancy leave. Deciding otherwise would, in the adjudicator's view, create a "startling proposition" in that it would "place relatively young male or female employees off on parental leave in a vastly superior position to any other employee during a downsizing, including very senior workers or employees off on sick or disability leave" (Smith, 2013). The test is whether or not the employee would have lost his job if he had not taken leave. Because pregnancy and parental leaves can last for up to one year, employers may be required to hold a position open for several years in a row. An employee or the employee's spouse may become pregnant while on leave, and leaves may be taken back-to-back. An employee who is not reinstated as required under the ESA, or who is terminated shortly after reinstatement, may file a claim with the Ministry of Labour, and the employer may be ordered to immediately reinstate the individual to the pre-leave position.

The following case of *P.S.S. Professional Salon Services* illustrates the high standard that an employer has to meet to justify a decision not to reinstate an employee after a statutory leave. Although the employee chose to pursue her claim under human rights legislation, rather than employment standards legislation, the employer's onus of proof and the issues involved are similar.

CASE IN POINT

"But For" the Leave Would She Have Been Dismissed?

P.S.S. Professional Salon Services Inc. v. Saskatchewan (Human Rights Commission), 2007 SKCA 149

Facts

Hitchings worked for P.S.S., a small distributor of hair care products. She performed her job duties fairly well but a few months after she started work other employees began to complain about working with her. A co-worker came to the owner, Campbell, in tears to say she found working with Hitchings stressful; Hitchings' own supervisor confided that Hitchings' attitude was giving her stomach aches. Campbell chose not to bring the matter up with her at that time because Hitchings was just about to go on pregnancy leave. He later admitted that had he spoken to her then, he would have disciplined, rather than terminated, her.

However, after Hitchings went on her leave, Campbell heard about more incidents of misconduct. He was told that she had often tried to undermine his authority, had used crude language when referring to him, and had insulted other employees. He was also told that she encouraged employees to leave work an hour early because that's when her supervisor left. Months later, when Hitchings contacted Campbell with her return date, her supervisor told him that she did not want Hitchings back and a co-worker said that if Hitchings returned she would quit. Campbell decided not to let Hitchings return to work; instead, he terminated her employment with two weeks' pay in lieu of notice.

Hitchings filed a human rights complaint based on gender discrimination. The employer responded that her termination was in no way related to her leave. Many employees in its female-dominated workplace had taken leaves and returned without incident and her replacement had been hired on a temporary basis. Her dismissal, Campbell argued, was entirely due to the negative reports he had received while she was on leave.

The Saskatchewan Human Rights Tribunal found for Hitchings. It stated that the onus was on the employer to show that Hitchings' dismissal was totally unrelated to her leave and that it had not met this burden of proof. The Tribunal did not believe that the employer would have dismissed her without any investigation or warnings had she been at work rather than on pregnancy leave. Hitchings was awarded approximately $4,400 for loss of income and for injury to her feelings.

The employer's appeal to the Saskatchewan Court of Queen's Bench was denied; it then appealed to the Saskatchewan Court of Appeal.

Relevant Issue

Whether the employer's refusal to reinstate was justified.

Decision

In a **majority decision**, the employer's appeal was allowed. The court noted that even Hitchings testified that it was likely that she was dismissed because she "rocked the boat," rather than because she went on pregnancy leave. The majority noted that the employer's decision to dismiss, rather than discipline, Hitchings was based on the information it received *after* Hitchings began her leave.

However, in a dissenting opinion, one appeal judge agreed with the Tribunal's finding that the employer's refusal to reinstate was unjustified. Although Hitchings' leave may not have been the primary reason for her termination, "but for" her leave she would not have been dismissed, especially not before she had been given an opportunity to give her side of the story. The fact that Hitchings was no longer in the workplace made it easier for the employer to simply dismiss her rather than deal with her alleged misconduct, and therefore the leave was relevant to her dismissal.

Although in this case the employer was eventually successful, the rulings described above show that a refusal to reinstate an employee after a statutory leave will attract a high degree of scrutiny. Certainly in relying on pre-leave misconduct an employer will have to explain why it failed to deal with the misconduct before the leave began. In *P.S.S. Professional Salon Services*, the fact that the employer only found out about certain behaviour after the employee's leave began was crucial in the appeal court's decision.

2. *Right to salary plus increases.* The returning employee must be paid at least as much as she was earning before the leave, plus any raises that she would have received if she had worked throughout the leave.

3. *Right to retain benefits.* During the leave, the employer must continue to pay its share of the premiums for benefit plans, such as pension plans, life insurance, accidental death benefits, extended health insurance plans, and dental plans, offered before the leave. The only exception arises when an employee elects, in writing, not to pay her share of the premiums required by these plans. A birth mother may be able to collect disability benefits during the part of the leave when she would otherwise have been absent from work for health reasons related to the pregnancy or birth. The one leave where the requirement to continue benefits does not apply is reservist leave. The employer does not have to continue any benefit plans unless it chooses to postpone the employee's return date, in which case it must continue benefits for the (maximum two-week) period of postponement.

4. *Right to accrue seniority.* Employees on statutory leave continue to accrue seniority and earn credit for service and length of employment as if they had not taken leave. For example, an employee who works for three years and then takes a year's leave is considered to have four years' service. However, the period of leave is not included for the purpose of completing a probationary period. Therefore, if an employee was on probation at the start of a leave, he must complete the probationary period after returning to work.

5. *Right to vacation entitlement.* An employee on leave does not lose any vacation time entitlement; she may defer vacation until after the leave ends or later, if the employer agrees.

6. *Right to be free from reprisals.* Employees cannot be penalized in any way for taking, planning to take, or being eligible to take a statutory leave.

7. Lie Detector Tests

Sections 68 to 71 of the ESA govern lie detector tests. Employees, including job applicants, have the right not to

- take a lie detector test,
- be asked to take a lie detector test, or
- be required to take a lie detector test.

Disclosing to an employer whether an employee or job applicant has taken a lie detector test, or disclosing the results of such a test, is also prohibited.

These are the only provisions of the ESA that apply to police officers or applicants for a police officer's job. However, they do not apply when the request to take a lie detector test is made by a police officer as part of an investigation of an offence.

8. Termination Notice and Severance Pay

Minimum statutory requirements for termination notice or pay in lieu of notice and severance pay are dealt with in Chapter 14.

9. Temporary Employment Agencies

Sometimes an organization may choose to "hire" an individual through a temporary employment agency. This individual is often referred to as an "agency employee" or a "temp." Unlike the situation where an executive search firm is used to recruit a new employee, agency employees are not actually hired by the organization where they work. They remain employees of the temporary employment agency. They are recruited, hired, and paid by the agency, and the agency is liable for employment standards, such as vacation and public holiday pay. The client organization simply pays the agency.

Protection of Agency Employees by Legislation

Over the past decade there has been a dramatic increase in the use of agency employees. Today, an estimated 20 percent of new hires in Canada are hired through temporary employment agencies, double the figure in 2001. The temporary employment industry in Ontario has gone from a small number of agencies, focusing largely on short-term clerical jobs, to about 1,000 agencies providing workers for a wide range of occupations in the manufacturing, construction, service, health, legal, and information technology sectors. Furthermore, although the typical assignment lasts three weeks, many agency employees are now assigned for several months or even years, usually working side by side with full-time staff.

As the use of agency employees has increased, questions have been raised about whether this group of employees is adequately protected by legislated employment standards, which were formulated with "standard" full-time, permanent employment in mind. For example, until 2009 the ESA exempted "elect-to-work" workers—those who can accept or refuse an agency assignment without negative consequences—from statutory holiday, termination, and severance entitlements. Arguments were made that a second-tier workforce, with significantly fewer legislative protections, was developing. Moreover, people hired through temporary employment agencies are typically paid much less than permanent employees doing the same work because they are paid only a portion of the hourly amount that the temporary employment agency receives from the client organization.

To address some of these concerns, the Ontario government made several changes in 2009. The right to holiday pay, termination notice or pay in lieu of notice, and severance pay is now extended to all elect-to-work employees. Furthermore, the ESA now imposes specific obligations and restrictions on temporary employment agencies. These include:

- Temporary employment agencies must provide their assignment employees with the agency's legal name (and business name, if different) and contact information, in writing.
- When offering a work assignment with a client organization, temporary employment agencies now have to provide to the employee, in writing, client contact information, as well as information on key elements of the assignment, including the wage rate, the hours of work, a general description of the work, and the term of the assignment, if known. They also have to provide an information sheet prepared by the Ministry outlining an agency employee's employment standards rights.
- Temporary employment agencies are prevented from charging agency employees fees for becoming an assignment employee, for finding or helping them find work, for resumé and interview preparation, or for accepting direct employment with a client.
- A temporary employment agency can no longer prevent agency employees from becoming permanent employees of the client organization. It can charge the client in this situation but only if the client hires the agency employee in the first six months of the assignment, beginning on the first day the employee first started to work for the client. It also cannot prevent the client from providing the assignment employee with a letter of reference.
- Neither the agency nor the client organization can penalize an agency employee for asking about, or asserting, his rights under the ESA.

In addition, under proposed amendments to the ESA (Bill 18, *Stronger Workplaces for a Stronger Economy Act, 2014*), client organizations would be jointly and severally liable with temporary agencies for any unpaid "wages" (but not termination and severance pay) of temporary workers. As a result, a client firm could possibly pay twice for the same services: it could pay the temporary agency for the services of the workers and then pay the workers if the temporary agency fails to pay the workers.

The Growing Trend Toward Non-Standard Work: Proposed Amendments to the ESA

Over the past decade there has been a significant trend toward non-standard work. The shift to contract (fixed-term), part-time, and temporary work, as well as to self-employment, means that a stable, permanent job with full-time hours and benefits is no longer the pre-dominant form of employment (Law Commission of Ontario, 2012, p. 7). From an employer's point of view, there are significant benefits to these non-traditional employment relationships. For example, by hiring someone through a temporary employment agency or as a contract employee, the employer achieves greater flexibility, including the ability to cover leaves of absences or peak work periods or to hire people with specialized skills for special projects. Moreover, hiring employees on contract can meet the varying preferences of the four generations now in the work-force. Employees with young children or older parents may not want a full-time, ongoing commitment; new workforce entrants may want to test out a variety of employers and positions before taking on a permanent position; and older employees may be looking for the scheduling flexibility that contract work provides.

That said, for many employees in lower-paying jobs, non-standard work equates to "precarious work" where they receive few, if any, benefits (Silliker, 2012) and there is little job or financial security. Moreover, instead of viewing non-standard work as a short-term means of meeting a temporary need, some employers now see it as a permanent strategy for maintaining a flexi-ble, less costly workforce (Law Commission of Ontario, 2012, p. 16). Just as concerns about agency employees

have led to specific changes in the ESA, questions are being raised about whether the trend away from full-time, permanent employment should lead to a change in the current regulatory framework.

In 2012, the Law Commission of Ontario released *Vulnerable Workers and Precarious Work: Final Report*. Several of the report's recommendations for amend-ing the ESA are found in Bill 18, which received second reading in October 2014. Proposed changes include removing the $10,000 cap on the amount of unpaid wages that an individual can currently recover through the Ministry of Labour; extending the time limit for recovery of wages from 6–12 months to two years; empowering employment standards officers to order employers to conduct a detailed self-audit regarding their ESA compliance, at the employer's expense; and requiring employers to provide each employee with a copy of the ESA poster (as opposed to only posting it in the workplace), in the language of their choice—if available from the Ministry in that language. The Bill would also make temporary employment agencies and their clients jointly responsible for unpaid wages.

Two other proposed changes under Bill 18 are that employers would be prohibited from charging recruit-ment fees to temporary foreign workers and from with-holding personal documents, such as passports. Moreover, young people on co-op placements or unpaid internships approved by a school board or post-secondary institution would be covered under the *Occupational Health and Safety Act*.

Employee Rights Where Employer Is Insolvent

Under s. 14(1) of the ESA, unpaid wages have priority over, and will be paid before, the claims of all other unsecured creditors of an employer up to the amount of $10,000 per employee. This means that if an employer still has assets left over after secured creditors (such as a bank that holds the mortgage on the employer's property) are paid, the Ontario Ministry of Labour will be able to retrieve, on the employees' behalf, up to $10,000 per employee for wages owed before any other unsecured creditor is paid. "Unpaid wages" include vacation pay but not termination or severance pay.

Where an employer has filed for bankruptcy or is in receivership, this priority en-titlement under the ESA no longer applies because bankruptcy and insolvency come under federal jurisdiction. However, in 2008 the federal government implemented a new program called the Wage Earner Protection Program (WEPP) that provides some compensation to employees whose employer goes bankrupt or files for receivership while owing them money for unpaid wages, vacation pay, termination pay, or severance pay.

Under the WEPP, employees are entitled to compensation of up to approximately $3,700 for moneys they became entitled to in the last six months before the bankruptcy or receivership. The claim must be filed with Service Canada within 56 days of the bankruptcy or receivership although late claims may be accepted if a reasonable explanation for the delay is given.

Initially, the WEPP did not cover termination or severance pay. However, as of January 27, 2009, it covers those entitlements as long as they arose no more than six months prior to the date of the bankruptcy or receivership. Employees who think they may be eligible for a WEPP payment should contact the trustee in bankruptcy or the court-appointed receiver acting for the employer for information about the WEPP. Proof of claim, which is a written statement that the employee submits to prove her claim, should be filed with the trustee as soon as possible. The trustee or receiver will send documentation on what the employee is owed to both the employee and Service Canada. The employee then applies for payment online, or in person to Service Canada.

The amounts owing to employees after the bankruptcy or insolvency of their employer will, in many cases, far exceed the approximate $3,700 limit provided for under the WEPP, especially now that termination and severance pay are included. It is therefore relevant to note that filing a WEPP claim does not prevent an employee from filing an employment standards claim with the Ministry of Labour for moneys that remain owing.

Administration and Enforcement

Filing a Complaint

An employee who believes that her rights under the ESA have been infringed may file a claim with the Ministry of Labour. It should be noted, however, that as part of Bill 68, the *Open for Business Act, 2010* amendments in 2011, the claims process has been changed so that, in most circumstances, an employment standards officer will only be assigned to a complaint after an employee has contacted (or tried to contact) her employer (or the client of a temporary help agency, if applicable) about an employment standard she believes has been violated and the amount of money she is owed. If the issue remains unresolved, a complaint may be filed but it must include an explanation of the way in which the information was provided to the employer, as well as the employer's response. The purpose of these requirements is to encourage early settlement of claims and ensure that the employer has an opportunity to deal with a claim before it escalates to the Ministry of Labour (Sherrard Kuzz LLP, 2011, p. 3). However, in appropriate circumstances, such as where the employee has a language difficulty or a disability, or is afraid of the employer, the Director of Employment Standards has the discretion to assign an employment standards officer to the complaint even where the employee has not taken these steps. Claimants are also encouraged to file their claims online.

There are time limits for establishing a claim, depending on the type of claim:

1. Under s. 111, six months is the time limit for recovering unpaid wages. However, if an employer has repeatedly violated the same section of the ESA and one of the violations occurred in the 6 months before the claim was filed, the employee can recover all wages due in the 12 months before the complaint was filed. For example, if an employee who has not been paid for public holidays over the past year files a claim for unpaid public holidays within 6 months of an unpaid public holiday, he may recover unpaid wages for all public holidays within the previous 12 months.

2. Unpaid vacation pay may be recovered if the claim is filed within 12 months of the date the vacation pay came due.

3. Under s. 96(3), two years is the time limit for claims related to leaves of absence, retail business establishments, lie detectors, and reprisals. Extensions may be given where the employee has been misled by the employer regarding her entitlements under the ESA and the employee acted promptly after finding out that the information given was incorrect.

    Under s. 74, reprisals refer to situations where an employee is penalized or threatened with a penalty for

    a. asking the employer to comply with the ESA;
    b. asking questions about rights under the ESA;
    c. filing a complaint under the ESA;
    d. exercising or trying to exercise a right under the ESA;
    e. taking, planning to take, or being eligible to take a leave, such as a pregnancy, parental, emergency, or family medical leave;
    f. being the subject of a garnishment order; or
    g. participating in a proceeding under the ESA.

    The two-year limit also applies to other non-monetary claims under the ESA, such as failure to provide adequate meal breaks or wage statements. It should be noted as well that the ESA limitation periods do not apply if the ESA right is claimed in a civil action—in that case, a two-year limitation period applies regardless of the type of claim.

An employee cannot file a claim with the Ministry of Labour for an employer's failure to pay wages or for discrimination in benefit plans *and* go to court against the employer for the same matter.

Similarly, an employee cannot file a claim for termination or severance pay *and* sue an employer for wrongful dismissal relating to the same termination. If an employee decides to start a court action after filing a claim with the Ministry, the employee must withdraw the claim within two weeks of filing, or the court action will be barred. However, as established in *Scarlett v. Wolfe Transmission Ltd.*, this rule is tempered by a court's inherent jurisdiction to do justice in the case before it.

In most circumstances, the maximum amount that can be ordered to be paid by an officer under the ESA is $10,000 (although Bill 18 proposes to remove that cap).

Therefore, being barred from conducting a wrongful dismissal action in court, where there is no such monetary ceiling, may have serious financial consequences.

Reprisals

The ESA protects employees who assert their rights under the Act against employer reprisals. As shown in the *Mucollari* decision, the onus is on the employer to demonstrate that its actions did not constitute a reprisal.

CASE IN POINT

Employer Has Onus of Proving Actions Were *Not* a Reprisal

Mucollari v. 1196811 Ontario Limited (Il Gabbiano Ristorante), 2013 CanLII 21009 (Ont. LRB)

Facts

The owner of the restaurant had a heated argument with an employee, Mucollari. Shortly after that, the owner told him his hours would be cut in half the following week for not following directions. A few days later, Mucollari told the owner that he had filed a complaint under the ESA regarding overtime pay. Although the owner eventually paid the overtime claim, Mucollari continued to be given significantly reduced hours on the schedule. Tensions between the two were brought to a head after the employee requested vacation time. Although he followed the restaurant's usual practice for requesting vacation time by leaving a note on the schedule for the manager, when he returned from vacation he was advised that his name was no longer on the schedule because he had gone on vacation without permission. In effect, he was terminated.

Relevant Issues

1. Whether the employer's actions constituted a reprisal contrary to s. 74 of the ESA.
2. Whether the award of termination pay should be increased since it was based on the 12 weeks prior to his termination when his hours had been reduced.

Decision

The Ontario Labour Relations Board found that the employer had engaged in a reprisal. The onus is on the employer to show that its actions were not, even in part, intended to punish the employee for asserting his rights under the ESA and it had failed to do so. The employer testified that the employee was terminated for going on vacation without permission. However, the employee had followed the employer's usual procedure of leaving the request on the schedule and his vacation request had not been denied. The Board awarded damages for the period between the employee's termination and when he started a new job.

With respect to the calculation of termination pay, the Board held that it should be based on his schedule prior to the initial reduction in his hours. Otherwise, the employer would benefit from his reprisal by having the employee's termination pay calculated on the basis of hours that had been illegally reduced. The employer was ordered to pay an additional $1,320.47.

As the Board found in *Mucollari*, where a termination or other negative employment consequence takes place shortly after an employee exercises her rights under the ESA, it raises suspicions that a reprisal has taken place. This presumption is only rebuttable by the employer's adducing clear evidence that its decision had nothing whatsoever to do with the exercise of the employee's rights under the ESA.

The Investigative Process

Ministry of Labour inspectors (ESOs) have wide-ranging powers to both investigate complaints and conduct proactive inspections. These powers include the ability to:

- enter the employer's premises and investigate without a warrant,
- examine company records (for example, payroll records, time sheets, and tax documentation),
- require production for inspection of relevant documents,
- remove records or other relevant documentation, and
- question anyone, including employees.

Failure of any party to comply with an order to attend a meeting or to provide certain evidence or information within a specified time frame may result in the ESA deciding the claim in the absence of that party or documentation. In addition to gathering information and making a decision, ESOs may also assist the parties to settle through voluntary mediation. Any resulting settlement is binding on the parties.

Officer's Decision

If, after investigating a claim, the employment standards officer does not find a contravention of the ESA, the employee will be notified of this finding in writing, and may apply for a review of the decision within 30 days. If the officer finds a contravention and the employer does not voluntarily comply with the officer's decision, the officer can issue one or more of the following orders.

1. Order to Pay Wages

Where wages are found owing to an employee, the officer may order the employer to pay wages of up to $10,000 per employee plus an administration fee of 10 percent of the money that is owing or $100, whichever is greater. If the employer decides to appeal this order, it must do so within 30 days. Orders to pay are the most common enforcement mechanism under the ESA. As noted above, the government has proposed legislation (Bill 18) that would remove the $10,000 cap on awards for unpaid wages and extend the limitation period on complaints from 6–12 months to two years. If passed, Bill 18 also would require a client of a temporary help agency to possibly pay twice for the same services: it could pay the temporary agency for the services of the workers, and then pay the workers if the temporary agency fails to pay the workers. If such a situation were to arise, the client would likely be in a position to sue the temporary help agency for recovery.

2. Compliance Order

Compliance orders require individuals to perform, or cease performing, actions that are contrary to the ESA. They are designed to enforce non-monetary violations, such as requiring employees to work excess hours, failing to keep accurate records, or failing to post material required by the ESA.

3. Tickets

Tickets are generally issued for less serious ESA violations. These offences fall into three categories: administrative and enforcement offences (for example, failure to provide meal breaks); contraventions of wage-based standards (for example, failure to pay overtime pay); and contraventions of non-wage-based standards (for example, requiring employees to work excess weekly hours without approval). Tickets carry set fines of $295, with a victim fine surcharge added to each set fine, plus court costs. An employer may either pay the fine or appear in a provincial court to dispute the offence (Ontario Ministry of Labour, 2013).

These fines are in addition to moneys the employer must pay to employees for amounts owed, including unpaid wages, overtime, and vacation pay.

4. Notice of Contravention

Employment standards officers also have the power to issue notices of contravention setting out a prescribed penalty when they believe that someone has contravened the ESA. The party receiving the notice must pay the penalty within 30 days of the date that the notice was issued or appeal it within 30 days of the date that it was served. Penalties for not complying with mandatory posting requirements or for failing to keep or make available to an employment standards officer adequate payroll records range from $250 for a first contravention to $1,000 for a third contravention in a three-year period.

Where the employer contravenes any other provision of the ESA, the penalties range from $250 for a first contravention, multiplied by the number of employees affected, to $1,000 for a third contravention in a three-year period, multiplied by the number of employees affected. For example, where an employer has received a compliance order requiring it to give adequate meal breaks to 10 employees, and it fails to comply with the order, the officer may issue a notice of contravention, including a penalty of $2,500 ($250 × 10). For a second offence, the sum would be $5,000 ($500 × 10), and for a third it would be $10,000 ($1,000 × 10).

5. Order to Reinstate or Compensate an Employee

For some violations of the ESA, an officer can order the employer to reinstate or compensate an employee, or both. Compensation in these cases is not limited to a $10,000 maximum but can cover the full amount owing, including back pay for wages lost. Violations that attract an order to reinstate can arise in the context of

- statutory leaves, including pregnancy, parental, family medical, and emergency leaves;
- lie detectors;
- the right of retail employees to refuse certain work; and
- reprisal when an employee exercises her rights under the ESA.

Appeals of Officer's Decision

Either party may apply for a review of an employment standards officer's decision to the Ontario Labour Relations Board as long as the application is made within a certain time frame—generally 30 days from the date of service of an order or notice of contravention. If an employer does not apply for a review within the time specified, the order or notice is final and binding on the employer. The Director of Employment Standards may use a private collection agency to collect unpaid amounts, and the employer must pay the collection agency's fees.

Before an employer can appeal an order to pay wages, it must pay the full amount of the order, plus the administrative fees, to the Director in trust. At the hearing, the onus is on the Director and/or the complainant's representative to establish, on a balance of probabilities, that the person against whom the order or notice of contravention was issued contravened the relevant ESA provision. There is no appeal from the Board's decision. However, the parties may apply to the Divisional Court of the Ontario Superior Court of Justice for judicial review of the decision. Because the Divisional Court will overturn the Board's decision only if it was unreasonable, rather than merely wrong, applications for judicial review are rarely successful.

Offences and Penalties

In addition to specific offences under the ESA, s. 132 states that it is an offence to contravene the ESA or its regulations or to fail to comply with an order. The ESA also sets out the specific offences of making, keeping, or producing false records or other documents required under the ESA or providing false or misleading information. Under amendments to the Act made in 2000, corporations may now be fined up to $100,000 for a first offence, $250,000 for a second offence, and $500,000 for a third or subsequent offence. An individual can be fined up to $50,000 for each offence or sentenced to up to 12 months in jail or both. Although imposing a jail sentence is uncommon, it is not unheard of. For example, in 2013 an employer, Peter Check, was sentenced to 90 days in jail for repeatedly failing to pay his employees their wages. His *modus operandi* was to hire students to work as lifeguards each year during summer school breaks and then to disappear or claim bankruptcy before all of their wages were paid. In addition to the jail sentence, Peter Check was ordered to pay the wages owing, plus a $15,000 fine (Doorey, 2013). An individual who is convicted of an offence may also find her name and other information about the offence, conviction, and sentence published on the Internet or elsewhere.

Ministry of Labour Information Bulletins and Fact Sheets

The Ministry of Labour has prepared information bulletins and fact sheets outlining its perspective on a number of statutory and regulatory requirements. Although these bulletins and fact sheets do not bind the courts, they provide valuable interpretive information.

Regulatory Powers to Share Information Between Ministries

With the passage of the Ontario *Regulatory Modernization Act, 2007* (RMA), Ontario's government regulators can now share compliance and complaint-related information among 15 different ministries. For example, information given to a Ministry of Labour health and safety inspector during an investigation or random audit may end up in the files of a Ministry of the Environment inspector or vice versa. This is possible even though the ministries involved may have different investigative rules. Moreover, under the RMA, ministries may form teams to target repeat offenders and publish (on the Internet) consolidated information about the organization's complaint and compliance record. Past convictions under one law will be considered in setting fines and penalties under another, unrelated law.

As a result, all inspections by the Ontario government should be considered multi-ministry inspections. It may be advisable to designate a single person to coordinate compliance with all provincial regulation.

REFERENCES

Allison, Gwendoline. The BlackBerry Dilemma: Paying for "24/7" Work Culture. *Canadian Employment Law Today*. Issue no. 523, December 3, 2008, p. 4.

Bank of Nova Scotia v. Cindy Fulawka. 2012 ONCA 443; 2013 CanLII 14307 (SCC).

Bill 18, *Stronger Workplaces for a Stronger Economy Act, 2014*. 1st Session, 41st Legislature, Ontario, 2014.

Bill 68, *Open for Business Act, 2010*. SO 2010, c. 16.

Bongarde Media Co. Paying Wages: Are You at Risk of an Overtime Class Action? *HR Compliance Insider*. Volume 5, no. 3, March 2009.

Campbell, Adrienne, and Ross Peigi. Maternity and Parental Leave: Implications for Employers. *Canadian HR Reporter*. September 9, 2002, p. G8.

Canada Labour Code. RSC 1985, c. L-2.

Canadian Imperial Bank of Commerce v. Dara Fresco. 2012 ONCA 444; 2013 CanLII 14331 (SCC).

Canadian Press. Court OKs Overtime Class Action Settlement for Scotiabank Front-Line Sales Staff. *Vancouver Sun*. August 13, 2014. http://www.vancouversun.com/business/court +overtime+class+action+settlement+scotiabank +frontline/10115591/story.html.

Doorey, David. Deadbeat Employer Gets Jail Time. April 9, 2013. http://lawofwork.ca/?p=6482.

Doorey, David. Did Mayor Ford's Office Violate the Employment Standards Act. December 2, 2010. http://lawofwork.ca/?p=2488.

Echlin, Randall, and Christine Thomlinson. *For Better or For Worse: A Practical Guide to Canadian Employment Law*, 3rd ed. Toronto: Canada Law Book, 2011.

Emergency Management and Civil Protection Act. RSO 1990, c. E.9.

Emond Harnden. Ontario Proposes Sweeping Legislation to Protect Vulnerable Workers. *What's New*. December 2013. http://www.ehlaw.ca/whatsnew.shtml.

Employment Insurance Act. SC 1996, c. 23.

Employment Standards Act 2000—Policy and Interpretation Manual. Ontario Ministry of Labour, Employment Practices Branch. Toronto: Thomson Carswell (looseleaf).

Employment Standards Act, 2000. SO 2000, c. 41.

Fitzgibbon, Michael. Reprisals Under the Employment Standards Act, 2000. May 9, 2013. http://labourlawblog .typepad.com/managementupdates/2013/05/reprisals -under-the-employment-standards-act-2000.html.

Gilbert, Douglas, Brian Burkett, and Moira McCaskill. *Canadian Labour and Employment Law for the US Practitioner*. Washington DC: Bureau of National Affairs, 2000.

Hutchins v. Atlantic Provincial Security Guard Service Ltd. 1995 CanLII 8876, [1995] NBLEBD no. 24.

Israel, Peter. Ask an Expert: Can a Claim Be Brought Under the ESA in Addition to Starting an Action for Wrongful Dismissal? *Canadian Employment Law Today*. Issue no. 387, April 16, 2003, p. 3020.

Israel, Peter. Ask an Expert: Can an Employer Withhold Pay from an Employee's Final Paycheque? *Canadian Employment Law Today*. Issue no. 306, April 2, 2003, p. 3012.

Johnston, Brian. Ask an Expert: Employment Standards— Recouping Used but Unearned Vacation Time. *Canadian Employment Law Today*. August 21, 2013, p. 1. http://www.stewartmckelvey.com/site/media/ stewartmckelvey/Ask%20an%20Expert_Brian%20 Johnston.pdf.

Law Commission of Ontario. *Vulnerable Workers and Precarious Work: Final Report*. December 2012. http:// www.lco-cdo.org/vulnerable-workers-final-report.pdf.

Loewenberg, Madeleine, and Lorenzo Lisi. Going into Overtime. *Canadian Employment Law Today*. Issue no. 520, October 22, 2008, p. 4.

McCracken v. Canadian National Railway Company. 2012 ONSC 6838.

Moday and Bell Mobility Inc. [2013] CLAD No. 48.

Mucollari v. 1196811 Ontario Limited (Il Gabbiano Ristorante). 2013 CanLII 21009 (Ont. LRB).

Ontario Budget 2014: Fostering a Fair Society. May 1, 2014. http://www.fin.gov.on.ca/en/budget/ ontariobudgets/2014/bk3.html.

Ontario Ministry of Labour. Are Unpaid Internships Legal in Ontario? June 2011. http://www.labour.gov.on.ca/ english/es/pubs/internships.php.

Ontario Ministry of Labour. Fact Sheets and Guides: Personal Emergency Leave, May 2013; Family Medical Leave, May 2013; Hours of Work and Overtime, May 2013; Minimum Wage, May 2013. http://www.labour.gov.on.ca/english/ es/pubs/index.php/factsheets/factsheets/guide/forms/ tools/factsheets/brochures/guide/pdf.

Ontario Ministry of Labour. Federal Wage Earner Protection Program. June 22, 2012. http://www.labour.gov.on.ca/ english/es//pubs/wepp.php.

Ontario Ministry of Labour. *Information Bulletins: Agreement to Vary from Certain Employment Standards*. December 10, 2004.

Ontario Ministry of Labour. *Your Guide to the Employment Standards Act, 2000*. May 2013. http://www.labour.gov .on.ca/english/es/pdf/es_guide.pdf.

P.S.S. Professional Salon Services Inc. v. Saskatchewan (Human Rights Commission). 2007 SKCA 149.

Piccolo, Patrizia. Lessons Learned from Being Involved in Several of the 468 Payroll Audits That Took Place Last Year. *RT Blog*. August 27, 2013. Rubin Thomlinson LLP. http://www.rubinthomlinson.com/blog/lessons-learned-from-being-involved-in-several-of-the-468-payroll-audits-that-took-place-last-year/.

Pugen, Daniel. Overtime Exempt or Non-Exempt? Issue May Be Certified as a Class Action. *Ontario Employer Advisor*. September 3, 2013. McCarthy Tétrault. http://www.ontarioemployerlaw.com/2013/09/03/investment-advisors-at-bmo-nesbitt-burns-can-proceed-with-a-class-action-for-overtime-pay/.

Regulatory Modernization Act, 2007. SO 2007, c. 4.

Roher, Eric, and Melanie Warner. *Ontario Employment Standards Act: Quick Reference*. Toronto: Carswell, 2002.

Rosen v. BMO Nesbitt Burns Inc. 2013 ONSC 2144.

Rousseau, Aaron. Overview of Overtime in Canada. April 1, 2009. Martindale-Hubbell. http://www.martindale.com/legal-management/article__657678.htm.

Rudner, Stuart. Understanding Different Types of Leaves. *Canadian Employment Law Today*. Issue no. 409, March 17, 2004, p. 3198.

Rudner, Stuart. Who Is Entitled to Overtime Pay? *Canadian Employment Law Today*. Issue no. 405, January 21, 2004, p. 3166.

Scarlett v. Wolfe Transmission Ltd. 2002 CanLII 53229 (Ont. SC).

Schiller v. P & L Corporation Ltd. 2012 CanLII 12611 (Ont. LRB).

Sherrard Kuzz LLP. Changes to the Employment Standards Act Mean Ontario Is Open for Business. *Management Counsel: Employment and Labour Law Update*. Volume X, no. 1, February 2011, p. 3. http://www.sherrardkuzz.com/pdf/Vol_X_1.pdf.

Sherrard Kuzz LLP. Family Day: Are Your Employees Entitled? *Management Counsel: Employment and Labour Law Update*. Volume VIII, no. 1, February 2009, p. 2. http://www.sherrardkuzz.com/pdf/Vol_VIII_1.pdf.

Sherrard Kuzz LLP. What's in a Name? *Management Counsel: Employment and Labour Law Update*. Volume XI, no. 6, December 2012, p. 1. http://www.sherrardkuzz.com/pdf/Vol_XI_6.pdf.

Silliker, Amanda. More Firms Hiring Contract Workers. *Canadian HR Reporter*. May 7, 2012. http://www.hrreporter.com/articleview/13016-more-firms-hiring-contract-workers.

Smith, Jeff. No Reinstatement for Employee Downsized While on Parental Leave. *Canadian Employment Law Today*. April 17, 2013, p. 3.

Smith, Jeffrey. Office Troublemaker Fired upon Return from Maternity Leave. *Canadian Employment Law Today*. Issue no. 500, January 2, 2008, p. 4.

Statistics Canada. *Employment Insurance Coverage Survey*. 2006. Catalogue no. 89M0025XCB.

Tri Roc Electric Ltd. v. Butler. 2003 CanLII 11390 (Ont. LRB), [2003] OESAD no. 1002.

Whitten & Lublin Employment Lawyers. More Statutory Leaves of Absence Are Coming to Ontario—Are You Ready? *WL Update*. Issue no. 43, June 2014, p. 1. http://www.toronto-employmentlawyer.com/wordpress/wp-content/uploads/June-2014.pdf.

Whitten, David. Unpaid Internships Can Carry Costly Risk. *Canadian HR Reporter*. September 23, 2013, p. 23.

Willms & Shier Environmental Lawyers LLP. Regulatory Modernization Act: Big Brother Is Watching. *Willms & Shier Report*. April 2008. http://www.willmsshier.com/docs/newsletters/willms-shier-report-april-2008.pdf?sfvrsn=8.

Wilson, Peter, and Allison Taylor. *The Corporate Counsel Guide to Employment Law*, 2nd ed. Aurora, ON: Canada Law Book, 2003.

RELATED WEBSITES

- http://www.labour.gov.on.ca/english
  The Ontario Ministry of Labour's website.
- http://www.servicecanada.gc.ca/eng/home.shtml
  Service Canada's website.

REVIEW AND DISCUSSION QUESTIONS

1. You want to improve your company's hiring process. Is it legal to require a job applicant to go to the worksite and perform the job for two or three hours to get a firsthand look at what the job entails? Would you need to pay the applicant, or could you consider the exercise to be part of the hiring process? Discuss.

2. Your employer asks your opinion on the following situation. An employee has been on pregnancy/parental leave for the past year and is scheduled to return next month. However, this employee's performance has been very unsatisfactory and she has received numerous verbal and written warnings in the past. He wants to know whether he can offer this employee a voluntary severance package. Discuss.

3. How does the ESA define "parents"? Can two parents take the full period of parental leave? What if they work for the same employer?

4. Under what three circumstances can an employer make deductions from an employee's wages?

5. Are the protections provided under the ESA available to employees regardless of the size of the employer?

6. Who determines when vacation time is taken: the employer or the employee?

7. Discuss six key protections available to employees who take statutory leave under the ESA.

8. Sponge Bob works part-time as a dishwasher at KrustyKrab Restaurant, where he earns $12 an hour. He works the same hours every week: four hours on Thursdays, three hours on Fridays, and five hours on Saturdays. Sponge Bob took Family Day off. Calculate how much public holiday pay Sponge Bob is entitled to receive for Family Day, not including vacation pay.

9. You are approached by a friend, Chantel, who manages a local shoe store in Toronto. She explains to you that she is working very long hours (50 to 60 hours a week) because she does everything in the store—hiring, firing, preparing shift schedules, serving customers, etc. She is paid an annual salary. At the time she was hired, Chantel understood that there would be no additional compensation for overtime but now she does not think this is fair. Chantel wants to know whether her employer has to give her overtime pay. Based on your knowledge of employment law, is Chantel entitled to receive overtime pay in these circumstances? Explain your answer.

10. Jason, a university student, was hired as a part-time sales clerk in a retail store on October 26, 2014. His spouse is ill and she needs Jason to drive her to the hospital for an important medical procedure. Jason wants to know the following information:

    a. Is he entitled to take a leave in these circumstances under Ontario's employment standards legislation? Explain your answer.

    b. Assuming for this part of the question that Jason *is* eligible for this leave, is he entitled under Ontario's ESA to be paid by the employer for this time off from work?

    c. Again, assuming that Jason is eligible for this leave, under Ontario's ESA how many more days (or partial days) from work can Jason take off for personal emergencies in 2014?

11. Allison worked as a bartender and cashier in a bar. She occasionally had to leave the bar, but would lock the till before doing so and leave the key between two registers. One evening, Allison's cash was short $300. She urged the employer to call the police but the employer did not. The next week her till was short

$1,000 and she was fired. The employer withheld her last paycheque as compensation for its losses. Allison filed a complaint with the Ministry of Labour for the deduction from her wages. The employer pointed to a form Allison had signed when she was hired that stated: "If a shortage occurs, full payment is due immediately. If for any reason this agreement cannot be met, I authorize the employer to deduct the shortage in full from my next pay." Did the employer violate the *Employment Standards Act* by deducting the till shortages from Allison's final pay in these circumstances? Explain your answer.

12. A friend, Elwyn, comes to you with a question. He has submitted an application for employment with a temporary employment agency. On the reverse side of the application there is a policy statement that states the applicant understands that he or she is not required to work on any particular day and retains the choice of whether to report to the agency's office to indicate availability for an assignment. He wants to know whether, and if so how, this statement could affect his rights under employment legislation. Describe to Elwyn the legal effect of this policy statement.

13. Should there be a formal mechanism for setting the minimum wage?

14. Your friend who owns a beauty shop tells you that one of her employees has just resigned, after taking more vacation days than she has earned to that point in the year. She wants to know whether the value of the excess days can be recovered. What do you tell her?

15. Happy Days Marketing regularly uses recent college graduates as unpaid "interns." The company sees it as a win–win: the students gain experience, skills, and connections that help them find that "first job," and the company gets free labour. Happy Days also tells these individuals that if a paid position comes up, they will be the first to be considered for it. Based on the information given, are these unpaid "internships" a breach of the ESA?

16. In the tough new economy, one employer brags that she hires students because she can pay them $400 a week and get 50 to 60 hours of work out of them each week.

    Is this a violation of the ESA? If so, calculate how much the employer owes each employee per week.

Occupational Health and Safety Act

7

LEARNING OUTCOMES

After completing this chapter, you will be able to:

- Understand the internal responsibility system that underlies Ontario's health and safety legislation.

- Outline the health and safety duties of the parties in the workplace.

- Identify workers' rights under the Ontario *Occupational Health and Safety Act* (OHSA).

- Understand the legal requirements surrounding workplace violence and harassment.

- State the accident-reporting requirements under the Act.

- Explain how the OHSA and its regulations are administered and enforced, and describe the test of due diligence.

- Identify the provisions in the *Criminal Code* related to an employer's health and safety obligations.

Introduction

Workplace health and safety needs to be a top priority for employers because the cost of on-the-job accidents—in terms of human suffering, lost time and production, workplace safety and insurance claims, fines, and other penalties—is extremely high. Current health and safety laws impose rigorous requirements on everyone in the workplace in an effort to avoid accidents. Failure to comply with statutory standards can result in fines of up to $500,000 and terms of imprisonment. A Brantford company that ignored a Ministry order to stop using a particular machine until it was fitted with proper guards was fined $50,000 even though no worker had been injured by it (Keith and Chandler, 2014, p. 7). These fines, even in the absence of a workplace accident or injury, are increasingly common.

Two major Ontario statutes address health and safety in the Ontario workplace: the *Occupational Health and Safety Act* (OHSA) and the *Workplace Safety and Insurance Act, 1997*. The OHSA focuses on promoting a safe and healthy workplace and preventing work-related accidents and diseases. The *Workplace Safety and Insurance Act* (formerly the *Workers' Compensation Act*), which also focuses on enhancing safety, covers the compensation and reintegration of workers who are injured or who contract a disease related to the workplace. Chapter 7 deals with the OHSA, and Chapter 8 covers the *Workplace Safety and Insurance Act*.

FYI

Tragic Consequences of Health and Safety Violations: The Story of Lewis Wheelan

In the summer of 2001, Lewis Wheelan, a 19-year-old student, got a summer job clearing overgrown bush around hydro lines near his hometown of Sault Ste. Marie. On his second day on the job, Wheelan was working near a hydro line when a tree broke through the line, which swung down and sent 7,200 volts of power through his body. He was so badly burned that doctors had to amputate both of his legs as well as his right arm and shoulder.

The power lines were owned by Great Lakes Power, a subsidiary of Brascan Corporation. Charges under the *Occupational Health and Safety Act* were laid against a co-worker, the contractor who hired Wheelan, and a Great Lakes safety inspector. Also charged were a former president of Great Lakes Power and several directors of Brascan under s. 32 of the *Occupational Health and Safety Act*. However, in September 2003, the Ministry of Labour dropped all charges against the directors and instead charged the company a $250,000 tax-deductible fine.

Wheelan's badly scarred flesh required constant air conditioning to keep his body from overheating. During the massive power blackout that struck Ontario in August 2003, the air conditioning stopped and he died alone in his apartment, unable to reach help. He would have been 22 in December 2003.

The Internal Responsibility System

Since 1977, Ontario's health and safety legislation has been based on a system of joint responsibility, which is referred to as the **internal responsibility system**. This system is based on the premise that government alone cannot effectively regulate all workplace risks. Instead, the law emphasizes participation by all parties in the workplace to ensure a healthy and safe environment.

In the internal responsibility system, **joint health and safety committees (JHSCs)** play a pivotal role. Generally required in workplaces with 20 or more workers, a JHSC is composed of equal numbers of management and worker representatives, who collectively exercise specific powers. In workplaces with 6 to 19 workers, a single **health and safety representative** exercises most of the same powers.

The OHSA gives workers the right to refuse unsafe work. Ontario Ministry of Labour inspectors may be called in where the workplace parties are unable to resolve an issue. Parties who fail to fulfill their obligations are subject to significant fines and even imprisonment.

Who Is Covered?

Ontario's OHSA covers almost every worker and workplace in Ontario. Because the OHSA applies to "workers," an individual need not be an "employee" in the legal sense of the term to be covered by the legislation. Anyone paid to perform work or supply services, including an independent contractor or a temporary agency employee, is protected. (Note that under Bill 18, which received second reading in October 2014, the definition of "worker" would expand to cover unpaid workers, including unpaid interns and co-op students.)

"Workplace" is defined broadly in s. 1 as "any land, premises, location or thing at, upon, in or near which a worker works." The only Ontario workplaces that are not covered by the OHSA are workplaces under federal jurisdiction, which are subject to the *Canada Labour Code*, or workplaces where work is done by an owner, occupant, or servant in a private residence or its connected land. In other words, the only provincially regulated workers not covered by the OHSA are individuals who come into a residence and are directly employed by the occupant, as in the case of a nanny.

It should be noted that in *Blue Mountain Resorts Limited v. Ontario (Labour)*, discussed below, the Ontario Court of Appeal found that for a site to constitute a "workplace" for purposes of requiring an employer to report a critical injury or death, there must be some reasonable connection between the hazard giving rise to the death or critical injury and a realistic risk to worker safety at the workplace.

FYI

Key Features of Ontario's OHSA

1. The OHSA focuses on *prevention* of workplace accidents and diseases.

2. The premise behind the legislation is that the workplace parties share the responsibility for occupational health and safety because they are best placed to identify health and safety problems and to develop solutions. This approach is called the "internal responsibility system."

3. The OHSA specifies the general rights and responsibilities of the workplace parties. However, specific requirements related to particular industries and hazards are contained in over 20 regulations enacted in support of the legislation.

4. All "workers," not just employees, are covered by the OHSA. This includes independent contractors, workers engaged in subtrades, and employees or workers of other employers who happen to be in the workplace.

5. The OHSA applies to provincially regulated workplaces in Ontario.

6. Under the OHSA, workers have three core rights:

    a. the right to participate in identifying and resolving health and safety concerns, primarily through the JHSC or, in smaller workplaces, the health and safety representative;

b. the right to refuse work they believe is dangerous to themselves or another worker, and in the case of a certified member of a JHSC, the right to stop work that is dangerous to any worker in specified circumstances; and

c. the right to know about potential hazards to which they may be exposed through training and the Workplace Hazardous Materials Information System (WHMIS).

7. Penalties for violating the OHSA include fines of up to $500,000 and terms of imprisonment.

8. The OHSA is administered by the Ministry of Labour, which also has legal responsibility for the prevention of workplace injuries and diseases through the Office of the Chief Prevention Officer, supported by the Prevention Council.

Duties of the Workplace Parties

The OHSA places duties on everyone involved with the workplace: employers, constructors, supervisors, owners, suppliers, licensees, officers of a corporation, and workers. An "owner" includes a tenant, trustee, receiver, or occupier of the land on which the workplace is situated. Where the OHSA is breached, several workplace parties, including supervisors and workers, may be found personally liable along with the employer and may be fined for breaching their duties under the OHSA. These duties are set out in ss. 23 to 32.

Employers' Duties

Under the OHSA, employers have an overriding general duty to take every reasonable precaution to protect the health and safety of workers (s. 25(2)(h)). In addition, employers have numerous specific obligations, including the duty to

1. appoint competent supervisors who are familiar with health and safety requirements;
2. maintain equipment in good condition;
3. ensure that workers use protective equipment;
4. prepare a written occupational health and safety policy, review it annually, and maintain a program to implement it (workplaces that regularly employ five or fewer workers are exempt from this requirement);
5. post the occupational health and safety policy in a conspicuous spot in the workplace, such as the lunchroom or on a safety bulletin board (it is a good idea to have workers sign to indicate that they have received a copy of the policy (Keith and Chandler, 2014, p. 44));
6. acquaint workers with any hazards associated with their work;
7. identify and take inventory of hazardous materials, and inform and train employees regarding these materials;
8. help JHSCs and health and safety representatives carry out their duties;
9. post the OHSA and explanatory material (including a prescribed poster) prepared by the Ministry that outlines the rights, responsibilities, and duties of workers in English and the majority language in the workplace (the best posting spots are the workers' lunchroom and the safety bulletin board);

10. refuse to employ underage workers (minimum age requirements depend on the workplace: a person must be at least 16 to work on a construction or logging project, 15 to work in a factory, and 14 to work elsewhere);

11. keep accurate records of biological, chemical, or physical agents as required by the regulations under the OHSA;

12. consider accident prevention and safety performance when evaluating supervisors and workers (Keith and Chandler, 2014, p. 43);

13. report work-related accidents, injury, or illness to the Ministry of Labour; and

14. ensure that workers and supervisors complete a basic occupational health and safety awareness training program.

Note that this training obligation, which became effective on July 1, 2014, is meant to provide workers and supervisors with a basic understanding of the OHSA. It does not replace any sector-specific training (for example, modular training for mining or logging), hazard-specific training (for example, training for WHMIS or work in confined spaces), or competency-specific training. It is also in addition to the employer's general duty under s. 25(2)(a) of the Act to provide information, instruction, and supervision to a worker to protect his or her health and safety (Ontario Ministry of Labour, 2014, p. 9).

All workers and supervisors, not just those in safety-sensitive jobs, must receive this basic training. Similarly, the obligation applies regardless of employment status (for example, full-time, part-time, and seasonal workers are all included).

Basic worker training, which must be completed "*as soon as practicable*" after a worker is hired, needs to cover the following topics, as set out in the *Occupational Health and Safety Awareness Training* regulation:

- the duties and rights of workers, supervisors, and employers under the OHSA;
- the roles of health and safety representatives and joint health and safety committees under the OHSA;
- the role of the Ministry of Labour, the Workplace Safety and Insurance Board (WSIB), and entities designated under s. 22.5 of the OHSA such as health and safety associations;
- common workplace hazards;
- the Workplace Hazardous Materials Information System; and
- occupational illness, including latency.

Basic supervisor training, which must be completed within *one week* of performing work as a supervisor, needs to also include the following additional topics:

- how to recognize, assess, and control workplace hazards;
- how to evaluate controls designed to prevent workplace accidents; and
- sources of information on occupational health and safety.

Note that "supervisor" is defined as anyone who is in charge of a workplace or has authority over a worker. This could include, for example, lead hands who direct work but do not have disciplinary authority.

Upon completion of the training program, both workers and supervisors receive a compliance certificate, which is valid for their working lives. Those who change employers do not have to retake the program but they must provide the new employer with proof that training was previously completed, and the *new employer must verify* that their training covered the minimum content requirements set out in the regulation. Similar requirements apply to individuals who completed a comparable awareness training program before the regulation came into force in July 2014. Although employers may develop or purchase comparable training materials, training workbooks and e-learning modules are available from the Ministry free of charge and in multiple languages. These can be found at www.labour.gov.on.ca/english/hs/training/workers.php. The basic worker training modules take approximately one hour to complete.

Finally, an employer is required to maintain records that prove that all of its workers and supervisors either have completed the safety awareness training or are exempt because they have received comparable training. These records must be retained for up to six months after a worker or supervisor stops being employed by that employer.

FYI

Bill 160—"Largest Revamp of Ontario's Worker Safety System in 30 Years"

As a result of the tragic deaths of four workers who fell to their deaths on Christmas Eve 2009 after a high-rise scaffold they were on collapsed, the Ontario government established an expert panel to recommend changes to Ontario's health and safety system. Those recommendations resulted in Bill 160—referred to by the Ministry of Labour as "the largest revamp of Ontario's worker safety system in 30 years"—and many of those changes have been gradually phased in since its passage in June 2011. The key changes include the following:

- Effective April 1, 2012, responsibility for prevention of accidents is transferred from the Workplace Safety and Insurance Board (WSIB) to the Ministry of Labour. This includes transferring oversight of the province's safety associations and training centres.
- Responding to concerns that there needs to be a single authority accountable for health and safety, the amendments created the Office of the Chief Prevention Officer (CPO). The CPO, operating within the Ministry of Labour but separate from its enforcement division, is responsible for establishing standards for legislatively required health and safety training and approves training providers.
- The Prevention Council, whose members represent labour, non-unionized workers, employers, and safety experts, was established to advise the CPO on prevention and health and safety strategy.
- Either co-chair of a JHSC may now make a unilateral written recommendation to the employer (which the

employer must respond to) if the committee fails to reach consensus on a recommendation after good-faith attempts to do so. Before this change, no single member of the committee had this authority.
- Reflecting concerns with the number of reprisals against workers who report unsafe conditions—including termination of employment—a Ministry of Labour inspector may now file a reprisal complaint on behalf of an employee, as long as that employee consents.
- Employers must post, in a conspicuous location in the workplace, a poster that tells workers their rights relating to safety and how to contact a Ministry of Labour inspector. There is now a single, toll-free number (1-877-202-0008) for reporting workplace health and safety incidents or unsafe work practices ("One Number for Workplace Health and Safety Calls," 2010, p. 4).
- Employers are responsible for ensuring that all of their workers and supervisors have basic health and safety awareness training—in addition to any required sector-specific or hazard-specific training.
- The Office of the Worker Adviser and the Office of the Employer Adviser may now advise non-unionized workers and employers (with under 50 employees), respectively, on health and safety matters (Miedema, 2011, p. 29). (Previously, their mandate was limited to workers' compensation issues.)

Workers' Duties

The OHSA imposes obligations on workers, including the duty to

1. comply with the OHSA and its regulations;
2. use any equipment, protective device, or clothing required by the employer;
3. report any missing or defective equipment or protective device that may be dangerous;
4. report any known workplace hazard; and
5. refuse to engage in any prank, contest, feat of strength, unnecessary running, or rough and boisterous conduct (such as racing forklifts in a warehouse).

The Ministry of Labour rarely charges a worker for violating the OHSA (Keith and Chandler, 2014, p. 51). Employers, however, should appropriately discipline employees who fail to comply with health and safety requirements. An employer who fails to do so is arguably condoning an employee's breach and therefore in violation of its obligations.

Unless a breach is serious, an employer should respond with progressive discipline. This involves the use of gradually escalating levels of discipline, starting with a verbal warning and counselling, and moving to a written warning, possibly a suspension, and, where warranted, dismissal. Appropriate discipline for a minor breach might entail a mandatory safety talk and counselling regarding the violation (Keith and Chandler, 2014, p. 17). However, if, for example, a worker intentionally disables a safety device in an effort to make his job go faster, the breach is serious enough to warrant a written warning or suspension, assuming that the worker previously received safety training and the employer consistently enforces safety rules. *USWA Local 862 v. Canadian General Tower Ltd.* involved an employee who grieved his dismissal for tampering with the safety button on a machine.

CASE IN POINT

Employee Dismissed for Tampering with Machinery

USWA Local 862 v. Canadian General Tower Ltd., [2003] OLAA no. 801

Facts

The employer's poor safety record had resulted in several accidents and charges from the Ministry of Labour. After an accident involving a paper rewinder, a Ministry inspector issued an order that directed the employer to ensure that a safety button on the rewinder was not taped down. Taping the button did not improve productivity, but it allowed the machine to run without an operator's finger on the button. The employer posted the order in the workplace and presented a letter to each operator at individual meetings called to discuss the matter.

Despite these discussions, an employee, Schramm, taped down the button. The machine operator on the next shift, unaware that the button was taped down, was slightly injured

as a result. Schramm apologized for the incident but was fired the next day. The employer claimed that it had taken every reasonable precaution but could not protect itself from an employee who knowingly put himself and others at risk. Schramm grieved the dismissal.

Relevant Issue

Whether the employer had just cause to dismiss the employee for tampering with the safety button.

Decision

The arbitrator refused to reinstate Schramm. He found that the company must be armed with the right to discharge employees for safety violations of the kind discussed here or it will not be able to meet its due diligence obligations. He noted Schramm's view that it was not a safety infraction because the button was not a safety mechanism. The arbitrator stated: "The accelerator pedal on an automobile would not normally be a 'safety' device but tying it down in some way could have significant consequences for the safe operation of a vehicle."

Supervisors' Duties

Because supervisors fall within the OHSA's definition of "workers," workers' duties apply to supervisors. Additionally, supervisors' duties include

1. ensuring that workers comply with the OHSA and regulations by using protective devices and wearing protective clothing as required by the employer;
2. advising a worker of potential or actual health or safety dangers;
3. providing workers with written instructions concerning protective measures; and
4. taking every reasonable precaution in all circumstances.

An individual need not have the title "supervisor" or "manager" to be a supervisor. A lead hand who is covered by a **collective agreement** may qualify if she has supervisory functions.

Constructors' Duties

Under the OHSA, constructors have responsibilities similar to those outlined for employers (Kelloway et al., 2014, p. 30). Constructors' duties include

1. ensuring that every employer and worker on the project complies with the OHSA and its regulations;
2. protecting the health and safety of workers on the project;
3. providing a Notice of Project to the Ministry of Labour, where required;
4. monitoring subcontractors for compliance with the OHSA and the *Construction Projects* regulation; and
5. appointing a competent supervisor, where the constructor has five or more workers at a project.

Owners' Duties

Owners' duties include

1. ensuring that facilities and workplaces comply with the OHSA and its regulations; and
2. where a construction project is involved, determining whether there are any designated substances (for example, arsenic or asbestos) at the project site and, if so, preparing a list of them for the constructor.

Suppliers' Duties

Every person who supplies workplace equipment under a *rental or leasing arrangement* must ensure that it is in good condition and complies with the OHSA and its regulations. This duty does not apply if the equipment is sold to the workplace.

Duties of Corporate Officers and Directors

Corporate officers and directors must take all reasonable care to ensure that their company complies with the OHSA and its regulations and with any orders and requirements of the Ministry of Labour. By placing duties directly on officers and directors, the OHSA encourages senior management to take a serious interest in compliance with health and safety requirements.

Duties of Architects and Engineers

Architects and engineers are liable under the OHSA if they negligently or incompetently give advice or certification required under the Act and a worker is endangered as a result.

Workers' Rights

Under the OHSA, workers have three key rights:

1. to participate in the health and safety process, mostly through the JHSC;
2. to refuse unsafe work and, in the case of a certified member of a JHSC, to stop work that endangers workers in certain circumstances; and
3. to know about workplace hazards.

1. The Right to Participate in the Health and Safety Process

The JHSC and Health and Safety Representatives (Sections 8 to 12)

The JHSC is one of the cornerstones of the internal responsibility system. It is an advisory group of worker and management representatives that has statutory powers. Members meet regularly to discuss health and safety concerns, review progress, and make recommendations on health and safety issues.

A JHSC is required in every workplace where 20 or more *workers* are regularly employed, where a designated substance regulation applies (these regulations cover substances such as arsenic and asbestos), or where a toxic substance order is in effect. Special rules apply to joint committees on construction projects. Prescribed farming operations with 20 or more workers must also have a JHSC (Keith and Chandler, 2014, p. 31). The relevant consideration is the number of *workers* regularly employed at the workplace, not the number of employees. Independent contractors must be included in the count (see *Ontario (Labour) v. United Independent Operators Limited*).

In workplaces with between 6 and 19 workers, a health and safety representative takes the place of a JHSC, exercising most of the powers and responsibilities of a JHSC. An employer cannot interfere in the choice of the health and safety representative; she must be selected by workers who do not exercise managerial functions. Where the workers are unionized, the union selects the representative.

Structure of the JHSC

The employer is responsible for ensuring that a JHSC is established in accordance with the requirements of the OHSA. These requirements are set out below.

1. A JHSC in a workplace with between 20 and 49 workers must have at least two members.
2. A JHSC in a workplace with 50 or more workers must have at least four members.
3. Worker members must be employed in the workplace covered by the JHSC. Management members may be chosen from another of the employer's workplaces if there are no managerial employees at the workplace covered by the JHSC.
4. At least half of the JHSC members must be worker representatives selected by workers. An employer is prohibited from having any involvement in the selection of the worker members. If a trade union represents the workers, the worker members must be selected by the union.
5. A JHSC must be co-chaired by one member selected by the worker representatives and one member selected by the management representatives.
6. There is no maximum number of JHSC members. The committee should be large enough to address the health and safety concerns of the entire workplace. For example, where the workplace includes a plant, office, laboratory, warehouse, and delivery service, the committee should be large enough to represent the health and safety issues in each department.
7. The names and work locations of the JHSC members must be posted in a conspicuous location in the workplace.
8. The JHSC must meet at the workplace at least once every three months. It may choose to meet more often, depending on the nature and size of the workplace.
9. The employer must pay JHSC members for at least one hour's preparation before each meeting, for time spent at JHSC meetings, and for time spent performing certain other committee duties, such as conducting monthly inspections.
10. The JHSC must keep minutes of its meetings, and these minutes must be available, if requested, by a Ministry of Labour inspector. It is also a good idea to post the minutes of meetings with the names of JHSC members and to distribute them to all first-line managers and senior management (Keith and Chandler, 2014, p. 24).
11. The employer or constructor must ensure that at least one management representative and at least one worker representative on the committee are trained in health and safety matters. These are "certified members," and their training is certified by the Chief Prevention Officer under the OHSA.

(Certifications granted by the Ontario Workplace Safety and Insurance Board (WSIB) before April 2012 are still recognized.) Construction projects that regularly employ fewer than 50 workers or that are expected to last less than three months are exempt from this requirement. Similarly, for farming operations, these requirements only apply if 50 or more workers are regularly employed (Keith and Chandler, 2014, p. 30).

Powers and Duties of the JHSC

An effective JHSC plays a central role in spotting dangers in the workplace and looking for solutions to health and safety problems. The main functions of the JHSC include the following:

1. *Identifying potentially dangerous situations in the workplace.* Machinery that lacks protective devices, harmful substances, and dangerous working conditions are some of the matters that should alert JHSC members. The workplace should be inspected at least once a month, preferably by a certified member who is a worker representative. Where the size of the workplace makes this impractical, the JHSC should set up an inspection schedule that ensures that part of the workplace is inspected each month and the entire workplace is inspected at least once a year.

2. *Obtaining information from the employer regarding workplace hazards.* The JHSC should obtain information from the employer regarding actual or potential hazards in the workplace, as well as the health and safety experience and standards in similar workplaces of which the employer is aware. It can also ask the employer for information concerning health and safety–related testing and have a worker committee member present at the beginning of the testing to validate the procedures and results.

3. *Making recommendations to the employer for improving workplace health and safety.* Recommendations could cover anything from new or modified safety training programs to additional protective devices. Although an employer need not comply with JHSC recommendations, it must respond in writing to any written recommendations within 21 days. A positive response must include a timetable for implementing the recommendation. A negative response must state the employer's reasons for rejecting it.

4. *Investigating work refusals.*

5. *Investigating serious injuries in the workplace.*

6. *Obtaining information from the Workplace Safety and Insurance Board regarding compensation claims.*

7. *Participating in the development, implementation, and annual review of training programs for workers related to hazardous materials or agents.*

8. *Selecting the committee co-chairs.*

9. *Appointing a designated member to represent the workers at the beginning of industrial hygiene testing.*

10. *Participating in the preparation of compliance notices and plans to be developed and filed with the Ministry of Labour* (Keith and Chandler, 2014, p. 23).

As noted above, where the JHSC is unable to reach consensus concerning a recommendation after attempting in good faith to do so, either co-chair may make a unilateral written recommendation and, as with other written JHSC recommendations, the employer or constructor has 21 days in which to respond.

Certified Members

WHAT IS A CERTIFIED MEMBER?

The "certified" members of the JHSC play a crucial role under the OHSA. A certified member is someone who has received specialized health and safety training approved by the CPO (previously, the WSIB gave approval) and, as such, has the knowledge to identify sources of danger, assess risks, and recommend elimination or control of those dangers (Keith and Chandler, 2014, p. 30). Certification is a two-step process that consists of "basic" certification and "workplace-specific" hazard training. Basic certification includes training on health and safety law; hazard identification and control; investigation techniques; and prevention resources. Workplace-specific hazard training is designed specifically for each workplace to reflect the results of the employer's workplace hazard assessment (Keith and Chandler, 2014, p. 33). Basic certification is transferable between employers whereas the workplace-specific certification may not be (Keith and Chandler, 2014, p. 36).

RIGHTS AND DUTIES OF CERTIFIED MEMBERS

Because of their specialized training, certified members have unique responsibilities under the OHSA:

1. to conduct monthly workplace inspections, where possible;
2. to investigate work refusals, where possible;
3. to investigate complaints about dangerous workplace conditions; and
4. to stop work that endangers workers in certain circumstances.

Workplaces with 20 or more workers must have certified committee members. The employer is responsible for ensuring that the JHSC has at least two certified members, one representing workers and one representing the employer. Where there is more than one certified worker member, the workers or union must designate at least one member to exercise the rights and duties of a certified member. Similarly, the employer must designate at least one certified management member to exercise the rights and duties of a certified member.

2. The Right to Refuse Unsafe Work/The Right to Stop Work

The Right to Refuse Unsafe Work (Section 43)

Under s. 43 of the OHSA, every worker has the right to refuse unsafe work. This right is restricted for some occupations, either because danger is an inherent part of the job or because exercising the right would expose others to danger. Restrictions apply to police officers, firefighters, and persons employed in operating a correctional facility, a hospital, a nursing home, or an ambulance service. For example, a police officer cannot refuse to follow a suspect carrying a gun on the ground that the situation is dangerous. An officer can, however, refuse to operate a police car that he believes has faulty brakes because driving a defective vehicle is not a danger inherent to his job.

WHEN CAN THE RIGHT TO REFUSE UNSAFE WORK BE EXERCISED?

Any worker may refuse work when she has reason to believe that

- the equipment she is to use,
- the physical condition of her workplace,
- a contravention of the legislation relating to her equipment or workplace, or
- workplace violence

is "likely to endanger" herself or another worker.

PROCEDURE FOR EXERCISING THE RIGHT TO REFUSE UNSAFE WORK

The procedure for exercising the right to refuse unsafe work is set out in s. 43 of the OHSA.

FIRST STAGE OF REFUSAL

Initially, the right to refuse work is based on the worker's personal belief. As long as a worker sincerely believes that a work situation is "likely to endanger" herself or another worker, she may refuse to work. The perceived danger need not be imminent or likely to result in serious bodily injury. The refusal need not be based on reasonable grounds. It must simply be based on an honest belief.

A worker who is exercising this right must immediately tell her supervisor that she is refusing to work and state her reasons. The supervisor must immediately investigate the refusal in the presence of the worker *and* a certified worker member of the JHSC (or the health and safety representative) or another worker with safety experience chosen by the union or workers to represent them.

The worker must remain in a safe place near the workstation until the investigation is completed. The employer must pay the worker during the first stage of refusal.

SECOND STAGE OF REFUSAL

If the worker who refused unsafe work is not satisfied with the results of the supervisor's investigation, she may continue to refuse to work if she has "reasonable grounds" for believing that the work continues to be unsafe. This is a higher standard than the "honest belief" required at the first stage. The standard is now objective: would a reasonable person, with knowledge of the workplace, reasonably believe that it is unsafe?

At this stage, the employer must call a Ministry of Labour inspector to investigate the work refusal. This investigation must be done in the presence of the employer's representative, the worker, a certified worker member of the JHSC (or a health and safety representative), or a person experienced in health and safety selected by the union or workers. While waiting for the results of the investigation, the worker must remain at a safe place near her workstation unless the employer assigns her other work. Alternatively, subject to an applicable collective agreement or employment contract, the employer may send the worker home if no other work is available and the inspection takes considerable time to complete. The employer must not send the employee home as a form of reprisal.

Pending the inspector's decision, the employer may ask another employee to do the disputed work only if that employee is advised of the work refusal and the reasons for it. This explanation must be given in the presence of a certified worker member of the JHSC (if possible) (or the health and safety representative) or a worker representative chosen because of his knowledge, experience, and training in health and safety. The replacement worker has the same rights of refusal as the first worker.

The Ministry of Labour inspector must make a decision in writing. If the inspector concurs that the situation is unsafe, he may issue an order requiring the employer to take the necessary corrective measures. Conversely, if the inspector agrees with the employer's position, no order will be made. The inspector's decision may be appealed to the Ontario Labour Relations Board (OLRB) by the party who disagrees with it.

NO REPRISAL

The employer may not penalize a worker in any way for exercising his rights under the OHSA, including this right to refuse unsafe work. An employee who believes he has suffered a reprisal may file a complaint with the Ontario Labour Relations Board. The onus is on the employer to show that the refusal was improper.

The right to refuse unsafe work is broad but not unlimited. Employees cannot refuse to work for reasons unrelated to their own safety, such as pressuring the employer on a collective bargaining issue or retaliating for their belief that another employee is being required to perform unsafe work. Employees who refuse work must have a sufficiently close relationship to the perceived danger to justify their belief that they are in danger or that they would put another employee in danger by performing the work. An employee who refuses unsafe work cannot subsequently refuse other work that is not unsafe (Gilbert et al., 2000, p. 295). *Doupagne v. Baltimore Aircoil*, *Pharand v. Inco Metals, Lennox Industries*, and *Battle Mountain* are all cases involving alleged employer reprisals for work refusals. Generally speaking, the OHSA work refusal provisions have received a broad interpretation, provided that the refusal is based on genuine health and safety concerns.

CASE IN POINT

Insubordination Justifies Discipline

Doupagne v. Baltimore Aircoil of Canada, 1982 CanLII 846, [1982] OLRB Rep. March 327

Facts

The employee, who worked as a lead hand in an area where a lot of welding was done, was disciplined for insubordination on two occasions. The first incident related to the employee's refusal to shut off a fan while a smoke extractor was in operation. Employees had been told not to use the fan at that time because it blew smoke away from the nozzle of the extractor, thus making it less effective in removing fumes. The employee received a two-day suspension for refusing a direct instruction to turn off the fan.

The second incident related to the employee's refusal to use new reusable earplugs instead of the old disposable kind. He insisted that the employer's storekeeper provide him and his crew with a box of disposable earplugs, stating that these earplugs were better. Management pointed out that the decibel ratings for the two types of earplugs were the same, but the employee continued to refuse to use the new earplugs. After receiving a two-week suspension, he filed a complaint with the Ontario Labour Relations Board, arguing that these disciplinary measures were reprisals for exercising his rights under the OHSA.

Relevant Issue

Whether the disciplinary actions taken by the employer contravened the OHSA.

Decision

The Ontario Labour Relations Board found that the employer's discipline of the employee was not a reprisal for exercising his rights under the OHSA. His failure to follow the employer's directions was not based on health and safety concerns. Rather, he was asserting that he should be able to do things his own way based on personal preference and comfort issues. He therefore was not acting within the scope of the OHSA and could be disciplined for insubordination (Gilbert et al., 2000, p. 296).

In *Pharand v. Inco Metals*, the Ontario Labour Relations Board held that valid employee refusals can arise in a group setting if each employee shares a common safety-related concern. Moreover, if the employees genuinely and reasonably believe that the work is unsafe, it is irrelevant that subsequent investigation reveals that no real danger existed.

CASE IN POINT

Employees Entitled to Act in Concert

Pharand v. Inco Metals Co., 1980 CanLII 966, [1980] OLRB Rep. July 981

Facts

The employees, who worked in a copper refinery, saw a hole in the ceiling of an anode furnace. Shortly after they finished their shift, the hole was patched, but fire was later seen coming through the ceiling of the furnace, and two other employees refused to "tap" the furnace (that is, tilt the furnace to extract the molten copper) because they believed it would be unsafe. Management called Ministry of Labour inspectors, but copper sheeting and fireproof cloth prevented their determining whether the problem was serious. Members of management who were familiar with anode furnaces assured them that the roof was unlikely to collapse, and the inspectors accepted their opinion that the furnace was safe. The inspectors directed that work proceed with an additional employee to detect any surges of molten copper.

When the employees returned for their shift, they found a patch over the hole and flames coming out the edges. They were informed that the tapper on the preceding shift had exercised his right to refuse work and that safety inspectors had been called in. The crew refused to tap the furnace. The foreman brought in a member of the JHSC, who called the inspector. The inspector, who had less experience than members of management, adopted their view and made an order allowing work to continue. However, the employees continued to refuse to work. The employer sent them home for the rest of their shift and placed a disciplinary note on their files. Employees on the subsequent shift agreed to tap the furnace, and after that job was safely done, the furnace was shut down and the hole was fixed.

The employees filed a complaint with the Ontario Labour Relations Board, alleging that they had been disciplined for exercising their right to refuse work under the OHSA. The employer argued that by acting as a group, they were engaging in an action akin to an unlawful strike, and that they lacked reasonable grounds for believing that the work was unsafe.

Relevant Issue

Whether the employer's disciplinary actions were unlawful under the OHSA.

Decision

The Ontario Labour Relations Board ruled in favour of the employees. It held that legitimate work refusals can occur where several employees share a common safety concern. The issue is whether the employees had reasonable cause to believe that the work was unsafe when they exercised their right to refuse to work. It is irrelevant that subsequent events proved that there was no danger when the employees exercised their right. Moreover, the Board found that the employees were still acting within their rights when they refused to return to work after the inspector ordered that work proceed. Because they knew that the inspector was basing his decision on the assurances of management, they had no confidence that this order reflected a neutral assessment of the situation.

As a result of these findings, the employer was ordered to reimburse the employees for the hours of work they lost when they were sent home and to eliminate disciplinary notes from their records (Gilbert et al., 2000, p. 293).

In *Lennox Industries*, the employer was found to be in violation of the OHSA anti-reprisal sections when it disciplined a worker whose concern about safety originated because of his reaction to the supervisor's proximity during an argument. The arbitrator found that the work refusal provisions of the OHSA applied because the worker's belief that he was in danger of being hurt was genuine.

CASE IN POINT

Reaction to Supervisor's Proximity Justifies Work Refusal

Lennox Industries (Canada) Limited v. United Steelworkers of America, Local 7235, 1999 CanLII 20394 (Ont. LA), [1999] OLAA no. 158

Facts

On investigating a work slowdown, a production supervisor found that the problem stemmed from the fact that a worker was away from his workstation, talking to a co-worker. The supervisor told the worker to return to work, but the worker indicated that there were "no parts" to work on in his area. The discussion developed into an unpleasant confrontation, with the worker asking the supervisor, "Are you intimidating me?" and stating to the co-worker, "I can't work like this. Can you work like this?" The worker said that he felt unsafe and wanted a health and safety representative to be called. The supervisor did not call the health and safety representative. Instead, he removed the worker from the line because production was backed up and gave him a two-day suspension for insubordination. In the log book, the supervisor wrote that the worker "refused to get back to work stating that it was unsafe to resume working *my being so close to him.*"

The worker grieved the imposition of discipline, arguing that it constituted a reprisal for asserting his right under the OHSA to refuse unsafe work. The basis for his refusal was that the supervisor was standing one foot away "hollering, coercing and intimidating him," his hands were shaking, and he was afraid that he would slip and cut himself on the steel edge of the materials he was handling. The employer argued that the worker did not fit within any of the protections allowed in the OHSA because he was making no claim that any "equipment, machine, device or thing" that he was "using or operating" was likely to endanger him.

Relevant Issue

Whether the employer violated the OHSA by disciplining the worker in these circumstances.

Decision

The arbitrator found in favour of the worker. During the first stage of a work refusal, a worker may refuse to work "where he has reason to believe" that danger exists. On the evidence, the worker had a subjective belief that he was in an unsafe situation. Once the worker communicated his concern about the supervisor's proximity, the supervisor was obliged to investigate the complaint in the presence of the health and safety representative. The arbitrator ordered that the worker's suspension be rescinded, that he be compensated for all wages lost, and that his personnel record be amended by removing all references to this incident.

Battle Mountain considers the actions of an employee who allegedly invoked the work refusal provisions of the OHSA without a bona fide belief that the work he refused was dangerous. The employee's termination for misusing the OHSA in this manner, and causing serious consequences for the employer and other employees, was upheld.

CASE IN POINT

Employee Lacks Honest Belief in Mineshaft Danger

Battle Mountain Canada Ltd. v. United Steelworkers of America, Local 9364, [2001] OLAA no. 722

Facts

The worker was employed by a mining company between 1989 and 1998 and had been a member of the JHSC since 1995. On December 14, 1998, he refused to take the "cage," which transported workers underground, to his assigned work area, alleging that it was unsafe. His action closed down the mineshaft. The worker's refusal was based on an allegation that pits designed to catch loose rocks were full and therefore presented a danger.

Later in the afternoon, the worker revoked his work refusal after the employer provided him with the documentation that he requested. It was therefore unnecessary for a Ministry of Labour inspector to investigate. However, shortly after the work refusal, the employer discharged the worker on the basis that his work refusal was unlawful and constituted serious culpable misconduct. The worker grieved his dismissal, arguing that it was a reprisal for exercising his rights under the OHSA and the collective agreement.

Relevant Issue

Whether the employer's termination of the worker violated the OHSA.

Decision

The arbitrator found that the employer's dismissal of the worker was justified. The "catch pits" were not situated on the side of the shaft that workers used and presented no danger. The employee's evidence was inconsistent and lacked credibility. The employee did not have an honest belief that his health and safety—or that of other workers—would be endangered by using the shaft cage. Instead, the evidence supported the view that the employee used the work refusal to "put forward his own personal agenda."

The arbitrator ruled that, as remedial legislation, the OHSA must be given a fair and liberal interpretation. However, to receive the protection of the OHSA, workers must comply with its legislative requirements, including having an honest, genuine, and bona fide belief that the refused work posed a danger. Misusing the right to refuse unsafe work was culpable misconduct that had significant negative effects for both the employer and his co-workers, who lost four hours' pay and their bonus. The arbitrator refused to reinstate the worker despite his 11 years' service, citing his lack of candour and noting that his prospects for rehabilitation were poor.

The Right to Stop Work (Sections 44 to 49)

In addition to the general right to refuse unsafe work, the OHSA also allows certified members of the JHSC to stop work in "dangerous circumstances." There are two kinds of work stoppages that may be initiated by certified members of the JHSC under the OHSA: the bilateral (two-party) work stoppage and the unilateral (single-party) work stoppage.

BILATERAL WORK STOPPAGES

Under s. 45 of the OHSA, a bilateral work stoppage starts when a certified member of a JHSC has reason to believe that "dangerous circumstances" exist at the workplace and the member requests a supervisor to investigate the matter. Dangerous circumstances require all three of the following:

1. the OHSA or its regulations are being contravened,
2. the contravention poses a danger or hazard to a worker, and
3. any delay in controlling the situation may seriously endanger a worker.

To trigger a bilateral work stoppage, there must be a *current* contravention of the law and the potential danger to a worker must be *serious*. Once dangerous circumstances are identified, a supervisor must investigate immediately. A certified member who is unsatisfied with the investigation may ask another certified member, representing the other workplace party, to investigate. For example, if the first certified member represents workers, the member next called must represent management.

If, after conducting his own investigation, the second certified member agrees with the first certified member, the two members may jointly direct the employer to stop work, and the employer must comply immediately. After taking steps to remedy the problem, the employer can ask the two certified members or a Ministry inspector to cancel the stop-work direction.

If the two certified members cannot agree about the necessity of a work stoppage, either of them may call a Ministry inspector to investigate the problem and issue a written decision.

UNILATERAL WORK STOPPAGES

Under the unilateral work stoppage provisions in s. 47 of the OHSA, any certified member of the JHSC may direct a work stoppage if he finds that dangerous circumstances exist. There are two situations in which a unilateral work stoppage can occur:

1. where the Ontario Labour Relations Board has issued a declaration that the unilateral work stoppage provisions will apply; and
2. where an employer voluntarily informs the JHSC in writing that it consents to the adoption of this procedure.

The first situation usually occurs where a certified member or a Ministry inspector has reason to believe that the bilateral work stoppage procedure is insufficient to protect workers. Either party may apply to the Ontario Labour Relations Board for a declaration that unilateral work stoppage procedures apply in that workplace. In making its decision, the Board considers such factors as the employer's record of accidents, work refusals, and non-compliance with inspectors' orders. The Board may also recommend to the Ministry that an inspector be assigned to oversee the employer's health and safety practices, at the employer's expense.

Where unilateral work stoppage procedures apply in a workplace and a single certified member directs a work stoppage, the employer must comply immediately. The stop-work order may direct the employer to stop specific work or stop the use of any part of the workplace or any equipment or device. The employer's investigation, started after work has stopped, must be conducted in the presence of the certified member who gave the work stoppage direction. Either party may request that a Ministry inspector investigate the issue, and the inspector will issue her decision in writing. In a unilateral work stoppage, the single certified member has the right to stop work before an investigation occurs; however, in a bilateral work stoppage, there must be an investigation and management must be alerted before work is stopped (Keith and Chandler, 2014, p. 106).

Employers are prohibited from retaliating against a certified member for exercising her powers to stop work. However, certified members are accountable for the responsible use of their authority; they may be named personally in a complaint to the Ontario Labour Relations Board if they exercise their power recklessly or in **bad faith**. Such a complaint must be filed within 14 days of the event in question, and the Board has the power to decertify the member.

Police, firefighters, and those employed in correctional facilities have no work stoppage rights. As well, the right to stop work is limited in certain workplaces, such as hospitals, residential group homes, or medical laboratories, if the stoppage would directly endanger another person.

Any work refusal or work stoppage under the Act should be documented and accurate records should be retained (Keith and Chandler, 2014, p. 108).

3. The Right to Know

Under the OHSA, workers have the right to know about potential hazards to which they may be exposed. This includes the right to receive training about the safe use of machinery, equipment, and processes. A significant part of this right relates to the right to know about hazardous substances at the workplace.

Designated Substances

In 2009, 11 of the 12 designated substance regulations (that is, for acrylonitrile, arsenic, asbestos, benzene, coke oven emissions, ethylene oxide, isocyanates, lead, mercury, silica, and vinyl chloride) were consolidated into one *Designated Substances* regulation (Keith and Chandler, 2014, p. 75).

In workplaces where these designated substances are present, processed, used, or stored and where workers are likely to come into contact with, inhale, or absorb them, employers are required to take specific measures. These include limiting the amount of the designated substance that workers can be exposed to in a given time period and recording this exposure. Use of personal protective equipment is not factored in when determining exposure to airborne concentrations of these substances (Keith and Chandler, 2014, p. 79).

The general hazardous substances regulation is the *Control of Exposure to Biological or Chemical Agents* regulation. It sets maximum exposure limits for about 725 listed biological and chemical substances or agents. Exposure means inhalation, ingestion, or skin contact. Measures to control exposure include engineering controls, special work practices, and hygiene facilities; personal protective equipment may, in limited circumstances, also be used.

These hazardous substances regulations incorporate maximum exposure limits. Their requirements are separate from those of the Workplace Hazardous Materials Information System, discussed below, that focuses on the rights of the worker to know and be educated about hazardous substances in the workplace.

Workplace Hazardous Materials Information System

WHAT IS WHMIS?

The **Workplace Hazardous Materials Information System (WHMIS)** is a national information system that applies to all industries and workplaces in Canada. It is Canada's first "right to know" legislation and is designed to provide workers and employers with essential information about using, handling, and storing hazardous materials in the workplace. As a national system, it provides a uniform level of protection throughout the country. The term "controlled products" used by the federal WHMIS legislation is essentially equivalent to the term "hazardous materials" in Ontario's OHSA. Examples of controlled products are compressed gas, flammable aerosols, and corrosive material.

EMPLOYERS' RESPONSIBILITIES

Under WHMIS, an employer has the following responsibilities:

1. *Prepare and maintain an inventory of hazardous materials.* Employers must take and maintain an inventory of all hazardous materials and physical agents present in the workplace.
2. *Label hazardous materials.* Employers must ensure that every hazardous material in or out of a container in the workplace is labelled with a supplier or a workplace label. Labels must contain certain information and hazard symbols. Labels that are illegible or removed must be replaced.
3. *Prepare or obtain material safety data sheets (MSDSs).* Employers must prepare or obtain from the supplier MSDSs for every hazardous material in the workplace. MSDSs must contain precautionary and first aid measures, and identify the product and supplier. They must be updated whenever there is a change to the relevant information, and they expire every three years. MSDSs must be readily available to workers who may be exposed to the hazardous material and to JHSC members or to the health and safety representative. They must be in English as well as in the majority language of the workplace.
4. *Provide worker training.* Employers must ensure that workers who are exposed or likely to be exposed to a hazardous material or physical agent are trained concerning its safe use, handling, and storage (s. 42(1) of the OHSA). Employers must consult the JHSC or health and safety representative concerning the content and delivery of training programs and must review the program at least annually to see whether retraining is necessary. Safety training must begin with the orientation of new employees.

Employers who are concerned that the requirement to provide information on the label or MSDS may result in the disclosure of confidential business information and trade secrets may request an exemption from disclosure by filing a claim with Health Canada. Even if this exemption is granted, the employer must still disclose the confidential information in a medical emergency.

FYI

Globally Harmonized System of Classification and Labelling of Chemicals (GHS)

Just as WHMIS is a way to standardize and harmonize the classification and labelling of chemicals throughout Canada, the GHS establishes a common system internationally (Keith and Chandler, 2014, p. 69). A voluntary system, the GHS is being implemented by Canada, which will require that WHMIS-related laws be updated. Although this is not expected to change the roles of suppliers, employers, and workers under WHMIS, it will affect how chemicals are classified and also affect supplier labelling requirements. The expected completion date is June 2016 (Keith and Chandler, 2014, p. 71).

FYI

Smoking in the Workplace

THE SMOKE-FREE ONTARIO ACT

In response to growing concerns about the effects of second-hand smoke, Ontario passed the *Smoke-Free Ontario Act*, which prohibits smoking in enclosed workplaces and enclosed public places throughout the province. This law, which replaced a patchwork of local municipal bylaws in 2006, makes employers responsible for ensuring that there is no smoking in an "enclosed workplace." This includes washrooms, lobbies, lunchrooms, parking garages, and transportable offices such as taxi cabs and company vehicles. The prohibition also applies during off-hours when people are not working. Under the legislation, employers are responsible for

- advising all workers that smoking is prohibited in the enclosed work environment;
- removing ashtrays or similar equipment;
- ensuring that anyone who refuses to comply does not remain in the enclosed workplace; and
- posting "no smoking" signs at all entrances, exits, washrooms, and other appropriate locations to ensure that everyone knows that smoking is prohibited. (The prescribed signs are available at: www.mhp.gov.on.ca/en/smoke-free/legislation/signs.asp.)

Under the Act, designated smoking rooms are not allowed. However, an employer may choose, but is not required, to accommodate employees who smoke by providing a smoking shelter outdoors as long as the structure consists of no more than two walls and/or a roof.

To enforce the law and investigate complaints, public health inspectors have broad powers to enter and inspect the workplace without a warrant. The maximum fine for an individual caught smoking in a non-smoking area is $5,000. There is no maximum fine for a corporation for contravening the legislation. Employers are also prohibited from committing any acts of reprisal against an employee who tries to have the provisions of the Act enforced. The maximum fine for violating this provision is $4,000 for an individual and $10,000 for a corporation.

Workplace Violence and Harassment

In the past, an Ontario employer's legal duty to address violence in its workplace stemmed from its general duty to take every precaution reasonable in the circumstances to protect the health and safety of its workers. However, as a result of the workplace murder of Lori Dupont and subsequent inquest (see the In the News box below), as well as other deaths related to workplace violence, in 2009 the Ontario legislature introduced amendments to the OHSA (Bill 168) that impose a *specific* duty on employers to take steps to address workplace violence.

IN THE NEWS

Lori Dupont—A Workplace Murder

Lori Dupont was a recovery room nurse at Hotel Dieu Grace Hospital who began a relationship in 2002 with Dr. Marc Daniel, an anesthesiologist at the hospital. After she broke off the relationship, he began making threats against her and her family. Following a suicide attempt, Daniel was required to take a medical leave and enroll in a health program. When he returned to work in May 2005, there were several conditions placed on his hospital privileges, including being monitored and restricted from working at the hospital during the weekends. However, by the fall, some of these restrictions had been removed and on Saturday, November 12, 2005 Daniel and Dupont were scheduled to work together. With only a skeletal staff in the operating room, Daniel took the opportunity to stab Lori Dupont to death. He committed suicide shortly thereafter. During the subsequent inquest, the coroner's jury heard that the hospital allowed Daniel to keep his hospital privileges, despite complaints about his threatening behaviour that included breaking a nurse's finger and destroying hospital equipment, as well as the ongoing harassment of Dupont.

SOURCE: Based on Doug Schmidt, "Why?: Family, Friends Ask," *Windsor Star*, Saturday, November 11, 2006.

The amendments to the OHSA introduced through Bill 168 have created a number of specific obligations for employers, including the requirement to assess the risk of workplace violence and to develop policies and implement programs to deal with workplace violence and harassment. "Workplace violence" is defined to include both the exercise of physical force and the *attempt or threat* to exercise physical force that causes or could cause physical injury to a worker. "Workplace harassment" refers to engaging in a course of vexatious comment or conduct against a worker in a workplace that is known or ought reasonably to be known to be unwelcome. This definition of "harassment" mirrors the one found in the Ontario *Human Rights Code*. Unlike the Code, however, which is only engaged when the harassing behaviour is based on one of the prohibited grounds of discrimination, the OHSA anti-harassment provisions apply regardless of the reasons for the harassment.

As noted, employers are required to conduct a violence risk assessment to determine the possibility or prevalence of violence in their workplace. For this assessment, employers must take into account circumstances that are common to other workplaces (such as whether the job involves handling money or working alone), as well as circumstances specific to their own workplace (for example, a poorly lit parking lot). The risk must be reassessed as often as necessary to protect the workers. Results of the assessment must be reported to the joint health and safety committee, or health and safety representative.

Employers are also required to prepare workplace policies aimed at preventing and addressing workplace violence and harassment. Those policies must be reviewed at least annually (and more frequently if necessary) and the employer must provide workers with information and instruction relating to those policies. Where there are six or more employees in a workplace, the employer must post the policies in a conspicuous location.

To implement its workplace *violence* program, an employer must

- take measures to control the risks identified in the assessment (such as improving lighting in poorly lit areas or controlling building access);

- implement procedures for summoning immediate assistance when violence occurs or is likely to occur, or when threats of violence are made;
- implement procedures for reporting incidents or threats of violence; and
- implement a process to investigate and address incidents, complaints, or threats of workplace violence.

Implementing the workplace *harassment* policy requires measures and procedures for reporting, investigating, and dealing with incidents of harassment.

It is noteworthy that Ontario's workplace anti-violence requirements also require employers to address domestic violence in the workplace—for example, when an abuser threatens or assaults a spouse at her place of work. Although employers are not required to uncover domestic violence (Klie, 2008, p. 8), if an employer is aware, or ought reasonably to be aware, that domestic violence may occur in the workplace, the employer must "take every precaution reasonable in the circumstances for the protection of a worker" (s. 25(2)(h)). An employer could, for example, develop a safety plan to ensure that a vulnerable person is protected while at the workplace or let the person know where she can go for assistance.

The Bill 168 provisions also extend the various health and safety duties of employers, supervisors, and workers to apply, as appropriate, to workplace violence (but not harassment). In certain circumstances, an employer must provide a worker with information about the risk of workplace violence from a person with a history of violence, including personal information as is reasonably necessary. This duty arises if the worker can be expected to encounter a person with a history of violent behaviour in the course of her work and if the risk of workplace violence is likely to result in physical injury. A worker who has reason to believe that workplace violence is likely to endanger her may exercise the right to refuse unsafe work and that worker must remain "in a safe place that is as near as reasonably possible to his or her work station."

If a worker is unable or refuses to work or requires medical attention because of workplace violence, an employer must report this to the Ministry of Labour and the Ministry must send investigators to the worksite.

Although the right to refuse work and report to the Ministry does not apply to workplace harassment, Ministry inspectors can visit workplaces to ensure that employers have a harassment policy and procedures.

Workplace violence and harassment are serious issues and employers need to keep apprised of best practices in these areas, as well as their legal obligations. These include:

- training all employees in violence prevention;
- making reporting mandatory;
- regularly inspecting the workplace to ensure standards are maintained;
- designating a response team;
- thoroughly investigating any and all incidents of workplace violence and harassment;
- maintaining accurate and detailed records of such incidents and the related investigations;
- disciplining employees for failing to adhere to policies; and
- contacting law enforcement as appropriate.

The WSIB (www.labour.gov.on.ca/english/hs/pubs/wvps_guide/index.php) and the Canadian Centre for Occupational Health and Safety (www.ccohs.ca/oshanswers/psychosocial/violence.html) are two of many websites that provide information on how to address workplace violence and harassment.

Since its passage, there have been a significant number of cases where the impact of Bill 168 has been considered. One of the first of these was *Kingston (City) v. Canadian Union of Public Employees, Local 109*. It signalled that adjudicators will indeed consider the Bill's requirements when determining the appropriate penalty for violence-related misconduct in the workplace.

CASE IN POINT

Bill 168 Provisions Raise the Ante on Verbal Threats

Kingston (City) v. Canadian Union of Public Employees, Local 109,
2011 CanLII 50313 (Ont. LA) (Arbitrator Newman)

Facts

Donna Hudson was an employee with 28 years' service who had a long history of anger-related misconduct, which included swearing at co-workers and arguing with her supervisor. Shortly after taking Bill 168-related training on workplace violence and harassment, as well as an anger-management program, Hudson made a verbal threat to her union representative. After he asked that she not talk about a friend of his who was dead, Hudson said, "Yes, and you will be too." The union reported the threat to the employer, who investigated the allegation. When interviewed, Hudson denied making a threat and did not apologize for what she said. The employer decided to terminate her employment for just cause and, as a unionized employee, Hudson grieved her dismissal.

Relevant Issue

Whether the employer had just cause for termination in these circumstances.

Decision

The arbitrator concluded that, despite the grievor's long service and the improbability of her carrying out her threat, the employer did have just cause to terminate her employment. In reaching her conclusion, the arbitrator noted the four ways in which the Bill 168 provisions on workplace violence and harassment have affected the appropriate penalty for verbal threats.

1. They clarify that while vexatious, unwelcome language is *harassment*, language that actually threatens to end someone's life falls into a category of its own. There does not need to be evidence of intent or ability to do immediate harm. The language itself is workplace *violence*.

2. They have changed the way employers react to a threat of harm: it now must be reported, investigated, and addressed. While an employer's response must still be proportionate and fair, the employer cannot turn a blind eye to such language.

3. They increase the weight to be given to one of the elements in determining the appropriate penalty: the seriousness of the incident.

4. They mean that workplace safety is now an additional factor that must be considered when assessing the reasonableness and proportionality of the discipline. The arbitrator noted, "If the offending employee is likely to render the employer incapable of fulfilling its obligation to provide a safe workplace under the Occupational Health and Safety Act," the employment relationship will be incapable of reparation. The question is this: "To what extent is it likely that this employee, if returned to the workplace, can be relied upon to conduct himself or herself in a way that is safe for others?"

In upholding the termination for cause, the arbitrator indicated that given all the circumstances, the employer had no reasonable reassurance that this behaviour would not be repeated. However, she noted that the result would have been different if the grievor had accepted responsibility for her statements and shown an understanding of how serious they were or what action she was going to take to gain control over her angry impulses (Minken, 2011).

Despite this early decision, there is some debate about how much Bill 168 has actually changed the law with respect to the seriousness of workplace threats and violence, which have always been considered very serious workplace offences, especially when compounded by denial and lack of remorse. However, it *is* clear that an employer that wants to rely on Bill 168 should follow its own investigation requirements.

In another decision related to the Bill 168 provisions, *International Brotherhood of Electrical Workers, Local 636 v. Niagara Peninsula Energy Inc.*, the arbitrator found that despite the employer's increased responsibilities related to maintaining a safe workplace, these responsibilities still have to be balanced with an employee's right to privacy. In *Niagara Peninsula*, the employer required one of its employees to obtain a psychiatric assessment before returning to work after he had engaged in several loud and angry outbursts. The arbitrator found that because the request was based on the employer's belief that the grievor had an anger problem (rather than a mental illness), the employer did not have reasonable and probable grounds to require the assessment. In the arbitrator's view, "the mere fact that an employee has engaged in conduct that engages Bill 168 does not mean that the employer may require a psychiatric examination. The pre-Bill 168 jurisprudence still applies in that there has to be a balancing of the employer's right and duty to maintain a safe workplace and the employee's privacy rights. The test for achieving that balance continues to be the 'reasonable and probable' test" (Groves, 2012).

With respect to workplace harassment, case law has noted the legal distinction between Bill 168's provisions related to it and those related to workplace violence. While employers are required to take every reasonable precaution against workplace violence, an employer's duty regarding harassment is more restricted, primarily requiring an employer to develop, educate employees about, and implement an anti-harassment policy that includes a complaint procedure (Sherrard Kuzz LLP, 2014, p. 3). However, as highlighted in the OLRB's decision in *Ljuboja v. Aim Group Inc.*, simply posting an anti-harassment policy is not sufficient; the employer has a duty to investigate a complaint. In *Ljuboja*, a temporary agency employee was placed in a supervisory position at a General Motors plant. During one end-of-shift meeting, his supervisor allegedly screamed at him for reassigning a relief worker so that there was no one available to stand in when other workers needed to take a washroom break. Ljuboja complained about this incident to GM's human resources department, and his employment was terminated shortly afterward. He filed a complaint with the OLRB, arguing that his termination was a reprisal for his workplace harassment complaint, contrary to s. 50(1) of the OHSA. The OLRB found for Ljuboja. It decided that, although there is no stand-alone right under the legislation for a worker to be free from workplace harassment, the employer's obligation to both implement a complaint mechanism and to investigate and deal with harassment complaints would have little meaning if the employer could retaliate against a worker for making such a harassment complaint (Stringer LLP, 2014).

This decision by the OLRB to consider reprisal complaints related to workplace harassment is important because, in reprisal cases, the onus is on the employer to show that the harassment complaint played *no part* in its decision to dismiss the complainant. Moreover, unlike in a common law wrongful dismissal action, reinstatement, with full back pay, is a possible remedy (Whitten & Lublin, 2014).

That said, the OLRB in *Ljuboja* reaffirmed that the Bill 168 provisions do not require an employer to provide a harassment-free workplace or to resolve a harassment complaint in a particular way. The employer's obligation is to have a complaint procedure, to investigate and deal with a complaint according to its policy, and to not punish a worker for making a harassment complaint (that is, no reprisal). How the complaint is investigated and resolved is left up to the employer (Sherrard Kuzz LLP, 2014, p. 3).

It should also be noted that not all language that a complainant finds unwelcome is "harassment." The test is an objective one: would a reasonable person in the complainant's position find the behaviour unwelcome? For example, in one case a single incident of rudeness—where a co-worker shouted at the complainant in the lunchroom—and in another, a supervisor's lack of tact in providing negative performance feedback, were both found *not* to constitute harassment. Similarly, a personality conflict between co-workers that resulted in tension but did not affect either worker's ability to perform the job was found not to fall under the workplace harassment provisions (Milne, 2013, p. 15). Additionally, normal supervision, counselling, and discipline are not harassment, regardless of whether the employee agrees with the actions taken.

Accidents

Accident Reporting

Separate accident-reporting obligations exist under the OHSA and the *Workplace Safety and Insurance Act*. Employers should avoid using the form relevant to the latter Act (Form 7) to satisfy their reporting obligations under the OHSA because this form does not provide them with an opportunity to outline the steps they took to prevent an injury (see Chapter 8 for discussion of reporting requirements under the WSIA).

Under s. 51 of the OHSA, employers must report all accidents in the workplace to the Ministry of Labour. For critical injuries or fatalities, the employer must notify the Ministry immediately and provide a written report within 48 hours. The employer must also immediately notify the JHSC or the health and safety representative and the injured worker's union, if any. The information required in these reports is set out in sector-specific regulations (for example, industrial, construction, and mining regulations). A critical injury is defined as including amputation of a limb or burns to a major portion of the body.

Under s. 52(1), employers must notify the Ministry, in writing, within four days of non-critical injuries, as well as the JHSC or the health and safety representative and the union, if any. A non-critical injury is a less serious injury that results in a worker's inability to perform his usual work or requires medical attention. Under ss. 52(2) and (3), employers must also give written notice to the Ministry within four days of being advised that a worker or former worker has an occupational illness or claim (Keith and Chandler, 2014, p. 111).

There are additional written notice requirements for unexpected explosions, fires, floods, or rock bursts in construction projects, mines, and mining plants.

The duty to report workplace injuries is taken seriously. In one case, an employer's failure to report a server's slip-and-fall accident in a restaurant and its cleanup of the accident site before the inspector arrived to investigate led to a $20,000 fine. For industrial establishments, notices of critical or fatal injuries must be kept for at least one year, while for some other sectors, including construction projects and mining, a permanent record must be kept (Keith and Chandler, 2014, p. 115).

CASE IN POINT

When Is the Duty to Report a Critical Injury or Death Triggered?

Blue Mountain Resorts Limited v. Ontario (Labour), 2013 ONCA 75

Facts

After Blue Mountain Resorts failed to report the drowning death of one of its hotel guests at its unattended swimming pool, a Ministry of Labour inspector issued an order under s. 51(1) for failure to report a death or critical injury at the workplace. The company had also failed to preserve the scene of the accident as required under s. 51(2). The employer appealed the order, arguing that the recreational facility was not predominantly a workplace, nor was a worker at the site when the drowning happened. Nonetheless, both the Ontario Labour Relations Board and the Ontario Divisional Court found that the duty to report was triggered because, although no employees were working there at the time, they did work there sometimes (for example, to clean the pool). In other words, in their view, a workplace includes all areas in or near where workers perform work, regardless of whether workers are present at the time of an injury. Blue Mountain Resorts appealed this decision to the Ontario Court of Appeal.

Relevant Issue

Whether the unattended swimming pool area constituted a "workplace," thereby triggering the s. 51(1) duty to report the guest's death by drowning.

Decision

The Court of Appeal held that the OLRB and Divisional Court's interpretation of the duty to report was too wide in that it would make virtually every place in the province a "workplace" simply because an employee could, at some time, work there. This could lead to absurd results. For example, if an NHL hockey player or spectator were critically injured during a game, the injury would have to be reported to the Ministry of Labour and the game would have to be suspended until a Ministry of Labour inspector allowed it to proceed. The appellate court found that the focus of the reporting requirement is on worker safety (Mills, 2013, p. 43). Therefore, while s. 51 *can* apply to the death or critical injury of a non-worker as well as a worker, the duty to report only arises when there is some reasonable connection between the hazard giving rise to the death or critical injury and worker safety in the workplace. Because there was nothing indicating that the guest's drowning death was caused by a hazard that could endanger a worker, the duty to notify and preserve the scene was not triggered.

In the event of any workplace accident, an employer should immediately

1. arrange for medical assistance for the injured worker;
2. lock out the machinery or equipment;
3. secure the accident site; and
4. notify the injured worker's family, the Ministry of Labour, the JHSC or health and safety representative, and its lawyer.

Accident Investigation Procedures

At least two managers should be trained in accident investigation techniques. One senior person should take charge of the investigation and the collection of all information and documents related to an accident. An employer should take the following actions:

1. Ensure that the investigation begins as soon as possible after an injured worker receives medical treatment. There should be a separate management investigation, apart from the investigation conducted by the Ministry inspector.
2. Prepare and file the requisite information for the Ministry of Labour.
3. Obtain a statement from the injured worker if possible.
4. Take photographs and, if relevant, samples of any hazardous materials. Examine the equipment or tools involved.
5. Interview all potential witnesses. Include questions about their observations of the incident; their training and knowledge of workplace hazards and rules and warnings; and the steps that were taken to prevent the accident (Sherrard Kuzz LLP, "12-Step Accident Checklist," 2014).
6. Ensure that all interviews are witnessed by a third party.
7. Prepare witness statements and have them signed by the witnesses.
8. Ensure that the site of the accident is not tampered with.
9. Develop a remedial action plan that identifies and addresses both the direct and the underlying causes of the accident. Have a senior executive review and approve the plan; then implement the plan (Keith and Chandler, 2014, p. 195).
10. Have a management representative accompany the Ministry inspector during her investigation and record her observations, comments, tests, and measurements. During the Ministry inspector's investigation, any person being questioned has the right to have counsel present and the right to remain silent.

Administration and Enforcement

Administration

Under Ontario's internal responsibility system, workplace parties share responsibility for ensuring a healthy and safe workplace. Ministry inspectors provide specialized safety advice and expertise, but they become involved in enforcement only when the self-regulatory system based on joint responsibility breaks down.

Ministry Inspections

In addition to investigating work refusals, work stoppages, and serious injuries or fatalities, inspectors also conduct random, unannounced inspections of workplaces. Employers are required to cooperate with these inspections. In one case, the owner of an automotive repair shop was sentenced to seven days in jail and placed on probation for six months for refusing to let health and safety inspectors onto the premises for a routine inspection (Government of Ontario, 2009). The owner, who was "verbally abusive and intimidating toward the inspectors," was convicted of obstructing an inspector contrary to s. 62(1) of the OHSA.

During a workplace inspection, the inspector must be accompanied by a worker representative from the JHSC, the health and safety representative, or a worker knowledgeable in the field.

Sections 54 to 56 of the OHSA give inspectors broad powers, including the power to:

1. enter any workplace without a search warrant, except where the workplace is also a personal dwelling;
2. conduct tests or have tests conducted at the employer's expense;
3. question anyone in the workplace;
4. speak privately to any worker;
5. compel the production of drawings, specifications, licences, or other documents for examination, and copy them, if necessary, before returning them to the employer; and
6. remove any equipment, machine, or device to test as necessary.

In certain circumstances, objects or other evidence may be seized, with the approval of a justice of the peace, if the inspector reasonably believes that a violation of the OHSA has occurred for which the object will provide evidence.

The employer should designate a member of senior management who is knowledgeable in health and safety matters to meet an inspector as soon as she arrives at the workplace. It is usually a good idea for the senior manager to accompany the inspector during the inspection to explain health and safety efforts and obtain feedback. However, an employer cannot insist on being present when a worker speaks to a Ministry of Labour inspector (Keith and Chandler, 2014, p. 118). The inspector should be debriefed at the end of the inspection so that management may benefit from her expertise and observations.

It is illegal to alter the scene of a serious workplace injury or fatality in any way without the permission of a Ministry inspector. Exceptions exist where alterations are necessary to relieve suffering, maintain an essential service, or prevent unnecessary damage to property.

Enforcement

Under s. 57 of the OHSA, an inspector who finds a contravention of the OHSA or its regulations may issue an order requiring the employer to comply with the law. If a contravention endangers the health or safety of a worker, the inspector has the authority to issue a stop-work order. A copy of an inspector's order must be posted in a conspicuous location in the workplace and given to the JHSC or the health and safety representative.

An inspector's order is binding as soon as it is issued. Any party may appeal an inspector's order to the Ontario Labour Relations Board within 30 days of the issuance of the order. This time limit is extended only in extraordinary circumstances. Launching an appeal does not suspend the order, although the Ontario Labour Relations Board has the discretion to suspend the order pending the appeal.

An employer may appeal an order if it requires more time to comply, perhaps because of the costs of compliance. A successful appeal may reduce the likelihood of charges being laid under the OHSA (Keith and Chandler, 2014, p. 132).

On an appeal, the Board may uphold or rescind the order or substitute its own findings. The Board's decision is effectively final because it will be overturned on judicial review only if it is "unreasonable" or without jurisdiction, not merely incorrect.

When an employer believes that it has complied with an inspector's order, it must submit a notice of compliance to the Ministry of Labour within three days of compliance. It must also include a statement from a worker member of the JHSC or the health and safety representative that indicates agreement or disagreement with the employer's notice. Alternatively, the employer must indicate that the worker member declined to sign such a statement. Ultimately, the inspector determines whether compliance has been achieved.

Due Diligence Defence

Offences under the OHSA are **strict liability offences** because the Ministry does not need to show that the employer intended to violate the legislation in order to obtain a conviction. Rather, if there is a workplace accident, the Ministry must prove beyond a reasonable doubt the act or omission (failure to act) that caused the danger to exist. The onus shifts to the accused employer to show, on a balance of probabilities, that it took every "precaution reasonable in the circumstances" to prevent the danger (s. 25(2)(h)). This is an objective standard; an employer's honest subjective belief that it has taken every reasonable precaution is not enough.

An attempt to show that every reasonable precaution was taken is a **due diligence defence**. For example, if a worker is injured because he removed safety guards (physical barriers that prevent injury) from a machine, the employer may successfully defend itself if it can prove that it took all reasonable care to ensure that the machinery was guarded, including training employees about the importance of guards and disciplining employees who removed them.

Although the due diligence defence is set out in s. 66(3) of the OHSA, it also exists at common law. Under this defence, an employer may also avoid liability if it reasonably believed in a mistaken set of facts that, if true, would have rendered its act innocent (Keith and Chandler, 2014, p. 12).

Employers are not held to a standard of perfection. The defence of due diligence does not require an employer to anticipate and solve every possible problem in advance of its arising. It does require an employer to proactively comply with the OHSA on an ongoing basis and anticipate reasonably foreseeable hazards. For example, in one case, an employer was charged when a Ministry inspector caught some workers not wearing the required safety belts. However, the charges were withdrawn when the employer was able to show, among other things, that it sent workers home whenever it caught them not wearing safety belts (Keith and Chandler, 2014, p. 14).

There is no list of factors that guarantees that a court will find that an employer was duly diligent. However, typically an employer's safety record, the foreseeability of the risk, and the hazards inherent in the industry are considered. Merely developing a health and safety program is not enough; a court assesses whether the employer had safety procedures in place that it implemented, monitored, and enforced (Keith and Chandler, 2014, p. 11).

Although the due diligence defence fails more often than it succeeds, the following two cases show that these decisions hinge on whether the employer took every reasonable precaution and on the specific facts in each case. In *Ontario (Ministry of Labour) v. Cementation Canada* the employer failed to prove that it exercised due diligence, while in *R v. King Paving & Materials* this defence was successful (Bongarde Media Co., November 2008, p. 1).

CASE IN POINT

Failure to Supervise Undermines Employer's Due Diligence Defence

Ontario (Ministry of Labour) v. Cementation Canada Inc. et al., 2008 ONCJ 135

Facts

A mine worker was given conflicting instructions on how to repair a machine called a cactus clam. Attempting to follow one set of instructions, the worker borrowed a forklift from another worker to flip over the machine to get access to the damaged part. While using the forklift, for which he had not been properly trained, the worker got into an accident and broke his leg. The employer was charged under the OHSA for several safety violations.

Relevant Issue

Whether the employer exercised due diligence in these circumstances.

Decision

The Ontario Court of Justice found that the employer had not exercised due diligence. Among other things, the injured worker had no direct supervision while he was repairing the damaged machine. It was clearly foreseeable that the worker had not been given enough information, instruction, or supervision to perform the task safely (Bongarde Media Co., December 2008, p. 4).

CASE IN POINT

Employer's Thorough Efforts Support Due Diligence Defence

R v. King Paving & Materials Company, A Division of KPM Industries Ltd., 2007 ONCJ 610

Facts

A water main project required that a pipe be pulled around a corner onto a side street. One worker, who was acting as a spotter, was specifically told by his supervisor and foreman to stand on the northeast corner of the street during the procedure for safety reasons. However, the worker did not remain there. Instead, he decided to walk in the westbound lane of the road, where he was struck from behind by the pipe. The worker's leg was broken and the employer, supervisor, and foreman were charged under the OHSA with failing to ensure that the material was moved in a way that did not endanger a worker.

Relevant Issue

Whether the company, supervisor, and foreman exercised due diligence in these circumstances.

Decision

The Ontario Court of Justice dismissed the charges, finding that all of the defendants had exercised due diligence. It found that the company, through its supervisor and foreman, took every precaution reasonable in the circumstances to ensure that the pipe would be moved in a manner that would not endanger the worker. In finding that the pull procedures were reasonable, the court noted that

- the employer had successfully performed the exact same pull with the same pipe and virtually the same crew a month before this pull;
- procedures specifically took into account the size and weight of the pipe;
- the employer conducted a "tool box" meeting before each of the pulls to explain the procedures fully, and the injured worker was present at both;
- the injured worker was extremely experienced and there was no reason why the employer should have kept him under surveillance in case he deviated from his instructions;
- a backhoe was placed in the intersection to prevent the pipe from rolling north;
- the injured worker acknowledged that he had been clearly instructed where to stand while conducting his spotter duties and had failed to stand there; and
- while the pipe was being moved, the foreman visually swept the area; the last time he saw the injured worker, he was standing as directed (Bongarde Media Co., December 2008, p. 6).

As part of exercising due diligence, an employer should document all of its efforts to prevent workplace accidents, including all discussions with employees regarding safety procedures. Specific steps that increase the credibility of a due diligence defence include the following:

1. Designate a senior manager to be responsible for OHSA compliance.
2. Prepare a *written* health and safety policy and develop and maintain safety procedures, as required by the OHSA.
3. Provide and maintain a record of safety orientations for new employees and for existing employees with new job assignments.
4. Have senior executives actively support the JHSC.
5. Identify workplace hazards through internal and external safety audits. An outside safety expert may identify "blind spots" in the program.
6. Hold monthly safety meetings in every department or work group, and forward all recommendations or concerns to the JHSC.
7. Support and respond to the JHSC.
8. Train workers and supervisors to perform their duties safely, and document all training. Make sure employees actively participate—doing is better than watching—and double-check that employees actually *understand* the procedures. Training should also be specific to the workplace and an employee's job.
9. Hold regular safety meetings to update workers.
10. Discipline all workers and managers who fail to follow safety requirements.
11. Have a corporate director chair a committee to address OHSA and environmental compliance, and place its concerns on the board of directors' agenda at every general meeting.
12. Have specialized legal counsel conduct an annual compliance audit.
13. Implement a system of recognition and rewards for individuals and departments that reach safety goals.
14. Conduct regular safety inspections and safety audits.
15. Prepare and use internal forms for reporting both critical and non-critical accidents to the Ministry of Labour.
16. Ensure that all managers and supervisors are instructed on the OHSA, applicable regulations, workplace hazards, and appropriate control measures.

17. Ensure that workers are instructed on the OHSA and the regulations and are properly trained on the work-related hazards. Retain confirming documentation (Keith and Chandler, 2014, p. 16).

18. Keep equipment in good order.

Offences and Penalties

Any person who contravenes the OHSA or who fails to comply with an order is potentially liable under s. 66 of the Act. An injury need not result from the contravention or failure for a penalty to be imposed; fines for violations that do not result in a workplace injury are often imposed as a deterrent. Maximum penalties for individuals, such as supervisors and managers, are $25,000 and/or imprisonment for up to 12 months, although imprisonment is extremely rare. Maximum fines for corporations are $500,000. In determining the amount of the fine, courts look at factors such as the employer's size; the scope of actual or potential harm; the maximum penalty; prior convictions; the organization's attitude toward safety generally; and subsequent action taken to correct the problem. There is also a 25 percent victim surcharge, under the *Provincial Offences Act*, added to the fine. To date, the highest fine, including the victim surcharge, has been $1,300,000; it was levied against Vale Canada in 2013 following the death of two workers (Keith and Chandler, 2014, p. 7).

In *R v. Corporation of the City of London*, the employer city was fined $400,000 for failing to meet the standard of care required under the OHSA when one of its employees was killed in a workplace accident.

CASE IN POINT

City Fined $400,000 for Failing to Provide for Workers' Safety

R v. Corporation of the City of London (2000), 11 MPLR (3d) 273 (Ont. CJ)

Facts

A city employee worked at a municipal hockey arena, where he maintained the ice resurfacing machine. While filling the machine with hot water, he heard a hissing sound coming from the machine's gas cap, opened the cap, and was severely burned in an ensuing explosion. He died a few days later in hospital. The employer was charged under the OHSA. At trial, experts were divided about the cause of the accident.

Relevant Issue

Whether the employer met its duty to provide for the safety of workers under the OHSA.

Decision

The justice of the peace found that the employer failed to meet its duties under the OHSA by installing water heaters at a height considerably below that required by the *Gas Utilization Code* and acted unreasonably in failing to install a mechanical ventilation system to disperse gasoline vapours. He fined the employer $50,000 on each of eight counts of failure to protect workers under the OHSA, for a total fine of $400,000.

The Ontario Court of Justice upheld the justice of the peace's decision, stating that the pilot light height regulation "raises a red flag about a hazardous situation and puts the employer on notice of the hazard." This regulatory "red flag" and the large warning notices on the heaters made it unreasonable for the employer to approve the design of the ice room. The court declined to review the fines because they were in the appropriate range.

As noted above, under the OHSA fines may also be awarded against individuals. In *R v. McKinley*, a company director was personally fined $10,000 for ordering painting to continue despite a Ministry-issued stop-work order that barred such work until certain safety modifications were made. This was in addition to a $25,000 fine against the corporation.

Reprisals

As noted above, under s. 50 employers are prohibited from dismissing, disciplining, or otherwise penalizing a worker for acting in compliance with the Act, the regulations, or orders made thereunder, or for seeking enforcement of the legislation. Non-unionized workers can obtain free and confidential advice, education, and representation concerning safety reprisals from the Office of the Worker Adviser (www.owa.gov.on.ca/en/Pages/default.aspx). Moreover, under the Bill 160 amendments, a Ministry of Labour inspector can, with the worker's consent, refer a reprisal complaint directly to the OLRB. At the same time, employers who employ fewer than 50 employees may seek assistance from the Office of the Employer Adviser (www.employeradviser.ca) in defending an unjust reprisal complaint before the OLRB.

Criminal Liability of Organizations

Amendments to Canada's *Criminal Code* in Bill C-45, which came into effect on March 31, 2004, impose a significant duty on organizations to ensure workplace health and safety. Because the *Criminal Code* is criminal legislation, rather than employment law, it applies to both federally and provincially regulated organizations and supplements occupational health and safety legislation.

The amendments do not set out specific requirements. Instead, they state that everyone who undertakes, or has the authority, to direct how another person does work or performs a task is under a legal duty to take "reasonable steps" to prevent bodily harm arising from that work or task. It is likely that "reasonable steps" entail compliance with provincial occupational health and safety legislation (Keith and O'Reilly, 2004, p. 3230).

The amendments were enacted in response to recommendations made by the inquiry into the Westray mine disaster in 1992, where serious safety violations resulted in the death of 26 Nova Scotia miners. The amendments are designed to make organizations more accountable for the safety of their workers.

Before these amendments, individuals could be held criminally liable for acts or omissions that caused workplace accidents. However, the new law strengthens the earlier provisions in a number of ways. Courts can now hold an organization liable for the combined effects of actions by several employees. For example, if two workers each turn off a safety mechanism in the belief that the other's safety mechanism is still operative, the organization can be held legally accountable for the collective failure of the safety system (Vu, 2003, p. 1).

IN THE NEWS

TTC Fined $165,000 in Subway Tunnel Incident

On February 7, 2006, seven Toronto Transit Commission workers and their foreman were repairing the concrete liner of some subway tunnels. To do this they used a flatbed subway car that held a gasoline generator and two gasoline-powered power washers. The workers were overcome by fumes and it was discovered that they were exposed to carbon dioxide levels 40 times the normal occupational exposure limit. The Ministry of Labour charged the TTC with violating the OHSA by allowing internal combustion engines to be operated in an enclosed structure without sufficient ventilation. All of the workers survived but the TTC pleaded guilty to the charge and was fined $165,000.

SOURCE: Ontario Ministry of Labour (December 10, 2007).

Earlier law was also limited because an organization's criminal liability depended on whether a senior member of the organization with policy-making authority committed an offence. For example, in the Westray mine disaster in Nova Scotia, proving criminal liability depended on establishing what the people at the head office in Toronto were aware of. Under the amendments, the net is cast much wider. The group of people whose acts or omissions can legally implicate an organization now includes anyone acting within the scope of his authority in directing work. This includes senior officers, directors, partners, members of an organization, co-workers, agents, and contractors.

The amendments also increase the maximum fine on **summary conviction** from $25,000 to $100,000. There is no limit on fines that can be imposed on conviction for **indictable offences**. Individuals who are convicted of serious health and safety violations now face the possibility of life imprisonment in addition to serious penalties under provincial health and safety legislation (Keith and O'Reilly, 2004, p. 3230). Factors in determining sentencing include the seriousness of the crime, the extent of the injury suffered, the degree of premeditation involved, and whether the individual has any previous convictions.

Although these amendments were designed to hold senior management more accountable for health and safety crimes, lower-level supervisors may face the greatest risk of being charged personally. In April 2004, less than a month after the amendments came into force, a 68-year-old construction supervisor became the first person charged under the new law. The supervisor was overseeing the repair of a drainage problem in the foundation of a house when a trench collapsed and a worker was trapped by heavy dirt. By the time an emergency crew reached the scene, the worker was dead. The supervisor was charged with criminal negligence causing death. Although the charges were later withdrawn as part of an apparent plea bargain, if the supervisor had been convicted, he would have faced the possibility of life in prison or a fine of an unlimited amount (Humber, 2004, p. 3291).

In 2008, a Quebec paving stone manufacturer, Transpavé Inc., became the first company to be convicted of criminal negligence under the *Criminal Code* amendments.

CASE IN POINT

Employer Found Criminally Negligent for Failing to Take Adequate Safety Measures

R c. Transpavé inc., 2008 QCCQ 1598

Facts

Steve L'Écuyer, a 23-year-old employee, worked for a small paving stone manufacturer. He was crushed to death by heavy machinery when he tried to remove a blockage in a jammed stacking machine. An investigation into his death found that the machinery was equipped with a safety device but it had been disabled at the time of the fatality.

Relevant Issue

Whether the employer was guilty of criminal negligence in the death of the employee.

Decision

Transpavé was found criminally negligent. The court noted that the employer did not have an adequate program to ensure that the safety device was operational and had not provided adequate safety training to employees. Transpavé was fined $100,000, plus a $10,000 victim surcharge (used to fund programs for victims of crime). In his ruling, the judge indicated the factors that the fine was based on. These included the relatively small size of the company (approximately 100 employees); the significant investments that the company had made to safety improvements since the fatality (over $500,000); and the employer's willingness to take responsibility for the fatality (Transpavé had pleaded guilty to the charges).

In the first Ontario conviction under the Bill C-45 provisions, *R v. Metron Construction Corporation*, the Ontario Court of Appeal almost quadrupled the fine levied by a lower court (from $200,000 to $750,000) against the employer for criminal negligence causing death. Characterizing the lower fine as "manifestly unfit," the Court of Appeal noted the culpability of the accused's actions in the death of four workers who fell to their deaths on Christmas Eve 2009, after a scaffold collapsed while they were doing repairs on the 14th floor of a high-rise building. The investigation revealed numerous health and safety violations, including the fact that six workers boarded scaffolding that only had two safety harnesses. The appellate court clarified that although the sentencing judge was entitled to consider the range of fines and sentences under the OHSA, those fines failed to "appreciate the higher degree of moral blameworthiness and gravity associated with the respondent's criminal conviction for criminal negligence causing death … . Denunciation and deterrence should have received greater emphasis" (paras. 89, 115).

In addition to the corporate fine, Metron's owner pleaded guilty to four charges under the OHSA and was sentenced to pay a fine of $90,000 (Miedema, 2013).

In another Ontario decision that reflects the seriousness of these criminal charges, *R v. Roofing Medics Ltd.*, the owner was sentenced to 15 days in jail, and the company to a fine of approximately $50,000, for failing to notify the Ministry of the death of a worker within 48 hours, for failing to ensure that the worker used a fall-arrest system, and for furnishing an inspector with false information (Catenacci, 2014).

Planning for a Pandemic

Planning for emergencies, such as widespread power outages and severe weather conditions, has always been recommended practice. However, the SARS outbreak and more recent concerns about the avian and H1N1 flu viruses have added a sense of urgency to the discussion surrounding emergency planning and the need to prepare specifically for a possible pandemic. Pandemic plans require special policies and procedures because widespread contagious diseases affect the workplace in unparalleled ways. Some experts have estimated that at an influenza pandemic's peak, companies may experience absentee rates between 15 percent and 30 percent because of sickness, quarantine, travel restrictions, family care obligations, and fear of contagion (Bongarde Media Co., "Making the Business Case for Safety," 2008, p. 15).

From a legal perspective, the OHSA does not specifically require pandemic preparedness measures. However, such measures are an important part of meeting an employer's general duty under the legislation to take every reasonable precaution to protect the health and safety of workers, as well as the employer's implied common law duty to ensure the safety of its employees. During a pandemic, an employer is responsible for taking all reasonable steps to ensure that the workplace is free from infection, and to prevent the spread of infection. Moreover, by taking all reasonable measures to reduce exposure to an infected person, an employer can reduce the likelihood of an employee successfully invoking the right to refuse unsafe work during a pandemic.

There is no "boilerplate" approach to pandemic planning because requirements depend on factors such as the organization's industry, size, and location. Generally, employers need to review all of their policies and procedures to assess and develop a policy that addresses the special conditions of a pandemic. This policy should be made available to employees.

Components of a pandemic plan could include

- ensuring that employees have credible, up-to-date details on what they should, and should not, do in the event of a pandemic.
- providing a channel such as a website that allows employees to post questions and comments.
- minimizing direct interaction among employees (social distancing) by, for example, limiting large gatherings or holding only essential meetings.
- altering the physical workspace to create distance between employees.
- allowing employees to work from home whenever possible because isolation is the best defence against a contagious disease. This will require identifying job responsibilities that can be performed from home and ensuring that those employees have the necessary training, as well as the hardware, software, bandwidth, and access to corporate information resources to work from home. It is important that employers *test the new infrastructure before it is needed*.
- adopting higher standards of cleanliness, including frequently disinfecting desks and computer equipment.
- maintaining an extra stock of critical supplies such as hygiene products, hand sanitizers, and disinfectants.

- preventing employees who are exhibiting symptoms of the influenza from coming to work or, if they are at work, sending them home. Employees should be required to complete a "fitness to work" questionnaire when they report to work.
- screening customers, suppliers, and the public and encouraging those who have symptoms not to enter.
- posting notices at entry points advising staff and visitors not to enter if they have symptoms of influenza.
- avoiding unnecessary travel.
- making personal protective equipment, such as masks or gloves, available to those at special risk.

Depending on the specific circumstances, employees who are made ill in the course of employment may be entitled to benefits under Ontario's *Workplace Safety and Insurance Act*. Otherwise, employees unable to work as a result of exposure or potential exposure to the flu may be entitled to employment insurance under the federal *Employment Insurance Act* (Torrance, 2009).

During a pandemic, several of the unpaid leave provisions under the *Employment Standards Act, 2000* (ESA) may come into play. As discussed in Chapter 6, declared emergency leave provides employees with unpaid, job-protected leave where there is a declared emergency and, for example, they are needed to stay home to take care of a sick relative. Employees will also be entitled to this leave where there is a declared emergency and an order of an authorized medical officer is made in relation to the employee or a member of the employee's family pursuant to the Ontario *Health Protection and Promotion Act*.

Family medical (up to eight weeks) and personal emergency leaves (up to ten days in a calendar year) under the ESA may also apply as a result of a pandemic.

While the ESA provides for unpaid leaves, contractual entitlements may allow employees to take leaves with pay, including through the use of sick pay or vacation pay (Torrance, 2009, p. 1).

REFERENCES

Alexandrowicz, G., et al. *Dimensions of Law: Canadian and International Law in the 21st Century*. Toronto: Emond Montgomery, 2004.

Angry Employee Digs Hole with Death Threat. *Canadian Employment Law Today*. July 25, 2012.

Battle Mountain Canada Ltd. v. United Steelworkers of America, Local 9364. [2001] OLAA no. 722.

Bill 160, *Occupational Health and Safety Statute Law Amendment Act, 2011*. SO 2011, c. 11.

Bill 168, *Occupational Health and Safety Amendment Act (Violence and Harassment in the Workplace), 2009*. SO 2009, c. 23.

Bill C-45, *An Act to amend the Criminal Code (criminal liability of organizations)*. SC 2003, c. 21.

Blue Mountain Resorts Limited v. Ontario (Labour). 2013 ONCA 75.

Bongarde Media Co. Due Diligence Scorecard. *Safety Compliance Insider: Your Plain Language Guide to C-45, OHS and Due Diligence*. Volume 4, no. 11, November 2008, p. 3.

Bongarde Media Co. Due Diligence Scorecard, Part 2. *Safety Compliance Insider: Your Plain Language Guide to C-45, OHS and Due Diligence*. Volume 4, no. 12, December 2008, p. 1.

Bongarde Media Co. Making the Business Case for Safety. *Safety Compliance Insider: Your Plain Language Guide to C-45, OHS and Due Diligence*. Volume 4, no. 10, October 2008, p. 15.

Bongarde Media Co. Workplace Violence. *Safety Compliance Insider: Your Plain Language Guide to C-45, OHS and Due Diligence*. Volume 4, no. 10, October 2008, p. 1.

Braithwaite, Colin. Creating a Pandemic "Shadow" Policy Manual. 2006. HRinfodesk. http://www.hrinfodesk.com/articles/pandemicelawarticle.htm.

Catenacci, Christina. Fatalities at Work: Are They Leading to Stiffer Sentences? January 27, 2014. First Reference Talks. http://blog.firstreference.com/2014/01/27/fatalities-at-work-are-they-leading-to-stiffer-consequences.

Constant Supervision of Employees Not Necessary: Court. *Canadian Employment Law Today*. January 3, 2013. http://www.employmentlawtoday.com/articleview/16995-constant-supervision-of-employees-not-necessary-court.

Construction Projects. O. reg. 213/91.

Control of Exposure to Biological or Chemical Agents. RRO 1990, reg. 833.

Corporation of the City of London, R v. (2000), 11 MPLR (3d) 273 (Ont. CJ).

Criminal Code. RSC 1985, c. C-46, as amended.

Designated Substances. O. reg. 490/09.

Dobson, Sara. Rona Case Raises Safety, Accommodation Issues. *Canadian HR Reporter*. September 24, 2012, p. 1.

Dobson, Sarah. Employers Prepare for Worst. *Canadian HR Reporter*. May 18, 2009, p. 1.

Doupagne v. Baltimore Aircoil of Canada. 1982 CanLII 846, [1982] OLRB Rep. March 327.

Driver Fired for Refusing to Drive Unsafe Truck. *Canadian Employment Law Today*. April 17, 2013, p. 1.

Edwards, Cheryl A., Jeremy Warning, and Samantha Seabrook. Charting OHS Change in Ontario: From Dean Panel to Bill 160, and Beyond. *Ultimate HR Manual*. Issue no. 79, December 2011. Ontario Hospital Association. https://www.oha.com/Services/HealthHumanResources/Documents/Ultimate%20HR%20Manual%20Newsletter%2079.pdf.

Emond Harnden. $100,000 Fine Imposed on First Corporation Convicted of Criminal Negligence in a Workplace Fatality. *What's New*. April 2008. http://www.emondharnden.com/whatsnew/0804/focus0804.shtml.

Emond Harnden. Bill 168 Amendments to the OHSA—Ontario Tackles Workplace Violence and Harassment. *What's New*. May 2009. http://www.emondharnden.com/whatsnew/0905a/focus0905a.shtml.

Employment Standards Act, 2000. SO 2000, c. 41.

Foulon, Chris. Ontario Targets Workplace Smoking. *Canadian Employment Law Today*. Issue no. 462, May 24, 2006, p. 3619.

Gilbert, Douglas, Brian Burkett, and Moira McCaskill. *Canadian Labour and Employment Law for the US Practitioner*. Washington, DC: Bureau of National Affairs, 2000.

Groves, Russell. Mental Health Assessments and Workplace Safety. July 2012. Filion Wakely Thorup Angeletti. http://filion.on.ca/july-2012-mental-health-assessments-and-workplace-safety.

Health Protection and Promotion Act. RSO 1990, c. H.7.

Humber, Todd. Supervisor Facing Criminal Charges. *Canadian Employment Law Today*. Issue no. 421, September 15, 2004, p. 3291.

Industrial Establishments. RRO 1990, reg. 851.

International Brotherhood of Electrical Workers, Local 636 v. Niagara Peninsula Energy Inc. 2012 CanLII 51862 (Ont. LA).

Keith, Norm, and Yvonne O'Reilly. The New Health and Safety Crime. *Canadian Employment Law Today*. Issue no. 413, May 12, 2004, p. 3230. http://www.employmentlawtoday.com/articleview/14081-the-new-health-and-safety-crime.

Keith, Norman, and Cathy Chandler. *A Practical Guide to Occupational Health and Safety Compliance in Ontario*, 4th ed. Toronto: Canada Law Book, 2014.

Kelloway, Kevin, Lori Francis, and Bernadette Gatien. *Management of Occupational Health and Safety*, 6th ed. Scarborough, ON: Nelson Education, 2014.

King Paving & Materials Company, A Division of KPM Industries Ltd., R v. 2007 ONCJ 610.

Kingston (City) v. Canadian Union of Public Employees, Local 109. 2011 CanLII 50313 (Ont. LA) (Arbitrator Newman).

Klie, Shannon. Domestic Violence Policies Needed. *Canadian HR Reporter.* April 7, 2008, p. 1.

Klie, Shannon. Ontario to Protect Workers from Violence. *Canadian HR Reporter.* May 18, 2009, p. 1.

Lennox Industries (Canada) Limited v. United Steelworkers of America, Local 7235. 1999 CanLII 20394 (Ont. LA), [1999] OLAA no. 158.

Ljuboja v. Aim Group Inc. 2013 CanLII 76529 (Ont. LRB).

MacKillop, M., and H. Nieuwland. Verbal Threats Cannot Be Tolerated. *Canadian HR Reporter.* June 18, 2012, p. 12.

McKechnie, Dave, and Ciaron Burke. "Training Day": The Ontario Occupational Health and Safety Awareness and Training Regulation. November 2013. McMillan LLP. http://www.mcmillan.ca/Training-Day-The-Ontario -Occupational-Health-and-Safety-Awareness-and -Training-Regulation.

McKinley, R v. Ontario Government News Release. December 6, 2007.

Metron Construction Corporation, R v. 2013 ONCA 541.

Miedema, Adrian. $750K Fine for "Extreme" Criminal Negligence: "More Serious" Than OHSA Offences, Says Appeal Court in Metron Construction Fatality Case. September 10, 2013. Canadian Occupational Health & Safety Law. http://www.occupationalhealthandsafetylaw .com/750k-fine-for-extreme-criminal-negligence-more -serious-than-ohsa-offences-says-appeal-court-in -metron-construction-fatality-case.

Miedema, Adrian. The Bill 160 "Revamp" of Ontario's Health and Safety System. *HR Professional.* November/December 2011, p. 29.

Mills, Mark D. Landmark Blue Mountain Decision Narrows Reporting Obligation Under OHSA. *HR Professional.* May/June 2013, p. 43.

Milne, Catherine. Is It Harassment, or Not? *HR Professional.* May/June 2013, p. 15.

Minken, Robert. Verbal Threat Considered Workplace Violence Resulting in Employee's Termination—Bill 168. October 25, 2011. Minken Employment Lawyers. http://www.minkenemploymentlawyers.com/blog/ verbal-threat-considered-workplace-violence-resulting -in-employee's-termination/.

Occupational Health and Safety Act. RSO 1990, c. O.1.

Occupational Health and Safety Awareness Training. O. reg. 297/13.

One Number for Workplace Health and Safety Calls. *Canadian Safety Reporter.* November 4, 2010, p. 4. http://www.safety-reporter.com/articleview/8390-one -number-for-workplace-health-and-safety-calls.

Ontario (Labour) v. United Independent Operators Limited. 2011 ONCA 33.

Ontario Ministry of Labour. Chesterville Painting Company & Director Found Guilty of Disobeying Health and Safety Order. December 6, 2007. http://www.labour.gov.on.ca/ english/news/pdf/2007/07-129.pdf.

Ontario Ministry of Labour. *A Guide to OHSA Requirements for Basic Awareness Training.* July 2014. http://www.labour. gov.on.ca/english/hs/pdf/ohsaguide_training.pdf.

Ontario Ministry of Labour. *A Guide to the Occupational Health and Safety Act.* October 2012. http://www.labour .gov.on.ca/english/hs/pdf/ohsa_guide.pdf.

Ontario Ministry of Labour. TTC Pleads Guilty to Failing to Protect Subway Workers, Fined $165,000. December 10, 2007. http://www.labor.gov.on.ca/english/news/ pdf/2007/07-131.pdf.

Ontario (Ministry of Labour) v. Cementation Canada Inc. et al. 2008 ONCJ 135.

Pharand v. Inco Metals Co. 1980 CanLII 966, [1980] OLRB Rep. July 981.

Provincial Offences Act. RSO 1990, c. P.33.

Roofing Medics Ltd., R v. 2013 ONCJ 646.

Saint-Cyr, Yosie. Coming into Force of Bill 160 and New Rules of Procedure for OHS Reprisals. *Employment Law at Work.* March 2012. HRPA and First Reference. http://www.hrpa.ca/Documents/elaw_October2012a _Corrina/ohsreprisalsandbill160elaw.pdf.

Saint-Cyr, Yosie. HRinfodesk Poll Result and Commentary: Does Safety Training Have to Be Multilingual? January 2, 2014. First Reference Talks. http://blog.firstreference.com/2014/01/02/hrinfodesk -poll-result-and-commentary-does-safety-training-have -to-be-multilingual.

Schmidt, Doug. Why?: Family, Friends Ask. *Windsor Star.* November 11, 2006. http://www2.canada.com/ windsorstar/features/dupont/news/story .html?id=1c328da8-20db-4c00-a3b9-eba818b38146.

Sherrard Kuzz LLP. 12-Step Accident Checklist [laminated seminar handout]. 2014.

Sherrard Kuzz LLP. Complaint of Harassment Cannot Be Reprised Against—So Says Ontario Labour Relations Board. *Management Counsel: Employment and Labour Law Update.* Volume XIII, no. 2, April 2014, p. 3. http://www.sherrardkuzz.com/pdf/Vol_XIII_2.pdf.

Sherrard Kuzz LLP. Sometimes a Swimming Pool Is Just a Swimming Pool. *Management Counsel: Employment and Labour Law Update*. Volume XII, no. 2, April 2013, p. 3. http://www.sherrardkuzz.com/pdf/Vol_XII_2.pdf.

Smoke-Free Ontario Act. SO 1994, c. 10.

Stringer LLP. OLRB Opens the Door to Harassment Reprisal Complaints Under the OHSA. *HR Blog*. January 8, 2014. http://www.stringerllp.com/hr-blog/olrb-opens-the-door-to-harassment-reprisal-complaints-under-the-ohsa-2.

Tanzola, Carissa, and Michael Sherrard. OHS Responsibilities When Employees Travel. *Canadian Safety Reporter*. November 2011, p. 7.

Torrance, Michael. A/H1N1 Flu and Pandemic Preparedness: An Employment and Labour Law Perspective. May 1, 2009. Norton Rose Fulbright. http://www.nortonrosefulbright.com/centre-du-savoir/publications/49167/ah1n1-flu-and-pandemic-preparedness-an-employment-and-labour-law-perspective.

Transpavé inc. , R c. 2008 QCCQ 1598.

USWA Local 862 v. Canadian General Tower Ltd. [2003] OLAA no. 801.

Vu, Uyen. Ottawa Proposes Corporate Killing Law. *Canadian HR Reporter*. July 14, 2003, p. 1.

Whitten & Lublin. You Can't Fire Me, I Complained About Workplace Harassment! *WL Update*. Issue no. 38, January 24, 2014, p. 1. http://www.toronto-employmentlawyer.com/wp-content/uploads/2014-01-employment-newsletter.pdf.

Wilson, Peter, and Allison Taylor. *The Corporate Counsel Guide to Employment Law*, 2nd ed. Aurora, ON: Canada Law Book, 2003.

Worker Fired for Unsafe Behaviour. *Canadian Employment Law Today*. Issue no. 413, May 12, 2004, p. 3229.

Workplace Safety and Insurance Act, 1997. SO 1997, c. 16, sched. A.

RELATED WEBSITES

- http://www.ccohs.ca/oshanswers/psychosocial/violence.html   The Canadian Centre for Occupational Health and Safety website contains an extensive list of questions and answers on workplace violence issues.
- http://www.labour.gov.on.ca/english/hs/pubs/wvps_guide/index.php   The Ontario Ministry of Labour website contains resources to help employers develop policies and programs to prevent and address workplace violence and harassment.

REVIEW AND DISCUSSION QUESTIONS

1. Ontario's health and safety legislation is based on an internal responsibility system. Explain this term. In your opinion, is it an effective approach to ensuring safety in the workplace? Give reasons for your answer.

2. Name and explain the three core worker rights under Ontario's OHSA.

3. What are the responsibilities of certified members of a JHSC?

4. Explain the due diligence defence. What steps can employers take to establish this defence?

5. You are the human resources manager in a small manufacturing firm. An operations supervisor, Habrim, comes to you with a problem. The plant has just started working on a rush order from a major customer and now one of his production workers (Bruce) has refused to work because he says that his machinery is unsafe. Habrim checked the machine and it looked safe to him. He then contacted the Ministry of Labour to further investigate the refusal but he is wondering whether, in the meantime, he can get another employee to work on the machine that Bruce says is unsafe. Advise Habrim by explaining to him what the law requires in these circumstances.

6. Thompson, an experienced operator of the bar bundler packager at ABC Steel Co., noticed that bars had fallen into the basement of the packager. Contrary to his training and the employer's safety protocol, Thompson did not lock out the machine. Instead he placed the machine on automatic and entered the basement area. To get there he had to push open a self-closing swing gate which displayed a sign warning that the packager had to be "locked out" before entry. Similar signage was on the guard rail fence. Nonetheless, Thompson continued into the basement area; within moments he was crushed to death by a movable portion of the bundler.

   The employer was charged with breaching s. 25 of the *Industrial Establishments* regulation under the OHSA, which requires machines with nip hazards to have a guard to prevent access to the pinch point—the point where moving machinery parts are strong enough to pull someone in and injure them. The employer argued that it had done everything reasonable in the circumstances—employee training, a gate that closed automatically, and ample signage. It claimed that it is impossible to foresee and therefore guard against "reckless" employees who do the totally unexpected—even a locked gate would not have deterred a "determined and intentioned" employee like Thompson.

On the basis of these facts, answer the following questions:

a. Is this a strict liability offence? If so, does the Ministry of Labour have to prove anything or does the entire burden of proof lie with the employer?

b. The employer may avoid liability if it shows that it exercised due diligence in attempting to carry out its duties. What is the standard of proof in making out a due diligence defence: "beyond a reasonable doubt" or "on a balance of probabilities"? Research what these two different standards of proof mean.

c. In light of all the circumstances, in your view did the employer exercise due diligence in the steps it took to protect employees from this hazard? If not, what additional steps should it have taken?

7. Wayne was hired as a truck driver for a steel transportation company in August 2012. In early November 2012 he brought his truck in for service and, on the way home, he noticed that his replacement truck was faulty: the steering wheel was loose, the mirrors had cracks in them, there was no engine brake, and fuel was leaking from the caps of both fuel tanks. The next morning Wayne called the dispatcher to say he would not drive the replacement truck to haul steel because it was unsafe. The dispatcher asked him to haul one final load back to Hamilton, which he refused to do, and his supervisor then called and, after a heated discussion, told him he was fired. Wayne filed a complaint, saying this was a reprisal for his exercising his right to refuse unsafe work. The employer countered that Wayne was still a probationary employee (and therefore could be terminated for any reason) and, in addition, he was fired for cause. The employer claimed Wayne swore at the dispatcher when he called in about the replacement truck (which Wayne denied) and that Wayne had failed to return another driver's CB radio in a truck he had started using.

Whose arguments do you think would be successful—Wayne's or the employer's? Support your answer.

8. The employer was a reconditioning centre that cleaned the interior and exterior of vehicles for leasing companies. Tom (aged 18), a recently hired cleaning employee, did not have a driver's licence and the employer made it clear—both verbally and through its safety policy—that employees without a licence were not allowed to drive any of the vehicles . Despite these warnings, Tom drove a car into the wash bay, where he collided with another vehicle. This set off a chain of events, which ultimately resulted in another employee breaking two arms. The employer was charged and convicted for failing to provide information, instruction, or supervision to a worker in the safe operation and parking of vehicles. It received a $50,000 fine, plus a 25 percent victim surcharge. The employer appealed the conviction. What do you think the employer's argument would be? What do you think a court would decide? Support your answer.

9. Kyle was an excavator operator with two years' service who became angry at a co-worker for allegedly driving his loader too fast and too close to his own excavator. After hearing Kyle's complaints, the assistant manager agreed to observe the load operator that morning. However, when he reported to Kyle that he had not seen anything wrong with the load operator's driving, Kyle became agitated. The load operator and manager were brought in and the others heard Kyle say, while pointing at the load operator, something like, "I could kill you six times over." Kyle was escorted out of the office and later terminated for uttering a verbal death threat against another employee. (Kyle's previous disciplinary record included a written warning and a three-day suspension for operating equipment improperly.)

Kyle grieved his dismissal, claiming that he had said, "I could have almost killed you six times," referring to the close calls he felt he'd had. Although he agreed that his outburst was wrong—and that it could be perceived as a threat—he did not apologize. What do you think the arbitrator decided? Explain your answer.

10. Employers have long been obligated to make reasonable efforts to ensure that the workplace is safe. How have the Bill 168 provisions added to, or enhanced, this obligation?

11. The employer decided to hold a training session on the second floor of the store, which was inaccessible to Ken because he used a wheelchair. To address this problem, Ken and a co-worker decided to use an order-picker truck to lift him to the second floor. When they told Barry, the assistant store manager, about this idea, Barry reminded them that Ken would be given the gist of the training by someone else later and that they should not go ahead with their plan. Nonetheless, on the day of the training—while Barry was away from the workplace—Ken and some friends used the order picker to lift him to the training session. After this incident was reported to HR, Barry was terminated for failing to follow safety rules. Barry, who had three and a half years' service and an unblemished disciplinary record, sued for wrongful dismissal.

What arguments might the employer put forward? What arguments might the employee present? Which arguments do you think would most likely be successful?

12. What are some ways that an employer can effectively communicate safety requirements to employees whose first language is not English?

Workplace Safety and Insurance Act

8

LEARNING OUTCOMES

After completing this chapter, you will be able to:

- Understand the historical trade-off that underlies the workers' compensation system.

- Identify the key features of the *Workplace Safety and Insurance Act, 1997*.

- Understand the eligibility requirements for statutory benefits.

- Explain the duty to cooperate and the purpose of worker reintegration and worker transition plans.

- Understand the system's funding and the assessment of employers.

- Understand effective claims management procedures.

- Describe the functions of the Workplace Safety and Insurance Board and appeals structure.

Introduction

The *Workplace Safety and Insurance Act, 1997* (WSIA), like the *Occupational Health and Safety Act*, relates to workplace health and safety in Ontario. While the focus of the *Occupational Health and Safety Act* is on prevention, the WSIA primarily deals with *compensating* and *reintegrating* workers who suffer work-related injuries and illnesses.

The principles that underlie Ontario's workers' compensation system are the same as they were when the system was devised more than 90 years ago. It is an insurance system financed by employers that guarantees compensation to workers for work-related injuries or diseases, regardless of who was at fault. In exchange for a no-fault system, workers have given up their right to sue employers for work-related injuries or disease. Thus, employers are relieved of the uncertainty of lawsuits and financially devastating claims.

The historical trade-off wherein workers relinquished the right to sue in exchange for guaranteed benefits has withstood occasional legal challenges from workers who have argued that preventing them from suing their employers infringed their rights under the *Canadian Charter of Rights and Freedoms*. In *Medwid v. Ontario*, the Ontario High Court of Justice held that any disadvantage to workers caused by this trade-off is offset by the advantage of immediate payment from an insurance fund on a no-fault basis. In fact, the principle underlying workers' compensation continues to be generally supported as benefiting both employers and workers.

However, the implementation of this general principle has generated a great deal of controversy over the years. Numerous government inquiries and legislative changes have grappled with the challenge of providing a compensation process and benefit structure that is both fair and financially sustainable. Questions related to benefit levels and eligibility criteria for claims based on such factors as stress, chronic pain, and environmental sensitivities continue to generate controversy.

The most recent significant change to the legislation occurred in 1997, when the statute was renamed and rewritten. Whereas previous versions of the statute focused on delivering benefits, the current version also emphasizes preventing injuries and reducing their effects. Similar to the internal responsibility system under the health and safety legislation discussed in Chapter 7, the current system requires workers and employers to take responsibility for and cooperate in getting the injured worker back to work. The Workplace Safety and Insurance Board (WSIB) plays the role of mediator in reintegration, stepping in only when the parties are unable or unwilling to resolve a situation.

FYI

Before There Was a Workers' Compensation System ...

The workers' compensation system was implemented in Ontario in 1914 to address the social and economic injustice that resulted from the treatment of injured workers under existing law.

Common law compensation for injured workers was based on the law of **negligence**. To receive com-pensation for an occupational injury, the worker would bring a negligence suit against the employer in court. However, an employer had several powerful defences to an employee's allegation of negligence.

The first of these was the defence of **contributory negligence**. If a court found that a worker had contributed in any way to his own injury, the employer was not liable. The second defence was **co-worker negligence**. If an employer could show that an injury was caused by the negligence of a co-worker, the employer was not liable. Finally, there was the defence of **voluntary assumption of risk**. If the work was inherently dangerous, an employer could argue that the worker voluntarily assumed the risk of injury by taking the job. If the defence succeeded, the employer was not liable.

Because the law was biased in favour of employers and because lawsuits were expensive and time-consuming, most workers who were injured on the job received no compensation, and many were left destitute if their injury rendered them unable to work. At the same time, employers occasionally faced ruinous damage awards. A royal commission was established to examine the situation, and in 1914 Ontario's workers' compensation system was established.

FYI

Key Features of Ontario's WSIA

1. The WSIA sets out a no-fault insurance system that compensates workers for work-related accidents or injuries that arise out of and in the course of employment, regardless of fault or negligence. Workers cannot sue employers for occupational injuries and illnesses.

2. Benefits for injured workers are funded entirely by employers in the province, who pay premiums that are based on their industry classification. The premium reflects the risks and rates of injury in a particular industry. However, employers with good safety records pay less, and employers with poor safety records pay more, than others in their industry group as a result of an experience-rating program.

3. It is against the law for workers to contribute to WSIA premiums.

4. Workers cannot waive their rights to benefits under the WSIA.

5. Most employees in Ontario are covered by the WSIA; they have no choice. In most industries, independent operators, sole proprietors, and executive officers may opt into the system if they pay their own premiums. The exception is the construction industry, where coverage for these groups is generally compulsory.

6. The current system focuses on the early and safe return of disabled workers to work. The WSIA requires workers and employers to cooperate in this effort. The worker must provide ongoing information concerning functional abilities, and the employer must look for suitable work to which she can return.

7. Employers with 20 or more employees are obliged to re-employ injured workers who have at least one year's service, wherever possible.

8. If an injured worker cannot return to his employer, the WSIB may prepare a work transition plan (formerly a labour market re-entry plan) to assist him in re-entering the workforce.

9. The system is administered by the WSIB, which adjudicates and pays compensation claims, collects employer premiums, sets employer assessment rates, and manages investments. The Board also enforces workers' rights to reinstatement. Private insurance companies play no role in compensating workers for occupational injuries and illnesses in Ontario, or elsewhere in Canada.

Worker Coverage

Most industries in the province—including manufacturing, construction, hospitals, hotels, restaurants, and theatres—are covered under the WSIA. Some industries are not compulsorily covered. These include financial institutions, recreational and social clubs, broadcasting stations, trade unions, law firms, barber shops, educational institutions, veterinary clinics, and dental offices (Gilbert and Liversidge, 2001, p. 7). However, many of these low-risk industries apply for coverage because it protects them from lawsuits for work-related injuries at a relatively low cost.

Similarly, certain workers—such as independent operators, sole proprietors, and executive officers—who are not automatically covered may opt into the system. In the construction industry, independent operators, sole proprietors, and executive officers *are typically* compulsorily covered. Independent operators are people who carry on a business in an industry covered by the WSIA and who do not employ any workers for that purpose (Knight et al., 2013, pp. 12, 17).

It should be noted that there is no federal workers' compensation board: workers' compensation benefits for federal public sector employees are administered by the workers' compensation board in the province in which they work. They also receive the same level of benefits as other workers in that province (Knight et al., 2013, p. 16).

WSIA Benefits

Who Is Eligible for WSIA Benefits?

The WSIA insures workers against only those injuries or diseases that relate to the workplace; non-occupational injuries or illnesses are not covered. The WSIB (formerly the Workers' Compensation Board) determines whether a worker qualifies for benefits on the basis of requirements set out in the WSIA. The following is a review of the general rules relating to WSIA benefit eligibility.

1. Wilful Misconduct

Assume that co-workers Vitaly and David get in a fight at work because Vitaly thinks that David wastes too much time on the job. Vitaly punches David, and David suffers a broken jaw as a result. Is David entitled to workers' compensation benefits?

In general, under s. 13, a worker is entitled to WSIA benefits if he suffers an injury or disability that arises "out of and in the course of his or her employment." However, the legislation does not cover an injury that is *solely* a consequence of the "serious and wilful misconduct of the worker," unless the injury results in death or serious impairment (s. 17). The rationale is that by reason of the misconduct, the worker has taken himself "out of the course of employment."

However, s. 17 has been narrowly interpreted. It is applied only to workers who are injured as a result of intentionally breaching a well-known rule, and not to workers who are injured because of carelessness or an impulsive action.

The WSIB may grant benefits if an injury is caused by fighting where the fighting involves work and the claimant does not provoke the fight. In *Decision no. 337*, upon which the David and Vitaly example is based, the WSIB found that David was eligible for WSIA benefits because horseplay was common in the workplace and tolerated by the employer (Gilbert and Liversidge, 2001, p. 27). Had the altercation been unrelated to the workplace, the result might have been different.

2. *"Arising out of and in the Course of His or Her Employment"*

Assume that Avivah, a flight attendant, is on layover in Amsterdam before returning to Toronto. Her purse is stolen while she is on her way to a café, and she suffers a concussion when she gives chase to the thief. Is Avivah entitled to WSIA benefits?

"Arising out of and in the course of his or her employment" is a broadly interpreted phrase. Benefits are paid as long as a worker is performing work-related duties anywhere on the employer's premises during her work hours. The injury need not result from the performance of a worker's job as long as the activities that result in the injury are reasonably incidental to the job. In one case, *Decision no. 339/91*, an employee who hurt her back when she reached around to do up a button while in the washroom before starting her shift was compensated because going to the washroom was reasonably incidental to her employment (Gilbert and Liversidge, 2001, p. 20).

Workers who travel on business are usually covered for injuries suffered while participating in predictable activities, such as dining in a hotel, but are not covered for personal or social activities, such as going to a movie theatre. In Avivah's case, the Tribunal recognized that there was a personal aspect to Avivah's activities but decided that the injury was compensable because, but for the layover, the incident would not have occurred, and the layover was an inherent part of her job (Gilbert and Liversidge, 2001, p. 24). Similarly, although a worker's regular drive to work does not likely occur in the course of employment, driving to a client's establishment for the purpose of work may be compensable. There is a **rebuttable presumption** that accidents sustained during employment arise out of and in the course of employment (s. 13(2)). If a worker suffers an injury while at work, an employer that wants to contest the worker's claim must prove that the injury did *not* arise out of employment. Where the evidence is inconclusive, the worker is given the benefit of the doubt, and the claim is resolved in the worker's favour.

The following case illustrates the application of this presumption.

CASE IN POINT

Was Fainting Spell Compensable?

Decision no. 413/07, 2007 ONWSIAT 1706

Facts

On December 21, 2001, a teacher was hurrying down the hallway to get to a photocopier when she fell, hitting her head first on a large door handle and then on the floor. She said she fell initially because she was feeling dizzy. Having sustained a closed head/skull fracture, the teacher returned to work on February 2, 2002 but only on a part-time basis. The teacher applied for, and was granted, WSIB benefits for loss of earnings and health care benefits for the period from December 22, 2001 to September 3, 2002. The employer appealed the granting of benefits, disputing that the accident "arose out of her employment." It argued that there needed to be a causal relationship between her work activities and her fall in order for it to be compensable. There were a number of other possible explanations for her dizziness, including the employee's rigorous jogging regime or cardiac problems.

Relevant Issue

Whether the worker suffered an accident arising out of and in the course of her employment.

Decision

The Tribunal found for the employee. The accident occurred *in the course of* her employment because it met the criteria of *place* (it happened in the workplace), *time* (during working hours), and most importantly, *activity* (while she was performing work-related duties or duties reasonably incidental to employment). The Tribunal found that the accident also *arose out of* her employment, based on the rebuttable presumption in s. 13(2). If an accident occurs in the course of employment, the onus is on the employer to persuasively demonstrate that the accident did *not* arise out of the employment. It is not sufficient for an employer to present a theory of non-employment relatedness as one of a number of possible theories of causation—the evidence must be sufficiently convincing for the Tribunal to conclude it is probable that the accident did *not* arise out of employment. In this case, the worker's representative submitted that the worker became dizzy and fainted because she leaned over quickly to retrieve a book, stood up quickly, and hurried to the photocopier. In the Tribunal's view, this theory was plausible and the presumption led to a finding in the worker's favour.

A worker who experiences a secondary injury that is causally linked to a work-related injury may receive benefits for the secondary injury. For example, someone who has a work-related injury to the right leg and then develops a problem with his left leg because of his increased reliance on it may be compensated for his left leg problem. Similarly, a second accident that is not work-related but that aggravates a compensable injury may be compensable. For example, in *Decision no. 327/96*, a worker who hurt his back in 1970 at work received a 10 percent pension. In 1992, he hurt his back again while playing baseball and was significantly disabled. The Workers' Compensation Appeals Tribunal found that because the compensable injury was a contributing factor to the worker's increased disability, the entire injury was compensable. Playing baseball did not break the causal link between the compensable injury and the increased disability suffered by the worker (Gilbert and Liversidge, 2001, p. 17).

Generally speaking, a worker is not entitled to benefits if the accident happens while she is working outside of Ontario. However, even then, coverage can be allowed where the worker lives and works in Ontario, the employer's place of business is in Ontario, and the employment outside of Ontario has lasted less than six months. Moreover, where the employment outside of Ontario is likely to last more than six months, the employer may apply to the Board for a declaration that WSIA coverage will continue for the worker throughout the period (Knight et al., 2013, p. 19).

3. Disability Claims

Assume that Francesco, a cashier in a grocery store, suffers from carpal tunnel syndrome in his wrist. Is he entitled to workers' compensation benefits?

The presumption of work-relatedness does not apply to disability cases. Where the onset of an injury is gradual—as in a repetitive strain injury—the onus is on the worker to show a relationship between the disability and the work. However, it is not necessary that the work be the primary or dominant cause of the injury. If the work contributed in a significant way to the injury, the worker is entitled to WSIA benefits. Francesco will probably find it easy to show a connection between the repetitive wrist motion required in his job and the disabling carpal tunnel syndrome that he suffers.

Where the worker has a pre-existing condition, he may receive benefits for his entire disability, although the employer may be relieved of part of the costs of the claim. For example, where a worker has a hereditary form of arthritis and his job contributes to the symptoms, the worker may receive full benefits, and the employer may ask the WSIB to charge part of the costs to the Second Injury and Enhancement Fund (discussed below).

4. Occupational Diseases

Occupational diseases are compensable if there is a causal relationship between the disease and the employment. Industrial diseases that are known to arise from specific industrial processes are set out in the schedules to the WSIA. If a worker in one of these industries contracts one of these diseases, there is a rebuttable presumption that the disease results from employment. For example, a miner who contracts silicosis is presumed to have a work-related disease. An employer that wishes to dispute the miner's claim must challenge this presumption by demonstrating that the silicosis was *not* related to the mining job. There are no minimum exposure requirements.

A few specified diseases create a non-rebuttable presumption of work-relatedness. In these cases, the disease is deemed to have been the result of a worker's employment, and the employer cannot attempt to allege otherwise. For example, a worker in one of the processes set out in Schedule 4 to the WSIA who contracts asbestosis is deemed to have contracted the disease as a result of employment (Gilbert and Liversidge, 2001, p. 28).

In all other circumstances, the WSIB must decide on the facts of a case whether a disease is work-related and therefore compensable. In *Decision no. 269/90*, a worker who operated some vibratory tools on an intermittent basis suffered from white finger disease. Because he did not use the tools for two continuous years, he did not meet the Board's policy guidelines for automatic recognition of the disease. However, the Workers' Compensation Appeals Tribunal found that on a balance of probabilities, the disease was related to the work that the worker performed. Because there was no reasonable alternative explanation as to how the worker acquired the disease, he was entitled to benefits (Gilbert and Liversidge, 2001, p. 30).

The following firefighter case provides another example of the Tribunal considering whether the worker's disease was work-related and thus compensable.

CASE IN POINT

Firefighter's Heart Disease Found to Be Not Work-Related

Decision no. 182/07, 2007 ONWSIAT 353

Facts

The worker became a firefighter in 1972. In the early 1980s, he began experiencing symptoms of coronary heart disease and in 1989 he had bypass surgery. In 1994, he was declared unfit to continue work and he went on disability pension. At age 70, the worker claimed that he was entitled to receive WSIA benefits because his ailment was work-related. He argued that on many occasions he had had to work without a proper breathing apparatus because one was not available. A few times he was given oxygen because he inhaled smoke and occasionally chemicals while fighting fires.

At the same time, the firefighter acknowledged that he had smoked for 37 years until he quit at age 52. A medical report also indicated the man's parents both died of heart disease and his brother had suffered a heart attack.

Relevant Issue

Whether the firefighter's coronary heart disease was compensable under the WSIA.

Decision

The Tribunal found that the worker's coronary heart disease was not compensable because he had failed to prove a causal connection between his work and his disease. Although he was exposed to smoke and fumes, there was no medical evidence that he ever required treatment after the incidents when breathing equipment was not available. Nor was there evidence that these incidents had a cumulative effect. The Tribunal found that it was more likely that the firefighter's condition was related to "non-compensable risk factors" such as his family's history of heart disease, decades of smoking, and his high levels of triglycerides (Smith, 2009, p. 7).

Hearing loss is compensable as an injury if it results from direct trauma to the ear, as in the case of an explosion. Hearing loss caused by hazardous noise levels over a long period of time may constitute an occupational disease, but the Board's guidelines require a history of such exposure, generally over a period of five years or more.

Disability benefits may be available to a worker who is not physically disabled but who must remain off work to avoid exposure to a hazardous substance or to avoid infecting others. For example, a hospital worker exposed to a communicable disease during employment is entitled to compensation if she is required to stay off the job to avoid infecting others (Gilbert and Liversidge, 2001, p. 31). Similarly, a worker who contracts a viral infection (for example, West Nile virus) while in the course of employment may be entitled to benefits, depending on the circumstances (Knight et al., 2013, p. 23).

5. *Mental Stress and Chronic Pain*

Claims for mental stress and chronic pain have long presented special challenges in determining eligibility for benefits. Section 13(5) provides that an employee's claim for mental stress can succeed only if it is "an acute reaction to a sudden and unexpected traumatic event arising out of and in the course of his or her employment." This would cover, for example, a bank teller who suffers mental stress as a result of an armed robbery but probably not a worker who suffers severe stress as a result of ongoing workload pressure.

However, in 2014 the Workplace Safety and Insurance Appeals Tribunal (WSIAT) released *Decision no. 2157/09*, which potentially expands the circumstances under which workers can receive compensation for mental stress resulting in psychological injury (Filion Wakely Thorup Angeletti, 2014). In that case, a nurse alleged that she had been mistreated by a doctor in the hospital where she had worked for many years. This included being yelled at and demeaned in front of colleagues. When she complained to her employer, not only did the employer fail to deal with the situation, but it also effectively demoted her. Eventually she was diagnosed with a psychological adjustment disorder resulting from workplace stressors and she left her job and applied for WSIA benefits. The WSIB denied her claim for benefits because she had not experienced a "sudden and unexpected traumatic event." However, on appeal, the WSIAT held that this requirement infringed the *Canadian Charter of Rights and Freedoms'* s. 15 equality guarantee. It did so by placing an additional hurdle in front of claimants with mental disabilities, an already historically disadvantaged group, compared with workers with physical disabilities.

Although the full impact of this decision is not yet known, it seems that for the first time, chronic mental stress claims are now potentially eligible for WSIA benefits. The potential extension of benefits to individuals suffering from non-traumatic mental stress claims could increase the number of claims in this area significantly. At the same time, acceptance of such claims by the WSIB could also make it easier for an employer to defend itself against a lawsuit for traumatic mental stress damages because the WSIA bars civil actions where that claim could be made in support of an application for workers' compensation benefits (Bolton and Shore, 2011, p. 5).

It should be noted that s. 13(5) also specifically excludes stress that arises from management decisions relating to the worker's employment. It states:

> The worker is not entitled to benefits for mental stress caused by his or her employer's decisions or actions relating to the worker's employment, including a decision to change the work to be performed or the working conditions, to discipline the worker or to terminate the employment.

For example, an employee who suffers depression or stress as a result of a management decision to terminate that individual is not eligible for benefits. The WSIAT declined to comment on the constitutionality of this part of s. 13(5) in *Decision no. 2157/09* (Cohen-Lyons, 2014).

Benefits for chronic pain usually are paid where the pain was initially caused by a work-related injury and continues for up to six months beyond the usual healing time for the injury. After that point, the WSIB will consider the worker's impairment of earning capacity, and may award a pension (Gilbert and Liversidge, 2001, p. 34).

What Benefits Can Eligible Workers Receive Under the WSIA?

Assume that Robert is a 38-year-old head mechanic at Otto's Auto Body Shop, a family-owned business that has 21 employees. Robert has worked at Otto's Auto for the last four years. At the beginning of his eight-hour shift on February 12, 2014, Robert tore a ligament in the thumb of his right hand. This is the same ligament he damaged several years before, when he worked for a previous employer. Robert is in a lot of pain, and he tells his employer he cannot work the remainder of his shift. The employer asks a co-worker to drive Robert to the hospital. This is a work-related injury, and the employer promptly files a Form 7 with the WSIB, as required by the legislation, to start a WSIA claim for Robert. (Employers have three calendar days to complete Form 7 and it must be received by the WSIB within seven business days after the employer learns of its reporting obligations (MacLeod Law Firm, 2013).) At the hospital, the attending physician advises Robert that he has badly injured his hand, and he will not be able to use it for at least four weeks. He will also need extensive physiotherapy if he hopes to recover its full use.

What benefits will Robert be entitled to under the WSIA? We use Robert's example in the sections below to illustrate the different benefits that a worker may be entitled to. Robert's after-tax earnings, including his benefit package, are approximately $200 per day ($1,000 per week).

1. Lost Earnings on the Day of Injury

In our example, Otto's Auto must pay Robert for the remainder of his February 12th shift. Section 24 of the WSIA provides that if a worker is unable to complete his scheduled hours of work because of a work-related injury or illness, the employer must pay the worker the wages and benefits that he would have earned for the day or shift on which the injury occurred.

2. Health Care Costs

Under s. 33, the WSIA system covers all health care costs that result from Robert's injury. Health care costs associated with a work-related injury or disease—such as chiropractic care, dental care, prescription drugs, and artificial limbs—are covered by the WSIB. Also covered are modifications to a worker's home or vehicle.

3. Loss of Earnings Benefits

In our example, the WSIB will compensate Robert for lost earnings after the day of his injury. Loss of earnings (LOE) benefits are calculated at 85 percent of an injured worker's *net* earnings—that is, earnings after income tax, Canada Pension Plan premiums, and employment insurance deductions are factored out. Robert will therefore receive $850 (85 percent of $1,000) per week while he is off work with his work-related injury. These benefits are non-taxable.

The maximum benefit level is 175 percent of the average industrial wage, which in 2014 was $84,100. Benefits are paid until the earliest of

- the day the loss of earnings ceases,
- the day the worker reaches age 65, and
- the day the worker is no longer impaired by the injury (s. 43).

If LOE benefits are paid for at least 72 months, they become permanent, subject to certain exceptions (s. 44).

Workers who were at least 63 years old at the time of their injury may be paid for up to two years. This legislated limit of age 65 remains despite changes in the Ontario *Human Rights Code* that prohibit age-based discrimination in employment beyond age 17.

Assume that after several weeks of physiotherapy, Robert's physician advises him that he can return to the workplace and to modified work if he does not use his right hand. Otto's Auto agrees that Robert can work in the office for a few weeks while one of the office employees is on holidays. However, the net earnings of this position are only $500 per week. In this situation, Robert will be paid 85 percent of the difference between his pre-injury net earnings ($1,000) and his net earnings in the office job ($500). Therefore, while Robert is performing modified work, his WSIB benefits will be $425 (85 percent of the $500 difference in pay between the two jobs). These partial benefits are also not subject to income tax. Robert would therefore receive a total of $925 (his $500 earnings plus $425 WSIB benefits) per week while performing this modified work.

While Robert is receiving WSIB benefits, he is required to notify the WSIB of any **material change** in his situation—that is, any change that would affect his entitlement to benefits and services. This could include a change in medical or employment status, earnings, or ability to cooperate with the Board. Failure to report a material change can result in disentitlement to benefits or being charged with an offence. Under s. 40 of the WSIA, Otto's Auto similarly has a duty to report material changes that may affect its obligations under the WSIA, including changes in business activity, assessable payroll, operations, or ownership.

Under s. 25 of the WSIA, Otto's Auto is also required to continue Robert's pre-injury employment benefits for the first year after his injury, provided that Robert continues to make any contributions he is responsible for during this year.

FYI

Which Benefit System Applies?

As a result of the numerous changes to the WSIA over the past 25 years, three different schemes for monetary benefits are now in place. The one that applies depends on the time that a worker was injured. The oldest system, which includes the notion of permanent pensions, applies to workers who were injured before January 1, 1990. The second system, which divides benefits into temporary and permanent, applies to injuries that occurred between January 2, 1990 and December 31, 1997. Future economic loss benefits only apply to permanent injuries that took place between these two dates. The third system, which compensates workers for loss of earnings and for non-economic losses, such as loss of the enjoyment of life, applies to workers who were injured on or after January 1, 1998. Only this system is discussed here.

4. Non-Economic Losses

In our example, if Robert's disability turns out to be a permanent impairment (PI), he may also be entitled to compensation for loss of enjoyment of life. This is referred to as a non-economic loss (NEL) benefit. A NEL benefit is calculated on the basis of the degree of permanent impairment multiplied by an amount based on the age of the worker. A younger worker receives a higher NEL award than an older worker would receive for the same injury because the younger worker will probably live with the disability for a longer time. As of 2014, for every year that a worker is under 45, $1,287.79 is added to the base amount of $57,929.41. Conversely, for every year a worker is over 45, $1,287.79 is subtracted from $57,929.41.

For example, Robert is 38 years old, or 7 years under the threshold age of 45. If his level of permanent impairment is determined to be, for example, 15 percent, Robert's NEL award is calculated as follows:

$$15\% \text{ (degree of permanent impairment)} \times [\$57{,}929.41 + (\$1{,}287.79 \times 7)]$$
$$= \$10{,}041.59$$

Effective March 30, 2011, all NEL benefits are payable, in the first instance, as a lump sum. If the benefits exceed a certain amount, the worker has the option of receiving them as a lump sum or as a monthly payment (Knight et al., 2013, p. 36). The NEL award is paid in addition to compensation for lost earnings. If a claimant has medical evidence that his condition has worsened significantly, he may ask the Board for a review 12 months after the date of the latest NEL decision. The 12-month rule may be waived in exceptional circumstances.

5. Loss of Retirement Income Benefits

In our example, if Robert continues receiving loss of earnings benefits for 12 consecutive months, the WSIB must set aside an amount equal to 5 percent of his benefits, in addition to his regular benefits, to provide him with a retirement pension (s. 45). Robert has the option of supplementing this amount by electing to deduct 5 percent of his loss of earnings benefits to make his own contributions to his retirement income.

6. Death and Survivor Benefits

Under s. 48 of the WSIA, a spouse who survives a worker who died from a compensable injury is entitled (a) to a lump-sum payment based on age, (b) to periodic payments based on the deceased worker's net average earnings and number of children, and (c) to vocational counselling. Where there is no eligible spouse, any surviving dependent children are entitled to dependants' benefits under the WSIA.

The Duty to Cooperate and the Right of Reinstatement

After an injury, the WSIB monitors the claim. The goal is to return a worker to the pre-accident employer, where possible, as soon as it is safe to do so. Therefore, Robert and Otto's Auto are expected to keep in touch throughout Robert's recovery period, sharing information necessary to facilitate Robert's return to work. Robert must cooperate by consenting to the disclosure of medical information indicating his functional abilities so that Otto's Auto can assess his ability to return to work. By identifying gaps between Robert's functional abilities and the physical demands of his job, Otto's Auto can make any necessary modifications to facilitate an early return.

Robert is required to let Otto's Auto know when he is fit to return to work and when there has been a material change in his circumstances. If he fails to provide information or consent for disclosure of medical information, his benefits may be suspended. *Koomson* illustrates the importance of timely disclosure of a material change.

CASE IN POINT

Failing to Disclose Material Change Has Serious Consequences

Ontario (Workplace Safety and Insurance Board) v. Koomson, 2011 ONCJ 755

Facts

In 2007, Koomson, a 30-year-old drywall taper, suffered apparent permanent cognitive impairment, as well as other injuries, after falling off a scaffold at work. His injuries also made him incapable of driving. Among the compensation he received from the WSIB were loss of earnings benefits, a lump-sum payment of $48,848.72 for non-economic losses, and support services for personal care (his wife became his personal care attendant). Although documentation received from the WSIB repeatedly reminded Koomson of his ongoing duty to report any material changes to his medical condition, he did not notify them of any changes. In 2009, the WSIB received information from the employer that Koomson was performing activities well beyond his stated functional abilities and so it hired private investigators to conduct surveillance. Over a three-week period, these investigators observed Koomson doing many activities on his own: driving, shopping, working out at a gym, conducting financial business at a store, retrieving mail, banking at two different banks, and lifting heavy objects. As a result, the WSIB not only suspended Koomson's benefits, but also charged him with wilfully failing to inform it of "a material change in circumstances in connection with [his] entitlement to benefits within 10 days after the change occurs." Koomson challenged the charge, arguing that there was no medical opinion that his condition had changed and that, even if it had, his failure to notify the WSIB of the

improvement was not "wilful" because his cognitive impairment undermined his decision-making ability.

Relevant Issue

Whether the defendant was guilty of wilfully failing to inform the WSIB of a material change in his condition related to his benefits as required by s. 149 of the Act.

Decision

The Court of Justice agreed with the WSIB that Koomson's failure to inform it of the material change in his condition was wilful. The range of activities seen during the surveillance proved conclusively that there had been a material change in his condition—for example, he was driving. No confirming medical opinion was necessary. Moreover, as the defendant showed no cognitive difficulties in performing a series of complex tasks, the court rejected his argument that his impairment rendered him unable to appreciate the nature of his obligations to report these changes (Smith, 2012, p. 5).

The employer has reporting obligations that must be taken seriously as well. Under s. 41, an employer such as Otto's Auto, which has 20 or more workers, has a statutory obligation to re-employ injured workers who have been continuously employed for at least one year before the accident, where possible (special rules apply to construction employers). Therefore, in our example, once Robert is physically able to perform the essential duties of his pre-injury job, Otto's Auto must reinstate him to the same or a comparable job with comparable earnings. This obligation expires on the earliest of

- two years after the accident date,
- one year after the date he is medically able to perform the essential duties of his pre-injury job, and
- the date he reaches age 65.

The WSIA requires Otto's Auto to accommodate Robert in performing the essential duties of his former job unless this results in undue hardship. Otto's Auto may need to change the way Robert does his work or reassign his non-essential duties. If Robert is unable to perform the essential duties of his pre-injury job, even with accommodation, Otto's Auto must offer him the first suitable comparable job that becomes available. (Employers with fewer than 20 employees, which have no statutory obligation under the WSIA to re-employ injured workers, are still subject to the duty to accommodate unless this causes them undue hardship under the *Human Rights Code*.)

Whether a job is suitable for a worker depends on the circumstances. In addition to the worker's physical ability, factors such as distance to work, wages, potential for advancement, shift time, the worker's age, and financial pressures are all considered relevant. Other factors may also be considered. In *Decision no. 118*, a worker refused an employer's job offer because the job was not covered by the worker's **bargaining unit**, and he was afraid he would lose seniority under his collective agreement. The Tribunal found that because the worker would have continued to have the right to bid for bargaining unit jobs that he was physically capable of performing, the job was suitable, and his benefits were reduced because he refused it. On the other hand, in *Decision no. 882/87*, where a worker refused an employer's job offer because it might have resulted in the loss of his 26 years' seniority, the Tribunal found that the job was not suitable and that the worker was entitled to full benefits (Gilbert and Liversidge, 2001, p. 76).

An employer who dismisses a worker within six months of her returning to work is presumed to be in contravention of its reinstatement obligations and is subject to a heavy financial penalty. The onus is on the employer to show that the dismissal was unrelated to the injury—for example, that it was part of a general layoff—and that the compensation claim played no part in the decision to dismiss the employee.

Worker Reintegration and Worker Transition Plans

Continuing with our example, assume that after six months of physiotherapy it becomes apparent that Robert will never recover sufficient use of his right thumb to perform his pre-injury mechanic's job. It is therefore unlikely that Otto's Auto will ever be able to re-employ him because all jobs comparable to Robert's require manual dexterity. As a result, the WSIB gets involved. It works with Robert to assess his skills and interests. It then prepares a **work transition (WT) plan** (formerly known as a labour market re-entry plan) to assist Robert in re-entering the labour market.

Based on Robert's personal, physical, and vocational abilities and interests, the Board and Robert agree that he should return to school to become a qualified auto mechanics instructor (a "suitable occupation" based on his transferable skills). In this way, he can build on his extensive experience and stay in a field he enjoys. With this additional qualification, Robert will probably eventually be able to earn a salary comparable to his pre-injury earnings.

A work transition plan may require many different approaches, such as work placements, workplace modifications, and formal retraining. The costs of a work transition plan are assessed against the employer's accident cost statement and can be extremely high. One of the indirect effects of a work transition plan is to encourage employers to find a position for an injured worker to avoid the expense of the plan. A worker who fails to cooperate in the work transition plan may have her benefits terminated. The Board may also provide a surviving spouse, where appropriate, with a work transition plan to facilitate the spouse's entry or re-entry into the labour market in an identified suitable occupation (Knight et al., 2013, p. 68).

Funding the WSIA System

Employer Assessments

Employers pay the full cost of the WSIA system by means of premiums. It is illegal for employers to recover any part of their premium from workers.

The WSIB's Unfunded Liability

There is currently a significant gap between the Board's annual revenue from employer premiums, plus investment returns on invested premiums, and the funds needed to meet its operating costs and the cost of benefits to workers. As of 2013, the unfunded liability was estimated to be over $13 billion. According to the Board, steps have been taken to address this issue, including a revamped return to work program, and the Board has indicated that it is on track to eliminate its unfunded liability by 2027 (Knight et al., 2013, pp. 115, 118).

A covered employer must register with the WSIB within ten days after becoming an employer. Failing to register can result in an employer's being assessed for periods during which it did not pay premiums, plus interest and penalties. If an accident occurs before an employer registers, all or part of the accident cost may be charged directly to the employer. Where a company hires a contractor or subcontractor for construction work, it *must* get a certificate issued by the Board confirming that the contractor or subcontractor is registered with the Board and has paid its WSIB premiums (Knight et al., 2013, p. 147).

For assessment purposes, there are two categories of employers: Schedule 1 and Schedule 2 employers. A few large employers—such as municipalities, schools, hospitals, railways, and airlines—are Schedule 2 employers. They are assessed individually on the basis of the actual (capitalized) cost of accidents suffered by their workers. Although the WSIB administers their claims in exchange for an administrative fee, Schedule 2 employers are essentially self-insured. The claims of federal public sector employees in Ontario are administered as if the federal government were a Schedule 2 employer (Knight et al., 2013, p. 16).

The majority of employers in Ontario are Schedule 1 employers. They pay assessment premiums to the WSIB on the basis of their industry class and rate group. As of 2014, there were approximately 240,000 employers registered with the WSIB that were divided among approximately 154 rate groups based on similarity of business activity and accident risk. The assessment rate for each group is set on the basis of the group's claims history and experience with frequency and length of claims; it is reviewed annually. The assessment rates range from a low of approximately 0.21 percent of payroll for a low-risk industry, such as legal and financial services, to a high of approximately 18.3 percent of payroll for a high-risk industry, such as demolition (Workplace Safety and Insurance Board, 2014).

An employer can have more than one rate classification unit, as long as it maintains segregated payrolls for each of those business activities (MacLeod Law Firm, 2013).

The employer's assessment is calculated as a percentage of the employer's payroll, up to a maximum amount per worker. (The maximum amount is subject to change.) The assessment for each worker can be calculated by multiplying the employer's assessment rate by the worker's annual earnings up to the maximum amount, which was $84,100 in 2014.

For example, assume that Robert's gross earnings were $90,000, which exceeds the maximum amount, and Otto's Auto's WSIA industry assessment rate is 3.5 percent of payroll. To calculate the assessment premium that Otto's Auto pays for Robert in one year, multiply $84,100 (the maximum amount) by 3.5 percent ($84,100 × 3.5% = $2,943.50).

To calculate Otto's Auto's total WSIA premiums for that year, multiply its total payroll (excluding amounts per individual worker that are above the earnings ceiling) by its assessment rate of 3.5 percent. For example, if the 21 employees at Otto's Auto earn a total of $630,000 (excluding earnings above the ceiling), the WSIA assessments for that year amount to $22,050 ($630,000 × 3.5%).

Experience Rating

While Schedule 1 employers are collectively liable for the benefits that their injured workers receive, the system also provides financial incentives to reduce the cost of injuries. The assessment rate is based on the industry group's accident cost record. However, an individual employer may receive a refund or a surcharge depending on how its experience measures up against the experience of others in its rate group.

The largest experience-rating program is the New Experimental Experience Rating (NEER) plan. It is based entirely on costs, including reserves for expected future costs plus administrative overhead. Frequency of accidents is not included as a measure of performance. CAD-7 (Council Amendment to Draft #7) is the experience-rating plan that covers all construction rate groups over a certain size, while the Merit Adjusted Premium program adjusts both construction and non-construction premium rates for employers that pay from $1,000 to $25,000 in average annual premiums (Knight et al., 2013, p. 102). Since March 10, 2008, the Board also has the discretion to apply a premium increase, equivalent to the NEER or CAD-7 refund that an employer is otherwise entitled to receive, to an employer that experiences a work-related traumatic fatality (Knight et al., 2013, p. 104).

Workwell Program

The Workwell Program operates by identifying employers with particularly poor accident records and/or high accident costs compared with other employers (of similar size) in their rate group, or who have a history of non-compliance with the *Occupational Health and Safety Act*. It charges a premium rate to those employers, in certain circumstances, that is independent of, and in addition to, surcharges from experience-rating programs. Identified employers are required to participate in a workplace health and safety evaluation; those who fail are given a specified time frame to make the necessary improvements. If those requirements are not met, an additional premium charge is levied that can ultimately be in a range from 10 percent to 75 percent of the employer's premiums (Knight et al., 2013, pp. 110–13).

Second Injury and Enhancement Fund

The Second Injury and Enhancement Fund (SIEF) is available where a pre-existing condition (a) contributes to a work-related accident, (b) increases the severity of the injury, or (c) prolongs a worker's recovery. In our example, Otto's Auto may apply for relief from the full cost of Robert's injury because its severity is partly the result of an injury that Robert sustained while working for a previous employer.

An employer that requests financial relief from the costs of a claim must justify its application by providing information such as a previous WSIB claim number or findings from a medical examination performed before the workplace accident that indicates a pre-existing condition. SIEF relief varies, but typical relief ranges from 25 to 90 percent of a claim. Its purpose is to make the distribution of costs more fair.

Effective Claims Management

To minimize the occurrence and costs of workplace accidents and illnesses, employers should, among other things, establish an effective claims management program. The following procedures are useful in this regard.

1. Establish procedures for investigating workplace injuries and train management in these procedures. Procedures include interviewing an injured worker, if possible, to obtain his recollection of an accident and any information about pre-existing medical conditions. Management should also interview witnesses about these matters, record the information, and photograph or sketch the accident scene without altering it, if possible.

2. Complete and file an accident report with the WSIB in the required Form 7. This initiates the claims process. The WSIB must receive the Form 7 report within seven calendar days of the time that the accident came to the employer's attention. There is a penalty for late filing. Provide all relevant data. Ask the injured worker to sign a medical release on the Form 7, which authorizes the employer to receive functional abilities information from the worker's physician.

3. Document all claims, even those that appear to be minor.

4. Where the worker's entitlement to benefits is clear, make every effort to ensure that the worker is able to claim benefits promptly. For example, respond promptly to Board inquiries.

5. Challenge only truly doubtful claims, and if you do challenge a claim, protest it from the outset because once a claim is established, it is difficult to question later. For example, an employer who fails to challenge a doubtful medical aid claim because the initial costs are minor will find it difficult to appeal the mounting costs later on. No injury should be underestimated. For example, an apparently minor back claim can result in long-term compensation and medical costs in the $100,000 range.

6. Keep notes concerning contacts with health and safety officials and the WSIB, including the date, time, and substance of any conversations, and the name of the WSIB contact person. Follow up on any conversations with the WSIB by letter, indicating any action or information that is required. Keep the file current.

7. Establish a return to work plan and make necessary accommodations short of undue hardship.

8. Do not contact the injured worker's physician. An employer may request clarification of a physician's report through the WSIB or the worker. An employer may also request an independent medical examination to verify the nature of the claim or to determine the worker's ability to participate in modified work.

9. Consider whether part or all of the costs may be covered by the SIEF. If so, obtain the requisite material to support a SIEF application.

10. Keep medical files separate from personnel files, and treat them in a confidential manner.

FYI

When Does an Employer Not Need to Report a Workplace Accident?

An employer is *not* required to report a work-related accident if the worker

- only receives first aid (as opposed to "health care" that requires the skills of a health care practitioner); or
- either does or does not receive first aid but requires modified work *at regular pay for seven calendar days or less* after the accident (Knight et al., 2013, p. 29).

Administration and Enforcement

The workers' compensation system is administered by the WSIB. The WSIB's approximately 4,500 employees perform many functions, including adjudicating and paying compensation claims to eligible workers. In 2014, the Board dealt with approximately 340,000 claims. In addition, the WSIB oversees workers' reintegration and re-employment, collects employer premiums, sets employer assessment rates, manages investments, and enforces reinstatement rights. The WSIB also prepares policies and guidelines for adjudicating claims to promote consistency. Medical specialists are available on staff to assist in complex claims, and outside specialists are used as required.

Appeals

A worker or employer who disagrees with a decision of the WSIB may file a written notice of objection, including reasons for the objection, with the WSIB. Issues raised on appeal are far ranging: examples include eligibility for benefits, health care issues, employer re-employment obligations, and the amount of premiums. If Robert or Otto's Auto disagreed with the WSIB's NEL award, for example, either party could appeal it.

The first level of appeal is handled by the same department of the WSIB that made the original decision. The next level is handled by the WSIB's Appeals Branch, where an appeals officer reviews the file, contacts the parties, and attempts to resolve the matter through telephone contacts, written inquiries, field investigations, medical assessments, and oral hearings, if necessary.

Either party may appeal the appeals officer's final decision to the Workplace Safety and Insurance Appeals Tribunal (WSIAT). The Tribunal is independent of the Board, although it is required under s. 126 of the WSIA to apply Board policy. Tribunal hearings are usually conducted before a single vice-chair. However, more complicated cases may be heard by a three-member panel that includes an employer and a worker representative. It is rare for workers' compensation issues to go to court, and few applications for judicial review of Tribunal decisions succeed (Gilbert et al., 2000, p. 300).

Related Agencies

Several other agencies are directly involved in the workers' compensation system. These include the Office of the Worker Adviser (OWA) and the Office of the Employer Adviser (OEA). The OWA advises injured workers who are not members of a trade union. The OEA advises employers with fewer than 100 employees.

The Right to Sue

Under s. 28 of the WSIA, Schedule 1 employers enjoy special protection from lawsuits. For example, if companies X and Y are Schedule 1 employers and their workers are involved in a motor vehicle accident while on the job, the workers cannot sue each other and cannot sue either company X or company Y.

In contrast, workers employed in a Schedule 2 industry who are injured in the course of employment are only prohibited from suing their own employers.

Furthermore, independent operators who have not opted for coverage under the WSIA may bring a lawsuit against the company with which they contract in the event they suffer a work-related injury. For this reason, employers may want independent operators to agree to opt for coverage. (Note that independent operators in the construction industry are now required to be covered.)

REFERENCES

Bolton, Lisa, and Stephen Shore. Challenging a Worker's Right to Sue. *Canadian HR Reporter*. January 31, 2011, p. 1. http://www.sherrardkuzz.com/pdf/BoltonShore.Challenging.pdf.

Canadian Charter of Rights and Freedoms. Part I of the *Constitution Act, 1982*, RSC 1985, app. II, no. 44.

Cohen-Lyons, Joseph. WSIAT Finds Limitations on Mental Stress Unconstitutional. *FTR Now*. May 15, 2014. Hicks Morley. http://www.hicksmorley.com/index.php?name=News&file=article&sid=2165&catid=6.

Decision no. 118. (October 3, 1986) (WCAT) [unreported].

Decision no. 182/07. 2007 ONWSIAT 353.

Decision no. 2157/09. 2014 ONWSIAT 938.

Decision no. 269/90. 1990 CanLII 4407 (Ont. WSIAT) [unreported].

Decision no. 327/96. 1997 CanLII 13384 (Ont. WSIAT), 41 WCATR 141.

Decision no. 337. 1986 CanLII 401 (Ont. WSIAT), 2 WCATR 141.

Decision no. 339/91. 1993 CanLII 6098 (Ont. WSIAT) [unreported].

Decision no. 413/07. 2007 ONWSIAT 1706.

Decision no. 882/87. 1990 CanLII 5011 (Ont. WSIAT), 15 WCATR 29.

Dee, G., N. McCombie, and G. Newhouse. *Workers' Compensation in Ontario Handbook*. Toronto: Butterworths, 1999.

Filion Wakely Thorup Angeletti. WSIAT Finds Provisions Restricting Compensation for Mental Stress Unconstitutional. *What's New in HR Law*. June 2014. http://filion.on.ca/uploads/ckeditor/attachment_files/1001/14-06-17_CLU.pdf.

Gilbert, Douglas, and Les Liversidge. *Workers' Compensation in Ontario: A Guide to the Workplace Safety and Insurance Act*, 3rd ed. Aurora, ON: Canada Law Book, 2001.

Gilbert, Douglas, Brian Burkett, and Moira McCaskill. *Canadian Labour and Employment Law for the US Practitioner*. Washington, DC: Bureau of National Affairs, 2000.

Guilbert, Sylvie, Carissa Tanzola, and Lisa Bolton. Is an Injury Work-Related? *Canadian HR Reporter*. April 25, 2011. http://www.sherrardkuzz.com/pdf/.GuilbertTanzolaBolton.Is_an_injury_worr-related.pdf.

Harder, D. Worker Assaulted in Parking Lot Denied Compensation. *Canadian Employment Law Today*. November 16, 2011.

Knight, J., B. Channe, L.C. MacLean, and C. Kontra. *Ontario Workplace Safety and Insurance Act: Quick Reference—2014 Edition*. Toronto: Carswell, 2013.

MacLeod Law Firm. WSIB—Three Issues for Employers to Consider. October 22, 2013. http://www.macleodlawfirm.ca/employers/2013/10/workplace-safety-insurance-board-wsib-three-issues-employers-consider.

McLarren, Philip. *Employment in Ontario*. Markham, ON: Butterworths Lexis Nexis, 2001.

Medwid v. Ontario. 1988 CanLII 193 (Ont. SC), 48 DLR (4th) 272.

Occupational Health and Safety Act. RSO 1990, c. O.1.

Ontario (Workplace Safety and Insurance Board) v. Koomson. 2011 ONCJ 755.

Police Dispatcher Can't Stay on the Line. *Canadian Employment Law Today*. Issue no. 563, August 25, 2010.

Shell, B., K. Coon, and S. Rashid. *Understanding the Workplace Safety and Insurance Act*. Aurora, ON: Canada Law Book, 1999.

Smith, Jeffrey. Bus Driver's Injuries Not from Driving a Bus. *Canadian Employment Law Today*. January 22, 2014, p. 7.

Smith, Jeffrey. Injured Worker Fails to Report Improvement. *Canadian HR Reporter*. March 12, 2012, p. 5.

Smith, Jeffrey. Worker on Modified Duty Fired, Reinstated After Surveillance of Activities. *Canadian Employment Law Today*. March 5, 2014.

Smith, Jeffrey. Workers' Compensation: Firefighter's Heart Disease the Result of Risk Factors, Not Job. *Canadian Employment Law Today*. Issue no. 525, January 14, 2009, p. 7.

Wilson, Peter, and Allison Taylor. *The Corporate Counsel Guide to Employment Law*, 2nd ed. Aurora, ON: Canada Law Book, 2003.

Workplace Safety and Insurance Act, 1997. SO 1997, c. 16, sched. A.

Workplace Safety and Insurance Board. 2014 Premium Rates Table. 2014. http://www.wsib.on.ca/WSIBPortal/faces/WSIBDetailPage?cGUID=WSIB013701&rDef=WSIB_RD_ARTICLE.

Workplace Safety and Insurance Board. *Workplace Safety and Insurance Board 2012 Annual Report*. 2013. http://www.wsib.on.ca/WSIBPortal/faces/WSIBArticlePage?fGUID=835502100635000459.

REVIEW AND DISCUSSION QUESTIONS

1. What have workers given up for their rights under the present injury compensation system? Do you think that they have benefited from this trade-off? Why?

2. Currently, there are three types of monetary benefits payable to injured workers, depending on the date of the initial claim. In your opinion, why have there been so many changes to the monetary benefit schemes under the WSIA and prior legislation over the past 25 years?

3. Why would an employer in an industry that is not required to be covered by the WSIA apply for coverage?

4. Why is it important for an employer to have an effective claims management program?

5. How is chronic pain treated under the current WSIA system?

6. Explain when injured employees have a statutory right to reinstatement under the WSIA.

7. Sameera, an employee who worked in one of the retail outlets in a mall, slipped and fell on a patch of ice in the mall parking lot on her way to work. She injured herself and then sued the owners of the mall for damages. The mall owners appealed to the WSIB, arguing that she was eligible for WSIB benefits. The parking lot was a "common area" owned by the mall's management company. The employee had parked in the portion of the lot designated by the employer for employees.

   a. Why would the mall owners want Sameera's injury to be covered by the WSIB?

   b. In your opinion, is Sameera eligible for WSIB benefits in these circumstances? Explain your answer.

8. Aisha sprains her ankle while she is on the picket line during a strike at her workplace. Is she entitled to workers' compensation benefits?

9. Pierre's job was marking locations for workers to build concrete building structures based on blueprints. One day his car was damaged while parked in the lot beside the construction site, which was fenced off for use by construction workers. A few days later, during normal working hours, Pierre approached the individual—an employee of a different firm working at the site—who he thought was responsible for the damage to his vehicle. That person swore at him and then attacked him. The perpetrator was charged and later convicted of assault for causing Pierre serious injuries. Pierre reported his injuries to his employer, who filed a WSIB Form 7 report on the basis that the parking lot was part of the workplace.

   In your opinion, is Pierre eligible for workers' compensation benefits?

10. Over the course of several years, Rick filed five WSIB claims related to back injuries. In February 2013 he hurt his back again. When Rick returned to work a month later, the functional abilities form (FAF) that his family physician provided indicated that his work duties had to be very restricted. He could not walk more than 100 metres at a time, stand for more than 15 to 30 minutes, or sit for more than 15 minutes. Over the course of the next two months his employer became suspicious concerning the extent of his injuries and it hired a private investigator to conduct surveillance. Initially, the PI did not notice Rick doing anything suspicious. However, when Rick went on a trip to Montreal to see a hockey game—which he told co-workers about—the PI followed and videotaped him doing a great deal that was beyond his stated physical restrictions: he loaded his car with luggage, drove for six hours with only two short breaks, rode a mechanical bull, danced, climbed stairs, and jumped down from a four foot high statute. When the PI reported his findings, the employer called Rick in for a meeting. The employer asked him how he was doing and he replied that although he was improving, his functional abilities had not increased much and he should remain with the same restrictions until his doctor gave him the go-ahead. After the meeting, the employer decided to terminate Rick for dishonesty for misrepresenting his restrictions. Several days later the employer brought Rick in for another meeting where he was shown and asked about the video. He downplayed his activities in Montreal: he'd been drunk and therefore did things he shouldn't have. Moreover, each activity was for a short period of time; it did not require him to exceed his restrictions on an ongoing basis. Not satisfied with this explanation, the employer proceeded to fire Rick. Rick, as a unionized employee, filed a grievance, challenging his dismissal and asking for reinstatement.

    Based on these facts, do you think Rick's grievance will be successful?

11. Sean had been a bus driver for six years when, rather suddenly, he began having serious back and knee pain in April 2008. After seeing his doctor, he filed a claim for WSIB benefits because he believed his physical problems were related to his job. He argued that the

jabbing pain in his lower back, and pain and numbness in his knees, stemmed from innumerable hours spent sitting while driving. These symptoms were compounded by his having to drive an older bus, which produced excessive vibration, the repeated pressure of holding the gas and brake pedals, and his having to drive along a route where there was considerable construction. Similarly, he believed the knee pain, for which he ended up having surgery, was caused in part by repeatedly hitting his knee on the fare box. Despite these arguments, Sean's WSIB claim was rejected by the first WSIB case manager, who did not believe his problems were related to his job duties. The employer put him on short-term disability benefits but Sean appealed the WSIB's denial of benefits to the WSIAT.

What type of factors do you think the WSIAT would consider relevant in deciding whether Sean's physical ailments arose "out of and in the course of" his employment, as required for Sean to receive benefits?

Equity in the Workplace

9

LEARNING OUTCOMES

After completing this chapter, you will be able to:

- Distinguish between equal pay for equal work, pay equity, and employment equity.

- Outline the steps for achieving pay equity.

- Identify the commonly overlooked features of work typically performed by women.

- Understand the challenges of maintaining pay equity in the workplace.

- Describe the requirements of the federal *Employment Equity Act* and the Federal Contractors Program.

Introduction

This chapter examines three laws related to equity in the workplace: the *Employment Standards Act* (Ontario), the *Pay Equity Act* (Ontario), and the *Employment Equity Act* (federal). The *Employment Standards Act*, which is the oldest of the three statutes, requires that women and men receive equal pay for equal work. The *Pay Equity Act* goes further by requiring employers to provide equal pay for work of equal value, based on a proactive model of compliance. The *Employment Equity Act* requires federally regulated companies with 100 employees or more to implement employment equity (also known as affirmative action) programs in the workplace.

Although these three equity concepts may sound similar, they place separate and distinct obligations on employers. Equal pay for equal work and pay equity are aimed at ensuring *gender* equality in the pay that employees receive for the jobs they perform. Employment equity focuses on improving job opportunities for women, people with disabilities, visible minorities, and Aboriginal people.

The *Employment Equity Act* is a federal statute and therefore directly affects only federal organizations and federally regulated employers. However, the federal government has a program that requires suppliers with contracts worth $1 million (previously $200,000) or more to commit to implementing employment equity. Provincially regulated companies that bid on sizable federal government contracts must therefore be aware of the requirements of the employment equity program.

In the mid-1990s, Ontario's legislature passed an *Employment Equity Act*, which was quickly repealed following a change in government. However, as the province's and country's workforce becomes ever more diverse, employment practices that remove systemic barriers and assist in making the workplace more inclusive are seen as playing a critical role in many Canadian organizations.

Employment Standards Act: Equal Pay for Equal Work

Section 42 of the *Employment Standards Act* makes it illegal to pay employees of one sex less money for doing the same work as employees of the other sex:

> No employer shall pay an employee of one sex at a rate of pay less than the rate paid to an employee of the other sex when,
>
>   (a) they perform substantially the same kind of work in the same establishment;
>   (b) their performance requires substantially the same skill, effort and responsibility; and
>   (c) their work is performed under similar working conditions.

This law requires employers to pay women and men at the same rate if they are performing substantially the same kind of work, in the same establishment, using substantially the same skills and effort, exercising substantially the same responsibility, and working under similar conditions. Exceptions are allowed only if the difference in compensation is based on seniority, merit, productivity, or any other factor not based on gender, such as a premium paid for working a night shift.

The requirement to provide **equal pay for equal work** has existed for over 60 years. Before this law was passed, it was common for men and women to receive different rates of pay even when they were performing the same job.

To fall within the protection provided by s. 42, the work of one employee must be substantially similar (but need not be identical) to the work of another. For example, male and female cooks working in the same restaurant must receive the same rate of pay, subject to the exceptions set out above, even though one makes salads and the other makes desserts. Similarly, a retail clothing store cannot reasonably argue that its female and male sales assistants receive different rates of pay because they work in separate sections of the store and therefore do different jobs.

To prove a violation of the equal pay for equal work provisions, there is no need to show that an employer intended to discriminate. The law applies wherever women and men perform similar work but receive different rates of pay for reasons other than the exceptions noted above. An employer may not reduce the rate of pay of the high-paid gender to comply with the law; under s. 42(3), it must raise the pay of the low-paid gender.

As with other standards under the ESA, equal pay for equal work is enforced by requiring individuals to file a claim with the Ministry of Labour. Although, historically, female employees have benefited most from equal pay laws, both men and women may file complaints with the Ministry. In practice, since the advent of the *Pay Equity Act*, few claims have been filed under s. 42 of the ESA.

Pay Equity Act: Equal Pay for Work of Equal Value

What Is Equal Pay for Work of Equal Value?

"Equal pay for work of equal value" is a relatively recent concept that requires employers to compare totally different jobs and ascertain whether they are equal in value. A comparison is made between the value of the jobs, not their content (that is, the job duties). While *equal pay for equal work* laws exist throughout Canada and are common elsewhere, *equal pay for work of equal value* laws are found only in some provinces (where they typically apply only to the public sector) and at the federal level. Ontario's (and Quebec's) equal pay for work of equal value law, on the other hand, goes further. In contrast to the traditional complaint-based model of enforcement, it places a positive obligation, on both public sector employers and private sector employers with ten or more employees, to proactively take certain steps to achieve "pay equity." Ontario's private sector pay equity legislation was the first of its kind.

A Comparison of Women's and Men's Earnings from 2002 to 2011

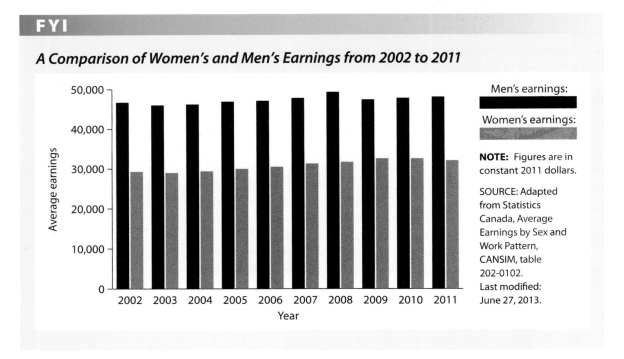

Men's earnings:

Women's earnings:

NOTE: Figures are in constant 2011 dollars.

SOURCE: Adapted from Statistics Canada, Average Earnings by Sex and Work Pattern, CANSIM, table 202-0102. Last modified: June 27, 2013.

Pay equity arose from the concern that equal pay for equal work laws would never be able to achieve gender equality in pay because men and women typically do not perform substantially similar work. Historically, women have tended to occupy a small number of relatively low-paying jobs collectively known as the "pink collar ghetto." Pay equity is premised on the idea that these jobs are poorly paid *because* they are primarily performed by women. In other words, the labour market has consistently undervalued jobs dominated by females. For example, parking lot attendants, who are usually men, are paid more than childcare workers, who are usually women.

The purpose of pay equity, therefore, is to reduce the wage gap between men and women by requiring employers to compare the underlying value of jobs performed predominantly by men with those performed predominantly by women. Pay for female-dominated jobs is then based on their value in relation to the value of male-dominated jobs, rather than on the value assigned to them by the external labour market. This can be a challenging task, and the process required by the legislation is necessarily technical and complex.

Key Features of Ontario's Pay Equity Act

1. The purpose of the *Pay Equity Act*, stated in s. 4(1), is to "redress systemic gender discrimination in compensation" for work that is predominantly performed by women. It applies to all private sector employers with ten or more employees in Ontario and all public sector employers.

2. The Act requires employers to evaluate and compare the value of jobs usually performed by women with the value of jobs usually performed by men in their establishment. If the jobs are of equal value, the employer must raise the pay for the women's job classes to match that of comparable men's job classes. (Note,

it is the job, and not the person doing the job, that is evaluated. Moreover, only the wage gap between male- and female-dominated jobs is covered; pay gaps based on other factors, such as ethnic group, would be covered by human rights, not pay equity, legislation.)

3. The job evaluation system used to compare jobs must be gender-neutral. It must not undervalue aspects of female-dominated jobs, such as multitasking, when comparing them to aspects of male-dominated jobs, such as physical effort.

4. In conducting its evaluation, an employer must base job value on requisite levels of skill, effort, and responsibility as well as on working conditions. These are the same four factors considered in assessing equal pay for equal work, but the evaluation process is more complex because different jobs—such as truck driver and librarian—are being compared. Private sector employers are required to compare only jobs that are performed within the same establishment.

5. Unlike the *Employment Standards Act*, Ontario's *Pay Equity Act* is enforced proactively. Enforcement does not rely solely on an individual's filing a complaint with the Ministry of Labour. The *Pay Equity Act* places a positive obligation on all covered employers to evaluate jobs in their workplaces and correct any discrimination in compensation.

6. Only people (both men and women) in a female job class or in a job traditionally performed by women can complain that their work is undervalued. The legislation is not available to members of a job class that is, and traditionally has been, male-dominated.

7. The Act is administered and enforced by the Pay Equity Commission, which consists of the Pay Equity Office and the Pay Equity Hearings Tribunal.

To Whom Does the Pay Equity Act Apply?

All Ontario public sector employers and all provincially regulated private sector employers with ten or more employees are covered by Ontario's *Pay Equity Act*. However, the Act distinguishes between employers that had ten or more employees in Ontario when the legislation was passed in 1987 and employers that were not in business or had fewer than ten employees at that time.

The rationale for this distinction is that the *Pay Equity Act* requires employers to set wage rates for jobs typically performed by women on the basis of the job's inherent value rather than rely on the market's evaluation. Because the wage rates of most employers in 1987 were based, at least in part, on the external labour market, the Act recognizes that rectifying long-standing wage inequalities takes time. To address this, the Act took the following approach. Employers with 100 or more employees as of January 1, 1988 were required to prepare and implement a plan for correcting unequal wages. Employers with 10 to 99 employees as of January 1, 1988 were not required to prepare a pay equity plan but were required to achieve pay equity within a specified time. The Act also provided for a phase-in period based on an employer's size that gave existing organizations time to perform the necessary job evaluations, make job comparisons, and prepare and implement their pay equity plans. Existing private sector employers who prepared a pay equity plan were allowed a ceiling of 1 percent of annual payroll in the annual pay adjustments that they were required to make to achieve pay equity. As of 2014, there are employers who are still making pay equity adjustments based on the 1 percent ceiling.

In contrast, new employers—those that were not operating in Ontario as of January 1, 1988 with ten or more employees, or those that reached the ten-employee threshold after January 1, 1988—are required to comply with the pay equity legislation *immediately*. There is no phase-in period and no 1 percent ceiling for these employers.

They are not required to create a pay equity plan because, as new employers, they have notice of the Act's requirements before they set wages and hire their first employees, so there are no existing wage inequities to "correct." However, they must be able to show that they have met the requirements of pay equity by setting wages according to a gender-neutral job evaluation system, rather than looking to the external labour market.

All phase-in periods have now ended and all employers that have ten or more employees have an ongoing obligation to maintain compensation practices that provide pay equity in their workplaces. Current or former employees who dispute an employer's pay equity plan or who believe that it is no longer appropriate because of changed circumstances may file a complaint with the Pay Equity Commission. The Commission may then undertake an investigation of the organization's pay equity practices. Similarly, current or former employees of employers that did not prepare a plan may file a complaint on the basis that the employer is not in compliance with its pay equity obligations.

Achieving Pay Equity

The Pay Equity Commission has identified six steps to achieving pay equity. These steps were written for employers in existence as of January 1, 1988 but new employers carry out many of the same analyses before hiring employees and setting wages, even though they are not required to prepare and post a plan.

1. *Identify establishments.* The employer begins by identifying how many establishments it has in Ontario and the number of pay equity plans it requires. All facilities in a regional municipality or county are considered to be one establishment. All of an employer's workplaces in the City of Toronto and certain other named cities and towns are considered to be a single establishment for pay equity purposes.

   The identification of establishments sets the boundaries for the plans that an employer must prepare and the job comparisons that it must make. A non-union employer's plan includes the entire establishment. An employer that has one or more unions must prepare a pay equity plan for each bargaining unit in an establishment and another for all other employees in the establishment. Plans for bargaining units must be negotiated with the bargaining agent. In organizations that are not unionized, an employer may unilaterally decide to treat two or more geographic areas as one establishment and therefore prepare a single plan, rather than have separate plans for each geographic area. In organizations that are unionized, an employer and bargaining agent can agree that an establishment includes employees in two or more geographic divisions.

2. *Identify gender-dominant job classes.* The employer (and union, if any) first must group jobs into job classes. These job classes form the foundation of any pay equity analysis. Positions with *similar* duties that (a) require similar qualifications, (b) are filled by similar recruiting procedures, *and* (c) have the same compensation schedule or range are considered to be part of the same job class. Note that to be in the same job class, the jobs must have the *same*

(not merely similar) compensation schedule, salary grade, or range of salary rates. Moreover, in looking at the similarity of qualifications, it is the qualifications required for the position, not the qualifications that the incumbent may happen to have, that are relevant.

The employer (and union, if any) must then identify which of these job classes is gender-dominant on the basis of rules set out in the Act. A job class is considered a **female job class** if at least 60 percent of the positions are held by women, have been held by women, or are perceived as being women's work as a result of gender stereotyping. For example, if historically the company nurse has always been a woman but currently the nursing position is held by a man, the job may fall within a female job class for the purposes of pay equity comparison. A job class is considered to be a **male job class** if at least 70 percent of the positions are held, or have traditionally been held, by men. The remaining job classes are gender-neutral job classes. Generally, they are not used for pay equity comparisons.

There is no minimum number of jobs in a job class; a single position may constitute a class.

3. *Select a gender-neutral job evaluation system.* The employer (and union, if any) must choose a **gender-neutral job evaluation system** that uses at least four designated factors in making its comparisons: skill, effort, responsibility, and working conditions. These factors are not defined, so the evaluation system may include its own subfactors that are relevant to a particular business. For example, the responsibility factor may include job complexity, decision-making authority, problem solving, and customer contact. Subfactors must give appropriate weight to aspects of jobs that are typically performed by females. For example, a job evaluation system that recognizes physical exertion under an effort category but fails to recognize the demands of working with numerous simultaneous deadlines may be biased in favour of jobs typically performed by men. Similarly, an evaluation system that awards points for working conditions that are dirty and noisy but ignores conditions that expose a worker to communicable diseases is probably not gender-neutral. The weighting of factors must also be gender-neutral. For example, a system that gives a lot of weight to working conditions may be biased in favour of jobs traditionally performed by men.

The goal of the job evaluation system is to recognize the contribution that a job makes to an organization, regardless of gender.

Therefore, the process of collecting accurate job information is a crucial one. In *Peterborough (City) v. Professional Fire Fighters Association, Local 519*, the Pay Equity Hearings Tribunal criticized a process whereby the organization's pay equity committee simply relied on the committee members' knowledge of the requirements of each of the jobs in making their evaluation. The Tribunal noted that job information is likely to be more accurate and complete if it is collected from incumbents rather than from the committee members who are doing the comparisons.

4. *Compare female and male job classes.* Once the jobs have been evaluated, the employer (and union, if any) must compare female job classes with male job

classes. There are two methods that private sector employers can use to make pay equity comparisons under the legislation: the direct job-to-job method and the proportional value method. Public sector employers may use both of these methods, but if a comparable male job class still cannot be found, the public sector employer must then use the proxy comparison method.

a. *Direct job-to-job comparison.* Under this method, the employer looks for a comparable male job class within the same bargaining unit as the female job class or, if the female job class is non-union, the employer looks for a comparator among the non-union male job classes in the establishment. If a comparable male job class is found, pay equity is achieved when the female job class and the male job class of comparable value have the same job rate. A job rate is defined as being the highest rate of compensation for a job class, including the value of benefits.

If there is no comparable male job class within the same bargaining unit or among the non-union male job classes to which the female job class can be compared, the female job class may be compared with all jobs in the establishment. This could involve making comparisons across bargaining units or between unionized and non-unionized employees.

Where there is still no male job class with which to compare the female job class, pay equity is achieved when the job rate of the female job class is at least equal to the job rate of a male job class anywhere in the establishment that has a higher job rate but that performs work of lower value than the female job class. Thus, the chosen male job class is not of equal or comparable value to the female job class, but it is used as a comparison because it is higher paid. For example, assume that a female receptionist position has been valued at 440 points under a gender-neutral job evaluation system and that there are no comparable male positions in the company. However, the male sweeper position is paid more than the receptionist position, although the sweeper job has been valued at only 400 points on the basis of its skills and responsibility. The receptionist's wage rate must be raised at least to that of the sweeper's, and arguably should be 10 percent higher (see the proportional value comparison system described below).

b. *Proportional value comparison.* This indirect method of comparison is used when an employer cannot find a direct match for one or more of its female job classes using the job-to-job comparison method. The most common method for making a proportional value comparison is for the employer to establish a "wage line" based on a representative group of male job classes. The same relationship between pay and job value found in that group is then applied to the female job classes. Employers who were required to use this method had to amend and repost their pay equity plans by January 1, 1993 or January 1, 1994, depending on the size of the organization.

c. *Proxy comparison.* Only the public sector is required to use this method. Where a public sector employer is unable to find a match for a female job class using the first two comparison methods, it must look outside its own organization for a comparable male job class in the same sector.

Different pay levels are permitted between comparable male- and female-dominated jobs if the pay differential results from a formal seniority system, a temporary training or development assignment, a merit pay system, red-circling (a practice of maintaining an incumbent employee's wage rate even though there is a change in circumstances that would usually justify reducing the rate), or a temporary skills shortage. This temporary shortage must be fully documented.

After pay equity has been achieved, the legislation allows differences in compensation that result from "differences in bargaining strength." This refers to the situation where unionized employees are able to negotiate increases that are higher than those paid to female job classes of comparable value that are not in the bargaining unit.

5. *Prepare and post the pay equity plan.* An employer that was required to prepare a pay equity plan (that is, an employer that was in existence before January 1, 1988 and had at least 100 employees) had to post its plan for review by employees.

In unionized workplaces, the employer had to negotiate the pay equity plan with the bargaining agent; once finalized, it was deemed approved, although bargaining unit members who believed the *Pay Equity Act* had been violated could voice their objections to the Commission.

Both employees and unions may file complaints with the Pay Equity Commission if, for example, they believe that a pay equity plan is not being implemented properly or that the plan is no longer appropriate for female job classes because of changes in the workplace. Complaints may be made to the Commission anonymously or on behalf of a group.

6. *Make pay adjustments.* Under the Act, private sector employers with ten or more employees in Ontario in 1988 who prepared and posted a plan could limit their annual pay adjustments to 1 percent of the previous year's payroll. For example, if the payroll of ABC Co. in 1992 was $3,000,000, the maximum amount that ABC Co. was required to pay toward its pay equity adjustments in 1993 was $30,000, and so on in subsequent years. In allocating this amount among employees, the Act provides that the greatest adjustments must be made to the employees in the female job class with the lowest job rate (s. 13(3)). "Job rate" is defined as the top rate of pay. Employers whose earlier payment practices reflected major discrepancies between male- and female-dominated jobs may take years to achieve pay equity.

Employers in the public sector who use the proxy method of comparison also may limit their pay equity adjustments to 1 percent of the previous year's payroll. In that case, there is no deadline for achieving pay equity. Otherwise, public sector employers were required to achieve pay equity by 1998.

Employers with ten or more employees that started doing business in Ontario after 1988 and employers that reach the ten-employee threshold after January 1, 1988 must achieve pay equity immediately. They are not required to create a pay equity plan but should document their pay equity decisions to defend themselves in the event that a worker or union files a complaint with the Commission.

FYI

Commonly Overlooked Features of Work Typically Performed by Women

SKILL

- applying analytical reasoning
- using manual dexterity for giving injections, typing, and graphic arts
- training and orienting new staff
- creating documents
- handling complaints
- communicating with upset, irate, or irrational people
- using a variety of computer software and database formats

RESPONSIBILITY

- caring for patients, children, and institutionalized people
- protecting confidentiality
- managing petty cash
- maintaining contact with others, internally or externally

EFFORT

- adjusting to rapid changes in office or plant technology
- concentrating for prolonged periods at computer terminals, lab benches, and manufacturing equipment
- having to perform frequent lifting and bending for childcare work
- performing complex sequences of hand–eye coordination

WORKING CONDITIONS

- stress from office noise and crowded conditions
- exposure to disease
- stress from caring for ill people
- stress from physical or verbal abuse from irrational clients or patients
- exposure to and disposal of body fluids
- exposure to eye strain from computer terminals

SOURCE: Based on Pay Equity Commission, *Commonly Overlooked Features of Work* (2003, pp. 1–2). © Queen's Printer for Ontario, 2003.

Maintaining Pay Equity

Once pay equity is achieved, employers have an ongoing obligation to maintain compensation practices that provide for pay equity. Job descriptions need to be kept up to date. All new jobs should be evaluated under the gender-neutral comparison system and paid accordingly. Also, when an incumbent changes, the employer may consider whether the gender of a job has changed, but must keep in mind that the gender of a job class is determined with reference to historical information as well (Blunt and Jeffery, 2012, p. 39).

An employer should also re-evaluate jobs in circumstances such as the following:

1. where a job eliminates a position by combining two jobs,
2. where a temporary skills shortage or red-circling procedure ends,
3. where the employer introduces new technology that affects the value of a job used for pay equity comparison,
4. where a sale or merger renders the current pay equity plan obsolete, and
5. where a union is certified to represent a group of employees, because this affects appropriate job comparisons under the plan.

Pay equity is also relevant when changes are made to benefit plans. An employer must ensure that the changes do not create a compensation inequity between female and male job classes. It is also relevant to unions and employers when negotiating wage increases, particularly where comparisons were made between union and non-union positions. If an employer has not yet achieved pay equity, it is critical that the parties identify whether negotiated wage increases go toward pay equity targets or economic targets.

The following case of *Canadian Union of Public Employees Local 1999 v. Lakeridge Health Corporation* illustrates that pay equity can remain a contentious issue years after a plan has been achieved. In *Lakeridge*, the union filed a complaint alleging that the plan failed to maintain pay equity because of the difference in the number of steps it took for employees in female-dominated job classes to reach the "job rate" (that is, the top rate) compared with employees in comparable male job classes (Silliker, 2012, p. 1).

CASE IN POINT

Does the Entire Wage Grid Have to Be Gender-Neutral?

Canadian Union of Public Employees Local 1999 v. Lakeridge Health Corporation, 2012 ONSC 2051

Facts

The employer, Lakeridge Health Corporation, was a large hospital that had finalized a pay equity plan with its union in 2006. The plan covered both its "service" (mostly male) and its "clerical" (mostly female) units. As required by law, the job rates (defined as the top rate) for comparable male- and female-dominated job classes within those two units were equal. However, the wage grid for the male job classes had fewer steps than the wage grid for the female job classes. As a result, employees in the former often had higher start rates and progressed more quickly through their grids to the top wage rate than did employees in comparably evaluated female jobs (9 months compared with 24 months). The resulting wage differential in the first two years of employment was as high as $4,000. The union, CUPE, applied to the Pay Equity Hearings Tribunal for an order that this arrangement violated the *Pay Equity Act*, arguing that the wage grids, as well as job rates, must be "harmonized." The employer countered that it met the requirements of the pay equity legislation and that the wage grids were negotiated in collective bargaining and therefore reflected the priorities of the different bargaining agents (Silliker, 2012, p. 16).

The Tribunal found for the employer on the basis that while the legislation requires pay equity to be achieved by adjusting job rates, its wording could not be extended to require an equalization of the wage grids as well. CUPE applied for judicial review.

Relevant Issue

Whether the *Pay Equity Act* requires equalization in the number of steps and amount of time it takes to reach the "job rate."

Decision

The Divisional Court dismissed the application, finding that the Tribunal's interpretation of the *Pay Equity Act* was reasonable—only the job rate needs to be equalized. While the legislation's purpose is to redress systemic gender discrimination in compensation, the legislative scheme relates the achievement of pay equity to the attainment of the same job rate. Referencing the Tribunal's decision, the court noted:

> The Act consistently refers to the achievement of pay equity in terms of the adjustment of job rates despite the fact that it also contains both explicit and implicit acknowledgement that job classes may have more than one rate of compensation attached to them. There is explicit acknowledgement of this fact in the definition of what positions may comprise a "job class": those with the same "compensation schedule, salary grade or range of salary rates." The use of the adjustment of "job rates" as the measure for when pay equity is achieved must be considered as a deliberate choice. Clearly the Act might have provided that pay equity is achieved when the "compensation schedule, salary grade or range of salary rates" for the male and female job classes are equalized.

However, the Act did not provide for such equalization; consequently, the Act does not require employers to harmonize wage grids to achieve pay equity (Greaves, 2012).

Although the employer was successful in *Lakeridge*, the case illustrates the on-going nature of the obligation to be able to show compliance with the law. Employers should review their pay equity plans at least once a year. They may need to prepare an amended plan for non-unionized employees or negotiate one with a union and post it in the workplace.

Unions are prohibited from bargaining for or agreeing to compensation that would violate pay equity requirements. Compensation adjustments under the pay equity plan are deemed to form part of the collective agreement.

In addition to responding to complaints, the Pay Equity Commission monitors compliance with the Act through two programs: the Monitoring Program and the Wage Gap Program. In the past, the Monitoring Program operated by selecting a particular industry each year and randomly visiting organizations within that sector and reviewing their compensation practices. For example, in 2008 the Pay Equity Office (discussed below) monitored the retail and hotel/motel sectors in Peel Region for compliance with the Act. More recently, the Monitoring Program has started to focus on employers who have been identified through the Wage Gap Program. This program, introduced in 2011, involves contacting workplaces (starting with those with over 500 employees, and now branching out to medium-sized and smaller businesses) to gather information concerning whether a gender wage gap still exists in those organizations. If a contacted employer does not respond to the Commission's request for wage data by the deadline set, or if the wage data show possible inequities, a review officer is assigned to the file (LeGault, 2013). Under the Monitoring Program, these identified employers are asked for three years of compensation data and information about jobs, locations, and the employer's pay equity process. Where concerns are raised, a review officer can require up to seven years of data and ultimately require compliance based on established timelines (LeGault, 2013).

It should be noted that there is no time limit on pay equity complaints; nor is there a limit on retroactive pay adjustments. An employer should therefore retain, indefinitely, everything used in developing its plan: for example, job descriptions, questionnaires, the job evaluation system, and payroll and benefits information (Blunt and Jeffery, 2012, p. 39).

IN THE NEWS

Epic Federal Equal Pay Battle

Despite being based on a less proactive model than Ontario's pay equity law, the federal law has seen some epic, decades-long battles. The following excerpts from a *Toronto Star* article recount the 30 years it took for a pay equity dispute between Canada Post and its union, the Public Service Alliance of Canada, to be resolved.

Canada Post, Union End 30-Year Pay Equity Fight

The cheques are finally going in the mail.

Canada Post and the Public Service Alliance of Canada have reached a settlement in the country's longest running pay equity dispute, which has spanned three decades.

"We are extremely happy about this. I'm very proud of our victory," said PSAC national president Robyn Benson in an interview. "It's a long time in coming. It's been 30 years."

Benson says as many as 30,000 people, predominantly women, could be eligible for a portion of the settlement, which is estimated at $250 million with interest. ...

When the union first filed the complaint in 1983, Pierre Trudeau was still prime minister and one of the biggest cultural events of the year was the final episode of the television show M*A*S*H. Over the years, the case wound its way through the

Canadian Human Rights Tribunal and through various courts, ending up at the Supreme Court in 2011. In a rare oral ruling, a mere 20 minutes after hearing arguments, the justices unanimously ordered the Crown corporation to pay up.

But payouts were never made because of a dispute over how much interest was owed. …

The complaint dates back to 1983, filed on behalf of 2,300 clerical workers. The union argued the mostly female clerical employees were doing comparable work to the mostly male letter-sorters and carriers, but earned substantially less.

The battle raged for years. In a 2005 decision, the tribunal sided with the union and the mostly female employees, ordering that Canada Post pay additional wages to close the gap, covering the period from 1982 to 2002, plus pre-judgment and post-judgment interest.

The Crown corporation appealed, and won at two levels before the Supreme Court's ruling.

Interest from Aug. 24, 1982 to Oct. 6, 2005 will be calculated using the Canada Savings Bond rate in effect on Sept. 1 of that year, and after that it will be 4 per cent per year until the date of payment.

SOURCE: Vanessa Lu, "Canada Post, Union End 30-Year Pay Equity Fight," *Toronto Star*, June 27, 2013. Reprinted with permission—TorStar Syndication Services.

Administration and Enforcement

The *Pay Equity Act* is administered and enforced by the Pay Equity Commission of Ontario. It consists of two bodies: the Pay Equity Office and the Pay Equity Hearings Tribunal. The Pay Equity Office receives and investigates complaints and attempts to bring about settlements. The majority of complaints are settled at this point (Blunt and Jeffery, 2012, p. 39). If necessary, a review officer from the Commission can issue orders that set out steps with which employers and unions are required to comply. A party named in an order can request the Pay Equity Hearings Tribunal to vary, confirm, or revoke that order. The Tribunal also has powers to enforce orders.

Fines for violating the *Pay Equity Act* go up to $5,000 for individuals and $50,000 for corporations. Offences include reprisals by employers against employees who exercise their rights under the Act, obstructing an officer of the Commission, and breaching an order of the Tribunal.

In addition, the Pay Equity Office provides resources to assist employers in complying with the legislation. Its extensive resource material can be found at www.payequity.gov.on.ca/en/resources/index.php.

FYI

Challenges to Achieving Pay Equity

January 2008 marked the 20th anniversary of Ontario's *Pay Equity Act*. Numerous articles covering that milestone have discussed what has, and has not, been accomplished by Ontario's groundbreaking legislation. Proponents of the law argue that pay equity has helped reduce the pay gap from 38 percent in 1988 to 29 percent two decades later. However, critics argue that its effectiveness has been limited by factors such as reduced funding for enforcement during the 1990s and the Ontario government's failure to continue pay equity adjustments to the female-dominated broader public sector (such as childcare centres and community agencies) after 2005. Many also argue that pay equity laws need to be bolstered by employment equity laws (discussed below) that remove systemic barriers to higher-paying male-dominated jobs (Cornish and Faraday, 2008).

Other critics argue that there are many reasons for the continuing gap between men's and women's earnings, including ones that cannot be readily cured by legislation. For example, women tend to bear an unequal share of childcare responsibilities and as a result they are more likely to have interruptions in their employment and to work fewer hours, on average, than men.

As illustrated by the following newspaper article excerpt concerning pay equity in Ontario's *public* sector, achieving the promise of pay equity is an ongoing issue.

Pay Equity Issue Still Simmers

The provincial government must acknowledge the importance of so-called "women's work" by investing half a billion dollars into pay equity so female workers earn an appropriate wage, advocates said today during a news conference at the legislature.

January will mark the 20th anniversary of the province's *Pay Equity Act*, but it's been an ongoing struggle to convince governments to recognize the legislation, said Irene Harris of the Ontario Federation of Labour.

The act was supposed to address pay inequity by comparing the wages of jobs predominantly held by women with the salaries of men with jobs deemed to be of similar importance or value. Government funding would then help subsidize increases in women's salaries.

The legislation helped secondary school secretaries get an annual raise of about $7,680 after their jobs were compared to the work of male audio-visual technicians, says the Equal Pay Coalition, and police dispatchers got a similar raise after their jobs were compared to radio technical supervisors.

But Harris said it's wrong that child-care workers and other skilled women working in social services and the health sector haven't benefited from the legislation and continue to be paid woefully inadequate salaries. ...

Advocates have long been frustrated by several government attempts to weaken or eliminate the *Pay Equity Act* as well as claims it shouldn't be a provincial responsibility to fund pay equity.

Unions and workers launched Charter fights in 1996 and 2001 to get more government funding and achieved successful results in each case.

A mediated settlement in 2003 provided $414 million to fund better pay equity through 2006, but there have been no government commitments since.

Hahn hopes the current government will commit to more funding without a fight, but he said another lawsuit isn't out of the question.

SOURCE: "Pay Equity Issue Still Simmers," *Toronto Star*, October 24, 2007. Reprinted with permission—TorStar Syndication Services.

Employment Equity

The term **employment equity** was coined by Judge Rosalie Abella in her landmark *Report of the Royal Commission on Equality in Employment*, which was prepared for the federal government in 1984. Created to avoid the negative connotations that the term "affirmative action" had acquired in the United States, "employment equity" is a Canadian phrase that refers to a range of measures, including affirmative action and other programs aimed at ensuring equality in employment.

Although human rights legislation prohibits discrimination in the workplace, it depends on the lodging of complaints and usually focuses on individual instances of unfairness. In contrast, employment equity addresses the broad social problem of the underrepresentation of certain groups of people, such as visible minorities and people with disabilities, in most workplaces, especially in better-paid and higher-level jobs.

In 1986, the federal government enacted the *Employment Equity Act*, which requires large federally regulated employers to implement employment equity programs in their workplaces. To encourage as broad an interest in employment equity as possible, the federal government has also introduced the Federal Contractors Program (FCP). Under the FCP, provincially regulated companies with 100 or more employees that contract with the federal government for business worth $1 million or more must commit to implementing employment equity.

Ontario's New Democratic Party government passed employment equity legislation in 1993, but it was repealed when the Ontario Progressive Conservative Party took office in 1995. They saw it as reverse discrimination. Currently, there is no provincial law requiring employers to implement employment equity. However, some provincially regulated employers in Ontario are implementing employment equity as a result of the FCP, while others are introducing it as a way of attracting and managing employees in a culturally diverse workforce.

The Employment Equity Act

Principles

Section 2 of the federal *Employment Equity Act* requires employers to identify workplace barriers and develop equity plans for four designated groups—women, Aboriginal peoples (including Indian, Inuit, and Métis), persons with disabilities, and visible minorities—to improve their representation in the workplace. Often, these barriers result from a particular employment practice. For example, one employment practice that adversely affects certain groups of employees is hiring on the basis of "word of mouth." This practice may result in perpetuating the current ethnic composition of a workforce and eliminating candidates who are equally, or better, qualified than those who are hired. An employment equity program identifies and removes this barrier, and replaces it with a practice that is more inclusive.

Who Is Covered?

The *Employment Equity Act* applies to federally regulated private sector companies— such as banks, transportation companies, communication companies, Crown corporations (for example, Canada Post), and other federal organizations with 100 or more employees. Approximately 500 private sector employers, 30 Crown corporations, and 5 other federal organizations with a combined workforce of over 760,000 employees are covered by this legislation (Government of Canada, 2014). These employers are known as Legislated Employment Equity Program (LEEP) employers.

What Are the Responsibilities of LEEP Employers?

LEEP employers must identify and eliminate barriers to the employment of members of the four designated groups. They must institute measures to ensure that group members are represented proportionately in the organization's workforce. This involves comparing a group's representation in the employer's workforce with that group's representation in the parts of the labour force from which the employer draws its employees. For example, if an employer's comparison shows that Aboriginal people are underrepresented in its workforce, the employer must take special measures to correct this. The employer might institute outreach programs, for example, to recruit more Aboriginal people.

Private sector employers who are covered by the Act must collect and analyze workforce data on each of the four designated groups and report this data annually to the federal government through the Labour Program of Employment and Social Development Canada. This report must specify the number of employees in each designated group, together with the number of both female and male employees in each of several occupational groups. LEEP employers must also provide information on salary ranges. These individual reports must be received by the Labour Program by June 1 of each year. Once compliance with the reporting requirements is verified, the individual reports are analyzed and consolidated into the *Employment Equity Act Annual Report*, which is tabled in Parliament. If an employer fails to comply with the reporting requirements, the Minister of Labour may issue a monetary penalty within two years of the violation.

In addition, the Canadian Human Rights Commission conducts compliance audits on LEEP employers, focusing primarily on those with more than 500 employees and a below-average employment equity result in comparison with their sector. Such audits include onsite visits and interviews with various parties; organizations are then provided with a report indicating any additional measures required to comply with the Act. If the organization fails to take these measures, the matter may be referred to the Employment Equity Review Tribunal (Canadian Human Rights Commission, 2013).

The Federal Contractors Program

Who Is Covered?

First established in 1986, the Federal Contractors Program applies to provincially regulated employers with 100 or more employees who wish to bid on federal government contracts for goods or services that are worth $1 million or more. As a condition for bidding, these employers must certify that they will implement an employment equity plan. It should be noted that this threshold for coverage was increased from $200,000 to $1 million, effective June 27, 2013, as part of a federal government initiative to reduce red tape for small to medium-sized employers (Labour Program, "Legislated Employment Equity Program," 2014). It effectively reduces the number of employers covered by the FCP from roughly 1,000 to 600 (Thompson, 2013).

What Are the Responsibilities of Employers Under the FCP?

The FCP covers the four designated groups under the *Employment Equity Act*—women, visible minorities, persons with disabilities, and Aboriginal peoples. An employer that wants to be on the list of potential contractors must file a certificate that commits it to implementing employment equity in its workplace. These commitments, which were also revamped effective June 2013, now are to:

1. *Collect workforce data.* The employer must survey its workforce to find out the representation of the four designated groups. The questionnaire used to collect the information, which is based on voluntary self-identification by employees, must meet prescribed standards. For example, it must include the appropriate definition for each designated group, and indicate that the information gathered is confidential and will only be shared with internal HR employees responsible for employment equity obligations. Although filling out the survey is voluntary, if the response rate is less than 80 percent, the employer must follow up with non-respondents. The employer must also maintain an up-to-date database of the collected information that includes the

following, where applicable: hire date; designated group membership; occupational group classification; salary and salary increases; promotion date(s); and termination date. To ensure that the database is current, the employer should provide the self-identification questionnaires to new employees and update survey results accordingly, as well as periodically remind employees that previously submitted information can be changed where circumstances warrant.

2. *Complete a workforce analysis .* An employer must analyze the representation of designated groups within the organization and compare it with the supply of qualified workers from which it could reasonably be expected to recruit employees to identify gaps in representation. The availability of qualified people is assessed on the basis of census data available from the Labour Program. This analysis must be done at least once every three years.

3. *Establish short-term and long-term numeric goals to correct gaps in representation (underrepresentation of designated groups).* The employer is required to set reasonable short-term goals (one to three years) and long-term goals for hiring and promoting designated group members to close any identified gaps. This often means making a commitment to hire a higher percentage of people from an underrepresented group. Consider, for example, an employer that finds that only 15 percent of its middle managers are female while census data in the relevant geographic area show that 25 percent of qualified middle managers are female. The employer could set the goal of hiring women to fill one-third of the middle management jobs available over the next three years to close this gap. Long-term goals are set to close gaps that are unlikely to be closed in under three years based on the degree of underrepresentation, the availability of qualified designated group members, the anticipated growth or reduction in the employer's workforce, and anticipated turnover (Labour Program, 2013).

4. *Make reasonable progress and reasonable efforts.* Some of the previous requirements that included consulting with unions or adopting reasonable accommodation measures to achieve employment equity have been eliminated. The Federal Contractors Program now calls on the employer to make "reasonable efforts" and "reasonable progress"—for example, meeting hiring and promotion goals by at least 80 percent. Reasonable efforts may be evidenced by demonstrating ongoing senior-level support for employment equity; establishing accountability mechanisms; providing the staffing and financial resources necessary to meet short-term goals; and developing a strategy to remove workplace barriers. As part of this commitment, an employer should review barriers that its employment systems may have created in hiring, promoting, and retaining members of the designated groups. For example, employers should ensure that staff who are responsible for recruiting, hiring, supervising, evaluating, or promoting employees eliminate discriminatory attitudes. The government's Federal Contractors Program website expressly states that "reasonable efforts" does not mean the contractor must, in order to comply, take action that would cause undue hardship, hire or promote unqualified persons, or create new positions (Labour Program, "Federal Contractors Program," 2014).

FCP employers must keep employment equity records for at least three years after the date to which the records relate.

Compliance assessments are conducted by the federal Labour Program's officers. A first-year compliance assessment is done after a contractor has been subject to the FCP for one year. It will involve an assessment of the self-identification questionnaire, the survey's response and return rates, the workforce analysis, and both short- and long-term goals. Third-year compliance assessments may be conducted after each finding of compliance. These assessments will look at whether reasonable efforts and progress were made toward implementing and maintaining employment equity (Labour Program, "Federal Contractors Program," 2014).

Employers that are found not to be in compliance with their employment equity obligations, and that are unsuccessful in appealing such a finding, will lose the right to bid on all federal contracts, regardless of their value. They also will be placed on a public list of non-compliant contractors.

The Labour Program provides consulting services to FCP employers and enforces compliance. Federal contractors need not report their statistics publicly, but their workforce data and results must be available to an FCP review officer on request.

FYI

Strategies for Making Workplaces More Inclusive

Organizations that are most successful with employment equity link the full participation of designated group members to their business strategy. For example, between 2003 and 2006, Scotiabank (a LEEP employer) increased its representation of women at the senior management level from 18.9 percent to 31.0 percent, and its representation at the most senior executive vice-president/corporate officer level from 26.7 percent to 36.8 percent. Its strategies included transparent accountability for people development and career advancement, as well as a series of programs that connected and developed women throughout the organization. Scotiabank was named Canada's Best Diversity Employer in 2009 and 2010 (Scotiabank, n.d.).

The following is a sampling of strategies that diversity award–winning employers in Canada have adopted:

- partnering with outside organizations to find job candidates who are hard to reach through traditional recruitment strategies;
- including a diversity statement on job postings;
- using a mentorship/buddy system to help a new hire feel comfortable in the workplace;

- holding equity-awareness sessions for recruiters;
- publishing and displaying recruitment materials in a variety of languages;
- providing tools to help employees with disabilities;
- surveying employees on whether they are treated respectfully and fairly at work;
- recognizing candidates who have obtained their qualifications and experience in non-traditional ways, such as doing volunteer work;
- building diversity training into management/supervisory preparation, including a training program on bias-free interviewing;
- focusing on retaining employees from designated groups by incorporating a diversity component into their succession planning program;
- hosting leadership seminars and networking breakfasts for senior-level female and minority employees; and
- providing paid internships to disabled individuals.

REFERENCES

Abella, R.A. *Report of the Royal Commission on Equality in Employment*. Ottawa: Supply and Services Canada, 1984.

Alexandrowicz, G., et al. *Dimensions of Law: Canadian and International Law in the 21st Century*. Toronto: Emond Montgomery, 2004.

Blunt, Antoinette, and Geoff Jeffery. Is Your Organization Maintaining Pay Equity Correctly? *HR Professional*. October 2012, p. 39.

Bowness, Suzanne. Dreaming of Diversity. *HR Professional*. May/June 2013, p. 24.

The Canadian Press. Pay Equity Issue Still Simmers. Reproduced in *Toronto Star*, October 24, 2007, http://www.thestar.com/news/ontario/2007/10/24/pay_equity_issue_still_simmers.html.

Canadian Human Rights Commission. Employment Equity: On Employment Equity Audits. Last modified January 9, 2013. http://www.chrc-ccdp.ca/eng/content/employment-equity#7.

Canadian Union of Public Employees Local 1999 v. Lakeridge Health Corporation. 2012 ONSC 2051.

Catalyst. Scotiabank—Unlocking Potential, Delivering Results: The Advancement of Women (AoW) Initiative. January 2007. http://www.catalyst.org/.

Conference Board of Canada. Women in Leadership: Perceptions and Priorities for Change. May 2013. http://www.conferenceboard.ca/e-library/default.aspx.

Cornish, Mary, and Fay Faraday. Ontario's Gender Pay Gap Cheats Women Workers. *Toronto Star*, September 17, 2008. http://www.thestar.com/comment/article/500415.

Dobson, Sarah. Employers Rewarded for Diversity. *Canadian HR Reporter*. March 9, 2009, p. 3.

Echlin, Randall S., and Christine M. Thomlinson. *For Better or For Worse: A Practical Guide to Canadian Employment Law*, 3rd ed. Aurora, ON: Thomson Reuters, 2011.

Elliott, Cheryl. *A Complete Guide to Pay and Employment Equity*. Aurora, ON: Canada Law Book, 2001.

Employment Equity Act. SC 1995, c. 44.

Employment Standards Act, 2000. SO 2000, c. 41.

Gerson, Jen. Visible Minorities in Just 3 Percent of Top Jobs. October 17, 2007. http://www.diversityworking.com/index.php.

Gilbert, Douglas, Brian Burkett, and Moira McCaskill. *Canadian Labour and Employment Law for the US Practitioner*. Washington, DC: Bureau of National Affairs, 2000.

Greaves, Carolyn. Divisional Court Affirms Pay Equity Wage Grids and Restricts Tribunal's Use of Human Rights Code. *FTR Now*. July 6, 2012. Hicks Morley. http://hicksmorley.com/index.php?name=News&file=article&sid=1282&catid=6.

Labour Program. Federal Contractors Program. 2014. http://www.labour.gc.ca/eng/standards_equity/eq/emp/fcp.

Labour Program. Federal Contractors Program: Compliance Assessment—OPD 700-14. 2013. http://www.labour.gc.ca/eng/resources/opd/700-14.shtml.

Labour Program. Legislated Employment Equity Program. 2014. http://www.labour.gc.ca/eng/standards_equity/eq/emp/leep/index.shtml.

LeGault, Anneli. Compliance Reminder—Ontario Pay Equity Commission Is Open for Business. November 25, 2013. Dentons. Mondaq. http://www.mondaq.com/canada/x/277110/employee+rights+labour+relations/Compliance+Reminder+Ontario+Pay+Equity+Commission+Is+Open+For+Business.

McLarren, Philip. *Employment in Ontario*, 2nd ed. Markham, ON: Lexis Nexis Canada, 2003.

Mediacorp Canada Inc. Canada's Best Diversity Employers. 2014. http://www.canadastop100.com/diversity/.

Patten, Rose. Linking Equity, Business Strategy. *Canadian HR Reporter*. December 16, 2002, p. 16.

Pay Equity Act. RSO 1990, c. P.7.

Pay Equity Commission. Commonly Overlooked Features of Work, June 16, 2003, http://www.payequity.gov.on.ca/en/pdf/over_look.pdf; Pay Equity: An Overview for Employees, May 25, 2004; Pay Equity and Equal Pay: What Is the Difference? June 16, 2003, http://www.payequity.gov.on.ca/en/pdf/difference.pdf; Pay Equity Plan: Amended for Proportional Value, June 16, 2003, http://www.payequity.gov.on.ca/en/resources/regression/pro_plan.php; Pay Equity Plan: Job-to-Job Comparison Method, June 16, 2003, http://www.payequity.gov.on.ca/en/pdf/job_to_job_plan.pdf.

Pay Equity Commission. Compliance Self-Assessment Checklist and Responses Guide—Private Sector. September 2012. http://www.payequity.gov.on.ca/en/resources/self_audit.php.

Pay Equity Commission. Wage Gap Pilot Program. April 8, 2014. http://www.payequity.gov.on.ca/en/about/wagegap_program.php.

Peterborough (City) v. Professional Fire Fighters Association, Local 519. 1997 CanLII 12087 (Ont. PEHT).

Scotiabank. Diversity Awards. (n.d.) http://www.scotiabank.com/ca/en/0,,5353,00.html.

Silliker, Amanda. Unequal Wage Grids Don't Violate Pay Equity. *Canadian HR Reporter*. July 16, 2012, p. 1.

Thompson, Elizabeth. Harper Government Reduces Employment Equity Requirements for Contractors. *iPolitics*. June 28, 2013. http://www.ipolitics.ca/2013/06/28/harper-government-reduces-employment-equity-requirements-for-contractors.

Women's Advancement to Senior Roles Stagnant, Says Conference Board Report. *HR Professional*. July/August 2013, p. 12.

RELATED WEBSITES

- http://www.payequity.gov.on.ca The Pay Equity Commission's website.
- http://www.labour.gc.ca/eng/standards_equity/eq/emp/fcp The Labour Program's website. Discusses the Federal Contractors Program.

REVIEW AND DISCUSSION QUESTIONS

1. What are the key differences between the requirements of Ontario's *Employment Standards Act* and those of its *Pay Equity Act*?

2. What is a gender-neutral evaluation system? Provide examples to illustrate your answer.

3. Ontario employers with 100 or more employees were required to prepare and implement a pay equity plan more than two decades ago. Are the pay equity plan provisions of the *Pay Equity Act* still relevant today? Why or why not?

4. Distinguish pay equity from employment equity.

5. According to the Cornish and Faraday article, "Ontario's Gender Pay Gap Cheats Women Workers":

   [W]hile women's increasing levels of education have helped, a gap remains regardless of education. Female high school graduates earn 27 per cent less than male graduates. Female university graduates earn 16 per cent less than male graduates. The lowest gap has long been found among women just starting work, but the gap widens as women age. Married women face the widest pay gap at 33 per cent, partly because they bear an unequal share of care responsibilities. The gap continues into retirement as a lifetime of unequal pay and benefits results in retired women receiving a median income just half that of retired men.

   Discuss the factors that contribute to the continuing wage gap between males and females despite increased levels of education (and unionization) among female employees. Consider ways that it can be best addressed.

6. XYZ Co. is a hair product company that has a factory (73 employees) and office (20 employees) in Guelph and a distribution outlet in Scarborough (9 employees). The factory employees are unionized; all of the other employees are non-union. XYZ Co. has been in business since 1987.

   a. Is this employer covered by Ontario's *Pay Equity Act*? Explain your answer.

   b. *Assuming that the employer is covered by the Pay Equity Act*, what is the greatest number of establishments that this employer can have under the legislation? How many pay equity plans should it have?

   c. Again, assuming that the employer is covered by the legislation, briefly explain the process that the employer needs to go through to achieve pay equity.

7. Beatrice works as a car mechanic at ABC Auto Inc. All of the other six mechanics at ABC Auto are male. Beatrice just found out that Ben, a mechanic who was hired two years after she was, makes more money per hour than she does. Does Beatrice have a pay equity issue? Does she have a legitimate equal pay for equal work claim under the ESA? Explain your answer.

8. To implement employment equity, an employer must first collect workforce data. The most common method in Canada is to design a self-identification questionnaire that is filled in by employees. Discuss some of the weaknesses as well as strengths of this approach. Identify ways in which those weaknesses might be addressed.

9. According to a Conference Board of Canada Study (2013), 86 percent of women believe there is still a "glass ceiling," while 68 percent of women managers think that organizations are still run by an "old-boys club."

   What do the terms "glass ceiling" and "old-boys club" refer to? Do you agree that they play a significant role in the low percentage of women found in senior management in many organizations? Discuss.

10. Watch the 10-minute YouTube video entitled "Business Owner Makes Money by Hiring Disabled Workers" at www.cacl.ca/news-stories/blog/cbc-story-benefits-hiring-disabled-employees. It features a Tim Hortons franchisee who promotes the economic benefits of hiring persons with disabilities. What are some of the advantages of hiring employees with disabilities pointed out in this video?

Privacy Inside and Outside the Workplace

10

LEARNING OUTCOMES

After completing this chapter, you will be able to:

- Understand the growing need for protection for personal information and other privacy rights.

- Identify the ten principles behind the *Personal Information Protection and Electronic Documents Act*.

- Understand how federal privacy legislation affects provincially regulated employers in Ontario.

- State the obligations of employers in handling employees' personal information where privacy legislation applies.

- Understand the requirements of Ontario's *Personal Health Information Protection Act*.

- Understand employee privacy rights in workplaces not covered by general privacy legislation, including an employer's ability to legally monitor computers and other devices that are used for personal, as well as work-related, purposes.

Introduction

Historically, the right to privacy has not been recognized as a separate right under the common law in Canada. In the past, the privacy of the average person has been protected by the practical difficulties of locating and compiling numerous records. However, in our increasingly electronic age, where personal information can be compiled and transferred in seconds, and an individual's activities monitored in unprecedented ways, privacy concerns are now paramount. These concerns are currently reflected in legislation to safeguard the privacy of personal information, in recent developments under the common law, and in legal decisions that, for example, restrict the admissibility of evidence gained through electronic means.

Canada's original privacy legislation related to personal information held only by governments. For example, Ontario's *Freedom of Information and Protection of Privacy Act*, enacted in 1991, allows individuals to file a request for information held by the Ontario government. It also provides privacy protection for the personal information of employees in Ontario's *public* sector. Every province and territory has privacy legislation governing the collection, use, and disclosure of personal information held by government agencies (Office of the Privacy Commissioner of Canada, "Privacy Legislation in Canada," 2014).

More recently, the federal government, followed by several provincial governments, has passed legislation that covers personal information held by organizations in the *private* sector. The federal law is called the *Personal Information Protection and Electronic Documents Act* (PIPEDA). Most recently, in 2012, the Ontario Court of Appeal became the first appellate court in Canada to recognize the common law tort of "intrusion upon seclusion."

In short, this is a developing area of the law and the privacy rights that an employee has in any given situation depend on a number of factors. These include:

- Whether the workplace is federally or provincially regulated.
- In the case of a provincially regulated workplace, whether the province has broad-based privacy legislation (for example, British Columbia, Alberta, and Quebec do; Ontario does not). (Note that Ontario, New Brunswick, and Newfoundland and Labrador now have privacy legislation that specifically protects personal *health* information. Recognized as being "substantially similar" to PIPEDA's requirements, these provincial laws apply where health-related information is involved. It should also be noted that in 2013 the Supreme Court of Canada declared Alberta's privacy legislation unconstitutional for failing to balance the right to privacy with a union's right to free expression under the *Canadian Charter of Rights and Freedoms*. The Alberta government was given one year to bring its privacy legislation into compliance with the Charter.)
- Whether the employee works in the public or the private sector.
- Whether the employee is unionized or non-union.

This chapter begins by looking at PIPEDA and the ways in which personal employee information is dealt with where broad-based privacy legislation applies. It then examines the privacy rights that exist in the absence of general privacy legislation for employees in Ontario's private sector workplaces, both union and non-union.

Personal Information Protection and Electronic Documents Act

As federal legislation, PIPEDA does not directly affect general personal *employee* information held by provincially regulated employers in Ontario. (For example, an employee of a provincially regulated employer in Ontario cannot make a claim under PIPEDA that her employer collected or used personal information, such as workplace video surveillance, without her consent.) However, PIPEDA's requirements are relevant to Ontario employers for a number of reasons that are discussed below.

How Wide Is PIPEDA's Application?

PIPEDA applies to all *federally regulated* organizations and affects how they collect, use, disclose, and retain personal information concerning their employees, customers, patients, and suppliers.

PIPEDA also applies to all personal information collected, used, or disclosed in *provincially regulated organizations in the course of commercial activity* unless the province in which the organizations are situated has implemented substantially similar legislation. Commercial activity refers to common commercial transactions and includes selling, bartering, or leasing donor, membership, or other fundraising lists. (The reason that PIPEDA applies to personal information collected in the commercial, but not the employment, context in provincially regulated organizations relates to the division of powers under Canada's Constitution, discussed in Chapter 1.)

FYI

Key Features of the Federal PIPEDA

1. The purpose of PIPEDA is to balance the individual's right to have personal information kept private with an organization's need to collect, use, and disclose personal information where necessary.

2. PIPEDA applies to all organizations—both federally and provincially regulated—in Canada that collect, use, or disclose personal information in the course of *commercial* activities (s. 4) unless the province in which the organization is situated has passed comparable legislation. In that case, the provincial law applies. Ontario currently has not passed comparable legislation for employers in the private sector except in the area of personal health-related information.

3. As federal legislation, PIPEDA does not apply directly to personal *employee* information in provincially regulated workplaces.

4. The term "personal information" is broadly defined to include any factual or subjective information about "an identifiable individual" (s. 2).

5. Subject to some limitations, PIPEDA requires an individual's consent before her personal information is collected, used, or disclosed. Information may be used only for the purpose for which consent was obtained. Further consent is necessary before the information can be used for any other purpose.

6. Organizations must take precautions to safeguard personal information in their possession.

7. With some limited exceptions, individuals have a right to gain access to their personal information and to challenge an employer's treatment of it or its accuracy.

8. An individual may make a complaint regarding the way an organization has handled his personal information to the Office of the Privacy Commissioner of Canada. The individual or the privacy commissioner may apply to the Federal Court for an order requiring the organization to change its practices. It may also award damages to the individual.

As noted, Ontario has not yet passed comparable privacy legislation (except in the area of personal health information; see the FYI feature below). Consequently, PIPEDA applies to all personal information collected, used, or disclosed in all provincially regulated private sector organizations in Ontario in the course of *commercial* activity (for example, customer, client, or supplier personal information) but not to personal information used in the course of *employment*. Therefore, employers should examine PIPEDA's requirements to ensure they are in compliance in their handling of personal information in the course of commercial activities. However, they should also consider extending PIPEDA's protections to personal employee information for the following reasons:

1. PIPEDA's principles are recognized in Canada and abroad as forming the basis of ethical personal information practices.
2. Quebec, British Columbia, and Alberta have already passed privacy laws related to employment. Employers that operate in several provinces would be wise to provide all employees with the same privacy protection.
3. At some point, Ontario will likely pass privacy legislation that is similar to PIPEDA, and employers that follow its requirements now will have a head start with compliance later. Some large organizations report that it takes approximately one year to examine practices and policies in preparation for the implementation of PIPEDA (Brown, 2003, p. 11).
4. Since PIPEDA currently applies to personal information collected by provincially regulated employers in the course of commercial activity, personal information collected about non-employees, such as independent contractors, is protected. To protect the personal information of independent contractors but not of employees is inconsistent.
5. As time goes on, employees will become increasingly aware of how their privacy is protected in many areas of their lives, and will expect their personal information to be treated similarly in the workplace.
6. Although Ontario's *Human Rights Code* does not expressly protect the right to privacy, the Ontario Human Rights Commission treats privacy as an important element of the right to "equal treatment" (Mediema, 2004, p. 13). Disclosure of personal information that relates to a prohibited ground, such as religious affiliation or marital status, can be the subject of a human rights complaint.
7. Employee health information is now subject to Ontario's *Personal Health Information Protection Act.*
8. With the recent recognition of the tort of intrusion upon seclusion by Ontario's appellate court, applying PIPEDA principles to the personal information of employees could reduce the risk of potential liability under the common law.

What Is Personal Information?

The term **personal information** is broadly defined in s. 2 of PIPEDA. It includes any factual or subjective information about "an identifiable individual," whether recorded or not. However, protection does not extend to the type of information that appears on a business card: an employee's name, title, business address, or business telephone number. Personal information that is protected under PIPEDA includes an individual's

- age, home address, and identification numbers (including social insurance number);
- residential telephone numbers and personal email address;
- sex, religion, ethnicity, social status, and marital status;
- employee files (formal and informal), performance appraisals, disciplinary actions, and evaluations;
- photographs, opinions, and income;
- relevant dates, such as a birth date;
- credit records, loan records, and purchasing and spending habits;
- blood type, genetic information, and medical records; and
- intentions (for example, to purchase goods or services, or change jobs).

According to the Office of the Privacy Commissioner, personal information also includes pay and benefit records, photographs, video and audiotapes, and records of Web browsing, email, and keystrokes. Personal information is collected in many forms: on paper, electronically, in a recording, or on a fax machine. Regardless of its form, the collection, use, protection, and disclosure of personal information should adhere to the ten PIPEDA principles set out under the heading "PIPEDA's Ten Principles" below.

FYI

Ontario's Personal Health Information Protection Act, 2004

Although Ontario does not have general privacy legislation comparable to PIPEDA that covers personal *employee* information, it does have comparable legislation covering personal *health* information. Ontario's *Personal Health Information Protection Act* (PHIPA) regulates how health information custodians (HICs) may collect, use, and disclose personal health information within the Ontario health-care system. The Act applies to this information if it is in the custody or control of a custodian, or in the custody or control of an individual or *organization* that received it from a custodian. As a result, although employers are not the target of the legislation, they are covered in certain circumstances, such as where they receive personal health information from HICs with respect to administering sick leaves. The PHIPA requires that HICs only disclose personal health information about an employee where that employee has given his express consent or where it is necessary to carry out a statutory or legal duty. For consent to be valid, it must be knowledgeable (informed), be given by the *individual*, relate to the information, and not be obtained through deception or coercion (Cavoukian, 2005). Moreover, once consent is given, the employer that receives the personal health information is restricted to using or disclosing the information strictly and solely for the purposes for which the employee authorized disclosure. Breach of the PHIPA could lead to a complaint with Ontario's Information and Privacy Commissioner and potentially to a court award for damages for breach of privacy and mental anguish (Thiffeault, 2005).

PIPEDA's Ten Principles

PIPEDA recognizes two fundamental facts. The first: individuals have a right to privacy concerning their personal information. The second: organizations have a need to collect, use, and disclose personal information for appropriate purposes. The aim of PIPEDA is to achieve a fair balance between these two valid requirements.

Schedule 1 of the legislation sets out ten **fair information principles** that underlie the collection, use, protection, and disclosure of personal information. The standard in applying these principles is one of reasonableness. Section 5(3) states that an organization may collect, use, or disclose personal information *only for purposes that a reasonable person* would consider are appropriate in the circumstances.

These ten principles, including some implementation suggestions in *Privacy Toolkit: A Guide for Businesses and Organizations* (Office of the Privacy Commissioner of Canada, 2014), are discussed below.

1. *Be accountable.* An organization that collects personal information must appoint one person to oversee its compliance with PIPEDA. The appointee should have the authority to intervene when a privacy issue arises, and employees should be aware of his name and title. The appointee is responsible for analyzing the organization's personal information handling practices: what personal information is collected and why; how it is collected; what it is used for; where it is kept; how it is secured; who has access to it; to whom it is disclosed; and when it is disposed of.

   The appointee must then develop and implement policies and procedures to protect personal information. Front-line staff should be trained about policies and procedures, and should know how to respond to inquiries. If personal information is transferred to a third party for processing, an organization should ensure, by contract or other means, that the information receives a comparable level of protection during processing.

2. *Identify the purpose of collection.* An organization must let an individual know why it is collecting personal information. Any forms or documents used to collect personal information must include

   a. an explanation of why it is needed and how it will be used—for example, to open an account, verify creditworthiness, provide benefits, or process a magazine subscription; and
   b. a list of those to whom it will be disclosed.

3. *Get consent.* With limited exceptions, the individual to whom the personal information relates must consent to its collection. Consent must be voluntarily given and the individual must be aware of what is being collected and for what reason. Consent clauses should be easy to find and understand. Consent should be obtained at the time or before the personal information is collected. The form of consent depends on the sensitivity of the personal information. Although consent must usually be express, it may be implied in some circumstances, such as where a magazine uses its subscription list to solicit a renewal. However, collection or use of medical, financial, or other sensitive data requires express consent. Similarly, employers should obtain the written consent of job applicants before contacting their references by including a request for consent on job application forms. All consents should be recorded by means of a note to file where consent is given orally, such as consent given over the phone, or by keeping a copy of emails or application forms where consent is given in writing.

   To continue using or disclosing information that was collected before PIPEDA came into effect, an organization must go back to the individual and obtain consent.

There are a number of exceptions to the need to obtain consent. Under s. 7, an organization may *collect* personal information without an individual's knowledge and consent in circumstances that include the following:

a. collection is in the interests of the individual and consent cannot be obtained in a timely manner, as in the case of a medical emergency;
b. obtaining the individual's consent would compromise the availability or accuracy of the information, which is relevant to an investigation of a breach of an agreement or a contravention of law;
c. collection is for journalistic, artistic, or literary purposes; or
d. the information is publicly available.

Providing consent should not be made a condition for supplying a product or service, unless the information is necessary to meet a legitimate purpose that is specifically identified.

4. *Limit collection.* The organization must collect only information that is necessary for its stated purposes. For example, in the course of conducting a credit check, an organization should not collect information related to an individual's religious affiliation. Moreover, as noted above, collection of personal information—as well as its use, retention, and disclosure—is subject to the test of "reasonableness." For example, the Privacy Commissioner in Alberta ordered an employer (Mark's Work Wearhouse) to stop collecting the personal credit information of job applicants, despite their consent, on the basis that such information was not reasonably necessary to evaluate prospective employees for retail positions. Mark's had argued that it required the information to assess whether an applicant posed a greater risk of committing in-store theft, but the Privacy Commissioner found that the information was not reasonably required to make this assessment ("Retailer Ordered to Stop Credit Checks," 2010).

5. *Limit use, disclosure, and retention.* Subject to the exceptions noted below, organizations cannot use the information collected for any purpose other than the one stated. They must not disclose the information to third parties unless they obtain a new consent that authorizes the new disclosure. For example, information regarding dependants gathered for life insurance purposes cannot be transferred to a medical insurer for the purpose of obtaining medical coverage without obtaining a specific new consent.

Personal information must be used only by those who need it and disposed of when it is no longer needed. If, for example, an employer provides personal information about employees to a payroll service provider, the service provider should commit to complying with PIPEDA and to using the information only for the purpose specified in its contract. For example, the information may not be used to create or sell mailing lists.

Under s. 7, there are a number of exceptions to the rule that an organization may not *use* personal information without an individual's knowledge and consent. An organization may use this information in circumstances that include the following:

a. obtaining the individual's consent would compromise the availability or accuracy of the information where the information is relevant to an investigation of a breach of an agreement or a contravention of law;

b. the information reasonably could be useful in investigating a contravention of law and it is used for that investigation;

c. the information is used in an emergency that threatens the life, health, or security of the individual;

d. the information is to be used for statistical or scholarly purposes, in which case the organization must notify the Privacy Commissioner of Canada before using it; or

e. the information is publicly available.

Under s. 7, organizations may also *disclose* personal information without an individual's knowledge or consent in certain circumstances. Personal information may be disclosed when the disclosure is made

a. to a lawyer who is representing the organization;

b. for the purpose of collecting a debt owed to the organization by the individual;

c. for journalistic, artistic, or literary purposes;

d. in circumstances where use or disclosure is required by law;

e. to assist in an emergency that threatens the life, health, or security of an individual (the organization must inform the individual of the disclosure);

f. for statistical or scholarly purposes, in which case the organization must notify the Privacy Commissioner of Canada before using the information; or

g. 20 years after the individual's death or 100 years after the record was created.

6. *Be accurate.* If use or disclosure of out-of-date or incomplete information would harm the individual, the employer should ensure that the information is accurate and current. Employees should also be given the opportunity to correct errors in information.

7. *Provide safeguards.* An organization should protect personal information against loss, theft, or unauthorized access. For example, written information should be kept in locked drawers with keys accessible only to those who need access. The most sensitive information should receive a higher level of protection through such devices as security clearances, passwords, and encrypted computerized data.

8. *Be open.* Privacy policies and procedures should be readily available to customers, clients, employees, and suppliers. Front-line supervisors should be familiar with them.

9. *Give individuals access.* Subject to the exceptions set out below, organizations must provide individuals with details about the personal information being held about them and the means to gain access to it, upon request. For

example, if a supervisor puts an informal note on an employee's file, the employee is entitled to gain access to the note on request. Employers should respond to employees' requests as soon as possible and no later than 30 days after the request is made.

Because the legislation is relatively new, it is impossible to know all the ways in which it may eventually affect organizations. However, case law suggests that there is little personal information that an employer can keep from an employee unless it falls within one of the exceptions in s. 9 of PIPEDA (Brown, 2003, p. 11). Section 9 provides that access *must* be denied

a. if the information would reveal personal information about another individual unless there is consent or a life-threatening situation (however, if the third-party information can be removed, the remaining information must be released); or
b. if the organization has disclosed information to a government institution for law enforcement or national security reasons and the organization is instructed by that institution to refuse access or not to reveal that the information has been released.

Access *may* be denied under s. 9 if

a. the information is protected by **solicitor–client privilege**;
b. disclosure could harm another individual's life or security (however, if the third-party information can be removed, the remaining information must be released);
c. disclosure would reveal confidential commercial information (however, if this information can be removed, the remaining information must be released);
d. the information was collected as part of an investigation into a breach of an agreement or a law; or
e. the information was generated in the course of a formal dispute resolution process.

Where access is denied, the organization should advise the individual in writing, provide reasons, and explain what recourse is available.

10. *Provide recourse.* Organizations must establish a procedure to deal with complaints about their compliance with PIPEDA. Organizations should investigate all complaints, notify the individual of the outcome of the investigation, correct any inaccuracies and instances of non-compliance, and record all decisions. If an organization refuses to provide the information or denies its existence, an individual may file a complaint with the **privacy commissioner**. The privacy commissioner has broad powers to investigate complaints and inquire into information practices. Although the privacy commissioner cannot issue a binding order against an organization, the commissioner or the individual may apply to the Federal Court under s. 14 for an order for damages and/or an order requiring the organization to change its practices related to personal information. Penalties for non-compliance include maximum fines of $100,000.

Although initially there was a reluctance to award damages for non-monetary losses resulting from a breach of privacy rights, in the 2013 case of *Chitrakar v. Bell TV*, an applicant was awarded $10,000 for a non-consensual credit check of a first-time customer of satellite TV. The court commented: "Privacy rights are being more broadly recognized as important rights in an era where information on an individual is so readily available even without consent. It is important that violations of those rights be recognized as properly compensable" (para. 25). While this case relates to personal information collected in a commercial context, its reasoning could apply within the employment context as well.

Note also that it is a criminal offence to obstruct the privacy commissioner, to "knowingly dispose" of personal information that could be requested, and to retaliate against employees for asserting their rights under PIPEDA.

PIPEDA Case Summary #2003-226 and *Eastmond v. Canadian Pacific Railway* illustrate the kinds of issues that can be raised under PIPEDA. Both cases involve federally regulated employers, which are required to follow PIPEDA's principles in handling personal employee information. *PIPEDA Case Summary #2003-226* involved a telecommunications industry employer's allegedly casual treatment of an employee's sensitive personal information. *Eastmond* involved an employer's use of non-surreptitious video surveillance in its workyard to deter theft and vandalism.

CASE IN POINT

Employer's Practices Regarding Medical Reports Too Lax

PIPEDA Case Summary #2003-226, CPCSF no. 114

Facts

While applying for long-term disability benefits, the employee received a letter from her employer asking her to provide all the medical information necessary for her application. The employer's intention was to expedite the application process; however, only the insurance company actually required the information in question. The employee objected to providing this sensitive information, including her diagnosis, to her employer. She also objected to the employer's use of a fax machine to transmit her medical reports to its human resources office because employees who had no need for this information might accidentally see it. The employee filed a complaint with the privacy commissioner.

The employer argued that the fax machine was a secure method of transferring personal information because the machine was designated for human resources personnel only. The human resources department was located at one end of a largely empty floor, and it required card access, although all human resources employees had cards. The fax machine room was locked when no employees were present, so it would be difficult (although not impossible) for other staff to enter the fax machine room when it was unlocked.

Relevant Issue

Whether the employer's conduct contravened PIPEDA's requirements to

1. limit collection and use of personal information to that which is necessary for the purposes identified by the organization; and
2. ensure that the information is properly secured, with more sensitive information being safeguarded by a higher level of protection.

Decision

The assistant privacy commissioner found that the employer contravened both PIPEDA requirements. With respect to the first issue, while a reasonable person might find nothing objectionable about the employer's facilitating the application process, it was unreasonable for the company to represent its collection of information as a requirement, rather than an option. Letters of notification concerning long-term disability should state that employees have the option of sending information directly to the insurance company.

With respect to the second issue, because of the sensitive nature of medical diagnoses, the level of protection provided was inadequate. Keeping a fax machine that receives personal information in an unlocked, accessible room was inappropriate. The assistant privacy commissioner also questioned the use of fax machines in general for relaying this sort of information and questioned the employer's practice of having human resources staff receive medical reports containing diagnoses.

She recommended that the employer inform all employees that they have the right to ensure that diagnostic information be kept confidential and that they have the option of sending reports to medical staff in health services rather than to human resources staff.

CASE IN POINT

Video Surveillance Cameras Justified in Workyard

Eastmond v. Canadian Pacific Railway, 2004 FC 852

Facts

The employer installed video cameras in one of its workyards to reduce vandalism and deter theft, to reduce its potential liability for property damage, and to improve security for employees. One of the employees, Eastmond, launched a complaint under PIPEDA on the basis that theft and security were not serious problems in the workyard and that the cameras could be used to monitor the performance and conduct of employees. The privacy commissioner applied the following four-part test to determine the reasonableness of the placement of cameras:

1. Is the measure demonstrably necessary to meet a specific need?
2. Is it likely to be effective in meeting that need?
3. Is the loss of privacy proportional to the benefit gained?
4. Is there a way of achieving this benefit that involves less invasion of privacy?

After applying these tests, the commissioner recommended that the employer remove the surveillance cameras. Because thefts were relatively rare and lack of security was not a serious issue among employees, the employer failed to show a need for surveillance. It should have looked for alternatives, such as better lighting, that were less likely to invade privacy. Because the employer did not comply with these recommendations, Eastmond applied to the Federal Court for an order.

Relevant Issue

Whether the employer's use of video surveillance cameras in the workyard violated the privacy rights of employees.

Decision

The Federal Court applied the four-part test set out by the commissioner, but it came to the opposite conclusion. In its view, the videotaping served a reasonable purpose. The cameras were not hidden from view, and they were placed in areas where employees had a low expectation of privacy. The tapes were reviewed only if there was a reported incident; otherwise, they were destroyed. The employer had considered alternatives, including fencing and security guards, but it had reasonably decided that these were not cost effective.

The employer was entitled to collect personal employee information through videotaping employees' movements without their knowledge and consent under the s. 7 exception in PIPEDA related to an investigation of a breach of the law. Because the employer looked at the tapes only after a reported incident, requiring consent to review them would compromise its investigation of such a breach.

Employees to whom PIPEDA applies have substantive privacy protections. However, the Federal Court in *Eastmond* showed a willingness to temper those rights where an employer demonstrates that it used the least intrusive means practicable to accomplish a reasonable purpose.

Similarly, where an employer conducts video surveillance of an employee outside the workplace, and that employee is covered by PIPEDA, arbitrators have generally applied the test of "reasonableness" to determine whether that evidence is admissible. In *Ross v. Rosedale Transport Inc.* a federally regulated employer had conducted video surveillance of an employee outside the workplace to establish whether the employee on sick leave was as disabled as he claimed to be. The surveillance was conducted while the employee was in full public view and thus had a "relatively low expectation of privacy." The video evidence showed the employee performing physical activities (carrying furniture) well beyond the capacity he claimed to have, and as a result, he was dismissed for just cause.

However, the videotaped evidence was ruled inadmissible because the employer had initiated the surveillance on the basis of a vague suspicion that the employee was exaggerating his injuries. Because there weren't "reasonable" grounds for conducting the surveillance in the first place, the resulting evidence could not be admitted. As a result, the employer lost the dismissal case because it was based on the video surveillance evidence.

The following two cases illustrate the application of PIPEDA (or comparable provincial legislation) where emerging technologies are used for the collection of personal information. *Parkland Regional Library* is an Alberta case where the employer used keystroke-logging computer software to monitor an employee's computer usage. In *Wansink v. TELUS Communications Inc.*, the employer sought to collect biometric data—in this case, voice prints—as part of its voice recognition remote access system.

CASE IN POINT

Is Monitoring Keystrokes Contrary to Privacy Legislation?

Parkland Regional Library, Order F2005-003, 2005 CanLII 78636 (Alta. OIPC)

Facts

The employer, a library, installed keystroke-logging software to monitor the computer use of one of its employees, an information technician, without his knowledge. It was concerned about his low productivity and what it thought might be an inappropriate use of his computer for personal purposes. When the employee discovered the software, he filed a complaint with the Office of the Information and Privacy Commissioner of Alberta.

Relevant Issues

1. Whether keystroke-logging data is "personal information."
2. Whether monitoring the complainant's keystrokes without consent violated the province's privacy legislation.

Decision

The Alberta privacy commissioner held that the data collected was personal information because it revealed how much work the employee did and how he did it. Moreover, it appeared that his use of the computer for personal reasons, including Internet banking, was done with the employer's permission, and this personal data was also captured.

The commissioner also decided that collection of this personal information infringed the privacy legislation. On the evidence, it was not clear that there was a legitimate reason for the monitoring, and the software was not a minimally intrusive means of gathering it. The employer could have, for example, simply asked the employee to explain his apparently low productivity.

Despite this decision, keystroke monitoring is frequently implemented by employers throughout the country in order to assess productivity and is typically unchallenged. In some cases, it will not be a breach of the applicable privacy legislation, especially where employees are notified of it ahead of time.

CASE IN POINT

Did Compulsory Speech Recognition Program Violate PIPEDA?

Wansink v. TELUS Communications Inc., 2007 FCA 21

Facts

To improve its security system, Telus asked employees who worked in the field to create a voice print that would be used to allow them to remotely access its internal computer network. Under this new e.Speak system, the employee's voice print would be converted into a matrix of numbers unique to that individual. The voice sample, upon which the voice print data were based, would be destroyed shortly after being taken and the voice print itself would be digitally stored in a secure database. Although most of the employees agreed to provide a voice sample for the new security system, four employees objected. Threatened with discipline, they filed a complaint with the privacy commissioner challenging the employer's right to force them to consent to the collection of this biometric information.

Relevant Issue

Whether requiring employees to provide voice samples in these circumstances infringed PIPEDA.

Decision

The privacy commissioner ruled in the employer's favour, finding that the system struck an appropriate balance between the employees' right to privacy and the employer's security needs. The process did not provide substantial information about an employee because the employer showed that it could only use the voice prints to verify the employee's identity. Appropriate security measures for the voice prints had been taken.

On appeal, both the Federal Court and the Federal Court of Appeal upheld the commissioner's decision. They confirmed that employee voice prints are "personal information" and thus governed by PIPEDA but stated that a "reasonable

person" would conclude that the collection and use of the voice prints for security purposes was appropriate in the circumstances. Factors considered included:

- the level of sensitivity of the personal information involved (here, the employee's voice sample was collected but only a voice print—a matrix of numbers—was used);
- the security measures implemented by the employer (this is critical);
- the bona fide business objectives (protecting sensitive customer data and other data);
- the effectiveness of the voice prints in meeting those objectives;
- the alternative methods of achieving the same levels of security at comparable cost and benefits (it replaced a less secure password system); and
- the proportionality of the loss of privacy as against the employer's costs and operational benefits in the level of security it provides.

The courts had more difficulty with the issue of consent. The Federal Court of Appeal confirmed that all of the exceptions to collection, use, and disclosure of personal information without consent are set out exhaustively in s. 7 of PIPEDA, and that none of them applied in these circumstances. However, the court noted that, by its very design, the employer's e.Speak system ensured that individual consent must be provided prior to collecting their voice prints, because without employees' active participation, the company could not create their voice print and forcibly enroll them into the system. The Court of Appeal left open the question of whether alleged threats of disciplinary measures against employees who refused to consent might negate meaningful consent under the Act.

Telus's success in the case suggests that employers covered by privacy legislation can collect biometric data if there is a significant business purpose for the collection and the employer implements strict security measures and protections against misuse. A central issue is proportionality: weighing the level of intrusion into an employee's privacy against its importance to the employer's operational needs in terms of what information it wants to collect, why it is collecting it, and how it will be used. Courts will also look at the alternatives available to see whether less privacy-intrusive measures are viable.

What Is Biometric Data?

Biometric technology uses an individual's unique physical attributes, such as a fingerprint or voice, to identify that individual. Typically, the technology involves scanning the physical attribute, reducing it to digital form, and storing it on a system so that it can be used for comparison purposes. For example, each time the individual wishes to gain access to the place or system protected by the biometric technology, the physical attribute is again scanned and the new scan is compared against the stored sample. If the two match within a preset threshold, the individual is granted access. Among other things, biometrics can now be used in time clocks to verify employee work hours, for security purposes in door locks, and in computer and telephone systems (York and Carty, 2006, p. 1).

Proposed Amendments to PIPEDA: Bill S-4, the Digital Privacy Act

At the time of writing, Bill S-4—a bill to amend PIPEDA—has received first reading in the House of Commons. The key proposed changes to PIPEDA are as follows:

- Where there has been a security breach (that is, loss of, or unauthorized access to, personal information resulting from a breach of an organization's security safeguards or failure to establish such safeguards), and there is risk of significant harm to an individual, the organization must report and keep records of the breach.
- The definition of "personal information" will be changed to eliminate the exception regarding name, title, business address, or telephone number of an employee.
- PIPEDA will cover job applicants as well as employees.

- Business contact information will be exempt where it is collected, used, and disclosed solely for the purpose of communicating with the individual for purposes related to her employment, business, or profession.
- The circumstances where personal information could be disclosed without the knowledge or consent of the individual with respect to breaches of agreements, illegality, fraud, and financial abuse would be broadened. Such disclosure could be to a third-party organization that is not a government institution or part thereof (Jacobs, 2014).
- The privacy commissioner will be able to enter into compliance agreements that include terms necessary for statutory compliance (Emond Harnden, 2014).

Privacy Rights in Private Sector Workplaces in Ontario

As discussed above, currently provincially regulated private sector employers in Ontario are not required to follow PIPEDA's principles in handling non-health-related personal *employee* information. However, even in the absence of legislation, privacy issues are increasingly being raised in the workplace as new technology makes it possible for employers to monitor employees' activities in unprecedented ways, such as through Web-browsing records, email and keystroke monitoring, and video surveillance. Moreover, as noted above, in 2012, Ontario's Court of Appeal issued its landmark decision in *Jones v. Tsige* wherein it became the first appellate court in Canada to recognize a common law right to sue for the tort of "intrusion upon seclusion." Although this case involved invasion of privacy by a co-worker rather than by an employer, it reflects a growing sense that the law needs to evolve to meet changes in both technology and in expectations surrounding privacy (Cameron, 2013).

Ontario's Appellate Court Recognizes New Tort: "Intrusion upon Seclusion"

Jones v. Tsige, 2012 ONCA 32

Facts

Jones, an employee of the Bank of Montreal, discovered that another bank employee, Tsige, had accessed her bank account at least 174 times over the previous four years. Tsige admitted doing this because she had been involved with Tsige's ex-husband and was checking to see whether Jones was receiving support payments from him. When the employer found out about this breach of its privacy policy, it suspended Tsige, without pay, for one week and denied her a bonus. However, Jones decided to also bring a court action directly against Tsige, suing her for damages for breach of privacy. Jones lost at trial on the basis that there was no independent tort action based on privacy. Jones appealed.

Relevant Issue

Whether there is an independent action for invasion of privacy under the common law.

Decision

Signalling that it was time for the common law to catch up with technological developments, the Ontario Court of Appeal awarded Jones $10,000 damages on the basis of a new tort called "intrusion upon seclusion." The court set out three elements that a plaintiff must prove to receive damages for this tort:

- the defendant's conduct must be intentional (which includes *reckless* conduct);
- the defendant must have invaded, without lawful justification, the plaintiff's private affairs or concerns; and
- a reasonable person would regard the invasion as highly offensive, causing distress, humiliation, or anguish (para. 71).

The court stressed that this tort will apply only where there are "deliberate and significant invasions" and that damages "will ordinarily be measured by a modest conventional sum." Where the plaintiff has suffered no monetary loss, as here, the award will be in a range up to $20,000. Relevant factors in determining the amount of damages include the nature, incidence, and occasion of the defendant's wrongful act; its effect; any relationship between the parties; any distress, annoyance, or embarrassment suffered by the plaintiff; and the conduct of the parties, including any apology or offer of amends (paras. 87–88) (Cameron and Johnston, 2013, p. 13). At $10,000, Jones's award was in the mid-range, reflecting the frequent and deliberate nature of the invasion, balanced against the fact that the information had not been disclosed publicly, there was no harm done to Jones's financial interests, and Tsige had apologized for her misconduct (Garber, 2012).

Interestingly, the employer (a bank) in *Jones v. Tsige* was federally regulated, and therefore Jones's personal information was covered by PIPEDA. However, PIPEDA provides remedies against organizations, not individuals, and Jones was seeking damages from the individual who had invaded her privacy, not her employer. Moreover, the court noted that because Tsige had acted as a "rogue" employee, violating the bank's own policies and being disciplined as a result, her employer may have had a complete defence to a PIPEDA-based complaint in any event. The court, therefore, was intent on creating a new remedy that would provide recourse whenever an individual's privacy is invaded in a serious and intentional (or reckless) way.

It is not yet known how far this new cause of action will be used to limit the actions of employers—including those in provinces such as Ontario for whom, up until the *Jones v. Tsige* decision, there were few legal constraints related to workplace monitoring. Will it, for example, create potential liability for employers who monitor emails or Internet use, or who use video surveillance without their employees' knowledge? Based on the three-part test set out in *Jones*, it appears that only intrusions into highly sensitive information will be protected (Harder, 2012, p. 6).

It is doubtful that, for example, use of publicly available social media content for a background check would be considered an invasion of someone's "private" affairs. On the other hand, as discussed below, an employer who hires a private investigator to investigate suspected malingering may have to ensure that the PI is retained for objectively reasonable purposes (Nieuwland, 2012). It also raises the question of whether an organization that allows its employees to take employees' sensitive medical or financial information home on unencrypted USB devices would be considered "reckless" for purposes of the tort if that information was then lost or stolen (Cameron and Johnston, 2013, p. 14).

It is interesting to note that the first case to apply this new tort against an employer, *Alberta v. Alberta Union of Provincial Employees*, resulted in 26 government employees being awarded $1,250 each after unauthorized credit checks were performed by an agent of their employer. This amount was awarded even though no actual harm was shown, the credit checks had not been authorized by the employer (they had been independently initiated by someone it had asked to investigate a case of suspected fraud), and upon notification the employer immediately acknowledged that the credit checks were improper and apologized (Avraam and Chow, 2013, p. 13-1).

Jones v. Tsige highlights the importance of an employer having policies that specifically address situations where an employee should have no expectation of privacy, such as email and Internet use. Similarly, any surveillance cameras should be well identified to employees to avoid any intrusion upon seclusion claims. That said, there still will be times where non-overt surveillance is appropriate and lawful (see below).

One point about the impact of this new tort is clear: employers need to have carefully drafted, well-communicated, and consistently enforced privacy policies that, among other things, reduce employee expectations of privacy (Harder, 2012, p. 6). This is especially true in light of *R v. Cole*, discussed below, which could be used by employees to argue that they do have a reasonable expectation of privacy in their workplace computers where personal use is allowed or reasonably expected. Furthermore, employers may want to warn employees who have access to other employees' personal information that it should only be accessed for legitimate purposes and that accessing another's personal information inappropriately could give rise to personal liability (Filion Wakely Thorup Angeletti, 2012).

To provide additional context to this discussion, the next section examines how some privacy issues are handled in unionized (provincially regulated private sector) workplaces in Ontario.

Unionized Workplaces in Ontario's Private Sector

In a unionized workplace, the collective agreement may restrict the use of video surveillance or other forms of employee monitoring, but such language is rare. An appropriate restriction would be to require the employer to notify the union and perhaps participate in discussions before implementing any decision to conduct such surveillance.

However, even in the absence of restrictions within the collective agreement, arbitrators have generally recognized a right to workplace privacy in unionized workplaces, although this right is not absolute (York and Carty, 2006, p. 2). Generally speaking, employee monitoring that is disclosed to the affected employees is allowed where it is a reasonable exercise of management rights, given all the circumstances.

For example, arbitrators have generally allowed video cameras to stay, provided they are trained on security points such as entrances and exits and not work areas or provided they are only turned on outside of working hours (Michaluk, 2007, p. 5).

Balancing the privacy interests of unionized employees with the interests of employers to run their businesses effectively is a subjective process and arbitration decisions in this area have often been divided, as the cases below show.

Use of Biometric Technology and Video Surveillance

In the following two cases, *IKO Industries Ltd. and U.S.W.A., loc. 8580* and *Re: Good Humour—Breyers and the United Food & Commercial Workers Union, Local 175*, the arbitrators reached opposite conclusions when considering whether the introduction of (Kronos) fingertip-scanning technology to replace card-swiping systems violated the management rights clause of their respective collective agreements.

CASE IN POINT

Union Challenges Finger Recognition Technology

IKO Industries Ltd. and U.S.W.A., loc. 8580 (2005), 140 LAC (4th) 393; 2006 CanLII 40103 (Ont. SCDC)

Facts

IKO Industries announced that it planned to implement fingertip-scanning technology to track payroll and attendance information. The union filed a grievance, alleging that this constituted a breach of employees' privacy. The employer argued that the new technology would improve the efficiency and accuracy of its timekeeping and payroll systems, as well as security.

Relevant Issue

Whether implementation of finger recognition technology was justified.

Decision

The arbitrator's decision, upheld by the Ontario Divisional Court, was that although the invasion of privacy was not substantial (only a mathematical representation of the fingerprint, not the fingerprint itself, was stored), the employer's interest in implementing the system did not outweigh the invasion of privacy in this case. In assessing the reasonableness of the employer's purpose, the arbitrator found that the old card-swiping system for timekeeping was equally efficient and accurate. Although the employer had argued that the old system allowed cheating ("buddy punching," where one employee punches in or out for another employee who is not at work), the arbitrator did not find evidence that such cheating was a problem. Therefore, the employer was not justified in implementing the fingertip-scanning technology.

In contrast, in *Re: Good Humour—Breyers and the United Food & Commercial Workers Union, Local 175*, the arbitrator dismissed the union's grievance on the basis that it had failed to prove that the fingertip-scanning technology was privacy-invasive. No expert testimony was heard, nor was any evidence adduced that suggested that the Kronos system (or systems like it) was somehow faulty or intrusive. As a result, the arbitrator held that the employer could adopt the biometric technology even though it had not demonstrated that buddy punching was a problem in the workplace. In his view, "If the employer believed that Kronos was state-of-the-art and met its needs why should it have to put up with second best absent any evidence that employee rights were being infringed?"

Another area where arbitral decisions have been divided relates to the admissibility of evidence obtained through video surveillance of employees outside the workplace. The main point of contention is whether the test for admissibility is one of "reasonableness" or "relevance." These differing perspectives are illustrated in the cases *Re Centre for Addiction and Mental Health v. Ontario Public Service Employees Union* and *Hôtel-Dieu Grace Hospital*.

Re Centre for Addiction and Mental Health provides an example of the issues raised by off-duty video surveillance of an employee.

CASE IN POINT

Employer Lacks Reasonable Basis for Intrusion: Surveillance Evidence Inadmissible

Re Centre for Addiction and Mental Health v. Ontario Public Service Employees Union
(2004), 133 LAC (4th) 178 (Nairn)

Facts

The employee, a full-time security guard at one of the employer's four mental health and addiction-related services, suffered from Tourette's syndrome, which causes uncontrollable motor or verbal tics. A co-worker lodged a complaint against the employee, resulting in the employee's suspension with pay pending an investigation of the complaint. The investigation began in late December 2002. In June 2003, the investigator submitted a report that recommended that the employee apologize, undertake harassment training, and return to work.

When the employee's co-workers strongly objected to his return, the employer decided to transfer him to the job of dietary assistant. The employee returned to work but after only one shift indicated that the new job was not an appropriate accommodation because, as a result of his disability, he had an aversion to water. The dietary assistant position involved washing dishes and other cleaning duties.

Shortly before the employee returned to work, a co-worker advised the employer that she believed he was working elsewhere while on paid suspension. The employer decided to engage the services of an investigator to determine whether the allegation was true.

The investigator conducted video surveillance at the employee's home. When the employer asked the investigator whether he had found any evidence that the employee was working elsewhere, the investigator reported that he had not. He had only seen the employee washing his car, hosing down his driveway, and watering a tree. He recorded these activities on videotape. The employer questioned the employee in the presence of union representatives about the extent of his alleged aversion to water. The employee denied being able to perform the tasks displayed on video. The employer dismissed

him for cause on the basis of the videotaped evidence and his responses during the interview.

The employee grieved his dismissal, and at the arbitration hearing, the union argued that the video surveillance evidence was inadmissible because the employer did not have reasonable grounds for surveillance. The employer countered that the videotaped evidence was admissible because the grievor was observed from the public street outside his home, where he had no reasonable expectation of privacy, and the evidence derived from the surveillance was relevant to the issues in dispute. It noted that if a neighbour had observed the employee washing his car in his front yard, the neighbour's evidence would be admissible.

Relevant Issue

Whether the evidence obtained through videotape surveillance was admissible.

Decision

The arbitrator ruled the evidence inadmissible. She reviewed three lines of arbitration decisions concerning an employer's right to use surveillance in respect of off-duty employees. The first line assesses the admissibility of surveillance evidence on the basis of its relevance and rejects the existence of an employee's right of privacy. The second line applies the reasonableness test: was the surveillance reasonable in the circumstances and was it conducted in a reasonable manner without being unduly intrusive? The third line adopts the view that an employee has no reasonable expectation of privacy in a public place, and therefore the relevance of surveillance evidence obtained in public "trumps any privacy concern."

After canvassing these three lines of cases, the arbitrator held that relevancy alone cannot justify video surveillance because in the absence of a legitimate interest in an employee's off-duty conduct, an employee's "private life" is "none of the employer's business." Therefore, an employer must be able to demonstrate that there is a reasonable basis for undertaking surveillance before it intrudes on an employee's privacy. This legitimate interest requirement does not change even if an employee is situated in full view in a public location.

In this case, the evidence obtained through surreptitious video surveillance was inadmissible because, in the arbitrator's opinion, the employer did not have a reasonable basis for undertaking the surveillance. The employee had not been told not to work while under suspension. The employer did not have a policy against "moonlighting." There was no evidence that the employee had been called in during the suspension and had failed or refused to attend work. Therefore, the employer did not have reasonable grounds for conducting the surveillance. Since the grounds for initiating surveillance were not reasonable, nothing uncovered during the surveillance—regardless of its relevance—was admissible.

In cases where the arbitrator applies the "reasonableness" standard, generally the following factors are considered:

1. Was it reasonable to conduct the surveillance?
2. Was the surveillance conducted in a reasonable manner—for example, by videotaping an employee in a street or public park rather than in his home?
3. Were there other alternatives open to the employer, such as seeking an independent medical opinion?

In contrast, in *Hôtel-Dieu Grace Hospital*, the arbitrator applied the test of "relevance."

CASE IN POINT

Applying a Standard of Relevance

Hôtel-Dieu Grace Hospital v. National Automobile, Aerospace, Transportation and General Workers Union of Canada (Caw-Canada, and Its Local 2458), 2004 CanLII 66320 (Ont. LA)

Facts

Bonello, a part-time worker at the employer hospital, was absent from work for medical reasons. The employer, after receiving a series of medical notes setting out varying lengths of time before Bonello would be fit to return to work, became suspicious and decided to place her under surveillance. The video surveillance recordings showed the grievor working in a family-owned restaurant. Bonello was discharged on the basis of the video evidence and the union grieved her dismissal. At the outset of the hearing, the union asked the arbitrator to rule that the video recording evidence was inadmissible on the basis of the "reasonableness" test.

Relevant Issue

Whether the video surveillance evidence was admissible.

Decision

The arbitrator ruled that the video evidence was admissible. Information is generally admissible as evidence in an arbitration if it is relevant to a material issue. Therefore, in the absence of a contractual (collective agreement) or statutory right to privacy, there is no "right" to privacy to balance against an employer's right to prove its case through relevant evidence. The arbitrator noted that the employer could have hired a detective to conduct similar surreptitious surveillance away from the workplace, make notes on what was observed and take still photographs, and then testify from memory aided by the notes and still photographs. Such evidence would not have been subjected to the reasonableness test and the arbitrator could see no reason to incorporate such a test when the evidence is electronic. The fact that video evidence is clearer, more detailed, and thus perhaps more persuasive should not change the usual test for the admissibility of evidence—the primary one being relevance.

Tracking Vehicle Use

The use of a Global Positioning System (GPS) or other tracking system in company vehicles has given rise to privacy-related disputes. In *Otis Canada*, the employer's use of a tracking system was found to be acceptable because it was for restricted, legitimate purposes.

CASE IN POINT

Vehicle Tracking "Reasonable"

International Union of Elevator Constructors, Local 50 v. Otis Canada Inc., 2013 CanLII 3574 (Ont. LRB)

Facts

As a result of a number of concerns, including excessive fuel consumption, Otis Elevator decided to adopt a vehicle-tracking technology called Telematics to monitor use of company vehicles for personal reasons. While employees had the option of driving the company vehicle to and from home, they were advised that personal use was prohibited and this new device would tell the employer *whether* the company vehicle was in use—but not *where* the vehicle was. The union protested that monitoring vehicle use outside of working hours infringed employee privacy. The employer countered that employees are not required to take a company vehicle home and that it was entitled to modernize its equipment and to introduce efficiencies in operation. The union filed a policy grievance.

Relevant Issue

Whether tracking use of company vehicles during off hours violated employee privacy.

Decision

The Labour Relations Board found for the employer. Otis had legitimate business reasons for installing Telematics in its vehicles and it was entitled to monitor its vehicles' use—although not their location—when they were driven by employees during off-duty hours. The Board noted that the "employer is responsible and indeed liable for that vehicle at all times. It is liable for its use and pays for its gas and maintenance. The Telematics device is a legitimate way to protect the employer's asset; an asset for which it has full responsibility." The Board found that, given the options that the employer had provided to its employees, the restriction on the use of the vehicle during off-duty hours was justified.

Although the *Otis* case did not involve a GPS device that could track location, as well as use, of company vehicles, use of such a device *during working hours* is generally acceptable if it is for legitimate reasons. The following principles should be kept in mind in considering a GPS surveillance policy:

- The information collected should be within the normal context of workday activities.
- Only information that is reasonably required for legitimate business reasons should be collected.
- The information collected should be effective in fulfilling the organization's objectives.
- Reasonable alternatives should have been considered.
- The policy and practice should be clear and understandable to employees.
- Employees should be made aware of the policy and practice (Sherrard Kuzz LLP, 2013).

Non-Union Workplaces in Ontario's Private Sector

As previously noted, until recently there were few legal restrictions on employee monitoring in non-union, provincially regulated workplaces in Ontario. If an employer openly installed a video camera, for example, employees had little recourse either under statute or at common law. Moreover, common law courts have usually applied a test of relevance in determining the admissibility of videotaped evidence; for example, in one wrongful dismissal case, *Richardson v. Davis Wire Industries Ltd.*, a video that showed an employee sleeping on the job was found to be relevant and therefore admissible. However, even before the 2012 *Jones v. Tsige* decision that recognized the tort of intrusion upon seclusion, there were signs that where employee monitoring takes a particularly intrusive form, courts may be willing to provide a remedy under the common law. This occurred in the 2008 case of *Colwell v. Cornerstone Properties Inc.*, where the court was asked to consider whether covert video surveillance of an employee's office for several months, without justification, constituted **constructive dismissal** under the common law. (As discussed in Chapter 15, constructive dismissal occurs where an employer breaches the employment contract in a fundamental way so that the employee is entitled to consider herself dismissed and to sue for wrongful dismissal.)

CASE IN POINT

Does Extended Secret Surveillance Breach the Employment Contract?

Colwell v. Cornerstone Properties Inc., 2008 CanLII 66139 (Ont. SC)

Facts

Colwell was a commercial mall manager who had worked for Cornerstone Properties for over seven years. In August 2004 Colwell was with Krauel, her immediate boss and the vice-president of finance, when she saw an image of her office on his monitor. Krauel seemed embarrassed but explained that a secret camera had been installed in the ceiling of her office in November 2003 to detect theft by the maintenance staff. Over the course of several subsequent meetings to discuss this matter, Krauel maintained that he had every confidence in her but that because he had the legal right to install the camera secretly in her office, there was no need for him to apologize. Colwell did not find Krauel's explanation for the camera credible since she never kept money in her office and had no knowledge of these thefts even though the maintenance staff reported to her.

Although the camera was removed, by September 2004 Colwell was seeing a doctor for stress and was on prescribed sedatives. Eventually Colwell left her job and sued her employer for breach of contract amounting to constructive dismissal.

Relevant Issue

Whether the employer's conduct constituted constructive dismissal under the common law.

Decision

The court found for the employee. The judge acknowledged that Ontario does not have any legislation protecting employee privacy and that the existence of a possible common law tort of invasion of privacy is still evolving. However, the court held that it was an implied term of Colwell's employment contract that each party would treat the other in good faith and fairly throughout the existence of the contract, and the employer's actions breached that duty. In the judge's words:

> A secret camera being installed in a trusted manager's office without her knowledge … coupled with a totally implausible explanation, renders the actions unacceptable. …
>
> The cost to human dignity caused by such surveillance, coupled with the unbelievable explanation subsequently provided, left Mrs. Colwell in a position of being unable to rely upon the honesty and trustworthiness of her immediate supervisor.

The court's finding that an employer has an implied duty to treat an employee in good faith and fairly *during the term of the contract*, and not just in the manner of termination as decided by the Supreme Court of Canada in *Wallace v. United Grain Growers Ltd.*, is an expansion of an employer's duties under the common law. As a result, it seems likely that, in future, these types of claims will be made under the new tort of intrusion upon seclusion. However, the *Colwell* decision is an indication that where particularly egregious invasions of privacy are involved, an employee may be able to successfully argue constructive dismissal as well.

Another interesting decision that directly touches upon privacy rights under the common law is *Poirier v. Wal-Mart Canada Corp.* Poirier was a store manager who was fired for his intentional manipulation of payroll accounts. After his abrupt dismissal, the employer still proceeded with a marketing campaign that included Poirier's image and words in promotional material to advertise the opening of a new store that he was originally designated to manage. In the subsequent wrongful dismissal action, the court upheld the dismissal for cause but found that the employer had violated Poirier's privacy because it could not assume that the consent given to the use of his picture before the dismissal still applied after his dismissal. The judge awarded Poirier $15,000 for damages for the violation of his privacy. This decision adds to a growing jurisprudence that recognizes a common law right to privacy.

Monitoring Computer, Email, and Internet Usage

As noted above, the monitoring of employee emails, Internet use, and technological devices is another area where the employee's right to privacy and the employer's need to manage the workplace may come into conflict. On the one hand, computer misuse can adversely affect an employer, as well as other employees, in a number of ways. These include reduced productivity if employees engage in personal activity on company time; the potential for defamatory statements to be made and widely disseminated or for confidential information to be leaked; and breaches of company policy against certain activities such as storing or viewing pornography at work. Computer misuse can facilitate harassment, either by creating a poisoned work environment through the circulation of offensive materials or by bombarding co-workers with objectionable email (Gilbert et al., 2000, p. 266). Employers have an obligation to maintain a workplace free from discrimination and harassment under the Ontario *Human Rights Code*.

On the other hand, as digitized technology becomes ever more portable and multi-purposed, and able to store and track personal information in unprecedented ways, courts are increasingly willing to protect sensitive personal employee data, even where the data are stored on employer-owned and -issued devices (Fletcher, 2013, p. 12-2). A key case in this area is the Supreme Court of Canada's decision in *R v. Cole.* Although grounded in criminal and constitutional law, this decision arguably signals that employees who are allowed to use employer property for personal purposes have a reasonable expectation of privacy in such use that can only be displaced (and even then perhaps not completely) with a clear and carefully drafted policy.

CASE IN POINT

Employee Privacy Expectations on Workplace Computers

R v. Cole, 2012 SCC 53; 2011 ONCA 218

Facts

Cole was a high school computer science teacher who, as a member of the school's technology committee, had an employer-issued laptop that he was expressly allowed to use for personal uses, including having a password to prevent others from accessing it. During routine maintenance, a computer technician discovered photographs of a nude, underage student on Cole's computer. He immediately reported his findings to the school's principal, who had the technician copy the photographs to a compact disc. The principal ordered Cole to return his laptop, which he did, although he refused to provide his password, saying the computer contained personal information. School board technicians then copied the temporary Internet files from the computer onto a second disc. The laptop and copied discs were handed over to the police, who examined them, without a warrant, and charged Cole with possession of child pornography. In his defence, Cole argued that the search of his computer violated his Charter rights against unreasonable search and seizure (s. 8) and therefore the photos should be excluded from evidence.

The trial court and, on appeal, the Ontario Court of Appeal found that, although the *employer* was justified in viewing the contents of the laptop (as part of its obligation to ensure student safety), the *police* could not do so without a warrant. This was because Cole had a reasonable expectation of privacy vis-à-vis the police on the basis of several factors:

- the employer had granted him permission to use the device for personal use, including taking it home on evenings, weekends, and vacation;
- the employer had allowed him to use a password to prevent others from accessing the device; and
- there was no "clear and unambiguous policy to monitor, search or police the teachers' use of their laptops."

Importantly, the courts found that the employer's voluntary handing over of the computer, which the employer owned, to the police did not change this result because an employer cannot waive an employee's Charter rights. The Crown appealed.

Relevant Issue

Whether the search of Cole's employer-owned computer, by any of the parties, infringed his Charter right to be free from unreasonable search and seizure.

Decision

The Supreme Court of Canada agreed with the Court of Appeal that the police violated Cole's Charter rights by not obtaining a search warrant before searching the laptop and discs. It held that where an individual reasonably uses a computer for personal purposes, at work or elsewhere, that person has a reasonable expectation of privacy. This is true regardless of the ownership of the device, because computers that are reasonably used for personal purposes "contain information that is meaningful, intimate, and touching on the user's biographical core" (Fletcher, 2013, p. 12-5). While ownership of the property is a relevant consideration, it is "not determinative."

At the same time, the Supreme Court also agreed with the lower courts that the *employer*'s search of the computer was justified: Cole's expectation of privacy vis-à-vis his employer was limited because he knew that a school technician could access the hard drive for technical purposes. Moreover, the employer had a statutory obligation to ensure student safety. Therefore, neither the technician, principal, nor employer school board had violated Cole's Charter rights.

Although in *Cole* the employer's search of the workplace-issued computer was vindicated (and Charter rights only directly apply to government actors, such as the police or public sector employers), this decision has potential significance for both public and private sector employers. It seems likely that, where personal information on company-issued devices is at issue, employees will try to use *Cole* to argue that they have a reasonable expectation of privacy where such personal use has been approved or allowed, notwithstanding that the Supreme Court was clear that Cole's expectation of privacy was limited vis-à-vis the employer. At the very least, *Cole* reinforces the importance of having written policies that clearly stipulate that the employer has a right to monitor these devices, including personal information stored on them, and that the employee should not have any expectation of privacy when using them.

A clear and carefully drafted information technology (IT) policy should do the following:

- Put employees on notice that they should not have an expectation of privacy when using employer technology and systems (including computers, cellphones, or other electronic devices).
- Provide an explanation of the purpose of the policy.
- Provide an explanation of how the policy will apply, including the types of technology and applications that are covered, and what the information may be used for.
- Provide guidance on what uses are permitted or not permitted. For example, an employer might stipulate that email is to be used for business purposes only. If personal emails are allowed, the policy should state any content restrictions. For instance, emails containing discriminatory, pornographic, or threatening content should be prohibited.
- Provide an explanation of the potential consequences for a breach of the policy (Jakibchuk, 2011, p. 5).

As with all workplace policies, they also must be effectively communicated and consistently enforced to be effective.

FYI

BYOD: The Newest Frontier

BYOD—Bring Your Own Device—refers to the trend of employees using their own personal devices for work-related, as well as personal, purposes (Dobson, 2012). While many employers are embracing this development, allowing employees to access corporate networks through their own smartphones, tablets, or laptops raises potential privacy and security issues. Many employers take the position that because the employee is connecting to the organization's network, the same rules that apply to an employer-owned device should apply to an employee-owned device. However, as discussed above, courts have found that employees have a reasonable expectation of privacy when they are allowed to use work-issued devices for personal data, and this expectation is arguably even stronger where the employee owns the device. Therefore, an employer's BYOD policy needs to clearly state that employer monitoring is allowed on such devices, explain the reason for it, and indicate how the information collected might be used. Employees may also be asked to sign an agreement that consents to the "remote wiping" of data where an employee-owned device is lost or stolen. Such an agreement should also release the employer from liability for the loss of any data, including personal data, from wiping activities (Dobson, 2012, p. 20). Some employers may decide that BYOD is more trouble than it is worth and prohibit the use of personal devices for work-related communication and data storage.

In addition to having an effective policy on the use of email, the Internet, and technological devices, employers should institute measures such as having lockdown codes on computers, laptops, photocopiers, printers, and all similar devices to prevent sensitive information from being misappropriated (Silliker, 2012, p. 7).

REFERENCES

Alberta (Information and Privacy Commissioner) v. United Food and Commercial Workers, Local 401. 2013 SCC 62.

Alberta v. Alberta Union of Provincial Employees. 2012 CanLII 47215 (Alta. GAA).

Anderson, Bill. Voiceprint Security: Is It Too Invasive? *Employment Notes*. October 2006, p. 1. Blaney McMurtry. http://www.blaney.com/sites/default/files/employnotes_oct06.pdf.

ATU (Local No. 569) v. Edmonton (City of). 2004 ABQB 280.

Avraam, George, and Cherrine Chow. Alberta v. Alberta Union of Provincial Employees (Privacy Rights Grievance): The Dangers of Employer Oversight. Presented at the Law Society of Upper Canada Six-Minute Employment Lawyer program, June 13, 2013, Toronto, p. 13-1.

Bill S-4, *Digital Privacy Act*. 2nd Session, 41st Parliament, 62-63 Elizabeth II, 2013-2014.

Brown, David. 10 Months to Get Ready. *Canadian HR Reporter*. February 24, 2003, p. 1.

Burgess, Bettina. Debunking Common Misconceptions Around Employee Privacy. August 15, 2011, p. 21.

Burkhardt, Keith. Privacy vs. Policy: Personal Use of Company Equipment. *Canadian Employment Law Today*. Issue no. 522, November 19, 2008, p. 4.

Cameron, Alex, and Michelle Johnston. Current Trends in Canadian Privacy Law: Damages Awards, Tort Claims and Class Actions. Presented at the Law Society of Upper Canada Six-Minute Employment Lawyer program, June 13, 2013, Toronto, p. 11-1.

Cameron, Alex. 2013. A Rising Tide of Liability Awards. *The Lawyers Weekly*. July 5, 2013. http://www.lawyersweekly.ca/index.php?section=article&articleid=1938.

Canada Safeway Ltd. and United Food and Commercial Workers, Local 401. [2005] AGAA no. 109.

Catenacci, Christina. Video Surveillance of Employees. *HRinfodesk—Canadian Payroll and Employment Law News*. May 2006. http://www.hrinfodesk.com/articles/videosurveillanceofemployeescc.htm.

Cavoukian, Ann. *Frequently Asked Questions: Personal Health Information Protection Act*. February 2005. Information and Privacy Commissioner of Ontario. http://www.ipc.on.ca/images/Resources/hfaq-e.pdf.

Centre for Addiction and Mental Health v. Ontario Public Service Employees Union, Re. (2004), 133 LAC (4th) 178 (Nairn).

Chitrakar v. Bell TV. 2013 FC 1103.

Cole, R v. 2012 SCC 53; 2011 ONCA 218.

Colwell v. Cornerstone Properties Inc. 2008 CanLII 66139 (Ont. SC).

Dobson, Sarah. Some Expectation of Privacy with Workplace Computers: SCC. *Canadian HR Reporter*. November 19, 2012, p. 1.

Doorey, David. Can a Law Firm Force Support Staff to Be Finger Scanned? http://lawofwork.ca/?p=5805.

Eastmond v. Canadian Pacific Railway. 2004 FC 852.

Echlin, Randall, and Christine Thomlinson. *For Better or For Worse: A Practical Guide to Canadian Employment Law*, 3rd ed. Toronto: Canada Law Book, 2011.

El Akkad, Omar. Watch What You Type. *Globe and Mail*, June 4, 2009, p. L1.

Emond Harnden. Canada Amends Privacy Law with Introduction of Bill S-4—Digital Privacy Act. *What's New*. May 2014. http://www.ehlaw.ca/whatsnew/1405/Focus1405_4.shtml.

Emond Harnden. Intrusion upon Seclusion—Ontario Court of Appeal Recognizes New Tort for Invasion of Privacy. January 2012. www.ehlaw.ca/whatsnew/1201/Focus1201.shtml.

Filion Wakely Thorup Angeletti. Ontario Court of Appeal Recognizes New Right to Privacy Tort. *What's New in HR Law*. February 2012. http://filion.on.ca/uploads/ckeditor/attachment_files/131/Tsige.pdf.

Fletcher, R. Mark. R v. Cole and Implications for Employee Privacy. Presented at the Law Society of Upper Canada Six-Minute Employment Lawyer program, June 13, 2013, Toronto, p. 12-1.

Focus on Canadian Employment and Equality Rights. Volume 6, no. 4. Toronto: CCH Canadian, October 2003.

Freedom of Information and Protection of Privacy Act. RSO 1990, c. F.31.

Garber, Anthony. Jones v. Tsige: How a Bizarre Love Triangle Inspired an Evolution in Privacy Law. *Canadian Labour & Employment Law Blog*. February 21, 2012. http://www.millerthomson.com/en/blog/canadian-labour-employment-law-blog/2012-archives/jones-v-tsige-how-a-bizarre-love-triangle.

Gibson, Colin G.M. An Employer's Right to Seek Medical Information. *Canadian Employment Law Today*. Issue no. 452, January 4, 2006, p. 3540.

Gilbert, Douglas, Brian Burkett, and Moira McCaskill. *Canadian Labour and Employment Law for the US Practitioner*. Washington, DC: Bureau of National Affairs, 2000.

Good Humour—Breyers and the United Food & Commercial Workers Union, Local 175, Re. [2007] OLAA no. 406 (Murray) (QL).

Gray, Helen. Employee Personal Information a Sensitive Area for Employers. *Canadian Employment Law Today*. Issue no. 488, June 7, 2007, p. 3.

Harder, Danielle. Court Ruling Opens Doors to Privacy Lawsuits. *Canadian HR Reporter*. February 27, 2012, p. 1.

Hôtel-Dieu Grace Hospital v. National Automobile, Aerospace, Transportation and General Workers Union of Canada (Caw-Canada, and Its Local 2458). 2004 CanLII 66320 (Ont. LA).

Human Rights Code. RSO 1990, c. H.19.

IKO Industries Ltd. and U.S.W.A., loc. 8580. (2005), 140 LAC (4th) 393; 2006 CanLII 40103 (Ont. SCDC).

International Union of Elevator Constructors, Local 50 v. Otis Canada Inc. 2013 CanLII 3574 (Ont. LRB).

Israel, Peter. Ask an Expert: Is a Threatening E-mail to a Co-worker Just Cause for Termination? *Canadian Employment Law Today*. Issue no. 382, February 5, 2003, p. 2980.

Israel, Peter. Ask an Expert: Surveillance Cameras. *Canadian Employment Law Today*. Issue no. 379, December 11, 2002, p. 2956.

Israel, Peter. Spying on Employees … and It's Perfectly Legal. *Canadian HR Reporter*. April 21, 2003, p. 5.

Jacobs, Adam. Canada: Updates to Canadian Privacy Law Ramping Up with the Introduction of the Digital Privacy Act (Bill S-4). June 12, 2014. Mondaq. http://www.mondaq.com/canada/x/320084/Data+Protection+Privacy/Updates+To+Canadian+Privacy+Law+Ramping+Up+With+The+Introduction+Of+The+Digital+Privacy+Act+Bill+S4.

Jakibchuk, Adrian. Whose Hard Drive Is It Anyway? *Canadian Employment Law Today*. June 15, 2011, p. 4. http://www.sherrardkuzz.com/pdf/Jakibchuk.Whose_Hard_Drive.pdf.

Jones v. Tsige. 2012 ONCA 32.

Kenny, Brian. Ask an Expert: Searching Employee's Locked Desk. *Canadian Employment Law Today*. February 19, 2014, p. 2.

Kenny, Brian. Privacy: Monitoring Employee Computer Use. *Canadian Employment Law Today*. Issue no. 482, March 28, 2007, p. 2.

Lawson, Philippa. Give Privacy Laws Teeth. *National Post*, August 5, 2009, p. A14. Available at Canadian Privacy Law Blog: http://blog.privacylawyer.ca/2009/08/opinion-give-privacy-laws-teeth.html.

Levitt, Howard A. Privacy vs. Security: Collecting Biometric Data and Such. *In Brief*. Winter 2006/2007. Lang Michener LLP.

MacDonald, Natalie. Technology Makes Passing Info Easy, Complying with Privacy Law Tough. *Canadian Employment Law Today*. Issue no. 410, March 31, 2004, p. 3205.

MacLeod Law Firm. Does Monitoring Emails Breach an Employee's Right to Privacy? March 25, 2013. http://www.macleodlawfirm.ca/employers/2013/03/does-monitoring-emails-breach-an-employees-right-to-privacy.

McEwen, Alan. Privacy Legislation and Payroll. *Canadian Employment Law Today*. Issue no. 402, November 26, 2003, p. 3139.

Mediema, Adrian. Privacy: The Unprotected Human Right? *Focus on Canadian Employment and Equality Rights*. Volume 7, no. 3, March 2004, p. 18.

Michaluk, Dan. Walking the Tightrope—Recent Developments in Employee Surveillance. April 20, 2007, p. 1. Hicks Morley. http://www.hicksmorley.com/images/SurveilancePaper_May07_DJM.pdf.

Nieuwland, Hendrik. New Tort of "Intrusion upon Seclusion" May Impact Employers. *HR Professional*. May/June 2012, p. 17.

Office of the Privacy Commissioner of Canada. Fact Sheets. Application of the Personal Information Protection and Electronic Documents Act to Employee Records, March 31, 2004, https://www.priv.gc.ca/resource/fs-fi/02_05_d_18_e.asp; Privacy in the Workplace, March 31, 2004, https://www.priv.gc.ca/resource/fs-fi/02_05_d_17_e.asp; and Privacy Legislation in Canada, updated May 2014, http://www.priv.gc.ca/resource/fs-fi/02_05_d_15_e.asp.

Office of the Privacy Commissioner of Canada. *Leading by Example: Key Developments in the First Seven Years of the Personal Information Protection and Electronic Documents Act (PIPEDA)*. 2008. https://www.priv.gc.ca/information/pub/lbe_080523_e.pdf.

Office of the Privacy Commissioner of Canada. *Privacy Toolkit: A Guide for Businesses and Organizations*. Updated March 2014. http://www.priv.gc.ca/information/guide_e.pdf.

Ogilvy Renault. Privacy and Access to Information Team, Labour and Employment Law Group. *Video Surveillance in the Workplace (Part 1)*. July 1, 2004. Norton Rose Fulbright. http://www.nortonrosefulbright.com/ca/en/knowledge/publications/55156/video-surveillance-in-the-workplace-part-1.

Parkland Regional Library, Order F2005-003. 2005 CanLII 78636 (Alta. OIPC).

Personal Health Information Protection Act, 2004. SO 2004, c. 3, sched. A.

Personal Information Protection and Electronic Documents Act. SC 2000, c. 5.

Phillips, Emma. Intrusion Upon Seclusion: Is an Employer's Request for Employee Medical Information an Invasion of Privacy? June 2013. Sack Goldblatt Mitchell LLP. http://www.sgmlaw.com/media/pdfs/intrusionuponseclusion.pdf.

PIPEDA Case Summary #2003-226. [2003] CPCSF no. 114.

PIPEDA Report of Findings #2012-003. Report of Findings: Job Seeker Not Adequately Informed About Purpose of Personal Information Collection. Office of the Privacy Commissioner of Canada. https://www.priv.gc.ca/cf-dc/2012/2012_003_0131_e.asp.

Poirier v. Wal-Mart Canada Corp. 2006 BCSC 1138.

Power Plant Workers Get Zapped for Email Porn. *Canadian Employment Law Today*. Issue no. 564, September 8, 2010.

Retailer Ordered to Stop Credit Checks. *Canadian HR Reporter*. February 24, 2010. http://www.hrreporter.com/articleview/7596-retailer-ordered-to-stop-credit-checks.

Richardson v. Davis Wire Industries Ltd. 1997 CanLII 4221 (BCSC).

Ross v. Rosedale Transport Inc. [2003] CLAD no. 237 (Ont.).

Rudner, Stuart. Dismissing Staff in "Employee-Friendly" Legal Environment. *Canadian Employment Law Today*. Issue no. 406, February 4, 2004, p. 3176.

Rudner, Stuart. Technically Easy, Legally Complicated. *Canadian HR Reporter*. June 5, 2006, p. 9.

Scallan, Niamh. Bay Street Law Firm Uses Fingerprint Technology to Monitor Employees' Comings and Goings. *Toronto Star*. November 1, 2012. http://www.thestar.com/news/gta/2012/11/01/bay_street_law_firm_uses_fingerprint_technology_to_monitor_employees_comings_and_goings.html.

Sherrard Kuzz LLP. Tracking the State of the Law on GPS Surveillance. *Management Counsel: Employment and Labour Law Update*. Volume XII, no. 3, June 2013, p. 3. http://www.sherrardkuzz.com/pdf/Vol_XII_3.pdf.

Silliker, Amanda. BC Ministry of Health Fires 5 for Privacy Breach. *Canadian HR Reporter*. October 8, 2012, p. 7.

Smith, J.R. Employer Has Right to Monitor Company Vehicle Use: Board. *Canadian Employment Law Today*. March 6, 2013, p. 3.

Smith, Jeffrey. Voiceprints Not a Violation of Privacy. *Canadian Employment Law Today*. Issue no. 477, January 17, 2007.

Surveillance an "Extraordinary" Step. *Canadian Employment Law Today*. Issue no. 417, July 7, 2004.

Surveillance Used to Fire Employee Violates Privacy Rights. *Focus on Canadian Employment and Equality Rights*. Volume 6, no. 33, September 2003, p. 265.

Thiffeault, Stéphane. Personal Health Information Act and Hours of Work. *Employee & Labour Relations Bulletin*. February 2005. McMillan Binch LLP. http://www.mcmillan.ca/Files/Health_and_Hours_of_Work_0205.pdf.

Wallace v. United Grain Growers Ltd. [1997] 3 SCR 701.

Wansink v. TELUS Communications Inc. 2007 FCA 21.

Wilson, Peter, and Allison Taylor. *The Corporate Counsel Guide to Employment Law*, 2nd ed. Aurora, ON: Canada Law Book, 2003.

York, Andrea, and Lisa Carty. Balancing Technology and Privacy at Work. *Blakes Bulletin on Privacy Law*. August 2006, p. 1.

RELATED WEBSITE

- http://www.priv.gc.ca/index_e.cfm The Office of the Privacy Commissioner of Canada's website.

REVIEW AND DISCUSSION QUESTIONS

1. Although PIPEDA does not apply to personal employee information in provincially regulated workplaces, Ontario employers should be aware of its requirements. Why?
2. In federally regulated workplaces, how might PIPEDA's requirements affect the following:
   a. checking references and retaining the information,
   b. taking witness statements for internal investigations, and
   c. conducting performance evaluations?
3. What are the ten privacy principles that underlie PIPEDA? Choose four that you consider significant and discuss them.
4. PIPEDA is intended to reflect a balance between an individual's need for privacy and an organization's need to use, collect, and disclose personal information in certain circumstances. Is this balance achieved by the legislation? Explain your answer.
5. Why should an organization have a policy on electronic monitoring? What should such a policy include?

6. George was a unionized car mechanic with 25 years' service in an auto body shop. On Thursday, May 12, 2005, he reported an injury while handling an air brake valve but he worked the balance of that day as well as the next. However, on the following Monday, George returned to work with a doctor's note stating he could only use his left arm. But because George was already doing modified work that required both arms, the employer said it could not offer him any modified work. The employer decided to undertake video surveillance of George off-duty. It was suspicious because George had a somewhat greater than average record of work-related incidents calling for medical attention and it wanted to see whether he was engaged in activities that went beyond the medical restrictions imposed upon him by his physician. The surveillance revealed him carrying objects of significant weight and digging up his garden. George was fired by his employer. He grieved his dismissal and an arbitrator had to rule on whether the surveillance evidence was admissible. If you were the arbitrator, how would you rule? Explain your decision.

7. In the *TELUS Communications* decision, the Federal Court and Federal Court of Appeal had some difficulty with the issue of employee consent. Discuss whether PIPEDA should be amended to remove the consent requirement with respect to personal *employee* information. In other words, should an employer be allowed to collect personal employee information without consent as long as the information is reasonably necessary for managing the employment relationship?

8. The employees of a transportation company complained to management that the men's washroom was very messy, despite regular cleaning. The employer implemented a log system that monitored the use and the state of the men's washroom. After three days of monitoring, the employer concluded that the facility required attention only after it was used by a particular employee, John. The employer gave John a disciplinary letter advising him that his behaviour had to stop; otherwise, progressive disciplinary actions would be taken. John filed a complaint with the federal privacy commissioner, alleging that management had monitored his washroom visits without his consent and used the collected personal information for disciplinary purposes. Did the employer infringe PIPEDA in this situation? Explain your answer.

9. An employee (in a federally funded organization) overheard a senior officer loudly tell others in the reception area what the employee's wage was and that his job performance did not measure up. The employee filed a complaint under PIPEDA for disclosure of his personal information without his consent. In response, the employer argued that the employee's consent for the disclosure was not necessary for two reasons. First, the wage rate disclosed was inaccurate (it was too high). Second, his salary was already publicly disclosed in the audited financial statements, which were available in the community library and, because he had not previously taken issue with this disclosure, he had already given his implied consent to its disclosure.

   Based on your knowledge of PIPEDA's provisions, what do you think the privacy commissioner decided?

10. The federal privacy commissioner is limited to making recommendations. Complainants must go to the Federal Court to get binding orders. Would Canada's privacy legislation be more effective if it "had more teeth"? Discuss.

11. The employer, a trucking company, had a conflict of interest policy whereby it reserved the right to assess potentially conflicting relationships on a case-by-case basis. Hearing rumours that its vice-president of human resources (Brian) was having a romantic relationship with Sarah, a woman who indirectly reported to him, the employer asked Brian whether they were romantically involved. Brian denied it. Over the next two years, the employer continued to receive information about a relationship, which Brian, when asked about, repeatedly denied. Finally, the company decided to hire a private investigator to look into the matter. When the five-day investigation confirmed that Brian and Sarah were cohabiting, the employer confronted Brian, who chose to resign.

    Around the same time, the employer underwent a cost-cutting restructuring and Sarah was told that her position had been eliminated. She filed a complaint with the privacy commissioner, alleging that under PIPEDA her employer needed her consent both to conduct its investigation and to use or disclose the resulting information.

    In your opinion, would Sarah's complaint be successful?

12. A representative from a Toronto company called Job Success contacted Ivan by email and invited him to attend an "interview." Before attending, Ivan asked for more details, including whether the meeting was for a specific job. However, the representative said the information was not available but that further details would be provided in person. During the meeting, the Job Success representative asked Ivan detailed questions about his background and professional experiences, including his career aspirations. After 45 minutes, the representative began listing the advantages of working with Job Success, which he finally acknowledged was a company that helped job seekers market themselves to prospective employers. At this point, Ivan realized he had been misled concerning the reasons why his information was being collected. Ivan filed a complaint with the privacy commissioner under PIPEDA.

    a. Does PIPEDA apply to this situation?
    b. Do you think Ivan's complaint under PIPEDA would be successful? Explain your answer.

13. A Toronto law firm has decided to implement finger-scanning technology as a way to monitor the location (and productivity) of its support staff, who are non-union. It announces that, from now on, all support staff will have to scan their fingerprints whenever they leave their work station. One of the administrative assistants asks you whether this is legal in Ontario. Advise her.

14. A large nuclear power plant's Code of Employee Conduct stated that its computer drives were for business use only and any inappropriate use (for example, the making of offensive, suggestive, or lewd comments) was unacceptable. It also stated that company email should not be used to "display, generate, or pass on to others material (whether in text, picture, or any other form) which may be regarded as offensive on the basis of race, sex, disability, or any other grounds." The Code was redistributed each year and reinforced through online quizzes and presentations.

    Prompted by an employee complaint, the employer initiated an investigation into its email system and discovered that 67 out of 90 supervisory staff in one department had sent inappropriate emails, as defined under the Code. The HR and IT departments decided to review the questionable emails and rate each of the 67 employees according to the number and seriousness of the emails distributed. There was a sliding scale: at the high end, those with 20 or more of the most explicit emails received a 12-day suspension, while at the low end, those with fewer than 5, less explicit emails received job counselling.

    Several employees grieved their suspension, arguing that they should have received a warning instead. They based their argument on several factors:

    - they did not realize the seriousness of the offence;
    - they had apologized; and
    - because the practice was common, there was a permissive culture in the workplace that led them to act in a way they otherwise would not have.

    In your opinion, were the suspensions warranted?

15. May an employer legally search an employee's locked desk at work without that employee's consent? (Assume this is a provincially regulated private sector workplace in Ontario.)

Navigating the Employment Relationship

LEARNING OUTCOMES

After completing this chapter, you will be able to:

- Understand the importance of a well-drafted employer policy manual.

- Explain the legal requirements for amending an employment contract.

- Understand ongoing management issues, including performance management, progressive discipline, and attendance management programs.

- Describe an employer's vicarious liability for damages caused by employees.

Introduction

While all of the statutes discussed in Part III affect the ongoing employee–employer relationship, for non-unionized employees the framework underlying that relationship remains the individual contract of employment. Whether written or oral, this contract contains the main terms and conditions governing employment, and the parties must always keep it in mind when dealing with both ongoing matters and significant changes to their relationship. As discussed in Chapter 4, an employment contract's terms include both those expressly agreed to by the parties and those that are implied into the agreement by the common law.

Common law principles of contract, such as the need for consideration to create a binding obligation, remain relevant throughout the employment relationship. They must be taken into account if either party seeks to change the contract or add terms that are disadvantageous to the other party after the employee starts work. Similarly, the parties must consider common law rules relating to constructive dismissal if an employer should attempt to change an employee's duties in any significant way or to impose certain types of discipline during the course of employment.

This chapter considers several common law issues and human resources practices that employers should keep in mind in navigating the ongoing employment relationship.

Employer Policy Manuals

All but the smallest organizations should have a policy manual that contains employment policies and procedures. Many large employers also have a more user-friendly version called an employee handbook that provides a quick reference guide to information about working for the organization. In general, an employee handbook answers the "when," "where," and "how" questions while an employer policy manual also provides insight into "why" things are done in a particular way in the workplace. Where a handbook is used, it should be sufficiently detailed to cover basic day-to-day rights and responsibilities and direct employees to where policies can be viewed in their entirety (Milne, 2005, p. 3-1). In the following discussion, reference to policy manuals includes employee handbooks.

A well-drafted employer policy manual serves several legal and communicative functions. It is an effective way for an employer to provide information to employees in a convenient, centralized location. It usually includes company rules concerning such matters as dress codes, probationary periods, benefit entitlements, disciplinary procedures, office procedures, computer and Internet use, sick leave policy, and the employer's harassment policy, and thus communicates an organization's expectations in these areas. A manual also provides a convenient means for making relatively minor changes to company rules, such as a slight alteration in coffee break times. In this case, it is sufficient that the employer amends the manual and notifies employees concerning the revised rule or procedure. However, in the case of significant changes, such as those that arguably affect fundamental terms of the employment agreement, the employer must take additional steps (discussed below under the heading "Changing Employment Terms and Conditions"). An employment policy manual also helps ensure consistency in an employer's treatment of employees. It provides managers with a set of pre-established rules to guide them in, for example, responding to various employee requests. Treating all employees consistently and predictably is a fundamental part of being a fair employer and being perceived as such by employees. By letting employees know what is expected of them and what they can expect from the employer in return, the manual helps reduce the potential for dissatisfaction and disputes.

Similarly, a policy manual that is clearly written and consistently applied can reduce the potential for wrongful dismissal litigation where the termination results from a breach of an employment policy. For example, an employee who is terminated for "padding" his expense account will be disinclined to argue that he was unaware of expense account procedures when they are clearly defined in the manual. On the other hand, an employer that does not have a clear, well-communicated policy on, for example, Internet and email use, or does not consistently enforce the one it has, will have a more difficult time defending a wrongful dismissal action where the alleged just cause involves the employee's inappropriate use of company Internet and email.

One word of caution: as shown in *Bennett v. Sears Canada Inc.*, even where a policy is clearly set out in the policy manual, it may not protect an employer when an employer representative misrepresents—even mistakenly—the contents of that policy (Sinclair, 2012).

CASE IN POINT

Employer Bound by HR Rep's Misrepresentation

Bennett v. Sears Canada Inc., 2012 ONCA 344; [2012] OJ no. 2288 (SCJ)

Facts

The employer's policy manual stated that to qualify for certain retirement benefits, the employee "must retire from active employment with 20 years or more *continuous full-time service*" (italics added). When Bennett, an employee who had worked 32 years for the employer (10 years full-time and 22 years part-time), made an inquiry about her eligibility for these benefits, she received an email from the HR department advising her that her part-time service would be prorated. As a result, she would need only three more years of service to qualify for the benefits. However, when Bennett was terminated four years later, she was told that this previous information was incorrect—the employer policy manual clearly indicated that 20 years or more of *continuous full-time service* was necessary. Bennett sued the employer for the denied post-retirement benefits on the basis of the information she had received from the HR department.

Relevant Issue

Whether the employer was bound by the misrepresentation of its HR representative.

Decision

The court found for the employee: the employer had to prorate the plaintiff's part-time service, resulting in Bennett being eligible for the retirement benefits. The information sent by email from the HR department became part of her contractual agreement with the employer and the employer was bound by it, even though it was incorrect and contrary to the plain language of the agreement.

This decision highlights the desirability of an employer's choosing an HR representative who is sufficiently trained and familiar with its benefit package or other policies to discuss entitlements with employees (Sinclair, 2012).

As noted in Chapter 4, a policy manual does not automatically bind the employee; the employer must take certain steps to ensure that it forms part of the employment contract.

An employer that wants to maximize the benefits of a policy manual should

1. ensure that the employment contract or letter of hire specifically incorporates the manual;
2. provide employees with a copy of the manual before they begin work;
3. ensure that the manual is clearly drafted;
4. apply the manual's policies consistently among employees;
5. ensure that all employees have up-to-date copies of the manual;
6. give as much notice as possible of significant changes to manual policy;
7. have employees indicate in writing (typically through a signed acknowledgment form) that they have reviewed the manual and any changes to it, perhaps on an annual basis (this form should note that employees are responsible for asking human resources staff or a supervisor about anything they do not understand in the manual (Leiper and Hall, 2006, p. 14));
8. ensure that employees are aware of the consequences of failing to adhere to the manual and that these consequences are fair;
9. include a statement advising employees that the organization retains the sole discretion to make changes to any of the policies, procedures, and guidelines contained in the manual; and
10. update the manual periodically to ensure compliance with current legislation.

Furthermore, the policy manual should contain a statement confirming the employer's commitment to complying with applicable legal requirements and indicating that, in the event that any part of the manual violates those requirements, the legislation will apply (Burkett, 2013).

A decision that aptly demonstrates the importance of effectively implementing an employment policy manual is *Daley v. Depco International Inc.* In that case, the employer's progressive discipline policy was at the heart of its defence that it had just cause to dismiss the employee. In finding for the employer, the court noted with approval that Depco not only distributed the employee handbook to its employees, but also obtained employee sign-offs that acknowledged receipt of the handbook and indicated agreement to abide by its rules, policies, terms, and conditions. Furthermore, the acknowledgment included an explicit statement that failure to abide by the handbook's policies "may result in disciplinary action and/or dismissal." The thorough way in which Depco implemented its progressive discipline policy played a crucial part in the court's ultimately finding in its favour.

It should be noted that for a breach of a company rule (or policy) to constitute just cause for dismissal, several factors must exist. In addition to being well-communicated and consistently enforced, the rule must be itself "reasonable," the implications of breaking the rule must be sufficiently serious to justify termination, and employees must be advised that they can be terminated for breaking it. Finally, the employee must not have had a reasonable excuse for breaking the rule (Saint-Cyr, 2012).

Changing Employment Terms and Conditions

Amending the Employment Contract

Chapter 4 discusses the benefits of having a written employment contract that sets out the rights and responsibilities of both parties during the employment relationship. However, what happens when, because of either changed circumstances or an oversight in negotiating the agreement, the employer wants to make changes to the contract after employment begins?

Introducing changes to an employment contract, whether oral or written, during the course of employment raises a number of issues. If an employer wishes to make a minor change, such as slightly modifying a procedure for applying for reimbursements, the employer can simply notify employees of the change and distribute amendments to the policy manual. However, an employer that wishes to introduce a change that is more significant faces two potential legal problems. First, if the change alters the employment agreement in a fundamental way, it may constitute constructive dismissal, thus allowing the employee to bring an action against it for damages for wrongful dismissal. Second, if the employer negotiates the change with the employee, the employer must provide consideration for the new term or the employee may subsequently argue that she is not bound by it. These two issues are discussed below.

Constructive Dismissal and Reasonable Notice

The first question that must be addressed is whether the change is so fundamental that it constitutes constructive dismissal. For example, an immediate 25 percent reduction in pay or a significant downgrade in job duties clearly goes to the heart of the employment agreement. It is a repudiation of the existing terms and conditions of employment. In cases such as these, an employee can either accept the change (or possibly negotiate changes of her own) and continue working under the new arrangement, or inform the employer that the change constitutes constructive dismissal. In the latter case, the employee may quit and sue the employer for pay in lieu of proper notice or stay in the position and sue the employer for the difference between the old and the new salary.

On the other hand, where an employer wants to introduce a more modest change, such as slightly modifying an employee's commission package or proposing a relatively small across-the-board salary decrease in response to difficult market conditions, the situation is less clear. Every case must be evaluated on its own facts to decide how essential the change is to that employee's job. Ultimately, if the issue ends up in court, it will be up to a court to decide whether the change is a fundamental one and therefore constitutes constructive dismissal.

Where a proposed change to an employment contract is arguably a fundamental one, an employer can generally meet its legal obligations by providing the employee with proper advance notice of the change. However, in 2008 the Ontario Court of Appeal issued a decision, *Wronko v. Western Inventory Service Ltd.*, that called into question the application of this general principle.

CASE IN POINT

Changing Employment Terms Mid-Stream

Wronko v. Western Inventory Service Ltd., 2008 ONCA 327; 2006 CanLII 34211 (Ont. SC)

Facts

Wronko began working for Western, a Toronto-based inventory service provider, in 1987 and by 2004 he was vice-president of sales. With each promotion he executed a new employment agreement. The last contract, signed in December 2000, provided for a generous severance package of a lump-sum payment of two years' salary upon termination without cause. In 2002, Western's new president decided that Wronko's contract should be amended and he presented Wronko with a draft agreement that provided him with only seven months' severance if terminated without cause. After seeking legal advice, Wronko refused to sign this amended agreement. On September 9, 2002, Western responded with a letter stating that the new contract would take effect in two years' time. Wronko made it clear that he still did not accept the change but he continued working. Two years later, Western wrote Wronko a letter that stated: "Effective September 9, 2004, the terms noted in the employment agreement ... apply and are in full force and effect. If you do not wish to accept the new terms and conditions of employment as outlined, then we do not have a job for you." Wronko again refused the new terms and, taking the position that the employer's letter effectively fired him, sued for wrongful dismissal.

At trial, the employer argued that it had met its legal obligations by giving Wronko two years' notice of the change and that by not attending work after that, Wronko had resigned. The trial judge agreed. Under the common law, Western had the legal right to vary even a fundamental term of the contract—in this case the termination clause—upon proper notice to the employee. The court therefore dismissed the wrongful dismissal claim. Wronko appealed.

Relevant Issue

Whether an employer is able to unilaterally change a fundamental term of an employment agreement simply by providing advance notice of the change to the employee.

Decision

The Ontario Court of Appeal unanimously found for Wronko. It held that where an employer attempts to make a unilateral and fundamental change to the terms of an existing employment agreement, and the employee clearly rejects that new term, the employer must do more than provide advance notice of the change. It must also advise the employee of the consequences of rejecting it. In this instance, Western could have done this by explicitly telling Wronko that if he refused to accept the new terms, employment under the terms of the *existing* contract would terminate at the end of the working notice period (September 2004). At the same time, it could have offered to rehire him under the *new* terms, starting at the end of the working notice period. However, because Western had allowed him to continue working in these circumstances without notifying him of the consequences of this decision, Wronko could legally insist that the notice was ineffective. Therefore, by the letter of September 2004 Western effectively terminated Wronko and he was entitled to wrongful dismissal damages. The Court of Appeal awarded Wronko two years' termination pay in lieu of notice ($286,000) pursuant to the terms of his existing employment contract. Western's leave to appeal to the Supreme Court of Canada was dismissed with costs.

It appears that the *Wronko* decision has changed the legal requirements surrounding an employer's ability to make a unilateral, fundamental change to an employment contract by simply providing advance notice. However, the extent of that change is still being considered. For example, in the 2012 case of *Kafka v. Allstate Insurance Company of Canada*, Allstate, an insurance company, had advised all of its insurance agents that significant changes to their compensation structure would take effect in 24 months' time. The agents who refused to accept the changes resigned and filed a motion to have their claim certified as a class action. Basing their argument on *Wronko*, these agents claimed that once they rejected the employer's proposed changes to their contract, the employer had to provide them with reasonable notice of termination and offer to rehire them on the new terms. However, the Ontario Divisional Court rejected this argument. It found that, unlike in *Wronko*, the employer's notice of the changes made it clear that the changes would take effect within 24 months, regardless of whether or not the employees accepted the change. The agents could therefore have no reasonable expectation that continuing under the previous compensation system at the end of the 24-month period remained an option.

The Ontario Divisional Court's decision in *Kafka* interprets *Wronko* quite narrowly. However, it is not entirely clear whether this approach will be consistently applied in the future. At the very least, an employer who wants to make a fundamental change to an employee's terms of employment by providing advance notice should clearly indicate that the change will take place at the end of the notice period regardless of the employee's acceptance or rejection of it. Without this clarity, where an employee rejects the change, the employer would be well advised to provide notice of termination of employment under the existing terms, which can be accompanied by an offer to rehire the employee on the new terms at the end of the notice period (Channe, 2012).

One important question that arises from this discussion is: how does an employer determine the amount of advance notice required? The answer is: what constitutes proper notice depends on the particular circumstances. First, the employer looks at the terms of the employment contract to see whether it sets out a period for notice of termination. In the absence of an enforceable termination clause, the common law implies a duty to provide reasonable notice, which, as is discussed in Chapter 15, depends on a number of factors, including the employee's age, position, and length of service. Where more than one employee is affected by a significant change, an employer probably should provide the same notice to all employees based on the longest notice period to which any of the employees is entitled. The main difficulty with this approach is that the notice required under the common law is often extensive, ranging from periods of several months to periods of up to two years for long-term employees. If the change being proposed by the employer is urgent, such as an immediate 15 percent across-the-board salary decrease to keep itself solvent, the employer may be unable to provide sufficient notice to meet its common law obligations. An employer may also be faced with resentment and declining morale if it chooses to institute significant unilateral changes in the terms and conditions of employment. This is especially true after the *Wronko* decision because, to make a change effective in the face of an employee's rejection of it, the advance notice now must be accompanied by rather direct statements regarding the consequences of the rejection. In short, significant changes to the employment contract can be made unilaterally by the employer if the proper steps are taken, but they should not be made lightly.

Even where proposed changes to the terms of employment involve the promotion of an employee, the employer must keep the common law notion of constructive dismissal in mind. An employee who is unhappy in a new position may successfully argue that his promotion constitutes constructive dismissal by affecting the foundation of his contract. In this case, an employer may be liable for damages for wrongful dismissal. Consequently, employers should never force employees to accept promotions. The decision must be mutual. Employers must be prepared to assist employees in performing new jobs. If an employee accepts a promotion but is unable to perform the new job satisfactorily, in the absence of just cause an employer should be prepared to re-employ him in his previous job or provide proper notice of dismissal or pay in lieu.

Providing Consideration

Another way to amend an employment contract is through negotiation. This approach is especially useful where the employer wants the new term, such as a non-competition clause, to be added immediately.

However, there is one legal requirement that an employer must keep in mind when negotiating a fundamental change to an employment contract. As discussed in Chapter 4, to create a binding contract under the common law, both parties must receive consideration—something of value—in exchange for the promise given. Without consideration, the agreement is unenforceable. The same requirement applies to the amendment of a contract. If an employer places a contract containing a disadvantageous new contractual term in front of an employee and simply asks her to sign it, a court may refuse to enforce the new term because it lacked consideration. This is what happened in *Kohler Canada Co. v. Porter*.

CASE IN POINT

Lack of Consideration Makes Non-Competition Clause Unenforceable

Kohler Canada Co. v. Porter, 2002 CanLII 49614 (Ont. SC)

Facts

Porter began working for the employer in 1988 as a customer service representative; by 1999 he occupied a management position. He did not have a written employment agreement until 2001, when the employer presented him with one and asked him to sign it. Believing it was a routine document, Porter signed it without obtaining legal advice. In fact, the agreement included a non-competition clause that prohibited him from working anywhere in North America for one year after the termination of his employment in a business that competed with the employer's business. It also stated that the consideration for the agreement was Porter's "employment status with Kohler and the payment of salary during such employment." Shortly after signing the rewritten contract, Porter was offered a position as regional sales manager with a company that competed with Kohler. Kohler sought an injunction restraining Porter from working for the new employer on the basis of the non-competition clause in the employment agreement.

Relevant Issue

Whether the employment contract and its non-competition clause were enforceable.

Decision

The Ontario Superior Court held that the non-competition clause was unenforceable because it covered an overly broad geographic area. However, even had this not been so, the entire employment contract was unenforceable because the employee had received no new consideration for signing it. The mere offer of continued employment is not consideration for a new promise that is disadvantageous to an employee. This situation differs from one in which an employer tells an employee that if the employee does not sign the new agreement, he will be dismissed in accordance with the terms of his existing contract. In this case, there was no evidence that the employer intended to dismiss Porter if he did not sign. Furthermore, the employer could not have dismissed him for failing to sign the agreement without providing reasonable notice, which would have been approximately 12 months, owing to Porter's 13 years of service. The court therefore refused to grant an injunction to prevent the employee from working for the employer's competitor.

In *Kohler*, the employer attempted to define the consideration for the new agreement as the employee's "employment status with [the employer] and the payment of salary during such employment." However, the court did not accept this because the employer had offered nothing of value to the employee in exchange for the new obligation. Because the employer could not dismiss the employee without reasonable notice, its promise of continued employment did not constitute consideration because it was merely offering to provide a benefit that it was already obligated to provide.

On the other hand, courts have found that where an employer is in a position to terminate an agreement with little or no notice, and clearly intends to do so if the new terms of the agreement are not accepted, a promise not to terminate if the employee agrees to a new term may constitute consideration. In *Techform Products Ltd. v. Wolda*, the employer successfully advanced such an argument. The employer was able to establish that it intended to terminate the employee under the terms of his agreement if he did not accept the amendment, and that forbearing from doing so was sufficient consideration.

To ensure that a negotiated amendment to an employment contract is enforceable, the employer should follow many of the same steps discussed in Chapter 4 with respect to drafting the initial employment contract. The employee should be given time to review the proposed changes and to seek independent legal advice before signing the amended contract. To address the issue of consideration, an employer might introduce an amendment when another aspect of a contract is changing as well, such as when an employee is promoted or given a pay increase. Alternatively, it might give the employee a signing bonus or increased annual vacation, for example. If the amendment is crucial and the employee refuses to sign, the employer may be faced with the last resort of telling the employee that she will be dismissed *with reasonable notice or pay in lieu* if she does not sign. (An employee's refusal to sign a disadvantageous new agreement does not usually constitute just cause for dismissal; therefore, notice or pay in lieu is required.) This last option should be considered an option of last resort because its effect on employee morale may be significant.

Monitoring the Contract

Employment contracts sometimes contain important dates. For example, many employers have probationary periods, during which they observe an employee's performance to ensure they have chosen the appropriate candidate for the job. To benefit from a probationary term, an employer must be prepared to take action before the end of the term, if necessary. Once the contractual probationary period has expired, it will probably be more difficult and costly to dismiss the now non-probationary employee. The employer should therefore adopt a reminder system that provides advance warning of all upcoming critical dates.

Similarly, if an employment contract is for a fixed term, it is important that the employer monitor the date that the contract expires. Under a fixed-term contract, an employer need not provide notice of termination, or an employee notice of resignation, if employment ends when the fixed task or term is completed. However, the employer risks losing the benefit of the fixed term if it inadvertently allows an employee to continue work beyond the expiry date. Should this occur, the employee automatically becomes covered by an indefinite-term contract. (Also note that *statutory* notice under the *Employment Standards Act* (ESA), discussed in Chapter 14, is required if the term or task extends beyond 12 months.)

To avoid this result, employers should use some form of a reminder system so that they do not inadvertently let a fixed-term employment contract lapse. Moreover, even fixed-term contracts should contain a termination provision that allows either party to terminate the contract on a certain amount of notice. The notice period is typically two to four weeks, but can be longer for more senior positions.

Finally, it is good practice to periodically revisit *all* employment contracts to ensure they reflect the current employment relationship. Courts will refuse to enforce contracts that they find obsolete, because obsolete contracts no longer reflect the employment relationship; the employer then will lose the protections contained in the original contract. This typically means that the termination clause negotiated by the parties at the outset of the employment relationship can be held not to apply. To avoid this result, the contract could contain a clause that allows it to be reopened and updated periodically. Alternatively, amendment of the existing employment contract could be a condition of all promotions and significant changes in duties.

Managing Employee Performance and Conduct

1. Performance Appraisals

Performance appraisals are a key tool in an employer's ongoing management of the employment relationship. Performance evaluation is not a form of discipline. It gives the employer an opportunity to provide regular feedback to an employee about his performance.

Performance appraisals serve several purposes. Done well, they motivate employees and foster an atmosphere of openness within an organization. They provide encouragement to strong performers and alert poor performers to problems at an early stage, thus providing an opportunity for improvement. Alternatively, performance appraisals may help an employee realize that his skills and aptitudes do not fit well with the current position, and that it is time to look elsewhere for a suitable job.

Even if a poorly performing employee remains on the job and the problems continue, the employer has laid the legal foundation for dismissing the employee with cause. As discussed in Chapter 13, it is particularly difficult for an employer to dismiss an employee on performance-related grounds. However, an employer that has created a paper trail by consistently documenting performance problems and efforts at providing assistance is in a stronger legal position than an employer that has failed to do so.

That being said, performance appraisals are useful only if they reflect the actual performance of an employee. Many supervisors have a natural reluctance to raise performance problems with employees for fear of a hostile response. They may therefore note only the more positive aspects of the employee's performance and remain silent on problematic areas. A series of inappropriately positive reviews makes it difficult for an employer to allege just cause for dismissing an employee. Therefore, supervisors should be trained to conduct fair and effective performance appraisals.

In small organizations, performance appraisals tend to be less formal than in larger ones. However, in either case, appraisals should be conducted regularly and objectively, based on the following principles:

1. Be honest and balanced. Identify both strengths and weaknesses.
2. Clearly communicate job standards to each employee.
3. Use a standard form to ensure that employees are evaluated consistently.
4. Allow the employee an opportunity to respond to an evaluation, both on the form and orally.
5. Document the evaluation.
6. Provide employees with a copy of the evaluation and have them acknowledge in writing that they have received it. The acknowledgment should indicate that an employee's signature does *not* mean that she agrees with the contents of the appraisal, simply that she has read it.
7. Set goals for the future and revisit these goals at the next performance review.
8. Conduct performance appraisals separately from salary reviews. An across-the-board salary increase, for example, may send a mixed message to someone who has received a poor performance review.

2. Progressive Discipline

The practice of **progressive discipline** first arose in unionized workplaces. It is based on the idea that discipline for less serious infractions should be imposed in a series of increasing steps. For example, where an employee is absent from work without leave, an employer may be required to give a verbal warning for a first occurrence, a written warning for a second occurrence, and suspensions of increasing lengths for subsequent occurrences, with a final written warning that the employee's job is in jeopardy. Each of these steps must be documented. If the misconduct continues despite these disciplinary actions, an employer may eventually be entitled to dismiss the employee for cause.

Generally speaking, when applying its progressive discipline policy, an employer considers the type of misconduct, as well as any previous misconduct, the discipline applied, and the length of time over which all of the incidents took place. The level of discipline applied must be proportionate to the employee's misconduct. An employer may skip steps in the disciplinary process as long as the policy allows it this discretion and the incident is sufficiently serious to warrant this action.

Progressive discipline is now common in many non-unionized workplaces as well. Although there are some incidents, such as acts of violence, for which immediate dismissal is appropriate, most incidents of misconduct warrant a less severe response. Applying discipline in a series of steps allows an employer to respond to an employee's inappropriate conduct in a measured way and allows an employee the opportunity to improve. Moreover, where rules are clear and consistently applied, employees are less likely to resent discipline or see it as unfair. An employee who is eventually dismissed for cause after being subjected to progressive disciplinary measures is less likely to challenge her dismissal in court or elsewhere (for example, before human rights or employment standards tribunals). Moreover, where a progressive discipline policy is in place and consistently applied, any such challenge is less likely to be successful.

FYI

Progressive Discipline: A Step-by-Step Guide for Employers

An employer may choose to include some of the following steps in a progressive discipline program:

1. Outline acceptable standards of conduct and the consequences of misconduct in the policy manual or elsewhere.

2. Describe the steps that may be taken as part of a disciplinary action: coaching, a verbal warning, a written warning, suspension(s) with or without pay, a final written warning that the employee's job is in jeopardy, and dismissal. (However, employers should be cautious when applying suspensions without pay to non-unionized employees. Unless an employer has a well-known policy regarding suspensions, suspensions without pay may constitute constructive dismissal, because under the common law an employer has no inherent right to suspend an employee for any reason.)

3. Retain the right to disregard these steps and proceed immediately to suspension or dismissal where serious misconduct is involved.

4. Clarify that progressive discipline is a disciplinary procedure, not merely performance feedback.

5. Document every step of the process, including verbal warnings, and indicate the time, date, and reason the step was taken. Be sure to indicate the type of discipline (for example, verbal warning or final written warning) at the top of the document (Dusti, 2013, p. 56).

6. Explain to the employee the problem, the acceptable standard, and the action necessary to meet this standard at every step.

7. Ensure that plans devised to correct the problem are realistic, including timelines for making the necessary improvements.

8. Ask employees whether they have any comments to add to the disciplinary form. Employees should sign the form to prove that they have received a copy of it. If an employee refuses to sign, this should be noted on the document.

9. Set a date for a follow-up meeting but state that management will respond immediately if further problems arise before the meeting.

10. Train managers to deal with performance issues and monitor employee performance.

11. If problems persist after taking other disciplinary action, give the employee a final written warning before termination. In the final warning, put the employee on notice that unless there is an improvement, he will be subject to immediate termination for cause and note the measures that management has taken to help the employee meet the job standards. A final written warning usually accompanies a suspension letter, which concludes with the following warning: "Should you repeat or continue any of the above conduct in the future, you will be subject to further discipline, up to and including termination of your employment."

Another benefit of consistently applying a progressive discipline policy is that the employer avoids condoning misconduct. **Condonation** occurs when an employer is aware of misconduct and takes no disciplinary action within a reasonable time. An employer that condones misconduct arguably cannot later use the misconduct as a basis for discipline or dismissal. For example, an employer that fails to react within a reasonable time after becoming aware of an employee's contravention of a company policy against borrowing money from suppliers arguably has condoned the employee's behaviour.

The aforementioned case of *Daley v. Depco International Inc.* shows the value of adopting clear disciplinary procedures and then following those procedures consistently.

Employer Argues "Cumulative Just Cause"

Daley v. Depco International Inc., 2004 CanLII 11310 (Ont. SC)

Facts

Daley was 58 years old and had worked for Depco for 13 years as an extrusion operator on a production line when, in December 2002, he was fired on the basis of "cumulative just cause." In the previous 28 months there had been nine documented incidents of misconduct. Depco, a non-union employer, had applied the five-step progressive discipline policy set out in its employee handbook. The steps were (1) counselling, (2) verbal warning, (3) written warning, (4) suspension, and (5) termination. It disciplined Daley as follows:

- August 21, 2000—Counselling for using the wrong materials in production, causing the production line to be shut down for hours.
- February 1, 2001—Written warning for failing to call in to report absence.
- August 17, 2001—Verbal warning for causing the production line to go down by failing to "drop the coil."
- October 2, 2001—Suspended for two and a half days for not setting the correct pressure and causing the production line to shut down.
- May 8, 2002—Suspended for one day for challenging a fellow employee to a fight in the parking lot following a disagreement.
- July 24, 2002—Suspended for five days and warned that his job was in jeopardy for showing up for work with alcohol on his breath.
- September 26, 2002—No disciplinary action but investigation undertaken for improperly inserting a part that resulted in 56 scrapped parts and the line being shut down for two hours.
- December 6, 2002—Termination for two culminating incidents—not dropping the coil (a very rare occurrence but done by Daley twice) and causing lubricant to be spilled onto the floor in a safety-sensitive area.

Daley sued for wrongful dismissal.

Relevant Issue

Whether the employer had just cause to terminate Daley on the basis of his cumulative misconduct.

Decision

The court found that Depco had just cause. It noted that in deciding a case of cumulative just cause it is the quality, and not the similarity, of the accumulated misconduct that matters. In this case, while each of the incidents (although serious) might not be sufficient to amount to just cause by themselves, "when viewed collectively … the series of acts cumulatively do amount to enough bricks to constitute a just cause wall." The court concluded that Daley's performance fell below any reasonable standard of conduct that his employer was entitled to expect.

The court made it clear that the thorough way in which the employer implemented its progressive discipline policy was crucial to its finding. It noted that

> Depco took care to clearly lay out the facts, the penalty if any, and notably, as the employee proceeded through the various progressive discipline steps, specific reference was made to the prior warnings given, the dates of the offences, and the prior transgressions. By doing this, the employee was clearly reminded of prior warnings, while at the same time advised as to the consequences of future violations of company policy. The employee was also asked to acknowledge receipt of copies of such notices in writing, while not necessarily being asked to admit an error. The employee's additional comments were also solicited. …
>
> This Court encourages employers to adopt clear and forthright disciplinary procedures and to apply them fairly.

Daley's wrongful dismissal action was dismissed and the employer was awarded $11,000 in legal costs.

One of the contentious issues in *Daley* was whether the first four incidents could be taken into consideration by the court because Depco's progressive discipline policy stated that "[a]ny disciplinary action will be removed from the employee's record after one year." Although the employer argued that the words "incident free" should be read into this line of the policy, the court refused to do so because this would have created a restriction that did not exist in the employer's own clearly written policy.

As a result, the court only considered the last five incidents because only these took place in the 12 months before the termination. However, the court found that these five incidents were sufficient to support a finding of cumulative just cause and praised the non-union employer's general approach to progressive discipline.

Progressive discipline is less applicable in the context of statutory termination or severance pay requirements than it is under the common law. Under the *Employment Standards Act*, misconduct must be "wilful" or intentional before an employer is exempt from notice or pay in lieu requirements. Employees who are terminated for ongoing performance problems that are not "wilful," as opposed to intentional misconduct, are therefore usually entitled to statutory termination or severance pay under the Act. (Chapter 14 contains a discussion of statutory termination and severance pay requirements.)

FYI

Dealing Effectively with Poor Performance

The following is a list of things to keep in mind when dealing with an underperforming employee.

- Meet with the employee in private.
- Give the employee some notice of the meeting so that he does not feel ambushed.
- Take the time to clarify your expectations of the employee (make sure the job description that this discussion is based on is up to date).
- Be prepared for different possible outcomes and reactions (anger, disbelief, upset) (Bell, 2010).
- Address shortcomings professionally—and promptly (keep in mind the negative impact, on everyone, of not dealing with them).
- Describe the behaviour, not the person, and quantify your observations (for example, "You have missed the last three deadlines" rather than "I notice you've been slacking off").
- Conduct regular performance "chats"; discuss progress and areas for continuous improvement on an ongoing basis.

- Arrange a follow-up meeting where improvements can be acknowledged.
- Consider a performance improvement plan—but do it with integrity and not simply to "build a case" for dismissal.
- Build a basis for discussion by familiarizing yourself with the employee's background, career path, and track record.
- Differentiate between problematic performance and problematic behaviour. Look at your organization's code of conduct to determine what is acceptable versus unacceptable behaviour.
- Be honest yet tactful in your discussion with the employee.
- Don't personalize the discussion—use the job description and code of conduct to guide it.

SOURCE: Based, in part, on Fiorella Callocchia, "Rehabilitating Underperformers," *Financial Post*, April 1, 2010.

---

3. Suspensions Without Pay

Despite the important benefits of progressive discipline, there is some question whether an employer has the right to suspend a non-unionized employee without pay. Unless there is an express or implied term in the employment contract allowing this form of discipline, a suspension without pay, even for a few days, may constitute constructive dismissal under the common law. This is because the right to work in exchange for pay is seen as a fundamental part of the employment contract. For example, in *Carscallen v. FRI Corp.*, the court found that a week-long unpaid suspension of a marketing executive, along with several other disciplinary measures, amounted to constructive dismissal. Unpaid suspensions were not, either explicitly or implicitly, a part of that employee's employment terms.

In *Haldane v. Shelbar Enterprises Limited*, the Ontario Court of Appeal stated that the right to suspend an employee may be an implied term of an employment contract based on custom and usage or based on the presumed intention of the parties. However, the onus is on the employer to prove that this implied term applies in the circumstances. An employer may therefore choose to include a contractual term that allows it to suspend employees without pay for cause. A clear, well-communicated, and consistently enforced progressive discipline process that specifically includes an unpaid suspension as one of the disciplinary steps probably also meets this requirement.

Alternatively, to avoid the possibility of a finding of constructive dismissal, many employers with non-unionized employees in Ontario have adopted a discipline policy with only three or four steps:

1. verbal warning,
2. written warning (optional),
3. final written warning, and
4. termination.

Even if an employer is able to suspend an employee without pay, the employer must act reasonably because an unreasonable suspension may constitute constructive dismissal under the common law. In *Reininger v. Unique Personnel Canada Inc.*, an unreasonably long suspension led to a finding that the employer had constructively dismissed the employee.

CASE IN POINT

Lengthy Suspension Without Pay Constitutes Constructive Dismissal

Reininger v. Unique Personnel Canada Inc., [2002] OJ no. 2826 (SCJ)

Facts

Reininger was a non-unionized long-haul driver who had been employed for more than 12 years with an above-average performance record. In July 2000, he was charged with impaired driving and driving with a prohibited blood alcohol level while operating his own car. His licence was immediately suspended for 90 days. As a result, the employer suspended his employment without pay pending the trial verdict, which was not rendered until May 2001. Reininger did not contest the employer's right to suspend him without pay, but he argued that suspending him beyond the 90 days was unreasonable and amounted to constructive dismissal. He sued the employer for damages in lieu of notice. On May 9, 2001, he was convicted on the blood alcohol charge only.

Relevant Issue

Whether the suspension until trial constituted constructive dismissal.

Decision

The Ontario Superior Court of Justice determined that the suspension constituted constructive dismissal. Generally, an employer does not have a right to suspend a non-unionized employee without pay. However, because the loss of a driver's licence affected Reininger's basic job functions, the employer had an implied contractual right to suspend him. However, this right must be exercised in a reasonable fashion, and in this case the suspension was unreasonably long. Suspension during the 90-day period was reasonable because Reininger was legally unable to perform his job. However, the employer did not act reasonably in suspending him from the end of the 90-day period until the criminal trial. Reininger had a 12-year clean driving record, and the employer was never concerned that he had a substance abuse problem. The employer could have taken less drastic measures, such as random alcohol testing, to protect its interests.

4. Probation

Another form of corrective action that some employers take with regard to an under-performing employee is to place the individual on **probation**. This puts the employee on notice that her performance is being watched for signs of significant improvement. In the absence of a contractual provision authorizing this action, the imposition of probation may constitute a fundamental change to the employment contract and give the employee the right to sue for damages for constructive dismissal. An employer may reduce the likelihood of this result if it imposes a probationary period as part of a progressive discipline program and provides the employee with a reasonable opportunity to meet its performance requirements. It cannot cut short the probationary period without leaving itself open to a claim for wrongful dismissal. Placing employees on probation is increasingly uncommon among employers because it is often not effective either at remediating employee performance or at protecting the employer from wrongful dismissal claims.

5. Temporary Layoffs

Although a temporary layoff is not a form of discipline, an employer that places a non-unionized employee on temporary layoff for economic reasons must consider the possibility that the employee will bring an action for damages for constructive dismissal. Unless the employment contract expressly or implicitly allows for layoffs, a layoff may constitute a fundamental change in the terms and conditions of employment that triggers wrongful dismissal damages.

Generally speaking, a short-term layoff will not amount to constructive dismissal but a longer-term layoff is more problematic. In Ontario, the terms of the ESA are impliedly included in every contract of employment. The ESA recognizes the concept of temporary layoffs and defines the circumstances under which a layoff is "temporary": layoffs that fall within this definition do not require advance notice under the ESA (see the discussion in Chapter 14 under the heading "Temporary Layoffs (Section 56)"). By extension, it is arguable that layoffs that fall within this statutory definition of "temporary" ought not to constitute constructive dismissal. This argument was, in fact, successful in *Trites v. Renin Corp*, where the court found that, because a layoff only becomes a termination under the ESA if it continues beyond the statutory limit of 13 weeks (or 35 weeks, in some situations), there is no constructive dismissal under the common law in those circumstances. The judge stated: "In my view, there is no room remaining at law for a common law claim for a finding of constructive dismissal in circumstances where a temporary layoff has been rolled out in accordance with the terms of the ESA" (para. 29).

Although this decision suggests a possible loosening of the common law constraints against temporary layoffs, it is not yet known whether this reasoning will be consistently adopted in the future (Thomlinson, 2013). The safest approach therefore is to include clear language in the employment contract and/or employer policy manual that gives the employer the right to temporarily lay off an employee in accordance with the ESA (Westlake, 2013).

In any event, wrongful dismissal actions based on temporary layoffs have been rare. Typically, an employee will accept a temporary layoff rather than quit and make a tenuous claim for constructive dismissal.

6. Attendance Management

Culpable Absenteeism

Under the common law there are two kinds of absenteeism: culpable and innocent. Culpable absences involve a blameworthy act such as being late without good reason, leaving work without permission, or failing to follow absence notification procedures. An employer may apply progressive discipline for culpable absenteeism. For example, if an employee leaves work without permission to watch a soccer game, the employer may issue a verbal or written warning for a first occurrence and apply increasing levels of discipline for any subsequent instances of culpable absenteeism. It may not always be obvious whether an absence is innocent or culpable. However, where there is a consistent pattern—as when absences usually occur on Mondays and Fridays—an employer may wish to pursue the matter.

Innocent Absenteeism

Innocent absences arise as a result of a legitimate medical or other cause, and they can never be subject to disciplinary measures. However, even non-blameworthy absences may cause an employer difficulty if they occur frequently or over a long period of time. Therefore, for frequent or lengthy absences, an employer should attempt to find out whether they relate to a "disability" as that term is broadly defined in s. 10 of the *Human Rights Code*. If an employee is absent owing to a disability, she is entitled to accommodation from the employer, unless this constitutes undue hardship. This usually means that the employer must accept such absences for a reasonable period of time, especially if an employee's prognosis is good and her attendance is likely to improve to an acceptable level. An employee has additional protections under the *Workplace Safety and Insurance Act* if the absences relate to a workplace injury. (See Chapter 8 for a discussion of the duty under s. 41 to re-employ injured workers.)

If an employee's absenteeism is likely to continue and there is little chance that he will ever return to regular attendance, an employer may consider dismissing the employee on a non-disciplinary basis for frustration of contract. However, this step cannot be taken lightly; it may take years to establish that the employment contract has been frustrated because the employee has no realistic chance of returning to regular attendance. Furthermore, the existence of long-term disability benefits must be considered if terminating the employee will lead to disentitlement to benefits (Gilbert et al., 2000, p. 132). Given the requirements of human rights legislation and the difficulty of establishing just cause under the common law, non-disciplinary termination is a last resort.

Sample letters relating to the management of an employee's non-culpable absences appear in Appendix C.

Attendance Management Programs

An employment policy manual should include an attendance policy that sets out the employee's basic responsibilities, such as being on time for work. It should also cover the following matters:

1. the person and/or number to call about being late or absent, such as a supervisor, a department head, the human resources department, or a 24-hour answering service;
2. the requirement to give as much notice as possible;

3. the requirement to give an anticipated date of return and, if relevant, the date that the employer can expect an update;

4. the circumstances when a doctor's note is required, such as on request (this allows maximum flexibility), for absences of three or more days, or when the employee's absenteeism record warrants it;

5. the form that a doctor's note should take and the type of information that should be included (that is, functional abilities information describing what the employee can and cannot do and her prognosis for recovery, but not other medical information);

6. information about the employer's contact program (an employer should keep in touch with absent employees to remind them that they are still part of the organization and that their return is welcomed, but contact should not be so frequent or aggressive that an employee feels harassed); and

7. the procedure for returning employees who have been off work for an extended period of time, including rules about when a written medical clearance is required (the medical clearance details employees' functional abilities and confirms their fitness to return to work).

A goal of an attendance management program is to promote good attendance by identifying and motivating employees with a poor attendance record. This can be done by making employees aware that their attendance level is being measured against a certain standard. Employees whose absenteeism record significantly exceeds this standard are brought into a program that includes interviews and counselling. Although this process may eventually lead to termination for cause, that final decision must always be made on a case-by-case basis and should not follow automatically based on attendance alone. Moreover, absences caused by disabilities should be dealt with outside any attendance management program.

FYI

What Medical (or Functional Abilities) Information May an Employer Ask For?

Subject to the terms of a collective agreement, employment contract, or policy, employers may generally ask for certain types of medical (more properly referred to as functional abilities) information where it is necessary for the proper management of their operations. For example, an employer may request information

- to determine whether a temporary absence due to illness or injury is bona fide;
- to determine whether an employee is fit to return to work after an absence due to illness or injury if there are reasonable grounds to question the employee's fitness or ability to work safely; or
- to respond to a request for accommodation.

Generally speaking, the information should disclose the general nature of the illness or disability (but *not* the diagnosis); the prognosis; the expected date when the employee will be fit to return to work (on a full or modified basis); any limitations or restrictions on that return; an assessment of duties that the employee is able to perform; information on whether the employee is receiving treatment; and evidence of fitness to return to work, where that is at issue.

Where the employee is seeking an extended sick leave, the employer may be entitled to additional information such as confirmation that the medical opinion is based on a current examination; confirmation that a treatment plan has been prescribed and is being followed; and information concerning medical follow-up.

A request for the specific diagnosis will not be considered reasonable unless there are compelling reasons to make such a request (Gibson, 2006, p. 3540). Also, under the Ontario *Personal Health Information Protection Act* employers must ensure that employees are specifically notified of the reasons, purposes, and subsequent uses for which their personal health information is being requested and must provide express consent for its disclosure and collection. One approach is to give the employee an authorization form that consents to the physician's releasing information to one designated employer representative. The information requested must be limited to that necessary for the accommodation process, kept confidential, and only used for the purpose for which it was disclosed (Williams, 2012, p. 17).

Employers' Vicarious Liability for Employees' Actions

Employers have a duty to take reasonable care to ensure the safety of their employees and others who come into contact with them. The common law makes employers vicariously liable—that is, legally responsible for the conduct of another—for damages caused by the actions of their employees if those actions fall within the course and scope of their employment. As noted in *Bazley v. Curry*, an action is deemed to be in the course of employment if it is either

- authorized by the employer or
- unauthorized but so connected with authorized acts that it may be regarded as a mode (albeit an improper mode) of doing an authorized act.

Determining whether an employee's wrongful act is so closely connected to his employment that the employer should be held vicariously liable for it is often difficult. The following two cases provide examples of how courts approach this issue.

CASE IN POINT

Vicarious Liability Not Dependent on Fault

John Doe v. Avalon East School Board, 2004 NLTD 239

Facts

John Doe (a pseudonym) was a grade 12 student at St. Michael's High School in Newfoundland. Neary, his computer teacher, accompanied him to a separate room for a test he had missed. Once there, Neary fondled John Doe's chest and genitals. John Doe immediately told him to stop. Neary then placed $20 on the table and told him not to tell anyone what had happened. A few days later John told another teacher about this incident; that teacher contacted the school board and the board called the police the same day. Neary was relieved of his duties later that day and he subsequently was charged with a single count of sexual assault. John Doe sued the school board, arguing it should be vicariously liable for Neary's actions.

Relevant Issue

Whether the employer was vicariously liable for the teacher's sexual assault on the student.

Decision

The court found that although the employer did nothing to cause the assault, and acted promptly when it found out about it, it was nonetheless vicariously liable for it. The court stated:

> It was the employer's mandate as a school board which placed in the hands of its teachers significant power and authority over the students: quite properly to carry out their teaching roles, but also enhancing the risk of something going wrong if that power was abused. It was the school board which gave Neary, as a trusted professional employee, the authority to set up the circumstances wherein this offence was committed.

In contrast, as the following case shows, an employer will not be held vicariously liable for an employee's wrongful acts where they arise independently of the employment relationship or where the workplace merely provided the opportunity for the wrongful act.

CASE IN POINT

Was Employer Vicariously Liable for Employee's Theft?

Royal Bank of Canada v. Intercon Security Ltd., 2005 CanLII 40376 (Ont. SC)

Facts

Hornett began working for Intercon as a security guard in 1991. At the beginning of each shift, Hornett was given a box of keys in numbered envelopes and only told which envelope to open when a client's alarm went off. During one of his shifts, an ATM alarm was accidentally set off by staff at a Royal Bank branch. While responding to this alarm, Hornett noticed some weaknesses in the branch's security system (for example, there were no door or motion alarms). He also correctly guessed how to get the combination for the ATM locks from a nearby mini-safe because of similar colour-coding. A week later Hornett went with a friend to the same branch and entered using a key (the evidence was inconclusive concerning where the key came from). They retrieved the lock combination from the mini-safe and then found a manual for the locked ATMs (helpfully) sitting on a nearby shelf. They successfully opened the lock and stole the money inside. Hornett resigned from his job shortly thereafter and over the course of the next two and a half years he and his friend committed a series of similar thefts in 11 Royal Bank branches. They stole over $1 million in total. Some of these branches were not serviced by Intercon and no key was used. Hornett and his accomplice later confessed, pleaded guilty, and served their sentences. The Royal Bank sued Intercon on the basis of vicarious liability.

Relevant Issue

Whether the employer was vicariously liable for the thefts committed by Hornett.

Decision

The court found that Intercon was not vicariously liable for Hornett's actions. Intercon did not authorize him to be on Royal Bank's premises when not responding to an alarm or when off-duty. Although Hornett's employment may have given him the idea to steal from the ATMs, it did not provide him with the means. Therefore, his conduct was not sufficiently connected to his employment to make his employer vicariously liable. In making its determination, the court also considered the following factors:

- the wrongful conduct did not further the employer's interests;
- there was not a great deal of power conferred on Hornett; and
- the bank was vulnerable because of its own negligence—there were gaps in its security systems, the combinations to the ATM locks were usually retrievable, and the ATM manual was located beside the ATMs.

Many of the cases where an employer has been found vicariously liable for the actions of its employees have related to intoxication. The employer's responsibility is greatest when it serves alcohol to an employee at a work-related event. However, it may also be liable if it is aware that an employee is intoxicated and takes no steps to protect the employee and others when it might have done so. In *Jacobsen v. Nike Canada Ltd.*, the employer was found liable after it served alcohol to an employee it knew would be driving home.

CASE IN POINT

Employer Liable for Employee's Impaired Driving

Jacobsen v. Nike Canada Ltd., 1996 CanLII 3429 (BCSC)

Facts

The employer, Nike, asked the 19-year-old employee, Jacobsen, to bring his vehicle to an annual trade show to transport merchandise and equipment. The show took many hours to set up, and around 7:00 p.m. and again at 8:30 p.m., the project manager brought beer to the crew. Members of the crew—including Jacobsen—were told not to consume more than they could handle, but when they were finished for the night, neither the foreman nor the project manager assessed their ability to drive home. After leaving work, Jacobsen stopped at another pub, where he consumed several more drinks. While driving home, he was involved in an accident that rendered him a quadriplegic. He sued his employer for failing in its duty of care to him.

Relevant Issue

Whether the employer was liable to the employee for negligence in these circumstances.

Decision

The British Columbia Supreme Court found the employer 75 percent liable and Jacobsen 25 percent liable for an award of approximately $2.5 million in total damages. It based its decision on several factors. The employer required Jacobsen to bring his car to work and therefore knew he would be driving home. By providing him with unlimited amounts of alcohol on the job, the employer failed in its duty to provide a safe work environment. It should have monitored Jacobsen's alcohol consumption and taken steps to prevent him from driving while impaired.

John v. Flynn presents a contrasting situation. In *John*, the Ontario Court of Appeal reversed a lower court's decision by finding that the employer was not liable where it was unaware that the employee was drinking on its premises.

CASE IN POINT

Employer Not Liable Despite Knowledge of Employee's Alcohol Abuse

John v. Flynn, 2001 CanLII 2985 (Ont. CA)

Facts

Flynn worked in the employer's forge department. One night, he drank for several hours before reporting for his overnight shift. During his breaks, he drank in his truck in the employer's parking lot, and he continued drinking after his shift before he drove home. Shortly after he got home, he went out again. While driving with an open beer bottle between his legs, he was involved in an accident in which the plaintiff, John, was seriously injured. At trial, the jury found Flynn 70 percent responsible and the employer 30 percent responsible for the plaintiff's damages. The employer appealed.

Relevant Issue

Whether the employer was vicariously liable to the plaintiff for the actions of its employee.

Decision

The Ontario Court of Appeal found that the employer was not liable. The employer neither provided Flynn with liquor nor knew that he was drinking on its premises during his breaks. When the accident occurred, Flynn was not at work, was not going to or leaving work, and was not travelling during working hours. An employer's duty of care does not extend to all members of the driving public who might come into contact with its employees.

The court acknowledged that the employer was aware that drinking occurred in its parking lot because it found empty beer bottles there. It also knew that Flynn had a substance abuse problem; he had participated in its employee assistance program and signed a "last chance agreement" some years before, wherein he agreed to abstain from alcohol consumption. However, the employer had no duty to monitor his compliance with this agreement. To hold the employer liable to a third party in these circumstances would discourage employers from setting up employee assistance programs. It was Flynn's responsibility to comply with the agreement, not the employer's duty to monitor it.

In *John*, the employer neither provided alcohol nor condoned its consumption. Employers who provide alcohol at work-related events are in a different legal situation. Consider the case of *Hunt v. Sutton Group Incentive Realty Inc.* in this regard.

CASE IN POINT

Employer Liable After Serving Alcohol to Employee

Hunt v. Sutton Group Incentive Realty Inc., 2001 CanLII 28027 (Ont. SC)

Facts

Hunt worked as a receptionist and secretary for a real estate sales office. The employer held an afternoon Christmas party on its premises for employees, agents, brokers, and customers. Hunt attended this party both as an employee and as a guest. Guests served themselves from an open bar, and no one was designated to monitor alcohol consumption.

After helping with the cleanup, Hunt went to a nearby pub with some co-workers at 6:30 p.m. She left the pub at approximately 8:00 p.m. At 9:45 p.m., she was involved in a car accident while driving home. The roads were slippery, and she appears to have slid into the opposite lane, where she was hit by an oncoming vehicle. Blood samples showed that she was driving with levels of alcohol in excess of the legal limit. Hunt sued both the employer and the pub for negligence in failing to fulfill their duty of care to her.

Relevant Issue

Whether the employer was in breach of its duty of care to the employee.

Decision

The trial judge found Hunt 75 percent responsible for the accident, and the pub and the employer 25 percent responsible for damages, which were assessed at $1,124,916. The employer knew or ought to have known that Hunt was intoxicated and intended to drive; it should have taken steps to protect her. The employer did not adequately discharge its duty of care to her by offering a cab to its employees generally or offering to drive her home. It should have ensured that Hunt did not drive herself home by taking her car keys or insisting that she take a cab. The employer should have foreseen or anticipated that some employees would stop for a drink on the way home.

The employer appealed this verdict and the Ontario Court of Appeal ordered a new trial on the basis that the trial judge failed to consider evidence that suggested that the employee was not intoxicated when she left the party. However, the case underscores the need for an employer to exercise caution when alcohol is served at employer-sponsored events. It may be prudent to make company functions alcohol-free events. If alcohol is served, an employer should consider adopting some of the following measures:

1. Limit alcohol intake by providing a small number of drink tickets to each guest.
2. Hire professional servers and instruct them to refuse to serve alcohol to anyone who appears to be intoxicated.
3. Serve meals or appetizers with alcohol.
4. Provide free transportation from office parties by means of taxi vouchers, and insist that guests use them.

5. Provide designated drivers.
6. Keep contact numbers of employees' family members.
7. Appoint people to monitor alcohol consumption.

One emerging area of potential vicarious liability for employers relates to the use of hand-held electronic devices by employees while driving. Assume that an employee gets into an accident while performing work duties and evidence shows that she was using, for example, a cellphone at the time. Just as an employer can be liable for allowing employees to drive impaired from a work event, employers can now be liable for letting employees use a cellphone for business purposes while driving (Zinn, 2008, p. 4). Those injured could sue the employer, as well as the driver, where the employee is acting in the course of employment, including checking voicemail, texting, or contacting the office.

Although there have not yet been any decided cases in Canada in this area, in the United States employers have been held vicariously liable as a result of car accidents caused by employees using mobile devices. In *Yoon v. Wagner*, a Virginia lawyer accidentally struck and killed a 15-year-old girl while allegedly speaking to a client on her cellphone. Following a jury trial, the court awarded the plaintiffs $1.9 million. The defendant lawyer lost her job and served one year in jail. Her employer was held vicariously liable and settled for an undisclosed amount.

FYI

Ontario Bans Use of Electronic Devices While Driving

A 2003 study by the University of Utah found that people are as impaired when they talk on a cellphone while driving as they are when they drive intoxicated at the legal blood alcohol limit (Strayer et al., 2006).

In response to growing safety concerns, on October 26, 2009, Ontario became the fourth province to pass a law that bans the use of cellphones and similar electronic devices while driving. Bill 118, *Countering Distracted Driving and Promoting Green Transportation Act, 2009* prohibits driving a motor vehicle while holding or using a hand-held wireless communication device (such as a cellphone or smartphone) or an entertainment device such as an MP3 player. It also bans driving if the display screen of a television, computer, DVD player, or other device in the vehicle is visible to the driver.

There are a few exceptions to this prohibition such as where the device is in hands-free mode (for example, Bluetooth) or where the device is a global positioning navigation or collision avoidance system. The rules also do not apply to emergency vehicles such as ambulances, fire department vehicles, or police vehicles, or to drivers using their cellphone to call emergency services.

A driver who breaches the Act may be fined from up to $500. In addition, a careless driving conviction can result in six demerit points, a fine of up to $2,000 and/or up to six months in jail.

Although the focus of the legislation is the driver of the vehicle, many employers will be affected by the ban. This is especially true for employers whose employees are regularly on the road as part of their job, such as truckers or travelling sales representatives.

In light of the above, Ontario employers should take every reasonable step to ensure that employees comply with the province's ban on the use of cellphones and similar electronic devices while driving. This law generally makes it illegal to use cellphones and most other hand-held personal electronic devices with display screens while behind the wheel of a moving vehicle. Employees should be educated about the dangers of driving with such distractions and about the requirements of the legislation. A workplace policy should also be developed. Such policies may expressly prohibit any use of wireless communication or electronic devices while driving and require the driver to pull over to take or make any calls (Fitzgibbon and Zavitz, 2009, p. 5). Others may allow for the use of hands-free devices where necessary, with the employer providing the required equipment and training for hands-free use. These policies must be strictly monitored and enforced.

REFERENCES

Bazley v. Curry. [1999] 2 SCR 534.

Bell, Sabine. Motivation a Goal of Progressive Discipline. *Canadian HR Reporter*. May 31, 2010, p. 16.

Bennett v. Sears Canada Inc. 2012 ONCA 344; OJ no. 2288 (SCJ).

Bill 118, *Countering Distracted Driving and Promoting Green Transportation Act, 2009*. SO 2009, c. 4.

Bowes, Barbara. Dressing for Success—Not Stress. *Canadian HR Reporter*. May 21, 2012, p. 1. http://www.legacybowes .com/images/stories/PDF/Dressingforsuccess.pdf.

Burkett, Megan. A Handbook for Handbooks: Tips for Ensuring Employee Handbooks Are Effective, Legal and up to Date. *Canadian HR Reporter*. January 14, 2013, p. 12.

Callocchia, Fiorella. Rehabilitating Underperformers. *Financial Post*. April 1, 2010. http://www.financialpost .com/executive/hr/story.html?id=2754213.

Carscallen v. FRI Corp. 2006 CanLII 31723 (Ont. CA); 2005 CanLII 20815 (Ont. SC).

Catenacci, Christina. Recent Case Clarifies Vicarious Liability of the Employer for Wrongful Employee Acts. *HRinfodesk—Canadian Payroll and Employment Law News*. October 2006. http://www.hrinfodesk.com/ articles/vicariousliabilitywrongulacts.htm.

Channe, Bonnea. Update on Constructive Dismissal: Is It Sufficient for Employers to Provide Reasonable Notice of a Fundamental Change? *What's New in HR Law*. May 2012. Filion Wakely Thorup Angeletti. http://filion.on.ca/ uploads/ckeditor/attachment_files/125/Kafka.pdf.

Daley v. Depco International Inc. 2004 CanLII 11310 (Ont. SC).

Deep Pockets Make a Prime Target. *Canadian Employment Law Today*. Issue no. 435, April 13, 2005, p. 3406.

Dusti, Courtney. HR 101: Document, Document, Document: How to Properly Handle Employee Discipline Reports. *HR Professional*. Volume 30, no. 2, February 2013, p. 56.

Echlin, Randall, and Christine Thomlinson. *For Better or For Worse: A Practical Guide to Canadian Employment Law*, 3rd ed. Toronto: Canada Law Book, 2011.

Farahani, Sheri. Employee Use of Blogging and Social Networking Sites: Understanding and Managing Threats to Employers. Presented at the Law Society of Upper Canada Six-Minute Employment Lawyer 2009 program, June 17, 2009, Toronto.

Fitzgibbon, Michael P., and Kate A. Zavitz. Employers Impacted by Cellphone Ban for Drivers. *Canadian Employment Law Today*. Issue no. 536, June 17, 2009, p. 4.

Foulon, Chris. Amending Contracts of Existing Staff. *Canadian Employment Law Today*. Issue no. 383, February 19, 2003, p. 2990.

Foulon, Chris. Finding the Disciplinary Middle Ground. *Canadian Employment Law Today*. Issue no. 506, March 26, 2008, p. 4.

Gibson, Colin. Ask an Expert: An Employer's Right to Seek Medical Information. *Canadian Employment Law Today*. Issue no. 452, January 4, 2006, p. 3540.

Gilbert, Douglas, Brian Burkett, and Moira McCaskill. *Canadian Labour and Employment Law for the US Practitioner*. Washington, DC: Bureau of National Affairs, 2000.

Gupta, Neena. Do Employers Have the Right to Suspend Staff? *Canadian Employment Law Today*. Issue no. 384, March 5, 2003, p. 2995.

Haldane v. Shelbar Enterprises Limited. 1999 CanLII 9248 (Ont. CA), 46 OR (3d) 206.

Hunt v. Sutton Group Incentive Realty Inc. 2001 CanLII 28027 (Ont. SC), [2001] OJ no. 374 (SCJ); reversed by 2002 CanLII 45019 (Ont. CA), 60 OR (3d) 665.

Intercon Not Liable for $1 Million Robber. *Canadian Employment Law Today*. Issue no. 453, January 18, 2006, p. 3547.

Israel, Peter. Employer Responsibility for Alcohol. *Canadian Employment Law Today*. Issue no. 385, March 19, 2003, p. 3004.

Israel, Peter. Ten Steps to Manage Employee Performance Problems. *Canadian Employment Law Today*. Issue no. 379, December 11, 2002, p. 2957.

Israel, Peter. The Case for a Policy Manual: It Causes More Good Than Harm. *Canadian Employment Law Today*. Issue no. 389, May 14, 2003, p. 3037.

Israel, Peter, and Chris Foulon. How to Create a Sound Progressive Discipline Policy. *Canadian Employment Law Today*. Issue no. 383, February 19, 2003, p. 2989.

Israel, Peter, and Chris Foulon. How to Implement an Employment Contract. *Canadian Employment Law Today*. Issue no. 391, June 11, 2003, p. 3053.

Jacobsen v. Nike Canada Ltd. 1996 CanLII 3429 (BCSC), 133 DLR (4th) 377.

Jakibchuk, Adrian, and Matthew Badrov. Crossing the Line with Off-Duty Online Posts. *Canadian Employment Law Today*. March 20, 2013, p. 1. http://www.sherrardkuzz .com/pdf/eCELT_March_20_2013.pdf.

John Doe v. Avalon East School Board. 2004 NLTD 239.

John v. Flynn. 2001 CanLII 2985 (Ont. CA), 54 OR (3d) 774.

Kafka v. Allstate Insurance Company of Canada. 2012 ONSC 1035.

Kohler Canada Co. v. Porter. 2002 CanLII 49614 (Ont. SC).

Leiper, Pamela, and Christina Hall. User-Friendly Employee Handbooks. *Workplace News*. November/December 2006, p. 14.

Levitt, Howard. Be Clear over Changes to Employment. *National Post*. February 11, 2009. Levitt & Grosman LLP. http://www.levittgrosman.com/resources/articles/be-clear-over-changes-to-employment.

Milne, Catherine. *Canadian Forms & Precedents: Employment*. Volume 1, p. 3-1. Markham, ON: LexisNexis Canada, 2005

Mitchell, Tim. Ask an Expert: Employment Standards: Delaying or Cancelling a Promised Raise. *Canadian Employment Law Today*. Issue no. 552, March 10, 2010, p. 2.

Nieuwland, Hendrik. Changing Employment Contracts. *HR Professional*. October/November 2008, p. 21.

O'Donohue, M. Christine, and Michael W. Kerr. When Termination Is Not an Option: How to Change Terms of Employment Post Wronko. Presented at the Law Society of Upper Canada Six-Minute Employment Lawyer 2009 program, June 17, 2009, Toronto, p. 7-1.

Personal Health Information Protection Act. SO 2004, c. 3.

Pugen, Daniel. Your Organization Needs a Social Media Policy. *Ontario Employer Advisor*. September 16, 2013. http://www.ontarioemployerlaw.com/2013/09/16/drafting-a-social-media-policy.

Reininger v. Unique Personnel Canada Inc. [2002] OJ no. 2826, 21 CCEL (3d) 278 (SCJ).

Royal Bank of Canada v. Intercon Security Ltd. 2005 CanLII 40376 (Ont. SC).

Rudner, Stuart. Changing the Employment Contract. *Canadian Employment Law Today*. Issue no. 399, October 15, 2003, p. 3115.

Rudner, Stuart. How to Amend an Employment Contract. *Canadian Employment Law Today*. Issue no. 400, October 29, 2003, p. 3123.

Rudner, Stuart. If You Can't Fire Him, Can He Be Suspended? *Canadian Employment Law Today*. Issue no. 412, April 28, 2004, p. 3219.

Rudner, Stuart. When a Plan Comes Together. *Canadian Employment Law Today*. Issue no. 567, October 20, 2010, p. 3.

Saint-Cyr, Yosie. Relying on Breach of Policy to Discipline Employees. February 23, 2012. First Reference Talks. http://blog.firstreference.com/2012/02/23/relying-on-breach-of-policy-to-discipline-employees.

Seale, Donna. The Dangers of Facebook in the Workplace. September 13, 2007. http://donnaseale.ca/the-dangers-of-facebook-in-the-workplace.

Sherrard Kuzz LLP. Hands Off! Ontario Bans Use of Electronic Devices While Driving. *Management Counsel: Employment and Labour Law Update*. Volume VIII, no. 4, August 2009, p. 1. http://www.sherrardkuzz.com/pdf/Vol_VIII_4.pdf.

Sinclair, Alex. Ontario Court of Appeal Holds Employer to Misinterpretation of Benefits Plan by Human Resources Representative. *What's New in HR Law*. September 2012. Filion Wakely Thorup Angeletti. http://filion.on.ca/uploads/ckeditor/attachment_files/236/Bennett.pdf.

Smith, Jeffrey R. Cellphone Ban Opens Door to Liability. *Canadian Employment Law Today*. Issue no. 534, May 20, 2009, p. 1.

Strayer, David L., Frank S. Drews, and Denis Crouch. A Comparison of the Cell Phone Driver and the Drunk Driver. *Human Factors*. Volume 48, no. 2, 2006. http://www.hfes.org/web/pubpages/celldrunk.pdf.

Techform Products Ltd. v. Wolda. 2001 CanLII 8604 (Ont. CA), 56 OR (3d) 1.

Thiffeault, Stéphane. Personal Health Information Act and Hours of Work. *Employee & Labour Relations Bulletin*. February 2005. McMillan Binch LLP. http://www.mcmillan.ca/Files/Health_and_Hours_of_Work_0205.pdf.

Thomlinson, Chris. A Temporary Layoff Can't Be a Constructive Dismissal? *RT Blog*. May 15, 2013. Rubin Thomlinson LLP. http://www.rubinthomlinson.com/blog/a-temporary-layoff-cant-be-a-constructive-dismissal.

Trites v. Renin Corp. 2013 ONSC 2715.

Westlake, Christine. Can an Employer Lay-Off an Employee Without a Term in the Employment Contract to That Effect? *Employment Law Blog*. November 6, 2013. Koskie Minsky LLP. http://blog.kmlaw.ca/can-an-employer-lay-off.

Williams, Laura. Reduce Disability Costs with Meaningful Medical Information. *HR Professional*. Volume 29, no. 3, March/April 2012, p. 17.

Wilson, Peter, and Allison Taylor. *The Corporate Counsel Guide to Employment Law*, 2nd ed. Aurora, ON: Canada Law Book, 2003.

Wronko v. Western Inventory Service Ltd. 2008 ONCA 327.

Yoon v. Wagner. United States District Court, Central District of Illinois, Urbana Division, action #05-2122.

Zinn, Russel. Employees Driving Under the Influence—Of a Cellphone. *Canadian Employment Law Today*. Issue no. 503, February 13, 2008, p. 4.

REVIEW AND DISCUSSION QUESTIONS

1. Describe the legal position of both parties to an employment contract when an employer wishes to make an amendment after the employee has started work.

2. What are some of the benefits of conducting regular employee performance appraisals?

3. What steps can an employer take to ensure that its policy manual becomes and remains part of the employment contract?

4. What is condonation? How can it be avoided?

5. Workplace romances, even where they are consensual relationships between co-workers, can create some difficult issues in the workplace. From a strictly legal perspective, employers may want to discourage workplace romances but from a practical point of view, it is virtually impossible to prevent them. Discuss some of the risks that a workplace romance poses from various perspectives—to the couple involved, to co-workers, and to the employer. Is a policy on workplace romances a good idea and, if so, what should it include? Are there any disadvantages to having such a policy?

6. The employer is a college campus that has several establishments that serve alcohol, such as pubs and bars. If an employee consumes alcohol during lunch at one of the campus bars and then returns to work and injures someone or gets into an accident, would the employer bear the responsibility for any resulting loss or damages? Explain your answer.

7. The employer, Yummy Biscuits Inc., has decided that it needs to make significant changes to its benefits package to cut costs in an increasingly competitive marketplace. Yummy Biscuits wants to know the best way to introduce the changes so that employees will respond positively and so there won't be any legal problems. It has approximately 50 employees and there is no union. How would you advise this employer?

8. Systems Cycle hired John, an experienced computer programmer, in its IT department. Shortly after being hired, John used Systems Cycle's computer to register a domain name similar to that of his former employer and he redirected traffic from the new domain to a pornographic website. The former employer sued John and Systems Cycle, arguing that the latter should be vicariously liable for John's actions. How do you think a court would rule in this case? Support your answer.

9. What happens if an employer tells an employee that he will be receiving a raise on a certain date but then, because of changed economic circumstances, changes its mind and does not give him the raise?

10. After several verbal warnings about her lack of time management skills, Bev was placed on a performance improvement plan (PIP) that outlined detailed performance objectives and provided timelines for fulfilling those objectives. The PIP was framed as a "last chance agreement," and Bev was aware that her job was in jeopardy when she signed it—without improvement, she would be terminated. The PIP called for several managers to work with her to help her improve her performance. It was a busy time of year, however, and the managers did not follow up until several months later when, noting that there had been no improvement in Bev's performance, Bev was fired for cause on the ground of poor performance.

    Do you think the employer had just cause to dismiss Bev?

11. Your employer is concerned that some of the clothing its employees are wearing, especially in the summer, suggests a lack of professionalism. The employer has asked you to implement a dress code policy. What are some of the considerations you should keep in mind in addressing this issue?

12. What kinds of issues can or should be covered in an organization's social media policy?

PART IV

The End of the Employment Relationship and Beyond

Part IV explores the legal implications of the many different ways in which an employment relationship can come to an end. Chapter 12 examines resignation and retirement. Subsequent chapters consider the implications of terminations initiated by employers. Chapter 13 looks at dismissal based on "just cause" under the common law. Chapter 14 reviews the requirements under the *Employment Standards Act, 2000* related to temporary and indefinite layoffs and terminations. Chapter 15 deals with common law requirements when dismissal is without just cause, while Chapter 16 examines employee obligations that survive the end of the employment relationship.

Generally speaking, the common law distinguishes between two kinds of dismissals: dismissals with just cause and dismissals without just cause—that is, wrongful dismissals. This distinction is an "all or nothing" proposition. If an employer cannot establish just cause for dismissing an employee—which is usually difficult to do—the employee has been wrongfully dismissed and is entitled to all the legal remedies that are available in the circumstances. On the other hand, if an employer can establish just cause for dismissing an employee, it can dismiss the employee without notice or pay in lieu of notice.

Chapter 13 considers issues related to dismissals for just cause, including the types of misconduct that constitute just cause under the common law. Chapter 15 explores dismissals, including constructive dismissals, in the absence of just cause and considers the remedies available to employees in these circumstances. It also looks at ways in which an employer can minimize the possibility of wrongful dismissal lawsuits.

An employer that dismisses an employee without just cause must consider both statutory and common law reasonable notice requirements. In most circumstances, the notice period considered reasonable under the common law is more generous than the notice period required under the *Employment Standards Act, 2000*. However, although an employer and employee may not agree to terms that are less advantageous to the employee than those set out in the Act, the parties may contract out of common law notice requirements by specifying an alternative notice period in their employment contract. In this case, if the contractual notice period at least matches the notice requirements in the Act, the employer need provide only the amount of notice specified in the contract.

Chapter 16 looks at employee obligations that survive the end of the employment relationship. These obligations include the common law duty not to disclose confidential information or, in some circumstances, not to solicit customers of the former employer.

Resignation and Retirement

12

LEARNING OUTCOMES

After completing this chapter, you will be able to:

- Explain why an employer should formally accept an employee's resignation in writing.

- Understand why a resignation must be voluntary and unequivocal.

- State why an employer should not dismiss an employee who gives notice of resignation.

- Explain an employee's obligation to provide notice of resignation.

- Understand the implications of the elimination of mandatory retirement at age 65 in Ontario.

Introduction

Two of the ways that the employment relationship may come to an end are when the employee resigns or retires. Although they may seem, and usually are, straightforward events, there are some potential legal issues that an employer should be aware of.

Resignation

Resignation Should Be Formally Accepted

Absent coercion, a letter of resignation is typically binding on an employee. However, there are some cases that suggest that an employee may retract a written resignation up to the time that the employer formally communicates its acceptance of the letter. It is therefore good practice for an employer who wishes to accept a letter of resignation to send a letter to the employee confirming its acceptance of the employee's letter as soon as possible after receiving it. This generally prevents an employee who changes his mind after submitting a letter of resignation from trying to argue that the letter is not binding because the employer has not formally accepted it.

Resignation Must Be Voluntary

Generally speaking, an employee who gives an employer notice of resignation is not legally entitled to **wrongful dismissal** damages. In that case, the only amounts owing to the employee are outstanding wages and vacation pay. However, to be valid, the resignation must be voluntarily and freely given. For example, if an employer gives an employee a "choice" between resigning or being dismissed, the courts usually find that the resignation is not voluntary, and the employer is obliged to provide pay in lieu of reasonable notice or show just cause for the dismissal. The legal test is an objective one: would a reasonable person believe that the employee resigned?

An employee also may allege that she resigned from her job because the employer changed a fundamental term of her employment contract. If a court determines that a reasonable person would believe that the employee resigned in response to such a contractual breach, the employee is entitled to damages for constructive dismissal. (See the discussion in Chapter 15 under the heading "Constructive Dismissal.")

Inferring Resignation from an Employee's Conduct

Resignation may be inferred from an employee's conduct. For example, if an employee expresses the intention to stop work and then returns a uniform and keys or tells co-workers that he will not be back, the employer generally may conclude that the employee has resigned. To ensure that the resignation becomes binding, the employer should send the employee a letter formally accepting it.

Courts will not infer resignation when an employee's words are vague or equivocal. For example, if an employee tells an employer that she plans to leave as soon as she can or that she is looking for another job and cannot wait to leave, the courts will not find that she voluntarily resigned. To be effective, a resignation must be "clear and unequivocal": both the employee's subjective intention to resign and the employee's words and actions, objectively viewed, must support a finding of resignation (David Brown, 2013).

Pollock v. First Heritage Financial and *Gilbert and Tandet Transport Inc.* illustrate the requirement that an employee's intention be clear and unequivocal before an employer can treat an employee's conduct as a resignation.

CASE IN POINT

Notice of Resignation Must Be Clear

Pollock v. First Heritage Financial, 2002 BCSC 782

Facts

Six employees of a financial planning firm were unhappy with proposed changes to their employment, including changes to their compensation program. They wrote a memo to their employer asking for a meeting to discuss the matter. When the employer's representative refused, they sent a second memo stating that they interpreted his refusal as an indication that he did not want them to report for work under the existing terms of employment and that, unless they received written notice to the contrary, they would "proceed accordingly." The employer wrote to the employees individually, indicating that he accepted their resignation. He told them to return their keys and expense account cards, and they were escorted out of the building.

Relevant Issue

Whether the plaintiffs resigned or were wrongfully dismissed and therefore entitled to pay in lieu of reasonable notice.

Decision

The court found that the employees were wrongfully dismissed and were entitled to pay in lieu of notice. The memo was not an unequivocal notice of resignation; rather, the employees stated that they intended to continue working under the existing terms of employment. A reasonable person in the employer's position would not conclude that the employees were resigning from their jobs. The court awarded the employees, who had between two and six years of service, between four and eight months' pay in lieu of notice for wrongful dismissal.

CASE IN POINT

Employee Must Form an Intention to Resign

Gilbert and Tandet Transport Inc., [2002] CLAD no. 196 (Arb. Bd.)

Facts

After seven years of employment, Gilbert was temporarily laid off. During the layoff, he found a part-time job. On June 5, 2000, the employer issued a recall notice, which stated that if Gilbert failed to return by June 9, 2000, he would be treated as having resigned. Gilbert left several urgent telephone messages with the employer asking whether he would be returning to part-time or full-time employment. He needed to know this because he didn't want to give up his new job for another part-time position. The employer returned his calls but was unable to reach him. Later that month, he received notice that the employer had processed his resignation. The employee then filed a complaint against his former employer for statutory termination and severance pay.

Relevant Issue

Whether the employee resigned or was dismissed.

Decision

The arbitrator found that Gilbert was dismissed. He never formed an intention to resign because he never had enough information to make that decision. The employer's letter of recall that stated that failure to attend the workplace on June 9 would be treated as resignation was not sufficient to establish Gilbert's intention to resign. Gilbert was therefore entitled to statutory termination and severance pay.

Even where an employee utters the words "I quit" or words to that effect, but does so while clearly distressed, the employer should not treat that as a resignation without allowing the employee a cooling-off period. In *Robinson v. Team Cooperheat-MQS Canada Inc.*, the plaintiff was a long-service employee who became very upset during a meeting when he was unexpectedly accused by several of his staff of being "a bully." He repeatedly stated that if the accusations were not withdrawn, he would be "forced to resign." The next morning Robinson met with his boss and tried to retract his resignation. His boss refused. Robinson sued, arguing that he had been wrongfully dismissed, and the court agreed. The court found that Robinson had not expressed a clear and unequivocal intention to resign. Moreover, even if he had said, "I quit," this would not necessarily constitute a valid resignation. A resignation given when emotions are running high can be withdrawn later, when emotions have cooled off. The court found that a reasonable employer would not have concluded that Robinson had quit. Robinson was awarded one year's salary and costs in damages.

As the *Robinson* case shows, employers that receive a resignation from an employee who is emotionally upset should realize that it may not be binding. They need to consider all of the circumstances surrounding it. Was it expressed unambiguously? Was the resignation put into writing? Was it accepted verbally or in writing? Did the employee try to retract the resignation? Are there special circumstances that suggest the employee was under emotional duress at the time? Has the employer already acted in reliance on the resignation? (Levitt, 2009).

Reid v. Stratford General Hospital, below, further underscores the importance of considering the entire context in which a resignation is offered—both before and after it is tendered—in deciding whether or not it is binding. Although this decision may be a bit of an outlier in the extent to which it allowed a retraction, it is worth noting.

CASE IN POINT

Court Sympathetic to Long-Service Employee Who Quit Impulsively

Reid v. Stratford General Hospital, 2007 CanLII 58483 (Ont. SC)

Facts

Reid was an employee with 20 years of service who was under a lot of stress due to personal family issues, as well as workload demands that she believed were unreasonable. After a particularly frustrating day when she had tried, unsuccessfully, to discuss the work-related issues with her boss, she wrote the following resignation letter.

> To All Concerned:
>
> After almost twenty years of dedicated service, it is with deep regret that I feel I must resign from my position as Executive Assistant/Administrative Assistant to the Vice-President, Multi-Site Administration at Stratford General Hospital effective Friday, March 16 at 17:00.
>
> I will be taking my two weeks' notice period as vacation days.
>
> Sincerely,
> Susan Reid

Reid placed this letter, along with her keys, on her supervisor's desk and then left. The next day the employer accepted her resignation in writing. However, before Reid received the employer's letter, she changed her mind and wrote a letter rescinding her resignation, two days after she wrote and submitted her first letter. It began, "The letter of resignation is hereby withdrawn. I have absolutely no intention of resigning from a job in which I have invested 20 years. I am under a Doctor's care and as soon as I am in a position to discuss returning to work, I will be in contact with you." However, the employer refused to accept Reid's withdrawal of her resignation. Reid, contending that this refusal constituted termination of her employment without notice, sued for wrongful dismissal. The employer argued that it was under no obligation to accept this withdrawal, because the plaintiff's resignation was given freely and voluntarily.

Relevant Issue

Whether the employer's refusal to accept the employee's withdrawal of her resignation constituted termination without notice.

Decision

The court found for the employee. Although the initial resignation letter conveyed a clear and unequivocal intention to resign, Reid gave notice that she was withdrawing her resignation before the defendant had relied upon it to its detri-

ment. In finding for the employee, the court referenced the power imbalance that "informs virtually all facets of the employment relationship" (*Wallace v. United Grain Growers Ltd.*, para. 92). The court noted that the plaintiff was a valued employee who, during a period of emotional vulnerability due to a series of personal setbacks, came to see resignation as the only course of action available to her. In contrast, the court had more difficulty understanding the supervisor's response, noting that he made no attempt to contact the plaintiff to secure an explanation for her abrupt and unexpected departure.

It should be noted that, although in *Reid* the court found that the "entire context" pointed to the employee not being bound by her resignation, in cases where the resignation decision appears to be well thought out and not impulsive, the opposite result has been reached. These cases are highly fact-specific (Kent Employment Law, 2014). Therefore, where the circumstances of a "quit" are ambiguous in any way, the employer may choose to ask the employee to clarify her intentions. As noted above, if the resignation is given while the employee is upset, an employer should be prepared for a possible retraction that may be found to be valid. Finally, if the employee tries to retract her resignation, the employer should hear the employee out and seek expert legal advice.

Dismissing a Resigning Employee

Sometimes an employer who receives advance notice of an employee's resignation does not want the employee to work during the notice period because, for example, the employee may have access to sensitive business information or have extensive contact with customers. However, the employer must be cautious in these circumstances. If the employer reacts by dismissing the employee, it has effectively fired that individual and may be liable for wrongful dismissal damages. The damages will likely be limited to the notice period provided by the employee on the principle that no wages are owing after the resignation date. However, where the employee has no other position to go to, there is a small risk that the employer will be held liable for full wrongful dismissal damages. Therefore, an employer that does not want a resigning employee to continue working during the notice period should accept the employee's resignation and advise the employee that he will be paid throughout the notice period but should not attend work. This subtle but important distinction may avoid potentially costly litigation.

Wrongful Resignation

Unlike several other provinces, Ontario has no legislated requirement that an employee provide advance notice of resignation except in special circumstances that are described in Chapter 14 under the headings "Mass Termination Requirements" and "Severance Pay." However, under the common law, just as an employer has an implied obligation to provide reasonable notice of termination or pay in lieu, the employee has a reciprocal obligation to provide reasonable notice of resignation. Reasonable notice of resignation can range from two weeks to significantly longer. The length depends on the employee's duties, the expected length of time it will take the employer to recruit and train a replacement, the timing of the resignation in relation to the employer's peak periods, and the custom in the workplace and industry (Sherrard Kuzz LLP, 2012). In practice, employers rarely sue employees for failure to provide reasonable notice because in most situations it is difficult for an employer to show that it suffered damage as a result of the employee's failure. It usually takes an employer less time to replace an employee than it takes a dismissed employee to find new employment.

However, there are situations in which an employee's specialized expertise or key role in an organization will lead a court to award damages to an employer for wrongful resignation. In *Tree Savers International Ltd. v. Savoy*, for example, two employees who left their employer on only two weeks' notice to set up a competing business were held liable for failing to provide reasonable notice of resignation. Damages, which included the cost of retraining and replacing employees on short notice, totalled $73,100. More recently, in *GasTOPS Ltd. v. Forsyth*, four software executives who quit and started a competing business using the former employer's confidential software information were ordered to pay their former employer almost $20 million for, among other things, failure to provide reasonable notice of resignation. The court found that, given all of the circumstances, including the fact that the executives were key employees with technical expertise and intimate knowledge of the business, the employer was entitled to 10 months' notice of resignation, rather than the two weeks each employee provided. The court noted that during that 10-month period they would have continued to owe the employer a duty of loyalty and good faith, thereby preventing them from starting their own company and competing with their former employer within that period. This decision was upheld on appeal.

It is important to note that if the length of notice being offered by an employee is inadequate, the employer should indicate this—in writing—at the time the notice is offered. Failing to object makes a subsequent claim for greater notice more difficult (Sherrard Kuzz LLP, 2012). In addition, as with a dismissed employee, an employer has a responsibility to lessen or mitigate its losses—in this case, by attempting to find a replacement for the employee, and it should document these efforts.

To reduce uncertainty, an employer may choose to include a policy in its employment manual or to negotiate a term in the individual contract of employment that sets out the notice of resignation that an employee is required to provide. In most cases, this is a period of approximately two weeks and written notice is required. However, as seen in the *Tree Savers* and *GasTOPS* decisions, the period can be much longer. In *Blackberry Limited v. Marineau-Mes* the court upheld a six-month notice of resignation requirement in a senior employee's employment contract. The employee had argued that the lengthy notice period amounted to a non-compete covenant. However, the court found that such a lengthy notice period was not equivalent to a comparably long non-competition agreement because the employee continued to be paid and the notice requirement was fair and standard in the industry.

Exit Interviews

Interviewing employees who resign may be useful in a number of ways. It can provide an employer with valuable information, including feedback about why an employee has chosen to leave. These insights can be used to identify causes of turnover and to develop improved retention programs. They may also identify issues that, left unaddressed, could lead to harassment or discrimination claims. As well, it provides an opportunity to gather "competitive intelligence" on what other companies are offering their employees (DiFlorio, 2012). To encourage an open discussion, someone other than the employee's direct supervisor should be involved. At an exit interview, an employer can ensure that all company property is returned and that the employee understands the outstanding legal obligations of both parties. Such obligations might include the employee's duty not to disclose confidential business information and the employer's duty to provide the employee's record of employment for employment insurance purposes.

Retirement

Abolition of Mandatory Retirement at Age 65

Although public and most private pension plans are based on a retirement age of 65, there has never been legislation requiring employees to retire at age 65 in Canada. However, until 2006, Ontario law allowed, but did not require, employers to have mandatory retirement policies if the age of retirement was 65 or higher. This resulted from the fact that Ontario's *Human Rights Code* limited protection against age-based discrimination in employment to people between the ages of 18 and 64. In effect, as long as the employer had a clear, consistently enforced, and properly communicated mandatory retirement policy, it could require an employee to retire at age 65.

However, in December 2006 the Ontario legislature removed the ceiling on the Code's definition of age completely, thereby effectively putting an end to mandatory retirement at age 65 in most workplaces. This brought Ontario into line with a majority of other provinces that had already eliminated mandatory retirement. There are arguments both in favour of and against the abolition of mandatory retirement at age 65. Making retirement a matter of employee choice rather than employer policy, however, raises a number of challenges to human resources practices.

Impact of Abolishing Mandatory Retirement at Age 65

Now that the *Human Rights Code* has been amended to effectively eliminate mandatory retirement at age 65, an Ontario employer is no longer able to maintain a mandatory retirement policy unless it can show that mandatory retirement is a bona fide occupational requirement. Under the test in *Meiorin*, the employer must show not only that the policy is reasonably necessary but also that it is impossible to accommodate the employees affected without creating undue hardship for itself. Very few occupations will be able to satisfy this test.

Without a mandatory retirement policy, employers must accommodate an aging workforce on a case-by-case basis. Although the effects of aging differ, in time they can be expected to influence the ability of many employees to meet the physical and mental demands of their jobs. Because employers have a legal obligation under the *Human Rights Code* to accommodate disabilities—including age-related disabilities— up to the point of undue hardship, the abolition of mandatory retirement will lead to increased demands for accommodation.

Employers also need to reconsider their approach to performance management as it relates to their older workers. Previously, with mandatory retirement policies in place, employers were often willing to accept decreased productivity as employees edged toward their retirement. With the removal of this option, employers now have to use the same approach with older workers that they use with all workers: a consistent and formal performance management program with all relevant documentation.

Employers need to carefully document the reasons for terminating an older employee because, with the elimination of the ceiling on the definition of age in the Code, they face the possibility of both an age discrimination complaint and a claim for damages for wrongful dismissal. Should a human rights tribunal conclude that age was a factor in an employer's decision to dismiss an employee, the employee may be entitled to a significant damages award, including possible reinstatement and/or compensation for lost wages and an award for mental anguish. Typically, anyone who raises a wrongful dismissal complaint will include any allegations of a breach of the Code and will not pursue a separate human rights complaint. This is especially true in light of *Wilson v. Solis Mexican Foods Inc.*, where a court awarded a wrongfully dismissed employee an additional $20,000 in damages for the employer's violation of the Code. At the same time, if an individual receives pay in lieu of notice through a court action, it is very likely that any damages awarded pursuant to a concurrent human rights complaint will be limited to damages for breach of the Code.

As noted above, under the previous law, employers with well-communicated mandatory retirement policies did not need to give employees advance notice that their employment would end when they reached age 65. However, now the common law rules that require an employer to give proper notice of termination, in the absence of just cause, apply to all employees. Employers should also be aware that, because many older employees also have lengthy service with the employer, if an employer terminates an employee who is entitled to receive a separation package upon termination, the amount of money involved may be significant.

The following case of *Filiatrault v. Tri-County Welding Supplies Ltd.* highlights the importance of not making assumptions about an employee's intention to retire, regardless of age.

CASE IN POINT

Age of Mandatory Retirement Truly Gone

Filiatrault v. Tri-County Welding Supplies Ltd., 2013 ONSC 3091

Facts

Paul Filiatrault and his wife Shirley (both in their 80s), as well as their three sons, worked at Tri-County Welding Supplies, which the couple owned. Pursuant to a buyout agreement, Air Liquide purchased Tri-County's shares in 2009 (for around $11 million) and agreed to employ the three sons. After the purchase, Air Liquide issued termination letters to Paul and Shirley. The couple sued for wrongful dismissal, arguing that they were

still actively employed there and had no intention of resigning. Air Liquide countered that, among other things, it was implied in the purchase agreement that the Filiatrault couple would resign or retire when they exercised the option to sell their company.

Relevant Issue

Whether the plaintiffs, both in their 80s, were entitled to receive reasonable notice of termination and therefore wrongful dismissal damages in these circumstances.

Decision

The court found that, despite receiving a lucrative sum for selling their company's shares, the Filiatraults were still entitled to reasonable notice of termination. Although they were in their 80s, the couple were "spirited, clear minded and enthusiastic individuals" who wanted to continue to work: following their termination they sent out resumés to

over 40 companies. The court awarded both Paul and Shirley reasonable notice damages based on 18 months' notice for a total award of $1,161,450. The trial judge stated: "I do not think there is a place in this social reality for an automatic presumption that persons should or would naturally retire on reaching senior age. … [E]mployers should be disinclined to ask a court, where there is no express agreement, to imply such a term in an employment contract based simply on that now time-worn presumption."

Finally, many employers have reviewed their pension and benefit plans to see how they are affected by the abolition of mandatory retirement. Some benefit plans limit benefits to employees over the age of 64. Whether this creates a legal problem depends on the terms of the employment contract or collective agreement. However, the limitation of benefits is not contrary to the Code. This is because, when the Code was changed to remove the age ceiling for age-based discrimination, amendments were also made to provide that the right to equal treatment on the basis of age is not infringed by benefit, pension, superannuation or group insurance plans, or funds that comply with the *Employment Standards Act, 2000*. Although the ESA prohibits employers from discriminating against employees on the basis of age in providing benefits, the definition of "age" means employees aged 18 to 64. As such, the regulations allow, but do not require, employers to extend workplace benefits to employees over 64. Therefore, an employer's ability to discontinue benefits to employees over the age of 64 is subject to the terms of any employment contract or collective agreement (Johnston, 2009, p. 2). Employers are commonly extending medical and dental benefits to 70 years of age, but anything beyond that is rare.

It should be noted that the Ontario Human Rights Tribunal has found that simply making an early retirement incentive available to older workers does not, in and of itself, constitute age discrimination (Ashley Brown, 2013). However, the employer must ensure that the way in which those incentives are presented does not place undue pressure on those eligible to accept. In *Deane v. Ontario (Community Safety and Correctional Services)* an employee was awarded $7,000 for injury to dignity, feelings, and self-respect because her supervisor's actions, while well-intentioned, pressured her into accepting the early retirement option. These actions included multiple meetings and arranging an unsolicited teleconference with two of the supervisor's retired acquaintances to discuss the advantages of retirement. The Tribunal found that these actions amounted to discrimination on the basis of age.

To prevent outcomes such as this, employers should ensure that early retirement offers are presented in a neutral way, focusing on contents and eligibility, not on whether the employee should accept it. Any threats or promises should be avoided. The contact person should be neutral—not the individual's immediate supervisor (Sherrard Kuzz LLP, 2013).

REFERENCES

BlackBerry Limited v. Marineau-Mes. 2014 ONSC 1790.

British Columbia (Public Service Employee Relations Commission) v. BCGSEU. [1999] 3 SCR 3.

Brown, Ashley. Early Retirement Decision Is Employee's Only. *Canadian Employment Law Today*. January 23, 2013, p. 1. http://sherrardkuzz.com/pdf/kuzz_eCELT_jan_2013_retirement.pdf.

Brown, David. "Did He Just Quit?": The Rules on Resignations. *The Barristers' Lounge*. November 18, 2013. http://barristerslounge.wordpress.com/2013/11/18/did-he-just-quit-the-rules-on-resignations.

Deane v. Ontario (Community Safety and Correctional Services). 2012 HRTO 1753.

DiFlorio, Laura. 9 Risks of Neglecting to Conduct Exit Interviews. *Canadian HR Reporter*. March 12, 2012, p. 19.

Echlin, Randall, and Christine Thomlinson. *For Better or For Worse: A Practical Guide to Canadian Employment Law*, 3rd ed. Toronto: Canada Law Book, 2011.

Employment Standards Act, 2000. SO 2000, c. 41.

Filiatrault v. Tri-County Welding Supplies Ltd. 2013 ONSC 3091.

GasTOPS Ltd. v. Forsyth. 2012 ONCA 134.

Gilbert and Tandet Transport Inc. [2002] CLAD no. 196 (Arb. Bd.).

Gilbert, Douglas, Brian Burkett, and Moira McCaskill. *Canadian Labour and Employment Law for the US Practitioner*. Washington, DC: Bureau of National Affairs, 2000.

Gupta, Neena, and Shawn Pulver. Mandatory Retirement Revisited. *Canadian Employment Law Today*. Issue no. 393, July 9, 2003, p. 3070.

Human Rights Code. RSO 1990, c. H.19.

Israel, Peter. Ask an Expert: "Wrongful Resignation." *Canadian Employment Law Today*. Issue no. 379, December 11, 2002, p. 2956.

Johnston, Brian. Human Rights: Cutting Off LTD at 65. *Canadian Employment Law Today*. Issue no. 533, May 6, 2009, p. 2.

Kent Employment Law. Employee Resignations: Not as Straightforward as They Seem. March 18, 2014. http://kentemploymentlaw.com/2014/employee-resignations-straightforward-seem/.

Keyser, John B. Employer's Rights: Key Employee's Duty of Reasonable Notice. September 20, 2012. Keyser Mason Ball LLP. http://www.kmblaw.com/employers-rights-key-employees-duty-of-reasonable-notice.

Levitt, Howard. Resigning Worker Entitled to Cooling-Off Period. March 10, 2009. Lexology. http://www.lexology.com/library/detail.aspx?g=dfc7db55-a5c2-412a-ac03-f298e6d217db.

Mackie, Richard. Ontario Turns Its Sights on Mandatory Retirement. *Globe and Mail*, August 18, 2004, p. A7.

Pollock v. First Heritage Financial. 2002 BCSC 782.

Reid v. Stratford General Hospital. 2007 CanLII 58483 (Ont. SC).

Robinson v. Team Cooperheat-MQS Canada Inc. 2008 ABQB 409, 67 CCEL (3d) 219.

Roher, E., and M. Henry. Age Discrimination in the Workplace. *Canadian Employment Law Today*. Issue no. 410, March 31, 2004, p. 3206.

Sherrard Kuzz LLP. Early Retirement Incentives Are Not Discriminatory. Volume XII, no. 1, February 2013, p. 3. http://www.sherrardkuzz.com/pdf/Vol_XII_1.pdf.

Sherrard Kuzz LLP. Quitting Time. *Management Counsel: Employment and Labour Law Update*. Volume XI, no. 3, June 2012, p. 2. http://www.sherrardkuzz.com/pdf/Vol_XI_3.pdf.

Smith, Jeffrey R. Depressed Employee's Resignation Upheld. Canadian Employment Law Today. April 18, 2012, p. 3. http://www.minkenemploymentlawyers.com/wp-content/uploads/2012/04/eCELT-April-18-2012-19.6-million.pdf.

Smith, Jeffrey R. Family Business Owners Get More Than $1.1 Million for Wrongful Dismissal. *Canadian Employment Law Today*. September 18, 2013. http://www.employmentlawtoday.com/articleview/18851-family-business-owners-get-more-than-11-million-for-wrongful-dismissal.

Tree Savers International Ltd. v. Savoy. 1991 CanLII 3952 (Alta. QB), 37 CCEL 116; var'd. but aff'd. on this point 1992 CanLII 2828 (Alta. CA), 87 DLR (4th) 202.

Wallace v. United Grain Growers Ltd. [1997] 3 SCR 701.

Wilson v. Solis Mexican Foods Inc. 2013 ONSC 5799.

REVIEW AND DISCUSSION QUESTIONS

1. Why should an employer inform an employee in writing of its acceptance of her resignation?

2. What should an employer do if it does not want an employee who has given notice of resignation to continue working during the notice period?

3. How might an employer benefit from an exit interview with a resigning employee?

4. From the point of view of society as a whole, is the elimination of mandatory retirement at age 65 a good idea?

5. You return to your office to find a letter of resignation on your desk from Stuart. This letter indicates that Stuart will be leaving in four weeks' time. You are actually pleased with the resignation because Stuart has been a poor performer for some time. However, you are concerned that his performance will deteriorate even further during the notice period, so you would like Stuart to leave immediately. What should you do?

6. You are an HR consultant. One of your clients, an employer (Joseph), has contacted you about the following situation. He has just finished a performance evaluation meeting with one of his employees, Allan. Allan became very upset during the meeting and at the end of it got up and shouted: "Okay, if that's the way you feel about me, I quit!" Joseph is delighted with the resignation because Allan has been a difficult employee from the time he was hired three years ago, but he wonders whether there's anything he needs to know about the law in this area before he starts hiring a replacement for Allan. Advise Joseph.

7. Janyce, aged 52, had worked at the employer's food market for ten years when a fire destroyed her house. The next day she called her employer, indicating that she did not know when she would be able to return to work. When a month went by without hearing from Janyce, the employer had its payroll department prepare a record of employment (ROE), which indicated that Janyce had "quit" her job. Several weeks later, Janyce was diagnosed with anxiety and depression, stemming from the fire and its surrounding circumstances, and she called the employer for her ROE, because she needed it to claim sick leave employment insurance benefits. When she picked it up, she discovered that the ROE indicated that she had quit her job. Janyce sued the employer for wrongful dismissal. The employer countered that Janyce had resigned.

   Do you think that Janyce was wrongfully dismissed? Support your answer.

Dismissal With Cause 13

LEARNING OUTCOMES

After completing this chapter, you will be able to:

• Differentiate between a good reason for dismissal and just cause for dismissal under the common law.

• Explain the contextual approach to determining just cause for dismissal.

• Understand the elements of procedural fairness in dismissals for just cause.

• Identify specific grounds for just cause, including dishonesty, insolence and insubordination, off-duty conduct, conflict of interest, disobedience, absenteeism, sexual harassment, intoxication, and incompetence.

• Understand related concepts, such as condonation.

Introduction

Generally speaking, under the common law in Canada, an employee may be dismissed without advance notice or pay in lieu if the dismissal is for "just cause." All other terminations require reasonable notice or pay in lieu, unless there is a clearly expressed and enforceable term in an employment contract that establishes an alternative notice requirement.

Under the common law, the term "just cause" has a particular meaning in the context of dismissal: it does not simply mean that an employer had a good reason, such as a need to downsize, for dismissing an employee. The essential legal question is whether an employee breached the employment contract in such a fundamental way that the employer is no longer bound by the common law obligation to provide reasonable notice of termination or pay in lieu of reasonable notice.

This is a very difficult standard for employers to meet, and the existence of just cause is decided on a case-by-case basis. Whether an employer has demonstrated just cause will ultimately be determined by a court, assisted by legal precedent—that is, previous cases involving similar fact situations in which other courts have decided what constitutes just cause. Unfortunately for the parties, this determination is made only after the matter comes before a court in a wrongful dismissal action brought by a dismissed employee. At the time that the employer makes the decision to dismiss the employee, the employer can rarely be certain that the employee's conduct constitutes just cause for dismissal under the common law.

However, by reviewing previous cases that have dealt with misconduct similar to that of the employee, the employer often will be able to get a sense of whether or not it can successfully defend a wrongful dismissal action in a particular situation. Furthermore, an employer can take certain measures, such as using progressive discipline and ensuring procedural fairness, to improve its chances of a successful defence.

Generally speaking, in determining just cause under the common law, the courts apply roughly the same standards as arbitrators apply to unionized workers under the just cause provision found in most collective agreements ("Common-Law Doctrine," 2004, p. 3200). Therefore, where there are few wrongful dismissal decisions that relate to a particular type of misconduct, courts sometimes make reference to relevant arbitration decisions.

Overview of Just Cause Requirements

Onus of Proof

Because the consequence of a finding of just cause—dismissal without notice or pay in lieu of notice—is severe, the courts are reluctant to reach this result. The **onus of proof** is on an employer to show, on a balance of probabilities, that an employee breached an employment contract in a fundamental way. As shown in *Billingsley v. Saint John Shipbuilding Ltd.*, in which the employer alleged illegal drug use at work, an employer that alleges dishonest or criminal acts to justify a dismissal may be required to meet an even higher standard of proof than a balance of probabilities.

Unfortunately for employers, just cause is an "all or nothing" proposition. In the past, a few courts have accepted the notion that misconduct or incompetence that falls short of just cause may reduce the length of the required notice period. However, more recently courts have rejected this notion of **near cause**; if an employee's misconduct or incompetence fails to meet the threshold for establishing just cause, an employer is obliged to provide reasonable notice or pay in lieu under the common law. There is no reduction in the notice period owed to that employee.

Proportionality and the Contextual Approach

Over the past three decades, courts have increasingly recognized the unequal bargaining relationship that exists between most employers and employees, especially at the time of dismissal, and they have adopted several ways to protect employees. One relevant development is the concept of **proportionality**—that is, the idea that any sanction must be proportional to the conduct to which it relates. There are a few acts of misconduct—such as theft, assault, breach of trust where a high level of trust is required, or a significant incident of sexual harassment—that may warrant **dismissal for cause** even if they occur only once because they go to the heart of the employment relationship. However, most other types of misconduct or performance-related incidents must usually occur more than once to constitute just cause.

Thus, even where a single instance of misconduct is relatively serious, such as refusing to follow direct instructions, courts are increasingly requiring employers to substitute penalties less severe than dismissal. This has led the courts to consider the application of progressive discipline in non-union workplaces. Courts generally support the use of progressive discipline, including verbal warnings, written warnings, and final written warnings. However, as discussed in Chapter 11, traditionally the common law has not recognized an employer's right to impose unpaid suspensions as part of that process. In fact, unpaid suspensions usually constitute constructive dismissal. More recently, however, a number of cases have suggested that in certain exceptional circumstances even unpaid suspensions may be an acceptable response to misconduct in a non-union workplace. This is an evolving area of the law.

A related development is the adoption by courts of a **contextual approach** in determining just cause. In the past, courts often focused on the nature and seriousness of an employee's conduct to determine whether it warranted dismissal without notice. Using a contextual approach, courts now consider the nature and seriousness of an alleged offence in the context of the overall employment relationship. The court in *McKinley v. BC Tel* determined that relevant contextual matters include the employee's length of service, her performance and disciplinary history, and any mitigating circumstances, such as personal factors that influenced the employee's conduct or performance. Under this contextual approach, where an employee has a substantial length of service and an otherwise good work and disciplinary record with an employer, courts rarely find that a single act of misconduct warrants dismissal.

Procedural Fairness

Regardless of what type of misconduct or incompetence it alleges, an employer improves its chances of successfully demonstrating just cause under the common law if it follows certain rules of **procedural fairness**. As a general rule, an employee should be given ample opportunity to respond to the allegations against him before an employer makes the decision to terminate. The employee may have a reasonable explanation for his actions or may describe extenuating circumstances that an employer should consider in determining a fair disciplinary response. Allegations should be investigated in good faith, thoroughly, and promptly. The investigation should remain confidential. A decision must be made in good faith—that is, not arbitrarily or for an ulterior motive.

If an allegation of misconduct is substantiated, the employer should ensure that the sanction is proportionate to the misconduct within the overall context of the employment relationship. For example, the employer should

1. consider whether the misconduct was planned and deliberate or a momentary error in judgment;
2. assess the misconduct in the context of the employee's position, length of service, performance record, and previous conduct;
3. consider extenuating circumstances, such as provocation, mistreatment, or external circumstances such as a serious illness in the family that may have prompted the incident; and
4. consider the employee's response to the allegations, such as admission, remorse, denial, or further challenge. For example, if the employee denies that his actions constitute misconduct, there is less chance that his behaviour will change.

An employee's response to allegations of wrongdoing is important for another reason. Under the contextual approach, courts look not only at the employment relationship up to the date of the alleged misconduct but also at how the employee responds to those allegations (Rudner, 2009, p. 6). A court may uphold a dismissal for just cause based not upon the seriousness of the alleged misconduct but on the fact that the employee lied or tried to conceal material information during the investigation. The case of *Obeng v. Canada Safeway Limited* underscores the importance of how an employee responds to allegations of wrongdoing during an investigation.

CASE IN POINT

Employee's Failure to Be Truthful During Investigation Justifies Dismissal

Obeng v. Canada Safeway Limited, 2009 BCSC 8

Facts

Obeng was assistant manager at a Vancouver-area Safeway store whose actions one day, as observed by several other staff members, raised suspicions that he was stealing groceries. When asked for an explanation, Obeng became very upset and denied all of the allegations made. For example, he vehemently denied placing groceries in a shopping basket or even having a basket in his arms that afternoon. As a result of Obeng's failure, during several investigatory meetings, to provide any alternative explanation for his actions, Obeng was dismissed for theft. He sued the employer for wrongful dismissal damages.

Relevant Issue

Whether the employer had just cause for dismissal.

Decision

The court held that Safeway had just cause for termination, not based on the alleged theft of groceries for which there was insufficient proof, but on Obeng's failure to be totally honest and forthright during the employer's investigation. Crucial to this finding was Obeng's admission at trial that he did have a grocery basket in his hands on the day in question, which he had used to collect misplaced merchandise for later reshelving. Although this was a reasonable explanation for his actions, his failure to provide it during the employer's investigation was a breach of his obligation to provide full and truthful disclosure. Referring to the contextual approach laid out in *McKinley*, the court stated:

> Mr. Obeng was well aware that theft was endemic in the grocery business and a serious problem, and he knew that Safeway considered it grounds for dismissal. He appreciated that, as a manager, his behaviour must be seen to be beyond reproach, and he knew that Safeway's Code of Business Conduct required that he make full and truthful disclosure in the course of an investigation. … A denial is not an explanation, nor was it full and truthful disclosure … .
>
> Mr. Obeng's dishonesty in relation to the investigation of his conduct on August 28 justifies his termination.

In short, Obeng's failure to provide a complete and truthful explanation for his behaviour during the employer's investigation was a breach of his implied duty of honesty, which constituted just cause for his dismissal.

Stating Grounds of Dismissal

On occasion, an employer may dismiss an employee without alleging just cause and later, when the employee sues for wrongful dismissal, assert that it actually had just cause. The employer is not necessarily prevented from changing its position, especially when it can show that the original decision was motivated by a desire to spare the employee's feelings, as in *Giancola v. Jo-Del Investments Ltd.* However, in most cases, it is sensible for an employer to allege just cause in its termination letter if it intends to do so in the event of litigation.

CASE IN POINT

Employer Fails to State True Reason for Discharge

Giancola v. Jo-Del Investments Ltd., [2001] OJ no. 4093 (SCJ); **2003 CanLII 48118 (Ont. CA)**

Facts

Giancola worked for the employer banquet hall for 18 years. After giving his employer one hour's notice, he took a five-week vacation without arranging for a replacement. He had done this previously, and the employer had warned him not to do it again. The employer terminated his employment several weeks after he returned from vacation. However, rather than indicating the real reason for dismissal, the termination letter said that Giancola was being dismissed as a result of restructuring. Giancola sued for wrongful dismissal.

Relevant Issue

Whether the employer could allege dismissal for just cause when the termination letter indicated dismissal without just cause.

Decision

The judge found that Giancola's misconduct was the real reason for termination. The termination letter cited restructuring and the dismissal was delayed for several weeks after Giancola's vacation to avoid an unpleasant confrontation with him. On the basis of all the evidence, the employer had just cause for termination.

The Ontario Court of Appeal upheld this decision, finding that the employer's delay in dismissing the employee reflected lack of resolve rather than condonation (see the discussion of condonation below).

Despite the positive result for the employer in *Giancola*, it is rarely worthwhile for an employer to take the risk that a court will interpret this failure to allege cause as favourably as the court did in *Giancola*. That being said, justification for dismissal can be based on facts discovered after dismissal ("after-acquired cause") or on grounds that differ from those alleged at the time of dismissal.

Sometimes an employer dismisses an employee for cause but still wants to provide her with some money as a gesture of goodwill. In this situation the employer should clarify in writing that the payment is made on a "without prejudice" basis— that is, the payment does not imply that the employer owes the employee reasonable notice of termination. Such a goodwill payment may also help to avoid litigation if it is comparable to the amount that an employee would be awarded in a successful suit for wrongful dismissal.

Condonation

An employer must be careful not to condone misconduct that it intends to rely on as just cause for termination. Condonation occurs when an employer who discovers an employee's misconduct or poor performance fails to respond within a reasonable time. If, for example, an employer discovers that an employee lied about his expense account and the employer fails to respond until two years later, the courts will not allow the employer to rely on the expense account incident in terminating the employee for cause.

In considering whether an employer has condoned an employee's behaviour, courts allow the employer a reasonable amount of time to consider its response to an incident. It is entitled to time to investigate the matter and decide how best to handle the situation. It must also know the full nature and extent of the misconduct in order to be held accountable for having condoned it.

Establishing Just Cause Under the Common Law

There are two general types of employee conduct that can justify dismissal without notice: misconduct, such as acts of theft or insubordination, and problems related to job performance. The following is a review of the more common grounds for dismissal for cause and their treatment in the courts.

Dishonesty

Dishonesty in the workplace is one of the most serious acts of misconduct because it undermines the crucial element of trust that should exist between an employee and an employer. Some examples of dishonesty include fraud, such as submitting inaccurate claims for overtime pay or sick leave benefits; accepting kickbacks from suppliers; or stealing company property.

However, an employer's ability to dismiss an employee for dishonesty is no longer a cut-and-dried issue. In the past, employers could assume that virtually any dishonest conduct constituted grounds for dismissal without notice (or pay in lieu of notice), because the employer could no longer be expected to trust the employee. However, recently courts have applied the contextual approach to assess whether an employee's dishonest conduct was serious enough to warrant dismissal without notice (or pay in lieu of notice) in light of all the relevant factors, including the employee's length of service and work record. If a single act of theft is seen as an error in judgment rather than a reflection of an untrustworthy character, the courts will probably find that dismissal without notice (or pay in lieu of notice) was unjustified and that progressive discipline should have been applied instead. This contextual approach to dishonesty was highlighted in the landmark case of *McKinley v. BC Tel*, where the Supreme Court of Canada found that dishonesty that does not go to the root of an employment relationship does not constitute just cause for dismissal.

CASE IN POINT

Employee's Dishonesty Must Be Assessed in Context

McKinley v. BC Tel, 2001 SCC 38

Facts

McKinley occupied a senior financial position with the employer when he began suffering from high blood pressure. In mid-June 1994, he took a leave of absence. He told his supervisor that he wanted to return to work in a position that involved less responsibility than the position he left. In August 1994, he was dismissed. The employer offered him a separation package that he found unsatisfactory, and he sued for damages for wrongful dismissal. Shortly after the trial started, the employer applied to the court to include the defence of just cause based on dishonesty. The alleged dishonesty related to the fact that McKinley's doctor had advised him that taking a certain medication would help to control his blood pressure and thus assist him in returning to his former position. The employer alleged that McKinley was dishonest in failing to reveal this possibility.

Relevant Issue

Whether McKinley's failure to reveal the doctor's information constituted dishonesty that warranted dismissal for cause.

Decision

The Supreme Court of Canada found that although McKinley had been dishonest, the nature and extent of the dishonesty in the circumstances did not fundamentally undermine the employee–employer relationship. The employer's response should have been proportional to McKinley's conduct, taking into account its nature and seriousness and the context of his situation, including length of service, work history, and other relevant factors. In these circumstances, McKinley's dishonesty was not so fundamentally inconsistent with his obligations to the employer that it violated an essential condition of the employment contract. The employer was required to provide McKinley with pay in lieu of reasonable notice of termination (approximately $110,000).

Although the Supreme Court found for the employee in *McKinley*, it set out circumstances in which dishonest conduct would warrant dismissal without notice (or pay in lieu of notice). It would do so if the dishonest conduct violated an essential condition of the employment contract, breached the bond of trust between the parties, and was fundamentally or directly inconsistent with an employee's obligations to an employer. Theft of money from a cash register or an elaborate scheme to defraud an employer, for example, would likely justify dismissal without notice (or pay in lieu of notice).

Litster v. British Columbia Ferry Corp. highlights another issue that an employer must keep in mind when dismissing an employee for conduct that it alleges is dishonest: the employer must be able to prove its case. In *Litster*, the employee was successful in her wrongful dismissal action because her credible explanation for her conduct defeated the employer's allegations of theft.

CASE IN POINT

Employee's Credible Explanation Defeats Allegations of Theft

Litster v. British Columbia Ferry Corp., 2003 BCSC 557

Facts

Litster, age 44, had worked for the British Columbia Ferry Corporation for more than 20 years when she was terminated for cause for removing paints from the employer's premises without permission. Litster admitted removing the paints for the purpose of taking them to a recycling depot. However, for various personal and work-related reasons, she stored the paints in the shed at her home for several months. When the employer became aware that Litster had its paints in her possession, it investigated and decided that the six months' delay was not reasonable. It concluded that Litster had stolen the paints, and dismissed her. Her termination letter—which was sent to several other employees, including the payroll manager—outlined the alleged theft. The employee sued the employer for wrongful dismissal. She also sued the author of the termination letter personally for **defamation**.

Relevant Issues

1. Whether the employer had just cause for dismissal based on dishonesty.
2. Whether the termination letter constituted defamation and, if so, whether the employer had a defence.

Decision

The British Columbia Supreme Court found that the employer did not have just cause to terminate Litster, because her explanation for the delay in taking the paints to a recycling depot was credible. Allegations of theft "must be proven on clear and cogent evidence and withstand the strict scrutiny appropriate for such a serious allegation." She was awarded 15 months' salary in lieu of reasonable notice. However, the court did not find that the employer acted in bad faith and therefore no additional damages were awarded.

With respect to the claim of defamation, the court decided that the letter was defamatory because alleging theft had "the effect of lowering Ms. Litster in the estimation of others." The defence of "justification"—that is, that the statements were true—was not available to the author of the letter because the court expressly found that Litster had not committed theft. The defence of "qualified privilege" was accepted, however. This defence applies where a person who makes a statement honestly and reasonably believes that the statement is true and has an interest in making it or a duty to make it; the recipient must have a corresponding interest in receiving it or a duty to receive it for the defence to succeed.

Despite the issues noted above, courts continue to view dishonesty as serious misconduct and where a court is satisfied that an employee was intentionally dishonest and the dishonesty was of such a nature that it fundamentally undermined the employer's trust, just cause for dismissal exists. As *Weisenberger v. Marsh Canada Limited* shows, just cause may exist even where an employee does not benefit personally from the misconduct and it was authorized by the employee's supervisor.

Dishonesty from Which Employee Does Not Personally Benefit Constitutes Just Cause

Weisenberger v. Marsh Canada Limited, 2004 MBQB 14

Facts

Weisenberger worked for the employer insurance broker for almost nine years. He regularly added a fee to the premium quoted by the Toronto office, without the client's knowledge, and the extra income went to the local branch. This practice, which involved an elaborate false invoice scheme, was apparently encouraged by the manager of the local branch. When the employer's head office discovered this practice, it reimbursed its clients $3.7 million in extra billings. Weisenberger was dismissed, and he sued for wrongful dismissal. He claimed he did not know that what he was doing was wrong because he was acting on his supervisor's instructions.

Relevant Issue

Whether the employer had just cause for dismissing the employee.

Decision

The Manitoba Court of Queen's Bench found that the employer had just cause for dismissing Weisenberger. He had worked in the industry for many years and it was not credible that he did not know that what he was doing was wrong. His employer was the company, not his supervisor, and Weisenberger knew that head office would not have condoned the practice had it been aware of it. The court found that his participation in the dishonest scheme constituted just cause for dismissal despite the fact that he did so on the directions of his immediate supervisor and derived no personal benefit from his participation. In the court's view, Weisenberger's conduct was fundamentally incompatible with his duties to his employer, and his dismissal was justified.

If an employee's dishonesty involves theft, the value of the stolen article need not be significant to warrant dismissal for just cause if the employee is aware that such conduct is prohibited. In *Mutton v. AOT Canada Ltd.*, the court found that an employee with less than a year's service was justifiably terminated for cause when he took stretch wrap from the employer for personal use without permission. Although the value of the item stolen was insignificant, the employee was aware that this behaviour could lead to termination, so the court found that his misconduct violated the trust necessary in an employment relationship. Citing the contextual approach used in *McKinley*, the court also took into account the employee's short length of service.

In dealing with instances of employee dishonesty, an employer can put itself in the strongest legal position possible by following the three steps outlined below.

1. *Provide clear written policies that outline required behaviour.* Key policies should state that violations will be cause for dismissal. To be effective, the policies must also be clearly communicated to employees and consistently enforced.

2. *Get the facts.* An employer must ensure that it has its facts right. Not only is there arguably a higher standard of proof required in cases where dishonesty is alleged, but the employer may also be required to pay additional compensation to an employee if it makes harmful accusations without sufficient evidence to support them. Employers should investigate incidents thoroughly—obtaining witness statements and listening to an employee's explanation—before

deciding whether or not to dismiss the employee for dishonesty. If the employee has a reasonable explanation for her actions, such as taking computer equipment home to finish a report on the weekend, a court will probably not find that the employer had just cause for dismissing the employee. Proving that an employee committed fraud or was dishonest requires convincing evidence.

3. *When allegations cannot be proven, provide a reasonable separation package.* If the employer cannot prove that the employee committed the dishonest act, but no longer wishes to retain the employee's services, it should dismiss the employee "without cause" and provide a reasonable separation package. This will protect the employer against additional damages that it could be required to pay an employee if it makes unsubstantiated allegations of dishonesty in a wrongful dismissal suit.

Insolence and Insubordination

It is rare, but not impossible, that a single act of insubordination provides just cause for termination. Such an act might be, for example, an assault on a supervisor or a deliberate contravention of an important employment policy that results in a significant loss for an employer. In *Donaldson v. Philippine Airlines Inc.*, the employee disobeyed a directive from management by extending credit to a certain customer and deliberately withholding information from the employer. The employer lost money as a result. The court found just cause for dismissal.

Usually, however, an employer must show a pattern of insubordinate or insolent behaviour that continues despite clear warnings before it can establish just cause. Courts will consider the context in which all conduct occurs. For example, if arguments are common in a workplace, a court will take into account "shop talk" in deciding whether an employee's behaviour is acceptable. In the case of an argument between an employee and a supervisor, courts will also consider whether the employee was provoked by the supervisor.

Henry v. Foxco Ltd. and *Mothersele v. Gulf Canada Resources Ltd.* demonstrate the courts' reluctance to disentitle an employee to reasonable notice for a single episode of insolence, even where the insolence was serious.

CASE IN POINT

Single Episode of Insolence Rarely Justifies Dismissal

Henry v. Foxco Ltd., 2004 NBCA 22

Facts

Henry had worked for the employer as a body repair technician for nearly eight years when, one day, his supervisor asked him to remove decals from two vans. Several hours later, his supervisor said that he hoped Henry was working on the second van, not the first. Henry became angry and, according to the employer's evidence, said several times, "If you want to fire me, go ahead and fire me." The supervisor tried to calm Henry down, but eventually said, "OK, you're fired." Henry sued for wrongful dismissal. The trial judge held that the supervisor was justified in firing Henry because the supervisor's comments were part of his duties as manager, Henry became abusive to the supervisor, and the incident took place in front of other employees whom the supervisor supervised. In these circumstances, the employee's insolence went to the heart of the employment relationship. Henry appealed this decision.

Relevant Issue

Whether the single episode of insolence constituted just cause for dismissal.

Decision

The New Brunswick Court of Appeal found that the employer wrongfully dismissed Henry. While a single incident may completely undermine an employment relationship, the circumstances in this case were insufficiently extreme to do so. A court must apply the principle of proportionality. Termination would be warranted where

1. the employee and supervisor could no longer maintain a working relationship;
2. the incident undermined the supervisor's credibility in the workplace; and
3. as a result of the incident, the employer suffered a material financial loss or loss of reputation, or its business interests were seriously prejudiced.

In Henry's case, these factors were not present. The incident did not occur in front of customers or the public. The employer should have imposed a "cooling-off period" before deciding on an appropriate penalty. Henry was awarded $14,200 plus interest as wrongful dismissal damages.

In *Mothersele*, the court found that even threats to destroy company property did not justify dismissal without notice (or pay in lieu of notice) where a long-term employee had an excellent performance record with the employer.

CASE IN POINT

Employee Threats Must Be Viewed in Context of Employment History

Mothersele v. Gulf Canada Resources Ltd., **2003 ABQB 2**

Facts

Mothersele was a senior engineer who had worked for the employer for 19 years. He had access to sensitive information concerning the employer's operations. His performance was generally good, but management was concerned about his attitude toward the company. He was highly critical of the company's methods of storing computer data and stored it on his own computer, backing it up onto the company's systems annually. He sent numerous memos to senior management expressing his concerns.

Management eventually called a meeting with Mothersele to discuss its concerns about his attitude and a possible need to transfer him. Upset by this discussion, Mothersele wrote another memo on December 17, 1999 that concluded with the remark that he would delete his files and "leave no tracks." His manager interpreted this to mean that Mothersele was threatening to destroy files belonging to the employer. Senior management concluded that this was a security threat. On December 20, 1999, the employer instructed the computer department to protect the information on Mothersele's system. Mothersele worked on December 20 and 21, having full access to his computer and company data. He was dismissed on the afternoon of December 21 for cause.

Relevant Issue

Whether Mothersele's conduct constituted just cause for dismissal without reasonable notice or pay in lieu.

Decision

The Alberta Court of Queen's Bench found that the employer did not have just cause for dismissal because the threat contained in Mothersele's memo should have been assessed in the context of his employment relationship. His history of complaints, the care he took with his data, and the employer's delay of several days before dismissing him all undermined the employer's claim of just cause. He had been a valued and trusted employee for many years, and in this context it was unreasonable that the employer failed to give him an opportunity to explain his intentions in writing the memo.

The court awarded Mothersele 15 months' pay in lieu of notice. After his termination, Mothersele became a consultant. Because he earned as much money as a consultant as he was making with the employer, he received no award for loss of earnings. However, he was awarded damages of approximately $80,000 for loss of medical benefits, bonus, and stock options.

It is clear from these cases that an isolated instance of insubordination by a long-term employee usually requires an employer to impose a form of discipline that is less severe than immediate dismissal without notice (or pay in lieu of notice). Only if an employee repeats the behaviour despite several warnings, including one that advises her that her job is in jeopardy if her insubordination continues, is termination for just cause likely sustainable.

Incompatibility

Generally speaking, it is difficult for an employer to dismiss an employee for cause simply because he does not fit in or has personal habits that are considered somewhat unpleasant in the workplace. General incompatibility is usually too vague to constitute just cause for termination without notice. However, in certain situations courts have upheld dismissals based on an employee's incompatibility with the dominant workplace culture. For example, in *Essery v. John Lecky & Co.*, the dismissed employee was a hairdresser who had greasy hair, smoked heavily, and neglected his appearance. The employer successfully defended itself against a claim for wrongful dismissal by showing that the employee's personal habits harmed its business.

Off-Duty Conduct

Generally speaking, conduct that takes place outside the workplace cannot provide just cause for termination. However, an exception arises if an employer can demonstrate that an employee's off-duty conduct harmed its business or reputation.

Much will depend on the employee's position, the nature of the off-duty conduct, and how the matter reflects on the employer's business. For example, in *Pliniussen v. University of Western Ontario*, a university professor was dismissed for cause after being convicted of insurance fraud. The court held that the employer had just cause for termination because dishonest behaviour on the part of faculty could affect the university's reputation. The employer was able to show a substantial and real connection between the off-duty conduct and its well-being.

This connection was also the key issue in *Kelly v. Linamar Corporation*. In that case a court had to decide whether a well-respected manager, with 14 years' service, could be dismissed for just cause for being charged with possessing child pornography on his home computer.

CASE IN POINT

Is Possession of Child Pornography on Home Computer Just Cause?

Kelly v. Linamar Corporation, 2005 CanLII 42487 (Ont. SC)

Facts

Kelly was the materials manager at Emtol, a subsidiary of Linamar, Guelph's largest employer. His duties included supervising 10 to 12 employees, as well as being in regular contact with suppliers and customers. On January 21, 2002, Kelly was arrested and charged with possession of child pornography (on his home computer). Although he was a well-respected and trusted manager with an unblemished 14-year work record, the employer decided to terminate his employment based on that charge. On January 24, 2002, it sent him the following termination letter:

Dear Mr. Kelly:

Subject: Termination of Employment

As you are aware you have been charged with a criminal offence, on or about Monday, January 21, 2002. Indeed, newspapers have published to the community that you have been criminally charged with possession of child pornography. As a result of our investigation, which includes statements made by yourself, you have been involved in inappropriate conduct in relation to the community at large and children in particular.

As you are also aware, Emtol Manufacturing and its parent company, Linamar Corporation, actively promote and contribute to the community and children's programs including a focus on elementary aged school children for the purpose of furthering a business and community reputation.

As a result of your misconduct, which has been published to the community at large, the Company's legitimate interests have been negatively affected. In addition, your conduct has impacted upon the workplace and employee morale to such an extent that employees have indicated a refusal to work with you.

Under these circumstances, and in light of your management position, you have left us no alternative but to terminate your employment effective immediately on a for cause basis.

Subsequently, Kelly pleaded guilty to the charge of possessing child pornography. He then brought an action against his employer for wrongful dismissal.

Relevant Issue

Whether the employer had just cause to terminate the employee on the basis of his off-duty misconduct.

Decision

The court found that the employer did have just cause to terminate Kelly because he had breached his duty to ensure that his off-duty conduct did not adversely affect his employer. In the judge's words:

> Linamar has over a long period of time built up a good reputation which it jealously protects. That reputation includes the promotion of its activities with young people outlined earlier. A company is entitled to take reasonable steps to protect such a reputation and the termination of Philip Kelly was just such a step.

The court noted that although at the time of dismissal Kelly had only been charged with the offence and had not yet pleaded guilty, he had admitted his guilt to the employer early on in the employer's investigation.

The court did caution that not every employee charged with possession of child pornography or a similar crime is subject to termination without compensation. Relevant factors include the employee's level of responsibilities and the degree to which the employer's reputation in the community will likely be affected. In this instance, dismissal was justified because Kelly was a senior manager with extensive contacts outside the organization. Moreover, his employer was a prominent and active member of the local community.

FYI

Can Blogging Get You Fired?

While "social networking" has been around since before the first water cooler was invented, employee use of personal blogs and online social networking websites is a more recent phenomenon. Should employers care about what an employee blogs, tweets, or posts on her own time?

In some respects, the issues raised by employee blogging are familiar ones. Concerns about employees leaking confidential data, making harassing or defamatory comments about co-workers or managers, or damaging the employer's reputation are not new. What has changed is the size of the potential audience, the permanence of the record created, and the (often mistaken) *perception* of anonymity by the author.

Can an employee be disciplined or fired for cause based on online postings, tweets, or blogs made outside of working hours? The same principle applies here as to other off-duty conduct. Usually, what an employee does on her own time is not relevant to the employment relationship. However, if the off-duty conduct seriously damages the employer's reputation or business, the employer has a right to take action. Generally speaking, simply complaining about the boss or employer online will not be considered just cause for termination. The comments must be so disparaging that they undermine the employment relationship. Although there have not yet been many common law decisions in Canada on when blogging can be just cause for dismissal, there are a number of arbitral decisions that provide some early guidance in this area.

One of the first Canadian arbitration decisions to deal with the termination of an employee for the contents of her blog is *Alberta v. Alberta Union of Provincial Employees*. Although the employee worked in a sensitive area of the provincial government (workers' compensation), her blog identified who she was, that she lived in Edmonton, and that she worked for the Alberta government. She made postings such as "I work in a lunatic asylum" and referred to being in an office populated by "imbeciles and idiot savants." She used aliases for her co-workers but they were easily identifiable by details given in her posting. One sample posting, under the heading "Aliens Around the Coffee Table," read:

> Roberta likes to talk—unfortunately she's menopausal—she might have short term memory problems—always forgets the people's names she's talking about, or the point of her story, or the ending—most of the time we just listen for a few minutes until we figure out who made eye contact with her, then we ditch the person from the conversation for the rest of the break. … If I had to choose a planet that she came from, I'd say it was some dark planet, with very little oxygen …

When confronted with printouts of blog entries, the employee stated that she was merely exercising her right to freedom of expression. The employer terminated her for cause, arguing that the employee's blogs had potentially damaged its reputation.

The arbitration board dismissed the employee's grievance, stating that although the employee had a right to create a personal blog, her public statements went well beyond what was permissible. Especially disturbing were her disparaging remarks about at least seven co-workers with whom she regularly worked. The board also considered several other factors. The frequency of her postings showed that it was not a momentary lack of judgment. She took no steps to prevent access to the general public. Perhaps most seriously, she failed to express serious regret over the effect that her behaviour had on her co-workers. This last point seems to have been especially important because a co-worker who had also written blogs criticizing the workplace but who later apologized to the people she had offended received only a two-day suspension (Harris, 2008, p. 18).

Although this decision was later struck down on judicial review, the court did so because of procedural concerns.

Another relevant arbitration decision is *Chatham-Kent (Municipality) v. CAW Local 217 (Clark Grievance)*. The grievor was a personal caregiver at a retirement home with eight years of service. She set up a personal, publicly accessible blog in which she made disparaging remarks about her employer, expressed her dislike for the residents, and posted several pictures of herself with residents. The arbitrator upheld her termination on two grounds: breach of confidentiality for posting residents' pictures and insubordination for the contemptuous comments made about management.

On the other hand, in *E.V. Logistics v. Retail Wholesale Union, Local 580 (Discharge Grievance)*, an arbitrator decided that a lengthy suspension was a more appropriate penalty than termination for a warehouse employee who was fired for the contents of his personal blog. The employee's publicly accessible blog contained a number of racist comments and violent fantasies. In reducing the penalty, the arbitrator noted several factors. These included the employee's personal problems, including a history of depression, and the fact that his violent fantasies were not directed at his employer. Nor were individual employees, customers, services, or products targeted. Finally, the employee had made a "sincere, complete, and without reservation" apology, as well as posting an apology on the blog's former site.

To minimize potential problems in this area, employers should develop a policy that sets out the ground rules on personal blogging, as well as the consequences for breaching those rules. A well-drafted policy will alert employees that online posts, even those done on their own time and posted under a pseudonym, can have an impact on their jobs. It will also encourage employees to think about how their co-workers, customers, or supervisors could be affected by inappropriate postings. The following are some points to address in a blogging policy:

- The employer's general code of conduct applies to employee blogs, even if the employee posts under a pseudonym.
- Any confidentiality or non-disclosure obligations to the employer apply to the Internet in general, and specifically to blogs, tweets, and social networking sites.
- The posting of defamatory or derogatory comments about fellow employees, customers, or management is expressly prohibited. Author anonymity, use of aliases, or omitting the names of people or organizations does not change this requirement.

- A blogger who identifies himself as an employee or who discusses substantive work issues in his blog should include a disclaimer stating that the opinions expressed are those of the author only (Pigott, 2005).
- Employees must use their own equipment and time for personal blogging purposes.
- Published materials that are damaging to the employer's business or reputation are expressly prohibited (employees should be reminded of their implied duty of good faith and loyalty to the employer) (Mitchell, 2013, p. 3).
- Failure to follow the policy will, depending on the circumstances, result in disciplinary measures up to and including dismissal (Smithson, 2006).

As always, an employer should ensure that its policy is clearly drafted, regularly brought to the attention of its current employees (at least annually), as well as its new employees, and applied consistently. Where relevant, employees should be made aware that the employer regularly reviews online journals and blogs for defamatory or other inappropriate material.

When investigating a suspected breach of its blogging policy, an employer should start by gathering as much information about the online conduct as possible. The employee should be shown the offending postings and instructed to remove them, within a reasonable time frame, and to apologize to the individuals affected. If the employee then refuses or fails to follow through with these measures, the employer is in a better position to justify the level of discipline imposed (Farahani, 2009, p. 16-6).

Conflict of Interest

As mentioned above, one of the implied duties that employees owe to their employers is the duty of loyalty. Consequently, engaging in activities that create a conflict of interest with the employer's interests may justify dismissal for cause (Echlin and Thomlinson, 2011, p. 206).

For example, an employee's moonlighting may adversely affect an employer. Moonlighting does not usually constitute just cause unless it harms an employer's interests, as it can, for example, if an employee moonlights for a competitor or at a job that involves the employer's customers. As shown in the *Patterson* decision below, in these circumstances, it is important for the employer to have a clearly communicated conflict of interest policy that sets out the conduct that will justify dismissal. Moreover, the potential harm to the employer must be significant to justify dismissal for cause.

CASE IN POINT

Conflict of Interest Justifies Dismissal for Cause

Patterson v. The Bank of Nova Scotia, 2011 BCPC 120

Facts

Patterson was a customer service supervisor whose job occasionally involved her dealing with customers and recommending various types of services. When first hired, Patterson had signed Scotiabank's guidelines for business conduct, which required her to inform her manager if there was a risk of a conflict of interest. It also stated that she "should not commence or continue a business which competes with the Bank or engage in *any activity likely to compromise the position of the Bank*" (italics added). About 12 years after Patterson started with the bank, she got her real estate licence and began working with a realtor on evenings and weekends. When the bank found out about this (Patterson had distributed her realtor business cards within the office), it insisted she either change positions within the bank or leave, because it was concerned about a perceived conflict of interest. Assuring the bank that she would not abuse her position, Patterson refused to make a change. The bank terminated her employment, alleging just cause.

Relevant Issue

Whether the employer had just cause to dismiss the employee.

Decision

The court found that the employer had just cause. The employer's guidelines were reasonable and clear, requiring employees to discuss outside business interests with it where a potential conflict of interest was involved, and the employee was aware of those guidelines. Moreover, the employer gave Patterson an opportunity to remedy the conflict before dismissing her; when she refused, the employer was entitled to enforce the terms of its employment agreement ("Employer Can't Bank on Moonlighting Employee," 2011).

Disobedience

Disobedience—like most other potential grounds for dismissal—is usually best dealt with through progressive discipline. A single act of disobedience will not constitute just cause for dismissal unless it is deliberate, entails no element of misunderstanding on the part of the employee, and causes substantial harm to the employer. It is also relevant whether the act of disobedience relates directly or incidentally to the employee's job. *Chaba v. Ensign Drilling Inc.* shows a court's reluctance to find just cause where an act of disobedience is an isolated occurrence and reflects poor judgment rather than an intention to disobey an employer's policies.

CASE IN POINT

Single Incident of Disobedience Rarely Creates Just Cause for Dismissal

Chaba v. Ensign Drilling Inc., 2002 ABPC 131

Facts

Chaba, age 21, worked as a roughneck on the employer's drilling rig. The employer instructed him to remove a buildup of ice using a crowbar and pickaxe. After using these tools unsuccessfully for 30 minutes, Chaba decided to remove the ice with a front-end loader, although he was not authorized to operate this machinery. In the process, he caused approximately $750 damage to the loader. He reported the mishap to his supervisor and offered to pay for the damage. The employer gave him a written warning. The next day, he was dismissed for failing to follow instructions and damaging equipment. The employer's safety manual prohibited roughnecks from operating heavy equipment without authorization and stated that non-compliance could result in immediate termination.

Relevant Issue

Whether the employee's failure to follow instructions constituted just cause for dismissal.

Decision

The Alberta Provincial Court found that Chaba's failure to follow specific instructions did not warrant dismissal without notice because it was an error in judgment rather than a wilful act of disobedience or defiance. Although Chaba was aware that he was not authorized to operate the equipment, ice had been removed with a front-end loader before, and he had experience using this equipment. The safety risk was minimal. Discipline short of dismissal was appropriate. The employee's misconduct was not sufficiently serious to eliminate his common law right to reasonable notice or pay in lieu. Based on his age and the character of his employment (involving frequent layoffs), Chaba was awarded one month's pay in lieu of notice in the amount of $5,000.

There have been cases in which employers have been unable to establish just cause for dismissing employees who fail to follow specific instructions because of the nature of the instructions. In *Dooley v. C.N. Weber Ltd.*, an employer instructed an employee not to have sexual relations with co-workers. The employee defied this directive and was consequently fired. In the resulting wrongful dismissal action, the court found that the sexual activity was consensual, did not involve a subordinate, and occurred outside the workplace and outside business hours. Therefore the employer's instructions were inappropriate and the employee's failure to comply with them did not constitute just cause.

Absenteeism and Lateness

As discussed in Chapter 11, there are two types of absenteeism under the common law: culpable (blameworthy) and innocent (blameless). They are treated differently under the law.

Culpable Absenteeism

Culpable absenteeism occurs when an employee is absent from work without a good reason. For example, if an employee sleeps in or decides not to go to work because he prefers to do something else, his absence is culpable. An employer is entitled to impose disciplinary action for culpable absenteeism or lateness. However, a single incident rarely justifies dismissal. Culpable absenteeism or repeated lateness is best addressed through a clear, communicated, and consistently enforced policy and the application of progressive discipline to breaches of that policy.

In assessing whether ongoing lateness or absenteeism constitutes just cause for dismissal, an employer should consider the context of the employment relationship, including

1. how long the employee has worked for the employer,
2. whether the lateness or absenteeism started suddenly or has been chronic since employment began,
3. how frequently the employee is late or absent,
4. what reasons the employee gives for his lateness or absences,
5. whether the lateness or absenteeism harms the employer, and
6. whether the employer consistently enforces its attendance policy. For example, if it tolerates the repeated lateness of other employees, the employer has little chance of justifying the dismissal of a particular employee on this basis.

Innocent Absenteeism

Innocent absenteeism occurs when an employee cannot come to work for reasons that are beyond the employee's control. In these circumstances, an employer cannot impose discipline. Under human rights legislation, where absenteeism results from a disability, an employer has a duty to accommodate the employee unless this causes it undue hardship. (See the discussion of the duty to accommodate disability in Chapter 5.)

Not all instances of innocent absenteeism resulting from sickness are protected under the disability provisions of the *Human Rights Code*. In *Ouimette v. Lily Cups Ltd.*, an employee was dismissed after a series of absences during her probationary period. The absence that led to her termination was a three-day absence arising from an asthmatic reaction to aspirin (one day) and the flu (two days). The employee filed a complaint with the Ontario Human Rights Commission, alleging that because she had been absent because of illness, her termination violated the Code. The Board of

Inquiry found that minor illnesses do not qualify as disabilities under the Code. To treat temporary illnesses that are common to the general population as "disabilities" would trivialize the purpose behind this prohibited ground of discrimination. As a result of this decision, minor temporary illnesses are not protected as disabilities, and human rights legislation does not apply.

However, *Ontario (Human Rights Comm.) v. Gaines Pet Foods Corp.* demonstrates that if *any part* of an employee's absences results from a disability, an employer cannot rely on these absences in determining whether it has just cause to dismiss an employee for excessive absenteeism.

CASE IN POINT

Employer Cannot Rely on Absences That Result from Disability in Dismissals

Ontario (Human Rights Comm.) v. Gaines Pet Foods Corp., 1993 CanLII 5605 (Ont. SC)

Facts

The employee had an extremely poor attendance record for several years before she was away from work for six months because of cancer. When she returned, the employer gave her a letter stating that she must maintain, over the next 12-month period, a level of attendance equal to or better than the average for the hourly-rated employees in the plant. When she failed to do so, the employer dismissed her for excessive absenteeism. She filed a human rights complaint. The Board of Inquiry held that because she had a serious absenteeism record, even without the six months off for cancer, the termination did not constitute discrimination on the basis of disability. The employee appealed.

Relevant Issue

Whether termination for excessive absenteeism in these circumstances constituted discrimination under the Ontario *Human Rights Code.*

Decision

The Ontario Divisional Court held that the employer contravened the *Human Rights Code* in dismissing the employee for excessive absenteeism. The 12-month attendance condition that it imposed was a direct result of her absence because of cancer, which is a disability. Her disability was therefore a proximate cause of her termination.

The court noted that because of the employee's poor record of absenteeism unrelated to disability (only 25 percent of the total days off related to cancer), the employer could have dismissed her without reference to her cancer absences. However, the employer had admitted that it included those days in deciding that termination was appropriate. To constitute discrimination under the Code, the prohibited ground of discrimination need not be the only reason for termination, as long as it is one of the reasons.

In determining the appropriate remedy, the court found that the employer had not acted in bad faith. It had been patient and given the employee several chances to improve her absenteeism record over the years. In the mid-1980s, when the employer decided to dismiss the employee, it may not have been clear that cancer was a disability under the Code. Therefore the employee was awarded six months' pay for loss of earnings but no further damages.

For absences that relate to disabilities, the *Human Rights Code* requires employers to accommodate employees up to the point of undue hardship. This may require them to accept irregular attendance or tolerate lengthy absences over a long period of time. However, where there is no realistic chance that an employee will ever be able to return to work on a regular basis, even with accommodation, an employer may eventually be able to prove undue hardship and thus dismiss the employee. This will depend on the employer's circumstances, the employee's prognosis, and the employee's attendance record over time.

Under the common law, a permanent illness that prevents an employee from returning to the workplace can result in a finding of frustration of contract. This principle of contract law applies when an employment contract becomes impossible to perform. However, findings of frustration are rare, particularly if the employee is not central to the employer's operation and has been employed for a long time. (See Chapter 15 under the heading "Frustration of Contract.")

In addition, where there is a long-term disability plan in the workplace and dismissing an employee would disqualify him or her from receiving benefits, such dismissal may be seen as a breach of the employment contract.

Sexual Harassment

Many types of sexual harassment, such as offensive humour or comments, warrant progressive discipline. However, in more serious cases of sexual harassment, especially those involving supervisors, courts have upheld employers' decisions to dismiss employees for just cause even in the absence of progressive discipline. The courts' concerns in these types of cases are set out in *Bannister v. General Motors*.

CASE IN POINT

Sexual Harassment and Abuse of Power by Supervisor Constitutes Just Cause for Dismissal

Bannister v. General Motors of Canada Ltd., **1994 CanLII 7390 (Ont. SC);** rev'd. **1998 CanLII 7151 (Ont. CA)**

Facts

Bannister worked as a security supervisor during the evening and night shifts. Most of the female staff in his department were summer students between 18 and 23 years of age. Bannister, who was in his late 40s, had worked for General Motors for 23 years when one of the summer students complained about his unwanted sexual approaches and comments. GM's investigation revealed that at least five women had similar complaints, alleging that he tried to kiss them, asked them to sit on his knee and give him a kiss, and described pornographic movies using sexual gestures.

During its investigation, the employer interviewed Bannister four times, and each time he denied any wrongdoing. He remembered some of the alleged incidents but did not believe they constituted sexual harassment. The employer terminated him for cause, and Bannister sued for wrongful dismissal. The trial judge found that Bannister was not "beyond redemption," and in light of his 23 years' service, granted him 21 months' pay in lieu of reasonable notice (roughly $120,000). The employer appealed.

Relevant Issue

Whether Bannister's conduct constituted just cause for dismissal.

Decision

The Ontario Court of Appeal found that the employer had just cause to dismiss Bannister. It acted with "care, responsibility and sensitivity" in investigating the initial complaint. The trial judge erred in focusing on Bannister's length of service and good record because it ignored two important duties of the employer: the duty to protect the members of its workforce from offensive conduct and the duty to protect the corporation against civil suits.

The Court of Appeal emphasized Bannister's supervisory role. A supervisor who abuses his power by condoning or creating a poisoned working environment for women is not doing his job. As for the argument that a modern industrial plant is a rough work environment where offensive commentary is common, the court stated, "It is not a question of the strength or mettle of female employees, or their willingness to do battle. No female should be called upon to defend her dignity or to resist or turn away from unwanted approaches or comments which are gender or sexually oriented. It is an abuse of power for a supervisor to condone or participate in such conduct." As a result of its finding of just cause, Bannister was not entitled to any damages for wrongful dismissal.

In *Bannister*, the employer's proactive stance on the issue of sexual harassment and the procedural fairness it exhibited in its investigation helped it justify the dismissal. It had permanently posted a copy of its sexual harassment policy throughout the plant. The employee had attended a sexual harassment seminar designed for supervisors, where the employer informed supervisors that sexual harassment could result in dismissal for cause. The employer's investigation of the complaint was thorough and well documented. During the initial interviews with other employees, the name of the employee under investigation was not mentioned. The other employees were asked whether they had general information with respect to any human rights or sexual harassment issues. Bannister acknowledged that the employer had given him every opportunity to explain his side of the story and had interviewed everyone that he had asked to be interviewed about the situation. Furthermore, the fact that the employee repeatedly denied that his actions constituted misconduct raised a question as to whether his behaviour could change.

Another instructive case about sexual harassment as just cause is *Simpson v. Consumers' Assn. of Canada*, in which the executive director of an association was terminated for sexual harassment and sued for wrongful dismissal. Although he was successful at trial, the Ontario Court of Appeal allowed the employer's appeal on the basis that the trial judge erred by ignoring the power imbalance between the workplace parties in determining that sexual conduct had been consensual. The court also found that offsite business functions that include a social component remain within the employment relationship, and an employee can be disciplined for misconduct that occurs on those occasions.

CASE IN POINT

Sexual Conduct During Business Trips Subject to Sanction

Simpson v. Consumers' Assn. of Canada, 2001 CanLII 23994 (Ont. CA); leave to appeal to SCC refused [2002] SCCA no. 83

Facts

Simpson was the executive director of an association whose job involved business travel and offsite meetings. He had held this position for nearly four years when his employer terminated him for sexual harassment of several female employees. The allegations included the following:

1. Simpson indicated to his newly hired secretary that if she had a sexual relationship with him, career opportunities could arise. When she refused, he became unpleasant, and she resigned.
2. Simpson engaged in unwelcome sexual conversations with a lawyer for the association, and on a business trip tricked her into going to a strip bar with him.
3. Simpson had an affair with another secretary that was obvious to all employees. When the relationship ended, she resigned.

4. During the social component of a business trip, Simpson undressed and got into a hot tub in front of the other employees; the secretary took off her top and joined him.

The trial judge found that some of the allegations were not credible, and that allegations related to conduct that occurred after business meetings were outside the employment relationship. The prevailing culture in the workplace tolerated the sexual conduct, which was consensual, and therefore did not constitute sexual harassment. As a result, the trial court awarded Simpson 12 months' pay in lieu of notice for wrongful dismissal and a further 6 months' pay for bad faith on the part of the employer. The employer appealed.

Relevant Issue

Whether the employee's conduct constituted just cause for dismissal.

Decision

The Ontario Court of Appeal allowed the employer's appeal. It found that business meetings that include a social component are part of the employment relationship. There was a disparity in power between Simpson and the other employees who appeared to consent to his behaviour because they were afraid their jobs would be in jeopardy if they objected strongly. Simpson's conduct resulted in the loss of confidence of staff.

Furthermore, the Court of Appeal found that the trial judge erred in suggesting that Simpson should not be held accountable because the employer did not have a sexual harassment policy that put him on notice that his conduct was prohibited. As executive director of the association, Simpson had a responsibility to develop and implement such a policy, and he should not benefit from his failure to fulfill this responsibility.

Intoxication

The human rights issues that arise when an employee's substance abuse problem constitutes a disability are discussed in Chapter 5 under the heading "Accommodating Employees Who Abuse Drugs or Alcohol." Subject to these rights, violation of a policy that prohibits the use of alcohol or drugs or intoxication on the job or at lunch may constitute grounds for dismissing an employee. However, a single violation by an employee who is not in a safety-sensitive job will probably not be considered just cause for dismissal. *Ditchburn v. Landis & Gyr Powers Ltd.*, involving the intoxication during working hours of an employee with 27 years of service, underscores the need to view misconduct in the context of the entire employment relationship.

CASE IN POINT

Single Incident of Intoxication Not Just Cause in Context of Entire Employment Relationship

Ditchburn v. Landis & Gyr Powers Ltd., 1995 CanLII 7290 (Ont. SC); rev'd. in part 1997 CanLII 1500 (Ont. CA)

Facts

Ditchburn was a sales executive with 27 years of above-average performance. However, he began to have difficulty keeping up with a recent change in sales strategy that depended more on computers and less on strong interpersonal skills. The employer demoted him. As a result of the changes in his job, Ditchburn arranged a goodbye lunch with a long-time client, Deason. At lunch they drank several beers and then they drank some more at a local strip club. After Ditchburn drove Deason back to his workplace, they had an argument in the parking lot, and both men suffered minor injuries. Ditchburn reported the incident to the employer, and the employer dismissed him for cause on the basis that he had violated the company policy against intoxication at work and by driving a company car while impaired during work hours while engaged in company business.

Relevant Issue

Whether intoxication during work hours and fighting on the employer's premises constituted just cause for dismissal.

Decision

The trial judge found that although Ditchburn had engaged in a flagrant breach of company policy, the incident was isolated and reflected uncharacteristically bad judgment. In light of Ditchburn's age (60), his many years of loyal service, and the fact that the incident was an isolated event, the employer should have given him the "benefit of the doubt" and been less rigid in the application of its policy. Instead, the employer used the incident as an excuse to rid itself of an employee who was not keeping up with technology. Ditchburn was awarded pay in lieu of 22 months' reasonable notice, plus $15,000 damages for mental distress, because it was foreseeable that he would suffer significant stress in these circumstances. He was also awarded an additional 2 months' pay because the employer failed to provide him with an adequate letter of reference.

On appeal by the employer, the Court of Appeal upheld the 22 months' pay in lieu of notice and the $15,000 awarded for mental distress. However, it held that the extension of the notice period by 2 months as a result of the inadequate letter of reference was inappropriate because the inadequate letter did not impair Ditchburn's job search.

Despite the result in *Ditchburn*, the contrasting decision in *Dziecielski v. Lighting Dimensions Inc.* shows that long service and a good employment record alone will not insulate an employee from a finding of just cause where the consequences of a single incident of misconduct involving intoxication are especially serious.

CASE IN POINT

Dismissal for Single Incident of Intoxication Upheld

Dziecielski v. Lighting Dimensions Inc., 2012 ONSC 1877; aff'd. 2013 ONCA 565

Facts

Dziecielski was vice-president of quality control of a small, privately owned automotive supplier. He had worked for the employer for 23 years when, after taking the company's pickup truck without permission to a client meeting and later consuming four beers over a one-hour lunch, he was in a single-vehicle accident. The company truck was destroyed and he was left with life-threatening injuries. On the basis of blood samples taken at the hospital, Dziecielski was charged with, and later pleaded guilty to, a criminal offence related to drunk driving. Several weeks after the accident, while recuperating, Dziecielski received a letter from his employer terminating his employment. He sued for wrongful dismissal, claiming reasonable notice damages of 24 months, plus punitive, aggravated, and exemplary damages.

Relevant Issue

Whether the employer had just cause to dismiss the employee.

Decision

The trial court's decision, upheld on appeal, was that the employer had just cause. In reaching this conclusion, the court acknowledged that a single, isolated incident by a long-service employee with a clean record rarely justifies dismissal. Similarly, intoxication on the job does not automatically justify termination. However, in this case, summary dismissal was appropriate for a number of reasons. Drinking and driving is a very serious criminal offence and widely condemned by society. The misconduct was prejudicial to the employer's interests because it put the employer at risk of both reputational damage and of vicarious liability to third parties if the employee had injured or killed others. Moreover, despite pleading guilty to the criminal charge, Dziecielski maintained that he was "not drunk" at the time of the accident. This ongoing denial spoke to a failure to accept responsibility for his actions. As a result, his lawsuit was dismissed and the court awarded the employer legal costs of almost $29,000.

Dziecielski's appeal to the Ontario Court of Appeal was unsuccessful and that court awarded further legal costs of about $11,000 to the employer (Filion Wakely Thorup Angeletti, 2013).

It is not clear whether this case portends a more rigorous approach by the courts to workplace intoxication-related misconduct than that taken in the *Ditchburn* decision. Certainly the two cases can be distinguished based on the severity of the consequences of the misconduct, as well as other elements. What is clear is that when dismissal based on just cause is alleged, each case will be considered on its own facts by balancing the seriousness of the misconduct against the other contextual factors.

In light of these cases, an employer should consider the following factors in determining an appropriate response to an employee who is intoxicated at work:

1. Did the intoxication harm its business interests?
2. How has it treated intoxicated employees in the past?
3. Does the employee work in a safety-sensitive area? If so, did the intoxication endanger the employee or others?
4. Was the employee's performance affected by the intoxication?

5. Is there a company policy or a term in the employment contract that addresses intoxication in the workplace?

If alcohol is regularly consumed at business lunches as a means of engaging with customers, for example, an employer may have difficulty justifying the dismissal of an employee for being intoxicated during working hours.

Substance Abuse

As discussed in Chapters 2 and 5, substance abuse is considered to be a disability and thus a prohibited ground of discrimination. An employer therefore cannot discipline an employee for substance abuse; instead, it must accommodate the employee up to the point of undue hardship. In reality, accommodating an employee with a substance abuse problem means providing rehabilitation services or allowing time off work to attend these services. There is no rule of thumb concerning how long an employee must be given to overcome his disability: every case depends on its facts. At a certain point, however, if rehabilitation efforts are not successful and the employee's continued dependency adversely affects the workplace, an employer can dismiss an employee on the basis of just cause or frustration of contract.

It should also be noted that where an employee is suffering from an addiction and that addiction is causally connected to other misconduct (for example, theft of narcotics by a drug-addicted nurse), a finding of just cause may not be sufficient to justify dismissal. The employer may also be required to demonstrate that it is unable to accommodate the disability without undue hardship (Lisi and Brown, 2013, p. 3).

Incompetence

Although general incompetence is one of the most common reasons for dismissing an employee, it is also one of the most difficult grounds to prove. An employer must show that an employee has fallen below an objectively determined level of performance and that the problem lies with the employee, not with other factors, such as lack of adequate training.

However, it is possible for an employer to dismiss an employee for cause on the basis of incompetence if it has laid the necessary groundwork. This includes ensuring the following:

1. The requirements of the job are clear, reasonable, and applied fairly.
2. The employer has provided adequate training and support.
3. The quality of the employee's performance is demonstrably below the average level.
4. The employer warns the employee that she is failing to meet the job requirements and that her job is in jeopardy as a consequence.
5. The employee understands what is required to achieve satisfactory performance.
6. The employer gives the employee a reasonable length of time to improve.
7. The employer documents every aspect of its corrective action plan, including the standard the employee must reach, the time in which the employee must reach it, and the fact that the employee's continued employment is at risk if she fails to reach it.

In *Daley v. Depco*, discussed in Chapter 11, the employee's misconduct included a number of incidents related to poor job performance. By properly implementing its carefully laid out progressive discipline policy, the employer was able to demonstrate that the employee's performance fell below any reasonable standard of conduct that it was entitled to expect.

That being said, it will be difficult for an employer to demonstrate just cause for dismissing a long-term employee whose performance it has accepted for years. In these circumstances, employers usually provide pay in lieu of notice instead of attempting to dismiss such an employee for cause.

An employer may dismiss an employee for cause on the basis of a single instance of incompetence in only the most extreme of circumstances, such as recklessly incompetent behaviour that leads to serious financial losses for the employer.

Grounds That Cannot Constitute Just Cause

Ontario's employment-related statutes prohibit employers from dismissing employees on certain grounds, including an employee's assertion of her statutory rights. These grounds are set out in the list below.

1. *Human Rights Code.* An employer cannot dismiss or otherwise penalize an employee for asserting his or her rights under the Code.
2. *Employment Standards Act, 2000.* An employer cannot dismiss or otherwise penalize an employee for asserting his or her rights under the Act, including the right to pregnancy or parental leave.
3. *Occupational Health and Safety Act.* An employer cannot dismiss or otherwise penalize an employee for asserting his or her rights under the Act, including the right to refuse unsafe work.
4. *Workplace Safety and Insurance Act, 1997.* An employer cannot dismiss or otherwise penalize an employee who is absent from work for a work-related cause and has a right to be reinstated under the Act.
5. *Pay Equity Act.* An employer cannot dismiss or otherwise penalize an employee for asserting his or her rights under the Act.
6. *Labour Relations Act, 1995.* An employer cannot dismiss or otherwise penalize an employee for union-related activity.

If an employer dismisses an employee for asserting his or her rights under these employment-related statutes, a court or tribunal may order the employer to reinstate the employee and pay the employee a monetary award.

REFERENCES

Alberta Union of Provincial Employees v. Alberta. 2009 ABQB 208; 2008 CanLII 88488 (Alta. GAA).

Asurion Canada Inc. v. Brown and Cormier. 2013 NBCA 13.

Bannister v. General Motors of Canada Ltd. 1994 CanLII 7390 (Ont. SC); rev'd. 1998 CanLII 7151 (Ont. CA).

Billingsley v. Saint John Shipbuilding Ltd. (1989), 95 NBR (2d) 19 (QB).

Chaba v. Ensign Drilling Inc. 2002 ABPC 131.

Chatham-Kent (Municipality) v. CAW Local 217 (Clark Grievance). [2007] OLLA no. 135 (Williamson).

Common-Law Doctrine of Just Cause Provides a Blueprint for Employers. *Canadian Employment Law Today*. Issue no. 409, March 17, 2004, p. 3197.

Coulter, Catherine. Receipt of Pornographic Material Was Not Just Cause for Dismissal: Appeal Court. *Employment and Labour Law*. May 14, 2013. Dentons. http://www.employmentandlabour.com/receipt-of-pornographic-material-was-not-just-cause-for-dismissal-appeal-court.

Daley v. Depco International Inc. 2004 CanLII 11310 (Ont. SC).

Ditchburn v. Landis & Gyr Powers Ltd. 1995 CanLII 7290 (Ont. SC); rev'd. in part 1997 CanLII 1500 (Ont. CA).

Donaldson v. Philippine Airlines Inc. (1985), 10 OAC 217 (CA).

Dooley v. C.N. Weber Ltd. 1994 CanLII 7300 (Ont. SC); aff'd. 1995 CanLII 866 (Ont. CA); leave to appeal to SCC refused 89 OAC 318n.

Dziecielski v. Lighting Dimensions Inc. 2012 ONSC 1877; aff'd. 2013 ONCA 565.

E.V. Logistics v. Retail Wholesale Union, Local 580 (Discharge Grievance). [2008] BCCAAA no. 22 (Laing).

Echlin, Randall, and Christine Thomlinson. *For Better or For Worse: A Practical Guide to Canadian Employment Law*, 3rd ed. Toronto: Canada Law Book, 2011.

Employer Can't Bank on Moonlighting Employee. *Canadian Employment Law Today*. October 5, 2011, p. 8.

England, Geoffrey. *Individual Employment Law*, 2nd ed. Toronto: Irwin Law, 2008.

Ernst v. Destiny Software Productions Inc. 2012 BCSC 542.

Essery v. John Lecky & Co. (1986), 60 Nfld. & PEIR 219 (PEISC).

Farahani, Sheri. Employee Use of Blogging and Social Networking Sites: Understanding and Managing Threats to Employers. Presented at the Law Society of Upper Canada Six-Minute Employment Lawyer 2009 program, June 17, 2009, Toronto.

Filion Wakely Thorup Angeletti. Ontario Court of Appeal Upholds For Cause Dismissal of Employee Caught Driving Company Vehicle While Intoxicated. December 2013. http://filion.on.ca/uploads/ckeditor/attachment_files/380/2013-12-03_CLU.pdf.

Giancola v. Jo-Del Investments Ltd. [2001] OJ no. 4093 (SCJ); 2003 CanLII 48118 (Ont. CA).

Gilbert, Douglas, Brian Burkett, and Moira McCaskill. *Canadian Labour and Employment Law for the US Practitioner*. Washington, DC: Bureau of National Affairs, 2000.

Gleason, Mary, and Anthony Moffatt. Addressing Employee Web 2.0 Indiscretions: Stickier in Canada Than in the US. Spring 2009. Norton Rose Fulbright. http://www.nortonrosefulbright.com/files/or_passport_spring09_webindiscret-pdf-100kb-47533.pdf.

Gleason, Mary, and Anthony Moffatt. Employers Caught in a Tangled Web 2.0. *Canadian Employment Law Today*. Issue no. 505, March 12, 2008, p. 4. http://www.minkenemploymentlawyers.com/wp-content/uploads/2008/03/eCELT-505.pdf.

Guerin, Nicole. Dismissing Employees for Theft. *Canadian Employment Law Today*. Issue no. 394, July 23, 2003, p. 3078.

Harris, Lorna. Staff Fired After Bad-Mouthing Colleagues, Management in Blog. *Canadian HR Reporter*. September 8, 2008, p. 18.

Henry v. Foxco Ltd. 2004 NBCA 22.

Human Rights Code. RSO 1990, c. H.19.

Israel, Peter. Ask an Expert: Can an Employee Be Terminated for Showing Up to Work Drunk? *Canadian Employment Law Today*. Issue no. 410, March 31, 2004, p. 3204.

Israel, Peter. Ask an Expert: Dismissing an Employee for Lateness. *Canadian Employment Law Today*. Issue no. 409, March 17, 2004, p. 3196.

Israel, Peter. Ask an Expert: Is a Threatening E-mail to a Co-worker Just Cause for Termination? *Canadian Employment Law Today*. Issue no. 382, February 5, 2003, p. 2084.

Israel, Peter. Firing an Employee for Dishonesty? Put Things in Context First. *Canadian HR Reporter*. August 12, 2002, p. 5.

Kelly v. Linamar Corporation. 2005 CanLII 42487 (Ont. SC).

Lisi, Lorenzo, and Fiona Brown. Misconduct and Addiction: When Is Cause Enough? *Canadian Employment Law Today*. November 13, 2013, p. 3.

Litster v. British Columbia Ferry Corp. 2003 BCSC 557.

Lobo, Vita. Dealing with the Social Media Monster. *Canadian HR Reporter*. June 1, 2009, p. 27.

Lougheed Imports Ltd. (West Coast Mazda) v. United Food and Commercial Workers International Union, Local 1518. 2010 CanLII 62482 (BCLRB).

Lublin, Daniel. Beware of Workplace Blogging. *Canadian Employment Law Today*. Issue no. 483, April 11, 2007, p. 4.

McKinley v. BC Tel. 2001 SCC 38.

Mistry, Heena. Employee Threats Not a "Slam-Dunk" Case. *Canadian Employment Law Today*. Issue no. 391, June 11, 2003, p. 3051.

Mitchell, Tim. Ask an Expert: Privacy—Control over Employee Social Media Activities. *Canadian Employment Law Today*. October 16, 2013, p. 2.

Mothersele v. Gulf Canada Resources Ltd. 2003 ABQB 2.

Mutton v. AOT Canada Ltd. [2002] OJ no. 696 (SCJ).

Nursall, Kim. Toronto Firefighters Axed over Inappropriate Tweets. *Toronto Star*. September 16, 2013. http://www.thestar.com/news/gta/2013/09/16/toronto _firefighters_axed_over_inappropriate_tweets.html.

Obeng v. Canada Safeway Limited. 2009 BCSC 8.

Ontario (Human Rights Comm.) v. Gaines Pet Foods Corp. 1993 CanLII 5605 (Ont. SC).

Ouimette v. Lily Cups Ltd. (1990), 12 CHRR D/19 (Ont. Bd. Inq.).

Patterson v. The Bank of Nova Scotia. 2011 BCPC 120.

Pigott, Mary. Employers Need to Address Workplace Blogging. Provided by Great Library Digest from the Law Society of Upper Canada. May 2005. http://www.hrinfodesk.com/articles/ addressworkplaceblogginggl.htm.

Pliniussen v. University of Western Ontario. [1983] OJ no. 913 (Co. Ct.).

Rudner, Stuart. Digging a Deeper Hole. *Canadian Employment Law Today*. Issue no. 530, March 25, 2009, p. 1.

Rudner, Stuart. Legal Flip-Flop. *Canadian Employment Law Today*. Issue no. 403, December 10, 2003, p. 3152.

Rush, Curtis. Tim Hortons Rehires Mother Fired Over Timbit. *Toronto Star*, May 8, 2008. http://www.thestar.com/News/ Ontario/article/422936.

Sargeant, Karen. Slapping Another Employee Not Necessarily Cause. *Canadian Employment Law Today*. March 15, 2013. http://www.employmentlawtoday.com/ articleview/17506-slapping-another-employee-not -necessarily-cause.

Shakur v. Mitchell Plastics. 2012 ONSC 1008.

Simpson v. Consumers' Assn. of Canada. 2001 CanLII 23994 (Ont. CA); leave to appeal to SCC refused [2002] SCCA no. 83.

Smith, Jeffrey. Move to Mexico Gets Work-at-Home Exec Fired. *Canadian HR Reporter*. June 4, 2012, p. 5.

Smithson, Robert. Employers Addressing Employee Blogging. April 3, 2006. Pushor Mitchell LLP.

http://www.pushormitchell.com/law-library/article/ employers-addressing-employee-blogging.

Steel v. Coast Capital Savings Credit Union. 2013 BCSC 527.

Waggott, George. Even Off-Duty Blogging Can Lead to Discharge. June 2, 2009. McMillan LLP. http://www.mcmillan.ca/101398.

Weisenberger v. Marsh Canada Limited. 2004 MBQB 14.

Whitten & Lublin Employment Lawyers. Termination for Cause Highlights Significance of Confidentiality and Privacy. *WL Update*. Issue no. 31, June 2013, p. 1. http:// www.toronto-employmentlawyer.com/wp-content/ uploads/2013-06-employment-newsletter.pdf.

Wilson, Peter, and Allison Taylor. *The Corporate Counsel Guide to Employment Law*, 2nd ed. Aurora, ON: Canada Law Book, 2003.

REVIEW AND DISCUSSION QUESTIONS

1. Define the following terms:
   a. the contextual approach
   b. condonation
   c. without prejudice
   d. near cause

2. Why should an employer be cautious when alleging that an employee has acted dishonestly?

3. Explain the difference between culpable and innocent absenteeism. Give an example of each.

4. According to case law, what type of off-duty conduct justifies dismissal without notice (or pay in lieu of notice)?

5. Nicole, a 27-year-old mother of four, had worked at the counter of a Tim Hortons doughnut shop for three years. One day she was seen giving a Timbit to a crying child who came into the shop with a regular customer. When the manager of the store confronted her about it, Nicole readily admitted giving the Timbit away without paying for it. She was aware that this was against the employer's policy but she had been busy at the time and did not go to her purse to get the 16 cents at the time. Also, knowing that day-old Timbits were given away to small children in the store regularly, she expected to get a reprimand at most. However, the manager fired her on the spot. Nicole was so upset that she called her local newspaper when she got home and her firing became headline news. (A day later the

owner of the franchise called and offered Nicole a job at another of his franchises.) Given the media attention the story garnered, it is clear that in the "court of public opinion" the employer did *not* have just cause to dismiss Nicole. However, did the employer have just cause under the common law? Explain your answer by referring to the principles upon which just cause dismissal of non-union employees is based.

6. Bert owns a small five-person consulting firm. He wants to terminate one of the consultants, George, for performance-related problems. George, who is 38 years of age, has been with the firm six and a half years and the quality of his work is excellent. Furthermore, he's a really nice guy. The problem is that he is a perfectionist and is extremely slow getting anything done. He keeps missing crucial client deadlines, and clients are starting to take their business elsewhere. It has reached the point where none of the other consultants is willing to work with him. Bert has spoken to George about this many times over the years (and this problem has been noted in all his performance reviews) but there has been no improvement. George is just incapable of picking up the pace. Bert wants to know whether he has just cause under the common law to dismiss George. Discuss.

7. Greg had worked for two years as games supervisor at a casino. His job was to monitor the dealers. He enjoyed his job and he joked around with his boss, Michael, all the time. One day Michael saw Greg spending a lot of time with one dealer who had nobody at her table and he told Greg to do his job and keep his eyes on his tables. Greg started to make loud kissing sounds and, suggesting that Michael was "sucking up" to management, he started making very crude gestures. When Michael asked him to stop, Greg continued. All of this was witnessed by a security guard and customers at nearby card tables. A week later, Greg was brought into the office and terminated for just cause, with no pay in lieu of notice. This was not the first time Greg had been disciplined for a lack of etiquette and professionalism but it was the most serious incident. Greg sued for wrongful dismissal. In court he denied making the crude gestures, saying he only made kissing sounds and it was part of their ongoing banter. Did the employer have just cause under the common law to dismiss Greg? Explain your answer.

8. Max was a 35-year-old machine operator who had worked for the employer for six years when he was dismissed for cause for slapping a co-worker across the face during a verbal argument. Accordingly, he was not given notice or pay in lieu. Max sued the employer for wrongful dismissal, arguing that he was entitled to reasonable notice. What factors do you think the court would consider in deciding whether the employer had just cause in this situation?

9. Art and Brian had eight and nine years' service, respectively, with the employer call centre and both had good work records. However, they were dismissed for cause after it was discovered that they had received about a dozen adult pornographic emails from a mutual friend. While they did not solicit or distribute the emails, the employer based the dismissals on breach of its computer use and harassment policy that, among other things, prohibited "accessing, transmitting, receiving, or storing discriminatory, profane, harassing, or defamatory information." The employer argued that it had done everything it could do to reinforce the importance of this policy: employees were required to read and sign off on it, they were reminded of it upon logging in; and they were made aware of the company's network monitoring system implemented to enforce compliance.

Did the employer have just cause to dismiss Art and Brian? Explain your answer.

10. Dennis was hired in March 2010 as vice-president of operations for a software development company. At an annual salary of $125,000, he was the employer's highest paid executive and had a wide range of functions. Although the employer was located in Vancouver, it agreed when Dennis was hired that, for family reasons, he could work from his home in Alberta. However, the employment agreement indicated that the employer had the right to require him to move to Vancouver in the future. In December 2010, Dennis requested vacation time to go to Mexico (where he had recently bought a house), and several times over the next six months Dennis went to Mexico for short visits, sometimes claiming one or two sick days for those periods. In mid-August 2011, after arranging Internet and phone service and thereby confirming that he could work remotely from Mexico, Dennis advised his employer that he and his family had decided to move to Mexico. The CEO said he felt betrayed by this sudden

announcement and, uncertain about its tax and other implications, asked Dennis for a written proposal, which he would present to the board of directors to show how this arrangement would work. Dennis responded that he could work just as effectively from Mexico as from Alberta and his employment agreement allowed him to work from home without any country restriction. Upset by Dennis's position, the employer dismissed Dennis in late November 2011, with two months' severance pay, shortly after Dennis had finalized a major business deal for the employer. The termination letter stated that the dismissal was for cause for relocating to another country without permission, and for dishonesty related to falsely claiming sick leave. Dennis sued for wrongful dismissal damages equivalent to 12 months' salary. He denied that the employer had just cause and argued, in the alternative, that even if it did, by delaying his termination for several months, the employer had condoned his decision to move to Mexico.

Did the employer have just cause to dismiss Dennis? If so, did its three-and-a-half-month delay amount to condonation?

11. ABC Company had recently become unionized after a highly contentious organizing drive. Two employees (Bob and Jeff), who had been very active in the organizing campaign, started posting derogatory statements on their Facebook accounts about their supervisor. Over the course of two months, the comments became increasingly negative, implying violence and demonstrating homophobia. For example, one post said: "If somebody mentally attacks you, and you stab him in the face 14 or 16 times, … that constitutes self-defence doesn't it????" Another said: "Don't spend your money at ABC Company as they are crooks out to hose you."

Together, the employees had hundreds of "friends" on Facebook, including several co-workers and a manager at ABC, who alerted the employer about these postings. After monitoring the postings for several weeks, ABC spoke to Bob and Jeff to hear what they had to say. Both initially denied their involvement, saying that their accounts had been hacked. Finding their explanation not credible, ABC decided it had just cause to dismiss them, despite their previously clean disciplinary records. They filed a grievance with their union, challenging their dismissal for cause.

Describe the arguments that both the employer and the union, on behalf of Bob and Jeff, could make regarding the alleged just cause. Who do you think would be successful and why?

12. Three Toronto firefighters were fired in 2013 for making sexist tweets that were degrading to women. Examples of the tweets included the following:

   - One quote from the TV show *The Office* read: "Reject a woman and she will never let it go. One of the many defects of their kind. Also weak arms."
   - Another was a line from the TV show *South Park*: "I'd never let a woman kick my a—. If she tried something, I'd be like HEY! You get your b—— a— back in the kitchen and make me some pie!"
   - One tweet, referencing a woman ordering coffee and overusing the word "like," queried: "[W]ould [swatting] her in the back of the head be considered abuse or a way to reset the brain?"

City officials indicated that these and similar tweets violated the city's social media guidelines, which state that employees should "not engage in harassment, personal attacks or abuse toward individuals or organizations," and "not use language that is discriminatory, hateful, or violent towards identifiable groups or that incites others to discriminate [or] practise hate or violence."

The three unionized firefighters grieved their dismissal. Referring to the principles discussed in the chapter, discuss whether the employer had just cause to dismiss these employees.

13. Sasha was a bank employee with 21 years' service whose IT role entitled her to virtually unlimited access to confidential documents. One day Sasha decided to access sensitive information concerning priority parking, without permission, to satisfy her curiosity about where she was on the list for the most prized parking spots. As soon as the employer found out about this action, it dismissed Sasha for just cause. Sasha sued the employer for wrongful dismissal, arguing that as a long-service employee with an unblemished work record, dismissing her for just cause for a single, isolated act was a disproportionate response. Did the employer have just cause in your view?

Termination and Severance Pay Requirements Under the Employment Standards Act

14

LEARNING OUTCOMES

After completing this chapter, you will be able to:

- Understand the purpose of statutory notice of termination or pay in lieu requirements.

- Explain the relationship between statutory and common law notice of termination requirements.

- Define "temporary layoff" under the *Employment Standards Act, 2000*.

- Understand the statutory requirements for giving individual and mass notice of termination or pay in lieu of such notice.

- Identify statutory severance pay requirements and exceptions.

- Understand the "continuity of service" provisions that apply where there is a change of ownership of the employer organization.

Introduction

As discussed in Chapter 6, the *Employment Standards Act, 2000* (ESA) gives employees a basic level of protection in setting the terms and conditions of employment. Although the parties to an employment contract may negotiate standards that are more beneficial to an employee than those set out in the ESA, they may not agree to standards that are less generous. Under employment standards legislation in Ontario and elsewhere in Canada, employees are entitled to receive notice of termination or pay in lieu (that is, instead) of this notice, unless the termination falls within one of the limited statutory exceptions. The purpose of termination notice is to provide an employee with time, while still being paid, to look for another job.

The notice requirements of the ESA do not replace common law notice requirements. However, in Ontario, an employee cannot file a claim with the Ministry of Labour against an employer for failure to provide termination or severance pay under the ESA *and* sue the employer for damages for wrongful dismissal for the same termination. If an employee decides to begin a court action for wrongful dismissal after filing a claim under the ESA, she must withdraw the statutory claim within two weeks of filing the claim. Once the two-week period ends, an action for wrongful dismissal is barred.

In most situations, statutory termination requirements are modest compared with the common law obligation to provide reasonable notice of termination. For example, under the ESA, a middle manager with 20 years' service with an employer is entitled to 8 weeks' notice of termination (and severance pay of 20 weeks if the employer is over a certain size). This is far less than the 12 to 18 months' notice that the common law would probably consider reasonable. Generally speaking, an employee in this situation who felt that the employer had failed to offer an acceptable **separation package** would sue for wrongful dismissal rather than file a claim under the ESA. Such a decision is reinforced by the fact that currently the maximum amount an employer can be ordered to pay an employee under the ESA is $10,000 in most situations. (This limit does not apply where the termination results from an employee's exercising her rights under ESA provisions relating to statutory leaves, retail business establishments, lie detectors, or reprisals for asserting her statutory rights.)

For many employees, however, the ESA's termination and severance requirements provide the only meaningful entitlements. For example, an entry-level employee who is laid off after two years' service is entitled to two weeks' termination notice or pay in lieu under the ESA. If the employer fails to provide this notice or pay in lieu, the employee may enforce his statutory rights by filing a claim with the Ministry of Labour. It is unlikely that this employee would hire a lawyer and launch a time-consuming and expensive lawsuit in the hope of obtaining a few more weeks' pay in lieu of reasonable notice under the common law. That being said, an employee who is not intimidated by the court system could file a claim in Small Claims Court at a much reduced cost.

While most employees fall between these two extremes, generally speaking only relatively senior employees or those with many years of service with the employer choose to go to court to assert their right to reasonable notice under the common law.

It should be noted that many dismissed employees—as well as some employers—are unaware that more generous notice entitlements may be available under the common law. The difficulties that can result from this lack of awareness are illustrated in the In the News feature below.

Dismissed Employees Sue Ministry of Labour over Bad Advice

FORMER EMPLOYEES DESERVED BETTER, LAWSUIT SAYS

Two long-time former employees of a Pickering manufacturing company are suing the Ontario Ministry of Labour on the grounds they were given bad advice about their severance entitlement.

The two employees of Trillium Screw Manufacturing Co. Ltd. each settled for eight weeks' pay and benefits, despite many years of service, after consulting the ministry helpline on their rights, according to statements of claim filed in Ontario Superior Court of Justice on Wednesday.

The suits contend Michael Mosey could have got much more under common law, up to 24 months' severance, while Eileen Mary Tremblay could have claimed up to 16 months' pay based on their positions and years of service. The suits seek $104,000 in damages for Mosey and nearly $53,000 in damages for Tremblay.

The allegations have yet to be proved in court.

SOURCE: Dana Flavelle, "Former Employees Deserved Better, Lawsuit Says," *Toronto Star*, September 25, 2013. Reprinted with permission—TorStar Syndication Services.

Overview of ESA Termination Requirements

There are three main statutory requirements that relate to termination. The basic one, which is set out in s. 57, requires employers to provide dismissed employees with between one and eight weeks' notice of termination, or pay in lieu of notice, depending on the length of an employee's service. Exceptions to this requirement—for example, where an employer dismisses an employee for wilful misconduct—are limited and interpreted narrowly by the courts. A second termination requirement applies where many employees are dismissed within a short period of time; in this case, the mass notice provisions contained in s. 58 of the ESA and s. 3 of the ESA's *Termination and Severance of Employment* regulation (O. reg. 288/01) replace the individual notice requirements noted above.

As with common law notice, an employer has a choice under the ESA of providing an employee with advance notice of termination and letting the employee work throughout the notice period, or giving the employee pay in lieu of notice. Employers commonly give "working notice" when they dismiss many employees at the same time for economic reasons. When dismissing employees individually, however, they usually provide the departing employee with pay in lieu of notice in preference to having the employee work throughout the notice period.

Under ss. 63 to 66 of the ESA, the third statutory requirement that applies in certain situations is **severance pay**. This entitlement exists in addition to termination notice or pay. Although the term "severance pay" is commonly used to refer to all money paid to employees on termination, under the ESA it refers to a specific requirement that applies only in defined circumstances (described below under the heading "Severance Pay").

Under the ESA, employees who are temporarily laid off, as defined in the legislation, are not entitled to termination notice or pay in lieu or severance pay. However, employees who are laid off indefinitely or whose layoff exceeds the time limits for temporary layoffs are protected by the termination requirements described above. Note that there is no requirement under the ESA to base layoffs on an employee's length of service (that is, seniority). However, this is a central tenet of collective agreements in most unionized workplaces and it is common practice in many non-union workplaces as well.

Temporary Layoffs (Section 56)

Under s. 56 of the ESA, an employer is not required to provide notice of a temporary layoff, even if it offers no recall date. However, a temporary layoff can last only a certain length of time. If it lasts longer, an employer is considered to have terminated the employee on the first day of the layoff and must provide statutory termination pay.

There are several different circumstances in which a layoff is defined as "temporary." The common thread is that an employer is allowed longer layoff periods before triggering the termination provisions if it shows a continuing commitment to the employment relationship. It can show this commitment by, for example, continuing to contribute to the employees' benefit package or maintaining an insurance plan that supplements the employees' employment insurance benefits. Under the ESA, a layoff is temporary in the following circumstances:

1. It lasts no more than 13 weeks in a period of 20 consecutive weeks. For example, if Chandra is laid off for 4 weeks, returns to work for 2 weeks, and then is laid off for another 8 weeks before returning to work, she is not entitled to termination notice or pay in lieu because the layoff totalled only 12 weeks within a 20-week period. However, if there is a further layoff shortly after Chandra's return to work, any previous weeks of layoff within a 20-week period are counted toward the 13-week total.

2. It lasts more than 13 weeks in a period of 20 consecutive weeks but lasts less than 35 weeks in any period of 52 consecutive weeks where
   a. the employee continues to receive substantial payments from the employer;
   b. the employer continues to make payments for benefits—such as continuing dental, disability, or extended health benefits;
   c. the employee receives or is entitled to receive supplementary employment insurance benefits; or
   d. the non-unionized employee is recalled within a time approved by the Director of Employment Standards or a time agreed to by the employer and the employee.

3. It lasts longer than 35 weeks in a 52-week period, the employee is represented by a union, and the employer recalls the employee within the time set out in an agreement between the employer and the union.

Under s. 56(3) a week of layoff generally means a week in which an employee receives less than half of his regular earnings for a regular workweek (excluding overtime). It does not include a week where the employee is unavailable or unable to work, suspended for disciplinary reasons, or off work because of a strike in the workplace or elsewhere.

An employee who retains **recall rights** (a time-limited contractual right to return to work if a job becomes available) and who is also entitled to termination pay because of a layoff of 35 weeks or more must make a choice. Under s. 67, he may either keep the recall rights and not receive payment at that time (in which case the termination pay is paid to the director in trust for non-unionized employees) or give up recall rights and receive the termination pay immediately. An employee who chooses the first option is entitled to receive termination pay after his recall rights have expired.

Finally, as noted in Chapter 11, non-union employees may consider a *temporary layoff* to be constructive dismissal unless the employment contract expressly or implicitly allowed for such a layoff. However, the fact that the ESA, which in Ontario is an implied part of the employment contract, specifically provides for temporary layoffs arguably undermines any such claim if the layoff falls within the statutory definition for a temporary layoff. Recent case law adds support to this position (see *Trites v. Renin Corp.*, discussed in Chapter 11). In practice, lawsuits in these circumstances are rare.

The following case of *Gauthier v. Beresford Box* raises the further question of whether an employer can avoid liability under the termination provisions of the ESA by offering to re-employ an employee whose temporary layoff has turned into a deemed termination under the Act.

CASE IN POINT

Does an Offer of Re-employment Negate a Deemed Termination?

Gauthier v. Beresford Box Company Inc., **2012 CanLII 98521 (Ont. SCSM)**

Facts

Gauthier, who had worked for Beresford for 28 years, was placed on temporary layoff in May 2010. Because Gauthier had been temporarily laid off several times before, this layoff could not be seen as a constructive dismissal. Moreover, since the employer maintained benefits, the layoff remained a temporary layoff for a full 35 weeks. However, this time the layoff went beyond 35 weeks and, accordingly, Gauthier's employment was deemed terminated under the provisions of the ESA. At that point, Gauthier's lawyer sent a letter to Beresford, advising that it now owed Gauthier statutory termination and severance pay equalling 34 weeks' pay—8 weeks' termination pay and 26 weeks' severance pay. Beresford responded by offering to bring Gauthier back to work, and Gauthier agreed. However, despite his re-employment, Gauthier continued to insist that the employer pay him his ESA entitlements, and eventually he sued his employer in Small Claims Court for the amount. The employer countered that by returning to work Gauthier had exercised his right of recall under his employment contract and so no termination moneys were owing.

Relevant Issue

Whether re-employment of an employee whose employment has been deemed terminated under the temporary layoff provisions of the ESA nullifies the requirement to provide statutory termination and severance pay to that employee.

Decision

The court held that the employee is still entitled to statutory termination and severance pay because his employment contract had been terminated under the deemed termination provisions of the ESA *before* the employer offered to return him to work. As a result, he was not exercising any recall rights; rather, the employer had rehired him under a new employment contract. He was therefore entitled to 34 weeks' termination and severance pay under the ESA (Channe, 2012).

As underscored by this decision, an offer of re-employment does not negate a deemed termination pursuant to the ESA unless it is made prior to the deemed termination date. Moreover, in *Elsegood v. Cambridge Spring*, the Ontario Court of Appeal confirmed that once a termination is triggered under the ESA, the employee is also conclusively terminated for purposes of claiming common law damages. An employer cannot "contract out" of the ESA by attempting to negotiate a term in the employment contract that allows for a temporary layoff period that is longer than that provided under the ESA (Filion Wakely Thorup Angeletti, 2012).

Termination Notice or Pay in Lieu Requirements (Sections 54 to 61 and O. Reg. 288/01)

When Is an Employee "Terminated"?

To trigger the notice provisions in ss. 57 and 58 of the ESA, an employee's employment must be terminated. Termination occurs when an employer

1. dismisses or stops employing the employee (including as a result of bankruptcy or insolvency);
2. lays the employee off for a period exceeding that of a temporary layoff, as defined in the ESA; or
3. constructively dismisses the employee and the employee resigns in response within a reasonable period. Constructive dismissal occurs when an employer makes a significant change to an employee's job without providing reasonable notice and explaining the consequences of rejecting it, or obtaining the employee's consent. In these cases, the employee may be entitled to resign and claim pay in lieu of notice. According to the Ministry of Labour publication *Your Guide to the Employment Standards Act, 2000* a fundamental change includes the alteration of an employee's hours of work, salary, or responsibilities. Constructive dismissal also occurs if an employer's conduct is so unpleasant that it effectively forces an employee to resign because of the abusive treatment.

Individual Termination Requirements

Individual Notice or Pay in Lieu Entitlements

Individual notice periods range from one to eight weeks, depending on an employee's length of service. An employer may provide an employee with a combination of written notice and termination pay as long as together they equal the required number of weeks' notice. Alternatively, the employer may provide employees with payment in lieu of notice for the entire period. The ESA requires employers to provide the following minimum notice periods to employees who are being terminated (unless one of the limited exceptions discussed under the heading "Exceptions to Individual or Mass Notice of Termination Requirements" applies):

- less than 3 months' service: nil;
- 3 months but less than 1 year's service: 1 week;
- 1 year but less than 3 years' service: 2 weeks;
- 3 years but less than 4 years' service: 3 weeks;
- 4 years but less than 5 years' service: 4 weeks;
- 5 years but less than 6 years' service: 5 weeks;
- 6 years but less than 7 years' service: 6 weeks;
- 7 years but less than 8 years' service: 7 weeks; and
- 8 or more years' service: 8 weeks.

SAMPLE CALCULATION OF TERMINATION PAY

Assume that Caitlin earns $700 per week by working 35 hours at $20 per hour. After six years' employment, she is about to be laid off indefinitely. The employer wants to know how much notice or pay in lieu of notice she is entitled to. Since Caitlin has worked between six and seven years, she is entitled to six weeks' notice of termination or pay in lieu of notice. The employer has three choices: it can give her six weeks' notice and require her to work during the notice period; it can give her six weeks' termination pay and ask her to leave immediately; or it can provide a combination of pay and notice, provided that it accounts to Caitlin for the entire six-week period.

If the employer chooses to provide pay in lieu of notice for the entire amount, it calculates the pay as follows:

1. Caitlin's wages for six-week period: $700 per week × 6 weeks = $ 4,200

2. Caitlin's vacation pay, at 4% of wages
   for six-week period: $4,200 × 4% = $ 168

3. Caitlin's termination pay, at six weeks'
   wages plus 4% vacation pay: $4,200 + $168 = $ 4,368

Caitlin is therefore entitled to receive $4,368 pay in lieu of notice when her employment is terminated without notice.

The employer must continue paying the employee's benefits during the statutory notice period, including a situation in which the employee receives termination pay instead of working during all or part of the notice period. If an employer provides longer notice than the ESA requires, the "statutory notice period" is the last part of the period that ends on the termination date. Note that, as discussed in Chapter 4, a termination clause is void in its entirety if it fails to provide for continuation of benefits during the statutory notice period (ss. 60(1)(c) and 61(1)(b) of the ESA).

Termination pay must be paid seven days after termination or on the employee's next regular pay date, whichever is later.

Communicating Termination Notice

The notice of termination must be in writing, and generally it must be addressed to the employee and given in person or by mail, fax, or email, as long as delivery can be proven. An exception exists if an employee has **bumping rights** under a collective agreement or individual contract of employment. If a laid-off employee has the right to bump—displace—other employees on the basis of seniority, the notice of termination must be posted in the workplace. This notice must set out the names, seniority, and job classifications of the employees being laid off and the proposed date of layoff. If a named employee exercises bumping rights, the posting of the notice serves as the notice of termination to any employee who is bumped from her job by the employee named in the notice, effective from the date of the posting.

The employer does not have to provide reasons for the termination, either in the notice or elsewhere. However, some reasons for termination are actually against the law. For example, an employer may not terminate an employee for exercising her rights under the ESA, such as going on pregnancy leave. Similarly, dismissing an employee for exercising rights under health and safety or human rights legislation would be illegal.

Working Notice

An employer that provides notice rather than pay in lieu during the notice period must abide by the following rules:

1. the employer cannot reduce an employee's wage rate or alter the terms of employment;
2. the employer must continue to contribute to the employee's benefit plans; and
3. the employer must pay the employee the wages she is entitled to, and this amount cannot be less than her regular wages for a regular workweek. An employee who does not have a regular workweek is entitled to the average amount that she earned in the 12 weeks before notice was given.

Working After the Termination Date

The employer has some flexibility to temporarily bring back employees who have been given notice of termination without having the temporary recall affect the original date of termination. For example, an order may come in that the employer can fill only if it temporarily brings back some of the laid-off employees. As long as the recalled employees work within a 13-week period *after* their employment has been terminated, no further notice of termination is required when the temporary work ends. However, if an employee works beyond the 13-week period after the termination date, the employee is entitled to a new notice of termination as if the first one had never been given. Moreover, the employee's period of employment also includes the period of temporary work.

Mass Termination Requirements (Section 58 and O. Reg. 288/01, Section 3)

Background

Employees often find it especially difficult to obtain new jobs when they are terminated as part of a mass layoff, because so many other workers are seeking employment at the same time. During the mid-1980s, Ontario experienced a large number of plant closures, and the government responded by instituting special mass termination rules to govern these situations.

Mass Notice or Pay in Lieu

A mass termination is defined as one in which an employer terminates 50 or more employees at the employer's establishment in a period of four consecutive weeks. In this situation, mass notice requirements apply as follows:

- 8 weeks' notice where 50 to 199 employees are terminated,
- 12 weeks' notice where 200 to 499 employees are terminated, and
- 16 weeks' notice where 500 or more employees are terminated.

These requirements do not apply, however, if the employer is terminating 10 percent or less of its workforce at an establishment *and* none of the terminations is caused by the permanent discontinuance of part of the employer's business. In other words, where the mass layoff (involving 50 or more employees) represents a relatively small percentage of the total workforce and it is not part of a plant closure, the employer does not have to meet the mass notice requirements. An employer must, of course, provide individual notice or pay in lieu to any employees terminated in these circumstances.

Where a terminated employee has bumping rights, a notice listing the name, seniority, and job classification of the employee must be posted. This notice is deemed to be notice of termination to the employee who ultimately will be laid off, and it is effective on the date of the original posting.

Because mass notice requirements arise only when 50 or more employees are terminated within four consecutive weeks, an employer may avoid these special requirements by staggering layoffs so that no more than 49 employees are laid off within that period.

Notice to Director of Employment Standards

In mass termination situations, an employer has two other obligations: notifying the Director of Employment Standards and posting this notification in the workplace. Notification to the Director must be in the prescribed form. No notice to employees is effective until the employer submits the required form to the Director. Part of this form must be posted in a conspicuous place in the workplace for the duration of the statutory notice period.

Employees' Advance Notice of Resignation

Employees who have received mass notice of termination and who wish to leave before the end of their notice period must provide the employer with advance notice of resignation. They must give at least

- one week's written notice if they have been employed for less than two years, or
- two weeks' written notice if they have been employed for two years or more.

This obligation is meant to address employers' concerns that employees who find alternative employment during a lengthy 8- to 16-week mass notice period may leave their jobs with little advance notice, thereby making it difficult to continue operating during the notice period.

Exceptions to Individual or Mass Notice of Termination Requirements

In certain situations, an employer is not required to give either notice of termination or pay in lieu of notice to a dismissed employee. Some of these exceptions resemble the circumstances in which reasonable notice of termination or pay in lieu is not required at common law (these circumstances are discussed in Chapter 13 under the heading "Establishing Just Cause Under the Common Law"). The exemptions from statutory notice of termination requirements, which appear in the *Termination and Severance of Employment* regulation (O. reg. 288/01), are discussed below.

1. Term or Task Employee

An employer is not required to provide statutory notice of termination to an employee hired for a definite term of less than one year or for a specific task that will take less than a year to complete. This exception does not apply if employment ends before the end of the term or the completion of the task or if employment continues for three months or more after the end of the term or the completion of the task.

2. Temporary Layoffs

The employer need not provide notice of termination to an employee who is on temporary layoff, as it is defined in the ESA.

3. Wilful Misconduct, Disobedience, or Wilful Neglect of Duty

No notice of termination is required where the employee has been "guilty of wilful misconduct, disobedience or wilful neglect of duty that is not trivial and has not been condoned by the employer." The words "that is not trivial" were added in 2000, and they suggest that the misconduct must be fairly serious to fall within this exemption. The non-trivial misconduct must also be "wilful." In other words, an employer must show that the employee's misconduct was intentional. For example, a truck driver who is frequently involved in accidents because of his carelessness is probably entitled to statutory termination notice or pay in lieu, provided that the accidents are not intentional. On the other hand, in *Re Chart Industries Ltd.*, the actions of an employee who engaged in three incidents involving serious mistakes, including rewiring a machine to bypass the safety control, were found to fall within the definition of "wilful neglect of duty."

Another example of misconduct that was found to be "wilful" is seen in the case of *Marquis v. Arrow Games Corporation*. There, a printing press operator called his manager an idiot, swore at him, and refused to take direction from him following a work-related disagreement. In a subsequent disciplinary meeting two days later, Marquis continued swearing at the plant manager and interrupting him whenever he spoke. At that point he was fired. When the employer refused to provide him with statutory termination or severance pay, Marquis filed a complaint with the Ministry of Labour. The Ontario Labour Relations Board found that Marquis was not entitled to termination or severance pay because his insubordinate conduct, which occurred on more than one occasion, was not trivial and was not condoned by the employer. Moreover, his refusal to apologize after the initial incident and at the meeting two days later showed that he felt no remorse, thus damaging the employment relationship irreparably.

Although the common law concept of just cause is similar to this statutory exemption, the two are not identical. (See Chapter 13 for a detailed discussion of just cause at common law.) Under the ESA, the inquiry is focused on the misconduct itself, and a single act of wilful misconduct may be sufficient to eliminate the requirements for notice. Under the common law, while the element of wilfulness is not essential, a single act of misconduct rarely satisfies the standard of just cause. In fact, under the common law, the inquiry is much broader and a number of other factors are considered: was it an isolated incident, were there prior warnings, what is the employee's length of service, have other employees been disciplined for similar incidents, and are there any mitigating circumstances? In the context of these other factors, while wilful misconduct under the ESA is typically thought to be a higher standard than just cause under the common law, sometimes it may be more difficult to show just cause than if the inquiry is limited to the issue of wilfulness.

In summary, where the employee's misconduct is serious, such as in the case of major theft, the employer will probably allege cause for both statutory and common law purposes and not provide notice of termination or pay in lieu of notice. However, in situations where the misconduct is less serious or less clearcut, the employer may decide to meet statutory notice requirements, because these requirements are relatively modest. Note, though, that the employer's payment should be made on a **without prejudice** basis. This means that the payment is made on a voluntary basis and is not an admission that there is no just cause under the law. Thus, the payment cannot be used by the dismissed employee later in court to argue that the employer effectively admitted lack of just cause and must now provide reasonable notice under the common law. This "without prejudice" payment can even be made where an employer has a strong just cause case in order to decrease the chance of litigation.

4. Refusal of (Reasonable) Alternative Work

An employer is not required to provide notice of termination if an employee refuses an offer of "reasonable alternative employment" with the employer or refuses an offer of "alternative employment" that is available through a seniority system. In other words, an employee who has the right to bump a more junior employee in a layoff but chooses not to exercise that right forfeits the right to termination notice. The alternative employment does not have to be "reasonable."

However, where the alternative work does not involve bumping rights under a seniority system, an employer's offer of alternative employment must be reasonable. To be reasonable, the offered job must be comparable in terms of duties, salary, security, and reporting relationships. An employer that offers an employee a job that involves a significant demotion or wage reduction will probably be required to provide notice of termination because the job does not fall within the exemption.

5. Return After Recall

An employee who does not return to work within a reasonable time after being recalled from a temporary layoff is not entitled to statutory notice of termination.

6. Strikes

An employee who is terminated during or as a result of a **strike** or **lockout** at the workplace is not entitled to notice of termination. This exception applies both to employees in the striking or locked-out bargaining unit and to other employees in the workplace who are laid off as a result of the lockout or strike.

7. Construction and Certain Shipbuilding Employees

Employees who work in construction and certain types of shipbuilding are not entitled to statutory notice of termination.

8. *Frustration of Contract*

If a contract of employment is frustrated—that is, made impossible to perform—by an unforeseeable event or circumstance, an employer is not required to provide an employee with termination notice or pay in lieu. **Frustration of contract** may occur, for example, where a fire or flood destroys the workplace and an employer is no longer able to provide a job. According to the Ministry of Labour's employment standards guide, a contract cannot be frustrated by the bankruptcy or insolvency of an employer.

This exception does not apply where the contract of employment has become impossible to perform because of an employee's disability.

Severance Pay (Sections 63 to 66 and O. Reg. 288/01, Section 9)

What Is Severance Pay Under the ESA?

The term "severance pay" can be confusing because it is commonly used in two distinct ways. People often use the term when referring to any severance package that an employee receives on dismissal. However, in both the federal jurisdiction and in Ontario, the term "severance pay" refers to a specific statutory entitlement on termination. It is a one-time lump-sum payment that is made in defined circumstances and that is based on an employee's years of service. This payment is made in addition to any minimum notice or pay in lieu of notice requirements. Whereas notice or pay in lieu requirements are intended to provide an employee with income while he finds another job, severance pay is generally intended to compensate longer-term employees for their loyalty, loss of seniority, and loss of job-related benefits.

To qualify for severance pay, an employee must have worked for the employer for five or more years. In addition, the employer must have an Ontario payroll[1] of at least $2.5 million *or* must have severed the employment of 50 or more employees in a six-month period because all or part of the business closed. In other words, severance pay obligations target relatively long-term employees who work for medium to large employers. The public policy reason behind this is that employees with five or more years' service usually have the most to lose in seniority and benefit rights. Furthermore, by limiting severance pay obligations to employers with minimum payrolls of $2.5 million, the statutory provisions do not directly affect small businesses.

Qualifying employees are entitled to receive severance pay in the amount of one week's pay for each year's service, to a maximum of 26 weeks. Part years are credited, so that an employee with 14 years and three months' service is entitled to 14.25 weeks' severance pay. (See the detailed calculations below under the heading "Calculating Severance Pay.")

Although many of the following provisions relating to severance pay are similar to those relating to termination notice or pay in lieu, they are not identical. Employers must review relevant parts of the ESA when terminations are being considered. For example, under the termination provisions, a week of layoff is generally defined as one where the employee receives less than one-half of his regular earnings. In contrast, under the severance pay provisions, a week of layoff is generally defined as one in which an employee receives less than one-quarter of his regular earnings.

When Is Employment Severed?

A person's employment is severed when an employer

1. dismisses or stops employing the employee (including as a result of bankruptcy or insolvency);
2. constructively dismisses the employee, who resigns within a reasonable time as a result;
3. lays the employee off for 35 or more weeks in a period of 52 consecutive weeks (the 35 weeks need not be consecutive);
4. lays the employee off because of a permanent discontinuance of all of the employer's business at an establishment; or
5. gives the employee written notice of termination, the person resigns after giving two weeks' written notice, and the resignation takes effect during the statutory notice period. For example, assume that Guo is entitled to 8 weeks' statutory notice, his employer gives him 12 weeks' notice, and during the notice period he finds another job. Guo is entitled to severance pay only if he gives his employer 2 weeks' notice of resignation *and* the notice takes effect within the final 8 weeks of employment. If he leaves before the final 8 weeks or without providing the required notice, he loses his entitlement to statutory severance pay.

Exemptions from Severance Pay

Many of the exemptions to the severance pay requirements are similar, but not always identical, to the exemptions for termination notice or pay in lieu. An employee whose employment is severed is not entitled to severance pay in the following situations:

1. The employee is guilty of wilful misconduct, disobedience, or wilful neglect of duty that is not trivial or condoned by the employer (same as the termination provisions).
2. The employee refuses an offer of "reasonable alternative employment" with the employer (same as the termination provisions).
3. The employee refuses "reasonable alternative employment" available through a seniority system. Unlike the termination provisions related to bumping, this provision requires the alternative employment to be "reasonable." (Recall that alternative employment is deemed to be reasonable when it is comparable in terms of duties, salary, security, and reporting relationships.) Therefore, an employee retains severance pay rights even when the right to termination notice or pay in lieu has been forfeited because the employee refused to bump another employee if the new job does not constitute *reasonable* alternative employment.
4. The employee retires on a full pension, excluding Canada Pension Plan benefits (different from the termination provisions).
5. The employee is severed because of a strike, and the employer can show that the economic effects of the strike caused all or part of the business to close (this wording varies from the notice of termination exemptions).
6. The employee's contract of employment has become impossible to perform or has been frustrated. Again, this exemption does not apply where the

employee is unable to perform the employment contract because of disability. Similarly, it does not apply where the frustration results from a permanent discontinuance of all or part of the employer's business because of a fortuitous or unforeseen event, the employer's death, or the employee's death, if the employee received a notice of termination before his or her death (same as the termination provisions with respect to the disability qualifier).

7. The employee is employed in construction (same as the termination provisions).

8. The employee is engaged in the onsite maintenance of buildings, structures, roads, sewers, pipelines, mains, tunnels, or other works (different from the termination provisions).

Calculating Severance Pay

Statutory severance pay is calculated by multiplying the employee's regular wages for a regular workweek by the sum of

1. the number of completed years of employment, and

2. the number of completed months of employment divided by 12 for a year that is not completed.

This calculation means that an employee receives one week's severance pay for each year he has worked for an employer, plus a partial week for any year that is incomplete. The maximum amount of severance pay is 26 weeks' pay. For example:

SAMPLE CALCULATION OF SEVERANCE PAY

Assume that Francesco regularly works 40 hours a week at $20 per hour. His employer has a payroll of more than $2.5 million, and he has worked for the employer for 10 years and 6 months, so he qualifies for severance pay as well as termination notice or pay in lieu, as follows:

1. Francesco's regular wages for a regular
   workweek: 40 hours × $20 per hour = $800

2. Francesco's completed years' service: = 10 years

3. Francesco's partial year's service
   (completed months in the final year,
   divided by 12):   6 months ÷ 12 = 0.5 years

4. Francesco's total years' service
   (completed years' plus partial year's
   service):   10 + 0.5 = 10.5 years

5. Francesco's severence pay (regular
   wages for a regular workweek
   multiplied by total years' service): $800 × 10.5 = $8,400

Francesco is entitled to $8,400 in severance pay in addition to 8 weeks' notice of termination or pay in lieu of notice.

For employees who do not have a regular workweek, the employer averages the regular wages they received in the 12 weeks in which they worked immediately before the employment was severed. For example, if Ashley was paid on the basis of commission, the employer would calculate her earnings in the 12 weeks before severance and divide them by 12 to determine her average earnings over that period. It would then multiply that amount by the number of years and any partial year she worked for the employer.

An employer may make severance payments in installments with the written agreement of the employee or the approval of the Director of Employment Standards, provided that the installment period does not exceed three years.

As shown in the *Mattiassi* decision below, without this agreement, statutory severance pay must be paid in a lump sum. This case also underscores the point that statutory termination and severance pay are distinct and separate entitlements and cannot be used to offset one another.

CASE IN POINT

Court Rejects Employer's "Set-Off" Argument

Mattiassi v. Hathro Management Partnership, [2011] OJ no. 4774 (Small Claims Court)

Facts

Mattiassi had worked for Hathro Management for 26 years when, on November 16, 2009, she received notice that her job would come to an end on November 30, 2010—effectively giving her 54 weeks' working notice of termination. Two weeks before the end of her working notice period, the employer also provided her with a cheque equivalent to approximately 8 weeks' pay. However, when her job ended, Mattiassi sued the employer in Small Claims Court for statutory severance pay, arguing that while the working notice provided by the employer far exceeded the ESA's *termination* notice requirement of 8 weeks, the employer still had to provide her with statutory severance pay. The employer countered that the combined 62 weeks' notice and pay were well in excess of the total statutory termination and severance pay requirements of 34 weeks (that is, 8 weeks plus 26 weeks, respectively) and therefore she was not entitled to a further, separate amount of statutory severance pay.

Relevant Issue

Whether the employer had met its obligation to provide statutory severance pay.

Decision

The court found that Mattiassi was entitled to an additional lump-sum amount equal to 26 weeks' pay to cover her statutory severance pay. It stated that termination and severance pay under the ESA are two distinct and separate entitlements—serving different purposes—and that exceeding the requirements of the former does not eliminate the requirement to provide the latter. The court noted that, unlike termination pay, which is payable only where the employer has failed to provide the statutory notice of termination, statutory severance pay cannot be avoided by giving notice. The court did, however, deduct the approximately 8 weeks' pay that Mattiassi received upon termination from the amount owing for statutory severance pay (Minken, 2012).

Mattiassi underscores the importance of getting a full release from an employee that acknowledges that the working notice and/or payment in lieu of notice received is, itself, in lieu of statutory severance pay (and constitutes a greater benefit) when the employer provides common law notice and/or pay in excess of the combined ESA notice and severance entitlements. That said, ideally, the amount paid in lieu of notice will exceed the statutory severance entitlement, so as to avoid any argument that the release isn't binding because the severance provisions of the ESA cannot be met by providing an extended working notice period.

Where an Employee Has Recall Rights

As with termination pay, an employee who both retains recall rights and is entitled to severance pay must make a choice. She may either keep the recall rights and not receive severance pay at that time (in which case, the money is paid to the director in trust for non-union employees) *or* give up the recall rights and receive the severance pay immediately. If she chooses to retain recall rights, she is entitled to receive severance pay once the recall rights have expired.

If an employee is entitled to both termination pay and severance pay, she must make the same election for both. She must either forfeit her recall rights and collect both termination and severance pay, or retain her recall rights and have the termination and severance pay held in trust until either she returns to work or the recall rights expire.

When ESA Payments Must Be Made

Under the ESA, employers must pay dismissed employees outstanding wages, vacation pay, and termination and severance pay no later than seven days after employment ends or on the day that would have been the employee's next payday, whichever is later. However, as noted above, with the agreement of the employee or the approval of the Director of Employment Standards, the employer may make severance payments in installments over a period of up to three years.

Continuity of Employment

Section 9 of the ESA addresses the effect of a sale or transfer of an employer's business to a new owner on an employee's length of service. It states:

> If an employer sells a business or a part of a business and the purchaser employs an employee of the seller, the employment of the employee shall be deemed not to have been terminated or severed for the purposes of this Act and his or her employment with the seller shall be deemed to have been employment with the purchaser for the purpose of any subsequent calculation of the employee's length or period of employment.

This provision means that where an employee continues to work for a new owner of a former employer's business, the employee retains his rights and length of service as if there had been no sale or transfer. For example, an employee who worked for Seller Company for five years and continued working for Buyer Company for another four years is entitled to termination notice or pay in lieu and severance pay on the basis of nine years' service. Note that because the employee's employment continued under Buyer Company, Seller Company did not have a statutory obligation under the ESA to provide termination or severance at the time of the sale.

Consider the following example of the continuity of service rule. Assume that Sam worked three and a half years for his employer, Rachel. Rachel sold the business to Mahmoud, who continued Sam's employment. Four years later, Mahmoud decided to close the business and permanently lay off all employees. In this situation, Sam's length of employment with the "employer" is seven and a half years, because it includes three and a half years' work for Rachel and four years' work for Mahmoud.

Sam is entitled to seven weeks' notice of termination or pay in lieu of notice, since he worked between seven and eight years for the employer. Because Sam has at least five years' service with the employer, he is also entitled to severance pay if one of the other two statutory requirements are met, namely:

1. Mahmoud has an Ontario payroll of at least $2.5 million, or
2. Mahmoud dismisses 50 or more employees in a six-month period because of the closure of his business.

If either of these statutory requirements is met, Sam is entitled to seven and a half weeks' severance pay in addition to the seven weeks' termination notice or pay in lieu.

An exception to this rule arises if there is at least a 13-week gap in employment. For example, if Buyer Company hires an employee more than 13 weeks after either the employee's last day of work with Seller Company or the date of Seller Company's sale to Buyer Company (whichever is earlier), the employee does not retain his years of service with Seller Company. This affects the employee's length of service with Buyer Company for the purpose of calculating termination notice or pay entitlement and other employment standards rights that depend on length of service, such as vacation time. In this situation, Seller Company would be responsible for providing termination and any severance pay owing upon the sale of the business.

This 13-week rule can also apply in the absence of a sale: if a person works for an employer for three years, resigns, and is then rehired more than 13 weeks later, only the employment after rehiring is taken into account for the purpose of entitlements under the ESA.

The continuity of service rule was also at issue in *Abbott v. Bombardier Inc.* In that case, employees whose jobs at Bombardier had been outsourced to a new employer argued that Bombardier should pay them termination and severance pay under the ESA because s. 9 only applies where the business is sold as a "going concern." Upholding the trial judge's decision, the Ontario Court of Appeal found that the sale of part of a business under s. 9 applies to a broad range of transactions, including outsourcing and the transfer of assets. In its view, giving s. 9 a broad interpretation is more consistent with the intent of the provision, which is to ensure that an employee's previous service is recognized during times of corporate change.

The employees in *Bombardier* also argued that s. 9 should not apply because the terms of employment offered by the new employer were fundamentally different from their previous terms. As such, there could be no continuity of employment. The trial court disagreed; it found that there had not been a fundamental change of terms but that even if there had been, the new terms are irrelevant once the employee accepts the new employer's offer. The Court of Appeal agreed that the new terms were not fundamentally different. It declined to rule on whether s. 9 applies where the terms of employment are radically different under the successor employer.

NOTE

1   Note that as of the date of writing, there is one Superior Court of Justice trial decision—*Paquette c. Quadraspec Inc.*—that has determined that the payroll calculation is not limited to Ontario. For a discussion of this case, see Filion Wakely Thorup Angeletti, "Severance Pay Alert: Recent Ontario Superior Court Decision Challenges Long-Standing Approach to Calculating the Payroll Threshold," *What's New in HR Law*, July 2014.

REFERENCES

2058761 Ontario Ltd v. Caceres. 2007 CanLII 605 (Ont. LRB).

Abbott v. Bombardier Inc. 2005 CanLII 63771 (Ont. SC); 2007 ONCA 233.

Canning, Ed. Joe Stuck to His Employment Rights. *Hamilton Spectator*, February 1, 2013. http://www.thespec.com/news-story/2269984-joe-stuck-to-his-employment-rights.

Channe, Bonnea. Termination and Severance Pay Owed to Employee Recalled from Layoff. *What's New in HR Law*. September 2012. Filion Wakely Thorup Angeletti. http://filion.on.ca/uploads/ckeditor/attachment_files/197/Gauthier.pdf.

Chart Industries Ltd., Re. (1992), OESAD No. 28 (LRB).

Echlin, Randall, and Christine Thomlinson. *For Better or For Worse: A Practical Guide to Canadian Employment Law*, 3rd ed. Toronto: Canada Law Book, 2011.

Elsegood v. Cambridge Spring Service (2001) Ltd. 2011 ONCA 831.

Employee Fired for Cause Gets $25,000. *HR Professional*. Volume 28, no. 5, July/August 2011, p. 12. Moneyville.ca.

Employment Standards Act, 2000. SO 2000, c. 41.

Ferguson, Meghan. Seasonal Employees May Be Eligible for Severance Pay but Not Termination Pay. February 20, 2014. First Reference Talks. http://blog.firstreference.com/2014/02/20/seasonal-employees-may-be-eligible-for-severance-pay-but-not-termination-pay.

Filion Wakely Thorup Angeletti. Common Law Damages for a Temporary Layoff. *What's New in HR Law*. May 2012. http://filion.on.ca/uploads/ckeditor/attachment_files/109/Elsegood.pdf?1338223486.

Gauthier v. Beresford Box Company Inc. 2012 CanLII 98521 (Ont. SCSM).

Gilbert, Douglas, Brian Burkett, and Moira McCaskill. *Canadian Labour and Employment Law for the US Practitioner*. Washington, DC: Bureau of National Affairs, 2000.

Marquis v. Arrow Games Corporation. 2008 CanLII 51222 (Ont. LRB).

Mattiassi v. Hathro Management Partnership. [2011] OJ no. 4774 (Small Claims Court).

Minken, Ronald. 26 Weeks Severance Added to 54 Weeks Working Notice. *Canadian Employment Law Today.* April 4, 2012, p. 1. http://www.minkenemploymentlawyers.com/wp-content/uploads/2012/04/eCELT-April-4-2012-26-Weeks-Severence.pdf.

Ontario Ministry of Labour. *Your Guide to the Employment Standards Act, 2000*. Toronto: Queen's Printer for Ontario, 2013. http://www.labour.gov.on.ca/english/es/pdf/es_guide.pdf.

Ontario Nurses' Association v. Mount Sinai Hospital. 2005 CanLII 14437 (Ont. CA); 2004 CanLII 15351 (Ont. SCDC).

Oosterbosch v. FAG Aerospace Inc. 2011 ONSC 1538.

Paquette c. Quadraspec Inc. 2014 ONCS 2431.

Roher, Eric, and Melanie Warner. *Ontario Employment Standards Act Quick Reference*. Toronto: Carswell, 2002.

Sastri, Tara. Bombardier: Outsourcing Transactions and Severance Payment Obligations Under the Ontario Employment Standards Act, 2000. *Labour Relations: Labour Relations Section*. Volume 10, no. 2, December 2007.

Smith, Jeffrey. Just Cause: No Severance Required for Insubordinate Employee. *Canadian Employment Law Today*. Issue no. 528, February 25, 2008, p. 7.

Snow Valley Resorts (1987) Ltd. v. Barton. 2013 CanLII 8963 (Ont. LRB).

Termination and Severance of Employment. O. reg. 288/01.

Trites v. Renin Corp. 2013 ONSC 2715.

Whitten & Lublin Employment Lawyers. Just Cause at Common Law Might Not Be Enough. *WL Update*. Issue no. 28, March 2013, p. 1. http://www.toronto-employmentlawyer.com/wp-content/uploads/2013-04-employment-newsletter.pdf.

Wilson, Peter, and Allison Taylor. *The Corporate Counsel Guide to Employment Law*, 2nd ed. Aurora, ON: Canada Law Book, 2003.

REVIEW AND DISCUSSION QUESTIONS

1. Is an employer required to provide a recall date in order for a layoff to be considered temporary? Explain your answer.

2. Must notice of termination under the ESA be in writing? Must it indicate the reasons for termination?

3. Statutory notice of termination and severance pay requirements under the ESA serve different purposes. Describe those different purposes.

4. Identify and describe eight exceptions to the severance pay requirements.

5. Brenda has just received written notice from her employer, ABC Inc., that she is being terminated from her mid-level management sales position, effective eight weeks from now, because the firm has decided to downsize. Twelve other people are also being terminated for the same reason. Brenda earns $52,000 per year (including vacation pay) and has been with this firm for four years. ABC Inc. is a medium-sized company with an Ontario payroll of approximately $9 million. Based on your knowledge of Ontario employment law, answer the following questions:

   a. Is Brenda entitled to severance pay under the *Employment Standards Act*? Explain your answer.

   b. How many weeks' notice of termination is Brenda entitled to under the ESA? Is she also entitled to mass notice of termination? Explain your answer.

   c. Under the ESA, Brenda cannot file a claim with the Ministry of Labour *and* sue for wrongful dismissal damages under the common law. Identify and discuss the factors Brenda should consider in making the choice between these two avenues.

6. You are an HR consultant. You are approached by an employer that currently has 500 employees but that must, for economic reasons, permanently lay off 102 of these employees over the next several weeks. Explain to him how much statutory termination notice or pay in lieu of notice he must give to these employees. Describe the other requirements that apply in a mass notice situation.

7. Several jurisdictions in Canada have "unjust dismissal" provisions in their employment standards legislation that allow an employee (with a certain minimum length of service) to challenge her dismissal in front of a tribunal and to be reinstated if she was dismissed "without just cause." Should Ontario amend its *Employment Standards Act* to include such a provision? Discuss.

8. Stuart had worked for a large aerospace company (with an annual payroll greater than $2.5 million) for 17.5 years. Over the past several years, he had been frequently coached and had received written warnings, as well as a two-day suspension, for taking excessively long meal breaks and being late for shifts. More recently, Stuart had produced numerous faulty parts that did not meet with the precise specifications required in the employer's industry. Given his poor performance record, the employer decided to dismiss Stuart for "just cause." Accordingly, the employer did not provide him with notice of termination or pay in lieu under either the ESA or the common law. Stuart sued the employer for both common law and statutory notice.

   a. Do you think Stuart is entitled to notice under either the common law or the ESA? Support your answer.

   b. Assume for this part of the question that Stuart *is* entitled to termination notice and, in addition, to severance pay under the ESA. If he earns $1,000 per week including vacation pay, how much does his employer owe him?

9. Richard worked in the detailing section of the employer's small car wash and car detailing business. Paid strictly on commission, he earned approximately $50 per detailing job. However, around the beginning of June 2014 he noticed that he was only being paid $40 to $44 per job. Richard spoke to his employer about this change, but nothing was done and shortly thereafter Richard quit his job and filed a complaint with the Ministry of Labour, alleging constructive dismissal. Do you think his complaint would be successful?

10. Chloe was a seasonal employee who had worked for the employer's resort every winter for 21 years—for a combined total of 80 months. At the end of Chloe's 21st season, the employer laid her off permanently, without providing termination or severance pay under the ESA. The employer explained that seasonal employees are not covered by those provisions. Chloe filed a claim with the Ministry of Labour for both entitlements.

    a. In your opinion, is Chloe entitled to termination pay under the ESA?

    b. Assuming that the employer has an annual Ontario payroll of at least $2.5 million, is Chloe entitled to receive statutory severance pay under ss. 64 to 65 of the ESA?

Dismissal Without Cause

15

LEARNING OUTCOMES

After completing this chapter, you will be able to:

- Understand how reasonable notice periods under the common law are determined.

- Identify when frustration of contract occurs.

- Explain the benefits and drawbacks of providing working notice rather than pay in lieu of reasonable notice to a dismissed employee.

- Explain how to structure a separation package.

- Explain an employee's common law duty to mitigate his or her damages after dismissal (including constructive dismissal).

- Identify the types of damages that can be awarded to a wrongfully dismissed employee in light of the Supreme Court of Canada's decision in *Honda Canada Inc. v. Keays*.

- Identify strategies for avoiding wrongful dismissal claims.

- Understand issues related to providing employee references.

Introduction

As discussed in Chapter 13, unless an employer is able to prove that an employee fundamentally breached the terms of the employment contract, any dismissal must proceed on a without-just-cause basis. An employer does not need just cause to dismiss a non-unionized employee. Provided that the dismissal does not infringe a statute, an employer may dismiss such an employee as long as the employer provides notice of dismissal or payment in lieu of notice. There is no right of reinstatement for wrongful dismissal under the common law.

To determine what the notice period or payment in lieu of notice should be, an employer needs to look to three areas: the employment contract, the termination provisions in the Ontario *Employment Standards Act, 2000*, and the common law.

If the employment contract has an enforceable termination provision that sets out the employee's entitlements in the case of dismissal without cause, the employer is required to provide those entitlements. (Note that the provision will only be enforceable if it at least matches the entitlements under the *Employment Standards Act*.) However, if an employment contract lacks a provision that governs notice of termination or if such a provision is unenforceable, an employer has an implied duty to provide *reasonable* notice of termination or pay in lieu of reasonable notice under the common law. When the employment contract is oral, the employer also has an implied duty to provide the employee with reasonable notice. What is "reasonable" in a particular situation depends on the facts of the case, but courts have developed a number of factors to consider and weigh in determining the appropriate length of the notice period. The reasonable notice standard under the common law exists in addition to, and usually significantly exceeds, the minimum statutory standards for notice of termination and severance pay (see Chapter 14 for discussion of statutory termination and severance pay requirements).

It should be noted that dismissal for economic reasons is not considered just cause, and reasonable notice of termination is required if an employee is permanently laid off for lack of work. The only exception to an employer's obligation to give reasonable notice of termination in the absence of just cause under the common law is frustration of contract, discussed below.

Frustration of Contract

In unusual circumstances, an employment contract comes to an end without notice because the contract has become impossible to perform for reasons such as floods, fires, or explosions that prevent the work from being performed. A contract cannot become frustrated as a result of foreseeable problems, such as the breakdown of machinery, a strike or lockout, or an employer's economic difficulties. The onus of proving that an employment contract has become frustrated lies with the employer.

Frustration of employment may also occur if an employee goes to jail or loses professional credentials, thereby rendering him incapable of performing the job. For example, if a member of an engineering department loses his engineering designation, and the designation is needed to do the job, the employer could argue that the employment contract has been frustrated.

A more problematic example is when an employer alleges frustration of contract because of an employee's prolonged illness. As discussed in Chapters 2 and 5, an employee who is absent from work because of disability is protected under the Ontario *Human Rights Code*, and an employer must accommodate that employee unless this creates undue hardship. However, in exceptional circumstances, an employer might advance an argument that the employment contract has been frustrated. In *Demuynck v. Agentis Information Services Inc.*, a court found frustration of contract on the basis of an employee's disability.

CASE IN POINT

Contract Frustrated Because of Employee's Physical Incapacity

Demuynck v. Agentis Information Services Inc., 2003 BCSC 96

Facts

Demuynck worked for the employer as an accounts clerk for 18 years. In 1996, she injured her right elbow in a fall unrelated to work. She continued working until mid-1997, but then she left work and began to receive short-term disability benefits. Her doctor postponed her date of return four times. She returned to work for three weeks, but left and collected long-term disability benefits for the maximum two-year period, which ended in January 2000. In April 1999, the employer dismissed Demuynck. The letter of termination did not refer to frustration of the employment contract; instead, it stated that the employer was undergoing considerable change. It offered Demuynck the equivalent of 12 months' salary if she remained unemployed or a "top up" of her earnings if she became employed. She rejected this offer and sued for damages equivalent to 16 to 18 months of salary in lieu of notice. At trial, the employer alleged that the employment contract had become frustrated by Demuynck's physical incapacity.

Relevant Issue

Whether the contract of employment had become frustrated by the employee's physical incapacity.

Decision

The BC Supreme Court found that the employment contract had become frustrated. Frustration of contract occurs when an employee's incapacity is of such a nature, or is likely to continue for such a period of time, that the further performance of employment duties either is impossible or would be radically different from that originally contemplated in the employment contract. In making this determination, the court considered the following factors:

1. *The terms of the contract, including provisions relating to sick pay.* If an employee returns to work or is likely to return to work within the period during which sick pay is available, the contract is not frustrated.

2. *How long the contract was likely to last in the absence of sickness.* An employment contract of indefinite duration is less likely to become frustrated than a contract related to temporary employment.

3. *The nature of the employment.* If the employee is one of many employees who do the same job, the contract is more likely to survive than if the employee is a key individual who must be replaced quickly.

4. *The nature of the illness or injury.* The length of an employee's absence and her prospects for recovery are also relevant. For example, where an employee is expected to make a full recovery, it is unlikely that the employment contract will be frustrated even if the absence is prolonged.

5. *The employment history.* A contract covering a longstanding employment relationship is not as easily frustrated as one covering a short relationship.

In this case, the court concluded that an absence of between 18 and 24 months was the limit of a temporary absence. Demuynck had been off work for 20 months, and there was no evidence that she would be able to return to work in the future. She had exhausted her disability benefits. If her incapacity was not permanent, it was of such a duration that further performance was impossible or radically different from that contemplated in the original employment contract. The employment contract was therefore frustrated, and Demuynck was not entitled to wrongful dismissal damages.

Although the court in *Demuynck* determined that the employment contract had been frustrated by the employee's physical incapacity, findings of frustration of contract are rare. Where the impossibility of performance stems from a disability, the employer must accommodate the employee up to the point of undue hardship before considering any further steps. A court is less likely to find frustration of contract if an employee continues to be eligible for long-term disability benefits, because the existence of long-term benefits indicates that the parties to the employment contract contemplated and provided for the possibility of long-term disability. As a general rule of thumb, an employer should wait for two years before considering severance of an employment relationship on the basis of frustration caused by an employee's absence. Even after that time, as shown in *Naccarato v. Costco*, an employer should, before alleging frustration, obtain an up-to-date prognosis from an absent employee's physician to establish that there is no reasonable likelihood of a return to work in the foreseeable future.

CASE IN POINT

Five Years' Absence Not Frustration

Naccarato v. Costco, 2010 ONSC 2651

Facts

After being off work for five years with depression, Naccarato, an employee with 17 years' service, received notice from Costco that it considered his employment contract terminated due to frustration. Its position was based on several factors: the length of Naccarato's absence; his receipt of long-term disability benefits, which required him to declare himself totally disabled; and his physician's statement that he could not predict when Naccarato would be able to return to his job (although Naccarato was still in treatment and a new psychiatrist was being sought). Costco paid Naccarato his statutory entitlements under the *Employment Standards Act*, as required where the frustration is disability related, but no other termination moneys were provided. Naccarato countered that his employment contract was not frustrated, and he commenced a lawsuit for common law wrongful dismissal (reasonable notice) damages.

Relevant Issue

Whether the employee's employment contract was legally frustrated.

Decision

The court found that Naccarato's employment contract was not frustrated. First, his doctor had indicated that he was still attempting treatment through a referral to another psychiatrist. This suggested there was a possibility of improvement and therefore the employer had not met the burden of proving there was no reasonable likelihood that Naccarato would return to work in the foreseeable future. Second, given the nature of the employer's operations, there was no evidence that holding Naccarato's clerk position open was disruptive or created hardship. As a result, Naccarato was awarded ten months' reasonable notice damages, which were reduced by the amount of the statutory termination and severance pay already given (24.8 weeks' pay, less statutory deductions).

This decision highlights the importance of looking at each situation involving an employee with a prolonged illness on its own facts and of making certain that the medical documentation is unambiguous concerning the likelihood of a return to work. The judge in *Naccarato* noted that the employer could have asked his doctor a follow-up question with respect to the likelihood of a return to work in the foreseeable future, but failed to do so. Furthermore, where a doctor's responses to that question are inconclusive, it may be appropriate to ask for the employee to submit to an independent medical examination. Alternatively, where an employee's extended absence for health-related reasons does not materially affect the employer, it may make sense to let the situation continue as it is (Sherrard Kuzz LLP, 2010, p. 3).

Wrongful Dismissal

The following discussion relates to dismissals without cause where the employment contract does not contain an enforceable termination provision. In these circumstances, employers must comply with the common law requirement to provide reasonable notice or pay in lieu of reasonable notice. If they do not, they have wrongfully dismissed the employee.

How Much Notice Is Reasonable?

In determining the necessary notice period, the first consideration is the minimum statutory requirements of the *Employment Standards Act* (see the discussion in Chapter 14). Because employees terminated without cause under the common law are usually entitled to statutory termination notice or pay in lieu (and possibly statutory severance pay) as well as common law notice, an employer must ensure that its separation package at least meets the statutory minimum requirements. Otherwise, if an employee sues for wrongful dismissal, the employer could find itself paying additional compensatory damages for its improper conduct in the manner of termination—that is, failing to meet its statutory obligations.

After determining the minimum statutory requirements, an employer must assess what constitutes reasonable notice under the common law. The answer to this question *depends on the unique circumstances* of a particular employment relationship. The leading case is *Bardal v. The Globe and Mail Ltd.*, which highlights the main, although not the only, factors that affect the length of the reasonable notice period:

1. length of service;
2. character of employment;
3. the employee's age; and
4. the availability of similar employment, given the employee's experience, training, and qualifications.

Length of Service

Although *Bardal* lists a number of relevant considerations in determining the reasonable notice period, many employers think there is a "rule of thumb" that employees who are dismissed without just cause are generally entitled to—for example, one month's notice (or pay in lieu) for each year of service. However, in 1999 the Ontario Court of Appeal rejected this rule in *Minott v. O'Shanter Development Company*, stating that it undermined the flexibility of the *Bardal* test by overemphasizing the length-of-service factor. Moreover, case law demonstrates that employees who have been working for short periods often receive more than one month's notice for each year of service, while long-term employees frequently receive considerably less than that "standard." This point was highlighted in *Love v. Acuity Investment Management Inc.*, which dealt with a senior VP who was dismissed after only two and a half years of service.

CASE IN POINT

Short Service—Not Necessarily Short Notice

Love v. Acuity Investment Management Inc., 2011 ONCA 130

Facts

Love, aged 50, had worked for two and a half years as a senior VP when he was terminated without cause. Unhappy with the separation package offered, he sued for wrongful dismissal, and at trial was awarded five months' wrongful dismissal damages. Convinced that as a senior VP with a 2 percent equity share in the employer company he was entitled to more, he appealed this award.

Relevant Issue

Whether five months' reasonable notice damages were adequate in these circumstances.

Decision

The Ontario Court of Appeal held for the employee and replaced the five months' reasonable notice damages with nine months. In increasing the award, it noted that determining reasonable notice is very fact-specific and deference is generally given to trial judges' decisions. However, in this case, the trial judge had given disproportionate weight to length of service and insufficient weight to the senior nature of the employee's position, his high level of compensation, and his 2 percent equity interest in the business. The trial court had also failed to consider the "availability of other employment" factor. Love's high level of compensation, plus his equity interest, would make finding a comparable position more difficult (Rubin Thomlinson LLP, 2011).

While *Love* demonstrates the point that employees with short service often receive more than one month's notice for each year of service, it should be noted that it is rare for employees with fewer than three years of service to obtain in excess of six months of notice.

Character of Employment

Historically, senior, managerial, and executive employees generally have received longer notice periods than other employees. This reflected the traditional view that it was more difficult for them to find jobs comparable to those from which they were dismissed. In fact, in the past it took exceptional circumstances for a lower-level employee to be awarded more than 12 months' pay in lieu of notice. Similarly, there was an unofficial cap for senior or highly skilled employees of 24 months. More recently, however, courts have questioned these ceilings, as well as the emphasis given to the "character of employment" factor in determining reasonable notice damages. This is illustrated in the Ontario Court of Appeal decision in *Di Tomaso v. Crown Metal Packaging Canada LP.*

CASE IN POINT

Character of Employment Factor Not to Be Given Disproportionate Weight

Di Tomaso v. Crown Metal Packaging Canada LP, 2011 ONCA 469

Facts

Di Tomaso, a 62-year-old mechanic with 33 years' service at a metal packaging manufacturing plant, was terminated as a result of a plant closure. Dissatisfied with the employer's separation package offer, Di Tomaso sued the employer for 24 months' common law damages for wrongful dismissal (that is, failure to provide reasonable notice of termination or pay in lieu). The employer countered that, among other things, Di Tomaso's common law notice period should be 12 months because that was the recognized cap for non-managerial workers. The trial court rejected the employer's argument and awarded Di Tomaso 22 months' reasonable notice damages instead. The employer appealed this award.

Relevant Issue

Whether the plaintiff's reasonable notice period should be capped at 12 months because he was a lower-level, non-managerial worker.

Decision

In upholding the original award of 22 months, the Ontario Court of Appeal explicitly rejected the argument that, save in exceptional circumstances, a non-managerial employee's damage awards should be capped at 12 months. In its view, such a limit places disproportionate weight on what is only one of four *Bardal* factors. Moreover, the court stated (citing *Medis Health and Pharmaceutical Services Inc. v. Bramble*):

> The proposition that junior employees have an easier time finding suitable alternate employment is no longer, if it ever was, a matter of common knowledge. Indeed, it is an empirically challenged proposition that cannot be confirmed by resorting to sources of indisputable accuracy.

As a result of this decision and others, it is increasingly clear that there is no longer a cap of 12 months placed on reasonable notice damages for non-managerial employees. Ontario's appellate court has also "lifted" the 24-month cap for senior employees, although awards above that level are still extremely rare. An example of exceptional circumstances might be where a long-service senior employee has remained with an employer after being given assurances that he would be employed until retirement (Dion, 2014).

Age

Courts generally assume that the older an employee is when dismissed, the more difficult it will be for her to find comparable employment. Accordingly, an employee who is dismissed when she is in her 50s, for example, will often receive a longer notice period than a similarly placed employee who is much younger at the time of dismissal. Reasonable notice awards to older workers have also been affected by the end of mandatory retirement at age 65. For example, in *Kotecha v. Affinia ULC*, a 70-year-old machine operator with 20 years of service was initially awarded 24.5 months' notice in a summary judgment. The notice was later reduced to 18 months on appeal on the basis that there were no exceptional circumstances to justify the larger award. Nonetheless, this decision illustrates that being over 65 is no longer a barrier to receiving significant reasonable notice damages. It also reflects the declining importance given to "character of employment" in determining the reasonable notice period, as Kotecha was a non-managerial employee (Meehan, 2014).

Availability of Similar Employment

Cases have held that the reasonable notice period is not determined by the actual length of time it takes an employee to obtain a new position. *Bain v. I.C.B.C.* demonstrates that an employer is not required to fully compensate an employee for having the misfortune of entering the job market when comparable jobs are particularly difficult to find.

CASE IN POINT

Appropriate Notice Period Not Equivalent to Time It Takes to Find a New Job

Bain v. I.C.B.C., 2002 BCSC 1445

Facts

The 57-year-old Bain had worked as a junior manager for seven years in the employer's information technology department when the employer dismissed him as a result of restructuring. The employer gave him 7 months' pay in lieu of notice, but he felt this was inadequate and sued for additional damages. Because of the scarcity of IT positions in the current economic climate, he argued that he should receive 18 to 20 months' notice instead.

Relevant Issue

Whether wrongful dismissal damages should reflect the current economic climate.

Decision

The BC Supreme Court held that the appropriate notice period is not equivalent to the length of time that it takes a dismissed employee to find a new job. Otherwise, employers would be held solely responsible for the lack of positions available during an economic downturn. A court should consider a lack of job opportunities in determining reasonable notice, but this factor should not receive undue weight. In this case, the court held that Bain was entitled to 12 months' notice on the basis of his age, position, length of service, marketable skills, and—to some extent—the current economic climate.

Another factor that affects the availability of similar employment is the degree to which the employee's position was specialized. In *Jamieson v. Finning International Inc.* the court awarded an employee a longer notice period because his job skills as a millyard systems manager in the heavy equipment supply industry were so specialized that there were limited opportunities for him to find similar employment.

Secondary Factors

In addition to the primary factors listed in *Bardal*, there are several secondary factors that courts consider relevant in determining reasonable notice. For example, if an employer lures an employee away from a secure position, and later dismisses that employee without just cause, a court may require it to provide a longer notice period than would have been necessary without such an enticement. This is especially true for short-service employees.

The fact that an employee is pregnant at the time of dismissal is a "*Bardal*-type" factor that can be used to determine a reasonable notice period. Although an employee's pregnancy should not be an overriding consideration, the court in *Ivens v. Automodular Assemblies Inc.* found that being pregnant probably will affect an employee's ability to find a new job and therefore should be considered. The court awarded the 27-year-old pregnant employee, who had two months of service with the employer as an assembler, 8 weeks' pay in lieu of notice. It felt that this was the appropriate reasonable notice period when the factor of her pregnancy was balanced with her type of work, probationary status, age, and length of service.

Other factors that may be taken into consideration include an employee's poor health, an employee's poor language skills, and the employer's refusal, without justification, to provide a letter of reference. In *Ostrow v. Abacus Management Corporation Mergers and Acquisitions*, the court confirmed another relevant factor: the existence of a non-competition clause in the employment contract. In that case, the court cited the non-competition clause as one of the factors it considered in awarding the plaintiff, who had been employed by the defendant for only nine months, reasonable notice damages of six months. Rejecting the employer's argument that the non-compete provision should not be considered because it had not sought to enforce it, the court held that it was the fact that the plaintiff was *led to believe* that he was bound by the clause that made it relevant in establishing the reasonable notice period (para. 84).

In the past, some courts recognized the notion of "ballpark damages" in deciding the length of reasonable notice. This meant that where an employer offered an employee a separation package that was within the range of what a court considered reasonable and fair, it would defer to the employer's assessment. However, this notion has been rejected by several courts because it allows an employer to usurp the court's function of establishing notice periods. For example, in the 2003 case of *UPM-Kymmene Miramichi Inc. v. Walsh*, the New Brunswick Court of Appeal upheld an award of 28 months, even though it was not much higher than the employer's offer of 24 months' pay in lieu of notice.

What's Better for an Employer: Working Notice or Pay in Lieu of Notice?

An employer is entitled to choose whether to pay an employee while she works during the reasonable notice period (working notice) or to pay her a sum that is equal to the amount she would have earned during the reasonable notice period, including both wages and benefits, and to ask the employee to leave immediately. An employer may also combine these options, provided that the combination of payment and notice equals the notice period to which the employee is entitled under law.

Providing working notice by giving employees notice and requiring them to work through the notice period may seem more cost effective than providing pay in lieu of notice. In some situations, working notice is a sensible business decision for an employer. For example, where an employer indefinitely lays off many employees because of its economic circumstances, the affected employees may be able to remain productive and motivated throughout this period. It will help if the employer continues to treat these employees with respect and does not leave them "out of the loop" during the working notice period.

Employees who work during the notice period should be given generous opportunities to search for a new job during working hours by, for example, making telephone calls, sending faxes and emails, and going to interviews. Although there have been few cases in this area, *Kelly v. Monenco Consultants Ltd.* provides support for this practice. In that case, the employer gave the employee working notice while he was on assignment in Nigeria. The court found that the notice was illusory because he had no practical opportunity to look for a new job until he completed his Nigerian assignment. As a consequence, the employee was awarded pay in lieu of reasonable notice.

On the other hand, there are situations in which it is inappropriate for an employer to require an employee to work throughout the notice period. For example, where an employer dismisses an employee as a result of performance problems that fall short of just cause, it may be counterproductive to leave the employee in the workplace during the notice period. It is likely that the employee's efforts will, if anything, deteriorate further, and his attitude will affect the morale of the remaining staff. The case for providing pay in lieu of notice is even stronger where the employee works with sensitive business information, in sales, with customers, or with the public. *Elg v. Stirling Doors* is a cautionary tale for employers who decide to leave an employee, who is dismissed for having an antagonistic attitude, in the workplace during the statutory notice period.

CASE IN POINT

Working Notice Is Not Always Appropriate

Elg v. Stirling Doors, [2002] OJ no. 2995 (SCJ)

Facts

Elg, a 54-year-old manual labourer, had worked for a manufacturer of kitchen cupboards for approximately 14 years. She was one of eight employees. In late 1999, the employer sensed that morale in the workplace was deteriorating as a result of Elg's attitude. The problem worsened when the employer addressed it in a meeting with Elg. Several weeks later, the employer dismissed her, providing eight weeks' notice as required under the *Employment Standards Act*.

During the first two days of her working notice period, Elg did little work and attempted to slow production down. When the employer confronted her, she told him that her notice period would be "eight weeks of hell," and there was nothing he could do about it. She also said, "You are the kind of employer that employees shoot." The employer reported the statement to the police and immediately dismissed the employee on the ground of wilful misconduct. Elg sued for wrongful dismissal.

Relevant Issue

Whether Elg's conduct during the working notice period constituted just cause for immediate dismissal.

Decision

The Ontario Superior Court found that the employer lacked just cause for dismissal. In the court's view, "working notice is an institution almost invariably predestined to fail." Elg's conduct was a predictable consequence of the employer's decision to provide termination notice rather than pay in lieu. Before the controversy, Elg had been a competent worker. There was no criticism of her work or attitude before the 1999 meeting, and the employer had never disciplined her. The court found that eight weeks' notice was insufficient to satisfy the employer's common law obligation to provide reasonable notice. Elg was entitled to eight months' notice instead.

This decision appears to be somewhat anomalous because it effectively questions the concept of working notice, a strategy that can benefit both the employer and the employee, provided that both parties act in a reasonable manner. However, *Elg* underscores the need for an employer to exercise caution in deciding to provide working notice instead of pay in lieu to an employee who is dismissed for disruptive behaviour.

Structuring a Separation Package

An employer that decides to dismiss an employee immediately and provide a separation package instead of working notice must consider how best to structure the package. One option is to offer an employee a lump sum that reflects both minimum employment standards and common law notice requirements. This approach has both advantages and disadvantages.

One of the disadvantages for an employer is that it must pay the employee a potentially large sum of money at one time. Moreover, if the dismissed employee finds a new job quickly, the employer receives no benefit, whereas if the employer continues the employee's salary and benefits instead, and the employee finds a new job before the notice period has ended, usually the employer can then discontinue salary payments. On the other hand, because many employees prefer to receive lump-sum payments, they may be willing to settle for a smaller total amount than if the employer paid the parting settlement over time.

Alternatively, an employer may continue an employee's salary and benefits during the notice period. In this case, there should be a written statement specifically indicating that these payments must include any statutory entitlements under the *Employment Standards Act*. The termination letter or agreement should also state that if the employee finds new employment, or self-employment, during the notice period, these salary continuation payments will end. The arrangement could also provide that the dismissed employee will receive a final lump-sum payment equal to, for example, 50 percent of the amount that the employee would have received if his salary had been continued for the remainder of the reasonable notice period. This type of arrangement motivates an employee to find a new job because the employer is obliged to pay a lump sum even after the employee begins a new job. At the same time, it potentially lowers the total amount that the employer must pay the former employee.

Employers are required to continue to make benefit payments throughout the statutory notice period. (In fact, as discussed in Chapter 4, a termination clause that does not expressly require the employer to maintain benefit coverage during the statutory notice period is unenforceable.) It is important that employers check to make sure that coverage can be maintained after the employee is no longer working. Although an employee is entitled to receive regular employment benefits during the common law notice period, the parties may negotiate other arrangements—for example, the employer may compensate the ex-employee for any lost benefits.

In addition to salary and benefits, an employer must consider what else an employee would have received had she worked throughout the reasonable notice period. As discussed below, this can include bonus payments (where they are integral to the employee's compensation package), commissions (those the employee probably would have earned), stock options/equity compensation and pension plan contributions (based on the plans' provisions), and other benefits such as a company car (if personal use was allowed) or club memberships (Stehr, 2012, p. 20).

Employees who are entitled to statutory termination and severance pay under the *Employment Standards Act* cannot be required to sign a release before receiving their minimum statutory entitlements. However, an employer may withhold payments that relate to the common law reasonable notice period until the employee has signed a full and final release. In such a release, an employee expressly forfeits her right to bring any legal action against the employer that is related to her employment or dismissal in exchange for the monetary settlement she receives.

Employees who are entitled to statutory severance pay have the right to receive a lump-sum payment within seven days of the termination of employment or on what would have been the employee's next payday, whichever is later. A salary continuation separation package does not meet this requirement. Therefore, a salary continuation offer should state that it includes any statutory notice and severance entitlements. An employer should make no payment unless the parties agree in writing that the package constitutes a greater benefit than severance pay under the *Employment Standards Act*.

Finally, an employer should not give working notice to an employee who is unable to use the notice period to look for a new job, such as an employee who is on sick, pregnancy, or parental leave. This is because the purpose of the notice period is to give the employee a reasonable opportunity to find comparable employment. However, provided that an employer does not infringe human rights or employment standards legislation in terminating an employee, it may give the employee notice of termination or pay in lieu of notice once the leave has ended and the employee has come back to work.

The Duty to Mitigate

Under the common law, but not under the *Employment Standards Act*, an employee who has been wrongfully dismissed has a **duty to mitigate** his damages. This means that the employee must take all reasonable steps to find comparable alternative employment during the reasonable notice period. Earnings from an employee's new job are usually deducted from the amount that the employer is required to pay to the employee as damages for wrongful dismissal. This duty flows from the principle that wrongful dismissal damages are meant to compensate the employee for the employer's failure to provide the required notice and the employee's resulting losses, not to penalize the employer for the dismissal itself. (As noted in the FYI feature below, this duty does not automatically apply where there is an enforceable employment contract that establishes a fixed, or easily calculable, amount payable upon severance.)

FYI

The Duty to Mitigate and Fixed Termination Damages

As discussed in Chapter 4, it is now settled law in Ontario that while the duty to mitigate applies to reasonable notice damages, it does *not* automatically apply where the employment contract establishes a fixed (or easily calculable) amount payable upon severance. This is because the employer is essentially attempting to contract out of providing common law reasonable notice or pay in lieu by replacing it with a contractual right to a predetermined payment (or liquidated damages), which is not subject to the duty to mitigate. Moreover, as the Ontario Court of Appeal in *Bowes v. Goss Power Products Ltd.* noted:

> It would be unfair to permit an employer to opt for certainty by specifying a fixed amount of damages and then allow the employer to later seek to obtain a lower amount … by raising an issue of mitigation that was not mentioned in the employment agreement.

As a result, where there is a fixed—or easily calculable—notice period in the contract, the employee will only have a duty to mitigate where the contract expressly says so (Braithwaite, 2013, p. 10-12). Note that it is important that any mitigation provision be drafted to clearly state that the duty to mitigate does *not* apply to minimum statutory entitlements (that is, under the *Employment Standards Act*). Otherwise, the entire termination provision may be unenforceable because it fails to at least match statutory entitlements.

The attributes of a reasonable job search are based on what a reasonable person would do in the circumstances: it is an objective standard. Employees who have been dismissed without notice are entitled to a period of time to accustom themselves to the new situation before beginning their job search. They are not expected to start making phone calls to prospective employers the morning after they have been dismissed; however, after a reasonable time has passed, they must start to look for a new position.

An employer that alleges that an employee failed to adequately mitigate her damages bears the onus of proof. It must prove two things: that there were comparable jobs available during the notice period that were suitable for the former employee and that she did not make reasonable efforts to obtain one of those suitable jobs. Courts rarely scrutinize a dismissed employee's job search efforts carefully. However, on occasion courts have found that an employee's job search was insufficient, and this finding has affected the reasonable notice period. In *Chambers v. Axia Netmedia Corporation*, the trial judge reduced the reasonable notice period from 11 months to 8 months because, among other things, the employee had limited his job search almost entirely to the Internet. In the court's view, using only one job search approach was not taking "all reasonable steps" to mitigate damages.

Courts recognize that certain factors may affect an employee's ability to conduct an active job search, such as an employee's older age, poor health, or slow market conditions. An employer's unjustified refusal to provide a timely letter of reference, or the existence of a non-competition or non-solicitation provision in the employment contract that limits the opportunities an employee can legitimately pursue, may also be considered (Braithwaite, 2013, pp. 10-5, 10-10).

Dismissed employees are expected to look for and accept only work that is comparable to their former job. Whether a job is comparable depends on the specific facts of the case, but generally the courts look at similarity in salary, location, status, skill, and training. Where a potential job would require a former employee to move to a different city, the courts consider the employee's family circumstances and the housing market. For example, if the former employee's spouse has a job in the community, it is less likely that the duty to mitigate would require relocation.

On occasion, discharged employees decide to make a career change. For example, a person who is dismissed from a position as a computer technician may decide to go into the tourist industry as a matter of personal preference. If jobs in the new industry are lower paying than available jobs in the previous industry, the former employer could argue that it should not be required to compensate the employee for the salary difference during the notice period. On the other hand, courts may accept an employee's decision to mitigate by starting a new business or retraining where this approach is realistic and there are few job opportunities in the former employee's previous industry or field.

Employers are legally liable for a former employee's out-of-pocket job search expenses. These could include expenses for long distance telephone calls, resumé preparation, postage, and travelling to job interviews.

One important development in the employee's duty to mitigate wrongful dismissal damages arose from the Supreme Court of Canada's 2008 decision in *Evans v. Teamsters Local Union No. 31*. In that case, the Supreme Court was asked to consider whether a wrongfully dismissed employee's duty to mitigate could require him to return to work for the employer that dismissed him if certain conditions were met. Previously, this had only been considered where the employee had been constructively dismissed. (See the discussion under "The Duty of a Constructively Dismissed Employee to Mitigate Damages" below.)

CASE IN POINT

Does Duty to Mitigate Require Returning to Job Employee Was Fired From?

Evans v. Teamsters Local Union No. 31, 2008 SCC 20

Facts

Evans was employed for over 23 years as a business agent in the Teamsters union. After the election of a new union executive, Evans was terminated. During settlement negotiations, Evans indicated that he was prepared to accept 24 months' notice of termination, possibly through 12 months of continued employment followed by a payment of 12 months of salary in lieu of notice. When the parties still had not reached agreement after five months of negotiations, the employer offered Evans his job back so that he could work out the balance of his 24-month notice period. The employer also indicated that refusal would be treated as just cause for dismissal. Evans refused the offer and sued for wrongful dismissal. The trial court agreed with Evans and awarded him 22 months' pay in lieu of notice totalling $100,000. The employer appealed. The Court of Appeal set aside the award, finding that Evans had not acted reasonably in refusing the former employer's job offer.

Relevant Issue

Whether the employee failed to reasonably mitigate his damages when he refused to return to the job he was fired from.

Decision

In a majority decision, the Supreme Court held that Evans had failed to mitigate because his refusal was not reasonable in the circumstances. Whether a refusal is reasonable depends on the particular facts of each case. The court found that "where the salary offered is the same, where the working conditions are not substantially different or the work demeaning, and where the personal relationships involved are not acrimonious," the employee has a duty to accept the temporary work offered. Although an employee is not obliged to mitigate by returning to work in "an atmosphere of hostility, embarrassment or humiliation," an objective standard will be used to evaluate this factor. Would a reasonable person in the employee's position perceive it that way? The majority decision noted that at one point in negotiations Evans indicated that he was prepared to return to work if certain of his conditions (including one that involved his wife's employment) were met. In light of these findings, his refusal to resume work temporarily was not reasonable and constituted a failure to mitigate.

There was a single dissenting opinion from Justice Abella in this decision that is worth noting. She stated that requiring a dismissed employee to accept temporary employment with the same employer that wrongfully dismissed him disregards the uniqueness of an employment contract as one of "personal service." In her view, an employer can either offer working notice or provide pay in lieu of notice. What it cannot do is fire an employee and then, when negotiations fail, fire him again for failure to accept its subsequent offer to work out his notice period. In contrast, the majority decided that there is little practical difference between providing an employee with reasonable working notice of termination and terminating employment immediately but offering new employment for the same time period.

This decision represents a significant change in this area of the law. A dismissed employee's obligation to mitigate wrongful dismissal damages now includes returning to work for the employer that dismissed her where it is "reasonable" to do so. The most apparent effect of this decision on employers is that it offers an additional option in negotiating a settlement in wrongful dismissal actions. However, this option is only available where the conditions set out in *Evans* are met—the salary remains the same (or is comparable), the working conditions are not substantially different or the work demeaning, and the personal relationships involved are not acrimonious. In practice, meeting all of these conditions may be difficult; otherwise, the employer probably would have given working notice in the first place. Nonetheless, this decision underscores the desirability of maintaining as positive a relationship as possible with an employee who is being dismissed without cause throughout the dismissal process and in any subsequent negotiations. This point is illustrated in the decision in *Chevalier v. Active Tire & Auto Centre Inc.*

CASE IN POINT

Court Applies Evans v. Teamsters

Chevalier v. Active Tire & Auto Centre Inc., 2012 ONSC 4309; aff'd. 2013 ONCA 548

Facts

The employer, Active Tire, inadvertently triggered the dismissal of a non-union employee (Chevalier) when it laid him off under the mistaken belief that it could legally do so. A few days after receiving notice that Chevalier was launching a legal action for constructive dismissal damages, the employer sent him a letter apologizing for its mistake and offering him his job back on exactly the same terms as he had had previously. Chevalier refused, arguing that he would be subjected to an atmosphere of hostility, embarrassment, or humiliation if he returned to work. The trial judge decided that Chevalier's concerns about the work atmosphere were unreasonable because he honestly but incorrectly mistook job coaching (which he received after management identified performance issues) for harassment. Applying *Evans*, the court held that he should have accepted the employer's offer to return to work out the reasonable notice period as part of his duty to mitigate. Because he failed to do so, no damages were awarded,

despite his constructive dismissal. Chevalier appealed the trial court's decision.

Relevant Issue

Whether the constructively dismissed employee was required to accept the employer's offer to return to work as part of his duty to mitigate.

Decision

The Ontario Court of Appeal upheld the trial judge's decision. Referring to the court record, including the employer's immediate admission of its mistake, apology, and offer to have him return on the pre-dismissal terms, the court found that the employment relationship was not acrimonious and therefore Chevalier should have returned to his former job to mitigate his damages. As a result of his failure to do so, he was not entitled to damages for constructive dismissal.

Although the result in *Chevalier* is fact-specific, it is also illustrative. In successfully arguing that the employee should have returned to the job as part of his duty to mitigate, the employer clearly benefited from the approach it took. This included the speed with which it offered Chevalier his job back, the unequivocal nature of that offer, the courteous and professional tone of its offer letter, and the fact that the offered terms and conditions were identical to those the employee had enjoyed previously (Sherrard Kuzz LLP, 2013, p. 3).

Constructive Dismissal

As previously discussed, constructive dismissal is a type of dismissal without cause. In this situation, an employer does not explicitly dismiss an employee. Rather, constructive dismissal occurs under the common law when an employer unilaterally makes a fundamental (and unfavourable) change to the employment agreement without providing reasonable notice and explaining the consequences of rejecting the change. Generally speaking, this fundamental breach of contract by the employer entitles the employee to resign in response and claim damages from the employer for pay in lieu of reasonable notice. More recently, an Ontario court has sanctioned another option: an employee can reject the new terms and sue the employer for constructive dismissal while still remaining with that employer and working under the "new" terms and conditions as part of the duty to mitigate. (See *Russo v. Kerr* below.)

Sometimes an employer constructively dismisses an employee because it wants the employee to resign and believes that its actions will eliminate the need to formally terminate the employee and provide reasonable notice or pay in lieu. However, more often an employer makes the changes because of factors such as business necessity and hopes that the employee will accept the modified terms. In these situations, which are especially common during an economic downturn, the employer has no intention of repudiating the employment contract.

However, the employer's motives as well as the employee's perceptions are usually irrelevant. In its landmark decision in *Farber v. Royal Trust Company*, the Supreme Court of Canada stated that constructive dismissal depends on an objective comparison between the employee's current job and the job that the employer offers, based on the facts known at the time that the employer makes the fundamental change. The test is an objective one: would a reasonable person in the employee's position find the changes imposed by the employer unreasonable and unfair? Each case depends on its own particular facts.

What Constitutes Constructive Dismissal?

Changes to Compensation Package

As discussed in Chapter 11, a minor change to an employee's compensation package probably does not result in constructive dismissal. For example, a 5 percent reduction in the salaries of all employees because of difficult market conditions is unlikely to be sufficient. On the other hand, a 30 percent reduction in pay undoubtedly would amount to constructive dismissal. Changes between these two extremes would need to be examined by a court to determine whether, given all the circumstances, they constitute a fundamental breach of the employment contract. (Generally speaking, decreases in pay of greater than 10 percent will most often constitute constructive dismissal.) It is also worth bearing in mind that it is not just big changes but also the cumulative effect of several small changes that can result in a finding of constructive dismissal (Bongarde Media Co., 2009, p. 2).

One decision of particular note in this area is *Russo v. Kerr*, where the court confirmed that constructively dismissed employees do not have to resign to sue for damages.

CASE IN POINT

Court Confirms Option of Staying and Suing

Russo v. Kerr, 2010 ONSC 6053

Facts

Kerr Bros. was a candy manufacturer that instituted an across-the-board wage decrease due to ongoing financial losses. One employee who was particularly affected by the change was Russo, a warehouse manager with 37 years' service, whose total annual compensation package (including bonus and pension) fell from about $114,000 to $60,000. Russo made it clear that he did not accept this change and decided to sue his employer for constructive dismissal—while continuing to perform his job. Kerr Bros. admitted that the change in compensation constituted constructive dismissal but, relying on existing case law, argued that by staying to work at the new, reduced compensation level, Russo had condoned (agreed to) those changes.

Relevant Issue

Whether an employee can sue his employer for constructive dismissal while continuing to work under the new terms of employment.

Decision

The court held for the employee, stating that once an employee makes it clear that he does not agree to the changed terms, which Russo did, he is entitled to continue in employment to mitigate his damages. Where the employer allows the employee to stay, knowing he has not accepted the change, it is liable for the difference between his old and new terms throughout the reasonable notice period, which in this case the court found to be 22 months. However, an employee who stays beyond the reasonable notice period is deemed to have accepted the new terms from that point on (Mitchell, 2011).

The court in *Russo v. Kerr* confirmed that where an employer wants to make a fundamental, unilateral change to an employee's terms of employment, the proper approach is to give the employee reasonable working notice that the current contract will end and "offer" a new contract (with the changed terms) as of the end of the reasonable notice period. If the employee rejects the new contract, she may leave but she will not be owed constructive dismissal damages (only ESA severance pay, as applicable) (Coulter, 2011).

Changes in Duties

Proposed changes to an employee's duties constitute constructive dismissal if they are so significant that they represent a fundamental change to the employment contract. Increased job duties may fall into this category if, for example, the core responsibilities change—or just keep being added to—and the job becomes much more stressful as a result. More typically, however, claims of constructive dismissal arise where the change in duties represents a demotion—a downgrade in responsibilities, authority, or status. For example, in *Jodoin v. Nissan Canada*, the court found that Jodoin had been constructively dismissed, even though his salary was unchanged, when he quit after his role was reduced from that of a manager with significant responsibilities to that of an employee without a job description, a budget, or employees reporting to him. He was also moved out of his office and into a cubicle (Smith, 2013, p. 1). The employee was awarded over $100,000 in reasonable notice damages. Similarly, albeit less dramatically, in *Hainsworth v. World Peace Forum Society* an executive director who lost her title and had to report to one of her former co-directors was found to have been constructively dismissed. However, in *Carnegie v. Liberty Health* the court found that a new reporting relationship that did not affect an employee's duties did not alone constitute constructive dismissal.

New Reporting Relationship Does Not Create Demotion

Carnegie v. Liberty Health, 2003 CanLII 25428 (Ont. SCDC)

Facts

Carnegie had 13 years' service and an excellent performance record. She earned approximately $100,000 a year, plus bonuses, as a director reporting to the senior vice-president. In 2000, the employer changed its sales structure to create the position of assistant vice-president. Carnegie and another worker applied for the new position; the other worker was the successful candidate. The employer presented Carnegie with three choices: (1) continue in her present job and report to the new assistant vice-president instead of the senior vice-president as before, (2) take the position of director of underwriting, or (3) take a new position as director of special projects. She quit, stating that she was not prepared to report to the assistant vice-president or accept what she perceived to be a demotion. She sued the employer for constructive dismissal. At trial, she was successful; the employer appealed.

Relevant Issue

Whether Carnegie was constructively dismissed.

Decision

The Ontario Divisional Court determined that Carnegie was not constructively dismissed. The trial judge had misconstrued a change in reporting obligations as being a transfer of responsibility. In fact, there was no evidence of this. Had Carnegie accepted the employer's first option and reported to the new assistant vice-president, she would have remained in the same job and exercised the same duties as before the restructuring. The change in reporting relationships that required Carnegie to report to someone who was previously her corporate "equal" did not amount to constructive dismissal.

Geographic Relocations

Geographic relocations must be significant to constitute constructive dismissal. A minor geographic change, such as moving an office or plant from one part of a city to another part, generally does not qualify. However, if an original workplace was accessible by public transit and a new workplace is not, an employer may be found to have constructively dismissed employees who are dependent on public transit, even though the workplaces are as little as 20 kilometres apart. In contrast, it may be an implied term in the contracts of senior executives of national or international companies that the employer is entitled to require the employee to relocate, unless there is an express contractual provision to the contrary.

Significantly increasing the time that an employee has to travel in the course of a job may also be considered a fundamental change in the employment contract. In *Antworth v. Fabricville*, the court found that a newly imposed job requirement that increased the time a district manager was on the road and away from home from 9 to 20 days per month constituted constructive dismissal.

Changes to Hours and Scheduling

Depending on the circumstances, a significant reduction (or increase) in hours can be considered constructive dismissal. In *Pimenta v. Boermans*, an optometrist cut an employee's hours from 40 to 35 per week. The Ontario Labour Relations Board found that that change, in conjunction with reductions in salary and duties, constituted constructive dismissal. In another case, a court found that *increasing* the hours of a part-time bookkeeper from 20 to 30 hours a week, and requiring her to start her days one hour earlier, was constructive dismissal under the circumstances.

It is not just the number of hours added or subtracted but also changes to when those hours are scheduled (for example, from weekdays to weekends) that matter. Each case will be very fact-specific and will also depend on whether there was an express or implied term in the contract relating to when the hours will be worked.

Layoffs

Under Canadian common law, an employer does not have the right to lay off employees unless layoffs are authorized by an express or implied term in the employment contract or, as more recent case law indicates (see Chapter 11 under the heading "Temporary Layoffs"), the prevailing statutory scheme. If there is no such contractual agreement or statutory scheme, in certain circumstances a temporary layoff may constitute constructive dismissal, in which case the employee can sue the employer for wrongful dismissal. To be safest, an employer should ensure that its employment agreements give it the right to lay an employee off temporarily. To be considered temporary, the period of layoff must not go beyond that set out in employment standards legislation (see Chapter 14).

Untenable Work Environment

A different situation that can lead to a claim of constructive dismissal arises when an employer fails to protect an employee from harassment. Courts have found that employers have an implied duty to maintain a safe workplace and to treat employees with civility and respect. As set out by the Ontario Court of Appeal in *Shah v. Xerox Canada Ltd.*, where this duty is breached and the employer's treatment of the employee (or its tolerance of offensive conduct) makes continued employment intolerable, the employee has been constructively dismissed. In other words, employers have an obligation under the common law to prevent workplace bullying.

If bullying in the workplace relates to one of the prohibited grounds of discrimination under the *Human Rights Code*, such as disability, race, or sex, an employee may file a harassment complaint under the Code. However, similar to the workplace violence and harassment provisions of the *Occupational Health and Safety Act* (OHSA), a claim for constructive dismissal resulting from a hostile workplace can be made regardless of the underlying basis for the bullying. A constructive dismissal claim is based on the fact that an employer's failure to eliminate bullying repudiates the employment relationship. Examples of unacceptable conduct include ongoing rude, demeaning, abusive, and intimidating conduct directed against an employee that goes beyond a mere personality clash. If a reasonable person could not be expected to persevere with the job in the face of the conduct, the employee is entitled to resign and sue the employer for damages for constructive dismissal.

Constructive dismissal claims based on a hostile work environment usually involve abusive conduct by the claimant's supervisor. However, there have also been cases where a hostile work environment was created by the employee's co-workers. *Stamos v. Annuity Research & Marketing Service Ltd.*, a case involving a co-worker who was repeatedly rude and unpleasant to the plaintiff, illustrates an employer's common law obligation to respond fairly and quickly to harassment in the workplace.

CASE IN POINT

Workplace Bullying by Co-worker Results in Constructive Dismissal

Stamos v. Annuity Research & Marketing Service Ltd., 2002 CanLII 49618 (Ont. SC)

Facts

Stamos started as a claims adjudicator for a company that administered life, dental, and health benefit plans. She was often praised by the company's owner for her loyalty and hard work, and eventually the employer promoted her to senior administrator/adjudicator. The atmosphere in the office changed drastically when the owner's uncle was hired to administer disability claims. He had an explosive personality, took criticism badly, and was subject to outbursts several times a day. He made sexist and racist comments that created a stressful atmosphere for all six workers, but he was especially rude to Stamos. On one occasion, he shouted at her, accusing her of sabotaging the computer system and undermining his authority. When she complained, the owner reassured her that there was nothing to the accusation, but he suggested that she avoid his uncle and keep her office door closed and locked. He never disciplined his uncle or assured Stamos that he would deal with his uncle's abusive conduct.

The situation continued with repeated incidents in which the uncle aggressively confronted Stamos about various matters. Finally, Stamos resigned because her health had deteriorated and she dreaded going to work. She sued the employer for damages for constructive dismissal.

Relevant Issue

Whether constructive dismissal can arise if a co-worker, not an employer or a supervisory employee, creates intolerable working conditions.

Decision

The Ontario Superior Court of Justice ruled that the employer constructively dismissed Stamos. The employer had a duty to ensure that the work atmosphere allowed the employee to perform her job. The employer's failure to prevent harassment by a co-worker breached this duty and constituted constructive dismissal. Instead of reprimanding his uncle for his inappropriate conduct, the employer allowed the employee to suffer physically and emotionally from repeatedly abusive conduct and language. She was entitled to treat the employment relationship as terminated and was awarded six months' pay in lieu of notice plus $2,500 for mental distress.

The *Stamos* decision happens to pre-date the 2010 Bill 168 amendments to Ontario's *Occupational Health and Safety Act* (see Chapter 7 under the heading "Workplace Violence and Harassment"). Those amendments now provide employees with an additional option or avenue for seeking redress for workplace bullying. What the employee's best option is in pursuing a claim depends on the circumstances. On the one hand, constructive dismissal actions related to a hostile work environment essentially require an employee to quit in order to allege that the workplace was so untenable that she was forced to leave. In contrast, an employee may file a complaint under the employer's workplace violence or anti-harassment policies without having to effectively resign; furthermore, the employee has legal protection against an employer's reprisal for lodging a complaint. Moreover, pursuing a constructive dismissal action in court involves the risk of an adverse finding, a significant commitment in time, effort, and resources, and potential liability for the legal costs of the other party if the action is unsuccessful. In short, a constructive dismissal claim involves a much higher risk and will typically only be pursued if the employee feels that remaining at the workplace and asserting his or her rights under the OHSA is untenable.

The Duty of a Constructively Dismissed Employee to Mitigate Damages

As discussed above, the duty to mitigate requires a wrongfully dismissed employee to make bona fide efforts to find a new job to limit the damages she suffers as a result of a dismissal. This duty also applies in constructive dismissal situations where the employer makes a unilateral and fundamental change to the terms of the employment contract.

Traditionally, courts have held the view that employees who are constructively dismissed should not be required to mitigate their damages by continuing to work for an employer in a job that is inferior to the one from which they were constructively dismissed. However, the Ontario Court of Appeal in *Mifsud v. MacMillan Bathurst Inc.* (and more recently the Supreme Court of Canada in the *Evans* case discussed above) has held that the duty to mitigate requires the constructively dismissed employee to continue working if

1. the salary offered in the new position is the same as in the former position,
2. the working conditions are not substantially different or demeaning, and
3. the relevant personal relationships are not acrimonious.

In its 2014 decision in *Farwell v. Citair, Inc. (General Coach Canada)*, the Ontario Court of Appeal confirmed an additional requirement: where an employee rejects the "new" position, the employer must expressly re-offer it to her as a means of mitigating damages. Absent that step, an employer may not succeed in arguing a failure to mitigate.

Whether the duty to mitigate requires an employee to accept a new position offered by an employer depends on the circumstances of each case. Often the relationship between the parties has become hostile, or an employee would be humiliated by accepting the new position; in these cases, the employee is not required to mitigate damages by accepting the new job. However, where the situation meets the criteria in *Mifsud*, an employee may be required to work through the reasonable notice period while looking for alternative employment. Moreover, the Supreme Court of Canada in *Evans* indicated that determining whether the workplace relationships are acrimonious or hostile is not purely a subjective matter. The test is what a "reasonable" person would feel in the circumstances.

Thus an employee who is presented with significant changes in his employment contract faces a difficult legal dilemma and should seek expert legal advice. On the one hand, if the employee decides to continue working, he may be seen as condoning the change. Although an employee is allowed a reasonable amount of time in a new position to determine whether it represents a fundamental breach of contract or to negotiate further change with the employer, if he remains on the job for more time than is reasonable, he will be seen as accepting the new terms of employment. In these circumstances, the employee cannot subsequently leave and claim constructive dismissal.

On the other hand, if an employee resigns and alleges constructive dismissal, but a court subsequently finds that the change was not sufficiently fundamental to constitute constructive dismissal, as in *Carnegie*, or that he should have stayed to mitigate his losses, the employee is out of a job *and* unable to claim damages.

To avoid this result, an employee might advise the employer in writing, as the employee *in Russo v. Kerr* did, that he does not accept the proposed changes and does not condone the constructive dismissal, but is staying on the job under the new terms in an attempt to mitigate his damages. However, this option is also potentially difficult, as it requires an employee to sue the employer while he is still employed.

Probably because of the employee's difficult position, constructive dismissal suits are relatively rare (Gilbert et al., 2000, p. 158).

The following two cases, *Chandran v. National Bank* and *Gillis v. Sobeys Group Inc.*, illustrate some of these complexities and the difficult choices that constructive dismissal and the duty to mitigate can present to both employees and employers.

CASE IN POINT

Employers Need to Proceed with Caution When Insisting on Employee Transfers

Chandran v. National Bank, 2011 ONSC 777; 2012 ONCA 205

Facts

Chandran, aged 45, was a senior bank manager who had received excellent performance reviews throughout his 18 years at the employer bank. However, after the bank became aware of morale problems at Chandran's branch, the HR manager conducted one-on-one interviews with all 11 employees, 9 of whom complained of Chandran's bullying behaviour. Unprompted, they said he made condescending remarks, shouted, and criticized employees in front of others; a couple mentioned being so upset that they had considered seeking legal advice. The employer met with Chandran and told him about the general allegations. Chandran was shocked; he denied the allegations and asked for specific details so that he could better defend himself. The employer refused, believing Chandran had enough information to respond. A few days later, it issued a disciplinary letter advising him he was being transferred to one of two possible non-supervisory positions and stating he would be terminated for cause if there was any further bullying behaviour. Both of the positions reported to senior executives and had comparable pay for at least 14 months. The employer also told Chandran that he was still a valued employee and that either position would keep him on his career path to VP. One of the offered positions was manager of business development/special projects (a new position); the other was manager of national accounts. Chandran rejected both positions and sued the bank for constructive dismissal. The bank responded that both positions were comparable and therefore he was not constructively dismissed. In the alternative, even if Chandran had been constructively dismissed, he had a duty to accept one of the positions during the reasonable notice period to mitigate his losses. The bank noted that it had been prepared to communicate the transfer in a manner that reflected positively on Mr. Chandran, so staying would not have been humiliating or demeaning.

Relevant Issues

1. Whether the employee was constructively dismissed.
2. If so, whether the employee had an obligation to take one of the offered positions as part of his duty to mitigate.

Decision

The trial court (upheld on appeal) sided with the employee: despite the employer's assurances to the contrary, both transfers were demotions. The 14-month limit before salary re-evaluation, as well as the removal of supervisory responsibilities, undermined the bank's contention they were not. Moreover, the trial judge stated:

> I find that any reasonable person in Mr. Chandran's position being presented with the disciplinary letter concluding that he was guilty of serious misconduct, being removed from his position, and offered positions of lesser grades, where the supervisory duties were removed, would conclude that the essential terms and conditions of the employment contract were being substantially changed (para. 63).

The court also rejected the employer's contention that Chandran should have taken one of the offered positions to mitigate his damages. Chandran had already lost trust in the employer because, without allowing him a chance to respond to specific allegations, it had tried to force him to accept an inferior position. As a result, the employment relationship was too damaged to expect Chandran to remain with the employer. The trial court awarded Chandran 14 months' reasonable notice damages, and the amount was upheld on appeal (Smith, 2011).

Note that the employer's legal obligation to protect its employees (Chandran's subordinates) from workplace bullying did not relieve it of its common law duty related to constructive dismissal. A key difficulty with the employer's position in *Chandran* was its failure to properly investigate the serious misconduct it alleged, or to give, in the court's view, the employee sufficient details so that he could know and fully respond to the case against him. The employee was thereby unfairly burdened with a serious disciplinary record, which undermined the employer's arguments that there had not been a fundamental change to the employment contract or that the proposed transfer would not cause embarrassment or humiliation (Whitten & Lublin Employment Lawyers, 2013). Given the court's reasoning in *Chandran*, it seems likely that in a situation with similar facts, but where the employer conducts a thorough investigation—including letting the employee know the specific allegations being made and providing an opportunity to respond—a different result would be reached.

The second case, *Gillis v. Sobeys Group Inc.*, highlights the dilemma an employee can face when her employer makes changes to her employment contract that she believes constitute constructive dismissal.

CASE IN POINT

High Stakes for Employees in Constructive Dismissal Claims

Gillis v. Sobeys Group Inc., 2011 NSSC 443

Facts

Having worked for Sobeys, a large grocery chain, for over 28 years, Gillis was surprised when the VP of marketing told her that her management position as food experience manager at head office was being eliminated as part of its general restructuring efforts. The employer offered her a choice of two jobs: assistant store manager in a town 40 minutes away (Gillis had previously been a store manager), or demo coordinator at head office. While her vacation entitlements and benefits would remain the same, both jobs had lower salaries, especially the demo coordinator position. The employer offered a one-time lump-sum payment to cover the difference in salary in the first year but Gillis still saw both jobs as demotions. She was also concerned about how the assistant manager hours would affect her childcare arrangements because her current babysitter could not extend her hours. Moreover, at the same meeting, the employer chose to bring forward some performance issues (among them, poor prioritizing and less-than-expected results for her program) that it had never previously raised. This upset Gillis even more.

Gillis ended up rejecting both jobs and suing the employer for constructive dismissal. The employer countered that there was no constructive dismissal because the assistant manager position (although admittedly not the demo coordinator position) was a lateral move: the pay was less but, with the bonus, not a great deal less; most assistant store managers became store managers within a relatively short period, which would make up the pay difference; and transfers between head office and stores were common and would not be seen as a demotion.

Furthermore, even if the position was not comparable, Gillis should have accepted it during the reasonable notice period to mitigate her damages.

Relevant Issues

1. Whether the employee had been constructively dismissed.

2. If so, whether the employee should have taken the assistant manager position to mitigate her damages.

Decision

The court held for the employer. It found that the change was part of a restructuring driven by legitimate business needs and, in that context, the assistant store manager position was not a demotion. It was a lateral move and a "reasonable person, in a similar fact situation, would have accepted the assistant store manager position" because it did not represent a substantial change in the essential terms of the employment contract. The income was only slightly lower, she would receive an equalizing lump-sum payment for a year after the transfer, and it would most probably have led to a store manager position within a short period of time. Moreover, it was common for Sobeys to accommodate childcare needs and, as a former store manager, Gillis was well aware of this. Although the court commented that Sobeys used poor judgment in raising the performance issues at such a critical time, it did not excuse Gillis's refusal of that position; nor did it make the new

position demeaning or humiliating. Her response was emotional rather than pragmatic.

The court similarly applied an objective standard in finding that, even if Gillis had been constructively dismissed, her lawsuit could not succeed because she failed to mitigate her damages by taking the assistant manager position during the reasonable notice period (Lancaster House, 2012).

As noted above, the outcome of cases alleging constructive dismissal is often difficult to predict and very fact-specific; small changes in conduct can alter outcomes. This decision arguably could have gone the other way, based on the *Evans* criteria: the offered position was at a lower salary, the employee had held the same position previously, and the employer introduced performance-related concerns into discussions about the new job offer. The judge's acceptance of the employer's position that performance issues played no part in its decision to restructure Gillis's position was important because courts seem to give more latitude to job changes made to meet legitimate business needs than to those implemented, as in *Chandran*, in response to performance issues. Nonetheless, this remains a complex area of the law.

How Can an Employer Avoid Constructive Dismissal Claims?

As discussed in Chapter 11 under the heading "Changing Employment Terms and Conditions," an employer that wants to change an employment contract should, if possible, either obtain the employee's consent and provide the necessary consideration or provide the employee with reasonable notice of the change and offer a new contract, with the changed terms, at the end of the notice period. Reasonable notice is equivalent to the common law notice period to which an employee would be entitled if an employer dismissed her without just cause. When presenting a significant employment change to an employee, the employer should ensure that the employee knows that she is still a valuable member of the organization. The employer should explain the changes within the context of where the organization is headed and how the changed duties fit within the new structure.

An employment contract that clearly spells out that certain parts of the employment relationship are subject to change may reduce the chances of a successful constructive dismissal action. This is because changes anticipated by the agreement are not, by definition, breaches of it. On the other hand, broad wording that, for example, allows an employer to assign duties to an employee "as may be required from time to time" probably will not assist an employer if the changes proposed to an employee's job go to the heart of the employment relationship.

Wrongful Dismissal Damages

As previously noted, an employer that dismisses an employee without cause often provides the employee with pay in lieu of notice instead of requiring the employee to remain at work during the notice period. The payment made by the employer to the employee is sometimes referred to as wrongful dismissal (or reasonable notice) damages or a severance or separation package.

Reasonable Notice Damages—The Basic Entitlement

Under the common law, courts do not reinstate employees who are wrongfully dismissed. Instead, the remedy for wrongful dismissal is based on principles of contract law. Employers are required to compensate wrongfully dismissed employees for lost wages and benefits during the reasonable notice period in order to put them in the same position they would have been in had the employer not breached the contract by failing to provide reasonable notice.

Damages for wrongful dismissal are calculated from the date on which an employer breaches the contract. If an employer dismisses an employee, damages are calculated from the date of dismissal. If an employer constructively dismisses an employee, damages are calculated from the date the employer makes the unilateral change to the fundamental terms of the contract of employment.

The calculation of these damages can be complicated because, in addition to lost salary or wages, the employee is entitled to all benefits and other compensation that she would have received during the reasonable notice period. For example, if a former employee is entitled to a reasonable notice period of 12 months, she is entitled to have the employer maintain the entire benefit package for that period or to be compensated for its loss. With the exception of the statutory notice periods during which benefits *must* be maintained, the parties may negotiate the manner in which the employer will compensate the employee for benefits during the common law notice period.

The following is an overview of a wrongfully dismissed employee's entitlements during the reasonable notice period.

1. *Salary.* The employee is entitled to receive the amount of salary he will lose during the reasonable notice period as a result of the wrongful dismissal. This includes any increases in salary that would have occurred during this period. If overtime pay or commissions are a fundamental part of the employee's pay package, lost earnings include overtime pay or commissions that the employee was likely to receive during the notice period.

2. *Benefits.* Benefits to which an employee is entitled include club memberships, rent-free residences, room and board, meal expenses, subsidized mortgages, professional fees, loans, or employee discounts. The value of staff loans and employee discounts are calculated by determining the difference between the market value of these benefits and what an employee would have paid for them during the notice period. An employee is also entitled to the personal-use aspect of benefits such as car allowances and club memberships. He is not entitled to include benefits that relate to job performance only, such as use of a company vehicle provided for business purposes only, in calculating wrongful dismissal damages.

3. *Company vehicle.* An employer is not required to compensate an employee for the use of a company vehicle that was provided to him exclusively for company purposes. However, if an employee has use of a company vehicle for personal, as well as for company, purposes or if use of the vehicle forms part of the employee's total compensation, an employer must compensate the employee for loss of its use during the notice period.

4. *Insurance.* Benefits may be owing for the following types of insurance: life, accidental death and dismemberment, disability or medical, drug, and

dental. Employers should continue coverage for insured benefits throughout the reasonable notice period, if possible. However, sometimes this is impossible. For example, in Ontario, disability insurers are required to cover employees during the statutory notice period, but it is unusual for coverage to go beyond this period since eligibility is usually based on an employee's being actively employed with the employer that arranged the coverage. If an employee is no longer actively employed during a reasonable notice period, an employer can reimburse the employee for the cost of obtaining his own coverage during the remainder of the notice period. Failing to address this issue can result in a large damages award against an employer. In *Brito v. Canac Kitchens*, for example, the employer was ordered to pay its former employee, Olguin, over $200,000 (plus legal costs) for the short- and long-term disability (LTD) benefits he would have received had benefit coverage been maintained throughout the common law reasonable notice period. In that case, Olguin was diagnosed with and treated for cancer after the end of the eight-week statutory notice period when benefit coverage had been maintained, but before the end of the 22-month reasonable notice period (as later determined by the court). Because Olguin was permanently disabled because of his condition, the award also included the present value of the remainder of his LTD entitlements to his 65th birthday.

It is worth noting that, pursuant to *Sylvester v. British Columbia*, the value of the long-term disability benefits were not deducted from Olguin's reasonable notice damages. This was because Olguin had contributed to the costs of the disability coverage; they were not entirely paid for by the employer.

5. *Bonuses.* If an employer was required to pay bonuses to an employee as part of the employee's compensation package, the employee must be compensated for their loss during the period of reasonable notice. The amount is based on what the employee would probably have received if he had worked throughout the notice period. If the bonuses cannot be determined in this manner, the employer should calculate the average of past bonuses. Bonuses that were gratuitous payments made at the employer's discretion, and were not an integral part of the employee's compensation package, do not have to continue during the reasonable notice period.

6. *Stock options.* An employee who is dismissed without cause may continue to accrue and exercise stock options until the end of the reasonable notice period unless her employment contract or stock option plan unequivocally states otherwise.

7. *Pension entitlements.* An employer must compensate an employee for any loss of pension entitlement during the reasonable notice period, including the value of anticipated employer contributions. For pension purposes, the employee's length of service includes the reasonable notice period. The pension benefit calculation includes any salary increases that the employee would probably have received during the notice period.

In *IBM Canada Limited v. Waterman*, the Supreme Court of Canada held that employee pension payments generally should not be counted as "earnings" (or alternative income) that reduce the amount of reasonable notice damages otherwise owing. In other words, a dismissed employee who is entitled to start receiving pension benefit income is also entitled to receive a full severance package, undiscounted by the amount of that pension income.

Note that damages do not include work-related expenses, such as a car allowance based on work kilometres travelled, because they are not incurred unless an employee is working.

Generally speaking, employers should not dismiss employees when they are on disability leave. An employee who becomes disabled during the notice period typically is entitled to both pay in lieu of notice *and* disability benefits because these are separate legal rights.

Other Types of Wrongful Dismissal Damages

In addition to the basic entitlement to pay in lieu of reasonable notice, the common law allows for other damages against employers in certain circumstances. A key principle underlying these "special" damages is that they are not intended to compensate an employee for the hurt feelings and mental distress that can arise from the actual dismissal. This is because the right to dismiss an employee on reasonable notice is an implicit part of the employment contract, so the normal distress and hurt feelings resulting from dismissal are not compensable. However, special damages can be awarded based on the employer's poor conduct *in the course* of the dismissal. The following is a brief overview of these special damages, including some relevant background on how they have developed up to the current time.

Before Wallace (Pre-1997)

Historically, employees were able to obtain special damages in a wrongful dismissal claim only where the employer's actions during the dismissal were so severe or outrageous that they gave rise to an "independent actionable wrong." For example, if an employer acted maliciously, knowing that its actions were causing an employee serious distress, the employee would be able to recover **aggravated damages** on the basis of the tort of intentional infliction of mental suffering, which—like any other tort—is an independent actionable wrong. Another example would be where the employer spread lies to intentionally harm an employee's reputation, thereby committing the tort of defamation (HRInsider.ca, 2010). Aggravated damages, then, were designed to compensate employees for non-monetary losses, such as emotional pain or loss of self-esteem, that were caused by an employer's conduct during the dismissal, as long as the employee could prove that the employer had committed an independent actionable wrong.

In addition, **punitive damages** could be awarded in those rare cases where the employer's dismissal-related misconduct was so flagrant that the court felt it necessary to go beyond compensating the employee to punish the employer, as well as to act as a deterrent. However, because awarding either aggravated or punitive damages required finding that the employer had committed an independent actionable wrong—a difficult threshold to meet—before 1997 special damages were rarely given out in wrongful dismissal lawsuits (HRInsider.ca, 2010). Moreover, when they were awarded, the amounts were relatively small.

"Wallace Damages" (1997–2008)

In its 1997 landmark decision, *Wallace v. United Grain Growers Ltd.*, the Supreme Court of Canada created a new avenue for awarding damages to dismissed employees. It held that employers have a duty to act fairly and in good faith in the course of dismissal (by being "candid, reasonable, honest and forthright") and employers that breach this duty will be made liable for an extended notice period. For example, where a court found that, based on the *Bardal* factors, the reasonable notice period should be 15 months, it could extend that to 18 months to reflect the employer's bad-faith conduct (such as falsely claiming that the termination was for cause). Note that this extension did *not* require the employee to prove that the employer had committed an independent actionable wrong, only that it had acted in bad faith. Nor did employees have to show that the employer's dismissal-related misconduct affected their chances of obtaining new employment. Examples given of bad-faith conduct included attacking the employee's reputation at the time of dismissal, misrepresenting the reason for the dismissal, or dismissing the employee to deprive the employee of a pension benefit or other right.

In *Wallace*, the Supreme Court made it clear that it did not intend for plaintiffs to automatically claim bad-faith damages in every dismissal case. An element of intent, malice, or blatant disregard for the employee had to be involved, such as where the employer was untruthful, misleading, or unduly insensitive in the manner in which the employee was terminated. Nonetheless, after *Wallace* many employees in their statements of claim began adding a claim for bad-faith damages as a matter of course, and courts regularly tacked "*Wallace* extensions" of several months on to the reasonable notice period (HRInsider.ca, 2010).

FYI

Termination: Employees at Their Most Vulnerable

In *Wallace v. United Grain Growers*, the employee, aged 59, was a successful commissioned salesman who was dismissed after being told that his job was secure. The employer indicated that the dismissal was for "good cause" although it would not explain the cause and later withdrew its allegation at trial. The trial court found that the employer had alleged cause as part of its "hardball" negotiation strategy. The Supreme Court found this conduct, while short of constituting an independent actionable wrong, worthy of a damage award, which it decided to confer by extending the reasonable notice period (HRInsider.ca, 2010). This extension came to be known as "*Wallace*" or "bad-faith" damages. In explaining its decision, the Supreme Court spoke about the inherent power imbalance between employers and employees, especially at the time of termination. It stated:

The point at which the employment relationship ruptures is the time when the employee is most vulnerable and hence, most in need of protection. In recognition of this need, the law ought to encourage conduct that minimizes the damage and dislocation (both economic and personal) that result from dismissal. ... I note that the loss of one's job is always a traumatic event. However, when termination is accompanied by acts of bad faith in the manner of discharge, the results can be especially devastating.

As a result of *Wallace*, employers were put on notice that harshness or even insensitivity in the manner in which an employee was dismissed could result in an extension to the notice period.

Over time, growing concern about how frequently *Wallace* damages were being awarded resulted in the Supreme Court of Canada returning to the issue in *Honda Canada Inc. v. Keays*.

Honda Canada Inc. v. Keays (2008)

In 2008 the Supreme Court of Canada issued a landmark decision in *Honda Canada Inc. v. Keays* that revisited the law of wrongful dismissal damages.

The changes made by the Supreme Court in *Honda* are significant. They include reformulating when and how *Wallace*-type damages are awarded and clarifying the circumstances in which punitive damages are appropriate. The decision also provides guidance to employers concerning their ability to monitor and manage their workforce in the context of the duty to accommodate.

CASE IN POINT

Supreme Court of Canada Restates the Law of Damages for Wrongful Dismissal

Honda Canada Inc. v. Keays, 2008 SCC 39

Facts

Keays worked for Honda for 14 years, first on the assembly line and later in data entry. He received positive work assessments but he had a poor attendance record because he suffered from chronic fatigue syndrome (CFS). Keays was enrolled in Honda's disability program, which allowed employees to miss work if they provided doctor's notes confirming that their absences were disability related.

However, when Keays began missing more days of work than his doctor had predicted and his medical notes changed in tone, becoming more "cryptic," Honda began to question whether Keays' absences were being independently evaluated by his doctor. Honda decided to cancel Keays' accommodation and stop accepting doctor's notes. Instead, it asked Keays to meet with Dr. Brennan, an occupational medical specialist, so that they could decide how best to accommodate his disability. Keays had earlier met with another doctor at Honda's request and, fearing he was being "set up," he retained a lawyer. The lawyer advised Honda that Keays would meet with the specialist only if the purpose, methodology, and parameters of the consultation were provided. Honda did not respond to the lawyer; it later advised Keays that it had a practice of only dealing with associates directly. Instead, it sent Keays a letter that included a medical opinion from Dr. Brennan and the previous doctor that they could find no diagnosis indicating that he was disabled from working. It also stated that Honda supported his full return to work but that he would be dismissed if he continued to refuse to meet with Dr. Brennan. He did not change his mind and shortly thereafter he was ter-

minated for cause, on the ground of insubordination. Keays sued for wrongful dismissal damages, as well as for damages for discrimination and harassment.

The trial judge found Honda's actions not only unwarranted, but in fact outrageous. The judge held that Keays had been wrongfully dismissed and awarded him the following:

- 15 months' pay in lieu of reasonable notice.
- a 9-month extension to the notice period (for a total of 24 months) for the employer's bad-faith conduct in his dismissal (*Wallace* damages). Among other things, the trial judge criticized Honda for requiring a doctor's note for every absence for CFS whereas it did not for more traditional illnesses.
- punitive damages of $500,000. This was by far the largest punitive award ever given in a wrongful dismissal action. The trial judge justified the award by stating that it takes a "large whack to wake up a wealthy and powerful defendant to its responsibilities."

On appeal, the Ontario Court of Appeal reduced the punitive damages award to $100,000, on the basis that it was disproportionately large and there was no evidence to support the trial judge's finding of a "protracted corporate conspiracy." However, the Court of Appeal supported much of the lower court's reasoning under the other headings of damages. Honda appealed.

Relevant Issue

Whether the damages awarded were appropriate.

Decision

The Supreme Court of Canada struck down all of the damages awarded except the reasonable notice award of 15 months. It found that the trial judge made a number of "palpable and overriding" errors in his decision. Furthermore, in its words, the case presented an "opportunity to clarify and redefine some aspects of the law of damages in the context of employment." It made the following rulings:

1. It upheld the 15 months' general reasonable notice damages.
2. It struck down the 9-month extension of the notice period (*Wallace* damages) and made the following key findings:
   a. Honda did not deliberately misrepresent its doctor's views;
   b. an employer is entitled to rely on its doctors' medical opinions;
   c. there is nothing inappropriate about an employer using doctor's notes as a way to manage attendance; and
   d. an employer is entitled to seek confirmation of disability or request clarification of accommodation needs; stopping the accommodation process was not a reprisal because its purpose was to allow Dr. Brennan to confirm the disability.

   The Supreme Court went on to revisit when and how *Wallace* damages are awarded. If an employee can prove that the manner of dismissal caused actual damages (for example, for mental distress), he should be compensated for it. Moreover, this award should be based on the employee's actual losses rather than given as an extension of the wrongful dismissal notice period.
3. It struck down the $100,000 punitive damages award. Punitive damages are reserved for exceptional cases where the employer's conduct is so malicious and outrageous that it is deserving of punishment on its own. In this case Honda's conduct did not demonstrate "egregious bad faith." There was no discriminatory conduct here; the employer's disability program was designed to accommodate particular types of disabilities and was not itself discriminatory.

With *Honda* the Supreme Court of Canada has redefined many aspects of the law of wrongful dismissal damages.

Key Points Addressed in Honda

Determining Reasonable Notice

The Supreme Court confirmed that the main factors in determining "reasonable notice" are the nature of the job, the employee's age and length of service, and the availability of similar employment (that is, the *Bardal* factors). No particular factor should be given undue weight, and each case turns on its own facts. The court criticized the trial court for focusing on Honda's flat management structure to lengthen the notice period. The employer's non-hierarchical management structure "said nothing of Keays' employment." However, the Supreme Court considered several factors specific to Keays—he had spent his entire adult working life with the employer, he lacked formal education, and he suffered from an illness—in deciding not to overturn the 15-month award for reasonable notice.

Moral (Formerly Wallace) Damages/Aggravated Damages

As discussed above, the Supreme Court decided that damages attributable to bad-faith conduct in the manner of dismissal should be determined on the same basis as other compensatory damages. The test is: what damages were within the "reasonable expectation" of the parties as flowing from a breach of contract? Because *Wallace v. United Grain Growers* established that an employer has a duty of good faith and fairness in the *manner of dismissal*, damages for breach of that obligation are foreseeable and the employee is entitled to compensation. The court also held that *Wallace* damages should not be given through an arbitrary extension of the notice period. Instead, they should be given in the same manner as all compensatory damages—through a monetary award that reflects proven damages. Consequently, there must be proof of damages, such as treatment for mental distress, for a damage award to be made (Echlin and Thomlinson, 2011, p. 254).

In *Honda*, the Supreme Court also eliminated the distinction between *Wallace* (now moral) damages resulting from conduct in the manner of termination, and "aggravated damages" resulting from a separate cause of action. There is no longer a requirement for an independent actionable wrong to support an action for aggravated damages.

Punitive Damages

The Supreme Court confirmed that the bar for awarding punitive damages is a high one. They should only be awarded for advertent conduct that is harsh, vindictive, malicious, and reprehensible and when compensatory damages are not enough to punish, deter, and denounce the bad behaviour.

An award of punitive damages continues to require a finding that the employer committed an "actionable wrong." However, a breach of the contractual duty of good faith can serve as the actionable wrong: it does not have to be an independent tort (Echlin and Thomlinson, 2011, p. 255).

Finally, courts should not award multiple forms of damages arising out of the same facts. The Supreme Court found that the lower courts' decisions indicated some confusion between damages for the employer's conduct in dismissal and punitive damages. It clarified the distinction and underscored the fact that punitive damages are only to be awarded in extreme cases.

The Duty to Accommodate

In *Honda*, the Supreme Court made several findings related to the employer's duty to accommodate. First, the need to monitor the absences of employees who are regularly absent from work is a bona fide management responsibility in light of the very nature of the employment contract and responsibility of the employer for the management of its workforce. Second, an employer is entitled to rely on the medical information it receives from its doctors. Third, an employer is entitled to take steps to confirm the nature of the employee's medical condition to determine the accommodation required.

These findings are significant because the trial judge's decision and large punitive damages awarded dissuaded many employers from pressing attendance issues when disability was involved (Rudner, 2008, p. 15). The Supreme Court's decision significantly supports an employer's ability to monitor and manage the attendance of its employees and require doctor's notes as part of the accommodation process. Similarly, it confirmed that asking for clarification of an employee's disability before adapting the workplace or employee's schedule is legitimate.

Employer's Entitlement to Deal with Employee Directly

The Supreme Court held that an employer's refusal to deal with an employee's lawyer is not outrageous behaviour. As long as an employee is employed, the parties "are always entitled to deal with each other directly." This confirms that there is no legal obligation to allow an employee's lawyer to attend internal management investigations.

Since Honda (2008 On)

It appears that since *Honda*, moral (formerly *Wallace*) damages are being claimed less frequently and, where claimed, they are somewhat less likely to be awarded than in the past because courts are generally requiring proof of damages suffered (HRInsider.ca, 2010).

That said, as the case of *Boucher v. Wal-Mart* discussed below illustrates, where courts find compelling evidence of both bad-faith conduct on the part of the employer and compensable losses by the employee, the *amount* of the awards given seems to be increasing.

Moreover, there is an argument that, where an employee's damages include elements such as loss of reputation or reduction in income, the potential award for compensatory damages under *Honda* exceeds that previously available under *Wallace*. Although it was overturned on appeal, the trial court decision in *Soost v. Merrill Lynch Canada Inc.* is an example of this possibility. In that case, the trial court awarded a financial adviser $1.6 million for loss of his professional reputation after he was dismissed, allegedly for cause. It held that the employer's allegations of improper conduct, although made in good faith, damaged the employee's reputation in an industry where confidence is key to being successful. Because this damage was foreseeable, the employer was responsible for the employee's resulting losses. This decision was reversed on appeal on the basis that the employer had not shown bad faith in the manner of dismissal and therefore a moral damages award was not justified. However, the case points to the potential for higher awards where the employee meets the evidentiary threshold for proving both bad-faith conduct by the employer and significant actual losses suffered (HRInsider.ca, 2010).

It has been noted that since *Honda*, some parties continue to make separate claims for aggravated damages, moral damages, and damages for mental distress, reflecting some ongoing confusion concerning these additional damages (Echlin and Thomlinson, 2011, p. 253).

As noted above, *Boucher v. Wal-Mart* is an example of a decision rendered after the *Honda* decision, and therefore helps demonstrate how its principles are being applied. In this case, the Supreme Court of Canada was asked to consider whether a total award of $1.45 million in aggravated, punitive, and tort damages was appropriate given the employer's actions, and those of its manager, which led to an employee's constructive dismissal.

CASE IN POINT

Major Damages Awarded Against Wal-Mart and Its Manager

Boucher v. Wal-Mart Canada Corp., 2014 ONCA 419

Facts

Boucher, aged 43, was an assistant manager at a Wal-Mart store in Windsor. A good worker, Boucher got along well with her manager, Pinnock, until May 2009, when he asked her to falsify a temperature log and she refused. After this, Pinnock started belittling and humiliating her in front of co-workers. In June, Boucher availed herself of Wal-Mart's Open Door Communica-

tion Policy by asking to meet with the district people manager to discuss this issue; however, in breach of that policy, Pinnock was advised of the meeting and thereafter his behaviour toward Boucher became even worse. In October, Boucher asked to meet with senior management representatives, who said they would investigate her concerns. However, they warned her that she could suffer negative consequences if her concerns were found to be unjustified and, in mid-November, after finding that her complaints were "unsubstantiated," they told Boucher she would be "held accountable for making them." A few days later, Pinnock again humiliated her in front of other employees, this time by grabbing her by the elbow and telling her to prove to him that she could count to ten. He prompted her by initiating the count, then told her to count out loud along with him. Boucher was so humiliated that she left the store and soon after tendered her resignation. As one witness later testified, Pinnock seemed "overjoyed" when he heard she had quit.

Boucher sued Wal-Mart and Pinnock for constructive dismissal and related damages. In a jury trial, Boucher was awarded the following:

- 20 weeks' salary as required under her employment contract (2 weeks' salary per year of service);
- $1.2 million against Wal-Mart ($200,000 in aggravated damages for the manner in which she was dismissed, and $1 million in punitive damages); and
- $250,000 damages against Pinnock ($100,000 for the tort of intentional infliction of mental suffering, and $150,000 for punitive damages).

The defendants appealed both their liability and the amount of damages. Boucher cross-appealed for $726,691 for future income loss until retirement, arguing that, but for the defendants' wrongful conduct, she would have stayed at Wal-Mart until her retirement.

Relevant Issues

1. Whether the special damage awards against Pinnock and Wal-Mart should be set aside or reduced for being unnecessary or excessive.
2. Whether the employee is entitled to future income loss until retirement.

Decision

Pinnock

The court found that Boucher had proven all three elements of the tort of intentional infliction of mental suffering:

- the defendant's conduct was flagrant and outrageous (Pinnock continuously and publicly demeaned Boucher over a period of nearly six months);
- the defendant's conduct was calculated to harm the plaintiff (evidence showed that Pinnock was "overjoyed" at having accomplished his goal of getting Boucher to quit); and
- the defendant's conduct caused the plaintiff to suffer a visible and provable illness (Boucher's family doctor confirmed that her symptoms—abdominal pain, weight loss,

and inability to eat or sleep—arose from work-related stress).

The appellate court also upheld the amount of the award ($100,000) even though it was unprecedentedly high against an individual employee in a breach of employment contract case. As the court explained: "The jury represents the collective conscience of the community. The magnitude of their award shows that they were deeply offended by Pinnock's mistreatment of Boucher."

Regarding punitive damages, the court found that Pinnock's mistreatment of Boucher met the high standard required for such damages; however, it reduced the amount of the award from $150,000 to $10,000 on the basis that the high $100,000 damages award for the tort of intentional infliction of mental suffering already carried a "strong punitive component."

Wal-Mart

Similarly, the court upheld the $200,000 award for aggravated damages against Wal-Mart but reduced the punitive damages award from $1 million to $100,000.

The court held that the $200,000 aggravated damages award was justified on several grounds: Wal-Mart failed to take Boucher's complaints seriously; it failed to discipline Pinnock or stop his ongoing mistreatment of her; it failed to follow and enforce its own workplace policies; and it threatened Boucher with retaliation for making her complaints. These actions warranted a substantial award for aggravated damages, separate from Pinnock's tort of intentional infliction of mental suffering (for which Wal-Mart was also vicariously liable).

On the other hand, as with Pinnock, the court found that while the extent of Wal-Mart's misconduct warranted punitive damages, the amount of those damages should be reduced because the high aggravated damages award already contained an element of punishment and denunciation.

Boucher's Cross-Appeal

The appellate court upheld the trial judge's ruling that Boucher was *not* entitled to an award for future loss of income. The evidence showed that Boucher had recovered from the effects of the wrongdoer's action. She was able to work (although she had not found a job), and therefore she had not suffered a loss of earning capacity. Accordingly, Boucher was only entitled to the loss of income provided for in her employment contract, which was 20 weeks. (The court noted that Boucher did not have an employment contract that guaranteed her employment to age 65. Her entitlement was to be put in the position she would have been in if the contract had been performed—in other words, employment subject to dismissal in accordance with the terms of her contract.)

FYI

Employer Misconduct That Attracts Punitive Damages at the "High End of the Scale"

One of the reasons the Court of Appeal in *Boucher* cited for reducing the amount of punitive damages awarded against Wal-Mart was that its misconduct, while serious, fell far short of the "gravity and duration of the misconduct in other cases that have attracted high punitive damages awards." For example, the court contrasted this case to the employer's actions in *Pate Estate v. Galway-Cavendish and Harvey (Township)*, where a wrongfully dismissed employee was ultimately awarded $450,000 in punitive damages. In *Pate*, the employer alleged that the employee had engaged in criminal activity and threatened to call the police if the employee refused to resign. When that failed, the employer instigated a police investigation that led to criminal charges and a four-day trial at which the dismissed employee was acquitted and it was revealed that the employer had withheld exculpatory information from the police. Moreover, this case was widely publicized over several years, causing the employee ongoing humiliation within the community. By contrast, the court noted that Wal-Mart was already liable for compensatory damages, the misconduct lasted less than six months, and it (unlike its manager, Pinnock) did not set out to force Boucher's resignation.

Conclusions

Although the Supreme Court scaled back the historically high punitive damage awards against both Wal-Mart and its manager, Pinnock, the total amount awarded ($410,000 in special damages alone) remains a significant sum. In fact, it's been reported that the awards both for aggravated damages and for intentional infliction of mental distress are the highest of their type in employment law in Canadian history (Schwartz and Portman, 2014). Thus, this decision signals the Supreme Court of Canada's willingness to uphold large special damages awards where the circumstances are particularly egregious.

Lessons for Employers

Boucher v. Wal-Mart reinforces several important lessons for employers:

- create fair workplace anti-harassment policies *and follow them*;
- conduct workplace investigations promptly, thoroughly, and in an unbiased manner;
- deal effectively with all employees, including managers and supervisors, who breach the workplace's violence, harassment, or discrimination policies; and
- do not impose sanctions against an employee who lodges a complaint except in the most obvious cases of bad faith. Employees should be encouraged to use the employer's internal conflict resolution processes—not discouraged from using them (Schwartz and Portman, 2014).

FYI

Ontario Court of Appeal Rejects Tort of Negligent Infliction of Mental Suffering in Employment Context

In *Piresferreira v. Ayotte*, the Ontario Court of Appeal considered and rejected adding another possible heading of special damages for dismissed employees: the tort of "negligent infliction of mental suffering." Unlike the tort of *intentional* infliction of mental suffering, discussed above, this tort would *not* require defendants to intend the consequences of their actions. The tort would be found as long as the plaintiff could show that the defendant had a duty of care to another person, the defendant failed to meet the standard of care required, and the other person suffered emotional distress as a result ("Ontario Court of Appeal Bars Claims," 2010, p. 8).

The facts of the case in which the Court of Appeal considered this issue are as follows. Piresferreira was an account manager at Bell who left her position after ten years because of her manager's (Ayotte) troubling behaviour. Ayotte was loud, critical, intimidating, and aggressive, and on one occasion pushed Piresferreira backward and yelled at her to "get the hell out" of his office. Although Piresferreira returned to work after this incident, not only did she not receive an apology, but Ayotte presented her with a performance improvement plan (PIP). Piresferreira complained to her HR department, which conducted a very brief investigation—that is, by speaking with Ayotte—but then asked her to attend a meeting to discuss her PIP. Piresferreira refused and, unsatisfied with the employer's overall response, went on stress leave. Later diagnosed with post-traumatic stress disorder, major depressive disorder, and anxiety, Piresferreira sued Bell for constructive dismissal and both Bell and Ayotte for special damages.

The trial judge awarded Piresferreira 12 months in reasonable notice damages ($90,000) for constructive dismissal and $500,000 based on the tort of "negligent infliction of mental suffering." The defendants appealed.

The Ontario Court of Appeal explicitly decided not to recognize the tort of negligent infliction of mental suffering in the employment context. In its view, recognizing such a tort would be "undesirable because it would be a considerable intrusion by the courts into the workplace, it has a real potential to constrain efforts to achieve increased efficiencies, and the postulated duty of care is so general and broad it could apply indeterminately."

The Court of Appeal also rejected the trial court's finding that Ayotte (and, vicariously, Bell) were liable for the tort of *intentional* infliction of mental suffering. Their misconduct, while serious, was not calculated to harm the plaintiff in that they did not intend the consequences that followed, nor did they know that the consequences were "substantially certain to follow."

Having set aside the $500,000 award for negligent infliction of mental suffering, the Court of Appeal awarded Piresferreira $45,000 for mental distress damages based on the manner in which she was dismissed and upheld the award of $90,000 for reasonable notice damages (Lublin, 2010, p. 5).

Wrongful Dismissal Procedures

A dismissed employee has two years from the date of dismissal to bring an action for wrongful dismissal. In Ontario, effective January 1, 2010, wrongful dismissal claims for $25,000 or less may be heard in Small Claims Court, where the adjudication process is relatively fast and informal. This increase from the previous limit of $10,000 has resulted in more employees pursuing wrongful dismissal actions because Small Claims Court has simpler, less costly procedures and there is less responsibility for the losing side to pay legal costs.

An employee with a claim that exceeds the limits for Small Claims Court may begin an action for wrongful dismissal in the Ontario Superior Court of Justice by issuing a statement of claim. This document sets out the key elements of the claim and the damages sought. It must be served on the employer within six months after it is issued. If the employer is a Canadian defendant, it must serve and file a statement of defence within 20 days. This time limit may be extended an extra 10 days if the employer serves and files a notice of intent to defend within that period.

Also effective January 1, 2010, a claim for $100,000 or less is filed under Ontario's simplified rules. (The previous limit was $50,000.) These rules reduce the number of pretrial procedures available in an effort to minimize costs and delays in smaller claims. A claim for more than $100,000 proceeds under the regular rules.

If the dispute involves allegations of just cause, a trial is necessary. If, on the other hand, the only issue in dispute is the amount of reasonable notice or damages in lieu, a motion for summary judgment may be allowed. Summary judgment motions are most appropriate when the parties agree on the essential facts of the case but disagree on the amount of notice that is required given those facts. Jury trials are available for wrongful dismissal actions.

Generally speaking, a successful party is entitled to **costs** from the other party on a partial indemnity basis. More generous substantial indemnity costs are usually awarded only if one of the parties has acted poorly—for example, if an employer has made serious unjustified accusations in its pleadings—or if an employee has made an offer to settle that is more advantageous for the employer than the final result of the litigation.

If an employer serves an offer to settle before trial that is as good as or better than the judgment that an employee eventually obtains at trial, the employee recovers partial indemnity costs to the date the employer served the offer. However, the employer recovers partial indemnity costs from the date of its offer.

The unsuccessful party at trial can appeal to the Ontario Court of Appeal without leave as long as the dispute involves more than $50,000. Appeals to the Supreme Court of Canada on wrongful dismissal cases require leave of the court. To receive leave, the case must raise a question of public importance, a significant issue of law, or a significant issue of mixed fact and law.

Avoiding Wrongful Dismissal Claims

Given the time, cost, and impact on staff morale involved in wrongful dismissal actions, it makes sense for an employer to avoid such actions, if possible. A list of suggestions to minimize the potential for lawsuits from dismissed employees follows. Even if an employee proceeds with litigation, an employer that has followed these suggestions is less likely to face a court that is unsympathetic to its point of view.

1. Hire Intelligently

An employer should do its homework when hiring. Thorough reference checks and comprehensive interviews reduce an employer's chances of hiring an employee who is unsuitable or unqualified for a job.

2. Include and Update a Termination Clause in Employment Contracts

An employer should negotiate a termination provision in an employment contract that sets out the amount of advance notice, or pay in lieu, that it must provide in the event that it dismisses an employee. The notice period must meet the minimum requirements of employment standards legislation, but it need not be as generous as reasonable notice under the common law. As discussed in Chapter 4, termination provisions must be written carefully. For example, a termination clause that does not specifically require an employer to provide benefit coverage during the statutory notice period will be found null and void for contravening the *Employment Standards Act*.

An employer must ensure that its contracts are kept up to date so that termination provisions remain enforceable over time. Otherwise, changes in an employee's duties or title may render the contract obsolete and therefore unenforceable. The employer may update the contract by, for example, negotiating the update with the employee and providing additional legal consideration or planning the change to coincide with consideration such as a wage increase or promotion. Alternatively, the employer may make the change by giving the employee reasonable notice of it and offering employment under the new terms at the end of the notice period.

3.   Make Use of Probationary Periods

A written contract or employment policy should state that the employee acknowledges that employment is subject to a set probationary period. This provision or policy should provide that the employer may terminate the employee at any time and for any reason within the first three months of employment (or six months, if appropriate) without providing notice or pay in lieu of notice. If the probationary period is longer than three months, the employer is required to provide one week's notice or pay in lieu if it dismisses an employee after three months under the *Employment Standards Act*. The contract should expressly recognize this statutory obligation. An employer should monitor an employee's performance during the probationary period to identify any difficulties while its legal obligations are minimal.

4.   Create a Paper Trail

An employer should document problems with employees as soon as they occur and in a precise and chronological way. If an employer makes an employee aware of a problem, the way in which it can be corrected, and the consequences of not correcting it, the employer has helped the employee meet the job requirements. If eventually there is no improvement, the employer has created a paper trail to support a decision to dismiss the employee. Such a trail is critical because an employer bears the burden of proof in establishing just cause for dismissal.

5.   Provide Reasonable Notice of Changes

An employer may change even significant terms and conditions of employment unilaterally if it provides an employee with reasonable notice of the change and offers employment under the new terms at the end of the notice period. Reasonable notice may be several months or more, depending on an employee's age and other factors such as length of service and position.

6.   Determine Whether a Just Cause Claim Is Sustainable

An employer should apply progressive discipline to most types of misconduct—such as insolence or disobedience—before deciding to dismiss an employee. Where alleged misconduct is particularly serious, an employer has a duty to investigate any allegations fully and fairly before deciding to terminate. If, after such an investigation, an employer has compelling evidence of serious misconduct and no reasonable alternative explanation, it may dismiss for just cause. If, however, the evidence falls short of the required standard of proof, the employer should provide appropriate notice and/or a separation package.

7. Absent Just Cause, Determine the Appropriate Notice Period

Where there is no just cause under the common law for dismissing an employee and no enforceable termination clause in the employment contract, an employer should review reasonable notice periods determined by the courts in similar fact situations. There is no formula for establishing reasonable notice under the common law. Relevant factors include an employee's age, length of service, and character of employment, and the availability of similar employment. Other factors that may come into play are whether an employer lured an employee away from a secure job.

8. Handle Terminations Professionally

Callous conduct during the termination process can increase an employer's liability in a number of ways. It can cause a court to award compensatory damages for damages the employee actually suffered because of the manner of dismissal. In extreme cases, unprofessional conduct can also lead to punitive damages. Below are general guidelines for an employer to follow when dismissing an employee.

1. Hold the termination meeting in a private location, such as the employee's office or meeting room, preferably near an exit. This way, the employer controls the length of the meeting and is able to leave, while the employee can remain in a private place until she is ready to encounter other employees.

2. Hold the termination meeting early in the week so that the employee has time before the weekend to obtain legal advice and make any other necessary arrangements. Consider holding the meeting late in the afternoon or at another time when the employee can leave immediately afterward.

3. Investigate an employee's personal circumstances before terminating him. For example, do not terminate an employee on his birthday or around a holiday; lack of sensitivity may cause a court to increase the compensatory damage award.

4. Keep the meeting focused on the termination and keep the meeting brief: a maximum of 15 minutes. If the employee is being dismissed for cause, the employer should briefly state the reasons for dismissal but should not recite a litany of the employee's shortcomings. An employer cannot benefit from attacking an employee when or after she is terminated, and an attack will make negotiations more confrontational. However, be clear that the decision to dismiss is final.

5. Make no unsubstantiated allegations. In the past, bad-faith damages have most commonly been awarded when an employer makes allegations without strong factual support. Do not misrepresent the reasons for the dismissal.

6. Ensure that the employee's supervisor and another manager are at the meeting to show that management supports the decision to dismiss the employee. The additional manager can also act as a witness to what is discussed.

7. Ensure that all representatives of management at the meeting make notes, date them, and sign them.

8. Confirm the termination of employment in writing (written notice is required under the *Employment Standards Act*). The letter should include the effective date of the termination. It should briefly set out the reasons for the

termination and confirm the reasonable notice provided or the just cause alleged. An employer can also use the letter to remind an employee of any post-termination obligations, such as those contained in a non-competition clause in the employment contract.

9. Pay outstanding wages, commissions, expenses, and vacation pay. Failure to pay these amounts violates employment standards legislation and makes an employee more likely to sue. It also places the employer in an unsympathetic light if the matter ever comes before a judge.

10. Provide employment standards termination and severance payments immediately if the dismissal is without cause, whether or not an employee signs a release. Unless cause is alleged, the employee is entitled to these payments. Withholding them as a tactic to pressure an employee into signing a release could result in additional damages for bad-faith behaviour if the matter goes to court.

11. Where a separation package is provided, give the employee the name of a contact person who can answer any questions related to the separation package. The contact person must be knowledgeable about the package and related legal requirements.

12. Ask the employee to return all company property in his possession. Specify the items and a date by which they must be returned. Determine whether expense accounts are outstanding, and advise the employee to submit an expense claim as soon as possible.

13. Offer outplacement counselling services where appropriate. Do not make the offer conditional on whether the employee signs a release. These services usually help an employee find other work quickly, thereby reducing the amount an employer owes for wrongful dismissal damages. An offer of counselling also sets a positive tone for a potential hearing in court.

14. Let the employee know her entitlements under the law, such as those relating to benefits.

15. Be honest and forthright.

16. Do not offer a separation package if the termination is for just cause. An employer might offer the employee some money as a gesture of goodwill, but it must make the offer on a "without prejudice" basis so that it is clear that the offer is not an admission of liability.

17. Explain all terms of any separation package. List the support being offered: financial compensation, relocation counselling, letter of reference, and cooperation concerning references, for example. Leave the employee with two copies of the severance letter and a release to review. Provide the employee with a contact person for her response.

18. Do not accept the employee's agreement to a separation package, and do not accept a signed release, during the termination meeting. The employee needs time to consider her position and to seek independent legal advice. Otherwise, a court may find the agreement unenforceable.

19. Avoid humiliating the employee. For example, do not escort her out the door when others are present. Any conduct that unnecessarily undermines an ex-employee's dignity may encourage a court to increase the damage award if the dismissed employee suffers damages as a result.

20. Prepare the employee's record of employment within five days of the last day of work for employment insurance purposes. Unjustifiably delaying an employee's receipt of employment insurance benefits could lead to additional damages.

21. Allow the employee some input into the manner in which news of her dismissal is announced to other employees, clients, and suppliers, while retaining control of the situation. An employee, for example, may prefer to keep the reason for her dismissal confidential. Do not make critical remarks about the employee to co-workers.

22. Designate someone to meet the dismissed employee's immediate co-workers as soon as possible to let them know about the dismissal. Indicate the assistance that the employer is offering him in finding another job. Let them know how the employee's responsibilities will be handled and how clients or customers will be notified of his departure. Send an internal memo to other employees. Quick action can minimize rumours and misunderstandings.

23. If a letter of reference is being provided, provide it unconditionally. Do not tie it in with reaching a settlement.

9. Provide Outplacement Counselling

Providing dismissed employees with the services of an outplacement agency has become an important aspect of a separation package in many organizations. These agencies support the employee in finding another job and offer career counselling. Their services are paid for by the employee's former employer.

10. Get a Signed Release, Where Possible

An employer should not require employees to sign a release as a condition of receiving their minimum termination or severance pay entitlements under employment standards legislation. However, to receive amounts in excess of statutory entitlements, employees should be asked to sign documents in which they agree to release the employer from all legal claims related to their employment or its termination. Because the release is a "contract," this additional amount also acts as "consideration" for the employee's signing of the release. Furthermore, a release is enforceable only if a court is convinced that (a) an employee signed it willingly and without undue pressure from the employer, and (b) the employee understood its impact.

As with employment contracts, employers should provide employees with a reasonable opportunity to obtain independent legal advice before signing a release so that they cannot later argue that they were unaware of its implications or felt unduly pressured to sign it. For example, in *Cuba et. al. v. Global Egg Corporation*, the Ontario Human Rights Tribunal upheld a release that provided the employees with only two weeks' more pay than what was required under the *Employment Standards Act*. In supporting this decision, the adjudicator emphasized that the employer had urged the employees to seek independent legal advice, which they did, had not misled them concerning the contents of the release, and had provided a Spanish-speaking manager to translate the release letter to them. In contrast, in *Stephenson v. Hilti (Canada) Ltd.* the trial court found the release unenforceable on the basis of unconscionability.

In that case, a 61-year-old employee with nine years' service signed a release providing him with 3.5 months' notice damages when his common law entitlement was later found to be 11 months. The employer did not suggest he seek independent legal advice. Stephenson signed because he was distraught at the thought that his pay would be cut off, as he needed money to pay his rent. The court found that these facts fit the three-part test for unconscionability:

- there was inequality of bargaining position arising out of ignorance, need, or distress of the weaker party (*Stephenson was unsophisticated in business matters and was evidently feeling desperate*);
- the stronger party had unconscientiously used a position of power to achieve an advantage (*the employer did not intentionally mislead him, but neither did it give any real thought to his well-being*); and
- the agreement reached was substantially unfair to the weaker party or was "sufficiently divergent from community standards of commercial morality that it should be set aside" (*the settlement offer was one-third of the employee's common law entitlement*).

The judge in *Stephenson* acknowledged that even on these facts the decision was "a close call" (para. 143) and, generally speaking, releases are not readily set aside. However, it is important that employers be aware of the need to be clear, balanced, and honest when asking an employee to sign a release and to encourage the employee to seek independent legal advice.

It is important that releases specifically reference all possible claims relating to the employment relationship, including human rights and employment standards claims, although the ability of a release to effectively foreclose a subsequent human rights claim is questionable at law and at best partially dependent on the facts of the case.

11. Carefully Consider All Issues When Providing a Letter of Reference

The employer is not required by law to provide a letter of reference to a dismissed employee. However, an employee without such a reference will probably find it more difficult to find a new job, and this may increase the wrongful dismissal damages that the employer owes to the employee. Similarly, an employer that withholds a letter of reference to coerce an employee into signing a release may find itself paying additional damages if the employee suffers actual damages as a result of its tactics. This is especially true where withholding a letter of reference is part of a pattern of unfair conduct.

An employer that chooses to provide a reference has an obligation to avoid recklessness in doing so. As a general rule, a former employer is not liable for providing a negative reference if it sincerely believes that its statements are true and there is a reasonable basis for them. In other words, a claim will only succeed if the comments are not only inaccurate but also malicious (Rudner, 2009, p. 5). Although such claims are rare, negative statements made carelessly or maliciously may result in a successful claim against a former employer for defamation or negligence. *Miller v. Bank of Nova Scotia* demonstrates the matters that a court considers in determining an employer's liability for providing negative references.

CASE IN POINT

Employer Not Liable for Providing Negative Reference

Miller v. Bank of Nova Scotia, 2002 CanLII 22030 (Ont. SC)

Facts

Miller worked part-time for the employer bank but did not like working evenings. When she complained, the employer reminded her that she had been hired to work evening hours but stated that it would try to make alternative arrangements after its busy RRSP season ended. She agreed to wait, but shortly thereafter received a conditional offer of employment from another bank for daytime work. She accepted this position and resigned from the employer without giving notice. The new job offer was conditional on checking references.

When the new bank contacted the employer, Miller's supervisor was surprised; she did not know that Miller had given her name as a reference. She indicated that she was upset with the manner in which Miller had left her job and that she did not want to give a reference. When pressed, she stated that Miller had performed adequately as a trainee, but that she had left her job irresponsibly without providing advance notice. Notes taken by the reference checker

suggested that the supervisor said that she thought Miller was underhanded, uncooperative, and always complaining. The new employer did not hire Miller and Miller sued her former employer for slander.

Relevant Issue

Whether the former employer was liable for the tort of slander for comments made during the reference check.

Decision

The Ontario Superior Court of Justice dismissed Miller's action. It found the reference checker's notes to be unreliable, and it accepted the supervisor's evidence as to what she said about Miller. However, even if the statements recorded in the notes were made, they were protected by the defence of qualified privilege because they were genuine views based on reasonable grounds. There was no malice on the supervisor's part to undermine this defence.

The defence of qualified privilege also requires that the person giving the reference have an interest in giving the information (that is, it is given within the context of the person's job), as was the case in *Miller*.

In deciding whether or not to provide a job reference, an employer must consider several issues. If it dismisses an employee without cause, and there have been no serious performance issues, the former employer benefits from providing a reference letter: the sooner an employee finds an alternative job, the fewer damages the former employer will probably need to pay in lieu of reasonable notice. Similarly, an employer that provides a letter of reference will be in a better position to argue, where relevant, that the employee failed to make reasonable efforts to mitigate her damages by finding a new job. In these situations, it may be helpful to use a standard form reference letter that allows specific information concerning salary, position, dates of employment, and duties, to be added for each employee. This will ensure consistency and help avoid claims based on discrimination under human rights legislation. Comments concerning the contributions of individual employees to the employer's organization may then be added, as long as they are accurate.

On the other hand, if an employee is dismissed for cause, the former employer must proceed with caution. A former employer that provides too positive a reference could face a lawsuit for negligent misrepresentation from a new employer who relies on the reference to its own detriment. For example, if an employee was dismissed for theft and a new position involved handling cash, the new employer could potentially sue the former employer for losses it suffered when its new employee stole from it, if the information provided in the reference was untrue. That said, there does not appear to be a single instance in Canada in which a successful claim has been made by a new employer against a former employer on the basis of misrepresentation in a letter of reference that it relied on to its detriment (Rudner, 2009, p. 3).

An employer that dismisses an employee for just cause must also take care not to undermine its own position by providing an overly positive letter of reference that contradicts its allegations of cause. One approach is to give the employee a letter that confirms his period of employment, position, and salary but does not comment on his performance. This is the safest approach, although it may not be of much assistance in the employee's job search and therefore may potentially result in a longer notice period if the employer's just cause defence is not successful.

Letters of reference should be drafted with care. Where the employee has been dismissed without cause, the referee (the person who writes the reference letter) should try to portray the individual as positively as possible while at the same time being truthful. The information given should be supported by company records, such as performance reviews (Goulart, 2013, p. 9-3). Potential employers in search of a reference should be directed to an experienced staff member who is familiar with the employee's situation. This will assist an employer in ensuring a consistent approach in the treatment of former employees. When an employer is contacted for a reference, usually it is a good idea for the employer to get back to the person seeking the reference after the referee has had a chance to review the file. It also provides an opportunity to confirm the identity of the person or organization seeking the reference, if that issue is in question.

Employment Insurance

Record of Employment

A record of employment form must be issued for employment insurance purposes within five calendar days of an interruption of an employee's earnings or the date on which the employer becomes aware of the interruption. An interruption of earnings occurs when an employee resigns, is laid off, is dismissed, or generally has had, or is expected to have, seven consecutive calendar days without both work and insurable earnings from the employer. An interruption of earnings may also occur when an employee's salary falls below 60 percent of her usual weekly earnings as a result of illness, injury, quarantine, or one of the statutory leaves under the *Employment Standards Act*.

Separation Packages

Under the federal *Employment Insurance Act*, an employer must deduct and account to Employment Insurance at Service Canada for any amount of pay in lieu of notice that an employee receives during a period when the employee also receives employment insurance benefits. The employer and former employee are jointly responsible for the repayment of benefits to the receiver general. However, the employer's obligation arises only where it has reason to believe that the employee received employment insurance benefits.

If an employer has reason to believe that there may have been an overpayment of benefits to a dismissed employee, the employer has two choices. Before providing an employee with a separation package, an employer can either obtain an acknowledgment from the employee stating that he has not received employment insurance benefits or obtain a statement from Employment Insurance at Service Canada confirming that the employee has not received benefits during the relevant period. If Employment Insurance at Service Canada indicates that there has been an overpayment, the amount of the overpayment should be deducted from the separation package and remitted directly to the receiver general.

REFERENCES

Antworth v. Fabricville. 2009 NBQB 54.

Bain v. I.C.B.C. 2002 BCSC 1445.

Bardal v. The Globe and Mail Ltd. (1960), 24 DLR (2d) 140 (Ont. HC).

Bongarde Media Co. Layoffs & Restructuring: Beware of "Constructive Dismissal" Risks. *HR Compliance Insider: Your Plain Language Guide to Hiring, Firing, Human Rights, Payroll & Privacy.* Volume 5, no. 4, April 2009.

Boucher v. Wal-Mart Canada Corp. 2014 ONCA 419.

Bowes v. Goss Power Products Ltd. 2012 ONCA 425.

Braithwaite, Jack. Mitigation in Constructive Dismissal. Presented at the Law Society of Upper Canada Six-Minute Employment Lawyer program, June 13, 2013, Toronto.

Brito v. Canac Kitchens. 2011 ONSC 1011; 2012 ONCA 61.

Carnegie v. Liberty Health. 2003 CanLII 25428 (Ont. SCDC).

Chambers v. Axia Netmedia Corporation. 2004 NSSC 24.

Chandran v. National Bank. 2011 ONSC 777; 2012 ONCA 205.

Chevalier v. Active Tire & Auto Centre Inc. 2012 ONSC 4309; aff'd. 2013 ONCA 548.

Chsherbinin, Nikolay. Disability-Related Dismissals Can Be Frustrating. *Canadian Employment Law Today.* Issue no. 565, September 22, 2010. http://nclaw.ca/testing/wp-content/uploads/2011/08/16-Disability-related-Dismissals-May-be-Frustrating.pdf.

Chsherbinin, Nikolay. Unskilled Worker Gets 22 Months' Notice. *Canadian Employment Law Today.* September 7, 2011, p. 1. http://nclaw.ca/testing/wp-content/uploads/2011/09/2-Unskilled-Employee-Gets-22-Months-Notice.pdf.

Coulter, Catherine, et al. Active Employee Wins Constructive Dismissal Suit, Gets Damages for Pay Cut. *FMC Ontario Employment Law Bulletin.* March 2011. Dentons. http://www.mondaq.com/canada/x/126652/employee+rights+labour+relations/FMC+Ontario+Employment+Law+Bulletin++March+2011.

Crossley, Sarah C. The Supreme Court Revisits Attendance Management and Wallace Damages: Honda v. Keays. July 22, 2008. Norton Rose Fulbright. http://www.nortonrosefulbright.com/knowledge/publications/50241/the-supreme-court-revisits-attendance-management-and-wallace-damages-honda-v-keays.

Cuba et. al. v. Global Egg Corporation. 2011 HRTO 1121.

Davies v. Fraser Collection Services Limited. 2008 BCSC 942.

Demuynck v. Agentis Information Services Inc. 2003 BCSC 96.

Di Tomaso v. Crown Metal Packaging Canada LP. 2011 ONCA 469.

Dion, Karine. Cap or No Cap? *The Workplace Matters.* February 19, 2014. http://www.theworkplacematters.ca/e/cap-or-no-cap.cfm.

Doorey, David. Cuba v. Global Egg Corp: When Should a Release Signed by an Employee Bar a Legal Proceeding Against an Employer? June 13, 2011. http://development.lawofwork.ca/?p=3422.

Echlin, Randall, and Christine Thomlinson. *For Better or For Worse: A Practical Guide to Canadian Employment Law*, 3rd ed. Toronto: Canada Law Book, 2011.

Elg v. Stirling Doors. [2002] OJ no. 2995 (SCJ).

Emond Harnden. Supreme Court of Canada Overturns $100,000 Punitive Damages Award in Wrongful Dismissal and Restates Law of Damages in Employment Cases. *What's New.* July 2008. http://www.emondharnden.com/whatsnew/0807/focus0807.shtml.

Employee Constructed Own Dismissal: Board. *Canadian Employment Law Today.* February 8, 2012, p. 1.

Employment Insurance Act. SC 1996, c. 23.

Employment Standards Act, 2000. SO 2000, c. 41.

Evans v. Teamsters Local Union No. 31. 2008 SCC 20, [2008] 1 SCR 661.

Farber v. Royal Trust Company. [1997] 1 SCR 846, 145 DLR (4th) 1.

Farwell v. Citair, Inc. (General Coach Canada). 2014 ONCA 177.

Filion Wakely Thorup Angeletti. Ontario Court of Appeal Discusses an Employee's Duty to Mitigate in Situations of Constructive Dismissal. *What's New in HR Law.* June 6, 2014. http://filion.on.ca/uploads/ckeditor/attachment_files/407/14-06-06_CLU.pdf.

Filion Wakely Thorup Angeletti. Trial Judge Reduces Notice Period Entitlement Due to Employer's Business Slowdown. *What's New in HR Law.* May 2014. http://filion.on.ca/uploads/ckeditor/attachment_files/404/14-05-09_CLU.pdf.

Foulon, Chris. Court Clarifies Basis for Wallace Awards. *Canadian Employment Law Today.* Issue no. 390, May 28, 2003, p. 3043. Israel Foulon LLP. http://israelfoulon.com/court-clarifies-basis-for-wallace-awards.

Foulon, Chris. Keays v. Honda—How Have the Courts Implemented the New Approach to "Wallace" and Punitive Damages? Presented at the Law Society of Upper Canada Six-Minute Employment Lawyer 2009 program, June 17, 2009, Toronto, p. 1A.

Fraser Milner Casgrain. Employees May Have to Mitigate Damages by Continuing to Work for Dismissing Employer. *Focus on Employment, Labour and Pensions.* June 2008. http://www.industrymailout.com/industry/landingpage.aspx?id=241867&lm=13855605&.

Gallop, Frances. Employment Contracts and the Duty to Mitigate. *What's New in HR Law*. August 2012. http://filion.on.ca/uploads/ckeditor/attachment _files/196/EmploymentContracts.pdf.

Gilbert, Douglas, Brian Burkett, and Moira McCaskill. *Canadian Labour and Employment Law for the US Practitioner*. Washington, DC: Bureau of National Affairs, 2000.

Gillis v. Sobeys Group Inc. 2011 NSSC 443.

Gorsky, Tom. Employer's Rush to Judgment Leads to Judgment Against Employer. *Canadian Employment Law Today*. February 22, 2012. http://www.sherrardkuzz.com/ pdf/Gorsky.eCELT2012-02-22.pdf.

Gorsky, Tom. Sweet Deal for Candy Factory Employee. *Canadian Employment Law Today*. January 26, 2011. http://www.sherrardkuzz.com/pdf/Gorsky.Sweet_deal.pdf.

Goulart, Ruben. Mitigation: An Employer's Toolkit. Presented at the Law Society of Upper Canada Six-Minute Employment Lawyer program, June 13, 2013, Toronto.

Gristey v. Emke Schaab Climatecare Inc. 2014 ONSC 1798.

Hainsworth v. World Peace Forum Society. 2006 BCSC 809.

Honda Canada Inc. v. Keays. 2008 SCC 39, [2008] 2 SCR 362.

HRInsider.ca. Wrongful Dismissal: The New Face of Wallace Damages. November 23, 2010. http://hrinsider.ca/ homepage/wrongful-dismissal-the-new-face-of-wallace -damages.

IBM Canada Limited v. Waterman. 2013 SCC 70, [2013] 3 SCR 985.

Israel, Peter, and Chris Foulon. The Pitfalls, and Benefits, of Providing References. *Canadian Employment Law Today*. Issue no. 390, May 28, 2003, p. 3045. Israel Foulon LLP. http://israelfoulon.com/providing-references.

Israel, Peter. Ask an Expert: Does Poor Treatment Entitle an Employee to Resign and Seek Damages for Constructive Dismissal? *Canadian Employment Law Today*. Issue no. 403, December 10, 2003, p. 3148.

Israel, Peter. Ask an Expert: Employers EI Obligations from Severance and Termination Pay. *Canadian Employment Law Today*. Issue no. 383, February 19, 2003, p. 2988.

Israel, Peter. Ask an Expert: Human Rights Legislation and Releases. *Canadian Employment Law Today*. Issue no. 390, May 28, 2003, p. 3044. Israel Foulon LLP. http:// israelfoulon.com/human-rights-legislation-and-releases.

Israel, Peter. Can Employers Temporarily Lay Off Workers? *Canadian HR Reporter*. September 22, 2003, p. 5.

Israel, Peter. Cut Down on Lawsuits Just by Being Nice. *Canadian HR Reporter*. November 18, 2002, p. 5. Israel Foulon LLP. http://israelfoulon.com/cut-down-on -lawsuits-just-by-being-nice.

Israel, Peter. Providing References to Employees: Should You or Shouldn't You? *Canadian HR Reporter*. March 24, 2003, p. 5.

Israel, Peter. Severance Obligations to Dismissed Employees Receiving EI Benefits. *Canadian Employment Law Today*. Issue no. 391, June 11, 2003, p. 3052.

Israel, Peter. Termination Checklist. *Canadian Employment Law Today*. Issue no. 385, March 19, 2003, p. 3005.

Ivens v. Automodular Assemblies Inc. [2002] OJ no. 3129 (Div. Ct.); rev'g. [2000] OJ no. 2579 (SCJ).

Jamieson v. Finning International Inc. 2009 BCSC 861.

Jodoin v. Nissan Canada Inc. 2013 ONSC 4683.

Kelly v. Monenco Consultants Ltd. [1987] OJ no. 563, (1987), 5 ACWS (3d) 26 (Ont. HCJ).

Koskie Minsky LLP. Duty to Mitigate Damages: Does That Include Returning to the Employ of Your Prior Employer? *Employment News*. Winter 2014, p. 1. http://www.kmlaw.ca/upload/Employment%20 News%20-%20Winter%202014.pdf.

Kotecha v. Affinia ULC. 2014 ONCA 411.

Lancaster House. Employee's Refusal to Accept New Position with Company Amounted to Resignation, Judge Rules. *Wrongful Dismissal and Employment Law eNewsletter*. Issue no. 300, 2012.

Levitt, Howard. Hell Hath No Fury Like an Employee Scorned. *Financial Post*, January 5, 2004, p. 9.

Levitt, Howard. Take Fear Out of Firing. *Financial Post*, June 17, 2009. Canada.com. http://www2.canada.com/topics/ technology/science/story.html?id=1702899.

Little, Christopher. The Severance Balancing Act. *Canadian HR Reporter*. October 7, 2002, p. 7.

Love v. Acuity Investment Management Inc. 2011 ONCA 130.

Lublin, Daniel. Damages Slashed for Manager's Assault. *Canadian HR Reporter*. July 12, 2010, p. 5.

MacDonald, Natalie. Balancing Wallace and Mitigation. *Canadian Employment Law Today*. Issue no. 406, February 4, 2004, p. 3174.

Manning, Melanie. Pregnancy a Factor in Reasonable Notice. *Canadian Employment Law Today*. Issue no. 382, February 5, 2003, p. 2979.

Mason, Mark. Employers Can't Sit Back and Do Nothing. *Canadian Employment Law Today*. Issue no. 382, February 5, 2003, p. 2982.

Medis Health and Pharmaceutical Services Inc. v. Bramble. 1999 CanLII 13124 (NBCA).

Meehan, Kathryn. Court of Appeal Reduces 24.5 Months' Notice Granted to 70 Year Old Employee. *Case in Point: Legal Developments in Human Resources Law*. June 12, 2014. Hicks Morley. http://www.hicksmorleycaseinpoint .com/2014/06/12/oca-reduces-24-5-months-notice -granted-to-70-year-old-employee.

Mifsud v. MacMillan Bathurst Inc. 1989 CanLII 260 (Ont. CA); leave to appeal to SCC refused (1990), 68 DLR (4th) vii.

Miller v. Bank of Nova Scotia. 2002 CanLII 22030 (Ont. SC).

Minken, Ronald S. Scrapped Damages in Keays Good News for Employers. *Canadian Employment Law Today.* Issue no. 514, July 16, 2008, p. 4. http://www.minkenemploymentlawyers.com/wp-content/uploads/2008/07/celt-514.pdf.

Minott v. O'Shanter Development Company Ltd. 1999 CanLII 3686 (Ont. CA).

Mistry, Heena. Junior Employees, Substantial Notice. *Canadian Employment Law Today.* Issue no. 387, April 23, 2003, p. 3022.

Mitchell, T. Ask an Expert: Constructive Dismissal—Changing Reluctant Employee's Job Duties. *Canadian Employment Law Today.* June 15, 2011.

Naccarato v. Costco. 2010 ONSC 2651.

Occupational Health and Safety Act. RSO 1990, c. O.1.

Ontario Court of Appeal Bars Claims Against Employers for Negligent Infliction of Emotional Distress. *Human Resources Management in Canada*, Report Bulletin 328, June 2010, p. 7. Toronto: Carswell (looseleaf).

Ostrow v. Abacus Management Corporation Mergers and Acquisitions. 2014 BCSC 938.

Pate Estate v. Galway-Cavendish and Harvey (Township). 2013 ONCA 669.

Pimenta v. Boermans. 2003 CanLII 26300 (Ont. LRB).

Piresferreira v. Ayotte. 2010 ONCA 384.

Probation Wording Costs Employer. *Canadian Employment Law Today.* Issue no. 415, June 9, 2004, p. 3245.

Robinson Heeney LLP. No Duty to Mitigate Where Employment Contract Termination Provision Is Silent on Mitigation. *RH on HR.* January 23, 2013. http://www.robinsonheeney.com/wp-content/uploads/2013/10/01-2013.pdf.

Rubin Thomlinson LLP. Employees with Short Service: How Much Notice Is Appropriate? *Employers' Alert.* Issue no. 36, August 2011, p. 1. http://www.rubinthomlinson.com/employers-alerts/documents LovevAcuityInvestmentManagementIncEmployersAlert August2011_000.pdf.

Rubin Thomlinson LLP. Hard Lessons for Home Hardware. *Workplace Investigation Alert.* Issue no. 13, June 2012. http://www.rubinthomlinson.com/workplace-investigation-alerts/documents/ WorkplaceInvestigationAlertJune2012.pdf.

Rudner, Stuart. Courts Adopting "Moderate" Approach to HR. *Canadian HR Reporter.* August 11, 2008, p. 3.

Rudner, Stuart. Everyone Wants a Piece of Wallace. *Canadian Employment Law Today.* Issue no. 414, May 26, 2004, p. 3238.

Rudner, Stuart. Reference Letters Not So Risky. *Canadian Employment Law Today.* Issue no. 539, July 29, 2009, p. 3.

Rudner, Stuart. The Confusing Duty to Mitigate. *Canadian Employment Law Today.* Issue no. 401, November 12, 2003, p. 3133.

Rudner, Stuart. The Myth of the One-Month Rule. *Canadian Employment Law Today.* Issue no. 416, June 23, 2004, p. 3254. http://www.employmentlawtoday.com/articleview/14061-the-myth-of-the-one-month-rule.

Rudner, Stuart. The Perils of Working Notice of Termination. *Canadian HR Reporter.* July 14, 2003, p. 20.

Rudner, Stuart. What Is "Sufficient" Change? *Canadian Employment Law Today.* Issue no. 404, January 7, 2004, p. 3158.

Russo v. Kerr. 2010 ONSC 6053.

Schwartz, Jeremy, and Frank Portman. Court of Appeal in Wal-Mart Case Scales Back Historic Punitive Damages Award. *Update.* May 26, 2014. Stringer LLP. http://www.stringerllp.com/court-of-appeal-in-wal-mart-case-scales-back-historic-punitive-damages-award.

Shah v. Xerox Canada Ltd. 2000 CanLII 2317 (Ont. CA).

Sherrard Kuzz LLP. A "New Reality": Higher Reasonable Notice Awards for an Aging Population. *Management Counsel: Employment and Labour Law Update.* Volume XIII, no. 1, February 2014, p. 3. http://www.sherrardkuzz.com/pdf/Vol_XIII_1.pdf.

Sherrard Kuzz LLP. Costco Experiences Frustration with Judge's Generous Returns Policy. *Management Counsel: Employment and Labour Law Update.* Volume IX, no. 6, October 2010, p. 3. http://www.sherrardkuzz.com/pdf/Vol_IX_6.pdf.

Sherrard Kuzz LLP. Dismissed Employee Obliged to Return to Job to Mitigate Damages. *Management Counsel: Employment and Labour Law Update.* Volume VII, no. 3, June 2008, p. 1. http://www.sherrardkuzz.com/pdf/Vol_VII_No_3.pdf.

Sherrard Kuzz LLP. Honda v. Keays—Back to the Starting Line! *Management Counsel: Employment and Labour Law Update.* Volume VII, no. 4, July 2008 (Special Edition), p. 1. http://www.sherrardkuzz.com/pdf/Vol_VII_SE.pdf.

Sherrard Kuzz LLP. Never Too Late to Mitigate. *Management Counsel: Employment and Labour Law Update.* Volume XII, no. 6, December 2013, p. 3. http://www.sherrardkuzz.com/pdf/Vol_XII_6.pdf.

Smith, Jeffrey R. Bumped Exec Gets More Than $100,000. *Canadian Employment Law Today.* November 13, 2013, p. 1.

Smith, Jeffrey R. Constructive Dismissal: Employee Jumps Ship After Late Paycheques. *Canadian Employment Law Today*. September 22, 2010, p. 7.

Smith, Jeffrey R. Ont. Employers Could See Spike in Lawsuits. *Canadian HR Reporter*. October 19, 2009, p. 1.

Smith, Jeffrey R. Transfer of Bank Manager After Complaints Was Constructive Dismissal. *Canadian Employment Law Today*. November 16, 2011, p. 4.

Soost v. Merrill Lynch Canada Inc. 2009 ABQB 591.

Stamos v. Annuity Research & Marketing Service Ltd. 2002 CanLII 49618 (Ont. SC).

Stehr, Craig. Severance Pay Key Issue in Terminations. *Canadian HR Reporter*. August 13, 2012, p. 15.

Stephenson v. Hilti (Canada) Ltd. 1989 CanLII 191 (NSSC).

Sylvester v. British Columbia. 1997 CanLII 353 (SCC), 146 DLR (4th) 207.

Talbot, Jorge. Constructive Lessons in Dismissal. *Canadian Employment Law Today*. Issue no. 415, June 9, 2004, p. 3246.

Treash, Andrew. Appeal Court Overturns Huge Damage Award. *Canadian HR Reporter*. September 20, 2010, p. 5.

UPM-Kymmene Miramichi Inc. v. Walsh. 2003 NBCA 32.

Wallace v. United Grain Growers Ltd. [1997] 3 SCR 701.

Whitten & Lublin Employment Lawyers. Where Employee Discipline Crosses the Line. *WL Update*. Issue no. 27, February 2013. http://www.toronto-employmentlawyer.com/wp-content/uploads/2013-03-employment-newsletter.pdf.

Wilson, Eric, and Allison Taylor. *The Corporate Counsel Guide to Employment Law*, 2nd ed. Aurora, ON: Canada Law Book, 2003.

REVIEW AND DISCUSSION QUESTIONS

1. Discuss the legal remedies that are available to an employee who is bullied or harassed in the workplace.
2. Discuss the legal issues that arise when an employee who was not dismissed for cause but whose performance was less than satisfactory requests a letter of reference from an employer.
3. What are the factors that a court considers in determining reasonable notice when an employer dismisses an employee without just cause?
4. Discuss the legal dilemma of an employee whose employer makes a significant change in the terms of employment without providing reasonable advance notice.
5. Identify and discuss five ways in which an employer may reduce the potential for wrongful dismissal actions.
6. From an employer's point of view, what are some of the benefits and drawbacks of providing an employee with working notice rather than pay in lieu of notice?
7. What are the factors that a court considers in determining whether a contract of employment has been frustrated due to an employee's physical incapacity?
8. Suzanne owns a small restaurant. Robert, the restaurant's chef, is an excellent cook but he is very temperamental; he becomes angry and abusive with the other kitchen staff and waiters over the slightest mistake. It has reached the point that many members of staff dread working with him. Suzanne has spoken to Robert about this issue many times over the years but if anything it is getting worse. Robert simply tells her that he cannot tolerate "incompetence" among the staff and that shouting and yelling at them is just his way of coping with stress. Suzanne has decided that enough is enough—she is going to terminate Robert's employment. (Robert is 39 years old and has worked for the restaurant for seven and a half years. He earns $1,000 per week, including vacation pay. The restaurant's annual payroll is $850,000.)

   Answer the following questions related to this fact situation.

   a. Under Ontario's employment standards legislation, how many weeks' notice, or pay in lieu of notice, is owing to someone with Robert's length of service who is terminated?

b. Is it possible that Suzanne's restaurant could be liable to Robert for statutory severance pay in these circumstances? Explain your answer.

c. In your opinion, is it likely that a court would find that Suzanne had just cause *under the common law* to terminate Robert's employment? Explain your answer.

d. Suzanne wants to avoid a lawsuit, so she decides that she will offer Robert a package. In your opinion, what would be a reasonable offer in these circumstances? Explain your answer by identifying at least three factors that a court takes into consideration in determining the appropriate amount of reasonable notice of termination (or pay in lieu) required under the common law.

e. Suzanne feels very nervous about dismissing Robert (given his temper) and she would like to avoid having to tell him about it face-to-face. She's thinking of just leaving a message on Robert's answering machine telling him that his services are no longer required and making the severance offer. Is this a good idea? If not, does she have an alternative to telling him in person? Explain your answer.

9. In the Supreme Court of Canada decision of *Evans v. Teamsters Local Union No. 31*, the majority held that the duty to mitigate wrongful dismissal damages may, under certain circumstances, require an employee to return to his former job to work out the remainder of the notice period. However, there was a strong dissenting opinion in that decision by Justice Abella. Discuss which opinion you find most compelling and explain the reasons for your view.

10. Hussain, a 66-year-old lab technician with 36 years' service, was dismissed without cause. Assuming Hussain does not have an employment contract with an enforceable termination provision, what would be the amount of reasonable notice damages he would be entitled to receive? Support your answer.

11. Ramond, aged 46, was a chartering manager with a shipping company. His contract stipulated that he was to be paid $7,000 per month, paid semi-monthly. His employer was frequently late in paying him: his first paycheque was three days late; the next two were paid on time but the next five were all three to four weeks late. This put Ramond in a difficult position with his landlord and, because it happened around Christmas time, he was unable to buy gifts for his family. When he questioned his employer about the situation, the employer provided unhelpful responses, saying the delays related to problems with an offshore account. In January, Ramond resigned and sued the employer for constructive dismissal. Do you think his claim would be successful?

12. Tamara was an administrative assistant at a security services company. She worked for both the information technology and the human resources departments at head office. Pursuant to a restructuring of the business, Tamara's IT support duties were largely removed, and she lost the right to a bonus, although her salary was increased to reflect the amount lost (around $1,300). Her reporting relationship also changed: she was now reporting to a lower-level HR professional rather than to the IT and HR managers. Several months later, Tamara resigned and sued the employer for constructive dismissal. Do you think she would be successful? Support your answer.

13. Greg, aged 52, was one of nine heating technicians who was permanently laid off as a result of a work shortage. He had worked for the employer for 12 years and was paid on an hourly basis, averaging earnings of about $55,000 per year. The employer offered Greg 16 weeks of pay in lieu of notice in exchange for a signed release, which he rejected. He sued the employer, claiming that his reasonable notice period should be 12 months. The employer countered that, had Greg worked through his claimed notice period, there would have been little work to do because of the slowdown in business, and his entitlement should be correspondingly reduced.

Do you think this argument would be successful? Support your answer.

14. Ethan was 48 years old and had worked for Happy Hardware for 18 years as a supervisor when a sexual harassment complaint was lodged against him. One of the complainants was the daughter of his manager, Stephan. When he heard about the complaint, Stephan arranged for a friend and colleague, Kyle, to conduct the investigation. Kyle met with Ethan to advise him that he was doing an investigation, but he refused to tell Ethan what he was alleged to have done. Kyle simply said, "You know what you did." At one point, Ethan told Kyle he thought someone might be out to get him; however, this allegation was never pursued and the complainants were never questioned about their motives. Within a week, Ethan was suspended, escorted from the workplace, and dismissed for cause. Ethan sued for wrongful dismissal and other damages.

At the trial (by a jury) the jury heard evidence that one of the complainants had been overheard to say that she would "get even" with Ethan for having her transferred. On the basis of this and other evidence, the jury found that the complainants lacked credibility and that the employer had acted in bad faith in its investigation. The jury awarded Ethan 24 months' reasonable notice damages, aggravated damages of $200,000 (although no evidence of mental distress losses were put forward), and punitive damages of $300,000.

a. Do you agree that the employer acted in bad faith? Support your answer.

b. Do you think a court of appeal would support the award of damages?

15. Were the changes made to *Wallace* (bad-faith) damages by the Supreme Court in *Honda Canada Inc. v. Keays* generally a good or a bad idea?

Post-Employment Obligations

16

LEARNING OUTCOMES

After completing this chapter, you will be able to:

- Explain a former employee's duty not to disclose (or misuse) confidential information.

- Understand the additional post-employment duties of fiduciaries.

- Describe the implications of an employee's implied duty to provide reasonable notice of resignation.

- Understand the implications of an employee's implied duty to act in good faith, including a management employee's duty to try to retain employees.

Introduction

Under the common law, it is an implied term of every employment contract that an employee serve an employer honestly and loyally. Aspects of this obligation continue after the employment relationship ends.

Duty Not to Disclose Confidential Information

Regardless of whether an employee leaves his job voluntarily or through dismissal, he cannot use or disclose trade secrets or confidential information obtained as a result of his employment. For example, generally speaking an employee cannot copy or memorize a list of an employer's customers to use after his employment ends.

This duty not to disclose confidential or proprietary (owned by the employer) information applies equally to managerial and non-managerial employees. However, the amount of sensitive, confidential, and proprietary information to which a senior manager has access typically exceeds that to which other employees have access.

Duty Not to Solicit or Compete with a Former Employer

General Employees

The general prohibition against using or disclosing confidential information obtained during employment is the only restriction imposed on most former employees. Unless there is an enforceable restrictive covenant in their employment contract that provides otherwise, they may start a business that competes with their ex-employer, work for a competitor, or solicit clients of the former employer after they leave employment. In fact, as decided in *RBC Dominion Securities Inc. v. Merrill Lynch Canada Inc.*, non-fiduciary employees are free to compete against their former employer immediately following their departure, even if they fail to provide their employer with reasonable notice of resignation (though damages may arise from the failure to give reasonable notice of their resignation).

Fiduciary Employees

In contrast, a **fiduciary employee**—that is, a senior or key employee who holds a position of trust and who could significantly affect an employer's interests—has additional post-employment obligations to a former employer. Even without a written agreement, a fiduciary may not solicit a former employer's customers or prospective clients if the fiduciary took part in developing a relationship with these clients while employed. Restrictions on fiduciaries last for a reasonable time after their employment ends. What is reasonable depends on the type of industry and the length of time it usually takes an employer to form a relationship with customers after the fiduciary leaves employment. This period of time typically extends from 6 to 12 months, to as long as 18 months in extreme cases.

Whether or not an employee is a fiduciary depends on the employee's role within an organization, rather than her job title. Senior managers are usually considered fiduciaries, but other employees can also be fiduciaries if they hold discretionary power that can materially affect an employer's business or legal interests.

The term "fiduciary" is narrowly interpreted because the obligations it places on an individual employee so designated are considerable. Sales representatives are not generally treated as fiduciaries. However, if a sales representative resigns and starts a competitive business with a former senior manager who is a fiduciary, the sales representative becomes charged with the same fiduciary obligations as the former senior manager.

The leading Canadian case on fiduciary duties is *Can. Aero v. O'Malley*. In this decision, the Supreme Court of Canada held that fiduciaries owe a duty not to appropriate a corporate opportunity for their own benefit, and that this duty survives the employment relationship.

CASE IN POINT

Fiduciary Employees Cannot Usurp Corporate Opportunity for Own Benefit

Can. Aero v. O'Malley, [1974] SCR 592

Facts

The president and executive vice-president of the employer corporation were in charge of obtaining a contract for topographical mapping and aerial photography in Guyana. The employer had already spent a large sum of money pursuing this contract when these two employees resigned and bid on the contract themselves. Their bid was successful.

Relevant Issue

Whether the employees owed a duty to the employer not to take advantage of the employer's business opportunity.

Decision

The Supreme Court of Canada found that the employees were fiduciaries and therefore owed the employer a duty of loyalty and a duty to avoid conflict of interest. These obligations continued after the employment relationship ended. The employer was entitled to damages of $125,000, the amount that the employees gained under the contract.

The following factors are relevant in determining whether a fiduciary duty has been breached: the position held by the employees; the nature of the corporate opportunity; its "ripeness," its specificity, and the fiduciaries' relation to it; the amount of knowledge possessed by the employees; the circumstances in which the knowledge was obtained and whether it was special or private; and the circumstances under which the relationship was terminated: retirement, resignation, or discharge.

As this discussion shows, even without a restrictive covenant in an employment contract, a fiduciary cannot take advantage of corporate opportunities presented because of his employment. In the more recent case of *KJA Consultants Inc. v. Soberman*, the trial judge extended the duties of fiduciaries by finding that the fiduciary employee breached his duty by accepting a contract offered, *without* his solicitation, by a former client.

CASE IN POINT

Fiduciary Duty Extended to Unsolicited Contract with Former Client

KJA Consultants Inc. v. Soberman, 2003 CanLII 13546 (Ont. SC); aff'd. 2004 CanLII 36050 (Ont. CA)

Facts

Soberman worked for 13 years for an employer that specialized in providing personal consulting services to the elevator industry. With 11 employees, it was the largest firm of its type in Canada. Soberman had been its general manager for four years, when he resigned and set up a competing engineering consulting business. There was no non-competition or non-solicitation clause in his employment contract. Soberman gave notice of resignation on August 20, 2001, effective September 17, 2001. By the end of September, he had sent 70 to 80 letters to potential clients. He followed this mailing approximately one month later with 400 more letters to potential clients, this time intentionally including the former employer's clients.

Shortly before leaving his job, Soberman met with a client of his employer with whom he had worked closely as a consultant in putting together an elevator modernization project. At that meeting Soberman announced that he was leaving the employer to start his own consulting business and stated that the employer was capable of continuing the project without him. Later the client called Soberman to ask whether his new firm would submit a proposal for the project. When the client told the employer that his firm was taking its business to Soberman's new firm, the employer applied for an interim interlocutory injunction to prevent Soberman from soliciting its customers. The injunction was granted, and later the issue of breach of fiduciary duties went to trial.

Relevant Issue

Whether Soberman breached his fiduciary duties to the employer when

1. he took over the client's elevator modernization project, and
2. he wrote to the employer's clients in the fall of 2001.

Decision

The Ontario Superior Court of Justice found that Soberman breached his fiduciary duties on both accounts. Because Soberman was the person with whom the employer's clients dealt, a one year's prohibition against soliciting the employer's clients was reasonable. Furthermore, the court found that Soberman breached his fiduciary duties when he accepted the client's request that his new company present a proposal for the elevator project. There was no evidence that Soberman resigned in order to take over this project, and he did not approach the client; the client approached him. However, in the court's opinion, Soberman took the project away from the employer, not because of his innate abilities or reputation, but because of his detailed familiarity with the project, which he had obtained solely by virtue of his position with the employer.

The employer was entitled to damages for Soberman's breach of fiduciary duty in the amount of $68,400 for the loss of its contract with the client's firm and $57,954 for the loss of contracts with other clients that Soberman had solicited. The Ontario Court of Appeal dismissed his appeal.

This case suggests that former fiduciary employees of businesses that rely on personal services, such as consulting firms, may not compete against former employers for a reasonable period of time after leaving employment, even where a client of the former employer seeks them out.

It should be noted that where a court decides that an award of damages is not an adequate remedy, it may grant an *injunction*. An injunction is a legal remedy that actually prevents the other party from doing something; in this context, an injunction would bar employees from continuing their unlawful competition. To succeed in getting an injunction, the employer must prove three things:

- there exists a substantial issue, which should go to trial (*that is, the employer has a strong case*);

- irreparable harm is likely to occur to the employer if the injunction is not granted (*that is, harm would result that could not be adequately compensated for by a damage award, such as loss of protection of trade secrets*); and
- granting the injunction will result in a balance of convenience in favour of the employer (*that is, harm to the employer without an injunction is likely to be greater than harm to the employee if the injunction is granted*) (Echlin and Thomlinson, 2011, p. 281).

Implications of an Employee's Implied Duty of Good Faith

In 2008, the Supreme Court of Canada issued an important decision that deals with the duties that departed employees owe to their employer upon termination. The case arose when the local branch manager of a brokerage firm coordinated the departure of virtually his entire office to its main competitor. Among other things, the Supreme Court found that although none of the employees involved were fiduciaries or subject to a restrictive covenant, the branch manager's actions were a breach of the implied duty of good faith he owed to his employer. He was required to pay his former employer approximately $1.5 million in damages for lost profits that resulted from breach of this duty.

CASE IN POINT

Manager Breached Implied Duty of Good Faith

RBC Dominion Securities Inc. v. Merrill Lynch Canada Inc., 2008 SCC 54

Facts

In 2000, Delamont, the RBC branch manager in Cranbrook, BC helped orchestrate the exodus of almost all of RBC's investment advisers and assistants to Merrill Lynch, its local competitor. The investment advisers left without notice and took with them client records, documents, and files that they had surreptitiously copied over the course of several weeks. The mass departures resulted in the near-collapse of the employer's Cranbrook office. None of the employees, including Delamont, was bound by a restrictive covenant or was a fiduciary. RBC sued Merrill Lynch and its former employees.

The trial court made the following findings:

- The employees had breached the implied terms of their employment contracts. The contracts (1) required reasonable notice of departure (which the court set at two and a half weeks each or $40,000 in total) and (2) prohibited unfair competition with their employer.

- The brokers were jointly and severally liable for $225,000 in damages for lost profits for breaching their implied duty not to compete during the reasonable notice period. Merrill Lynch was also jointly and severally liable for this amount for inducing the brokers to breach this implied duty.

- As a manager, Delamont had breached his implied duty of good faith, which required him to attempt to retain employees under his supervision, and certainly not to coordinate their departure. The court awarded almost $1.5 million against Delamont for loss of profits during the notice period plus future loss of profits for a five-year period flowing from breach of his duty of good faith.

- Merrill Lynch should pay $250,000 and the investment advisers $5,000 each in punitive damages for removing the client records from the employer's office.

On appeal the BC Court of Appeal reversed the nearly $1.5 million award against Delamont and the $225,000 award against the other brokers and Merrill Lynch. RBC appealed to the Supreme Court of Canada.

Relevant Issue

Whether the Court of Appeal properly overturned those awards.

Decision

The Supreme Court of Canada restored the $1.5 million damages award against Delamont. By organizing the mass exodus, Delamont breached his implied duty to perform his employment duties in good faith. As a manager, it was part of his job to retain employees, not to facilitate their departure. Citing the *Hadley* principle, the court ruled that damages for loss of profits for breach of this duty were within the reasonable contemplation of the parties when they entered into the employment contract. Therefore, RBC was entitled to claim all of the losses flowing from that breach, not just losses that were associated with the period of notice of resignation he should have given. The court further found that, given the evidence at trial, the loss of profits was reasonably measured on the basis of five years.

The Supreme Court upheld the (total) $40,000 in damages awarded against the other employees for failing to provide reasonable notice of their departure. This amount was based on the profit that RBC lost by not having these brokers employed in the two and a half weeks after their departure. However, it rejected the trial judge's award of an additional (total) $225,000 against the brokers for unfairly competing with RBC during those two and a half weeks based on loss of profits flowing from that breach. It found that, in the absence of any non-competition agreement or fiduciary duty, once the brokers left, they were free to compete against their former employer, even during what should have been their notice period. The Supreme Court confirmed that there is no general duty not to compete.

The Supreme Court upheld the punitive awards related to removing the client records.

Several points concerning the duties of departing employees flow from, or are highlighted by, this decision:

- All employees, regardless of whether they are fiduciaries, have an implied duty of good faith in the performance of their job duties.
- A management employee's implied duty of good faith includes the duty to try to retain employees and certainly not to organize their departure. Significantly, damages for breach of this duty will be awarded to compensate for lost business beyond the reasonable notice period itself.
- All employees must provide their employers with advance notice of resignation. However, in most situations the required notice period will be short.
- A non-fiduciary employee who fails to give notice of resignation is not liable for competing against her former employer during the reasonable notice period. There is no general duty "not to compete" in such circumstances. Although it is difficult to enforce non-competition agreements, the result in this case highlights their desirability.
- Employees owe a duty of confidentiality to their employers. However, this duty does not necessarily extend to client contact lists (as opposed to client documents) in every industry. In this case, because of the nature of the relationship between investment advisers and clients, the court did not award damages for the removal of the actual client lists although punitive damages were awarded for removal of client documents.
- A new employer may be held liable for damages where it induces an employee to breach contractual duties (implied or explicit) owed to the former employer.

Recouping Investment in Training Costs

Occasionally an employer will agree to pay for training of a new employee on the basis that if the employee leaves before a certain date, she will have to repay a pro-rated portion of those training costs. This is sometimes known as a training bond. For example, in *North Cariboo Flying Services Ltd v. Goddard*, the employer agreed to pay between $25,000 and $40,000 for specialized training for an employee who was being hired as a chief pilot. When the employee resigned with one month's notice after only six months, the employer successfully sued that employee in Small Claims Court for a prorated portion of the training costs.

The following factors are key to ensuring the enforceability of this type of training agreement:

- the training must at least in part enhance the employee's own marketability in the industry—it cannot simply be for the employer's benefit;
- the terms must be made clear before the employee accepts the training;
- the obligations placed on the employee must be clearly set out in writing;
- the employee must have time to consider the commitment involved and the opportunity to negotiate the terms of the agreement;
- there must not be coercion or any suggestion that the commitment is "unlikely to be enforced"; and
- the terms should be fair (for example, any amount owed will be reduced on a prorated basis, depending on how long the employee works for the employer) (Mitchell, 2011, p. 13).

FYI

Employer Sues Employee for Theft—and Wins

While most post-dismissal lawsuits involve an employee suing an employer for damages, occasionally it's the other way around. One example of this is seen in the *North Cariboo* case; other examples include where an employer sues an employee for failure to provide reasonable notice of resignation (discussed in Chapter 12) or to enforce a restrictive covenant or protect its confidential information.

In *Canada Safeway Limited v. Brown*, the employer took the unusual step of suing an employee it had caught stealing—and it won. When Canada Safeway became aware of unexplained cash and inventory shortages at its grocery store, it undertook an extensive investigation that eventually pointed to Brown, a cashier and customer service representative, as the thief. Brown was charged with, and pleaded guilty to, theft over $5,000. In addition, the employer sued Brown for the amount stolen and for the cost of its investigation. The BC Supreme Court awarded the employer $31,000: $6,000 for the lost cash, plus $25,000 to compensate for the costs of its investigation (Mitchell, 2011, p. 14).

REFERENCES

889946 Alberta Ltd. v. Carter. 2002 ABPC 28.

Burgess, Bettina. RBC Dominion Securities Inc. v. Merrill Lynch Canada Inc. Case Summary. *Compliance @ Gowlings*. Volume 3, no. 4, October 14, 2008.

Can. Aero v. O'Malley. [1974] SCR 592, 40 DLR (3d) 371.

Canada Safeway Limited v. Brown. 2007 BCSC 1619.

Echlin, Randall, and Christine Thomlinson. *For Better or For Worse: A Practical Guide to Canadian Employment Law*, 3rd ed. Toronto: Canada Law Book, 2011.

Gilbert, Douglas, Brian Burkett, and Moira McCaskill. *Canadian Labour and Employment Law for the US Practitioner*. Washington, DC: Bureau of National Affairs, 2000.

Hadley v. Baxendale. [1854] EWHC J70.

KJA Consultants Inc. v. Soberman. 2003 CanLII 13546 (Ont. SC); aff'd. 2004 CanLII 36050 (Ont. CA).

Mitchell, Tim. When the Employer Is the Victim. *Canadian HR Reporter*. January 17, 2011, p. 13.

North Cariboo Flying Services Ltd v. Goddard. 2009 ABPC 219.

RBC Dominion Securities Inc. v. Merrill Lynch Canada Inc. 2008 SCC 54.

Sherrard Kuzz LLP. Employees: To Have and To Hold: RBC ats. Merrill Lynch. *Management Counsel: Employment and Labour Law Update*. Volume VII, no. 7, December 2008, p. 2. http://www.sherrardkuzz.com/pdf/Vol_VII_7.pdf.

Smith, Jeffrey R. Worker Ordered to Pay $1.5 Million. *Canadian HR Reporter*. December 1, 2008, p. 8.

Taylor, Kristin. The Role of Fiduciary Employees. *Canadian Employment Law Today*. Issue no. 400, October 29, 2003, p. 3126.

Wilson, Peter, and Allison Taylor. *The Corporate Counsel Guide to Employment Law*, 2nd ed. Aurora, ON: Canada Law Book, 2003.

REVIEW AND DISCUSSION QUESTIONS

1. Describe the difference between the post-employment obligations of fiduciaries and those of other employees.

2. In your opinion, does the *KJA Consultants Inc. v. Soberman* decision go too far in protecting the interests of employers by prohibiting a former employee from accepting work that he did not solicit from his former employer's client? Why or why not?

3. There was a dissenting opinion in the *RBC Dominion Securities Inc. v. Merrill Lynch Canada Inc.* case by Justice Abella. Locate the Supreme Court of Canada's decision on www.canlii.org and review Justice Abella's dissent. It begins on paragraph 26 with the statement:

   In the best of all possible worlds, employers and employees would treat each other with mutual respect, consideration and empathy. In the real world, however, as the dispute before us demonstrates, this aspiration is not always realized. The question, then, is at what point does the breakdown of an employment relationship cross the legal line from conduct that is disappointing to conduct that is compensable.

   Review the arguments that Justice Abella makes in her dissent. Do you agree or disagree with them? Support your position.

4. The employee, Abigail, signed a training agreement whereby she agreed to repay the employer (a Dairy Queen franchisee) the costs of her training as a store manager if she left before working there for two years. The subjects covered and assessed by Dairy Queen in this course included Leadership, Attitude, Customer Focus, Financial, Personnel Management, Product, Equipment, and Operations. Abigail resigned after only four months and the employer sued her to cover the $5,000 worth of training she had received. Do you think the employer would be successful?

Conclusion

Employers and employees are bound together by many legal obligations that begin before an employer makes a decision to hire and that may continue beyond the end of the employment relationship. At every stage, legal issues present ongoing challenges and opportunities for the human resources professional. The focus of this text has been to equip you with the legal knowledge you will need to perform your job and to keep you mindful of the requirements of the law as it tries to balance the rights and obligations of employers and employees.

It has been said that the study of law is not the learning of rules, but the continuing process of attempting to solve the problems of a changing society. Understanding the law as it tries to establish, maintain, and enforce fair and practical rules in the workplace, and respond to evolving needs, will undoubtedly be one of the most challenging and interesting aspects of your career.

Appendixes

Sample Indefinite-Term Contract

EMPLOYMENT AGREEMENT

B E T W E E N:

(the "Employer")

– and –

("Employee")

WHEREAS the Employer and Employee have agreed to enter into an employment relationship for their mutual benefit;

THE PARTIES agree that the terms and conditions of their employment relationship shall be as set forth below.

1. **Scope of Duties**

    1.1 The Employer agrees to employ Employee in the position of Plant Manager, to perform the duties inherent in the position, including the duties set out in the job description attached as Appendix "A" to this Agreement. Employee will report to _____.

    1.2 Employee agrees to devote his full-time efforts to the position and perform his duties to the best of his abilities. Employee further agrees not to engage in any other employment or self-employment.

2. **Term**

    2.1 The Employer agrees to employ Employee for an indefinite period of time, subject to the termination clause in paragraph 9 of this Agreement.

    2.2 During the first three months of his employment, Employee will be working in a probationary period. The Employer reserves the right to terminate the employment of Employee for any reason without notice or pay in lieu thereof during this probationary period, notwithstanding the provisions of paragraph 9 of this Agreement.

3. **Compensation**

    3.1 The Employer shall provide Employee with a gross salary of $_____ per week from which standard deductions will be made.

    3.2 Employee will also be entitled to earn an annual bonus not to exceed $_____. The payment of the annual bonus will be at the sole discretion of _____ and should not be considered to be an expected part of Employee's remuneration.

    3.3 Should Employee resign or have his employment terminated, he will not be entitled to any bonus for that year or any subsequent year.

4. **Benefits**

    4.1 Employee will be entitled to participate in all of the Employer's medical/dental benefit plans generally available to its management employees in accordance with the terms thereof.

    4.2 The Employer will provide Employee with a car allowance of $_____ per month. This allowance will include any and all vehicle operating costs.

5. **Vacation**

    5.1 During this Agreement, Employee shall be entitled to three weeks' vacation per year. Such vacation shall be taken at a time or times acceptable to the Employer having regard to its operations. Vacation may only be carried over from year to year with the written authorization of _____.

6. **Expenses**

    6.1 Employee shall be reimbursed for reasonable and authorized business expenses, including travel, parking, and other necessary business expenses incurred as a result of his work on behalf of the Employer. The Employer shall reimburse Employee for such expenses upon presentation of supporting documentation satisfactory to the Employer in accordance with the tax principles applicable in Canada for such reimbursement and the Employer's established reimbursement policies, as those policies may be modified from time to time in the Employer's discretion. Reimbursement for any such expenses will be at the sole discretion of the Employer.

7. **Confidentiality, Non-Competition and Non-Solicitation**

    7.1 Employee acknowledges that he is in a fiduciary position and, in the course of his employment, he will have access to and be entrusted with confidential information and trade secrets of the Employer and its subsidiaries.

    7.2 Employee agrees to sign Confidentiality, Non-Competition and Non-Solicitation Agreement attached as Appendix "B" to this Agreement and understands that it forms an integral part of his employment contract.

8.   **Return of Property**

   8.1   Upon the termination of Employee's employment under this Agreement, Employee shall at once deliver or cause to be delivered to the Employer all books, documents, effects, money, securities, or other property belonging to the Employer or for which the Employer is liable to others, which are in the possession, charge, control, or custody of Employee.

9.   **Termination**

   9.1   Employee may terminate this Agreement upon two weeks' notice at any time by providing a written notice of resignation. Upon such termination of this Agreement, Employee will not be entitled to any further compensation under this Agreement.

   9.2   The Employer may terminate the employment of Employee without notice or any payment at any time during the course of this Agreement with just cause. "Just cause" is defined as serious and wilful misconduct, and specifically includes but is not limited to theft, fraud, unauthorized absence without good reason, assault, gross insubordination, harassment, and breach of the attached confidentiality agreement.

   9.3   The Employer may terminate the employment of Employee without notice and without cause at any time by providing written notice of termination to Employee. If the Employer elects to terminate the employment of Employee without cause after the completion of his probationary period, Employee shall be entitled to a lump sum payment equivalent to two weeks' pay in lieu of notice plus an additional two weeks' pay in lieu of notice for each completed year of employment as well as benefit continuation for the Ontario *Employment Standards Act, 2000* (as amended) required period. This lump-sum payment and benefit continuation will be in lieu of and include all of Employee's entitlements under statute and common law and under this Agreement including all compensation, benefits, and perquisites of any kind whatsoever, and specifically including any entitlements to termination and/or severance pay under the Ontario *Employment Standards Act, 2000* (as amended).

10.   **Severability**

   10.1   If any provision of this Agreement is determined to be invalid or unenforceable in whole or in part, such invalidity or unenforceability shall attach only to such provision or part thereof and the remaining part of such provision and all other provisions thereof shall continue in full force and effect.

11.   **Modification of Agreement**

   11.1   Any modification to this Agreement must be in writing and signed by the parties or it shall have no effect and shall be void.

12. **Governing Law**

   12.1 This Agreement shall be governed by and construed in accordance with the laws of the Province of Ontario.

13. **Independent Legal Advice**

   13.1 Employee acknowledges that he has obtained or has had the opportunity to obtain independent legal advice with respect to the terms and conditions contained herein.

Signed this _____ day of _____, 20___, in the City of Toronto in the Province of Ontario.

_____   _____
Employee   Witness

_____
Employer

Sample Fixed-Term Contract

B

EMPLOYMENT AGREEMENT

B E T W E E N:

EMPLOYER

(the "Employer")

– and –

ROBERT

("Robert")

WHEREAS the Employer and Robert have agreed to enter into an employment relationship for their mutual benefit;

THE PARTIES agree that the terms and conditions of their employment relationship shall be as set forth below.

1. **Scope of Duties**

   1.1 The Employer agrees to employ Robert in the position of President, to perform the duties inherent in the position, including the full authority to deal with all operational issues of the Employer and its subsidiaries including staffing, bidding, customer and supplier approval, performance reviews, organization, hiring, firing, corporate acquisitions, and protection of the Employer's intellectual property rights. Robert will report to the Employer's Chair.

   1.2 Robert agrees to devote his full-time efforts to the position and perform his duties to the best of his abilities. Robert further agrees not to engage in any other employment or self-employment for the life of this Agreement.

   1.3 Notwithstanding paragraph 1.1 of this Agreement, Robert must obtain written authorization from the Employer's Chair in respect of any acquisition, expenditure, or contemplated acquisition or expenditure the cost of which exceeds or could potentially exceed $1 million.

2. **Term**

   2.1 The Employer agrees to employ Robert from _____ to _____, unless Robert's employment is terminated earlier pursuant to section 11 of this Agreement. Upon the expiry of this Agreement, Robert will not be entitled to any notice of termination or pay in lieu thereof.

3.   Compensation

3.1   The Employer shall provide Robert with a gross salary of $4,000.00 per week from which standard deductions will be made.

3.2   Robert will also be entitled to earn an annual bonus for the fiscal years ending on the last Saturday in September in each of 2015, 2016, and 2017. The annual bonus will be equivalent to 5% of the increase in the net profit of the Employer from one fiscal year to the next fiscal year. "Net profit" is the earnings before income taxes and the deduction for management fees reflecting the shareholder profit distribution as disclosed in the Employer's audited consolidated financial statements.

3.3   Robert's bonus entitlement each year, if any, will be paid within 150 days of the end of the fiscal year.

3.4   Should Robert resign or have his employment terminated during any fiscal year, he will not be entitled to any bonus for that fiscal year or any subsequent fiscal year.

4.   Benefits

4.1   Robert will be entitled to participate in all of the Employer's medical/dental benefit plans generally available to its executive employees in accordance with the terms thereof.

4.2   The Employer will provide Robert with a car allowance of $1,000.00 per month. This allowance will include any and all vehicle operating costs.

4.3   Robert will be entitled to the benefit of a golf club membership at the golf club of his choice for the period of this Agreement, the cost of which shall not exceed $30,000.00. The equity share or membership in the golf club will be owned by the Employer. The Employer will pay the annual golf club membership dues associated with the golf club membership on Robert's behalf. Before entering into any agreement with a golf club, Robert must satisfy the Employer that the golf club membership can and will revert back to the Employer upon the termination of Robert's employment or the expiry of this Agreement, whichever occurs first.

5.   Vacation

5.1   During this Agreement, Robert shall be entitled to three weeks' vacation per year. Such vacation shall be taken at a time or times acceptable to the Employer having regard to its operations. Vacation may be carried over from year to year only with the written authorization of the Employer's Chair.

6. **Professional Development and Expenses**

    6.1 Upon presentation of receipts, Robert shall be reimbursed for professional development expenses to a maximum of $5,000.00 per fiscal year commencing in Fiscal Year 2015.

    6.2 During the term of this Agreement, Robert shall be reimbursed by the Employer for approved expenses, including travel, parking, and other necessary business expenses incurred as a result of his work on behalf of the Employer. The Employer shall reimburse the executive for such expenses upon presentation of supporting documentation satisfactory to the Employer in accordance with the tax principles applicable in Canada for such reimbursement and the Employer's established reimbursement policies, as those policies may be modified from time to time in the Employer's discretion. Reimbursement for any such expenses will be at the sole discretion of the Employer.

7. **Confidentiality**

    7.1 Robert acknowledges that he is in a fiduciary position and, in the course of his employment, he will have access to and be entrusted with confidential information and trade secrets of the Employer and its subsidiaries.

    7.2 The term "confidential information" when used herein shall include all information of a confidential or proprietary nature that relates to the business of the Employer including, without limitation, trade or business secrets, formulae, designs and design methods, other methodologies, computer software programs and modifications and enhancements thereto, business plans and policies, sales and marketing information, training materials, business records, intellectual property, intellectual technology, and any other information not normally disclosed to the public.

    7.3 Robert acknowledges that all of the Employer's confidential information is its exclusive property and that all such property is held by Robert in trust. Except as his duties during his employment with the Employer may require, Robert shall keep secret and confidential and shall not make any copies of, and shall never disclose or use, either during or after his employment with the Employer, any confidential information of the Employer, except as required to fulfill his obligations to the Employer or as explicitly directed by law.

8.   Non-Solicitation

8.1   Robert agrees that he shall not, during the term of this Agreement or within one year after the date of the expiry of this Agreement or the termination or cessation of Robert's employment pursuant to this Agreement, either directly or indirectly, in partnership or jointly or in conjunction with any other person or persons, firm, association, syndicate, company, or corporation, whether as principal, agent, shareholder, director, officer, employee, consultant, or in any other manner whatsoever, at any time solicit or accept any business from or the patronage of, or render any services to, sell to, or contract or attempt to contract with any person, firm, or corporation who is a customer or prospective customer of the Employer or an employee or former employee of the Employer.

8.2   Robert confirms that the restrictions in paragraph 8.1 above are reasonable and valid and all defences, if any, to the strict enforcement thereof by the Employer are waived by Robert. Robert further agrees that any breach of paragraph 8.1 will entitle the Employer to injunctive relief, as monetary damages would not be an adequate remedy.

9.   Non-Competition

9.1   Robert shall not, at any time within one year of the expiry of this Agreement or the termination or cessation of Robert's employment pursuant to this Agreement, either individually or in partnership or jointly or in conjunction with any person as principal, consultant, agent, employee, shareholder, director, officer, or in any other manner whatsoever carry on, or be engaged in, or be concerned with, or interested in, or advise, lend money to, guarantee the debts or obligations of, or permit his name or any part thereof to be used or employed by, any person engaged in or concerned with or interested in a business similar to or in competition with the Employer in the Province of Ontario.

9.2   Robert confirms that the restrictions in paragraph 9.1 above are reasonable and valid and all defences, if any, to the strict enforcement thereof by the Employer are waived by Robert. Robert further agrees that any breach of paragraph 9.1 will entitle the Employer to injunctive relief, as monetary damages would not be an adequate remedy.

10.   Return of Property

10.1   Upon the termination of Robert's employment under this Agreement or the expiry of this Agreement, Robert shall at once deliver or cause to be delivered to the Employer all books, documents, effects, money, securities, or other property belonging to the Employer or for which the Employer is liable to others, which are in the possession, charge, control, or custody of Robert.

11. **Termination**

   11.1   Robert may terminate this Agreement upon one month's notice at any time by providing a written notice of resignation. Upon such termination of this Agreement, Robert will not be entitled to any further compensation under this Agreement.

   11.2   The Employer may terminate the employment of Robert without notice or any payment at any time during the course of this Agreement with just cause. "Just cause" is defined as serious and wilful misconduct.

   11.3   The Employer may terminate the employment of Robert without notice and without cause at any time during the course of this Agreement by providing written notice of termination to Robert. If the Employer elects to terminate the employment of Robert without cause in the first year of this contract, Robert shall be entitled to a lump-sum payment equivalent to two months of pay plus benefit continuation for the required period under Ontario's *Employment Standards Act* (as amended). This lump-sum payment will be in lieu of and include all of Robert's entitlements under statute and common law and under this Agreement including all compensation, benefits, and perquisites of any kind whatsoever, and specifically including any entitlements under the termination provisions of the Ontario *Employment Standards Act* (as amended).

   11.4   If the Employer elects to terminate the employment of Robert without cause after the first year of this contract, but before the expiry of this Agreement, Robert will be entitled to the lesser of a lump-sum payment equivalent to six months of pay or the remaining period of the contract plus benefit continuation for the required period under Ontario's *Employment Standards Act* (as amended). This lump-sum payment will be in lieu of and include all of Robert's entitlements under statute and common law and under this Agreement including all compensation, benefits, and perquisites of any kind whatsoever, and specifically including any entitlements under the termination provisions of the Ontario *Employment Standards Act* (as amended).

12. **Severability**

   12.1   If any provision of this Agreement is determined to be invalid or unenforceable in whole or in part, such invalidity or unenforceability shall attach only to such provision or part thereof and the remaining part of such provision and all other provisions thereof shall continue in full force and effect.

13. **Modification of Agreement**

   13.1   Any modification to this Agreement must be in writing and signed by the parties or it shall have no effect and shall be void.

14. **Governing Law**

    14.1 This Agreement shall be governed by and construed in accordance with the laws of the Province of Ontario.

15. **Independent Legal Advice**

    15.1 Robert acknowledges that he has obtained independent legal advice with respect to the terms and conditions contained herein.

Signed this _____ day of _____, 20___, in the City of Toronto in the Province of Ontario.

_____   _____

Robert   Witness

_____

Employer

Sample Absenteeism Letters

C

SAMPLE FIRST LETTER TO EMPLOYEE

Dear Mr./Ms. X:

Re: Poor Attendance Record

This letter is sent to express our concern over your poor attendance record.

We are aware of your health-related problems and we do realize that these problems are not your fault. Unfortunately, however, your attendance record with ABC Company has now become very poor. In this year alone, you have been absent from the workplace [since/on the following dates …]. Moreover, when someone is absent from work, ABC Company is less able to meet its obligations and an extra burden is placed on your fellow employees.

Unless your attendance record improves, your continued employment with ABC Company may not be possible. Furthermore, I wish to advise you that the Company will require you to produce a doctor's note to support any future absence in the next twelve months. This warning is not a disciplinary notation.

We look forward to your full recovery and sincerely hope that you can be a valued member of our work force.

Yours very truly,
ABC COMPANY

Per: _____

SAMPLE SECOND LETTER TO EMPLOYEE

Dear Mr./Ms. X:

Re: Continuing Attendance Problem

This letter is sent to express our continued concern over your poor attendance record.

As you are aware, your attendance record is extremely poor. Our concerns were first brought to your attention in our letter dated [insert date] and when we met with you on [insert date]. Unfortunately, however, your attendance record with ABC Company has still not improved. Our records indicate that you have been absent from the workplace for the following periods:

[set out updated history of employee absenteeism]

We realize that these health/illness problems are not your fault. However, the cost of your time off to ABC Company and your fellow employees is substantial. This letter is a further non-disciplinary warning that your attendance record is not acceptable and that your continued employment with ABC Company will not be possible unless your attendance record improves.

In view of your continuing attendance problem, we will meet with you again in [three/four/etc.] months' time to determine whether the necessary improvement has taken place.

We sincerely hope that your health/illness problems improve so that you can attend to work on a regular basis.

Yours very truly,
ABC COMPANY

Per: _____

SAMPLE SECOND LETTER TO EMPLOYEE WITH REQUEST FOR DETAILED MEDICAL ASSESSMENT

Dear Mr./Ms. X:

Re: Request for Detailed Medical Assessment

We are extremely concerned to see that your health/illness problems have again required you to take time off work. As you know, your attendance record is extremely poor. Our records indicate that you have now been absent from the workplace for the following periods:

[insert dates]

We realize that these health/illness problems are not your fault. However, the cost of your time off to ABC Company and your fellow employees is substantial. You previously received notice that ABC Company had a concern regarding your absenteeism on [insert dates]. We now wish to advise you that unless your attendance record improves, your continued employment with ABC Company will not be possible. This warning is a non-disciplinary notation.

In view of your ongoing attendance problems, we now require a more detailed medical certificate that addresses the following questions:

1. Are you fit to perform the essential duties of your regular position? In order for your physician to answer this question, please provide your doctor with the enclosed job description and physical demands analysis.

2. If you are not fit to perform the essential duties of your regular position, what limitations/restrictions exist on your ability to perform these essential duties? This information is required in order to determine whether suitable modified work can be made available to you.

3. What is the future prognosis on whether you will be able to maintain regular attendance in the foreseeable future, either with or without limitations/restrictions?

4.   What is the expected duration of any limitations/restrictions that may exist on your ability to perform the essential duties of your regular position?

Please provide the above-requested information no later than [insert date]. We are enclosing an extra copy of this letter for you to provide to your doctor. Would you kindly sign the consent to the release of this information found at the bottom of this letter. Thank you in advance for your immediate attention to this matter.

We sincerely hope that your health/illness problems improve so that you can attend at work on a regular basis.

Yours very truly,
ABC COMPANY

Per: _____

I, _____, hereby authorize and consent to Doctor _____ [name of doctor] releasing all of the above-requested information to my Employer at the following address: [insert name and address of information recipient].

DATED this _____ day of _____, 20___.

SAMPLE FINAL WARNING LETTER TO EMPLOYEE

Dear Mr./Ms. X:

Re: Unacceptable Absenteeism

This letter is sent to express our continuing concern over your extremely poor attendance record. As you are aware, our ongoing concern over your continuing attendance problems has been brought to your attention on numerous occasions, including [reference dates of previous letters and meetings].

Our most recent letter to you, dated [Y], indicated that we would review your attendance record in [X] months' time to determine whether the necessary improvement in your attendance had taken place. Regrettably, however, your attendance problems have still not improved to an acceptable standard. Our records indicate that in the most recent [X] months alone, you have been absent from the workplace on the following occasions: [insert dates].

We recognize that these ongoing health/illness problems are not your fault. However, the cost and disruption of your time off to ABC Company can no longer continue. Accordingly, this letter constitutes a final warning that your employment with ABC Company will be terminated in [X] months' time, unless there has been an improvement in your attendance record to minimum acceptable standards. This warning is a non-disciplinary notation.

We will review this matter with you again in [X] months' time. We sincerely hope that your attendance problems will improve in order that your employment at ABC Company may continue.

Yours very truly,
ABC COMPANY

Per: _____

SAMPLE TERMINATION LETTER TO EMPLOYEE

Dear Mr./Ms. X:

Re: Employment Termination

This letter will confirm our meeting of today's date wherein you were advised that your employment is being terminated effective [immediately/specify date] due to the frustration of your employment contract caused by ongoing attendance problems.

Our records indicate that you have been absent from the workplace for the following periods:

[outline history of employee absenteeism]

Our concern regarding your ongoing attendance problems has been brought to your attention on numerous occasions since [insert date]. Most recently, you were issued a final warning on [insert date] advising that unless your attendance record improved by [specify time frame], your continued employment would not be possible. Regrettably, the necessary improvement did not occur.

Your record of absenteeism is excessive and, in the circumstances, it does not appear that you will be capable of regular attendance in the foreseeable future.

We regret having to take this action. However, your ongoing attendance problems have reached the point where your continued employment is no longer possible.

[add appropriate paragraphs relating to any employee entitlements under applicable provisions of the *Employment Standards Act, 2000*]

Yours very truly,
ABC COMPANY

Canadian Charter of Rights and Freedoms

RSC 1985, app. II, no. 44

PART I OF THE CONSTITUTION ACT, 1982

Whereas Canada is founded upon principles that recognize the supremacy of God and the rule of law:

GUARANTEE OF RIGHTS AND FREEDOMS

Rights and freedoms in Canada

1. The *Canadian Charter of Rights and Freedoms* guarantees the rights and freedoms set out in it subject only to such reasonable limits prescribed by law as can be demonstrably justified in a free and democratic society.

Fundamental Freedoms

Fundamental freedoms

2. Everyone has the following fundamental freedoms:
    (a) freedom of conscience and religion;
    (b) freedom of thought, belief, opinion and expression, including freedom of the press and other media of communication;
    (c) freedom of peaceful assembly; and
    (d) freedom of association.

Democratic Rights

Democratic rights of citizens

3. Every citizen of Canada has the right to vote in an election of members of the House of Commons or of a legislative assembly and to be qualified for membership therein.

Maximum duration of legislative bodies

4(1) No House of Commons and no legislative assembly shall continue for longer than five years from the date fixed for the return of the writs at a general election of its members.

Continuation in special circumstances

(2) In time of real or apprehended war, invasion or insurrection, a House of Commons may be continued by Parliament and a legislative assembly may be continued by the legislature beyond five years if such continuation is not opposed by the votes of more than one-third of the members of the House of Commons or the legislative assembly, as the case may be.

Annual sitting of legislative bodies

5. There shall be a sitting of Parliament and of each legislature at least once every twelve months.

Mobility Rights

Mobility of citizens

6(1) Every citizen of Canada has the right to enter, remain in and leave Canada.

Rights to move and gain livelihood

(2) Every citizen of Canada and every person who has the status of a permanent resident of Canada has the right
> (a) to move to and take up residence in any province; and
> (b) to pursue the gaining of a livelihood in any province.

Limitation

(3) The rights specified in subsection (2) are subject to
> (a) any laws or practices of general application in force in a province other than those that discriminate among persons primarily on the basis of province of present or previous residence; and
> (b) any laws providing for reasonable residency requirements as a qualification for the receipt of publicly provided social services.

Affirmative action programs

(4) Subsections (2) and (3) do not preclude any law, program or activity that has as its object the amelioration in a province of conditions of individuals in that province who are socially or economically disadvantaged if the rate of employment in that province is below the rate of employment in Canada.

Legal Rights

Life, liberty and security of person

7. Everyone has the right to life, liberty and security of the person and the right not to be deprived thereof except in accordance with the principles of fundamental justice.

Search or seizure

   8. Everyone has the right to be secure against unreasonable search or seizure.

Detention or imprisonment

   9. Everyone has the right not to be arbitrarily detained or imprisoned.

Arrest or detention

  10. Everyone has the right on arrest or detention

     (a) to be informed promptly of the reasons therefor;

     (b) to retain and instruct counsel without delay and to be informed of that right; and

     (c) to have the validity of the detention determined by way of *habeas corpus* and to be released if the detention is not lawful.

Proceedings in criminal and penal matters

  11. Any person charged with an offence has the right

     (a) to be informed without unreasonable delay of the specific offence;

     (b) to be tried within a reasonable time;

     (c) not to be compelled to be a witness in proceedings against that person in respect of the offence;

     (d) to be presumed innocent until proven guilty according to law in a fair and public hearing by an independent and impartial tribunal;

     (e) not to be denied reasonable bail without just cause;

     (f) except in the case of an offence under military law tried before a military tribunal, to the benefit of trial by jury where the maximum punishment for the offence is imprisonment for five years or a more severe punishment;

     (g) not to be found guilty on account of any act or omission unless, at the time of the act or omission, it constituted an offence under Canadian or international law or was criminal according to the general principles of law recognized by the community of nations;

     (h) if finally acquitted of the offence, not to be tried for it again and, if finally found guilty and punished for the offence, not to be tried or punished for it again; and

     (i) if found guilty of the offence and if the punishment for the offence has been varied between the time of commission and the time of sentencing, to the benefit of the lesser punishment.

Treatment or punishment

  12. Everyone has the right not to be subjected to any cruel and unusual treatment or punishment.

Self-crimination

  13. A witness who testifies in any proceedings has the right not to have any incriminating evidence so given used to incriminate that witness in any other proceedings, except in a prosecution for perjury or for the giving of contradictory evidence.

Interpreter

14. A party or witness in any proceedings who does not understand or speak the language in which the proceedings are conducted or who is deaf has the right to the assistance of an interpreter.

Equality Rights

Equality before and under law and equal protection and benefit of law

15(1) Every individual is equal before and under the law and has the right to the equal protection and equal benefit of the law without discrimination and, in particular, without discrimination based on race, national or ethnic origin, colour, religion, sex, age or mental or physical disability.

Affirmative action programs

(2) Subsection (1) does not preclude any law, program or activity that has as its object the amelioration of conditions of disadvantaged individuals or groups including those that are disadvantaged because of race, national or ethnic origin, colour, religion, sex, age or mental or physical disability.

Official Languages of Canada

Official languages of Canada

16(1) English and French are the official languages of Canada and have equality of status and equal rights and privileges as to their use in all institutions of the Parliament and government of Canada.

Official languages of New Brunswick

(2) English and French are the official languages of New Brunswick and have equality of status and equal rights and privileges as to their use in all institutions of the legislature and government of New Brunswick.

Advancement of status and use

(3) Nothing in the Charter limits the authority of Parliament or a legislature to advance the equality of status or use of English and French.

English and French linguistic communities in New Brunswick

16.1(1) The English linguistic community and the French linguistic community in New Brunswick have equality of status and equal rights and privileges, including the right to distinct educational institutions and such distinct cultural institutions as are necessary for the preservation and promotion of those communities.

Role of the legislature and government of New Brunswick

(2) The role of the legislature and government of New Brunswick to preserve and promote the status, rights and privileges referred to in subsection (1) is affirmed.

Proceedings of Parliament

17(1) Everyone has the right to use English or French in any debates and other proceedings of Parliament.

Proceedings of New Brunswick legislature

(2) Everyone has the right to use English or French in any debates and other proceedings of the legislature of New Brunswick.

Parliamentary statutes and records

18(1) The statutes, records and journals of Parliament shall be printed and published in English and French and both language versions are equally authoritative.

New Brunswick statutes and records

(2) The statutes, records and journals of the legislature of New Brunswick shall be printed and published in English and French and both language versions are equally authoritative.

Proceedings in courts established by Parliament

19(1) Either English or French may be used by any person in, or in any pleading in or process issuing from, any court established by Parliament.

Proceedings in New Brunswick courts

(2) Either English or French may be used by any person in, or in any pleading in or process issuing from, any court of New Brunswick.

Communications by public with federal institutions

20(1) Any member of the public in Canada has the right to communicate with, and to receive available services from, any head or central office of an institution of the Parliament or government of Canada in English or French, and has the same right with respect to any other office of any such institution where

    (a) there is a significant demand for communications with and services from that office in such language; or

    (b) due to the nature of the office, it is reasonable that communications with and services from that office be available in both English and French.

Communications by public with New Brunswick institutions

(2) Any member of the public in New Brunswick has the right to communicate with, and to receive available services from, any office of an institution of the legislature or government of New Brunswick in English or French.

Continuation of existing constitutional provisions

21. Nothing in sections 16 to 20 abrogates or derogates from any right, privilege or obligation with respect to the English and French languages, or either of them, that exists or is continued by virtue of any other provision of the Constitution of Canada.

Rights and privileges preserved

22. Nothing in sections 16 to 20 abrogates or derogates from any legal or customary right or privilege acquired or enjoyed either before or after the coming into force of this Charter with respect to any language that is not English or French.

Minority Language Educational Rights

Language of instruction

23(1) Citizens of Canada
    (a) whose first language learned and still understood is that of the English or French linguistic minority population of the province in which they reside, or
    (b) who have received their primary school instruction in Canada in English or French and reside in a province where the language in which they received that instruction is the language of the English or French linguistic minority population of the province,
have the right to have their children receive primary and secondary school instruction in that language in that province.

Continuity of language instruction

(2) Citizens of Canada of whom any child has received or is receiving primary or secondary school instruction in English or French in Canada, have the right to have all their children receive primary and secondary school instruction in the same language.

Application where numbers warrant

(3) The right of citizens of Canada under subsections (1) and (2) to have their children receive primary and secondary school instruction in the language of the English or French linguistic minority population of a province
    (a) applies wherever in the province the number of children of citizens who have such a right is sufficient to warrant the provision to them out of public funds of minority language instruction; and
    (b) includes, where the number of those children so warrants, the right to have them receive that instruction in minority language educational facilities provided out of public funds.

Enforcement

Enforcement of guaranteed rights and freedoms

24(1) Anyone whose rights or freedoms, as guaranteed by this Charter, have been infringed or denied may apply to a court of competent jurisdiction to obtain such remedy as the court considers appropriate and just in the circumstances.

Exclusion of evidence bringing administration of justice into disrepute

(2) Where, in proceedings under subsection (1), a court concludes that evidence was obtained in a manner that infringed or denied any rights or freedoms guaranteed by this Charter, the evidence shall be excluded if it is established that, having regard to all the circumstances, the admission of it in the proceedings would bring the administration of justice into disrepute.

General

Aboriginal rights and freedoms not affected by Charter

25. The guarantee in this Charter of certain rights and freedoms shall not be construed so as to abrogate or derogate from any aboriginal, treaty or other rights or freedoms that pertain to the aboriginal peoples of Canada including

(a) any rights or freedoms that have been recognized by the Royal Proclamation of October 7, 1763; and

(b) any rights or freedoms that may be acquired by the aboriginal peoples of Canada by way of land claims settlement.

Other rights and freedoms not affected by Charter

26. The guarantee in this Charter of certain rights and freedoms shall not be construed as denying the existence of any other rights or freedoms that exist in Canada.

Multicultural heritage

27. This Charter shall be interpreted in a manner consistent with the preservation and enhancement of the multicultural heritage of Canadians.

Rights guaranteed equally to both sexes

28. Notwithstanding anything in this Charter, the rights and freedoms referred to in it are guaranteed equally to male and female persons.

Rights respecting certain schools preserved

29. Nothing in this Charter abrogates or derogates from any rights or privileges guaranteed by or under the Constitution of Canada in respect of denominational, separate or dissentient schools.

Application to territories and territorial authorities

30. A reference in this Charter to a province or to the legislative assembly or legislature of a province shall be deemed to include a reference to the Yukon Territory and the Northwest Territories, or to the appropriate legislative authority thereof, as the case may be.

Legislative powers not extended

31. Nothing in this Charter extends the legislative powers of any body or authority.

Application of Charter

Application of Charter

32(1) This Charter applies

(a) to the Parliament and government of Canada in respect of all matters within the authority of Parliament including all matters relating to the Yukon Territory and Northwest Territories; and

(b) to the legislature and government of each province in respect of all matters within the authority of the legislature of each province.

Exception

(2) Notwithstanding subsection (1), section 15 shall not have effect until three years after this section comes into force.

Exception where express declaration

33(1) Parliament or the legislature of a province may expressly declare in an Act of Parliament or of the legislature, as the case may be, that the Act or a provision thereof shall operate notwithstanding a provision included in section 2 or sections 7 to 15 of this Charter.

Operation of exception

(2) An Act or a provision of an Act in respect of which a declaration made under this section is in effect shall have such operation as it would have but for the provision of this Charter referred to in the declaration.

Five year limitation

(3) A declaration made under subsection (1) shall cease to have effect five years after it comes into force or on such earlier date as may be specified in the declaration.

Re-enactment

(4) Parliament or a legislature of a province may re-enact a declaration made under subsection (1).

Five year limitation

(5) Subsection (3) applies in respect of a re-enactment made under subsection (4).

Citation

Citation

34. This Part may be cited as the *Canadian Charter of Rights and Freedoms*.

Ontario Human Rights Code

RSO 1990, c. H.19

Preamble

Whereas recognition of the inherent dignity and the equal and inalienable rights of all members of the human family is the foundation of freedom, justice and peace in the world and is in accord with the Universal Declaration of Human Rights as proclaimed by the United Nations;

And Whereas it is public policy in Ontario to recognize the dignity and worth of every person and to provide for equal rights and opportunities without discrimination that is contrary to law, and having as its aim the creation of a climate of understanding and mutual respect for the dignity and worth of each person so that each person feels a part of the community and able to contribute fully to the development and well-being of the community and the Province;

And Whereas these principles have been confirmed in Ontario by a number of enactments of the Legislature and it is desirable to revise and extend the protection of human rights in Ontario;

Therefore, Her Majesty, by and with the advice and consent of the Legislative Assembly of the Province of Ontario, enacts as follows:

PART I   FREEDOM FROM DISCRIMINATION

Services

1. Every person has a right to equal treatment with respect to services, goods and facilities, without discrimination because of race, ancestry, place of origin, colour, ethnic origin, citizenship, creed, sex, sexual orientation, age, marital status, family status or disability.

Accommodation

2(1) Every person has a right to equal treatment with respect to the occupancy of accommodation, without discrimination because of race, ancestry, place of origin, colour, ethnic origin, citizenship, creed, sex, sexual orientation, age, marital status, family status, disability or the receipt of public assistance.

Harassment in accommodation

(2) Every person who occupies accommodation has a right to freedom from harassment by the landlord or agent of the landlord or by an occupant of the same building because of race, ancestry, place of origin, colour, ethnic origin, citizenship, creed, age, marital status, family status, disability or the receipt of public assistance.

Contracts

3. Every person having legal capacity has a right to contract on equal terms without discrimination because of race, ancestry, place of origin, colour, ethnic origin, citizenship, creed, sex, sexual orientation, age, marital status, family status or disability.

Accommodation of person under eighteen

4(1) Every sixteen or seventeen year old person who has withdrawn from parental control has a right to equal treatment with respect to occupancy of and contracting for accommodation without discrimination because the person is less than eighteen years old.

Idem

(2) A contract for accommodation entered into by a sixteen or seventeen year old person who has withdrawn from parental control is enforceable against that person as if the person were eighteen years old.

Employment

5(1) Every person has a right to equal treatment with respect to employment without discrimination because of race, ancestry, place of origin, colour, ethnic origin, citizenship, creed, sex, sexual orientation, gender identity, gender expression, age, record of offences, marital status, family status or disability.

Harassment in employment

(2) Every person who is an employee has a right to freedom from harassment in the workplace by the employer or agent of the employer or by another employee because of race, ancestry, place of origin, colour, ethnic origin, citizenship, creed, sexual orientation, gender identity, gender expression, age, record of offences, marital status, family status or disability.

Vocational associations

6. Every person has a right to equal treatment with respect to membership in any trade union, trade or occupational association or self-governing profession without discrimination because of race, ancestry, place of origin, colour, ethnic origin, citizenship, creed, sex, sexual orientation, gender identity, gender expression, age, marital status, family status or disability.

Sexual harassment

Harassment because of sex in accommodation

7(1) Every person who occupies accommodation has a right to freedom from harassment because of sex, sexual orientation, gender identity or gender expression by the landlord or agent of the landlord or by an occupant of the same building.

Harassment because of sex in workplaces

(2) Every person who is an employee has a right to freedom from harassment in the workplace because of sex, sexual orientation, gender identity or gender expression by his or her employer or agent of the employer or by another employee.

Sexual solicitation by a person in position to confer benefit, etc.

(3) Every person has a right to be free from,

(a) a sexual solicitation or advance made by a person in a position to confer, grant or deny a benefit or advancement to the person where the person making the solicitation or advance knows or ought reasonably to know that it is unwelcome; or

(b) a reprisal or a threat of reprisal for the rejection of a sexual solicitation or advance where the reprisal is made or threatened by a person in a position to confer, grant or deny a benefit or advancement to the person.

Reprisals

8. Every person has a right to claim and enforce his or her rights under this Act, to institute and participate in proceedings under this Act and to refuse to infringe a right of another person under this Act, without reprisal or threat of reprisal for so doing.

Infringement prohibited

9. No person shall infringe or do, directly or indirectly, anything that infringes a right under this Part.

PART II   INTERPRETATION AND APPLICATION

Definitions re: Parts I and II

10(1) In Part I and in this Part,

"age" means an age that is 18 years or more;

"disability" means,

(a) any degree of physical disability, infirmity, malformation or disfigurement that is caused by bodily injury, birth defect or illness and, without limiting the generality of the foregoing, includes diabetes mellitus, epilepsy, a brain injury, any degree of paralysis, amputation, lack of physical co-ordination, blindness or visual impediment, deafness or hearing impediment, muteness or speech impediment, or physical reliance on a guide dog or other animal or on a wheelchair or other remedial appliance or device,

    (b) a condition of mental impairment or a developmental disability,

    (c) a learning disability, or a dysfunction in one or more of the processes involved in understanding or using symbols or spoken language,

    (d) a mental disorder, or

    (e) an injury or disability for which benefits were claimed or received under the insurance plan established under the *Workplace Safety and Insurance Act, 1997*;

"equal" means subject to all requirements, qualifications and considerations that are not a prohibited ground of discrimination;

"family status" means the status of being in a parent and child relationship;

"group insurance" means insurance whereby the lives or well-being or the lives and well-being of a number of persons are insured severally under a single contract between an insurer and an association or an employer or other person;

"harassment" means engaging in a course of vexatious comment or conduct that is known or ought reasonably to be known to be unwelcome;

"marital status" means the status of being married, single, widowed, divorced or separated and includes the status of living with a person in a conjugal relationship outside marriage;

"record of offences" means a conviction for,

    (a) an offence in respect of which a pardon has been granted under the *Criminal Records Act* (Canada) and has not been revoked, or

    (b) an offence in respect of any provincial enactment;

"services" does not include a levy, fee, tax or periodic payment imposed by law;

"spouse" means the person to whom a person is married or with whom the person is living in a conjugal relationship outside marriage.

Pregnancy

(2) The right to equal treatment without discrimination because of sex includes the right to equal treatment without discrimination because a woman is or may become pregnant.

Past and presumed disabilities

(3) The right to equal treatment without discrimination because of disability includes the right to equal treatment without discrimination because a person has or has had a disability or is believed to have or to have had a disability.

Constructive discrimination

11(1) A right of a person under Part I is infringed where a requirement, qualification or factor exists that is not discrimination on a prohibited ground but that results in the exclusion, restriction or preference of a group of persons who are identified by a prohibited ground of discrimination and of whom the person is a member, except where,

(a) the requirement, qualification or factor is reasonable and *bona fide* in the circumstances; or

(b) it is declared in this Act, other than in section 17, that to discriminate because of such ground is not an infringement of a right.

Idem

(2) The Commission, the Tribunal or a court shall not find that a requirement, qualification or factor is reasonable and *bona fide* in the circumstances unless it is satisfied that the needs of the group of which the person is a member cannot be accommodated without undue hardship on the person responsible for accommodating those needs, considering the cost, outside sources of funding, if any, and health and safety requirements, if any.

Idem

(3) The Commission, the Tribunal or a court shall consider any standards prescribed by the regulations for assessing what is undue hardship.

Discrimination because of association

12. A right under Part I is infringed where the discrimination is because of relationship, association or dealings with a person or persons identified by a prohibited ground of discrimination.

Announced intention to discriminate

13(1) A right under Part I is infringed by a person who publishes or displays before the public or causes the publication or display before the public of any notice, sign, symbol, emblem, or other similar representation that indicates the intention of the person to infringe a right under Part I or that is intended by the person to incite the infringement of a right under Part I.

Opinion

(2) Subsection (1) shall not interfere with freedom of expression of opinion.

Special programs

14(1) A right under Part I is not infringed by the implementation of a special program designed to relieve hardship or economic disadvantage or to assist disadvantaged persons or groups to achieve or attempt to achieve equal opportunity or that is likely to contribute to the elimination of the infringement of rights under Part I.

Application to Commission

(2) A person may apply to the Commission for a designation of a program as a special program for the purposes of subsection (1).

Designation by Commission

(3) Upon receipt of an application, the Commission may,

(a) designate the program as a special program if, in its opinion, the program meets the requirements of subsection (1); or

(b) designate the program as a special program on the condition that the program make such modifications as are specified in the designation in order to meet the requirements of subsection (1).

Inquiries initiated by Commission

(4) The Commission may, on its own initiative, inquire into one or more programs to determine whether the programs are special programs for the purposes of subsection (1).

End of inquiry

(5) At the conclusion of an inquiry under subsection (4), the Commission may designate as a special program any of the programs under inquiry if, in its opinion, the programs meet the requirements of subsection (1).

Expiry of designation

(6) A designation under subsection (3) or (5) expires five years after the day it is issued or at such earlier time as may be specified by the Commission.

Renewal of designation

(7) If an application for renewal of a designation of a program as a special program is made to the Commission before its expiry under subsection (6), the Commission may,

(a) renew the designation if, in its opinion, the program continues to meet the requirements of subsection (1); or

(b) renew the designation on the condition that the program make such modifications as are specified in the designation in order to meet the requirements of subsection (1).

Effect of designation, etc.

(8) In a proceeding,

(a) evidence that a program has been designated as a special program under this section is proof, in the absence of evidence to the contrary, that the program is a special program for the purposes of subsection (1); and

(b) evidence that the Commission has considered and refused to designate a program as a special program under this section is proof, in the absence of evidence to the contrary, that the program is not a special program for the purposes of subsection (1).

Crown programs

(9) Subsections (2) to (8) do not apply to a program implemented by the Crown or an agency of the Crown.

Tribunal finding

(10) For the purposes of a proceeding before the Tribunal, the Tribunal may make a finding that a program meets the requirements of a special program under subsection (1), even though the program has not been designated as a special program by the Commission under this section, subject to clause (8)(b).

14.1 REPEALED.

Age sixty-five or over

15. A right under Part I to non-discrimination because of age is not infringed where an age of sixty-five years or over is a requirement, qualification or consideration for preferential treatment.

Canadian Citizenship

16(1) A right under Part I to non-discrimination because of citizenship is not infringed where Canadian citizenship is a requirement, qualification or consideration imposed or authorized by law.

Idem

(2) A right under Part I to non-discrimination because of citizenship is not infringed where Canadian citizenship or lawful admission to Canada for permanent residence is a requirement, qualification or consideration adopted for the purpose of fostering and developing participation in cultural, educational, trade union or athletic activities by Canadian citizens or persons lawfully admitted to Canada for permanent residence.

Idem

(3) A right under Part I to non-discrimination because of citizenship is not infringed where Canadian citizenship or domicile in Canada with the intention to obtain Canadian citizenship is a requirement, qualification or consideration adopted by an organization or enterprise for the holder of chief or senior executive positions.

Disability

17(1) A right of a person under this Act is not infringed for the reason only that the person is incapable of performing or fulfilling the essential duties or requirements attending the exercise of the right because of disability.

Accommodation

(2) No tribunal or court shall find a person incapable unless it is satisfied that the needs of the person cannot be accommodated without undue hardship on the person responsible for accommodating those needs, considering the cost, outside sources of funding, if any, and health and safety requirements, if any.

Determining if undue hardship

(3) In determining for the purposes of subsection (2) whether there would be undue hardship, a tribunal or court shall consider any standards prescribed by the regulations.

(4) REPEALED.

Special interest organizations

18. The rights under Part I to equal treatment with respect to services and facilities, with or without accommodation, are not infringed where membership or participation in a religious, philanthropic, educational, fraternal or social institution or organization that is primarily engaged in serving the interests of persons identified by a prohibited ground of discrimination is restricted to persons who are similarly identified.

Solemnization of marriage by religious officials

18.1(1) The rights under Part I to equal treatment with respect to services and facilities are not infringed where a person registered under section 20 of the *Marriage Act* refuses to solemnize a marriage, to allow a sacred place to be used for solemnizing a marriage or for an event related to the solemnization of a marriage, or to otherwise assist in the solemnization of a marriage, if to solemnize the marriage, allow the sacred place to be used or otherwise assist would be contrary to,

   (a) the person's religious beliefs; or

   (b) the doctrines, rites, usages or customs of the religious body to which the person belongs.

Same

(2) Nothing in subsection (1) limits the application of section 18.

Definition

(3) In this section,

"sacred place" includes a place of worship and any ancillary or accessory facilities.

Separate school rights preserved

19(1) This Act shall not be construed to adversely affect any right or privilege respecting separate schools enjoyed by separate school boards or their supporters under the *Constitution Act, 1867* and the *Education Act*.

Duties of teachers

(2) This Act does not apply to affect the application of the *Education Act* with respect to the duties of teachers.

Restriction of facilities by sex

20(1) The right under section 1 to equal treatment with respect to services and facilities without discrimination because of sex is not infringed where the use of the services or facilities is restricted to persons of the same sex on the ground of public decency.

Minimum drinking age

(2) The right under section 1 to equal treatment with respect to services, goods and facilities without discrimination because of age is not infringed by the provisions of the *Liquor Licence Act* and the regulations under it relating to providing for and enforcing a minimum drinking age of nineteen years.

Recreational clubs

(3) The right under section 1 to equal treatment with respect to services and facilities is not infringed where a recreational club restricts or qualifies access to its services or facilities or gives preferences with respect to membership dues and other fees because of age, sex, marital status or family status.

Tobacco and young persons

(4) The right under section 1 to equal treatment with respect to goods without discrimination because of age is not infringed by the provisions of the *Smoke-Free Ontario Act* and the regulations under it relating to selling or supplying tobacco to persons who are, or who appear to be, under the age of 19 years or 25 years, as the case may be.

Residential accommodation
Shared accommodation

21(1) The right under section 2 to equal treatment with respect to the occupancy of residential accommodation without discrimination is not infringed by discrimination where the residential accommodation is in a dwelling in which the owner or his or her family reside if the occupant or occupants of the residential accommodation are required to share a bathroom or kitchen facility with the owner or family of the owner.

Restrictions on accommodation, sex

(2) The right under section 2 to equal treatment with respect to the occupancy of residential accommodation without discrimination because of sex is not infringed by discrimination on that ground where the occupancy of all the residential accommodation in the building, other than the accommodation, if any, of the owner or family of the owner, is restricted to persons who are of the same sex.

Prescribing business practices

(3) The right under section 2 to equal treatment with respect to the occupancy of residential accommodation without discrimination is not infringed if a landlord uses in the manner prescribed under this Act income information, credit checks, credit references, rental history, guarantees or other similar business practices which are prescribed in the regulations made under this Act in selecting prospective tenants.

Restrictions for insurance contracts, etc.

22. The right under sections 1 and 3 to equal treatment with respect to services and to contract on equal terms, without discrimination because of age, sex, marital status, family status or disability, is not infringed where a contract of automobile, life, accident or sickness or disability insurance or a contract of group insurance between an insurer and an association or person other than an employer, or a life annuity, differentiates or makes a distinction, exclusion or preference on reasonable and *bona fide* grounds because of age, sex, marital status, family status or disability.

Employment

23(1) The right under section 5 to equal treatment with respect to employment is infringed where an invitation to apply for employment or an advertisement in connection with employment is published or displayed that directly or indirectly classifies or indicates qualifications by a prohibited ground of discrimination.

Application for employment

(2) The right under section 5 to equal treatment with respect to employment is infringed where a form of application for employment is used or a written or oral inquiry is made of an applicant that directly or indirectly classifies or indicates qualifications by a prohibited ground of discrimination.

Questions at interview

(3) Nothing in subsection (2) precludes the asking of questions at a personal employment interview concerning a prohibited ground of discrimination where discrimination on such ground is permitted under this Act.

Employment agencies

(4) The right under section 5 to equal treatment with respect to employment is infringed where an employment agency discriminates against a person because of a prohibited ground of discrimination in receiving, classifying, disposing of or otherwise acting upon applications for its services or in referring an applicant or applicants to an employer or agent of an employer.

Special employment

24(1) The right under section 5 to equal treatment with respect to employment is not infringed where,

(a) a religious, philanthropic, educational, fraternal or social institution or organization that is primarily engaged in serving the interests of persons identified by their race, ancestry, place of origin, colour, ethnic origin, creed, sex, age, marital status or disability employs only, or gives preference in employment to, persons similarly identified if the qualification is a reasonable and *bona fide* qualification because of the nature of the employment;

(b) the discrimination in employment is for reasons of age, sex, record of offences or marital status if the age, sex, record of offences or marital status of the applicant is a reasonable and *bona fide* qualification because of the nature of the employment;

(c) an individual person refuses to employ another for reasons of any prohibited ground of discrimination in section 5, where the primary duty of the employment is attending to the medical or personal needs of the person or of an ill child or an aged, infirm or ill spouse or other relative of the person;

(d) an employer grants or withholds employment or advancement in employment to a person who is the spouse, child or parent of the employer or an employee;

(e) a judge or master is required to retire or cease to continue in office on reaching a specified age under the *Courts of Justice Act*;

(f) a case management master is required to retire on reaching a specified age under the *Courts of Justice Act*;

(g) the term of reappointment of a case management master expires on the case management master reaching a specified age under the *Courts of Justice Act*; or

(h) a justice of the peace is required to retire on reaching a specified age under the *Justices of the Peace Act*.

Reasonable accommodation

(2) No tribunal or court shall find that a qualification under clause (1)(b) is reasonable and *bona fide* unless it is satisfied that the circumstances of the person cannot be accommodated without undue hardship on the person responsible for accommodating those circumstances considering the cost, outside sources of funding, if any, and health and safety requirements, if any.

Determining if undue hardship

(3) In determining for the purposes of subsection (2) whether there would be undue hardship, a tribunal or court shall consider any standards prescribed by the regulations.

Same

(4) Clauses 24(1)(e), (f), (g) and (h) shall not be interpreted to suggest that a judge, master, case management master or justice of the peace is an employee for the purposes of this Act or any other Act or law.

24.1 REPEALED.

Employee benefit and pension plans

25(1) The right under section 5 to equal treatment with respect to employment is infringed where employment is denied or made conditional because a term or condition of employment requires enrolment in an employee benefit, pension or superannuation plan or fund or a contract of group insurance between an insurer and an employer, that makes a distinction, preference or exclusion on a prohibited ground of discrimination.

Same

(2) The right under section 5 to equal treatment with respect to employment without discrimination because of sex, marital status or family status is not infringed by an employee superannuation or pension plan or fund or a contract of group insurance between an insurer and an employer that complies with the *Employment Standards Act,* 2000 and the regulations thereunder.

Same

(2.1) The right under section 5 to equal treatment with respect to employment without discrimination because of age is not infringed by an employee benefit, pension, superannuation or group insurance plan or fund that complies with the *Employment Standards Act, 2000* and the regulations thereunder.

Same

(2.2) Subsection (2.1) applies whether or not a plan or fund is the subject of a contract of insurance between an insurer and an employer.

Same

(2.3) For greater certainty, subsections (2) and (2.1) apply whether or not "age", "sex" or "marital status" in the *Employment Standards Act, 2000* or the regulations under it have the same meaning as those terms have in this Act.

Same

(3) The right under section 5 to equal treatment with respect to employment without discrimination because of disability is not infringed,

(a) where a reasonable and *bona fide* distinction, exclusion or preference is made in an employee disability or life insurance plan or benefit because of a pre-existing disability that substantially increases the risk;

(b) where a reasonable and *bona fide* distinction, exclusion or preference is made on the ground of a pre-existing disability in respect of an employee-pay-all or participant-pay-all benefit in an employee benefit, pension or superannuation plan or fund or a contract of group insurance between an insurer and an employer or in respect of a plan, fund or policy that is offered by an employer to employees if they are fewer than twenty-five in number.

Compensation

(4) An employer shall pay to an employee who is excluded because of a disability from an employee benefit, pension or superannuation plan or fund or a contract of group insurance between an insurer and the employer compensation equivalent to the contribution that the employer would make thereto on behalf of an employee who does not have a disability.

Discrimination in employment under government contracts

26(1) It shall be deemed to be a condition of every contract entered into by or on behalf of the Crown or any agency thereof and of every subcontract entered into in the performance thereof that no right under section 5 will be infringed in the course of performing the contract.

Idem: government grants and loans

(2) It shall be deemed to be a condition of every grant, contribution, loan or guarantee made by or on behalf of the Crown or any agency thereof that no right under section 5 will be infringed in the course of carrying out the purposes for which the grant, contribution, loan or guarantee was made.

Sanction

(3) Where an infringement of a right under section 5 is found by the Tribunal upon a complaint and constitutes a breach of a condition under this section, the breach of condition is sufficient grounds for cancellation of the contract, grant, contribution, loan or guarantee and refusal to enter into any further contract with or make any further grant, contribution, loan or guarantee to the same person.

PART III   THE ONTARIO HUMAN RIGHTS COMMISSION

The Commission

27(1) The Ontario Human Rights Commission is continued under the name Ontario Human Rights Commission in English and Commission ontarienne des droits de la personne in French.

Composition

(2) The Commission shall be composed of such persons as are appointed by the Lieutenant Governor in Council.

Appointment

(3) Every person appointed to the Commission shall have knowledge, experience or training with respect to human rights law and issues.

Criteria

(4) In the appointment of persons to the Commission under subsection (2), the importance of reflecting, in the composition of the Commission as a whole, the diversity of Ontario's population shall be recognized.

Chief Commissioner

(5) The Lieutenant Governor in Council shall designate a member of the Commission as Chief Commissioner.

Powers and duties of Chief Commissioner

(6) The Chief Commissioner shall direct the Commission and exercise the powers and perform the duties assigned to the Chief Commissioner by or under this Act.

Term of office

(7) The Chief Commissioner and other members of the Commission shall hold office for such term as may be specified by the Lieutenant Governor in Council.

Remuneration

(8) The Chief Commissioner and other members of the Commission shall be paid such remuneration and allowance for expenses as are fixed by the Lieutenant Governor in Council.

Employees

(9) The Commission may appoint such employees as it considers necessary for the proper conduct of its affairs and the employees shall be appointed under Part III of the *Public Service of Ontario Act, 2006.*

Evidence obtained in performance of duties

(10) A member of the Commission shall not be required to give testimony in a civil suit or any proceeding as to information obtained in the performance of duties under this Act.

Same, employees

(11) An employee of the Commission shall not be required to give testimony in a civil suit or any proceeding other than a proceeding under this Act as to information obtained in the performance of duties under this Act.

Delegation

(12) The Chief Commissioner may in writing delegate any of his or her powers, duties or functions under this Act to any member of the Anti-Racism Secretariat, the Disability Rights Secretariat or an advisory group or to any other member of the Commission, subject to such conditions as the Chief Commissioner may set out in the delegation.

Divisions

(13) The Commission may authorize any function of the Commission to be performed by a division of the Commission composed of at least three members of the Commission.

Acting Chief Commissioner

28(1) If the Chief Commissioner dies, resigns or is unable or neglects to perform his or her duties, the Lieutenant Governor in Council may appoint an Acting Chief Commissioner to hold office for such period as may be specified in the appointment.

Same

(2) An Acting Chief Commissioner shall perform the duties and have the powers of the Chief Commissioner and shall be paid such remuneration and allowance for expenses as are fixed by the Lieutenant Governor in Council.

Functions of Commission

29. The functions of the Commission are to promote and advance respect for human rights in Ontario, to protect human rights in Ontario and, recognizing that it is in the public interest to do so and that it is the Commission's duty to protect the public interest, to identify and promote the elimination of discriminatory practices and, more specifically,

(a) to forward the policy that the dignity and worth of every person be recognized and that equal rights and opportunities be provided without discrimination that is contrary to law;

(b) to develop and conduct programs of public information and education to,

(i) promote awareness and understanding of, respect for and compliance with this Act, and

(ii) prevent and eliminate discriminatory practices that infringe rights under Part I;

(c) to undertake, direct and encourage research into discriminatory practices and to make recommendations designed to prevent and eliminate such discriminatory practices;

(d) to examine and review any statute or regulation, and any program or policy made by or under a statute, and make recommendations on any provision, program or policy that in its opinion is inconsistent with the intent of this Act;

(e) to initiate reviews and inquiries into incidents of tension or conflict, or conditions that lead or may lead to incidents of tension or conflict, in a community, institution, industry or sector of the economy, and to make recommendations, and encourage and co-ordinate plans, programs and activities, to reduce or prevent such incidents or sources of tension or conflict;

(f) to promote, assist and encourage public, municipal or private agencies, organizations, groups or persons to engage in programs to alleviate tensions and conflicts based upon identification by a prohibited ground of discrimination;

(g) to designate programs as special programs in accordance with section 14;

(h) to approve policies under section 30;

(i) to make applications to the Tribunal under section 35;

(j) to report to the people of Ontario on the state of human rights in Ontario and on its affairs;

(k) to perform the functions assigned to the Commission under this or any other Act.

Commission policies

30. The Commission may approve policies prepared and published by the Commission to provide guidance in the application of Parts I and II.

Inquiries

31(1) The Commission may conduct an inquiry under this section for the purpose of carrying out its functions under this Act if the Commission believes it is in the public interest to do so.

Conduct of inquiry

(2) An inquiry may be conducted under this section by any person who is appointed by the Commission to carry out inquiries under this section.

Production of certificate

(3) A person conducting an inquiry under this section shall produce proof of their appointment upon request.

Entry

(4) A person conducting an inquiry under this section may, without warrant, enter any lands or any building, structure or premises where the person has reason to believe there may be documents, things or information relevant to the inquiry.

Time of entry

(5) The power to enter a place under subsection (4) may be exercised only during the place's regular business hours or, if it does not have regular business hours, during daylight hours.

Dwellings

(6) A person conducting an inquiry under this section shall not enter into a place or part of a place that is a dwelling without the consent of the occupant.

Powers on inquiry

(7) A person conducting an inquiry may,

(a) request the production for inspection and examination of documents or things that are or may be relevant to the inquiry;

(b) upon giving a receipt for it, remove from a place documents produced in response to a request under clause (a) for the purpose of making copies or extracts;

(c) question a person on matters that are or may be relevant to the inquiry, subject to the person's right to have counsel or a personal representative present during such questioning and exclude from the questioning any person who may be adverse in interest to the inquiry;

(d) use any data storage, processing or retrieval device or system used in carrying on business in the place in order to produce a document in readable form;

(e) take measurements or record by any means the physical dimensions of a place;

(f) take photographs, video recordings or other visual or audio recordings of the interior or exterior of a place; and

(g) require that a place or part thereof not be disturbed for a reasonable period of time for the purposes of carrying out an examination, inquiry or test.

Written demand

(8) A demand that a document or thing be produced must be in writing and must include a statement of the nature of the document or thing required.

Assistance

(9) A person conducting an inquiry may be accompanied by any person who has special, expert or professional knowledge and who may be of assistance in carrying out the inquiry.

Use of force prohibited

(10) A person conducting an inquiry shall not use force to enter and search premises under this section.

Obligation to produce and assist

(11) A person who is requested to produce a document or thing under clause (7)(a) shall produce it and shall, on request by the person conducting the inquiry, provide any assistance that is reasonably necessary, including assistance in using any data storage, processing or retrieval device or system, to produce a document in readable form.

Return of removed things

(12) A person conducting an inquiry who removes any document or thing from a place under clause (7)(b) shall,

(a) make it available to the person from whom it was removed, on request, at a time and place convenient for both that person and the person conducting the inquiry; and

(b) return it to the person from whom it was removed within a reasonable time.

Admissibility of copies

(13) A copy of a document certified by a person conducting an inquiry to be a true copy of the original is admissible in evidence to the same extent as the original and has the same evidentiary value.

Obstruction

(14) No person shall obstruct or interfere with a person conducting an inquiry under this section.

Search warrant

31.1(1) The Commission may authorize a person to apply to a justice of the peace for a warrant to enter a place and conduct a search of the place if,

(a) a person conducting an inquiry under section 31 has been denied entry to any place or asked to leave a place before concluding a search;

(b) a person conducting an inquiry under section 31 made a request for documents or things and the request was refused; or

(c) an inquiry under section 31 is otherwise obstructed or prevented.

Same

(2) Upon application by a person authorized under subsection (1) to do so, a justice of the peace may issue a warrant under this section if he or she is satisfied on information under oath or affirmation that the warrant is necessary for the purposes of carrying out the inquiry under section 31.

Powers

(3) A warrant obtained under subsection (2) may authorize a person named in the warrant, upon producing proof of his or her appointment,

(a) to enter any place specified in the warrant, including a dwelling; and

(b) to do any of the things specified in the warrant.

Conditions on search warrant

(4) A warrant obtained under subsection (2) shall contain such conditions as the justice of the peace considers advisable to ensure that any search authorized by the warrant is reasonable in the circumstances.

Time of execution

(5) An entry under a warrant issued under this section shall be made at such reasonable times as may be specified in the warrant.

Expiry of warrant

(6) A warrant issued under this section shall name a date of expiry, which shall be no later than 15 days after the warrant is issued, but a justice of the peace may extend the date of expiry for an additional period of no more than 15 days, upon application without notice by the person named in the warrant.

Use of force

(7) The person authorized to execute the warrant may call upon police officers for assistance in executing the warrant and the person may use whatever force is reasonably necessary to execute the warrant.

Obstruction prohibited

(8) No person shall obstruct or hinder a person in the execution of a warrant issued under this section.

Application

(9) Subsections 31(11), (12) and (13) apply with necessary modifications to an inquiry carried out pursuant to a warrant issued under this section.

Evidence used in Tribunal proceedings

31.2 Despite any other Act, evidence obtained on an inquiry under section 31 or 31.1 may be received into evidence in a proceeding before the Tribunal.

Anti-Racism Secretariat

31.3(1) The Chief Commissioner directs the Anti-Racism Secretariat which shall be established in accordance with subsection (2).

Composition

(2) The Anti-Racism Secretariat shall be composed of not more than six persons appointed by the Lieutenant Governor in Council on the advice of the Chief Commissioner.

Remuneration

(3) The Lieutenant Governor in Council may fix the remuneration and allowance for expenses of the members of the Anti-Racism Secretariat.

Functions of the Secretariat

(4) At the direction of the Chief Commissioner, the Anti-Racism Secretariat shall,

   (a) undertake, direct and encourage research into discriminatory practices that infringe rights under Part I on the basis of racism or a related ground and make recommendations to the Commission designed to prevent and eliminate such discriminatory practices;

   (b) facilitate the development and provision of programs of public information and education relating to the elimination of racism; and

   (c) undertake such tasks and responsibilities as may be assigned by the Chief Commissioner.

Disability Rights Secretariat

31.4(1) The Chief Commissioner directs the Disability Rights Secretariat which shall be established in accordance with subsection (2).

Composition

(2) The Disability Rights Secretariat shall be composed of not more than six persons appointed by the Lieutenant Governor in Council on the advice of the Chief Commissioner.

Remuneration

(3) The Lieutenant Governor in Council may fix the remuneration and allowance for expenses of the members of the Disability Rights Secretariat.

Functions of the Secretariat

(4) At the direction of the Chief Commissioner, the Disability Rights Secretariat shall,

(a) undertake, direct and encourage research into discriminatory practices that infringe rights under Part I on the basis of disability and make recommendations to the Commission designed to prevent and eliminate such discriminatory practices;

(b) facilitate the development and provision of programs of public information and education intended to promote the elimination of discriminatory practices that infringe rights under Part I on the basis of disability; and

(c) undertake such tasks and responsibilities as may be assigned by the Chief Commissioner.

Advisory groups

31.5 The Chief Commissioner may establish such advisory groups as he or she considers appropriate to advise the Commission about the elimination of discriminatory practices that infringe rights under this Act.

Annual report

31.6(1) Every year, the Commission shall prepare an annual report on the affairs of the Commission that occurred during the 12-month period ending on March 31 of each year.

Report to Speaker

(2) The Commission shall submit the report to the Speaker of the Assembly no later than on June 30 in each year who shall cause the report to be laid before the Assembly if it is in session or, if not, at the next session.

Copy to Minister

(3) The Commission shall give a copy of the report to the Minister at least 30 days before it is submitted to the Speaker under subsection (2).

Other reports

31.7 In addition to the annual report, the Commission may make any other reports respecting the state of human rights in Ontario and the affairs of the Commission as it considers appropriate, and may present such reports to the public or any other person it considers appropriate.

PART IV   HUMAN RIGHTS TRIBUNAL OF ONTARIO

Tribunal

32(1) The Tribunal known as the Human Rights Tribunal of Ontario in English and Tribunal des droits de la personne de l'Ontario in French is continued.

Composition

(2) The Tribunal shall be composed of such members as are appointed by the Lieutenant Governor in Council in accordance with the selection process described in subsection (3).

Selection process

(3) The selection process for the appointment of members of the Tribunal shall be a competitive process and the criteria to be applied in assessing candidates shall include the following:

1. Experience, knowledge or training with respect to human rights law and issues.
2. Aptitude for impartial adjudication.
3. Aptitude for applying the alternative adjudicative practices and procedures that may be set out in the Tribunal rules.

Remuneration

(4) The members of the Tribunal shall be paid such remuneration and allowance for expenses as are fixed by the Lieutenant Governor in Council.

Term of office

(5) A member of the Tribunal shall be appointed for such term as may be specified by the Lieutenant Governor in Council.

Chair, vice-chair

(6) The Lieutenant Governor in Council shall appoint a chair and may appoint one or more vice-chairs of the Tribunal from among the members of the Tribunal.

Alternate chair

(7) The Lieutenant Governor in Council shall designate one of the vice-chairs to be the alternate chair.

Same

(8) If the chair is unable to act, the alternate chair shall perform the duties of the chair and, for this purpose, has all the powers of the chair.

Employees

(9) The Tribunal may appoint such employees as it considers necessary for the proper conduct of its affairs and the employees shall be appointed under Part III of the *Public Service of Ontario Act, 2006.*

Evidence obtained in course of proceeding

(10) A member or employee of the Tribunal shall not be required to give testimony in a civil suit or any proceeding as to information obtained in the course of a proceeding before the Tribunal.

Same

(11) Despite subsection (10), an employee of the Tribunal may be required to give testimony in a proceeding before the Tribunal in the circumstances prescribed by the Tribunal rules.

Panels

33(1) The chair of the Tribunal may appoint panels composed of one or more members of the Tribunal to exercise and perform the powers and duties of the Tribunal.

Person designated to preside over panel

(2) If a panel of the Tribunal holds a hearing, the chair of the Tribunal shall designate one member of the panel to preside over the hearing.

Reassignment of panel

(3) If a panel of the Tribunal is unable for any reason to exercise or perform the powers or duties of the Tribunal, the chair of the Tribunal may assign another panel in its place.

Application by person

34(1) If a person believes that any of his or her rights under Part I have been infringed, the person may apply to the Tribunal for an order under section 45.2,

     (a) within one year after the incident to which the application relates; or

     (b) if there was a series of incidents, within one year after the last incident in the series.

Late applications

(2) A person may apply under subsection (1) after the expiry of the time limit under that subsection if the Tribunal is satisfied that the delay was incurred in good faith and no substantial prejudice will result to any person affected by the delay.

Form

(3) An application under subsection (1) shall be in a form approved by the Tribunal.

Two or more persons

(4) Two or more persons who are each entitled to make an application under subsection (1) may file the applications jointly, subject to any provision in the Tribunal rules that authorizes the Tribunal to direct that one or more of the applications be considered in a separate proceeding.

Application on behalf of another

(5) A person or organization, other than the Commission, may apply on behalf of another person to the Tribunal for an order under section 45.2 if the other person,

> (a) would have been entitled to bring an application under subsection (1); and
>
> (b) consents to the application.

Participation in proceedings

(6) If a person or organization makes an application on behalf of another person, the person or organization may participate in the proceeding in accordance with the Tribunal rules.

Consent form

(7) A consent under clause (5)(b) shall be in a form specified in the Tribunal rules.

Time of application

(8) An application under subsection (5) shall be made within the time period required for making an application under subsection (1).

Application

(9) Subsections (2) and (3) apply to an application made under subsection (5).

Withdrawal of application

(10) An application under subsection (5) may be withdrawn by the person on behalf of whom the application is made in accordance with the Tribunal rules.

Where application barred

(11) A person who believes that one of his or her rights under Part I has been infringed may not make an application under subsection (1) with respect to that right if,

> (a) a civil proceeding has been commenced in a court in which the person is seeking an order under section 46.1 with respect to the alleged infringement and the proceeding has not been finally determined or withdrawn; or
>
> (b) a court has finally determined the issue of whether the right has been infringed or the matter has been settled.

Final determination

(12) For the purpose of subsection (11), a proceeding or issue has not been finally determined if a right of appeal exists and the time for appealing has not expired.

Application by Commission

35(1) The Commission may apply to the Tribunal for an order under section 45.3 if the Commission is of the opinion that,

> (a) it is in the public interest to make an application; and
>
> (b) an order under section 45.3 could provide an appropriate remedy.

Form

(2) An application under subsection (1) shall be in a form approved by the Tribunal.

Effect of application

(3) An application made by the Commission does not affect the right of a person to make an application under section 34 in respect of the same matter.

Applications dealt with together

(4) If a person or organization makes an application under section 34 and the Commission makes an application under this section in respect of the same matter, the two applications shall be dealt with together in the same proceeding unless the Tribunal determines otherwise.

Parties

36. The parties to an application under section 34 or 35 are the following:
    1. In the case of an application under subsection 34(1), the person who made the application.
    2. In the case of an application under subsection 34(5), the person on behalf of whom the application is made.
    3. In the case of an application under section 35, the Commission.
    4. Any person against whom an order is sought in the application.
    5. Any other person or the Commission, if they are added as a party by the Tribunal.

Intervention by Commission

37(1) The Commission may intervene in an application under section 34 on such terms as the Tribunal may determine having regard to the role and mandate of the Commission under this Act.

Intervention as a party

(2) The Commission may intervene as a party to an application under section 34 if the person or organization who made the application consents to the intervention as a party.

Disclosure of information to Commission

38. Despite anything in the *Freedom of Information and Protection of Privacy Act*, at the request of the Commission, the Tribunal shall disclose to the Commission copies of applications and responses filed with the Tribunal and may disclose to the Commission other documents in its custody or in its control.

Powers of Tribunal

39. The Tribunal has the jurisdiction to exercise the powers conferred on it by or under this Act and to determine all questions of fact or law that arise in any application before it.

Disposition of applications

40. The Tribunal shall dispose of applications made under this Part by adopting the procedures and practices provided for in its rules or otherwise available to the Tribunal which, in its opinion, offer the best opportunity for a fair, just and expeditious resolution of the merits of the applications.

Interpretation of Part and rules

41. This Part and the Tribunal rules shall be liberally construed to permit the Tribunal to adopt practices and procedures, including alternatives to traditional adjudicative or adversarial procedures that, in the opinion of the Tribunal, will facilitate fair, just and expeditious resolutions of the merits of the matters before it.

Statutory Powers Procedure Act

42(1) The provisions of the *Statutory Powers Procedure Act* apply to a proceeding before the Tribunal unless they conflict with a provision of this Act, the regulations or the Tribunal rules.

Conflict

(2) Despite section 32 of the *Statutory Powers Procedure Act*, this Act, the regulations and the Tribunal rules prevail over the provisions of that Act with which they conflict.

Tribunal rules

43(1) The Tribunal may make rules governing the practice and procedure before it.

Required practices and procedures

(2) The rules shall ensure that the following requirements are met with respect to any proceeding before the Tribunal:

1. An application that is within the jurisdiction of the Tribunal shall not be finally disposed of without affording the parties an opportunity to make oral submissions in accordance with the rules.
2. An application may not be finally disposed of without written reasons.

Same

(3) Without limiting the generality of subsection (1), the Tribunal rules may,

(a) provide for and require the use of hearings or of practices and procedures that are provided for under the *Statutory Powers Procedure Act* or that are alternatives to traditional adjudicative or adversarial procedures;

(b) authorize the Tribunal to,

(i) define or narrow the issues required to dispose of an application and limit the evidence and submissions of the parties on such issues, and

(ii) determine the order in which the issues and evidence in a proceeding will be presented;

    (c) authorize the Tribunal to conduct examinations in chief or cross-examinations of a witness;

    (d) prescribe the stages of its processes at which preliminary, procedural or interlocutory matters will be determined;

    (e) authorize the Tribunal to make or cause to be made such examinations of records and such other inquiries as it considers necessary in the circumstances;

    (f) authorize the Tribunal to require a party to a proceeding or another person to,

        (i) produce any document, information or thing and provide such assistance as is reasonably necessary, including using any data storage, processing or retrieval device or system, to produce the information in any form,

        (ii) provide a statement or oral or affidavit evidence, or

        (iii) in the case of a party to the proceeding, adduce evidence or produce witnesses who are reasonably within the party's control; and

    (g) govern any matter prescribed by the regulations.

General or particular

    (4) The rules may be of general or particular application.

Consistency

    (5) The rules shall be consistent with this Part.

Not a regulation

    (6) The rules made under this section are not regulations for the purposes of Part III of the *Legislation Act, 2006.*

Public consultations

    (7) The Tribunal shall hold public consultations before making a rule under this section.

Failure to comply with rules

    (8) Failure on the part of the Tribunal to comply with the practices and procedures required by the rules or the exercise of a discretion under the rules by the Tribunal in a particular manner is not a ground for setting aside a decision of the Tribunal on an application for judicial review or any other form of relief, unless the failure or the exercise of a discretion caused a substantial wrong which affected the final disposition of the matter.

Adverse inference

    (9) The Tribunal may draw an adverse inference from the failure of a party to comply, in whole or in part, with an order of the Tribunal for the party to do anything under a rule made under clause (3)(f).

Tribunal inquiry

44(1) At the request of a party to an application under this Part, the Tribunal may appoint a person to conduct an inquiry under this section if the Tribunal is satisfied that,

(a) an inquiry is required in order to obtain evidence;

(b) the evidence obtained may assist in achieving a fair, just and expeditious resolution of the merits of the application; and

(c) it is appropriate to do so in the circumstances.

Production of certificate

(2) A person conducting an inquiry under this section shall produce proof of their appointment upon request.

Entry

(3) A person conducting an inquiry under this section may, without warrant, enter any lands or any building, structure or premises where the person has reason to believe there may be evidence relevant to the application.

Time of entry

(4) The power to enter a place under subsection (3) may be exercised only during the place's regular business hours or, if it does not have regular business hours, during daylight hours.

Dwellings

(5) A person conducting an inquiry shall not enter into a place or part of a place that is a dwelling without the consent of the occupant.

Powers on inquiry

(6) A person conducting an inquiry may,

(a) request the production for inspection and examination of documents or things that are or may be relevant to the inquiry;

(b) upon giving a receipt for it, remove from a place documents produced in response to a request under clause (a) for the purpose of making copies or extracts;

(c) question a person on matters that are or may be relevant to the inquiry, subject to the person's right to have counsel or a personal representative present during such questioning and exclude from the questioning any person who may be adverse in interest to the inquiry;

(d) use any data storage, processing or retrieval device or system used in carrying on business in the place in order to produce a document in readable form;

(e) take measurements or record by any means the physical dimensions of a place;

(f) take photographs, video recordings or other visual or audio recordings of the interior or exterior of a place; and

(g) require that a place or part thereof not be disturbed for a reasonable period of time for the purposes of carrying out an examination, inquiry or test.

Written demand

(7) A demand that a document or thing be produced must be in writing and must include a statement of the nature of the document or thing required.

Assistance

(8) A person conducting an inquiry may be accompanied by any person who has special, expert or professional knowledge and who may be of assistance in carrying out the inquiry.

Use of force prohibited

(9) A person conducting an inquiry shall not use force to enter and search premises under this section.

Obligation to produce and assist

(10) A person who is requested to produce a document or thing under clause (6)(a) shall produce it and shall, on request by the person conducting the inquiry, provide any assistance that is reasonably necessary, including assistance in using any data storage, processing or retrieval device or system, to produce a document in readable form.

Return of removed things

(11) A person conducting an inquiry who removes any document or thing from a place under clause (6)(b) shall,

(a) make it available to the person from whom it was removed, on request, at a time and place convenient for both that person and the person conducting the inquiry; and

(b) return it to the person from whom it was removed within a reasonable time.

Admissibility of copies

(12) A copy of a document certified by a person conducting an inquiry to be a true copy of the original is admissible in evidence to the same extent as the original and has the same evidentiary value.

Obstruction

(13) No person shall obstruct or interfere with a person conducting an inquiry under this section.

Inquiry report

(14) A person conducting an inquiry shall prepare a report and submit it to the Tribunal and the parties to the application that gave rise to the inquiry in accordance with the Tribunal rules.

Transfer of inquiry to Commission

(15) The Commission may, at the request of the Tribunal, appoint a person to conduct an inquiry under this section and the person so appointed has all of the powers of a person appointed by the Tribunal under this section and shall report to the Tribunal in accordance with subsection (14).

Deferral of application

45. The Tribunal may defer an application in accordance with the Tribunal rules.

Dismissal in accordance with rules

45.1 The Tribunal may dismiss an application, in whole or in part, in accordance with its rules if the Tribunal is of the opinion that another proceeding has appropriately dealt with the substance of the application.

Orders of Tribunal: applications under s. 34

45.2(1) On an application under section 34, the Tribunal may make one or more of the following orders if the Tribunal determines that a party to the application has infringed a right under Part I of another party to the application:

1. An order directing the party who infringed the right to pay monetary compensation to the party whose right was infringed for loss arising out of the infringement, including compensation for injury to dignity, feelings and self-respect.

2. An order directing the party who infringed the right to make restitution to the party whose right was infringed, other than through monetary compensation, for loss arising out of the infringement, including restitution for injury to dignity, feelings and self-respect.

3. An order directing any party to the application to do anything that, in the opinion of the Tribunal, the party ought to do to promote compliance with this Act.

Orders under par. 3 of subs. (1)

(2) For greater certainty, an order under paragraph 3 of subsection (1),

(a) may direct a person to do anything with respect to future practices; and

(b) may be made even if no order under that paragraph was requested.

Orders of Tribunal: applications under s. 35

45.3(1) If, on an application under section 35, the Tribunal determines that any one or more of the parties to the application have infringed a right under Part I, the Tribunal may make an order directing any party to the application to do anything that, in the opinion of the Tribunal, the party ought to do to promote compliance with this Act.

Same

(2) For greater certainty, an order under subsection (1) may direct a person to do anything with respect to future practices.

Matters referred to Commission

45.4(1) The Tribunal may refer any matters arising out of a proceeding before it to the Commission if, in the Tribunal's opinion, they are matters of public interest or are otherwise of interest to the Commission.

Same

(2) The Commission may, in its discretion, decide whether to deal with a matter referred to it by the Tribunal.

Documents published by Commission

45.5(1) In a proceeding under this Part, the Tribunal may consider policies approved by the Commission under section 30.

Same

(2) Despite subsection (1), the Tribunal shall consider a policy approved by the Commission under section 30 in a proceeding under this Part if a party to the proceeding or an intervenor requests that it do so.

Stated case to Divisional court

45.6(1) If the Tribunal makes a final decision or order in a proceeding in which the Commission was a party or an intervenor, and the Commission believes that the decision or order is not consistent with a policy that has been approved by the Commission under section 30, the Commission may apply to the Tribunal to have the Tribunal state a case to the Divisional Court.

Same

(2) If the Tribunal determines that the application of the Commission relates to a question of law and that it is appropriate to do so, it may state the case in writing for the opinion of the Divisional Court upon the question of law.

Parties

(3) The parties to a stated case under this section are the parties to the proceeding referred to in subsection (1) and, if the Commission was an intervenor in that proceeding, the Commission.

Submissions by Tribunal

(4) The Divisional Court may hear submissions from the Tribunal.

Powers of Divisional Court

(5) The Divisional Court shall hear and determine the stated case.

No stay

(6) Unless otherwise ordered by the Tribunal or the Divisional Court, an application by the Commission under subsection (1) or the stating of a case to the Divisional Court under subsection (2) does not operate as a stay of the final decision or order of the Tribunal.

Reconsideration of Tribunal decision

(7) Within 30 days of receipt of the decision of the Divisional Court, any party to the stated case proceeding may apply to the Tribunal for a reconsideration of its original decision or order in accordance with section 45.7.

Reconsideration of Tribunal decision

45.7(1) Any party to a proceeding before the Tribunal may request that the Tribunal reconsider its decision in accordance with the Tribunal rules.

Same

(2) Upon request under subsection (1) or on its own motion, the Tribunal may reconsider its decision in accordance with its rules.

Decisions final

45.8 Subject to section 45.6 of this Act, section 21.1 of the *Statutory Powers Procedure Act* and the Tribunal rules, a decision of the Tribunal is final and not subject to appeal and shall not be altered or set aside in an application for judicial review or in any other proceeding unless the decision is patently unreasonable.

Settlements

45.9(1) If a settlement of an application made under section 34 or 35 is agreed to in writing and signed by the parties, the settlement is binding on the parties.

Consent order

(2) If a settlement of an application made under section 34 or 35 is agreed to in writing and signed by the parties, the Tribunal may, on the joint motion of the parties, make an order requiring compliance with the settlement or any part of the settlement.

Application where contravention

(3) If a settlement of an application made under section 34 or 35 is agreed to in writing and signed by the parties, a party who believes that another party has contravened the settlement may make an application to the Tribunal for an order under subsection (8),

>   (a) within six months after the contravention to which the application relates; or
>
>   (b) if there was a series of contraventions, within six months after the last contravention in the series.

Late applications

(4) A person may apply under subsection (3) after the expiry of the time limit under that subsection if the Tribunal is satisfied that the delay was incurred in good faith and no substantial prejudice will result to any person affected by the delay.

Form of application

(5) An application under subsection (3) shall be in a form approved by the Tribunal.

Parties

(6) Subject to the Tribunal rules, the parties to an application under subsection (3) are the following:

>   1. The parties to the settlement.
>   2. Any other person or the Commission, if they are added as a party by the Tribunal.

Intervention by Commission

(7) Section 37 applies with necessary modifications to an application under subsection (3).

Order

(8) If, on an application under subsection (3), the Tribunal determines that a party has contravened the settlement, the Tribunal may make any order that it considers appropriate to remedy the contravention.

Annual report

45.10(1) The Tribunal shall make a report to the Minister not later than June 30 in each year upon the affairs of the Tribunal during the year ending on March 31 of that year.

Report laid in Assembly

(2) The Minister shall submit the report to the Lieutenant Governor in Council who shall cause the report to be laid before the Assembly if it is in session or, if not, at the next session.

PART IV.1   HUMAN RIGHTS LEGAL SUPPORT CENTRE

Centre established

45.11(1) A corporation without share capital is established under the name Human Rights Legal Support Centre in English and Centre d'assistance juridique en matière de droits de la personne in French.

Membership

(2) The members of the Centre shall consist of its board of directors.

Not a Crown agency

(3) The Centre is not an agent of Her Majesty nor a Crown agent for the purposes of the *Crown Agency Act*.

Powers of natural person

(4) The Centre has the capacity and the rights, powers and privileges of a natural person, subject to the limitations set out in this Act or the regulations.

Independent from but accountable to Ontario

(5) The Centre shall be independent from, but accountable to, the Government of Ontario as set out in this Act.

Objects

45.12 The objects of the Centre are,

(a) to establish and administer a cost-effective and efficient system for providing support services, including legal services, respecting applications to the Tribunal under Part IV;

(b) to establish policies and priorities for the provision of support services based on its financial resources.

Provision of support services

45.13(1) The Centre shall provide the following support services:

1. Advice and assistance, legal and otherwise, respecting the infringement of rights under Part I.
2. Legal services in relation to,
   i.   the making of applications to the Tribunal under Part IV,
   ii. proceedings before the Tribunal under Part IV,
   iii. applications for judicial review arising from Tribunal proceedings,
   iv. stated case proceedings,
   v.   the enforcement of Tribunal orders.
3. Such other services as may be prescribed by regulation.

Availability of services

(2) The Centre shall ensure that the support services are available throughout the Province, using such methods of delivering the services as the Centre believes are appropriate.

Board of directors

45.14(1) The affairs of the Centre shall be governed and managed by its board of directors.

Composition and appointment

(2) The board of directors of the Centre shall consist of no fewer than five and no more than nine members appointed by the Lieutenant Governor in Council in accordance with the regulations.

Appointment of Chair

(3) A Chair designated by the Lieutenant Governor in Council will preside at meetings.

Remuneration

(4) The board of directors may be remunerated as determined by the Lieutenant Governor in Council.

Duties

(5) The board of directors of the Centre shall be responsible for furthering the objects of the Centre.

Delegation

(6) The board of directors may delegate any power or duty to any committee, to any member of a committee or to any officer or employee of the Centre.

Same

(7) A delegation shall be in writing and shall be on the terms and subject to the limitations, conditions or requirements specified in it.

Board to act responsibly

(8) The board of directors shall act in a financially responsible and accountable manner in exercising its powers and performing its duties.

Standard of care

(9) Members of the board of directors shall act in good faith with a view to the objects of the Centre and shall exercise the care, diligence and skill of a reasonably prudent person.

Government funding

45.15(1) The Centre shall submit its annual budget to the Minister for approval every year in a manner and form, and at a time, specified in the regulations.

Approved budget included in estimates

(2) If approved by the Minister, the annual budget shall be submitted to Cabinet to be reviewed for inclusion in the estimates of the Ministry.

Appropriation by Legislature

(3) The money required for the purposes of this Act shall be paid out of such money as is appropriated therefor by the Legislature.

Centre's money not part of Consolidated Revenue Fund

45.16 The Centre's money and investments do not form part of the Consolidated Revenue Fund and shall be used by the Centre in carrying out its objects.

Annual report

45.17(1) The Centre shall submit an annual report to the Minister within four months after the end of its fiscal year.

Fiscal year

(2) The fiscal year of the Centre shall be from April 1 to March 31 of the following year.

Audit

45.18(1) The Centre must ensure that its books of financial account are audited annually in accordance with generally accepted accounting principles and a copy of the audit is given to the Minister.

Audit by Minister

(2) The Minister has the right to audit the Centre at any time that the Minister chooses.

PART V   GENERAL

Definitions, general

46. In this Act,

"Commission" means the Ontario Human Rights Commission;

"Minister" means the member of the Executive Council to whom the powers and duties of the Minister under this Act are assigned by the Lieutenant Governor in Council;

"person" in addition to the extended meaning given it by Part VI (Interpretation) of the *Legislation Act, 2006*, includes an employment agency, an employers' organization, an unincorporated association, a trade or occupational association, a trade union, a partnership, a municipality, a board of police commissioners established under the *Police Act*, being chapter 381 of the Revised Statutes of Ontario, 1980, and a police services board established under the *Police Services Act*;

"regulations" means the regulations made under this Act;

"Tribunal" means the Human Rights Tribunal of Ontario continued under section 32;

"Tribunal rules" means the rules governing practice and procedure that are made by the Tribunal under section 43.

Civil remedy

46.1(1) If, in a civil proceeding in a court, the court finds that a party to the proceeding has infringed a right under Part I of another party to the proceeding, the court may make either of the following orders, or both:

1. An order directing the party who infringed the right to pay monetary compensation to the party whose right was infringed for loss arising out of the infringement, including compensation for injury to dignity, feelings and self-respect.
2. An order directing the party who infringed the right to make restitution to the party whose right was infringed, other than through monetary compensation, for loss arising out of the infringement, including restitution for injury to dignity, feelings and self-respect.

Same

(2) Subsection (1) does not permit a person to commence an action based solely on an infringement of a right under Part I.

Penalty

46.2(1) Every person who contravenes section 9 or subsection 31(14), 31.1(8) or 44(13) or an order of the Tribunal is guilty of an offence and on conviction is liable to a fine of not more than $25,000.

Consent to prosecution

(2) No prosecution for an offence under this Act shall be instituted except with the consent in writing of the Attorney General.

Acts of officers, etc.

46.3(1) For the purposes of this Act, except subsection 2(2), subsection 5(2), section 7 and subsection 46.2(1), any act or thing done or omitted to be done in the course of his or her employment by an officer, official, employee or agent of a corporation, trade union, trade or occupational association, unincorporated association or employers' organization shall be deemed to be an act or thing done or omitted to be done by the corporation, trade union, trade or occupational association, unincorporated association or employers' organization.

Opinion re authority or acquiescence

(2) At the request of a corporation, trade union, trade or occupational association, unincorporated association or employers' organization, the Tribunal in its decision shall make known whether or not, in its opinion, an act or thing done or omitted to be done by an officer, official, employee or agent was done or omitted to be done with or without the authority or acquiescence of the corporation, trade union, trade or occupational association, unincorporated association or employers' organization, and the opinion does not affect the application of subsection (1).

Act binds Crown

47(1) This Act binds the Crown and every agency of the Crown.

Act has primacy over other Acts

(2) Where a provision in an Act or regulation purports to require or authorize conduct that is a contravention of Part I, this Act applies and prevails unless the Act or regulation specifically provides that it is to apply despite this Act.

Regulations

48(1) The Lieutenant Governor in Council may make regulations,

(a) prescribing standards for assessing what is undue hardship for the purposes of section 11, 17 or 24;

(a.1) prescribing the manner in which income information, credit checks, credit references, rental history, guarantees or other similar business practices may be used by a landlord in selecting prospective tenants without infringing section 2, and prescribing other similar business practices and the manner of their use, for the purposes of subsection 21(3);

(b) prescribing matters for the purposes of clause 43(3)(g);

(c) respecting the Human Rights Legal Support Centre;

(d) governing any matter that is necessary or advisable for the effective enforcement and administration of this Act.

(e) REPEALED.

Human Rights Legal Support Centre

(2) A regulation made under clause (1)(c) may,

(a) further define the Centre's constitution, management and structure as set out in Part IV.1;

(b) prescribe powers and duties of the Centre and its members;

(c) provide for limitations on the Centre's powers under subsection 45.11(4);

(d) prescribe services for the purposes of paragraph 3 of subsection 45.13(1);

(e) further define the nature and scope of support services referred to in subsection 45.13(1);

(f) provide for factors to be considered in appointing members and specify the circumstances and manner in which they are to be considered;

(g) provide for the term of appointment and reappointment of the Centre's members;

(h) provide for the nature and scope of the annual report required under section 45.17;

(i) provide for reporting requirements in addition to the annual report;

(j) provide for personal information to be collected by or on behalf of the Centre other than directly from the individual to whom the information relates, and for the manner in which the information is collected;

(k) provide for the transfer from specified persons or entities of information, including personal information, that is relevant to carrying out the functions of the Centre;

(l) provide for rules governing the confidentiality and security of information, including personal information, the collection, use and disclosure of such information, the retention and disposal of such information, and access to and correction of such information, including restrictions on any of these things, for the purposes of the carrying out of the functions of the Centre;

(m) specify requirements and conditions for the funding of the Centre and for the Centre's budget;

(n) provide for audits of the statements and records of the Centre;

(o) determine whether or not the *Business Corporations Act*, the *Corporations Information Act* or the *Corporations Act* or any provisions of those Acts apply to the Centre;

(p) provide for anything necessary or advisable for the purposes of Part IV.1.

PART VI   TRANSITIONAL PROVISIONS

Definitions

49. In this Part,

"effective date" means the day sections 4 and 5 of the *Human Rights Code Amendment Act, 2006* come into force;

"new Part IV" means Part IV as it reads on and after the effective date;

"old Part IV" means Part IV as it reads before the effective date.

Orders respecting special programs

50. On the fifth anniversary of the effective date, all orders that were made by the Commission under subsection 14(2) before the effective date shall be null and void.

Application of s. 32(3)

51. Subsection 32(3) applies to the selection and appointment of persons to the Tribunal on or after the day section 10 of the *Human Rights Code Amendment Act, 2006* comes into force.

Tribunal powers before effective date

52(1) Despite anything to the contrary in the old Part IV, the Tribunal may, before the effective date,

(a) make rules in accordance with the new Part IV, including rules with respect to the reconsideration of Tribunal decisions; and

(b) when dealing with complaints that are referred to it under section 36 of the old Part IV,

(i) deal with the complaint in accordance with the practices and procedures set out in the rules made under clause (a),

(ii) exercise the powers described in section 39 of the new Part IV, and

(iii) dispose of the complaint in accordance with section 40 of the new Part IV.

Application

(2) Sections 41 and 42 of the new Part IV apply to rules made under clause (1)(a).

Tribunal decisions made before effective date

(3) Despite anything in the old Part IV, the following applies before the effective date with respect to a complaint that is referred to the Tribunal by the Commission under section 36 of the old Part IV on or after the day section 10 of the *Human Rights Code Amendment Act, 2006* comes into force:

1. Section 42 of the old Part IV does not apply to a decision of the Tribunal made with respect to the complaint.

2. Sections 45.7 and 45.8 of the new Part IV apply to a decision of the Tribunal made with respect to the complaint.

Complaints before Commission on effective date

53(1) This section applies to a complaint filed with the Commission under subsection 32(1) of the old Part IV or initiated by the Commission under subsection 32(2) of the old Part IV before the effective date.

Commission powers continued for six months

(2) Subject to subsection (3) and despite the repeal of the old Part IV, during the six-month period that begins on the effective date, the Commission shall continue to deal with complaints referred to in subsection (1) in accordance with subsection 32(3) and sections 33, 34, 36, 37 and 43 of the old Part IV and, for that purpose,

(a) the Commission has all the powers described in subsection 32(3) and sections 33, 34, 36, 37 and 43 of the old Part IV; and

(b) the provisions referred to in clause (a) continue to apply with respect to the complaints, with necessary modifications.

Applications to Tribunal during six-month period

(3) Subject to subsection (4), at any time during the six-month period referred to in subsection (2), the person who made a complaint that is continued under that subsection may, in accordance with the Tribunal rules, elect to abandon the complaint and make an application to the Tribunal with respect to the subject-matter of the complaint.

Expedited process

(4) The Tribunal shall make rules with respect to the practices and procedures that apply to an application under subsection (3) in order to ensure that the applications are dealt with in an expeditious manner.

Applications to Tribunal after six-month period

(5) If, after the end of the six-month period referred to in subsection (2), the Commission has failed to deal with the merits of a complaint continued under that subsection and the complaint has not been withdrawn or settled, the complainant may make an application to the Tribunal with respect to the subject-matter of the complaint within a further six-month period after the end of the earlier six-month period.

New Part IV applies

(6) The new Part IV applies to an application made under subsections (3) and (5).

Disclosure of information

(7) Despite anything in the *Freedom of Information and Protection of Privacy Act*, at the request of a party to an application under subsection (3) or (5), the Commission may disclose to the party any information obtained by the Commission in the course of an investigation.

Application barred

(8) No application, other than an application under subsection (3) or (5), may be made to the Tribunal if the subject-matter of the application is the same or substantially the same as the subject-matter of a complaint that was filed with the Commission under the old Part IV.

Settlements effected by Commission

54. Section 45.9 of the new Part IV applies to the enforcement of a settlement that,
   (a) was effected by the Commission under the old Part IV before the effective date or during the six-month period referred to in subsection 53(2); and
   (b) was agreed to in writing, signed by the parties and approved by the Commission.

Where complaints referred to Tribunal

55(1) This section applies to complaints that are referred to the Tribunal by the Commission under section 36 of the old Part IV before the effective date or during the six-month period referred to in subsection 53(2).

New Part IV applies

(2) On and after the effective date, the new Part IV applies to a complaint described in subsection (1) as though it were an application made to the Tribunal under that Part and the Tribunal shall deal with the complaint in accordance with the new Part IV.

Parties

(3) The Commission,

(a) shall continue to be a party to a complaint that was referred to the Tribunal before the effective date; and

(b) subject to subsection (4), shall not be a party to a complaint referred to the Tribunal during the six-month period referred to in subsection 53(2).

Same, exceptions

(4) The Commission shall continue as a party to a complaint that was referred to the Tribunal during the six-month period referred to in subsection 53(2) if,

(a) the complaint was initiated by the Commission under subsection 32(2) of the old Part IV; or

(b) the Tribunal sets a date for the parties to appear before the Tribunal before the end of the six-month period.

Same

(5) Nothing in subsection (3) shall prevent,

(a) the Tribunal from adding the Commission as a party to a proceeding under section 36 of the new Part IV; or

(b) the Commission from intervening in a proceeding with respect to a complaint described in subsection (1).

Regulations, transitional matters

56(1) The Lieutenant Governor in Council may make regulations providing for transitional matters which, in the opinion of the Lieutenant Governor in Council, are necessary or desirable to facilitate the implementation of the *Human Rights Code Amendment Act, 2006.*

Same

(2) Without limiting the generality of subsection (1), the Lieutenant Governor in Council may make regulations,

(a) providing for transitional matters relating to the changes to the administration and functions of the Commission;

(b) dealing with any problems or issues arising as a result of the repeal or enactment of a provision of this Act by the *Human Rights Code Amendment Act, 2006.*

Same

(3) A regulation under this section may be general or specific in its application.

Conflicts

(4) If there is a conflict between a provision in a regulation under this section and any provision of this Act or of any other regulation made under this Act, the regulation under this section prevails.

Review

57(1) Three years after the effective date, the Minister shall appoint a person who shall undertake a review of the implementation and effectiveness of the changes resulting from the enactment of that Act.

Public consultations

(2) In conducting a review under this section, the person appointed under subsection (1) shall hold public consultations.

Report to Minister

(3) The person appointed under subsection (1) shall prepare a report on his or her findings and submit the report to the Minister within one year of his or her appointment.

Glossary

accommodation a human rights concept that refers to making changes that allow a person or group protected by the *Human Rights Code* to participate in the workplace; most often required with respect to disability, creed, and pregnancy; for example, accommodating a blind employee could involve providing a voice synthesizer on a computer

administrative agency a body created by a statute to administer that statute; administrative agencies are empowered to investigate complaints, make rulings, and sometimes issue orders

administrative tribunal a quasi-judicial authority whose rules are typically governed by a subject-specific statute

adverse impact discrimination unintentional discrimination that has an adverse effect on members of certain groups (also known as constructive discrimination)

affirmative action a policy designed to increase the representation of groups that have suffered discrimination

agent a party who has the capacity to bind another party in contracting with others

aggravated damages damages awarded to compensate a party for non-monetary losses intentionally or maliciously caused by the other party's conduct

agreements to vary agreements between employers and employees to vary from legislated minimum employment standards with respect to daily and weekly maximum hours of work, overtime hours and pay, and vacation time

appellant the party appealing from a previous decision of a lower court or tribunal

application a claim of a human rights violation

arbitrator a person who decides disputes on the basis of evidence submitted by the parties

attestation clause a clause on a job application form that states that the information provided is true and complete to the applicant's knowledge and that a false statement may disqualify the applicant from employment or be grounds for dismissal

bad faith improper motivation

balance of probabilities the degree of proof required in civil law cases wherein a proposition is established as fact if it is shown that the proposition is more likely than not to be true

bargaining unit a group of the employer's employees whom the trade union is entitled to represent

binding requiring a lower court to follow a precedent from a higher court in the same jurisdiction (see also *stare decisis*)

bona fide in good faith

bona fide occupational qualification (BFOQ) or requirement (BFOR) a reasonably necessary qualification or requirement imposed in a sincere belief that it is related to job performance

bumping rights on a layoff, the right of employees with greater seniority to displace more junior employees

case citation a reference for locating a specific case that includes style of cause (case title), year, volume number, series number (where applicable), page of the case report in which it appears, and court

case law law made by judges, rather than legislatures, that is usually based on the previous decisions of other judges

cause of action the factual basis on which a legal claim can be made

certify in a class action claim, have a civil court judge decide that there are common issues of law or fact involved, a representative plaintiff will adequately represent the class, and a class action is the preferred proceeding

civil law law that relates to private, non-criminal matters, such as property law, family law, and tort law; alternatively, law that evolved from Roman law, not English common law, and that is used in certain jurisdictions, such as Quebec

collective agreement a written agreement between an employer and its employees' bargaining agent that contains the terms and conditions of employment

common law law made by judges, rather than legislatures, that is usually based on the previous decisions of other judges

conditional offer of employment a job offer that is subject to certain requirements being met

condonation implied acceptance by one party of the conduct of another party; once misconduct is condoned, an employer cannot dismiss an employee for that misconduct without any new misconduct

consideration a mutual exchange of promises required, along with an offer and an acceptance, to create an enforceable contract; for example, in an employment contract, consideration is a promise of payment in exchange for a promise to perform the work

constitutional law in Canada, a body of written and unwritten laws that set out how the country will be governed, including the distribution of powers between the federal government and the provinces

constructive discrimination unintentional discrimination that has an adverse effect on members of certain groups

constructive dismissal fundamental breach by an employer of an employment contract that entitles an employee to consider herself dismissed and to sue the employer for wrongful dismissal

contextual approach the increasing tendency of courts to view employee misconduct within the overall context of the employment relationship, including length of service and work and disciplinary record, in determining whether the employer had just cause for dismissal

contra proferentem a doctrine for interpreting contracts; where the terms of a contract can bear two or more meanings, the ambiguity is interpreted against the party who drafted it

contract law an area of civil law that governs agreements between people or companies to purchase or provide goods or services

contributory negligence a common law defence in an action arising from negligence in which it is asserted that the plaintiff's own negligence directly caused or contributed to the injuries suffered

costs compensation for legal fees and expenses that the other party in a lawsuit is entitled to recover

co-worker negligence a common law defence in an action arising from negligence in which it is asserted that the plaintiff's injuries were caused by the negligence of the plaintiff's co-worker, not the employer

Crown a lawyer employed by the state to prosecute a criminal offence; also refers to the government

damages losses suffered as a result of the other party's actions

defamation something that tends to harm a person's reputation, either through slander (things said) or libel (things written)

defendant in civil law, the party against which an action is brought

discrimination treating a person or group differently or negatively, based on a prohibited ground of discrimination under the *Human Rights Code*

dismissal for cause dismissal without notice or pay in lieu of notice, based on just cause

distinguishable term used for a precedent from a higher court that a lower court decides not to follow, usually because the facts in the case differ

due diligence defence the onus on a party in certain circumstances to establish that it took all reasonable steps to avoid a particular event

duty of care a legal obligation to take reasonable care in the circumstances

duty to mitigate the obligation to take all reasonable steps to lessen the losses suffered as a result of a breach of contract

employee an individual who is in an employment relationship with an employer

employment equity a range of measures, including affirmative action and other programs, aimed at ensuring equality in employment for certain disadvantaged groups

equal pay for equal work the legal obligation to pay male and female employees who perform substantially the same kind of work in an establishment at the same rate, unless one of the legislated exceptions applies

essential job duties the core duties and requirements of a job

fair information principles the ten principles that underlie the *Personal Information Protection and Electronic Documents Act* for proper collection, use, and disclosure of personal information

female job class generally, a job class in which 60 percent or more of the positions are held by women

fiduciary employee an employee who holds a position of trust and could significantly affect the employer's interests, and who therefore has special obligations to the employer

frustration of contract where a contract becomes impossible to perform through the fault of neither party

gender-neutral job evaluation system a system that evaluates the relative value of positions in an organization in a way that does not favour factors found in jobs typically performed by men

health and safety representative a person who exercises rights and powers similar to those of the joint health and safety committee; required in workplaces with 6 to 19 employees

implied terms where the parties to a contract did not address a particular issue, the courts may deem certain contractual provisions to be part of the agreement; for example, the obligation of an employer to provide reasonable notice of termination to an employee is an implied term unless the parties expressly agreed otherwise

independent contractor a self-employed worker engaged by a principal to perform specific work

indictable offence a more serious offence than a summary offence

internal responsibility system an approach to health and safety that is based on the belief that healthy and safe workplaces require the participation of all the workplace parties

joint health and safety committee (JHSC) an advisory health and safety body that is composed of equal numbers of management and worker representatives; generally required in workplaces with 20 or more workers

judicial review the process where a party asks a court to reconsider a decision of an administrative tribunal to ensure that, for example, it observed the rules of natural justice

just cause very serious employee misconduct or incompetence that warrants dismissal without notice

litigation legal action

lockout an employer's refusal to let unionized employees into the workplace following the expiry of a collective agreement or a failure to reach a first collective agreement, typically while the employer and union are attempting to negotiate a new collective agreement

majority decision a decision reached by a majority of the judges hearing a case where a minority of the judges disagree, in whole or in part, with that decision

male job class generally, a job class in which 70 percent or more of the positions are held by men

material change a change that would have an impact on a decision or situation

natural justice a set of rules that provide due process to individuals involved in legal actions, including the duty of courts and tribunals to act in good faith and without bias, and the rights of affected parties to be heard

near cause the principle, now rejected by the courts, that misconduct that falls short of establishing just cause may be used to reduce the amount of reasonable notice owing

negligence an act or omission that involves no intention to cause harm but that a reasonable person would anticipate might cause harm

negligent hiring failing to take reasonable care in the hiring process that results in foreseeable injury to a third party

negligent misrepresentation failing to take reasonable care in providing information that results in foreseeable injury to a third party

nepotism policies employer policies that allow an employer to discriminate in favour of, or against, specified close relatives of employees

non-unionized employee an employee whose terms and conditions of employment are based on an individual employment contract rather than a collective agreement negotiated between an employer and a union

notwithstanding clause a clause in the *Canadian Charter of Rights and Freedoms* that may be invoked by Parliament or provincial legislatures to override Charter protections

onus of proof burden of proving a case or the facts involved in a dispute

pay equity equal pay for work of equal value

personal information information about an identifiable individual (other than name, title, or business address and number) as defined under the *Personal Information Protection and Electronic Documents Act*

persuasive of a precedent from another jurisdiction or from a lower court, convincing but not binding

plaintiff in civil law, the party that brings an action

precedent a legal decision that acts as a guide in subsequent cases

prima facie on the face of it

prima facie **case** a case in which the facts alleged by the plaintiff or complainant, if true, constitute a breach of law

principal the party who contracts for the services of an independent contractor; the party who can be bound by its agent

privacy commissioner the commissioner appointed to investigate complaints of failure to comply with the requirements of the *Personal Information Protection and Electronic Documents Act*

privative clause a term in a piece of legislation that attempts to restrict the right to review a tribunal's decision by a court

probation a period of time when an employee is monitored to determine his or her suitability for a job

procedural fairness certain process rights that one party provides to another, such as an employer giving an employee an opportunity to respond to allegations against him or her

progressive discipline discipline that is imposed in a series of increasing steps

proportionality the principle that the sanction must fit the offence

punitive damages damages awarded to punish the employer for its malicious or oppressive conduct, rather than to compensate the employee

rebuttable presumption an inference that a court will draw unless the contrary is proven

recall rights the right to be called back to work after a layoff according to seniority level

regulations rules made under the authority of an enabling statute

remedial legislation law intended to right a societal wrong and provide a remedy, rather than to punish an offender

respondent the party opposing an appeal of a previous decision by a lower court or tribunal

restrictive covenant an agreement that restricts an employee's activities or conduct during or after employment; for example, a non-solicitation clause is a restrictive covenant that prevents an employee from soliciting employees or customers of an employer for a specified period of time after the end of employment

separation package pay and benefits paid by an employer to a dismissed employee

severance pay in Ontario, a one-time lump-sum payment made to a terminated employee in certain circumstances as set out in the *Employment Standards Act*

sexual harassment a course of vexatious comment or conduct (based on sex or gender identity) that is known or ought reasonably to be known to be unwelcome

solicitor–client privilege a rule of evidence that protects a client from having to divulge confidential communications with his or her lawyer made for the purpose of obtaining legal advice

special program an employer program aimed at relieving hardship or promoting the employment status of disadvantaged groups

special service organization a non-profit social, religious, or other organization that serves the interests of a group that is protected under the *Human Rights Code*

standard of care the level of diligence that one is expected is exercise

standard of review the level of scrutiny that an appeal court will apply to the decision of a lower court or tribunal

stare decisis a common law principle that requires lower courts to follow precedents emanating from higher courts in the same jurisdiction

statute law law passed by a government legislative body

strict liability offence an offence where the doing of the prohibited act is sufficient proof of the offence and the accused has the burden of proving that it took all reasonable care to avoid the offence

strike a refusal to work by a group of unionized employees following the expiry of a collective agreement or a failure to reach a first collective agreement, typically while the employer and union are attempting to negotiate a new collective agreement

summary conviction offence a less serious offence that is tried summarily

third party someone other than the employer or the employee

tort law a branch of civil law (non-criminal law) that governs wrongs for which a legal remedy is available independent of any contractual relationship

trade union an association formed for the purpose of representing a group of employees in all aspects of their employment relationship with their employer

unconscionable unreasonably harsh or unreasonably one-sided

undue hardship difficulty exceeding that which an employer is required to endure when accommodating the needs of an individual or a protected group under the *Human Rights Code*; defined in the Ontario Human Rights Commission's policy as the point when accommodation would alter the essential nature of an enterprise, substantially affect the economic viability of an enterprise, or produce a substantial health and safety risk that outweighs the benefit of accommodating a group or individual worker

vicarious liability liability that arises when one party, such as an employer, is legally responsible for the acts or omissions of another party, such as an employee

voluntary assumption of risk a common law defence in which it is asserted that the plaintiff voluntarily assumed the risk of injury

***Wallace* damages** damages (given by extending the reasonable notice period) formerly awarded to a dismissed employee because of the employer's bad-faith conduct in the manner of dismissal

without prejudice without an admission of wrongdoing in a legal dispute

work transition (WT) plan a written agreement that sets out a plan for providing an injured worker with the necessary skills to mitigate the loss of earnings resulting from a workplace injury

Workplace Hazardous Materials Information System (WHMIS) a national information system designed to provide workers and employers with essential information about hazardous materials in the workplace

wrongful dismissal dismissal without just cause wherein an employer breaches its common law duty to provide reasonable notice of termination to an employee

Index